DAY HIKES IN THE
Santa Monica Mountains

From Los Angeles to Point Mugu
Including the entire Backbone Trail

Robert Stone

Day Hike Books, Inc.
RED LODGE, MONTANA

1st Edition
ISBN: 978-1-57342-065-5

Day Hike Books, Inc.
P.O. Box 865 · Red Lodge, Montana 59068
www.dayhikebooks.com

Distributed by The Globe Pequot Press
246 Goose Lane · P.O. Box 480
Guilford, CT 06437-0480
800-243-0495 (direct order) · 800-820-2329 (fax order)
www.globe-pequot.com

Photographs by Robert Stone
Layout/maps by Paula Doherty

The author has made every attempt to provide accurate information in this book. However, trail routes and features may change—please use common sense and forethought, and be mindful of your own capabilities. Let this book guide you, but be aware that each hiker assumes responsibility for their own safety. The author and publisher do not assume any responsibility for loss, damage, or injury caused through the use of this book.

Printed in the United States of America

Library of Congress Control Number: 2011940532

Cover photo:
Goat Buttes in Malibu Creek State Park, Hikes 67 and 72

Back cover photo:
Sandstone formations along Saddle Peak Trail,
Section 5 of the Backbone Trail

Also by Robert Stone

Day Hikes On the California Central Coast

Day Hikes On the California Southern Coast

Day Hikes Around Sonoma County

Day Hikes Around Napa Valley

Day Hikes Around Big Sur

Day Hikes Around Monterey and Carmel

Day Hikes In San Luis Obispo County, California

Day Hikes Around Santa Barbara

Day Hikes In the Santa Monica Mountains

Day Hikes Around Ventura County

Day Hikes Around Los Angeles

Day Hikes Around Orange County

Day Hikes In Sedona, Arizona

Day Hikes In Yosemite National Park

Day Hikes In Sequoia & Kings Canyon Nat'l. Parks

Day Hikes In Yellowstone National Park

Day Hikes In Grand Teton National Park

Day Hikes In the Beartooth Mountains

Day Hikes Around Bozeman, Montana

Day Hikes Around Missoula, Montana

I wish to thank the following people from the Santa Monica Mountains National Recreation Area. Their tireless dedication and achievements to the expanding Backbone Trail system is a gift to all of us that will remain for many years to come.

Thank you for your helpful assistance, trail updates, and clarifications:

Sheila Braden

Melanie Beck

Ken Low

LINDA STONE

Hiking partner, Kofax

Table of Contents

THE HIKES

Griffith Park and Hollywood Hills
Los Angeles

Beverly Hills to Santa Monica
East San Fernando Valley to 405 Freeway

Santa Monica and 405 Freeway to Topanga Canyon

Will Rogers State Historic Park • Topanga State Park

"Dirt" Mulholland Drive
East San Fernando Valley to Topanga Canyon

Topanga Canyon to Malibu Canyon

Cold Creek area

Malibu Canyon Road/Las Virgenes Road to Kanan Dume Road/Kanan Road

Point Dume • Kanan Dume Road/Kanan Road

Decker Road to Point Mugu State Park

Point Mugu State Park
Rancho Sierra Vista/Satwiwa

THE BACKBONE TRAIL

Santa Monica Mountains

The Santa Monica Mountains are a 50-mile-long range that parallels the coastline in Southern California, dividing the Pacific coast from the interior valleys. The mountains stretch from the Hollywood Hills in Los Angeles to Point Mugu at the Pacific Ocean, sloping into the Oxnard Plain in Ventura County. As the range travels northwest from Los Angeles to Point Mugu, the urban areas gradually get replaced by thousands of acres of undeveloped land.

The Santa Monica Range reaches a width of ten miles at its broadest and covers 200,000 acres. The altitude across most of the range is from 1,000—2,000 feet, although the highest peaks reach just over 3,000 feet. The southern half of the range divides the San Fernando Valley from the Los Angeles Basin, while the northern half of the mountains divides the Conejo Valley from Malibu and Santa Monica Bay.

Most of the range is located within the Santa Monica Mountains National Recreation Area, the largest urban national park in the world. The parkland, which covers 150,000 acres, is a patchwork of land managed by more than twenty federal, state and municipal parks, including the National Park Service, Santa Monica Mountains Conservancy, California State Parks, and numerous county and municipal agencies.

The Santa Monica Mountains have four centerpiece parks that anchor the major trail systems: Griffith Park, the nation's largest municipal park, covers 4,300 acres on the east end of the range. Topanga State Park, at 11,000 acres, is the largest park within city limits. The 7,000-acre Malibu Creek State Park is located near the middle of the range. Point Mugu State Park stretches across 16,000 acres on the western tip of the mountain range.

The Santa Monica Mountains are well-known for being the backdrop to Hollywood, Beverly Hills, and Malibu. Since the earliest days of Hollywood, the mountains have been used in making films (especially westerns). Paramount and Twentieth Century Fox even owned "movie ranches." The television and motion picture industry continues to film in these mountains.

A great route to experience the Santa Monica Mountains is the Mulholland Scenic Corridor. The road was built in the 1920s "to take Angelinos from the city to the ocean." The corridor runs 50 miles along the mountain crest, from Griffith Park to Leo Carrillo State Beach at Sequit

Point. The automobile route is comprised of Mulholland Drive (from Hollywood to the 405 Freeway) and Mulholland Highway (the western rural portion). An 11-mile unpaved stretch known as Dirt Mulholland (open only to pedestrians, equestrians, and cyclists) lies between the two sections. From the corridor are panoramic vistas of the ocean, access to the steep canyons and rocky ridges of the mountains, and views of the cities on both sides of the range.

This hiking guide includes 125 hikes throughout the mountain range. The 69-mile Backbone Trail, which runs along the crest, is completely covered in an additional section of 13 day hikes. A variety of hikes accommodates every level of hiking, from short strolls along boardwalks to all-day coast-to-peak hikes. Highlights include fantastic sandstone landscapes, cool retreats along stream-fed canyons, gorges, waterfalls, coastal bluffs, filming locations, historic sites, and numerous 360-degree overlooks. Several hikes are found in Los Angeles' Griffith Park, including a hike up to the famous "HOLLYWOOD" sign.

A map on the following page shows the main access roads to all of the hikes. The Santa Monica Range generally lies between Highway 1 (Pacific Coast Highway) and Highway 101 (Ventura Freeway). Major arteries that connect the two highways are Topanga Canyon Boulevard, Malibu Canyon Road/Las Virgenes Road, and Kanan Dume Road/Kanan Road. The roads follow along Topanga Canyon and Malibu Canyon, waterways which have cut gorges hundreds of feet deep en route to the Pacific. The western half of the mountain range contains a network of canyons that run south to the ocean, with rolling hills, live oak woodlands, and rocky peaks. The west end of the range is the most remote, least developed, and most dramatic, with secluded gorges, sycamore-lined streams, native grasslands, and the highest peaks.

All of these hikes can be completely within a day. A quick glance at the summaries will allow you to choose a hike that is appropriate to your ability and intentions. Wear supportive, comfortable hiking shoes and layered clothing. Take along hats, sunscreen, sunglasses, drinking water, snacks, and appropriate outerwear. Ticks may be prolific and poison oak flourishes in the canyons and shady moist areas. Exercise caution by using insect repellent and staying on the trails.

Use good judgement about your capabilities—reference the hiking statistics for an approximation of difficulty and allow extra time for exploration.

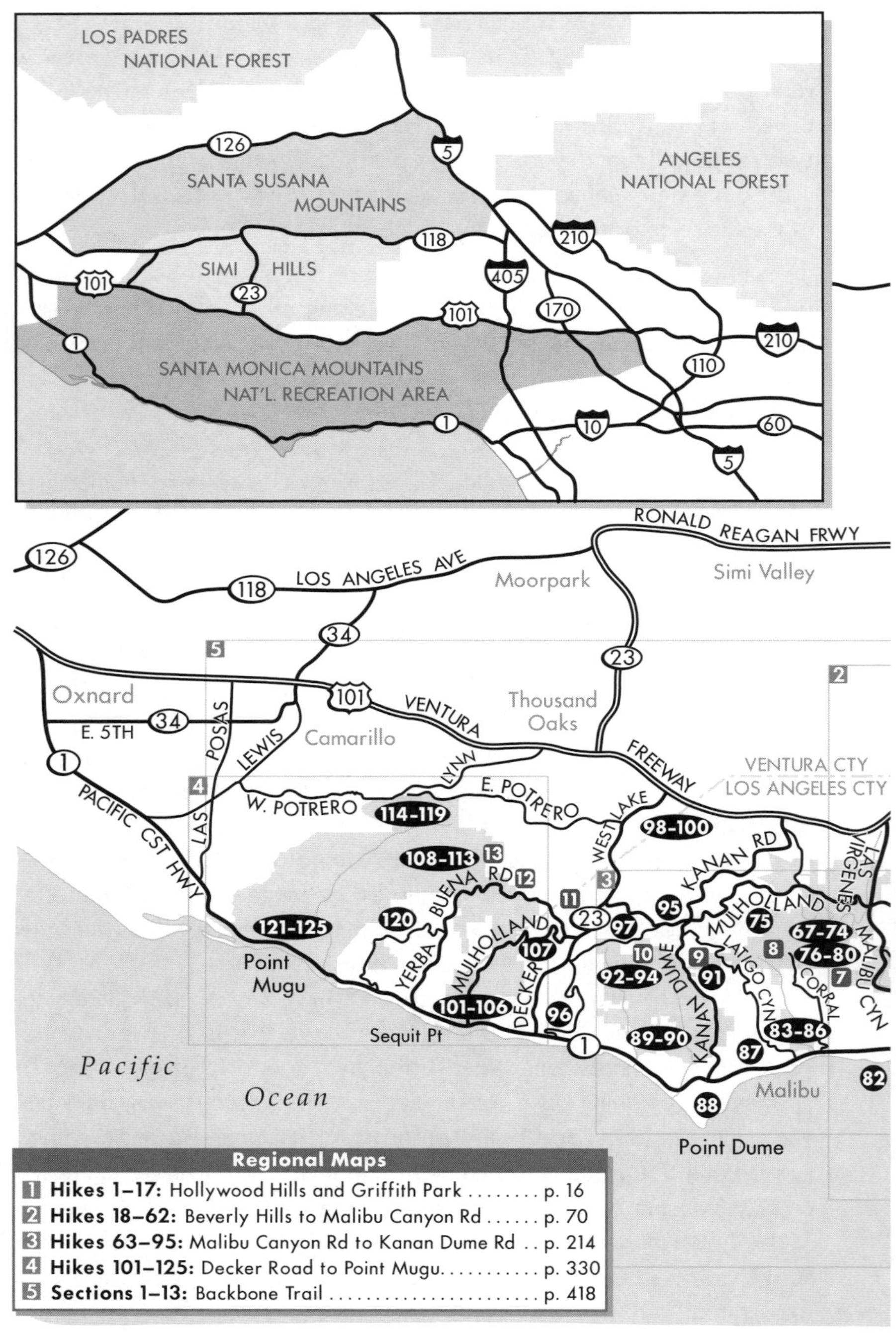
LOS PADRES
NATIONAL FOREST
ANGELES
NATIONAL FOREST
SANTA SUSANA
MOUNTAINS
SIMI
HILLS
SANTA MONICA MOUNTAINS
NAT'L. RECREATION AREA
126
5
118
210
405
101
23
170
1
110
10
60
RONALD REAGAN FRWY
LOS ANGELES AVE
Moorpark
Simi Valley
34
Oxnard
E. 5TH
LAS POSAS
LEWIS
Camarillo
VENTURA FREEWAY
Thousand
Oaks
LYNN
E. POTRERO
W. POTRERO
WESTLAKE
VENTURA CTY
LOS ANGELES CTY
PACIFIC CST HWY
KANAN RD
LAS VIRGENES
MULHOLLAND
YERBA BUENA RD
DECKER
KANAN DUME
LATIGO CYN
CORRAL
MALIBU CYN
Point
Mugu
Sequit Pt
Pacific
Ocean
Malibu
Point Dume
114-119
108-113
98-100
121-125
120
107
101-106
96
97
95
92-94
89-90
91
75
67-74
76-80
83-86
87
88
82
Regional Maps
1 Hikes 1–17: Hollywood Hills and Griffith Park . . . . p. 16
2 Hikes 18–62: Beverly Hills to Malibu Canyon Rd . . . . . . p. 70
3 Hikes 63–95: Malibu Canyon Rd to Kanan Dume Rd . . p. 214
4 Hikes 101–125: Decker Road to Point Mugu. . . . . p. 330
5 Sections 1–13: Backbone Trail . . . . p. 418

MAP of the HIKES

SANTA MONICA MOUNTAINS

N
W
E
S
126
5
Santa Clarita
LOS ANGELES NATIONAL FOREST
210
San Fernando
118
GOLDEN STATE FREEWAY
TOPOANGA CYN BLVD
405
170
1
VENTURA
FREEWAY
101
MULHOLLAND HWY
DIRT MULHOLLAND
MULHOLLAND DR
64-66
53
51
52
45-50
26
18-24
14-17
1-13
HOLLYWOOD FRWY
SAN DIEGO FRWY
25
54-62
3
2
37
STUNT
4
38
39-40
6
63
5
35-36
PIUMA RD
41-44
27-34
SUNSET BLVD
SUNSET
2
SANTA MONICA FRWY
1
10
81
Santa Monica
Santa Monica Bay
1
10 MILES
10 KILOMETERS

HIKES 1–17

Griffith Park and Hollywood Hills

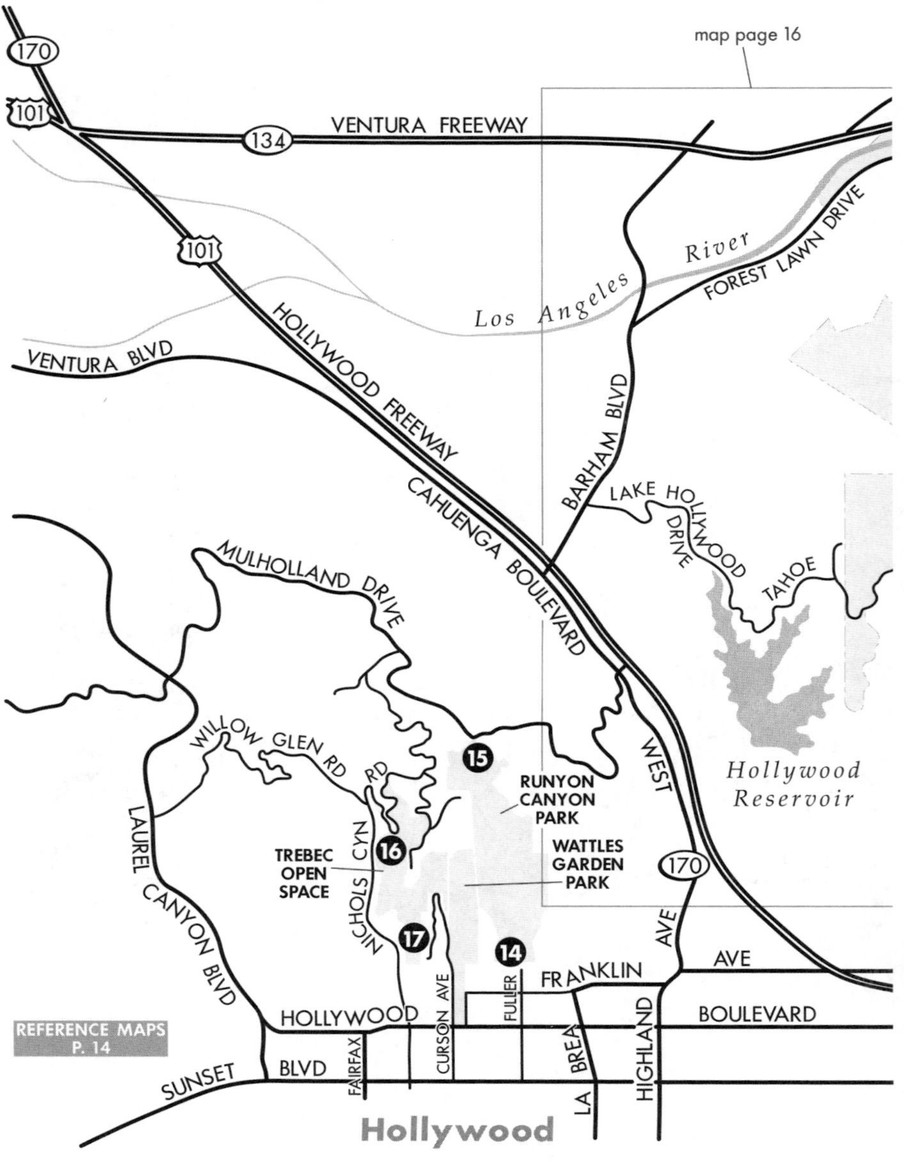

MAP of the HIKES

SANTA MONICA MOUNTAINS

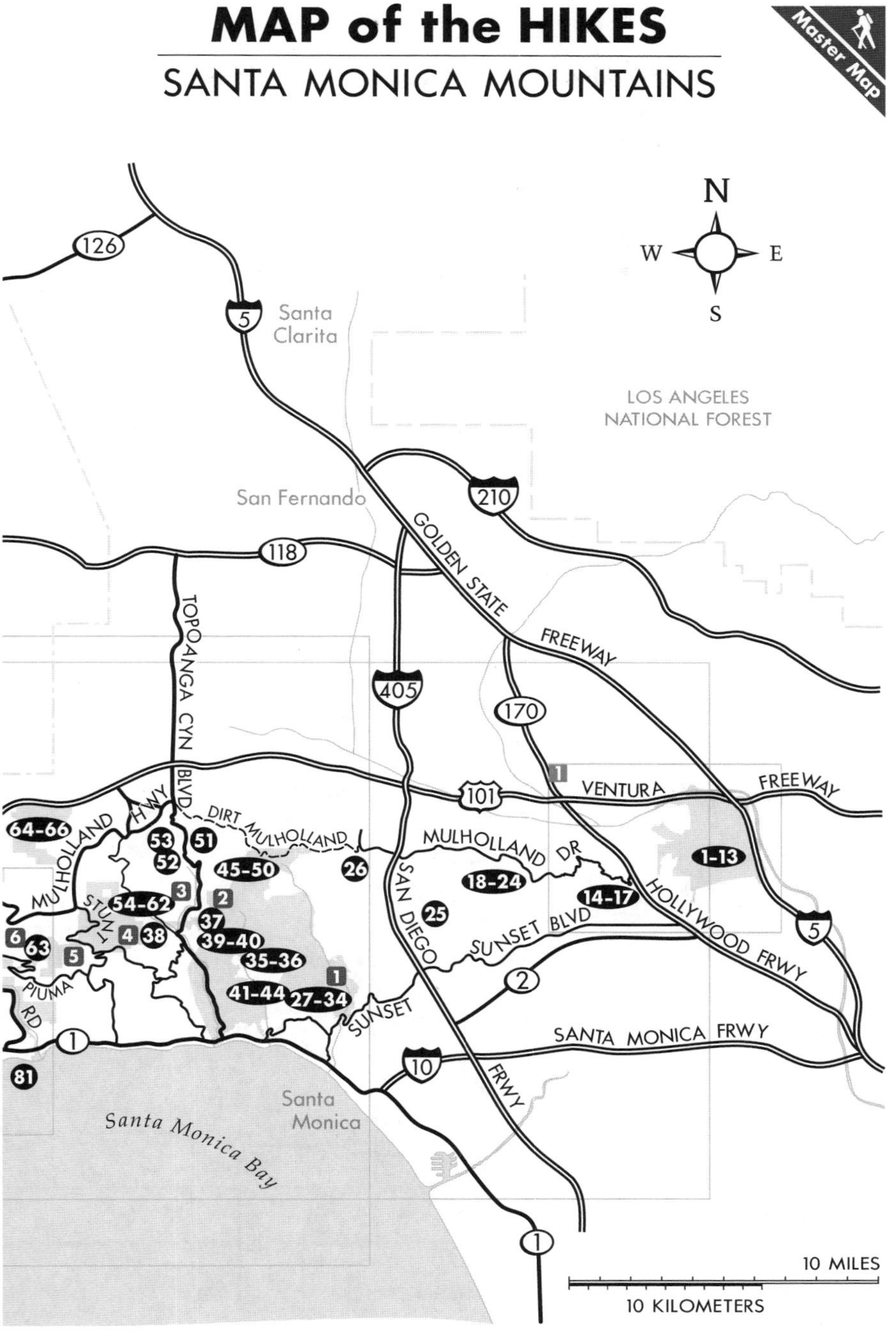

N
W
E
S

126
5
Santa Clarita
LOS ANGELES NATIONAL FOREST
San Fernando
210
118
GOLDEN STATE FREEWAY
TOPOANGA CYN BLVD
405
170
1
VENTURA FREEWAY
101
DIRT MULHOLLAND
MULHOLLAND HWY
MULHOLLAND DR
64-66
53
52
51
45-50
26
18-24
1-13
SAN DIEGO FRWY
25
14-17
HOLLYWOOD FRWY
STUNT
54-62
3
2
37
39-40
35-36
41-44
27-34
6
63
4
38
5
PIUMA RD
SUNSET BLVD
SUNSET
2
SANTA MONICA FRWY
1
10
81
Santa Monica
Santa Monica Bay
1
10 MILES
10 KILOMETERS

HIKES 1–17

Griffith Park and Hollywood Hills

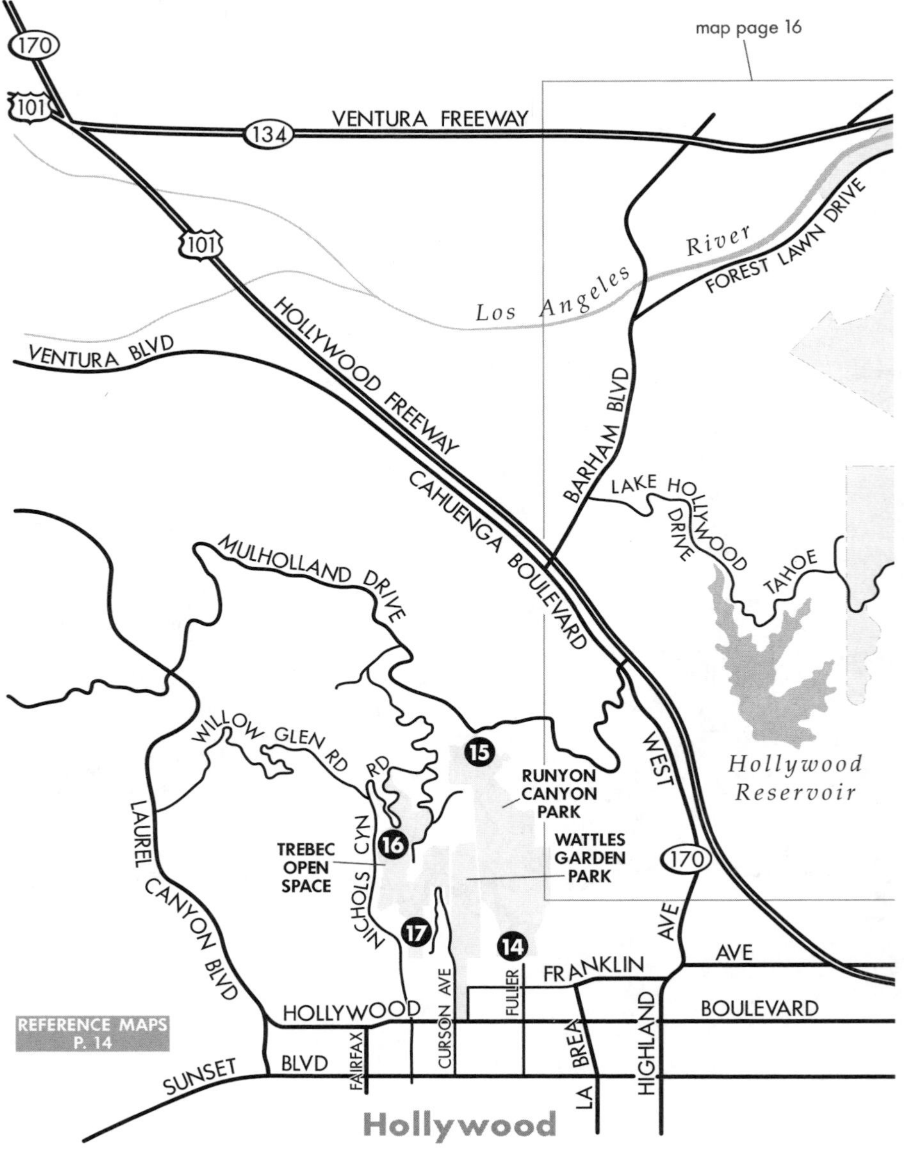

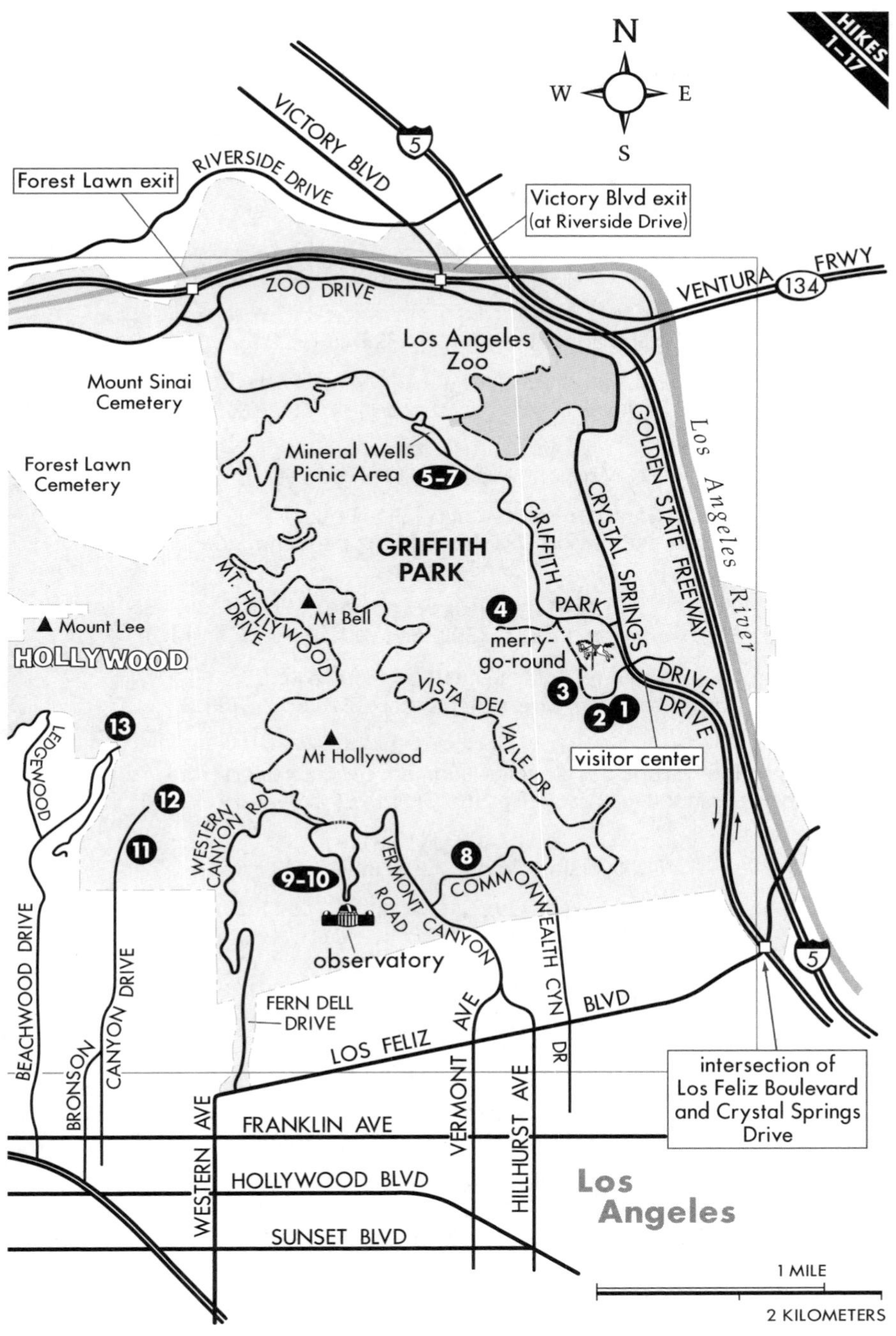
HIKES 1–17
N
W
E
S
VICTORY BLVD
5
RIVERSIDE DRIVE
Forest Lawn exit
Victory Blvd exit (at Riverside Drive)
ZOO DRIVE
VENTURA FRWY
134
Los Angeles Zoo
Mount Sinai Cemetery
Forest Lawn Cemetery
Mineral Wells Picnic Area
5-7
GRIFFITH PARK
GRIFFITH PARK DRIVE
CRYSTAL SPRINGS DRIVE
GOLDEN STATE FREEWAY
Los Angeles River
MT. HOLLYWOOD DRIVE
Mt Bell
Mount Lee
HOLLYWOOD
4
merry-go-round
3
2
1
VISTA DEL VALLE DR
visitor center
13
LEDGEWOOD
Mt Hollywood
12
11
WESTERN CANYON RD
9-10
8
VERMONT CANYON ROAD
COMMONWEALTH CYN DR
observatory
BEACHWOOD DRIVE
BRONSON CANYON DRIVE
FERN DELL DRIVE
LOS FELIZ BLVD
VERMONT AVE
HILLHURST AVE
WESTERN AVE
5
intersection of Los Feliz Boulevard and Crystal Springs Drive
FRANKLIN AVE
HOLLYWOOD BLVD
SUNSET BLVD
Los Angeles
1 MILE
2 KILOMETERS

ATTRACTIONS and ACTIVITIES

FACILITIES
athletic facilities • soccer • swimming • tennis • golf
picnicking • horseback riding • camping • hiking • jogging

AUTRY NATIONAL CENTER
4700 Western Heritage Drive • (323) 667-2000

BICYCLE RENTAL
4730 Crystal Springs Drive at ranger station • (323) 653-4099

BIRD SANTUARY
2900 N. Vermont Avenue • (323) 666-5046

FERNDELL NATURE MUSEUM • WESTERN CANYON
5375 Red Oak Drive • (323) 666-5046 (Hike 9)

GREEK THEATER
2700 N. Vermont Avenue • (323) 665-1927

GRIFFITH PARK MERRY-GO-ROUND
between the Los Angeles Zoo and the Los Feliz park entrance
(323) 665-3051

GRIFFITH OBSERVATORY
2800 E. Observatory Road • (323) 664-1191 (Hikes 9 and 10)

GRIFFITH PARK SOUTHERN RAILROAD
Corner Los Feliz/Riverside Drive • (323) 664-6788

HOLLYWOOD SIGN
Views of the historic Los Angeles landmark can be gained from many hiking trails in the Park as well as the Griffith Observatory (Hike 13)

L.A. EQUESTRIAN CENTER
480 Riverside Drive • (323) 840-9063

L.A. LIVE STEAMERS
5200 Zoo Dr • (323) 662-5874

L.A. ZOO
5333 Zoo Drive • (323) 666-4650

PONY RIDES
Corner Los Feliz/Riverside Drive • (323) 664-3266

STATUARY
Statues are found throughout Griffith Park

SYMPHONY IN THE GLEN
Free concert program has been based in Griffith Park at the Old Zoo Picnic Area • www.symphonyintheglen.org

TRAVEL TOWN
5200 Zoo Drive • (323) 662-5874

Griffith Park

Griffith Park is an emerald gem in the midst of the Los Angeles metropolis. The 4,217-acre park (equal to five square miles) is the largest municipal park in the United States. It is nearly three times the size of New York City's Central Park. This rugged urban wilderness contains ridges and peaks with overlooks, secluded canyons, creeks, springs, and gardens. Large portions of the park remain virtually unchanged from its original natural state. The mountains and steep interior canyons of Griffith Park, as well as the adjacent Hollywood Hills, are largely undeveloped and offer a natural haven for humans and animals.

Griffith Park lies on the easternmost tip of the Santa Monica Mountains. It is surrounded by the cities of Burbank, Hollywood, Glendale, and Los Angeles. To the east, the park faces the Verdugo Mountains and San Gabriel Mountains. The preserved parkland is bound along its borders by major thoroughfares as well as the Los Angeles River.

Colonel Griffith J. Griffith donated over 3,000 acres to create this parkland in 1896. Griffith was a Welsh immigrant who made his fortune in gold and silver mining speculation. He deeded the land as a Christmas gift to the people of Los Angeles as "a place of rest and relaxation for the masses." Additional land acquisitions since this time have expanded the park to 4,217 acres.

A 56-mile network of hiking and equestrian trails weaves across the semi-arid foothills, chaparral-cloaked hills, oak groves, and wooded glens. The trail system combines single-track footpaths, unpaved fire roads, and paved (but gated) roads. The park's elevation ranges from 384 feet to 1,625 feet at the summit of Mount Hollywood. From the trails are some of the best views of the Los Angeles basin.

Numerous attractions are located with the park, in addition to the Griffith Observatory and Greek Theater (see left). The next 13 hikes include some of these points of interest, including the historic merry-go-round, the Old Zoo, Mount Hollywood, Amir's Garden, Ferndell Park, the Bronson Caves, and the HOLLYWOOD sign (arguably the best-known site within the park). For a complete list of events and attractions, go the observatory (2800 East Observatory Road) or the visitor center (4730 Crystal Springs Drive).

Note: Leashed dogs are allowed on all the trails within the park.

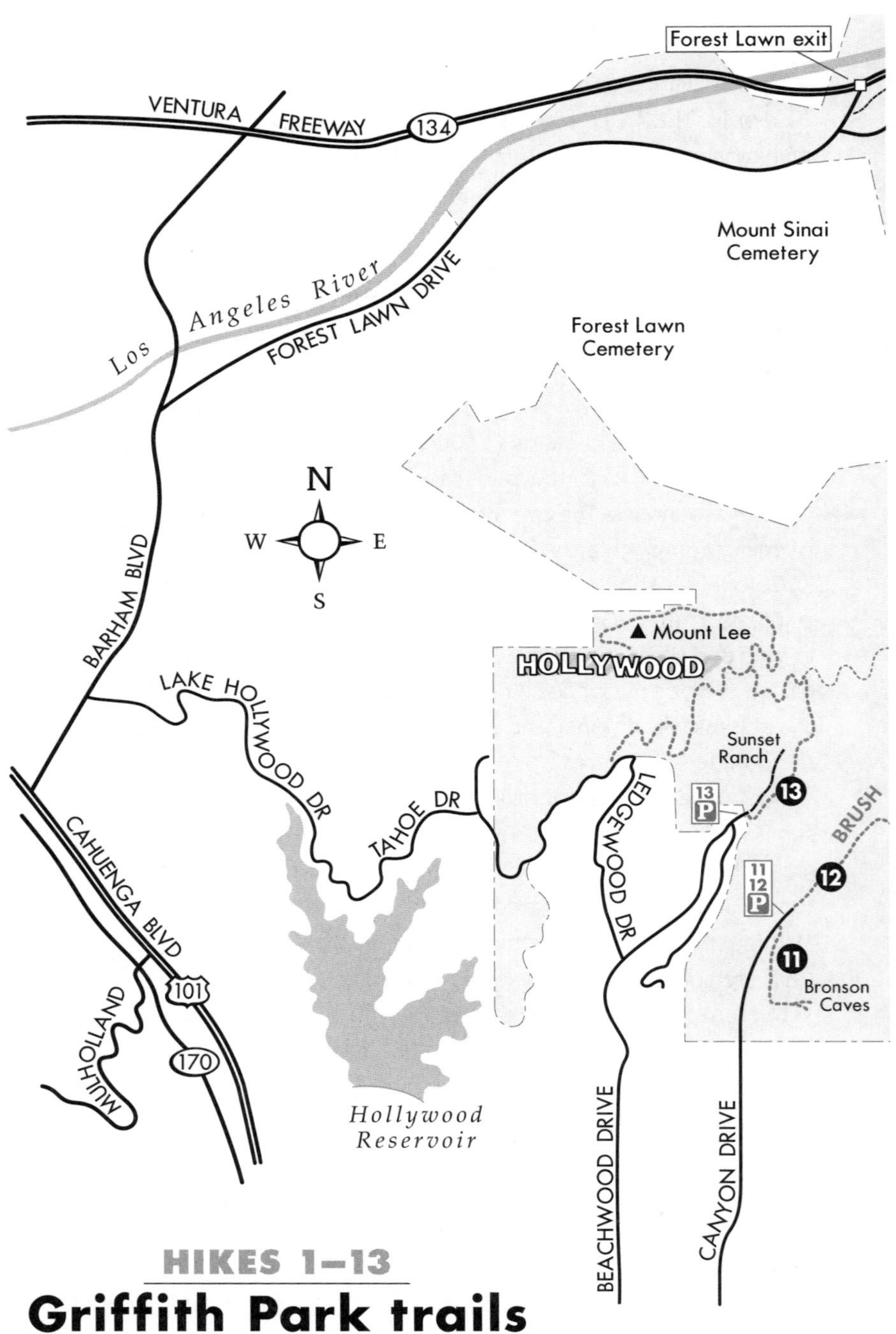

HIKES 1–13

Griffith Park trails

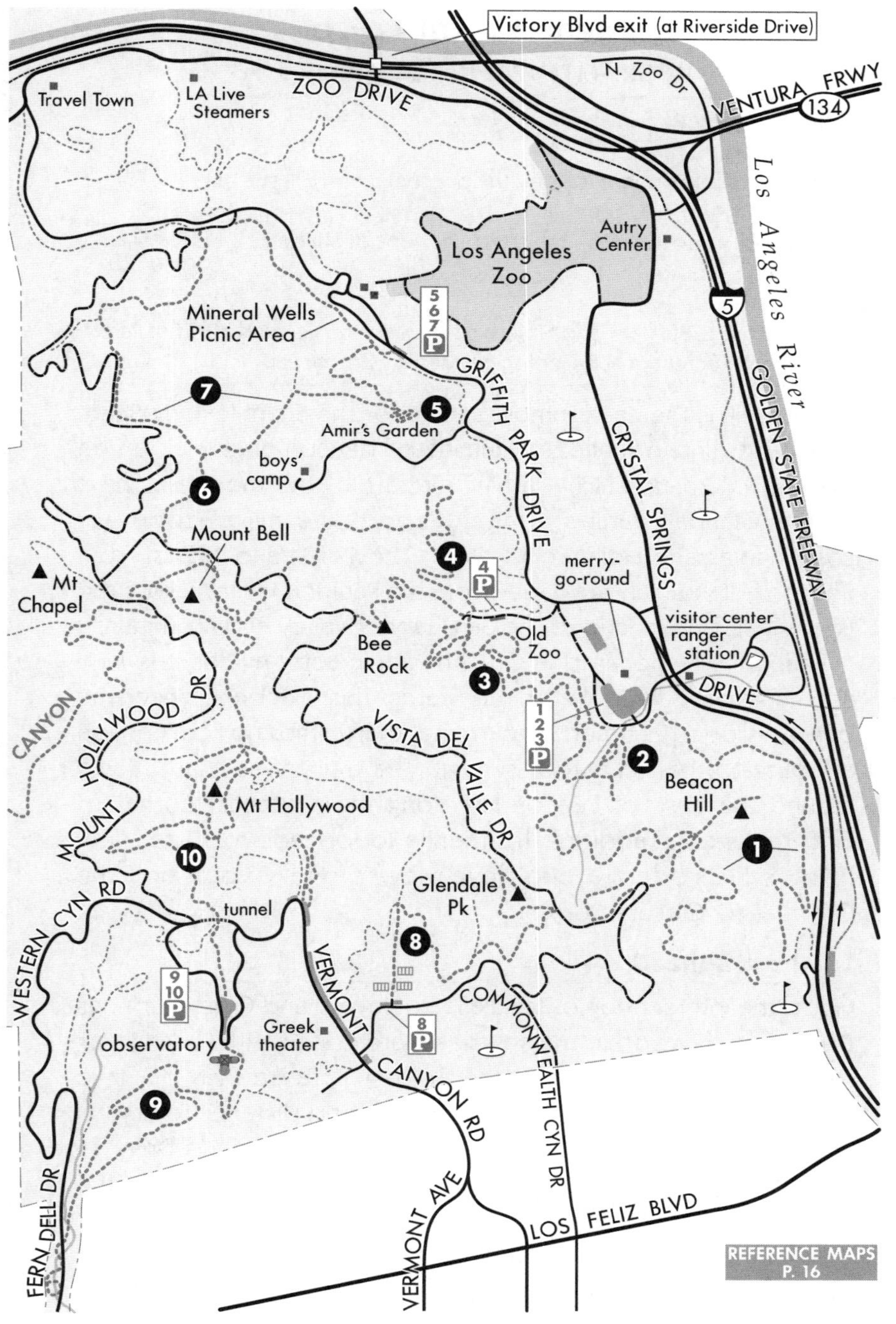

Victory Blvd exit (at Riverside Drive)
N. Zoo Dr
VENTURA FRWY
134
Travel Town
LA Live Steamers
ZOO DRIVE
Los Angeles River
Autry Center
Los Angeles Zoo
5
Mineral Wells Picnic Area
5 6 7 P
GRIFFITH PARK DRIVE
GOLDEN STATE FREEWAY
CRYSTAL SPRINGS
7
5
Amir's Garden
boys' camp
6
Mount Bell
4
4 P
merry-go-round
Mt Chapel
visitor center
ranger station
Bee Rock
Old Zoo
3
DRIVE
CANYON
HOLLYWOOD DR
VISTA DEL VALLE DR
1 2 3 P
2
Beacon Hill
MOUNT
Mt Hollywood
1
10
WESTERN CYN RD
Glendale Pk
tunnel
8
VERMONT
9 10 P
COMMONWEALTH CYN DR
Greek theater
8 P
observatory
CANYON RD
9
VERMONT AVE
LOS FELIZ BLVD
FERN DELL DR
REFERENCE MAPS P. 16

1. Beacon Hill Loop

GRIFFITH PARK: Los Angeles

Hiking distance: 5-mile double loop
Hiking time: 3 hours
Configuration: double loop with spur to Beacon Hill summit
Elevation gain: 650 feet
Exposure: exposed hills with short sections of shade
Difficulty: moderate
Dogs: allowed
Maps: U.S.G.S. Burbank and Hollywood · Map and Guide of Griffith Park
Hileman's Recreational & Geological Map of Griffith Park

map page 25

Beacon Hill is the easternmost summit of the 50-mile-long Santa Monica Mountain Range. An illuminated beacon once resided on the top of Beacon Hill, warning aircraft of the mountains next to the Glendale Grand Central Airport, the main airport for Los Angeles and Hollywood during the 1910s and 1920s. From Beacon Hill you can see it all—from the Pacific Ocean, across the Los Angeles Basin, and to the San Gabriel Valley and Mountains.

Beacon Hill is located in Griffith Park in Los Angeles, the largest municipal park in the United States. This hike begins near the park's historic 1926 merry-go-round, then climbs up Fern Canyon en route to the 1,001-foot summit. The trail forms a large loop around the base of Beacon Hill along the southeast corner of Griffith Park. An additional one-mile loop leads to Vista View Point, which offers a bird's-eye view of Hollywood and the Griffith Park Observatory.

To the trailhead

Go to the intersection of Los Feliz Boulevard and Crystal Springs Drive in Hollywood in the southeast area of Griffith Park. (To arrive at this intersection from the Golden State Freeway/I-5, take the Los Feliz Boulevard Exit. Drive west a short distance to Crystal Springs Drive.) Drive 1.3 miles north on Crystal Springs Drive to the merry-go-round turnoff on the left. Turn left and park in the first parking lot.

From Highway 134/Ventura Freeway in Burbank, take the Victory Boulevard exit. Drive south to a T-junction with Zoo Drive.

Turn left on Zoo Drive and continue 2.1 miles to the merry-go-round turnoff on the right. (En route, Zoo Drive becomes Griffith Park Drive.) Turn right and park in the first parking lot.

The hike

From the parking lot, walk back to the entrance road and the vehicle gate. The Lower Beacon Trail, our return route, is directly across the road. Walk 75 yards to the right on the paved road to the Fern Canyon Nature Trail on the left (Hike 2). Continue on the paved road for 55 yards (straight ahead) to a second junction. Leave the paved road and veer left on the Fern Canyon Trail, a dirt road. Pass two junctions on the right that form a loop through the Old Zoo (Hike 3). Pass a side path on the left that descends into Fern Canyon and the amphitheater. Steadily climb the west canyon wall, following the curvature of the mountains. Cross over to the east slope of Fern Canyon, reaching the 5-Points junction on a ridge overlooking the San Gabriel Valley and Los Angeles at one mile. Straight ahead is the Coolidge Trail, our return route. The two trails to the right form the smaller one-mile loop.

For now, bear left on a spur trail to the summit of Beacon Hill. Walk east along the eucalyptus-lined ridge at a near-level grade. Make a short but steep ascent to the rounded, 1,001-foot summit at 1.25 miles. Below is the Golden State (I-5) Freeway and the Los Angeles River. To the east and north are Glendale, Eagle Rock, Burbank, the Verdugo Mountains, and the San Gabriel Mountains. To the south and west are downtown Los Angeles and the entire Los Angeles basin to Palos Verdes.

Return to the 5-Points junction. To add a one-mile loop to the hike, take the second trail to the right. Traverse the mountain westward, perched on the steep slope. Climb to Vista Del Valle Drive, at the head of Fern Canyon and directly across from Vista View Point. The overlook offers more sweeping views of Hollywood, Los Angeles, and the Griffith Park Observatory. Across the road is the Hogback Trail and Riverside Trail (Hike 8). Follow the path to the left, above and parallel to Vista Del Valle Drive. The path joins the road along a U-bend in Vista Del Valle Drive. Pick up the posted trail on the outside bend. Descend east, completing the loop at 5-Points junction.

To continue on the large loop, take the Coolidge Trail to the right, descending on the south-facing slope. As the path nears the Marty Tregnan Golf Academy, look north to a great view of Beacon Hill. Descend to a trail split at the southeast corner of Griffith Park. The right fork drops down to Crystal Springs Drive. Veer left on the Lower Beacon Trail, skirting the east flank of Beacon Hill above the freeway on the undulating path. Curve left (west) and climb to northern park views. Descend to the park road, directly across from the trailhead parking area. ■

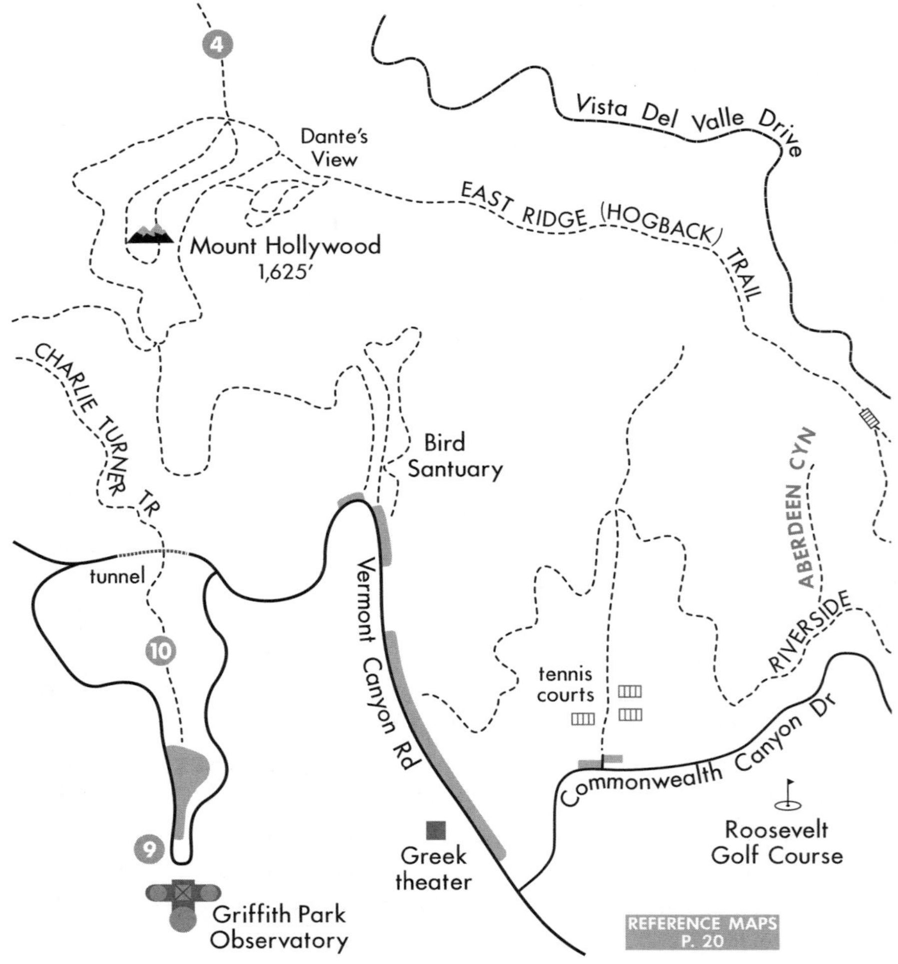

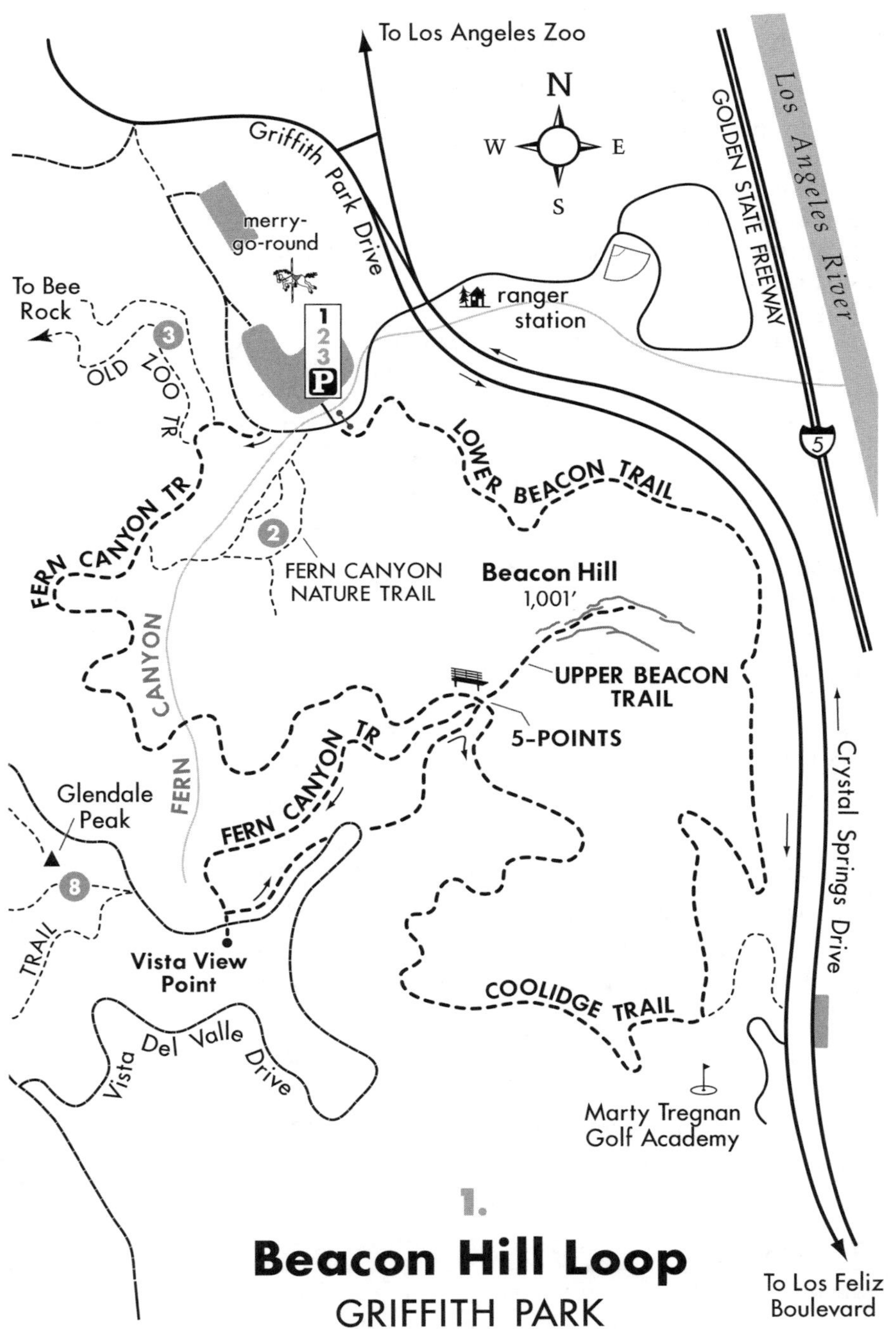

1.
Beacon Hill Loop
GRIFFITH PARK

2. Fern Canyon Nature Trail

GRIFFITH PARK: Los Angeles

Hiking distance: 0.6-mile loop
Hiking time: 0.5 hours
Configuration: loop with spur to amphitheater
Elevation gain: 150 feet
Exposure: a mix of exposed slopes and forested canyon
Difficulty: easy
Dogs: allowed
Maps: U.S.G.S. Burbank • Map and Guide of Griffith Park
Hileman's Recreational & Geological Map of Griffith Park

The Fern Canyon Nature Trail, near the eastern terminus of the Santa Monica Mountains, takes you through a forested canyon on a looping trail in Griffith Park. The self-guided nature trail meanders through dense pockets of streamside vegetation and winds through shady groves of oak, sycamore, black walnut, willow, toyon, and cedar. The path crosses a footbridge over the stream to an amphitheater. This quiet refuge on the lower slope of Fern Canyon is located minutes from the park's merry-go-round and the Old Zoo Park.

To the trailhead

Go to the intersection of Los Feliz Boulevard and Crystal Springs Drive in Hollywood in the southeast area of Griffith Park. (To arrive at this intersection from the Golden State Freeway/I-5, take the Los Feliz Boulevard Exit. Drive west a short distance to Crystal Springs Drive.) Drive north on Crystal Springs Drive for 1.3 miles to the merry-go-round turnoff on the left. Turn left and park in the first parking lot.

From Highway 134/Ventura Freeway in Burbank, take the Victory Boulevard exit. Drive south to a T-junction with Zoo Drive. Turn left on Zoo Drive and continue 2.1 miles to the merry-go-round turnoff on the right. (En route, Zoo Drive becomes Crystal Springs Drive.) Turn right and park in the first parking lot.

The hike

From the parking lot, walk back to the entrance road and the vehicle gate. The Lower Beacon Trail is directly across the road.

Walk 75 yards to the right on the paved road to the Fern Canyon Nature Trail on the left. Bear left and walk into the mouth of the canyon to a Y-fork. Begin the loop to the right, staying on the main trail along the east (left) side of the stream. Twenty yards from the first junction is a second trail split. The left fork climbs up and over a hill, reconnecting with the main trail a short distance ahead. Pass another junction (the return route), and cross a footbridge over the stream to the Fern Canyon Amphitheater. From the amphitheater, steps lead up the hill to the right and connect with the Fern Canyon Trail (Hike 1).

Retrace your steps back to the upper-most junction, and now take the footpath to the right. Climb over the hill and descend into the adjoining canyon. Continue down canyon, completing the loop. Head right for a short distance back to the entrance road. ■

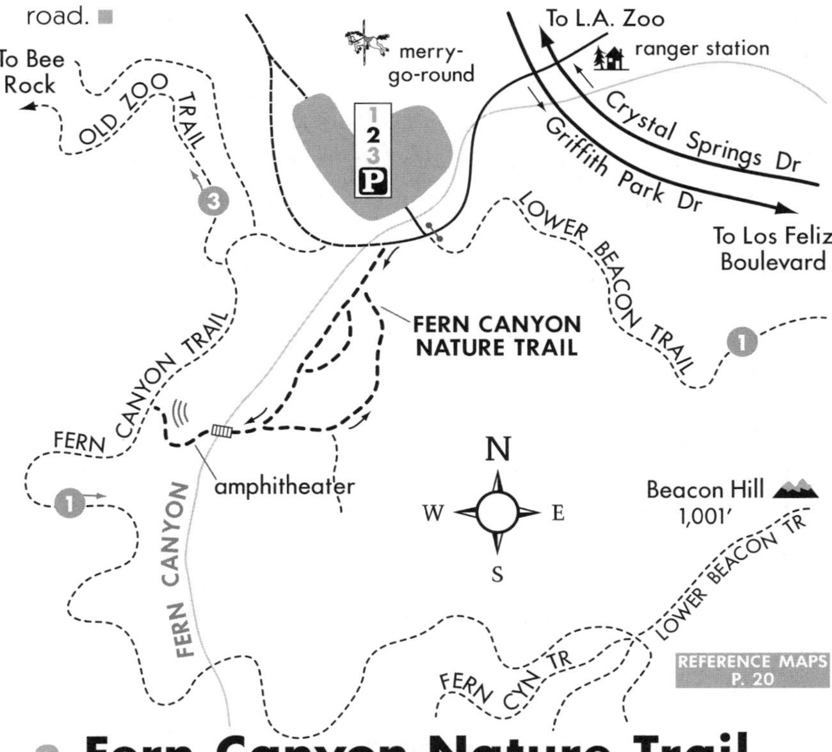

2. Fern Canyon Nature Trail

GRIFFITH PARK

3. Bee Rock and Old Zoo Park

GRIFFITH PARK: Los Angeles

Hiking distance: 2.2-mile loop
Hiking time: 1.5 hours
Configuration: loop with spur to Bee Rock
Elevation gain: 600 feet
Exposure: mostly exposed with sections of shade
Difficulty: easy with moderate ascent to Bee Rock
Dogs: allowed
Maps: U.S.G.S. Burbank • Map and Guide of Griffith Park
Hileman's Recreational & Geological Map of Griffith Park

Bee Rock is a large, cavernous sandstone outcropping that is naturally sculpted into the shape of a beehive near the center of Griffith Park. From atop the 1,056-foot rock formation are impressive views across the massive park. The hike returns through the Old Los Angeles Zoo, which was converted into a park after the new zoo was built. The Old Los Angeles Zoo operated from 1912 through 1965 at this location before moving to the current location two miles north. The historic enclosures, walls, and grottoes, built in the 1930s to house the animals, are still intact. The trail winds past the abandoned animal cages with an eerie animal ghost town atmosphere. The trails are on the old walking paths and expansive lawns. This hike begins at the at the merry-go-round and follows a dirt road that circles the back side of the Old Zoo to Bee Rock, then returns through the Old Zoo.

To the trailhead

Go to the intersection of Los Feliz Boulevard and Crystal Springs Drive in Hollywood in the southeast area of Griffith Park. (To arrive at this intersection from the Golden State Freeway/I-5, take the Los Feliz Boulevard exit. Drive west a short distance to Crystal Springs Drive.) Drive 1.3 miles north on Crystal Springs Drive to the merry-go-round turnoff on the left. Turn left and park in the first parking lot.

From Highway 134/Ventura Freeway in Burbank, take the Victory Boulevard exit. Drive south to a T-junction with Zoo Drive.

Turn left on Zoo Drive and continue 2.1 miles to the merry-go-round turnoff on the right. (En route, Zoo Drive becomes Crystal Springs Drive.) Turn right and park in the first parking lot.

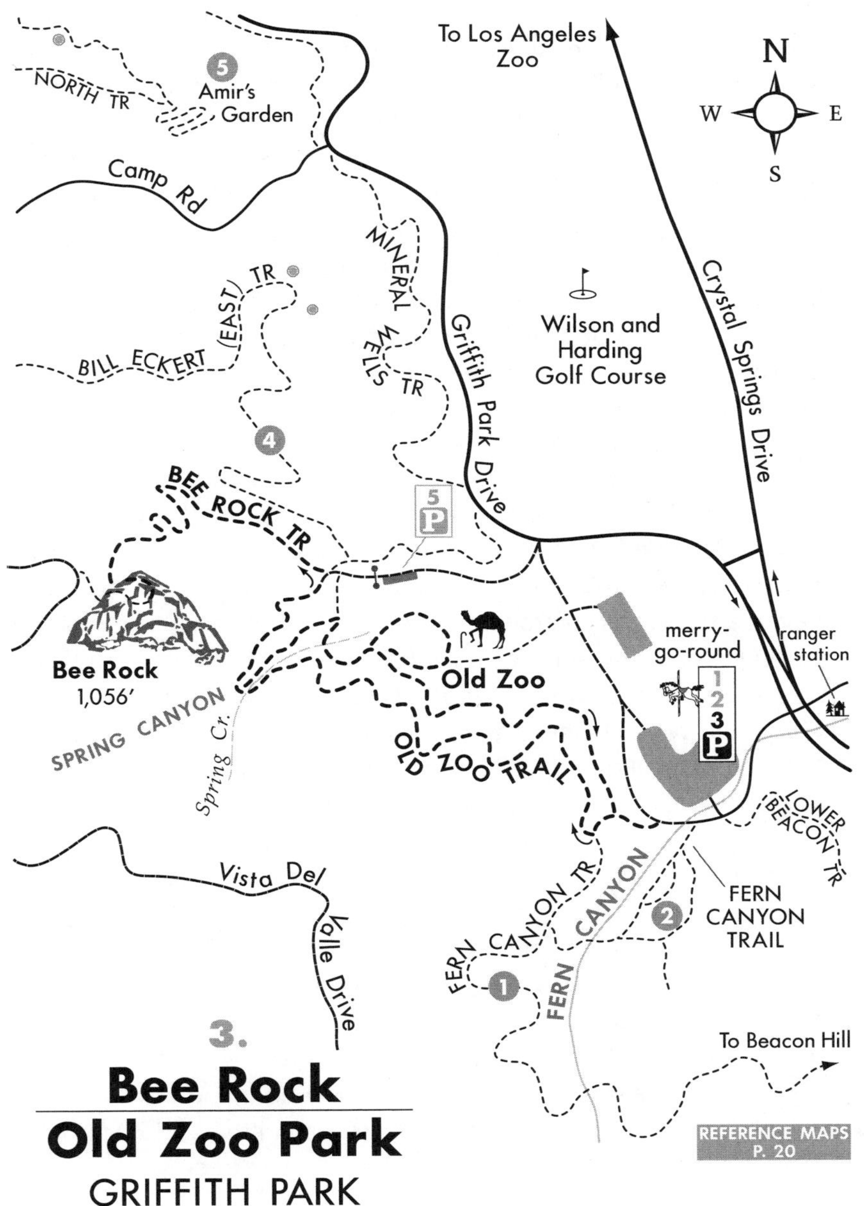

3.

Bee Rock

Old Zoo Park

GRIFFITH PARK

The hike

From the parking lot, walk back to the entrance road and the vehicle gate. The Lower Beacon Trail is directly across the road. Walk 75 yards to the right on the paved road to the Fern Canyon Nature Trail on the left (Hike 2). Continue on the paved road for 55 yards (straight ahead) to a second junction. Leave the paved road and veer left on the Fern Canyon Trail, a dirt road. Walk 80 yards to a Y-fork. Begin the loop to the left, staying on the Fern Canyon Trail for 60 yards to a junction with the Old Zoo Trail. The left fork (straight ahead) leads to Beacon Hill (Hike 1). Instead, veer right on the Old Zoo Trail and head uphill into the trees. Skirt the back (west) side of the Old Zoo as prominent Bee Rock comes into view at a half mile. Gently descend into the shade of pines and oaks. On a horseshoe right bend is seasonal Spring Creek and a rock grotto. Cross over the stream to an unsigned trail on the right, our return route.

For now, continue straight ahead and descend to a 4-way junction at 0.7 miles. The right fork descends to the Old Zoo Picnic Area. The Mineral Wells Trail continues straight ahead, then curves right. For this hike, take the Bee Rock Trail to the left, and traverse the south canyon slope with scattered oaks. The road/trail curves left and ends by a footpath. Bear left on the path and weave uphill at a steeper grade. Head generally south on the steep, narrow trail. Concrete steps lead up to the perch atop Bee Rock. From the fenced 1,056-foot summit are great vistas of the San Gabriel Mountains and the San Fernando Valley.

Return to the unsigned path at Spring Canyon. Descend to the left along the left side of the waterway to a paved path, part of the Old Zoo pathway. Go to the right, passing old cell-like cages built in the 1930s that once housed the animals. On the left are expansive lawns. At 100 yards is a junction. The main trail (straight head) weaves downhill, passing abandoned rock animal habitats and returning to the parking lots by the merry-go-round. Take the narrower paved path to the right. Wind along the contours of the hillside, passing more animal cages. Parallel the Old Zoo Trail, completing the loop at the Fern Canyon Trail. Retrace your steps back to the trailhead parking lot. ■

4. Mount Hollywood from Old Zoo Picnic Area

GRIFFITH PARK: Los Angeles

Hiking distance: 4.5 miles round trip
Hiking time: 2.5 hours
Configuration: out-and-back
Elevation gain: 1,175 feet
Exposure: exposed hills
Difficulty: moderately strenuous
Dogs: allowed
Maps: U.S.G.S. Burbank • Map and Guide of Griffith Park
Hileman's Recreational & Geological Map of Griffith Park

map page 33

Mount Hollywood, the highest peak in Griffith Park, sits at an elevation of 1,625 feet. The overlook atop the flattened summit looks down on the Griffith Park Observatory and across Hollywood and Los Angeles. The views span from the Pacific Ocean across the eastern San Fernando Valley. It is the most popular lookout in the park. Several routes lead up to Mount Hollywood. The most travelled route begins at the observatory and climbs north to the summit (Hike 10). This hike accesses Mount Hollywood from the opposite direction, beginning at the Old Zoo Picnic Area. The trail climbs the mountain via the Bill Eckert (East) Trail, a dirt fire road. It is named for Bill Eckert, a park ranger, hiking guide, Griffith Park historian, and self-taught botanist.

To the trailhead

Go to the intersection of Los Feliz Boulevard and Crystal Springs Drive in Hollywood in the southeast area of Griffith Park. (To arrive at this intersection from the Golden State Freeway/I-5, take the Los Feliz Boulevard exit. Drive west a short distance to Crystal Springs Drive.) Drive 1.5 miles north on Crystal Springs Drive to Griffith Park Drive—just past the merry-go-round—and turn left. Drive a quarter mile to the Old Zoo Picnic Area on the left. Turn left and go 0.2 miles to the parking spaces on the left.

From Highway 134/Ventura Freeway in Burbank, take the Victory Boulevard exit. Drive south to a T-junction with Zoo Drive. Turn left on Zoo Drive and continue 1.9 miles to Griffith Park Drive on the right. (En route, Zoo Drive becomes Crystal Springs Drive.) Turn right and go a quarter mile to the Old Zoo Picnic Area on the left. Turn left and go 0.2 miles to the parking spaces on the left.

The hike

Walk up the paved road towards towering Bee Rock, the cavernous sandstone formation. Pass the open gate to a left bend in the road at 0.2 miles. Leave the road and walk through the trail gate to an unpaved fire road and a junction. The trail straight ahead leads to Bee Rock (Hike 3). The Old Zoo Trail goes left and leads to Fern Canyon.

For this hike, bear right on the Mineral Wells Trail, and walk 50 yards to the posted Bill Eckert Trail on the left. Bear left and head up the slope along the north wall of the ravine, with a great view of Bee Rock across the canyon. At the second switchback is a bench at an overlook of Burbank, Glendale, the Verdugo Mountains, and the San Gabriel Mountains. The path levels out and follows the chaparral-covered contours of the hillside. Pass two water tanks on the right while overlooking the Wilson and Harding Golf Courses. Continue weaving up the hill to a view into the canyon of the Griffith Park Boys Camp on the right. At 1.8 miles, the trail ends at a junction with Vista Del Valle Drive, an old paved road. The left fork descends to Bee Rock, Glendale Peak, and Beacon Hill.

Bear right and walk 200 yards to a trail on the left as the road bends sharply to the right. Take the wide footpath, wending uphill to a trail split. Veer left and continue uphill along the northeast slope of Mount Bell. Cross a narrow ridge, with views of Los Angeles, the San Fernando Valley, and the San Gabriel Valley, to a 4-way junction. The East Ridge (Hogback) Trail goes to the left, leading to Dante's View and Glendale Peak. The 3-Mile Trail goes to the right, leading to Mount Hollywood Drive. For this hike, walk straight ahead to 1,625-foot Mount Hollywood, the highest point in the park. From the summit is a classic view of the Griffith Park Observatory, Hollywood, downtown Los Angeles, and the surrounding mountains. Return by retracing your steps. ■

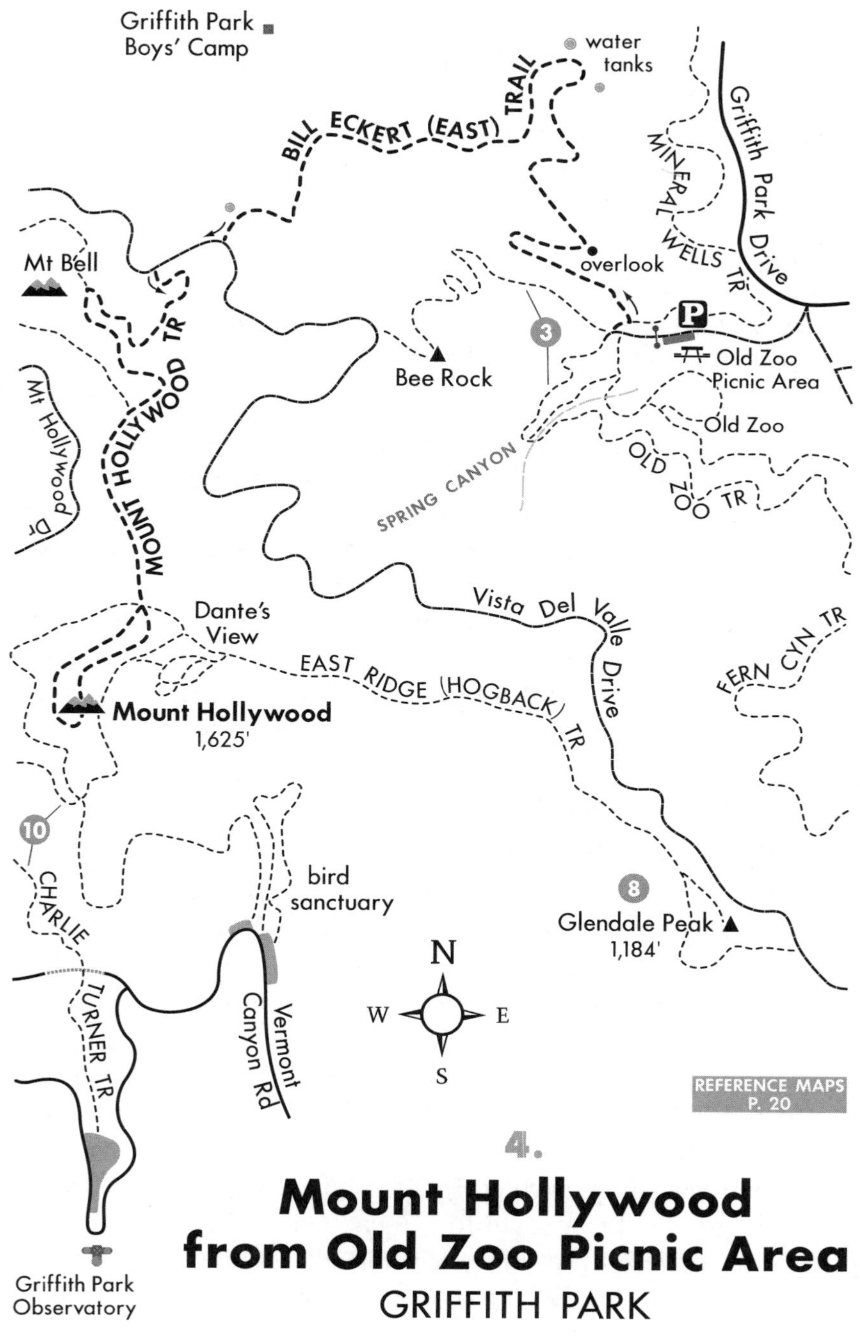

4. Mount Hollywood from Old Zoo Picnic Area

GRIFFITH PARK

5. Amir's Garden

GRIFFITH PARK: Los Angeles

Hiking distance: 1.5 miles round trip
Hiking time: 1 hour
Configuration: out-and-back with interconnected pathways in garden
Elevation gain: 300 feet
Exposure: exposed hills with shaded pockets
Difficulty: easy
Dogs: allowed
Maps: U.S.G.S. Burbank • Map and Guide of Griffith Park
Hileman's Recreational & Geological Map of Griffith Park

Amir's Garden is a beautifully landscaped garden with rock-lined paths, benches, and picnic tables on layered terraces in Griffith Park. The nearly five-acre oasis contains several species of trees (including pines, palm, eucalyptus, jacaranda, and pepper), ferns, ice plants, geraniums, rose bushes, yucca, and a wide variety of succulents. A network of trails and stairways lead through the lush, shaded grove. The garden was once a barren hillside. Amir Dialameh, a Persian immigrant, created, designed, planted, nurtured, and maintained this idyllic landscape as a labor of love from 1971 until his death in 2003. The garden is currently cared for by volunteers. This hike begins at the Mineral Wells Picnic Area and climbs the hillside to the tranquil garden.

To the trailhead

Go to the intersection of Los Feliz Boulevard and Crystal Springs Drive in Hollywood in the southeast area of Griffith Park. (To arrive at this intersection from the Golden State Freeway/I-5, take the Los Feliz Boulevard exit. Drive west a short distance to Crystal Springs Drive.) Drive 1.5 miles north on Crystal Springs Drive to Griffith Park Drive—just past the merry-go-round—and turn left. Drive 1.3 miles to the Mineral Wells Picnic Area and park alongside the road.

From Highway 134/Ventura Freeway in Burbank, take the Victory Boulevard exit. Drive south to a T-junction with Zoo Drive. Turn right and drive 2.3 miles to the Mineral Wells Picnic Area. (En route, Zoo Drive becomes Griffith Park Drive.) Park along the road.

The hike

At the trailhead is a 3-way junction. The Mineral Wells Trail heads left and right, connecting the Bill Eckert Trail by the Old Zoo with Mount Hollywood Drive. For this hike, bear right and immediately go left onto the unsigned North Trail. Switchback to the left and curve around a water tank to views of Burbank, Glendale, the Verdugo Mountains, and the majestic San Gabriel Mountains. At a half mile is a trail split. The North Trail continues to the right. Bear left into Amir's Garden, the lush oasis on the southeast mountain slope. Explore along your own route as the garden paths zigzag across the hillside. Stroll to overlooks and benches among the landscaped grounds. Return along the same route.

To extend the hike, continue up the hill on the North Trail, leading to Mount Bell and Mount Hollywood (Hike 6).

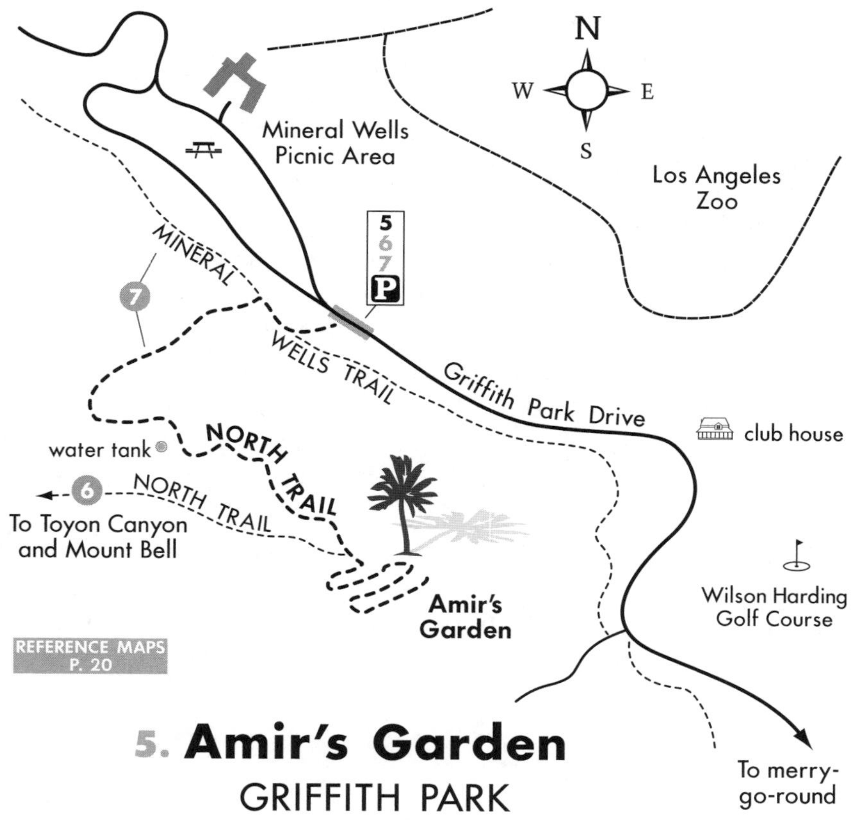

REFERENCE MAPS
P. 20

5. Amir's Garden

GRIFFITH PARK

6. Mount Bell from Mineral Wells Picnic Area

GRIFFITH PARK: Los Angeles

Hiking distance: 4.2-miles round trip
Hiking time: 2.5 hours
Configuration: out-and-back with loop; side-trip to Amir's Garden
Elevation gain: 900 feet
Exposure: exposed hills
Difficulty: moderate
Dogs: allowed
Maps: U.S.G.S. Burbank · Map and Guide of Griffith Park
Hileman's Recreational & Geological Map of Griffith Park

Mount Bell sits in the geographic center of Griffith Park at an elevation of 1,582 feet. It is less than a half mile north of Mount Hollywood, the highest peak in the park. This hike begins at the Mineral Wells Picnic Area and climbs high into the park's back-country to Mount Bell. The trail circles the summit, offering spectacular vistas in every direction. En route, the trail visits Amir's Garden, a 5-acre hillside oasis.

To the trailhead

Go to the intersection of Los Feliz Boulevard and Crystal Springs Drive in Hollywood in the southeast area of Griffith Park. (To arrive at this intersection from the Golden State Freeway/I-5, take the Los Feliz Boulevard exit. Drive west a short distance to Crystal Springs Drive.) Drive 1.5 miles north on Crystal Springs Drive to Griffith Park Drive—just past the merry-go-round—and turn left. Drive 1.3 miles to the Mineral Wells Picnic Area and park alongside the road.

From Highway 134/Ventura Freeway in Burbank, take the Forest Lawn Drive exit. Turn right and drive one block to Zoo Drive. Turn left and go 0.2 miles to Griffith Park Drive. Turn right and continue 1.4 miles to the signed Mineral Wells Picnic Area. Park alongside the road.

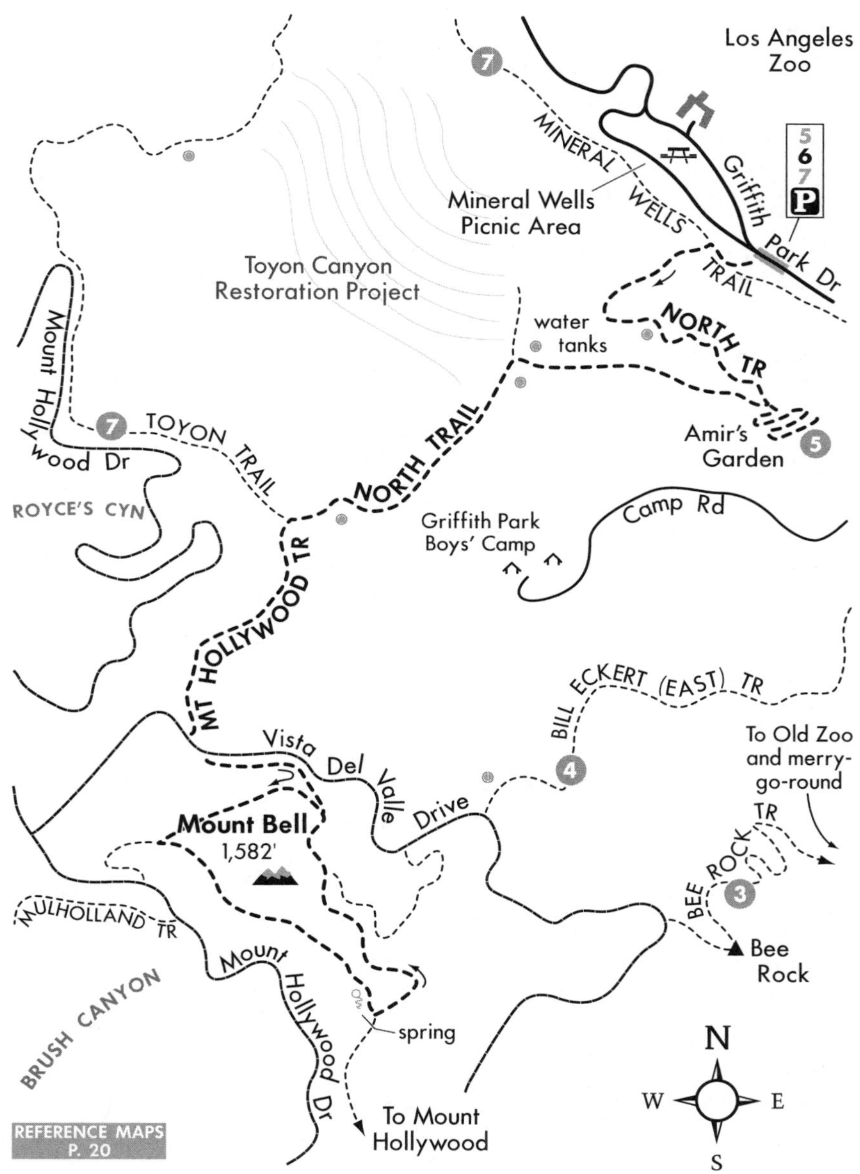

6. Mount Bell from Mineral Wells Picnic Area

GRIFFITH PARK

The hike

At the trailhead is a 3-way junction. The Mineral Wells Trail heads left and right, connecting the Bill Eckert Trail by the Old Zoo with Mount Hollywood Drive. For this hike, bear right and immediately go left onto the unsigned North Trail. Switchback to the left and curve around a water tank to views of Burbank, Glendale, the Verdugo Mountains, and the majestic San Gabriel Mountains. At a half mile is a trail split. The North Trail continues to the right. First, detour left into Amir's Garden, a lush oasis on the southeast mountain slope.

After exploring the garden, return to the North Trail and continue uphill. Follow the ridge overlooking the Griffith Park Boys Camp (in the canyon to the left) to a T-junction by a water tank. The right fork leads to an irrigated, terraced hillside, part of the Toyon Canyon Restoration Project. Go to the left, curving around the right side of the water tank. Walk 100 yards to an unmarked junction at one mile. The Toyon Trail, a footpath, goes to the right and heads downhill (Hike 7). Stay on the fire road to the left, now the Mount Hollywood Trail. Head south and climb to Vista Del Valle Drive as views open up across the San Fernando Valley. Walk 30 yards to the left on the paved road, and pick up the trail on the right. Traverse the slope above Vista Del Valle Drive, passing rock formations and admiring the far-reaching vistas, to a trail fork by power poles at 1.5 miles.

Begin the loop sharply to the right on the north flank of Mount Bell. Climb across the north face of Mount Bell to a T-junction. A view spans across Los Angeles, extending from the towering buildings of Hollywood, Century City, and Westwood to the Pacific Ocean. The right fork leads to Mount Hollywood Drive. Bear left and cross the south side of Mount Bell above Brush Canyon. Walk beyond Mount Bell to an overlook by a spring on the right, and drop down to another junction. The right fork leads to Mount Hollywood, which can be seen ahead, and Dante's View. Go to the left and descend to a trail on the right that leads to Bee Rock and the Old Zoo (Hike 3). Walk straight ahead and continue downhill, completing the loop. Return by retracing your steps. ■

7. Mineral Wells—Toyon Trail Loop

GRIFFITH PARK: Los Angeles

Hiking distance: 2.7-mile loop
Hiking time: 1.5 hours
Configuration: loop with side-trip to Amir's Garden
Elevation gain: 500 feet
Exposure: mostly exposed hills with shaded areas
Difficulty: easy to moderate
Dogs: allowed
Maps: U.S.G.S. Burbank • Map and Guide of Griffith Park
Hileman's Recreational & Geological Map of Griffith Park

map page 41

This loop hike circles Toyon Canyon in the upper end of Griffith Park. From 1957 through 1985, Toyon Canyon (originally called Mineral Wells Canyon) was the site of the Toyon Landfill, a controversial refuse site. It is now being restored as a landscaped green space. The hike incorporates a mix of footpaths and fire roads (including the North Trail, Toyon Trail, and Mineral Wells Trail) to form a loop. This hike begins at the Mineral Wells Picnic Area, winds through forested canyons, and offers magnificent vistas across Griffith Park from the canyon-top ridges.

To the trailhead

Go to the intersection of Los Feliz Boulevard and Crystal Springs Drive in Hollywood in the southeast area of Griffith Park. (To arrive at this intersection from the Golden State Freeway/I-5, take the Los Feliz Boulevard exit. Drive west a short distance to Crystal Springs Drive.) Drive 1.5 miles north on Crystal Springs Drive to Griffith Park Drive (just past the merry-go-round) and turn left. Drive 1.3 miles to the Mineral Wells Picnic Area and park alongside the road.

From Highway 134/Ventura Freeway in Burbank, take the Forest Lawn Drive exit. Turn right and drive one block to Zoo Drive. Turn left and go 0.2 miles to Griffith Park Drive. Turn right and continue 1.4 miles to the signed Mineral Wells Picnic Area. Park alongside the road.

The hike

At the trailhead is a 3-way junction. The Mineral Wells Trail heads left and right, connecting the Bill Eckert Trail by the Old Zoo with Mount Hollywood Drive. For this hike, bear right and immediately go left onto the unsigned North Trail. Switchback to the left and curve around a water tank to views of Burbank, Glendale, the Verdugo Mountains, and the majestic San Gabriel Mountains. At a half mile is a trail split. The North Trail continues to the right. For a short detour, head left into Amir's Garden, a lush oasis on the southeast mountain slope.

Return to the North Trail and continue uphill. Follow the ridge overlooking the Griffith Park Boys Camp (in the canyon to the left) to a T-junction by a water tank. The right fork leads to the terraced hillside of the Toyon Canyon Restoration Project. Go to the left, curving around the right side of the water tank. Walk 100 yards to an unmarked junction at one mile. The Mount Hollywood Trail continues straight ahead up the hill (Hike 6).

For this hike, veer right on the Toyon Trail, a footpath. Descend between Royce's Canyon on the left and Toyon Canyon on the right, dropping down to paved Mount Hollywood Drive. Stay on the dirt path, parallel to the road. As Mount Hollywood Drive makes a horseshoe left bend, continue straight on the footpath past eucalyptus, oak, and pine groves. Cross a utility road and take the signed bridle trail. Top a rise to a vista across the entire San Fernando Valley. At a fork, stay on the Toyon Trail to the right. Stroll along the toyon-covered hillside, and descend among pines, oaks, and bay laurel to a junction at 2 miles. The left fork leads 150 feet to gated Mount Hollywood Drive at Zoo Drive. Go to the right on the Mineral Wells Trail. Steadily loose elevation, following the old paved road for 200 yards. Stay to the left, picking up the dirt trail again. Cross a concrete spillway and meander through the forest above Mineral Wells Picnic Area, completing the loop at the trailhead. ■

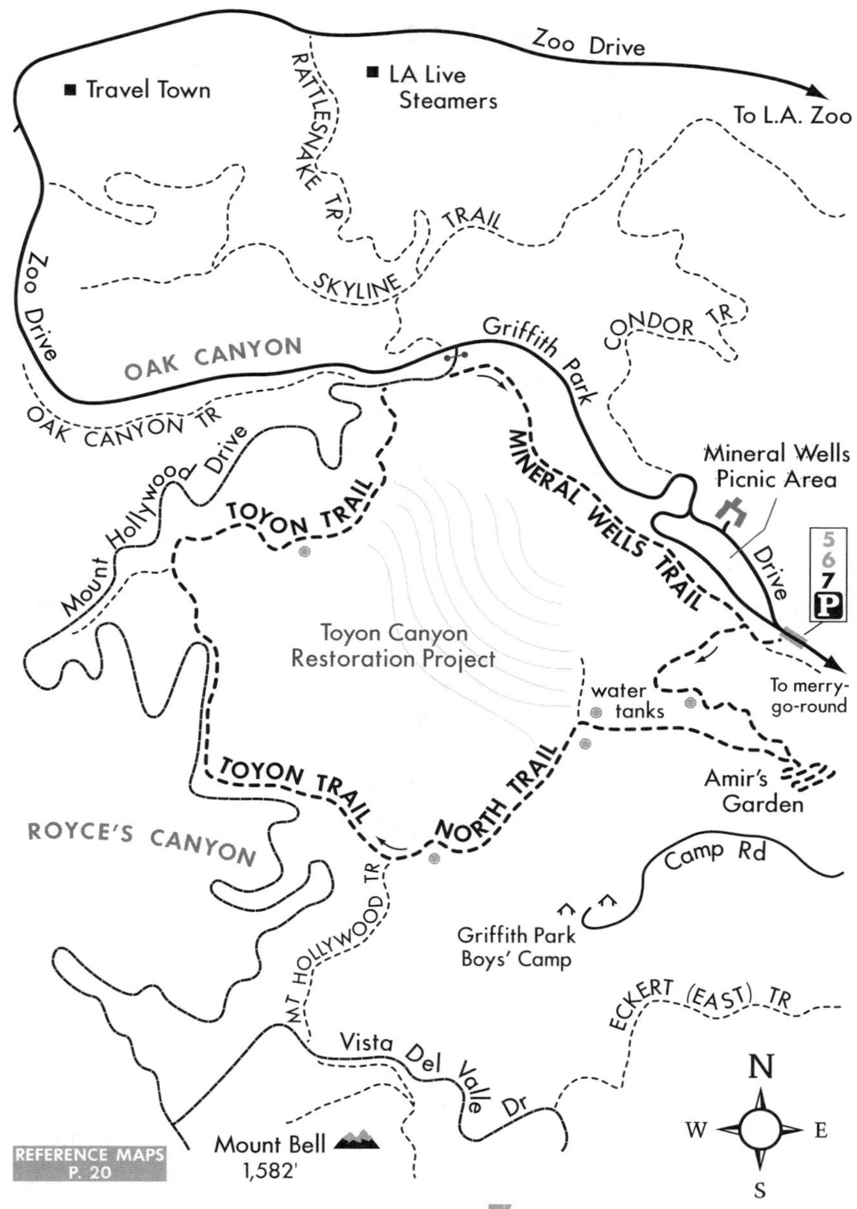

7.

Mineral Wells—Toyon Trail Loop

GRIFFITH PARK

8. Glendale Peak from the Riverside Trail

GRIFFITH PARK: Los Angeles

Hiking distance: 2.8 miles round trip
Hiking time: 1.5 hours
Configuration: out-and-back
Elevation gain: 400 feet
Exposure: exposed hills
Difficulty: easy to moderate
Dogs: allowed
Maps: U.S.G.S. Hollywood and Burbank • Map and Guide of Griffith Park
Hileman's Recreational & Geological Map of Griffith Park

Glendale Peak is a 1,184-foot mountain on the southeast corner of Griffith Park between Mount Hollywood and Beacon Hill. From the peak are sweeping vistas that span from downtown Los Angeles to Glendale and from the San Gabriel Valley to the Pacific Ocean. A short, quarter-mile memorial trail climbs to the summit of Glendale Peak. The narrow footpath—Henry's Trail—is named for the late Henry Shamma, former chairman of the Sierra Club. (He was also a long-time friend of Amir Dialameh, who created Amir's Garden from Hike 5.) Henry worked on many of Griffith Park's trails and gardens. This hike begins on the Riverside Trail, traversing the mountain slopes with views of the nearby Griffith Park Observatory. For an extended hike, the East Ridge (Hogback) Trail connects Glendale Peak to Dante's View and Mount Hollywood, following the ridge of the steep hillside.

To the trailhead

From the intersection of Los Feliz Boulevard and Vermont Avenue in Hollywood, drive 0.7 miles north on Vermont Avenue to Commonwealth Canyon Drive on the right. It is located just before the Greek Theatre. (En route, Vermont Avenue curves into Vermont Canyon Road.) Turn right on Commonwealth Canyon Drive, and go 0.15 miles to the parking lot for the Vermont Canyon tennis courts on the left. Turn left and park.

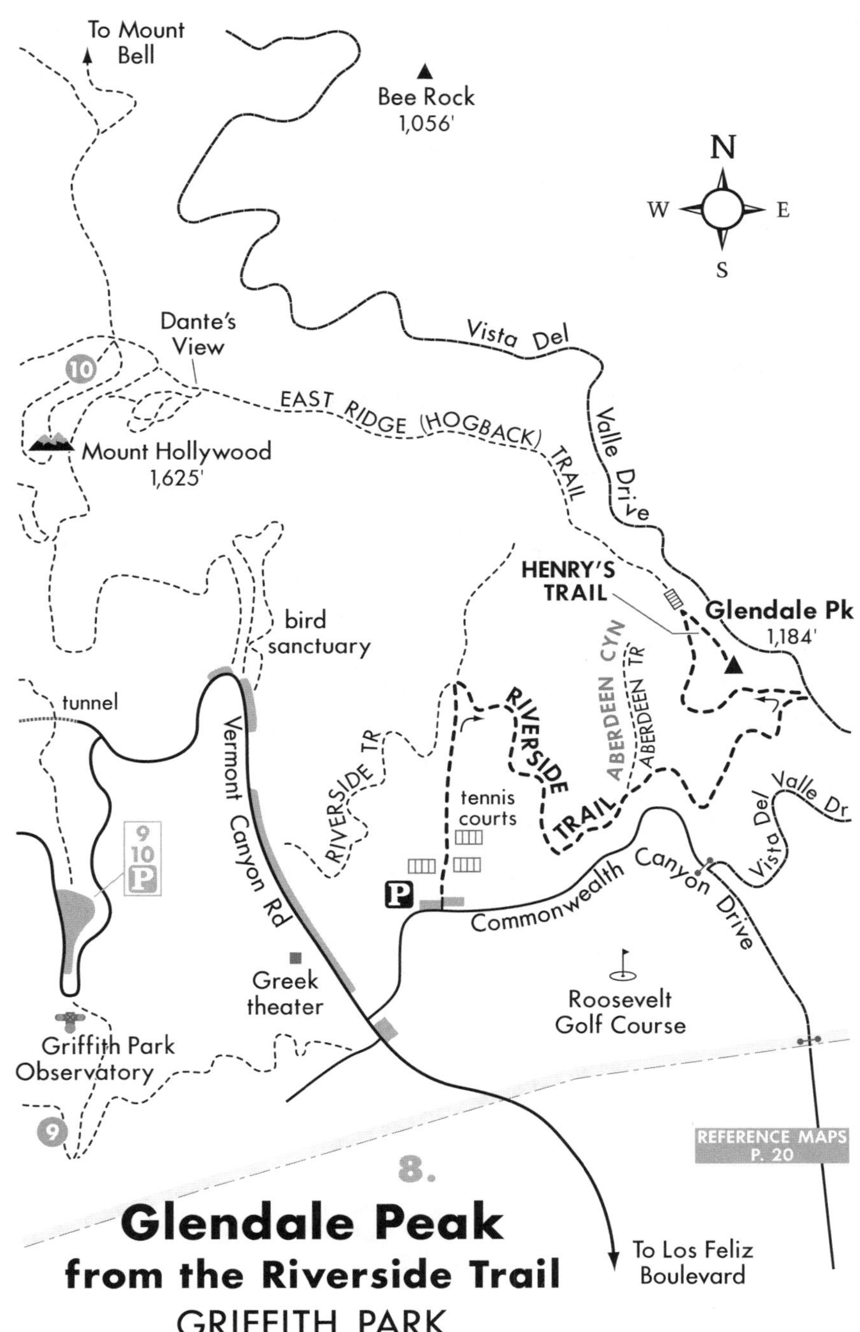

8. Glendale Peak from the Riverside Trail

GRIFFITH PARK

The hike

Walk up the paved lane between the tennis courts to a 3-way junction with the Riverside Trail (formerly called the Aberdeen Trail). The footpath straight ahead is a dead-end path that leads to the north end of the canyon. To the left, the Riverside Trail leads to Vermont Canyon Road south of the bird sanctuary.

Take the right fork of the Riverside Trail. Traverse the hillside slope on a gentle uphill grade to an overlook of downtown Los Angeles, Hollywood, the Hollywood Hills, and the Griffith Park Observatory. Follow the contours of the hillside, and slowly descend into Aberdeen Canyon. At the mouth of the canyon, the Aberdeen Trail, a narrow footpath spur, veers left up the canyon. Stay on the Riverside Trail straight ahead, and ascend the hillside to a junction with Vista Del Valle Drive at one mile. Take the switchback to the left on the East Ridge (Hogback) Trail, savoring the views overlooking the entire Los Angeles basin. Loop clockwise around Glendale Peak to a metal bridge over a narrow ridge at the head of Aberdeen Canyon. From the bridge is a view below of Fern Canyon, Beacon Hill, and the merry-go-round. Just before crossing the bridge, bear sharply right on Henry's Trail, the access trail to Glendale Peak. Take the footpath and follow the ridge south 0.1 mile to the 1,184-foot summit, where there are great 360-degree views. Return by retracing your route.

To extend the hike from the bridge, the East Ridge (Hogback) Trail steeply climbs the serpentine spine of the mountain 0.8 miles to Dante's View, then a short distance farther to the overlook atop Mount Hollywood. Throughout the hike are spectacular vistas. ■

9. Griffith Park Observatory to Ferndell Park

GRIFFITH PARK: Los Angeles

Hiking distance: 2.5 miles round trip
Hiking time: 1.5 hours
Configuration: out-and-back with central loop
Elevation gain: 500 feet
Exposure: exposed hills and sun-filtered shade in Ferndell Park
Difficulty: easy to slightly moderate
Dogs: allowed
Maps: U.S.G.S. Hollywood · Map and Guide of Griffith Park
Hileman's Recreational & Geological Map of Griffith Park

map page 47

The copper-domed Griffith Park Observatory is a Los Angeles landmark and one of Griffith Park's most popular attractions. The historic observatory is perched on the south-facing slope of Mount Hollywood overlooking the city. The facilities include a planetarium, laser programs, gift shop, and a variety of science displays. An observation deck with telescopes winds around the south side of this architectural landmark, with views across Hollywood and the expansive metropolitan area.

This hike begins at the observatory and descends the mountain slope to the waterway in Ferndell Park. The park is a lush, stream-fed oasis in Western Canyon down the hillside from the observatory. The upper portion of the park is a shaded glen with mature oaks, sycamores, spruce, alders, and coast redwoods. At the southern end of the park is an exotic tropical garden with a stone-lined path, a tree-shaded brook, charming footbridges, small waterfalls, stone retaining walls, a variety of ferns, succulents, and moss-covered rocks.

To the trailhead

OPTION 1: From Los Feliz Boulevard in Hollywood, take Fern Dell Drive north 2.3 miles to the Griffith Park Observatory parking lot. (Fern Dell Drive becomes Western Canyon Road after the hairpin turn.)

OPTION 2: From Los Feliz Boulevard in Hollywood, take Vermont Avenue north 1.8 miles to the observatory parking lot.

(En route, Vermont Avenue curves into Vermont Canyon Road.) Both directions offer a beautiful, curving drive through Griffith Park.

The hike

From the parking lot, walk towards the observatory. Take the unpaved trail to the left (east) of the magnificent structure to an overlook and trail split at a quarter mile. The left fork descends to the Greek Theater at Vermont Canyon Road. For this hike, bear right another quarter mile to a second junction. Begin the loop to the right on the West Observatory Trail, a dirt road. Continue down the hillside, leaving the chaparral-clad hillside into forested Western Canyon at Ferndell Park (also known as Fern Dell). At the canyon floor is an old adobe restroom and a junction with the East Observatory Trail, our return route.

For now, detour down canyon to the south through Ferndell Park under towering sycamore and oak trees. Pass through the picnic grounds to the brook. Stroll along the quarter-mile path, meandering along the park's stream, crossing over bridges, passing waterfalls and pools, and meandering through the lush gardens and glen.

Return to the trail junction by the adobe restroom, and now take the East Observatory Trail. Climb up the side canyon under the three domes of the observatory, completing the loop. Bear right and return a half mile to the trailhead at the observatory. ■

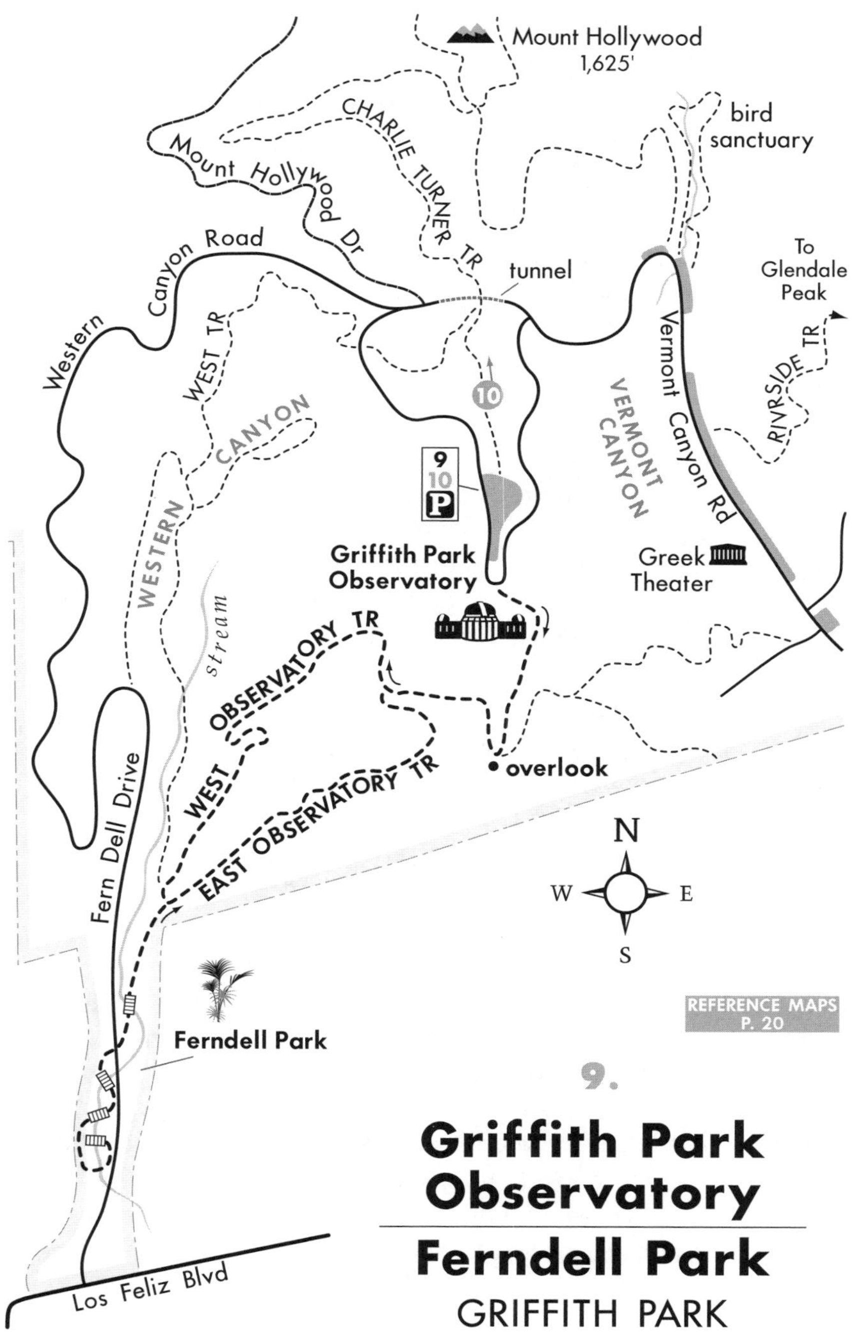

9.

Griffith Park Observatory

Ferndell Park

GRIFFITH PARK

10. Mount Hollywood and Dante's View

CHARLIE TURNER TRAIL from the GRIFFITH PARK OBSERVATORY

GRIFFITH PARK: Los Angeles

Hiking distance: 3 miles round trip
Hiking time: 1.5 hours
Configuration: out-and-back with loop
Elevation gain: 500 feet
Exposure: exposed hills
Difficulty: easy to moderate
Dogs: allowed
Maps: U.S.G.S. Hollywood and Burbank • Map and Guide of Griffith Park
Hileman's Recreational & Geological Map of Griffith Park

map page 51

Mount Hollywood, the highest peak in Griffith Park, is perched at 1,625 feet in elevation. From the bald, flat summit is an overlook with commanding vistas of the Los Angeles basin, the San Fernando Valley, the San Gabriel Mountains, the majestic Griffith Park Observatory, and a view of the landmark "HOLLYWOOD" sign.

East of Mount Hollywood is Dante's View, a terraced, two-acre garden oasis planted in 1964 by Dante Orgolini, a Brazilian-born Italian immigrant. Dante maintained and cared for the garden until he died in 1978. Charlie Turner became caretaker of the famed arboretum for 15 years until he passed away in 1997. The picturesque garden has been maintained since by volunteers. The south-facing Dante's View overlooks the observatory with picnic benches and shade trees along its intertwining trail.

The Charlie Turner Trail, arguably the most popular trail in the park, connects the Griffith Park Observatory with the lookout atop Mount Hollywood and Dante's View. This hike begins just north of the historic observatory, built in 1935. The triple-domed landmark has excellent science exhibits, a planetarium, gift shop, and an observation deck with telescopes. Throughout the hike are panoramic vistas. Mount Hollywood can also be accessed from the north via several other routes. (See Hike 4 for one option.)

To the trailhead

OPTION 1: From Los Feliz Boulevard in Hollywood, take Fern Dell Drive north 2.3 miles to the Griffith Park Observatory parking lot. (Fern Dell Drive becomes Western Canyon Road after the hairpin turn.)

OPTION 2: From Los Feliz Boulevard in Hollywood, take Vermont Avenue north 1.8 miles to the observatory parking lot. (En route, Vermont Avenue curves into Vermont Canyon Road.) Both directions offer a beautiful, curving drive through Griffith Park.

Griffith Park Observatory
2800 East Observatory Road • Los Angeles 213-473-0800 • general information
Hours:
Wednesday—Friday • Noon—10 p.m. Saturday—Sunday • 10 a.m.—10 p.m. Monday—Tuesday • closed closed on major holidays (call ahead to confirm)
Admission:
free to observatory • small admission to planetarium
History of Griffith Park:
Griffith J. Griffith donated over 3,000 acres to create this parkland in 1896. Griffith was a Welsh immigrant who made his fortune in mine speculation. Additional land acquisitions since this time have expanded the park to 4,217 acres, making it the largest municipal park in the United States.
Attractions within the Park:
Griffith Park Observatory • Greek Theater Los Angeles Zoo and Botanical Gardens Travel Town Transportation Museum • Los Angeles Live Steamers Griffith Park and Southern Railroad (miniature railroad) Autry National Center • Los Angeles Equestrian Center Historic 1926 Merry-Go-Round • golf courses Griffith Park Boys' Camp • Camp Hollywoodland (girls' camp) Bird Sanctuary • Amir's Garden • Ferndell Park The Hollywood Sign • Bronson Caves

The hike

From the parking lot, hike north (opposite from the observatory) to the well-marked and landscaped Charlie Turner trailhead. Climb the tree-lined ridge between Vermont Canyon and Western Canyon to the Berlin Forest, a friendship park between the people of Berlin and Los Angeles. From the pine-dotted knoll with picnic benches are great views across Los Angeles. Cross over the Vermont Canyon Road tunnel. Meander up the sage- and chaparral-covered hillside at an easy grade. At the hairpin right bend is a close-up view of the "HOLLYWOOD" sign.

At 0.8 miles is a 4-way junction on the ridge below Mount Hollywood. Begin a clockwise loop on the left fork. Pass Captain's Roost on the left by a row of towering palm trees. The landscaped plateau offers additional vistas across Los Angeles. Continue uphill to the north (back) side of Mount Hollywood to another 4-way junction. The two trails on the right form a short 0.2-mile loop to the 1,625-foot summit. From the flat, rounded peak are 360-degree vistas, including a picture-perfect view of the observatory.

After marveling at the views, return to the 4-way junction. Curve right (east), skirting the elevated picnic area on the knoll. Descend 100 yards to a junction at Dante's View. The Hogback (East Ridge) Trail continues straight ahead to Glendale Peak (Hike 8). The landscaped two-acre garden takes in the southeast corner, with access from both trails. After exploring the terraced slope, continue southwest on the loop around Mount Hollywood, completing the loop on the ridge below the summit. Return down the hill, retracing your route. ■

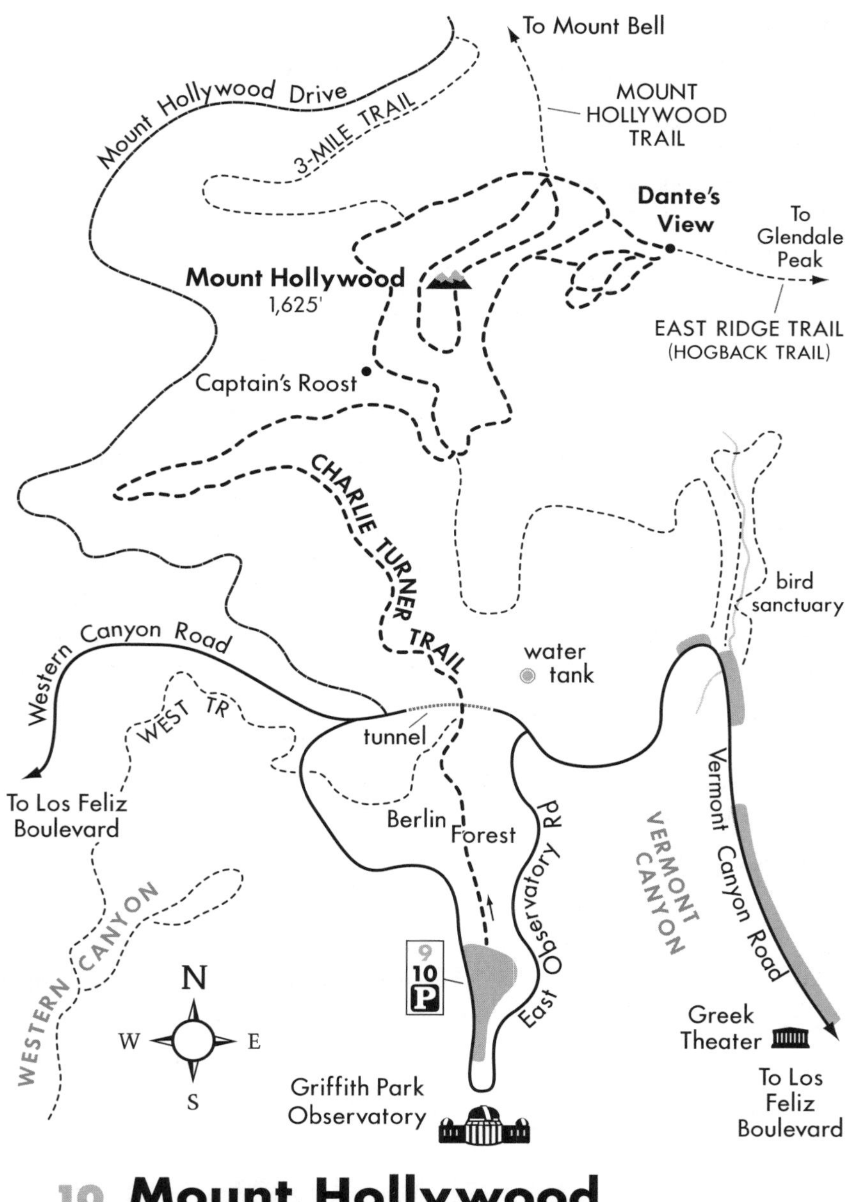

10. Mount Hollywood

Dante's View

GRIFFITH PARK

REFERENCE MAPS P. 20

11. Bronson Caves

GRIFFITH PARK: Los Angeles

Hiking distance: 0.6 miles round trip
Hiking time: 0.5 hours
Configuration: out-and-back
Elevation gain: 40 feet
Exposure: exposed
Difficulty: very easy
Dogs: allowed
Maps: U.S.G.S. Hollywood · Map and Guide of Griffith Park
Hileman's Recreational & Geological Map of Griffith Park

At the southwest corner of Griffith Park is a short, historical hike to one of Hollywood's most frequently filmed caves—the Bronson Caves. First used as a quarry in 1907, the crushed rock from the area was used to pave the streets of a growing Hollywood. The quarry ceased operation in the late 1920s, leaving the manmade caves. The two caves were originally made as an access tunnel through the huge rock, which sat within the abandoned quarry. The tunnels were used to reach the granite cliffs as a source for crushed rock. Many western and science fiction movies have shot on location at these caves, including *Star Trek*, *Mission Impossible*, *Gunsmoke*, *Bonanza*, *Little House on the Prairie*, and the *Batman* series.

To the trailhead

At the intersection of Hollywood Boulevard and Western Avenue in Hollywood, drive 0.5 miles west on Hollywood Boulevard to Bronson Avenue. Turn right (north) and continue 1.5 miles on Bronson Avenue (which merges with Canyon Drive) past Bronson Park to the end of the road. Park in the lot on the left.

The hike

From the parking lot, hike back along the park road 100 feet to the trailhead on the left (east) side of the road. The trail gently climbs a quarter mile to the caves backed by granite cliffs. From here you may walk through the caves and around the hill. Return along the same path.

To extend the hike, a trail heads north from the end of Canyon Drive into Brush Canyon (Hike 12). ■

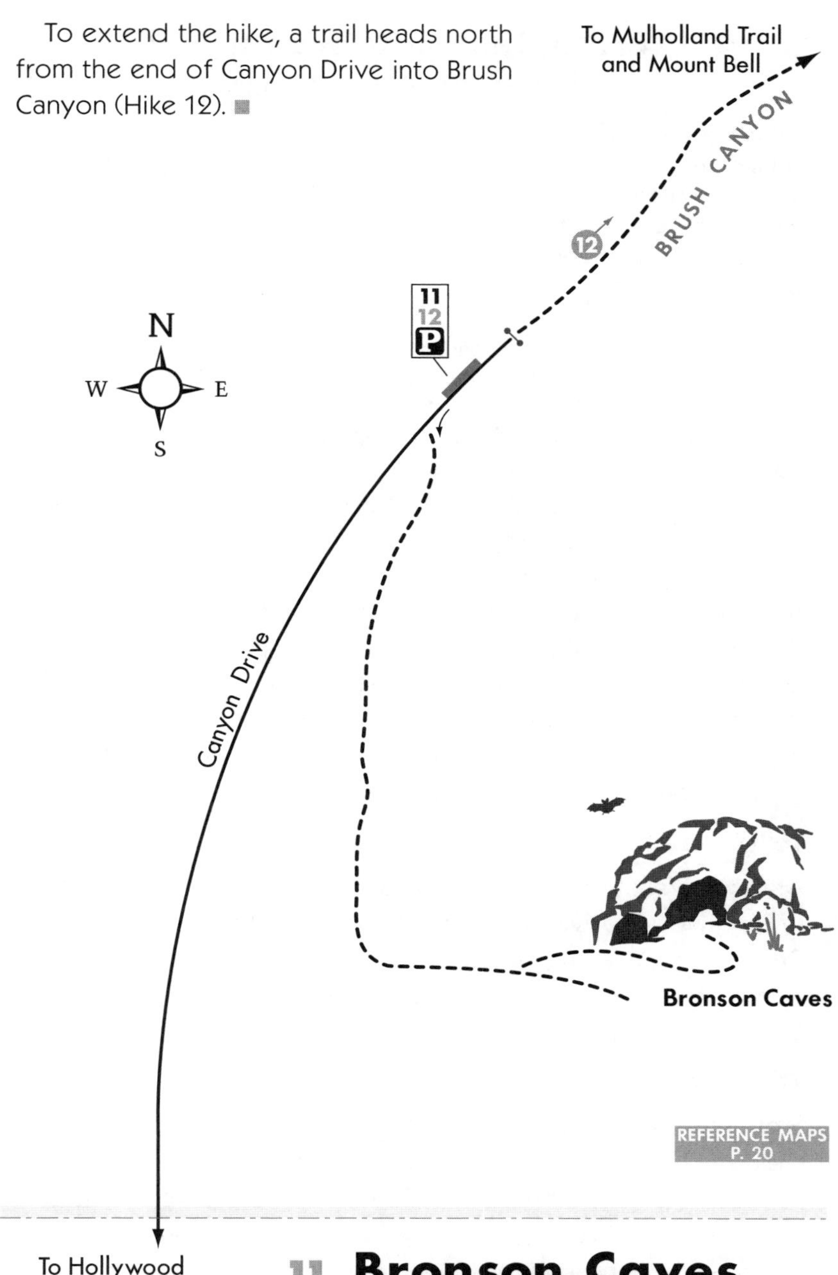

11. Bronson Caves

GRIFFITH PARK

12. Brush Canyon to Mount Bell

GRIFFITH PARK: Los Angeles

Hiking distance: 3.3 miles round trip
Hiking time: 2.5 hours
Configuration: out-and-back
Elevation gain: 850 feet
Exposure: shaded canyon and exposed hills
Difficulty: moderate
Dogs: allowed
Maps: U.S.G.S. Hollywood and Burbank • Map and Guide of Griffith Park
Hileman's Recreational & Geological Map of Griffith Park

map page 56

Brush Canyon is a beautiful yet lightly traveled trail from the southwest corner of Griffith Park. This hike begins from the north end of Canyon Drive and winds through a forest of large sycamore and oak trees in the canyon. The trail climbs into a drier chaparral and shrub terrain in the undeveloped mountainous interior of Griffith Park, leading up the southwest slope of Mount Bell. The 1,582-foot peak is located in the geographic center of Griffith Park. From the summit are fantastic views of secluded canyons, Hollywood, and the Los Angeles Basin. Mount Bell can also be accessed from the Mineral Wells Picnic Area (Hike 6) or from the park's merry-go-round.

To the trailhead

At the intersection of Hollywood Boulevard and Western Avenue in Hollywood, drive 0.5 miles west on Hollywood Boulevard to Bronson Avenue. Turn right and continue 1.5 miles on Bronson Avenue (which merges with Canyon Drive) past Bronson Park to the end of the road. Park in the lot on the left.

The hike

From the parking lot, walk uphill on the road to the north. Pass the vehicle gate and continue on the unpaved fire road parallel to Brush Creek. The fire road follows along the perennial stream in a thicket of oak, manzanita, and sage. Pass the Pacific Electric Quarry and bend right (east), crossing over the creek to an expansive park and picnic area on the right at a quarter mile. After passing the park, climb out of the canyon, leaving the shade of the forest for the drought-resistant shrubs and a view of Mount Lee and the "HOLLYWOOD" sign. Continue up the canyon wall, with views of Mount Hollywood and Mount Bell, reaching the Mulholland Trail junction at one mile. To the left, the Mulholland Trail heads 1.5 miles west to the "HOLLYWOOD" sign on Mount Lee (Hike 13). Take the Mulholland Trail to the right 0.3 miles to Mount Hollywood Drive, a paved and gated road.

To continue up the final ascent to Mount Bell, take Mount Hollywood Drive 0.1 mile to the left. Pick up the dirt path on the right, and head up the slope. Stay to the right at a junction on a saddle and skirt the south flank of Mount Bell. To ascend the 1,582-foot summit, watch for a narrow path that scrambles through brush to the peak. Return by retracing your steps. ■

13. Mount Lee and the "Hollywood" sign

GRIFFITH PARK: Los Angeles

Hiking distance: 3 miles round trip
Hiking time: 1.5 hours
Configuration: out-and-back
Elevation gain: 550 feet
Exposure: exposed hillside and ridges
Difficulty: easy to moderate
Dogs: allowed
Maps: U.S.G.S. Hollywood and Burbank • Map and Guide of Griffith Park

map page 56

This hike up the Hollyridge Trail leads to the famous "HOLLYWOOD" sign on the south slope of Mount Lee in the far west end of Griffith Park. The historic Los Angeles landmark was originally built in the 1920s to read "HOLLYWOODLAND" to promote real estate development in Beachwood Canyon. In 1978, entertainment celebrities donated money to replace the original sign, which was worn from time, weather, and vandalism. The sign now measures 50 feet high by 450 feet long. It sits just below the Mount Lee summit. The sign itself is fenced off from direct visitation, but the views from atop Mount Lee are superb. The vistas extend across the Los Angeles basin and the San Fernando Valley.

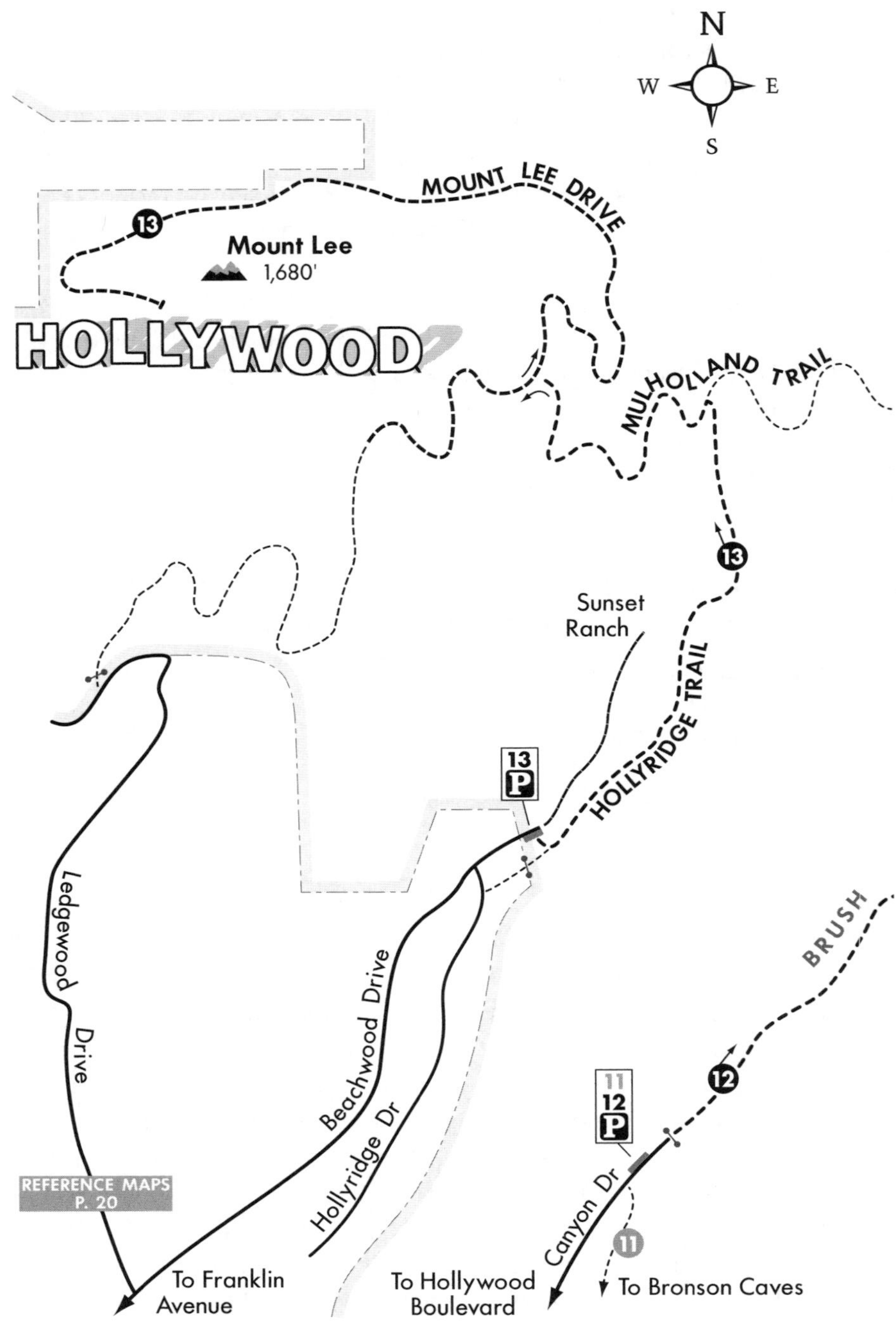
N
W
E
S
MOUNT LEE DRIVE
13
Mount Lee
1,680'
HOLLYWOOD
MULHOLLAND TRAIL
13
Sunset
Ranch
HOLLYRIDGE TRAIL
13
P
BRUSH
Ledgewood
Drive
Beachwood Drive
Hollyridge Dr
12
11
12
P
Canyon Dr
11
REFERENCE MAPS
P. 20
To Franklin
Avenue
To Hollywood
Boulevard
To Bronson Caves

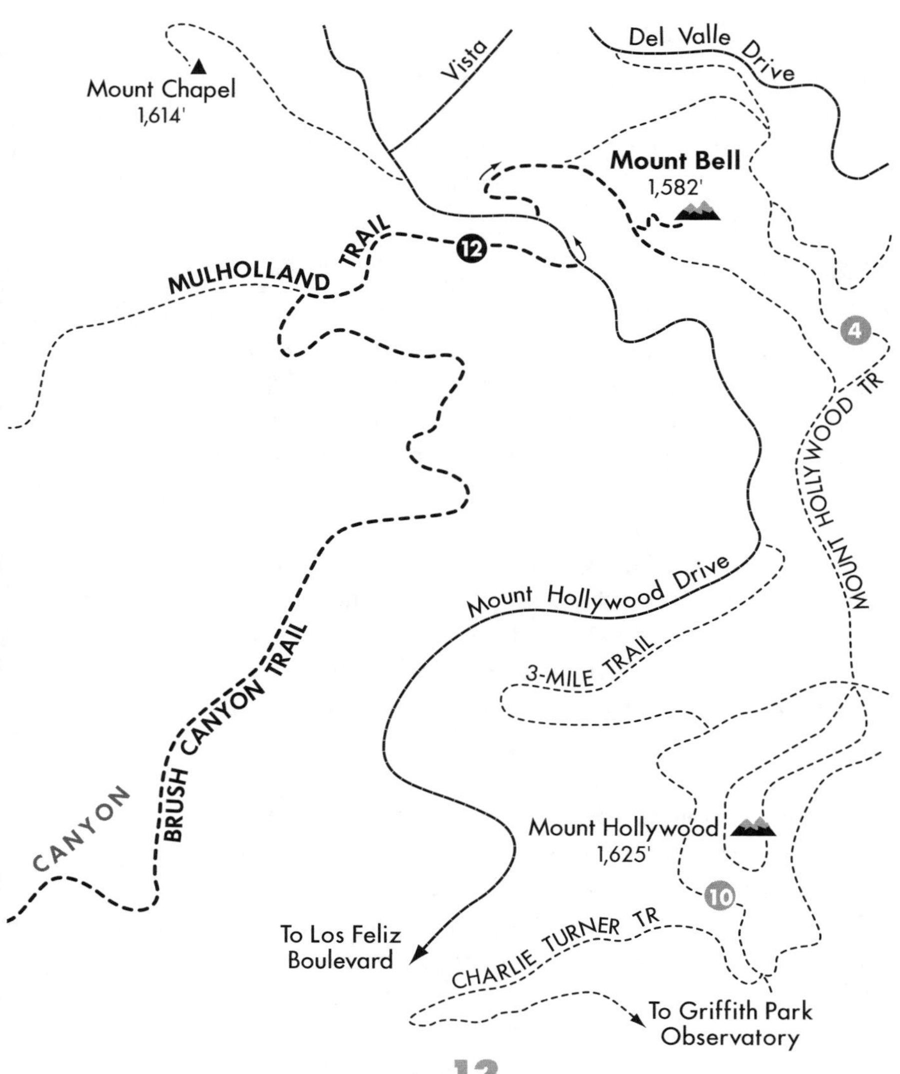

12.

Brush Canyon to Mount Bell

13.

Mount Lee and the "Hollywood" sign

GRIFFITH PARK

To the trailhead

At the intersection of Franklin Avenue and Western Avenue in Hollywood, drive 0.7 miles west on Franklin Avenue to Beachwood Drive. Turn right (north) and continue 1.8 miles up Beachwood Drive to the signed trailhead parking area on the right at the end of the public road.

The hike

Head up the signed slope to a T-junction on a ridge overlooking Hollywood and Los Angeles. From the ridge is a picture-perfect view of the "HOLLYWOOD" sign. The right fork descends to the old trailhead access, which is now fenced off. Bear left and follow the ridge northeast, overlooking the Sunset Horse Ranch on the left and a view of the Griffith Park Observatory to the right. Continue 0.5 miles to an intersection with the unmarked Mulholland Trail. The right fork leads to Brush Canyon and Mount Bell (Hike 12). Take a sharp left up the Mulholland Trail as it heads west. The winding fire road leads 0.3 miles to the paved and gated Mount Lee Drive. The left fork leads a short distance to an excellent frontal view of the sign. Go uphill to the right and steadily climb to the ridge. Head west along the north slope of Mount Lee, overlooking the San Fernando Valley. Pass below the telecommunication towers atop Mount Lee to a horseshoe left bend. Loop around the bend to the end of the road, perched above and 30 yards behind the "HOLLYWOOD" sign. A fence prohibits access to the sign (along with several warnings), but there is a view of the back of the towering letters and the skeletal support structure. The vistas extend across the Los Angeles basin to the south and the San Fernando Valley to the north. Return along the same route. ■

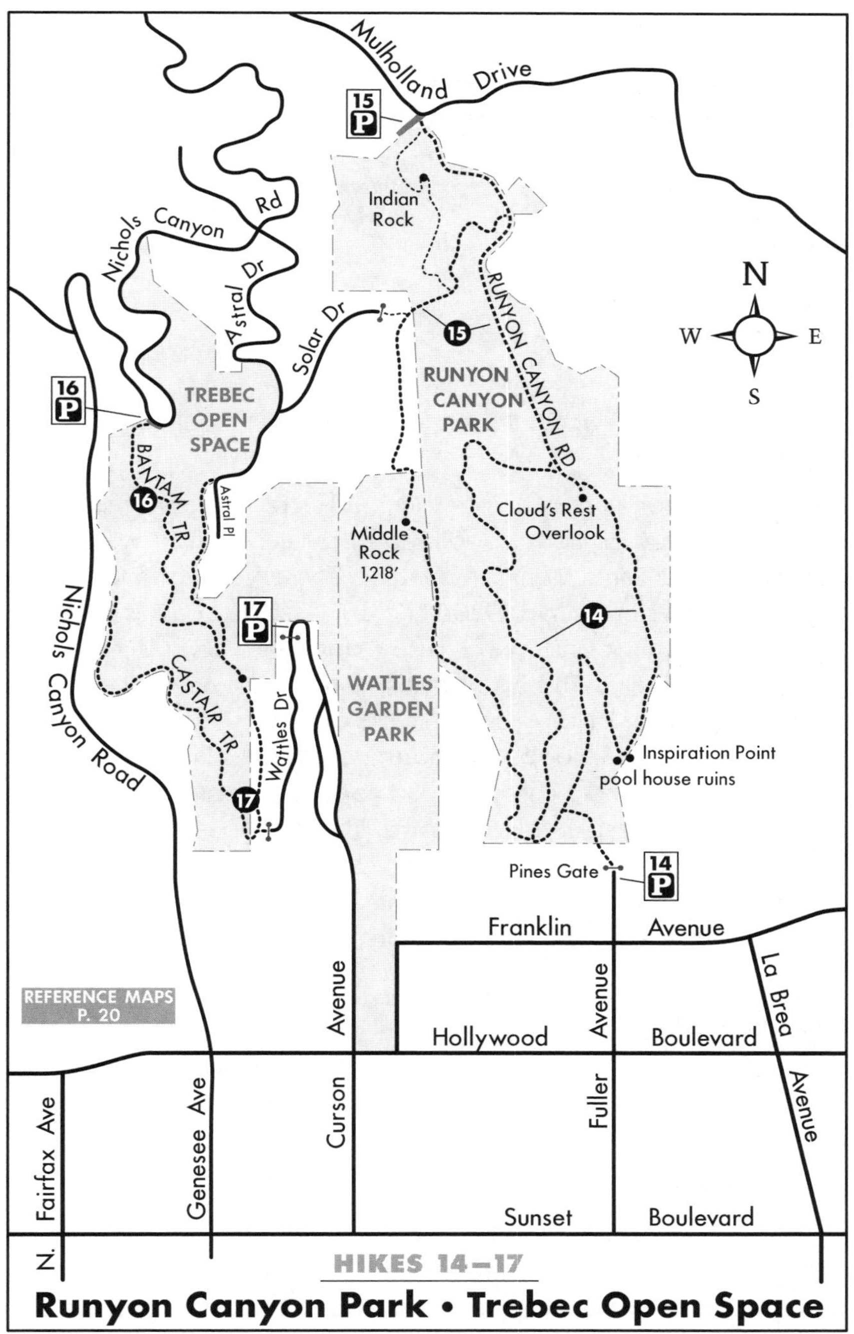
Mulholland Drive
15 P
Indian Rock
Nichols Canyon Rd
Astral Dr
Solar Dr
15
RUNYON CANYON RD
RUNYON CANYON PARK
N
W
E
S
16 P
TREBEC OPEN SPACE
BANTAM TR
16
Astral Pl
Cloud's Rest Overlook
Middle Rock 1,218′
17 P
14
CASTAIR TR
Wattles Dr
WATTLES GARDEN PARK
Nichols Canyon Road
Inspiration Point
pool house ruins
17
Pines Gate
14 P
Franklin Avenue
La Brea Avenue
REFERENCE MAPS P. 20
Avenue
Avenue
Hollywood Boulevard
N. Fairfax Ave
Genesee Ave
Curson
Fuller
Sunset Boulevard
HIKES 14—17
Runyon Canyon Park • Trebec Open Space

14. Runyon Canyon Loop from Fuller Avenue

RUNYON CANYON PARK: Lower Trailhead

Los Angeles

Hiking distance: 2-mile loop
Hiking time: 1 hour
Configuration: loop
Elevation gain: 500 feet
Exposure: exposed hills
Difficulty: easy
Dogs: allowed
Maps: U.S.G.S. Hollywood · Runyon Canyon Park map
Trails Illustrated Santa Monica Mountains Nat'l. Rec. Area

Runyon Canyon Park is a sprawling 130-acre preserve minutes from the heart of Hollywood. The popular preserve was purchased by the Santa Monica Mountains Conservancy and the city of Los Angeles in the mid 1980s. The off-leash dog park is among the most popular and heavily used open spaces in the Santa Monica Mountains. This hike begins from the lower trailhead at the north end of Fuller Ave, just two blocks north of Hollywood Boulevard. The trail loops around the chaparral-clad hillsides of Runyon Canyon and crosses a broad gorge overlooking the urban canyon wilderness and Hollywood. The loop passes the ruins of a pool house designed by Frank Lloyd Wright and occupied by Errol Flynn in the late 1950s. Remnants of the old foundation, tennis courts, and exotic landscaping are all that remain of the ruined oasis.

To the trailhead

At the intersection of Franklin Avenue and Highland Avenue in Hollywood, drive 0.3 miles west on Franklin to Fuller Avenue. Turn right (north) and continue 0.5 miles to The Pines gate at the end of the road. Park along the street where a space is available.

The hike

Walk through The Pines entrance gate at the north end of Fuller Avenue into Runyon Canyon Park. A short distance past the

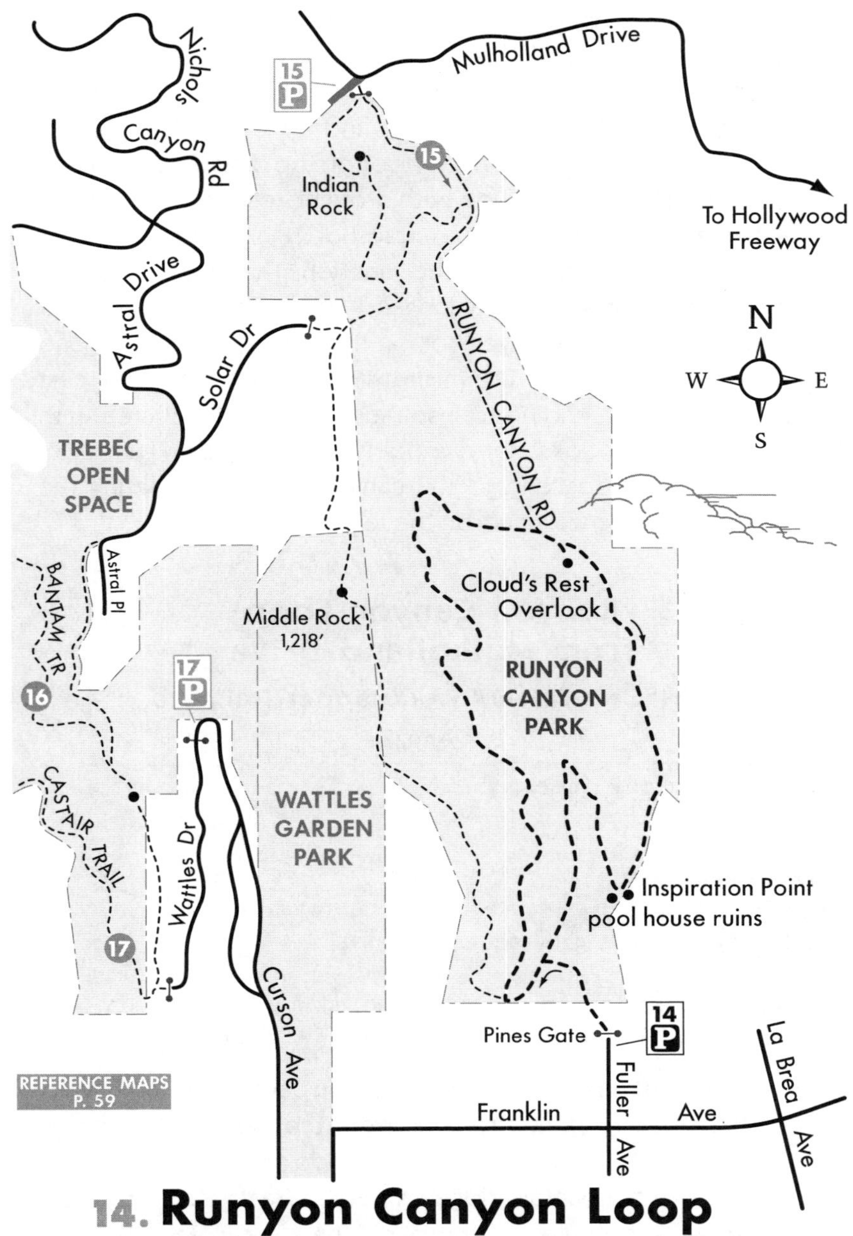

14. Runyon Canyon Loop from Fuller Avenue (Lower Trailhead)

RUNYON CANYON PARK

entrance is a trail junction. Begin the loop to the left, hiking clockwise. Curve along the south end of the park to a second trail split. The left fork, straight ahead, climbs the west ridge of Runyon Canyon (Hike 15). Instead, veer right and traverse the west canyon slope, parallel to the canyon floor on the paved path. Follow the chaparral-covered hillside with drought-resistant evergreens on a gentle uphill grade. Make a horseshoe right bend to the east side of the canyon and a posted junction. The left fork climbs to the upper trailhead at Mulholland Drive. For this hike, veer right to Cloud's Rest, an overlook on the right with benches and 360-degree panoramas. The main trail continues along the east canyon ridge, descending to Inspiration Point, a level area with a bench that overlooks Hollywood. Pass the Wright/Flynn pool house ruins, and descend to the canyon floor, completing the loop. Return to the trailhead on the left. ■

15. Runyon Canyon Loop from Mulholland Drive

RUNYON CANYON PARK: Upper Trailhead

Los Angeles

Hiking distance: 2.5-mile loop
Hiking time: 1.5 hours
Configuration: loop
Elevation gain: 500 feet
Exposure: exposed hills
Difficulty: easy to slightly moderate
Dogs: allowed
Maps: U.S.G.S. Hollywood • Runyon Canyon Park map
Trails Illustrated Santa Monica Mountains Nat'l Rec. Area

Runyon Canyon Park is a gorgeous mountain park in the Hollywood Hills. The 130-acre park stretches from the base of the mountains at the congested edge of Hollywood to Mulholland Drive atop the scenic mountain ridge. A vehicle-restricted fire road runs through the center of the park. The park is an extremely popular hiking, jogging, and off-leash dog-walking park. (It is especially crowded on weekends.) This hike begins from the upper

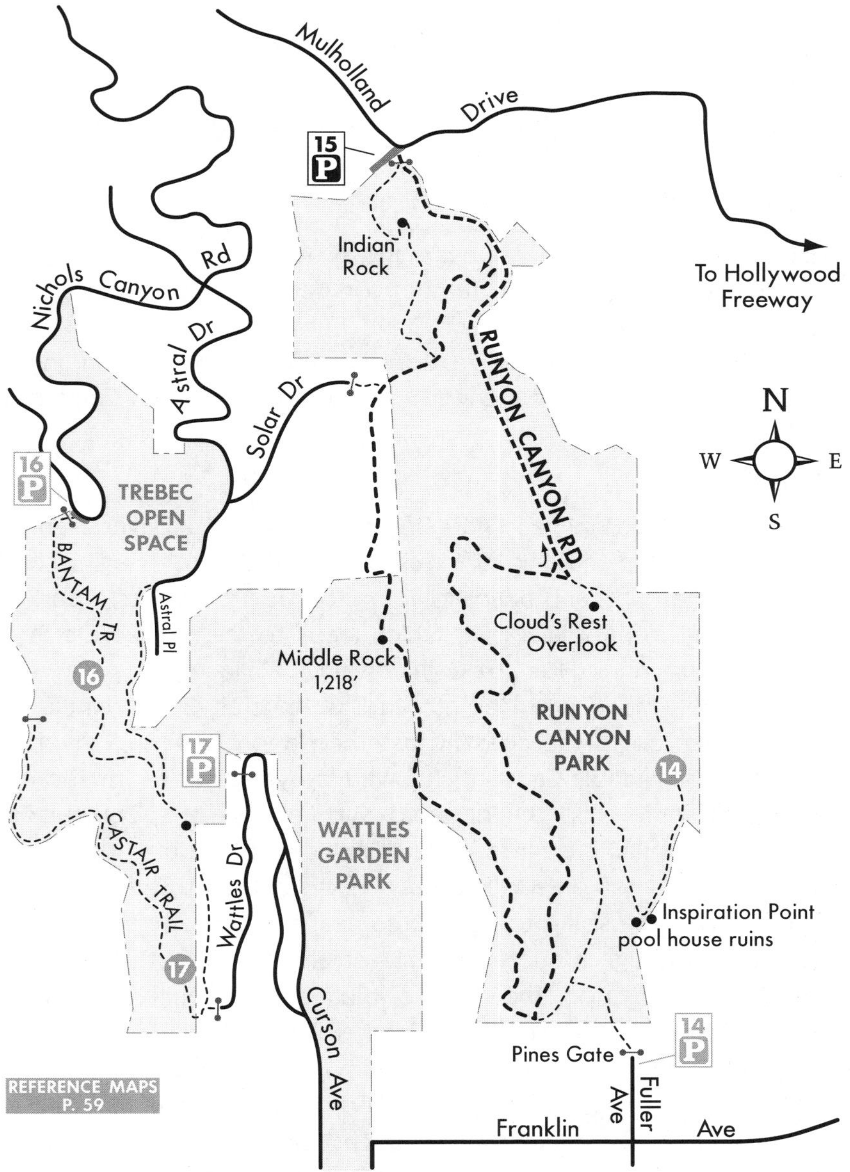

15. Runyon Canyon Loop from Mulholland Drive (Upper Trailhead)

RUNYON CANYON PARK

reaches of the park, with spectacular views of the surrounding hills, the "HOLLYWOOD" sign, Griffith Park Observatory, the San Gabriel Mountains, and the Los Angeles basin. The hike forms a loop along the west ridge of Runyon Canyon and returns up the canyon floor.

To the trailhead

From the Hollywood Freeway/Highway 101 in Hollywood, take the Barham Boulevard exit. Turn left on Cahuenga Boulevard and drive a half mile to Mulholland Drive. Turn right and an immediate left onto Mulholland Drive. Continue 1.5 miles on the winding road to the trailhead parking lot on the left at Runyon Canyon Road.

The hike

Pass through the trailhead gate and descend on the paved path. Skirt around Indian Rock to a trail split at 300 yards. Begin the loop to the right, and head uphill on the dirt road. Pass a park access trail from Solar Drive, which leads to the Trebec Open Space on the right (Hike 16). Gain elevation while enjoying views across Hollywood and downtown Los Angeles. Bend right as vistas open up to the coast. Cross the ridge between Runyon Canyon and Nichols Canyon, and weave over a rock formation. Continue south atop the ridge to Middle Rock, a spectacular overlook with 360-degree vistas. Using careful footing, sharply descend the knoll on a loose gravel and sand path. Steadily descend along the spine to a flat area near the bottom. Veer left and walk through a eucalyptus forest along the south face of the hill to a junction. The right fork leads to the Fuller Avenue Trailhead at the south end of the park (Hike 14).

Bear left on the paved path, and follow the west wall of Runyon Canyon on a gentle uphill grade. Wind up the canyon wall, and make a horseshoe right bend to the east side of the canyon and a posted junction. The right fork follows the lower loop, leading to Cloud's Rest and Inspiration Point. For this hike, curve left, staying on the paved path and completing the loop. Return to the trailhead 300 yards straight ahead. ■

16. Trebec Open Space

Upper Trailhead from NICHOLS CANYON ROAD

Los Angeles

Hiking distance: 2 miles round trip
Hiking time: 1 hour
Configuration: out-and-back
Elevation gain: 300 feet
Exposure: exposed hills
Difficulty: easy
Dogs: allowed
Maps: U.S.G.S. Hollywood • Trebec Open Space map

map page 67

What is Trebec Open Space? Answer: In 1998, Alex Trebec, host of the game show *Jeopardy*, donated these 62 undeveloped acres in the Hollywood Hills to the Santa Monica Mountains Conservancy. The pet-friendly open space has well-established fire roads and is open to hikers and mountain bikers. It is a great spot for a short hike without seeing crowds of people. This hike begins from the upper trailhead on Nichols Canyon Road and follows the Bantam Trail to an overlook. The knoll offers expansive views of the entire city, from the ocean to the San Gabriel Mountains. The hike can be easily extended into adjacent Runyon Canyon Park via Astral and Solar Drives.

To the trailhead

From Hollywood Boulevard and La Brea Avenue in Hollywood, drive 0.8 miles west on Hollywood Boulevard to Nichols Canyon Road. Turn right (north) and continue 1.3 miles to the dirt pullout on the right at a horseshoe left bend in the road. Park in the pullout by the trailhead.

The hike

Walk past the trailhead gate on the unsigned Bantam Trail, a fire road. Traverse the hillside slope on the east wall of Nichols Canyon. Bend left to a spectacular overlook of Los Angeles. Follow the trail south to a distinct junction at a half mile. Detour 100 yards straight ahead to an overlook of the entire city on a 1,000-foot knoll. The trail follows the ridge steeply downhill to Wattles

Drive (Hike 17) For this hike, return to the junction and take the horseshoe left bend. Continue uphill, staying on the west-facing cliff to the end of the trail at the corner of Astral Drive and Astral Place at one mile. Return by retracing your steps.

To extend the hike into Runyon Canyon Park, walk 250 yards up Astral Drive to Solar Drive. Go to the right and walk another 400 yards to the gated entrance of Runyon Canyon Park and a T-junction. The right fork descends to the lower (south) trailhead at Fuller Avenue (Hike 14). The left fork leads 0.4 miles to the upper (north) trailhead at Mulholland Drive (Hike 15). ■

17. Trebec Open Space

Lower Trailhead from WATTLES DRIVE

Los Angeles

Hiking distance: 1.9 miles round trip
Hiking time: 1 hour
Configuration: two out-and-back trails
Elevation gain: 250 feet
Exposure: exposed hills
Difficulty: easy
Dogs: allowed
Maps: U.S.G.S. Hollywood · Trebec Open Space map

map page 69

Trebec Open Space encompasses sixty-two acre of rolling terrain in the Hollywood Hills between Nichols Canyon and Runyon Canyon. The scenic land was generously donated by Alex Trebec, host of the game show *Jeopardy*. The pet-friendly parkland offers sweeping vistas across Los Angeles, including the downtown area, the Griffith Park Observatory, Santa Monica, and on clear days, the Palos Verdes Peninsula and Catalina Island. Although the open space abuts popular Runyon Canyon Park, it still provides privacy and solitude. The land contributes to the wildlife corridor for deer, coyotes, and other species to roam between the San Diego Freeway and Hollywood Freeway. This hike begins from the lower trailhead off of Curson Avenue and follows the

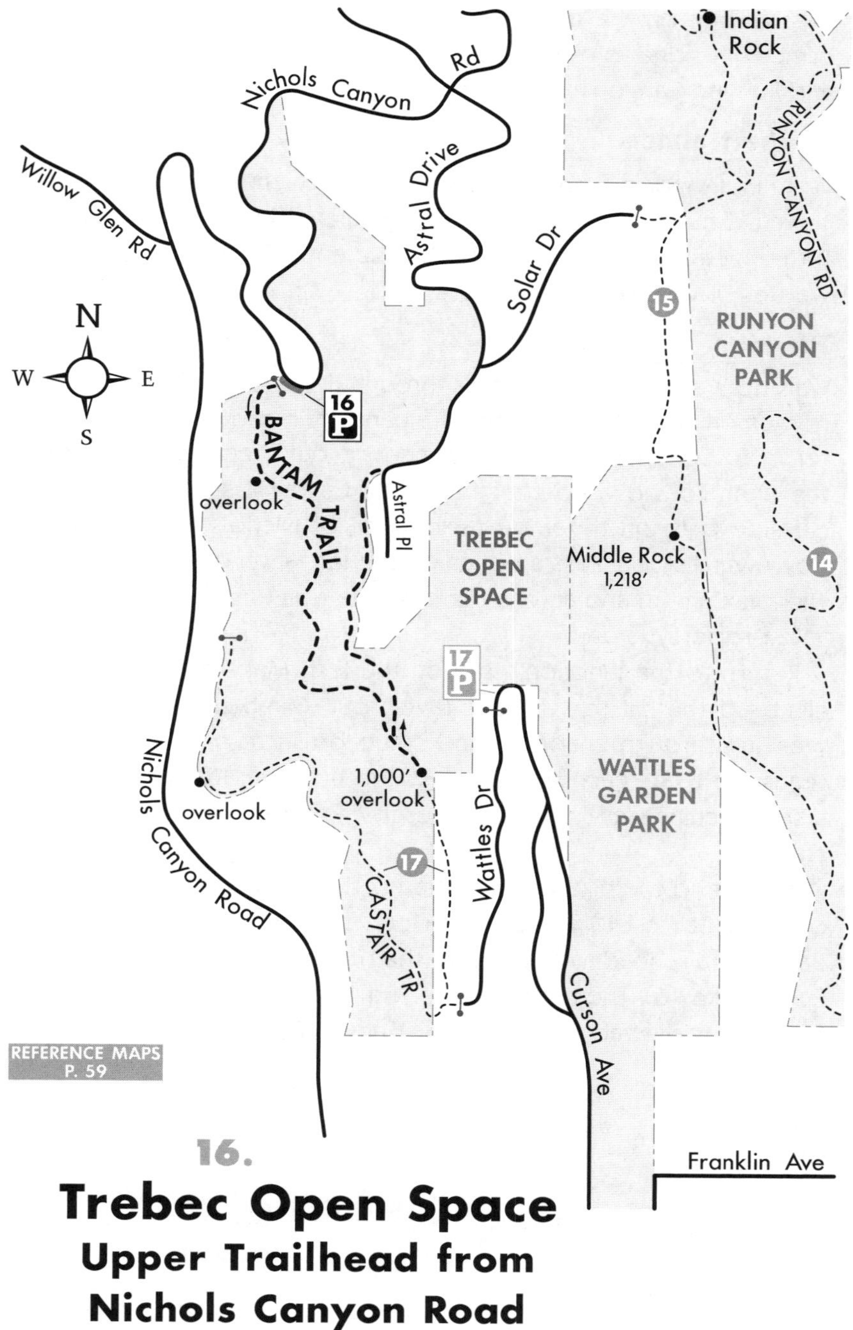

REFERENCE MAPS
P. 59

16.

Trebec Open Space

Upper Trailhead from Nichols Canyon Road

Castair Trail on the east wall of Nichols Canyon. The hike also climbs the ridge to overlooks and connects with the Bantam Trail and Runyon Canyon Park.

To the trailhead

From Hollywood Boulevard and La Brea Avenue in Hollywood, drive 0.6 miles west on Hollywood Boulevard to Curson Avenue. Turn right and continue 0.5 miles to the end of Curson Avenue at Wattles Drive. Park alongside the curb.

The hike

Walk up Wattles Drive and pass through the pedestrian gate. Pass homes on the left to the dirt trail and trailhead gate at a quarter mile. Continue 30 yards to a short, but steep footpath on the right. For now, go straight on the Castair Trail. Traverse the cliffside path on the west-facing wall of Nichols Canyon on a downward slope. Pass a bench on the left at an overlook down Nichols Canyon and across the city. The trail ends at fenced private property.

Return to the junction, now on the left. Make a short, steep climb up the hill to where it levels out. Climb the ridge again, weaving through chaparral and scrub brush to a series of plateaus with far-reaching vistas. At the upper 1,000-foot flat is a spectacular view of the entire city. Return by retracing your steps.

To extend the hike through the north end of the open space, continue north 100 yards to a Y-fork. The left (lower) fork—the Bantam Trail—leads a half mile to the trailhead on Nichols Canyon Road (Hike 16). The right (upper) fork leads a half mile to Astral Drive, providing access to Runyon Canyon Park. ■

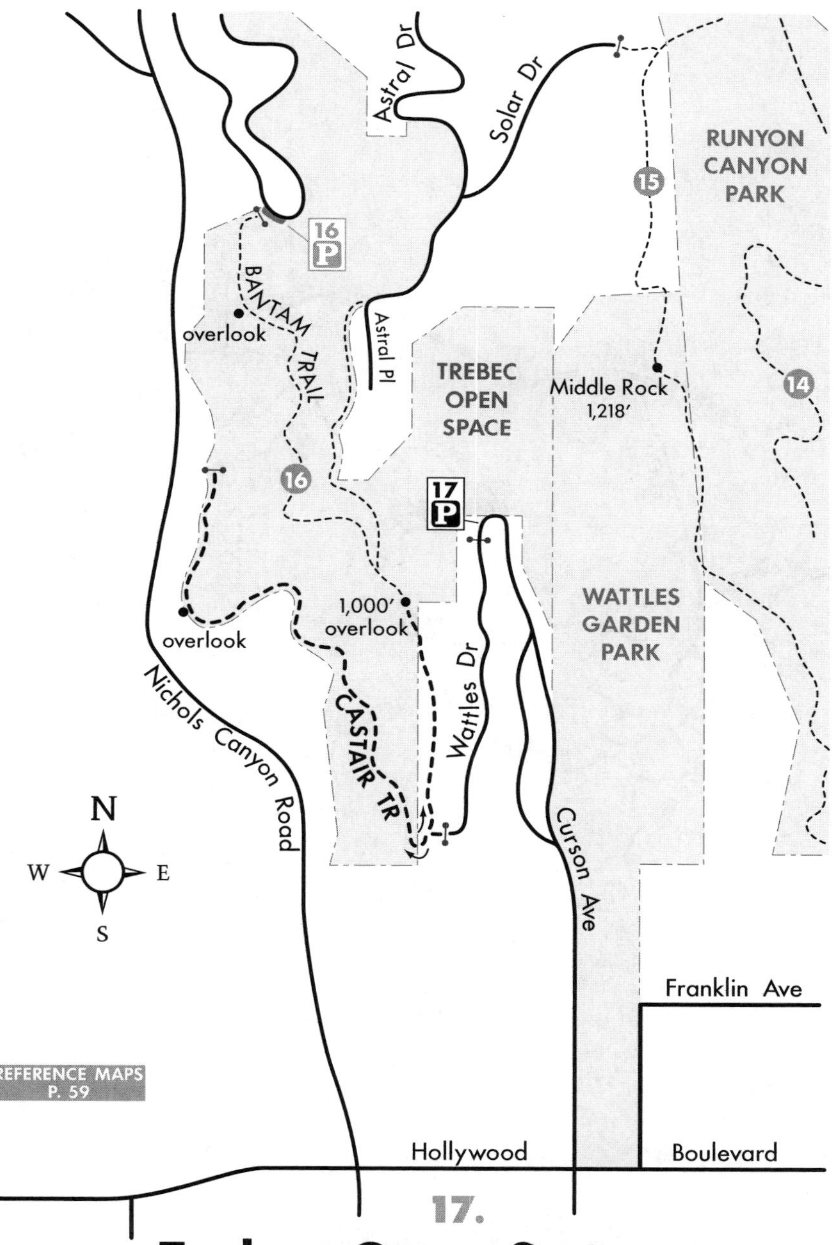

17. Trebec Open Space

Lower Trailhead from Wattles Drive

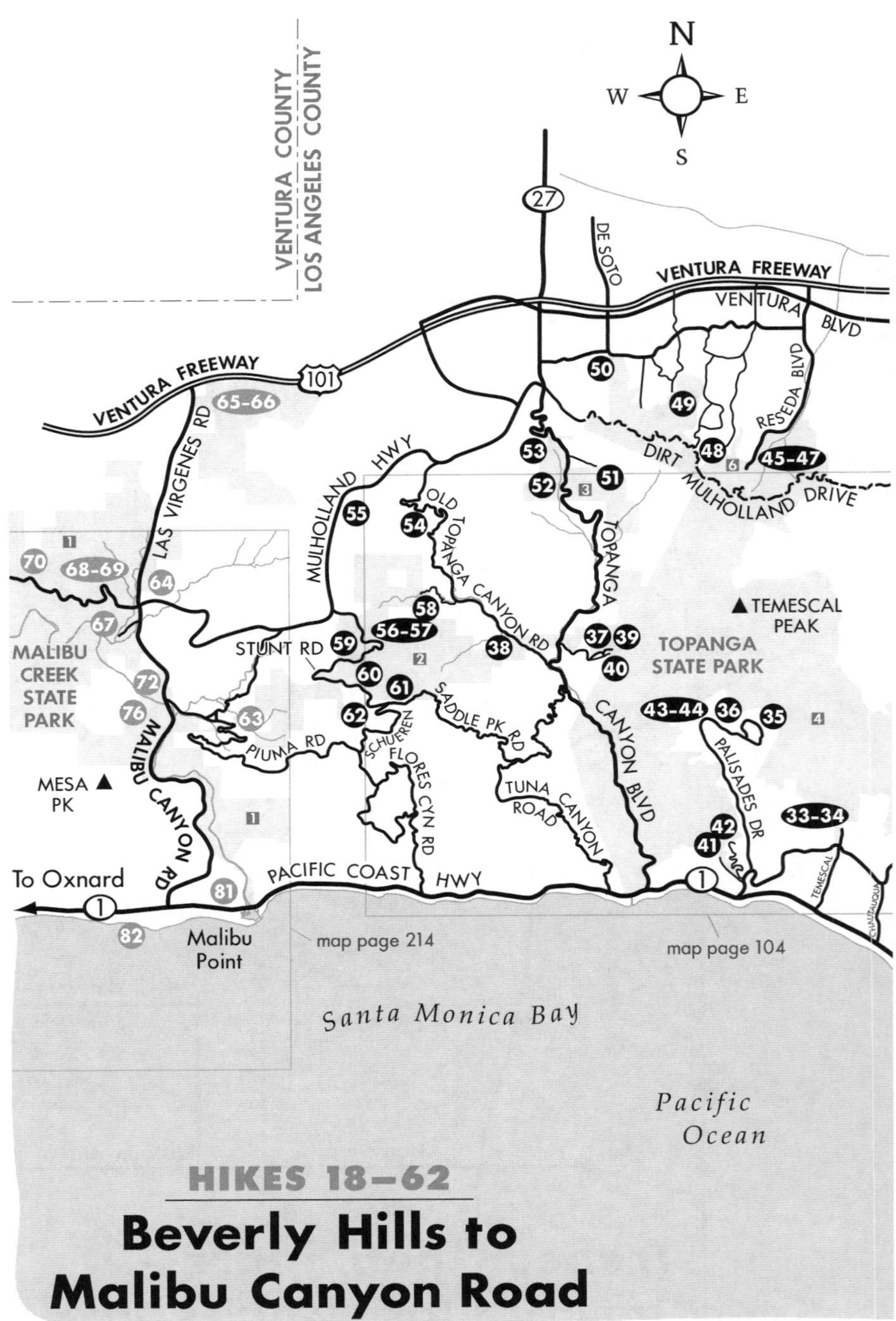

HIKES 18–62

Beverly Hills to Malibu Canyon Road

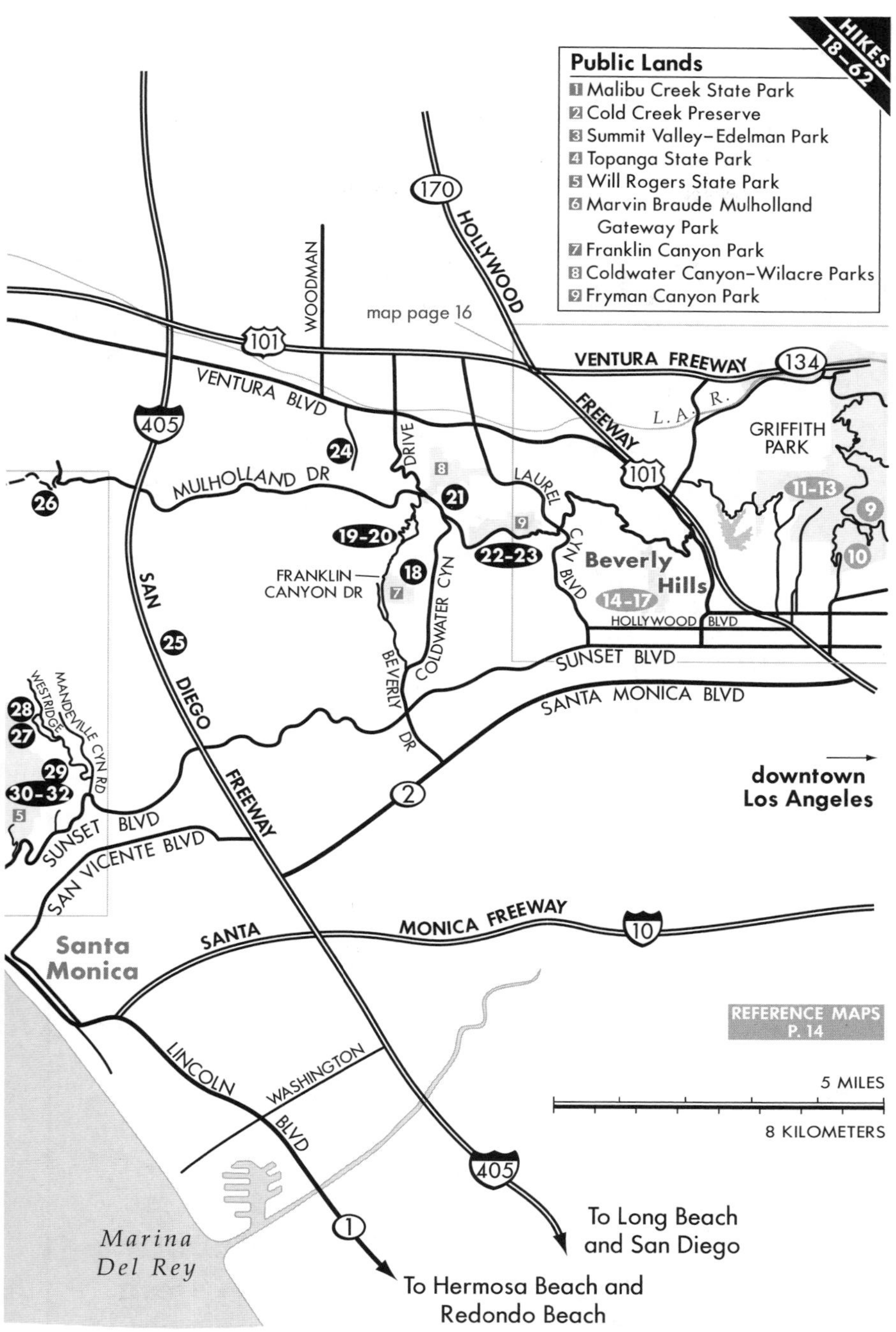
HIKES 18–62
Public Lands
1 Malibu Creek State Park
2 Cold Creek Preserve
3 Summit Valley–Edelman Park
4 Topanga State Park
5 Will Rogers State Park
6 Marvin Braude Mulholland Gateway Park
7 Franklin Canyon Park
8 Coldwater Canyon–Wilacre Parks
9 Fryman Canyon Park
170
HOLLYWOOD
WOODMAN
map page 16
101
VENTURA FREEWAY
134
VENTURA BLVD
FREEWAY
L. A. R.
GRIFFITH PARK
405
DRIVE
LAUREL
MULHOLLAND DR
24
26
21
11-13
9
19-20
22-23
CYN BLVD
Beverly Hills
10
FRANKLIN CANYON DR
18
COLDWATER CYN
14-17
HOLLYWOOD BLVD
SAN DIEGO FREEWAY
25
BEVERLY DR
SUNSET BLVD
SANTA MONICA BLVD
WESTRIDGE
MANDEVILLE CYN RD
28
27
29
30-32
downtown Los Angeles
2
SUNSET BLVD
SAN VICENTE BLVD
SANTA MONICA FREEWAY
10
Santa Monica
REFERENCE MAPS P. 14
LINCOLN BLVD
WASHINGTON
5 MILES
8 KILOMETERS
405
1
To Long Beach and San Diego
Marina Del Rey
To Hermosa Beach and Redondo Beach

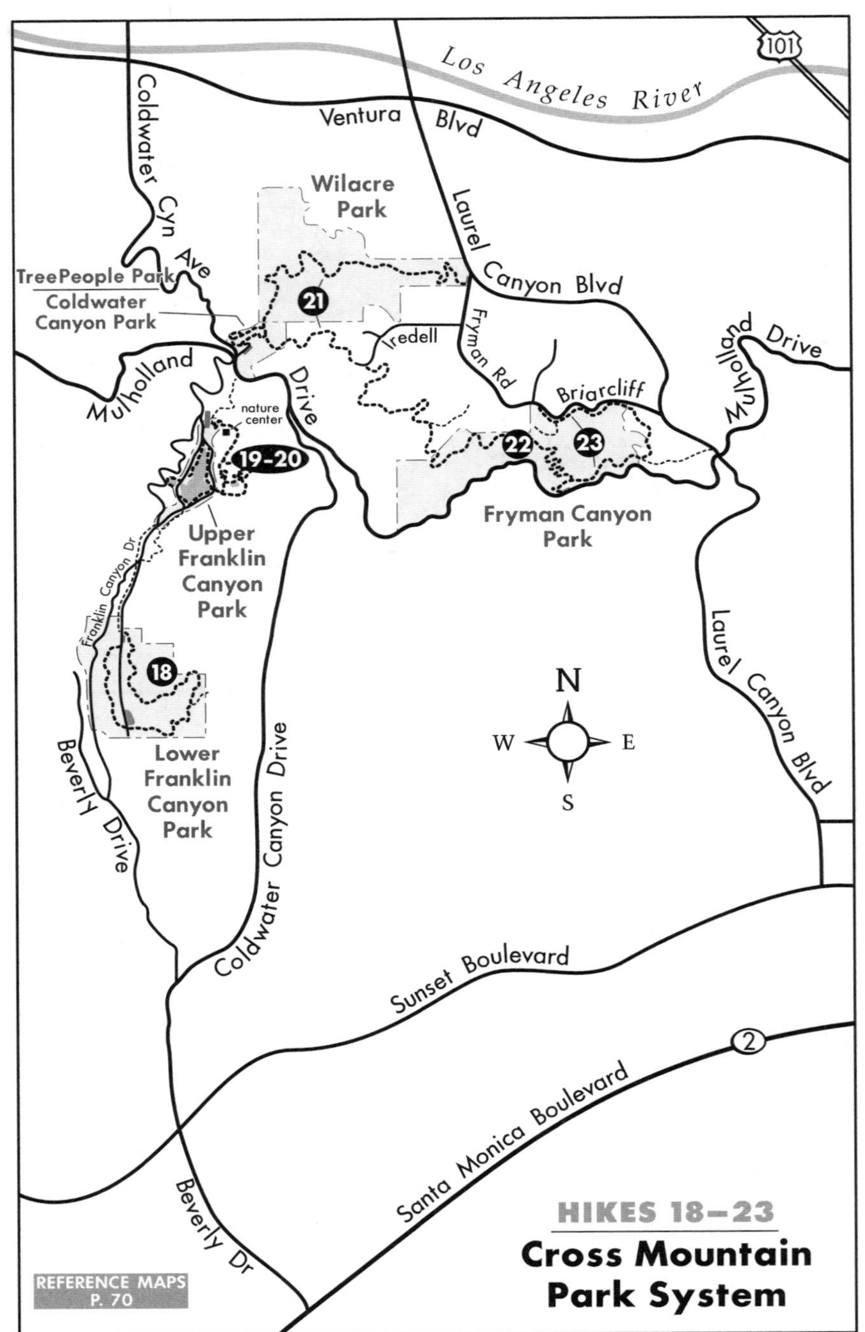
Los Angeles River
101
Ventura Blvd
Coldwater Cyn Ave
Wilacre Park
Laurel Canyon Blvd
TreePeople Park
Coldwater Canyon Park
21
Iredell
Fryman Rd
Mulholland Drive
Mulholland
Drive
nature center
19-20
Briarcliff
22
23
Fryman Canyon Park
Upper Franklin Canyon Park
Franklin Canyon Dr
18
Lower Franklin Canyon Park
Beverly Drive
Coldwater Canyon Drive
Laurel Canyon Blvd
N
W
E
S
Sunset Boulevard
2
Santa Monica Boulevard
Beverly Dr
HIKES 18–23
Cross Mountain Park System
REFERENCE MAPS P. 70

18. Hastian—Discovery Loop

LOWER FRANKLIN CANYON PARK

CROSS MOUNTAIN PARK SYSTEM: Beverly Hills

Hiking distance: 3-mile loop
Hiking time: 1.5 hours
Configuration: loop
Elevation gain: 400 feet
Difficulty: easy
Exposure: exposed slopes and shaded canyon
Dogs: allowed
Maps: U.S.G.S. Beverly Hills • Franklin Canyon Park Nature Trails map

map page 75

The Hastian–Discovery Loop in Lower Franklin Canyon Park winds through the 105-acre Franklin Canyon Ranch site. The ranch is nestled in a deep valley in the mountains above Beverly Hills. These two trails form a loop through the canyon bottom woodlands to the chaparral-covered slopes. The Hastian Trail climbs the east wall of Franklin Canyon on a fire road to spectacular vistas of the lower canyon, Franklin Canyon Reservoir, West Los Angeles, and the Pacific Ocean. The Discovery Trail follows the canyon floor through groves of sycamore, oak, and black walnut trees.

To the trailhead

From Sunset Boulevard in Beverly Hills, head north on Beverly Drive for 0.6 miles. At the fork, go left on Beverly Drive, where the main road continues as Coldwater Canyon Drive. Continue 0.8 miles and curve right onto Franklin Canyon Drive. Drive 1.1 mile to Lake Drive. Turn right and drive 0.3 miles to the posted trailhead parking area on the left.

From the Ventura Freeway/Highway 101 in Studio City, exit on Coldwater Canyon Drive. Head 2.5 miles south to the intersection with Mulholland Drive by the Coldwater Canyon Park/TreePeople Park. Make a 90-degree right turn onto Franklin Canyon Drive. Continue 1.4 miles to Lake Drive. Curve left onto Lake Drive, and go 0.3 miles to the posted trailhead parking area on the left.

The hike

Take the posted Hastian Trail (a fire road) past the trail gate. Traverse the hillside high above Lake Drive. The easy uphill grade climbs the east canyon wall. The trail curves left and makes a wide sweeping loop around a side canyon, steadily gaining elevation to an overlook of Lower Franklin Canyon, Westwood, Santa Monica, and the ocean. The main trail curves left and continues up to the ridge, leaving Franklin Canyon and the park. Take the narrow footpath on the right by the wood pole and wind down the hill. The serpentine path exits the hillside at 2.3 miles on a broad grassy lawn by the old Doheny ranch house, a Spanish-style stucco house built in 1935. Cross Lake Road to the Discovery Trail. Curve right and head north, parallel to the park road along the lower west canyon slope. The forested trail joins Lake Drive 50 yards south of the trailhead. Return to the left. ■

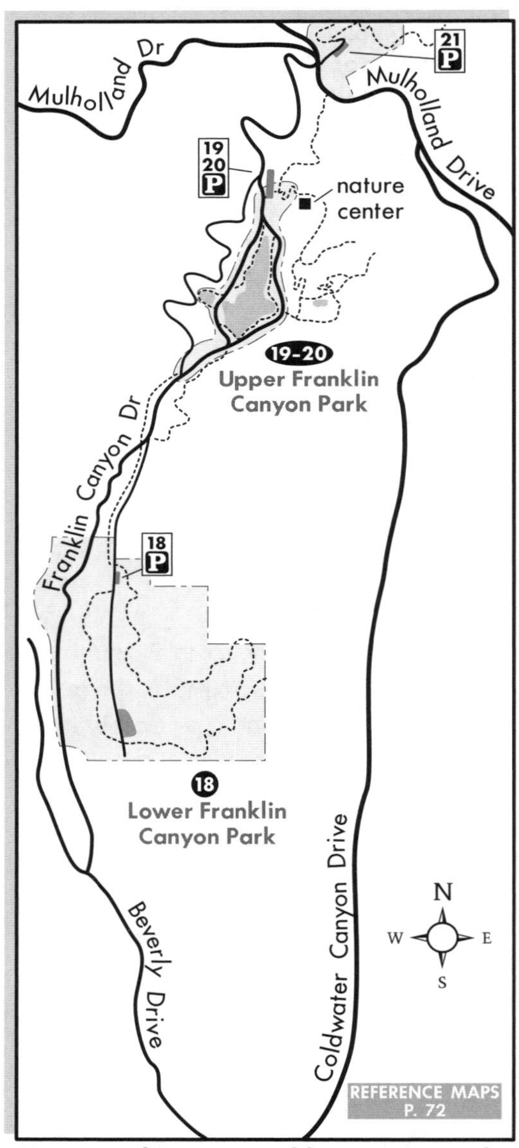

Upper and Lower Franklin Canyon Parks

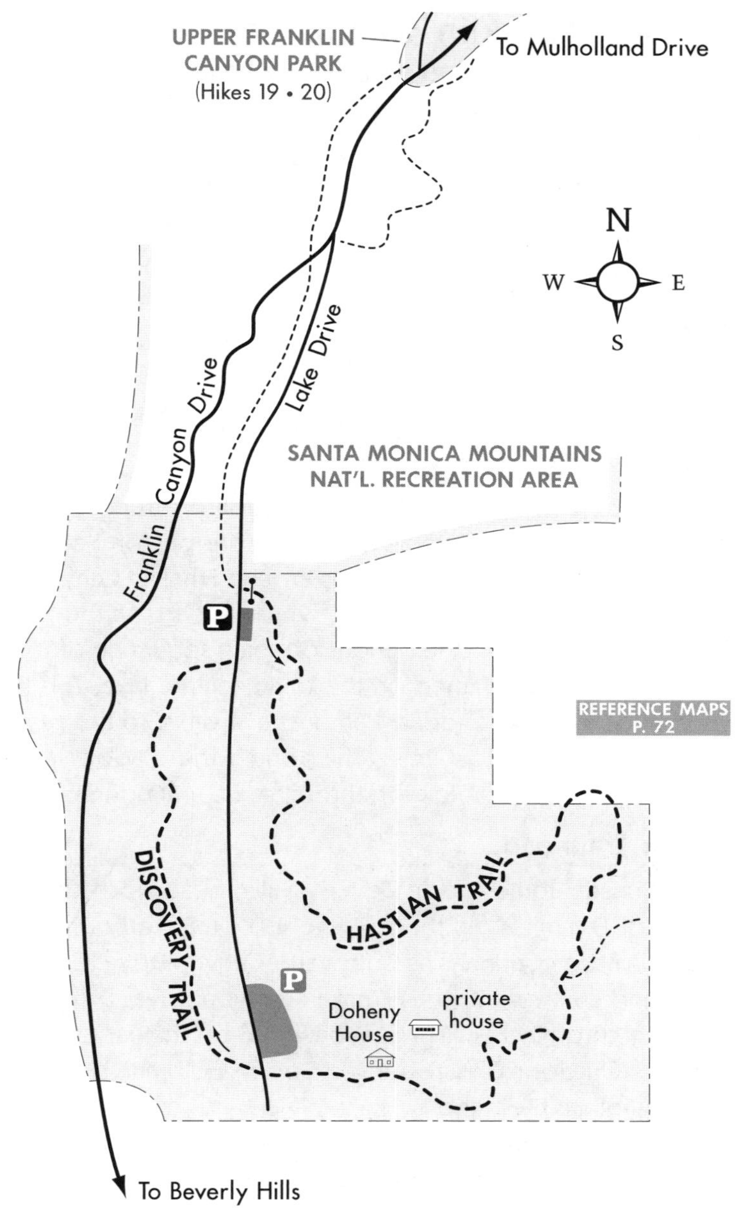

18. Hastian Discovery Loop

LOWER FRANKLIN CANYON PARK

19. Franklin Canyon Lake Loop

UPPER FRANKLIN CANYON PARK

CROSS MOUNTAIN PARK SYSTEM

1500 Franklin Canyon Drive · Beverly Hills

Hiking distance: 1-mile loop
Hiking time: 30 minutes
Configuration: loop
Elevation gain: 30 feet
Difficulty: very easy
Exposure: exposed hills and shaded canyon
Dogs: allowed
Maps: U.S.G.S. Beverly Hills · N.P.S. Franklin Canyon Site
Franklin Canyon Park Nature Trails map

Franklin Canyon Park is a 605-acre wildlife refuge and tranquil retreat just minutes from Beverly Hills. The pastoral open space of Upper Franklin Canyon centers around Franklin Canyon Lake, a beautiful, 9-acre manmade lake which is part of the California migratory bird route. The famous opening sequence of the *Andy Griffith Show* was filmed on the trail near the lake. This hike circles the serene lake under sycamores and oaks. To the east of the lake is Heavenly Pond. Circling the pond is the Wodoc Nature Trail, a wheelchair-accessible path through a natural riparian habitat.

To the trailhead

From Sunset Boulevard in Beverly Hills, head north on Beverly Drive for 0.6 miles. At the fork, go left on Beverly Drive, where the main road continues as Coldwater Canyon Drive. Continue 0.8 miles and curve right onto Franklin Canyon Drive. Drive 1.8 miles, winding through Franklin Canyon Park, to the large William O. Douglas Outdoor Classroom and Sooky Goldman Nature Center parking lot on the right.

From the Ventura Freeway/Highway 101 in Studio City, exit on Coldwater Canyon Drive. Head 2.5 miles south to the intersection with Mulholland Drive by the Coldwater Canyon Park/TreePeople Park. Make a 90-degree right turn onto Franklin Canyon Drive.

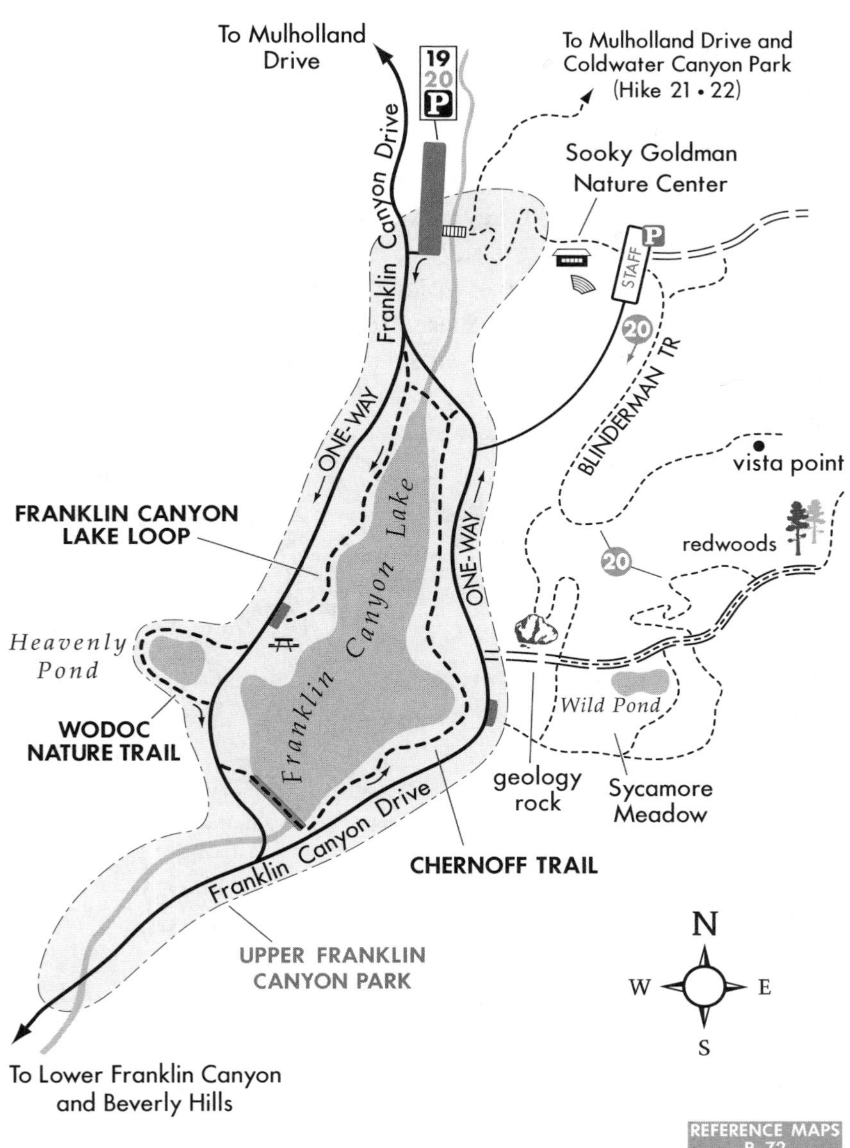

REFERENCE MAPS P. 72

19.

Franklin Canyon Lake Loop

UPPER FRANKLIN CANYON PARK

Continue 0.7 miles to the William O. Douglas Outdoor Classroom and Sooky Goldman Nature Center parking lot on the left.

The hike

Follow the park road to the left (south) for 30 yards to a road on the right by the maintenance shop. To hike counter-clockwise around Franklin Canyon Lake, curve right and descend steps on the left to the trail. Pass the surge basin to a trail split. Both paths parallel the lake and merge at a picnic area by the park road. (The left fork skirts the edge of the lake.) Follow the road to the left 50 yards to the Wodoc Nature Trail at Heavenly Pond. Loop around the serene pond on the paved path. Back at the road, continue south above the lake, and cross the dam at the end of the lake. After crossing, descend steps on the Chernoff Trail, and follow the east banks of the lake through a shady woodland and a picnic area. At the Franklin Lake spillway, curve right to the road, and bear left 100 yards, returning to the parking area. (If the spillway is dry, you may cross over it to complete the loop and return to the right.) ■

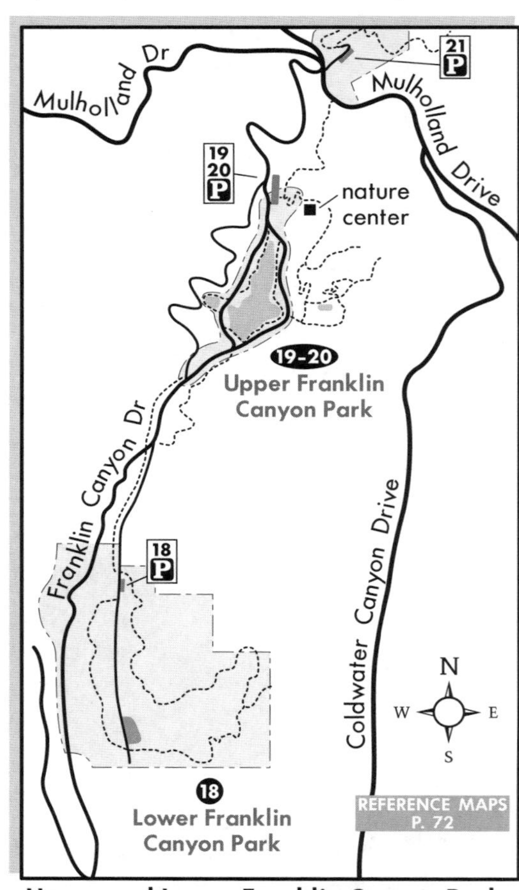

Upper and Lower Franklin Canyon Parks

20. Blinderman Trail

UPPER FRANKLIN CANYON PARK

CROSS MOUNTAIN PARK SYSTEM

1500 Franklin Canyon Drive • Beverly Hills

Hiking distance: 1.5-mile loop
Hiking time: 45 minutes
Configuration: loop with spur trail to overlook
Elevation gain: 200 feet
Difficulty: easy
Exposure: exposed hills and shaded canyon
Dogs: allowed
Maps: U.S.G.S. Beverly Hills and Van Nuys • N.P.S. Franklin Canyon Site Franklin Canyon Park Nature Trails map

map page 81

Upper Franklin Canyon Park is home to the Sooky Goldman Nature Center and the William O. Douglas Outdoor Classroom, providing educational programs to the public and local schools. The Blinderman Trail is adjacent to the nature center. The path traverses the canyon slopes through chaparral, strolls along stream-fed side canyons with meadows, and climbs to overlooks of Franklin Canyon Lake and the entire canyon oasis.

To the trailhead

From Sunset Boulevard in Beverly Hills, head north on Beverly Drive for 0.6 miles. At the fork, go left on Beverly Drive, where the main road continues as Coldwater Canyon Drive. Continue 0.8 miles and curve right onto Franklin Canyon Drive. Drive 1.8 miles, winding through Franklin Canyon Park, to the large William O. Douglas Outdoor Classroom and Sooky Goldman Nature Center parking lot on the right.

From the Ventura Freeway/Highway 101 in Studio City, exit on Coldwater Canyon Drive. Head 2.5 miles south to the intersection with Mulholland Drive by the Coldwater Canyon Park/TreePeople Park. Make a 90-degree right turn onto Franklin Canyon Drive. Continue 0.7 miles to the William O. Douglas Outdoor Classroom and Sooky Goldman Nature Center parking lot on the left.

The hike

Cross the wooden bridge to the information board. The left fork is a northbound connector trail to Coldwater Canyon Park (Hikes 21 and 22). Bear right and wind up the hill to the Sooky Goldman Nature Center. Walk through the courtyard to the back (east) side of the buildings and the posted Blinderman Trail. Twenty yards up the footpath is a trail fork. The left fork leads through walnut groves to a maintenance road. Head right and traverse the hillside, curving left to a trail split. Take the left fork and climb up the hillside to an overlook of Franklin Lake. Continue uphill to the ridge, with views down the entire length of Franklin Canyon. The ridge path leads to additional observation points.

Return to the main trail, and continue on the south fork to the canyon floor by Geology Rock. Bear left on the dirt road, passing Wild Pond on the right to a 4-way junction. (En route, a short side path loops around the pond to Sycamore Meadow.) Bear left and climb steps up the hillside. The undulating path crosses a wooden bridge and returns to the canyon floor at a T-junction. The left fork leads 100 yards to a large grassy flat with towering redwoods at the park boundary. The right fork returns to the 4-way junction. Take the left fork and climb the hill through a eucalyptus grove. Curve right to the park road by Franklin Canyon Lake. Follow the one-way road to the right, returning to the trailhead parking lot. ■

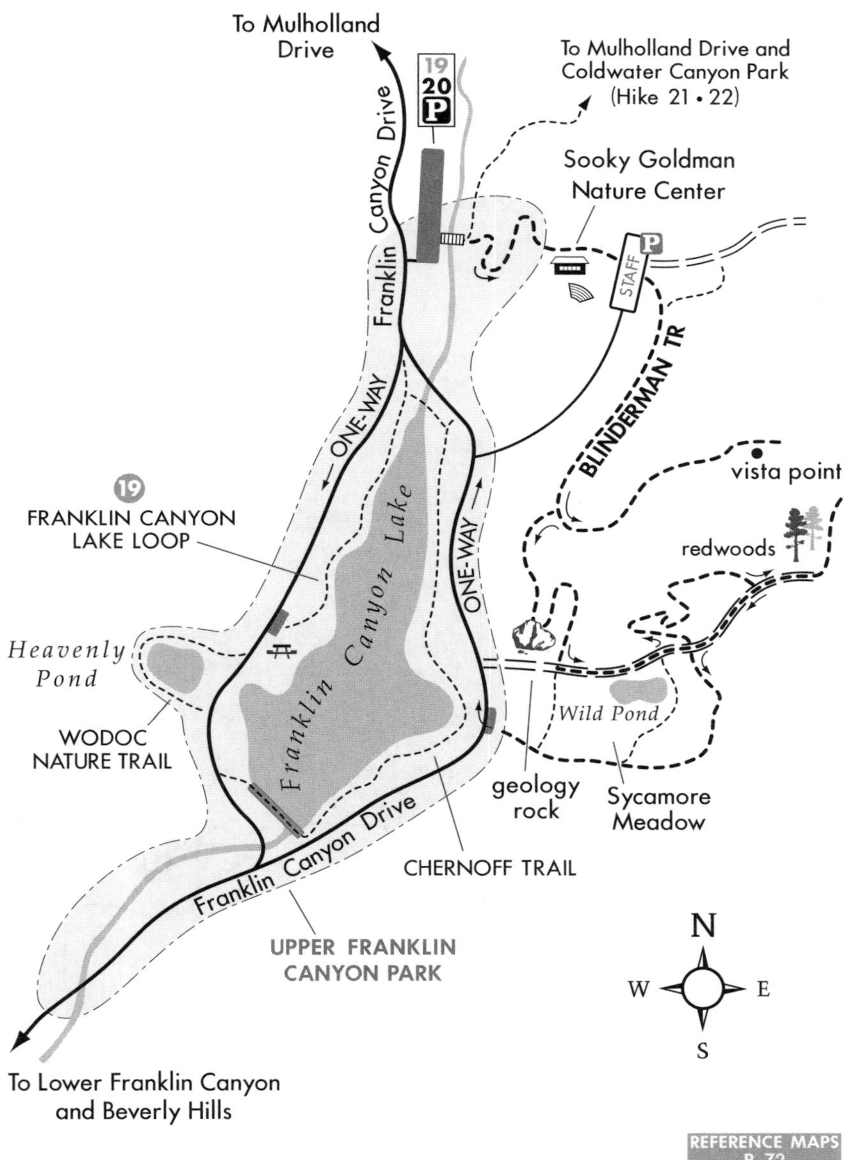

REFERENCE MAPS P. 72

20.

Blinderman Trail

UPPER FRANKLIN CANYON PARK

21. Coldwater Canyon Park—Wilacre Park Loop

CROSS MOUNTAIN PARK SYSTEM

12601 Mulholland Drive • Beverly Hills

Hiking distance: 2.7-mile loop
Hiking time: 1.5 hours
Configuration: loop (partially on residential streets)
Elevation gain: 500 feet
Difficulty: easy
Exposure: exposed slopes and shaded canyon
Dogs: allowed
Maps: U.S.G.S. Van Nuys
Trails Illustrated Santa Monica Mountains Nat'l Rec Area

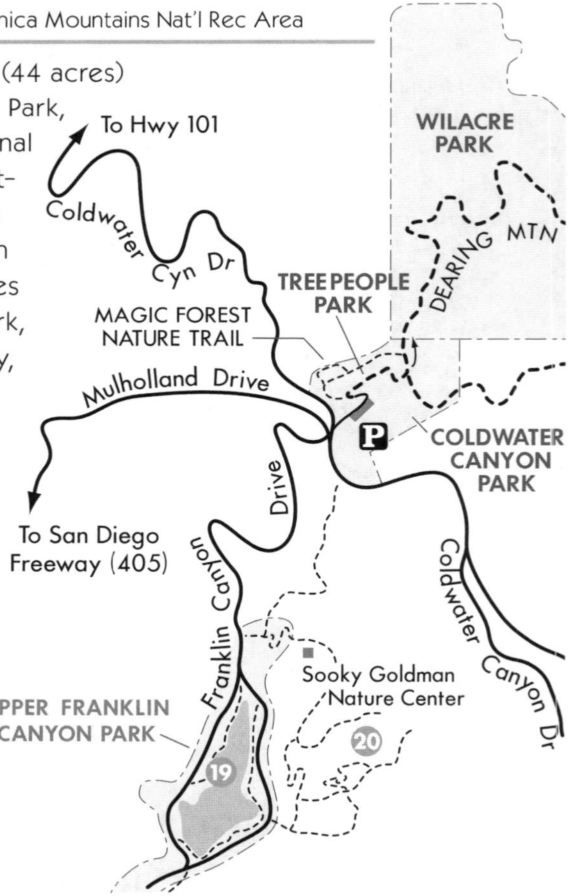

Coldwater Canyon Park (44 acres) is home to TreePeople Park, a non-profit educational facility known for planting more than a million trees. TreePeople, which maintains and improves Coldwater Canyon Park, includes a tree nursery, fruit orchard, organic garden, and the Magic Forest Nature Trail. The adjacent Wilacre Park is formerly the estate of silent film star Will Acres. The 128-acre greenbelt in Studio City contains chaparral-covered ridges and wooded canyons surrounded by residential homes. This

21. Coldwater Canyon– Wilacre Park Loop

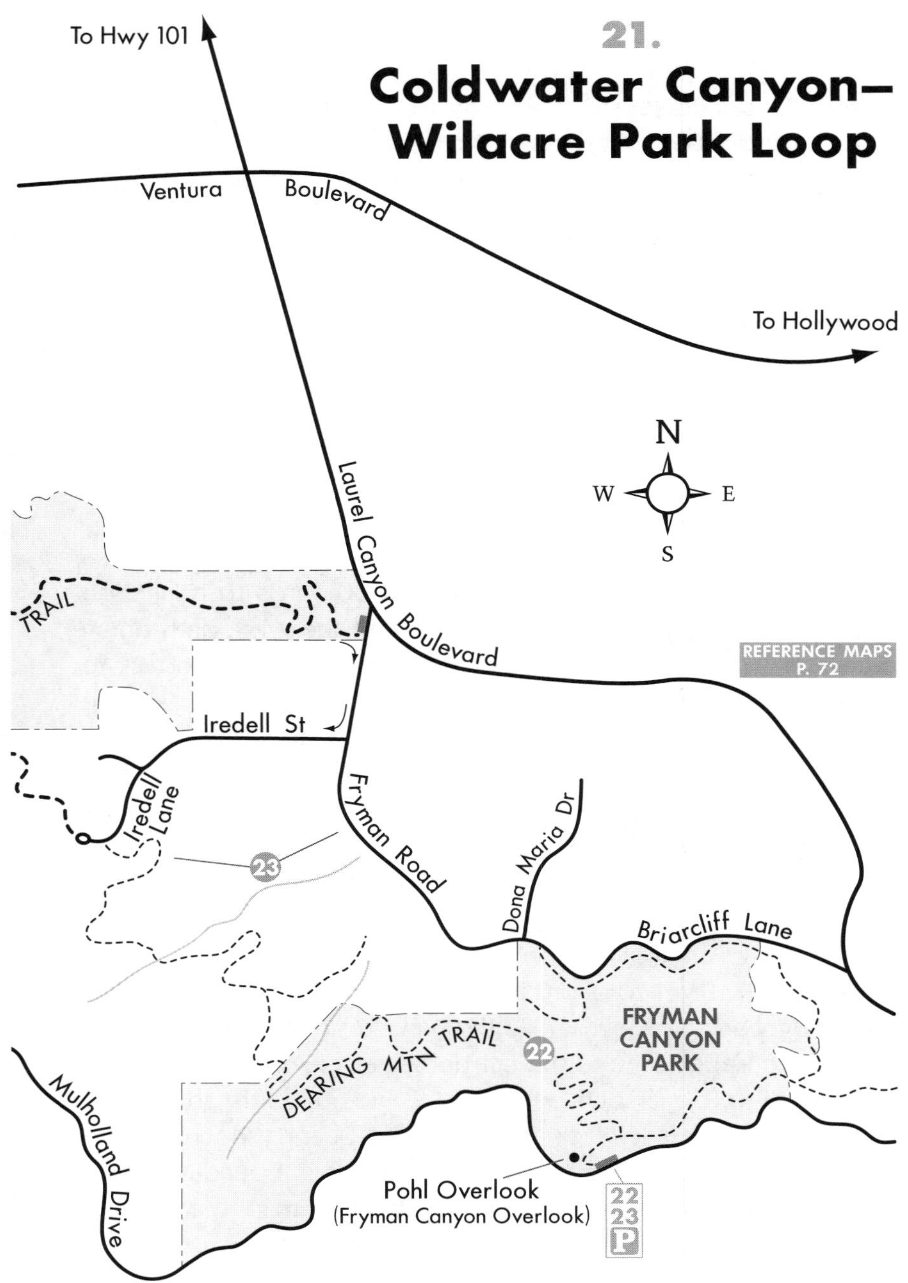

loop hike crosses Coldwater Canyon Park and Wilacre Park with panoramic views of the San Fernando Valley.

To the trailhead

From Sunset Boulevard in Beverly Hills, head north on Beverly Drive for 0.6 miles. At the fork, go right onto Coldwater Canyon Drive. Continue 3 miles to an intersection with Mulholland Drive. Go to the left, staying on Coldwater Canyon Drive, and drive 0.4 miles to the posted Coldwater Canyon/TreePeople Park on the right. Turn right into the parking area.

From the Ventura Freeway/Highway 101 in Studio City, exit on Coldwater Canyon Drive. Head 2.5 miles south to the intersection with Mulholland Drive. The posted Coldwater Canyon/TreePeople Park entrance is on the left (east) side of the intersection.

The hike

From the information kiosk at the far end of the parking area, bear left on the nature trail, and head 30 yards to a junction. Cut back sharply to the right, and follow the wide path on an easy downhill grade to the second hillside level. Switchback to the left and descend to the third level and a junction with the Dearing Mountain Trail. Begin the loop to the left, gaining elevation while crossing the head of Iredell Canyon. Cross a small saddle and curve around the hillside to sweeping bird's-eye views of the valley. Continue on a slow but steady descent with wide curves. Along the way, the trail becomes a narrow, paved path, winding through cypress and pine tree groves. The trail ends at the Wilacre Park trailhead on Fryman Road at 1.5 miles. For a loop hike, follow Fryman Road 0.15 miles to the right to Iredell Street. Bear right and walk a half mile through a residential area, curving left onto Iredell Lane to the cul-de-sac at the end of the street. (The trail to Fryman Canyon—Hike 22—is to the left, shortly before the cul-de-sac.) Pick up the posted Dearing Mountain Trail, and ascend the hillside along the open space boundary. Make a wide right curve, completing the loop. Return to the left and stroll through the Magic Forest Nature Trail. ■

22. Dearing Mountain Trail

Fryman Canyon Park to TreePeople Park

CROSS MOUNTAIN PARK SYSTEM: Beverly Hills

Hiking distance: 5 miles round trip
Hiking time: 2.5 hours
Configuration: out-and-back or loop on residential streets
Elevation gain: 500 feet
Difficulty: moderate
Exposure: exposed slopes and shaded canyon
Dogs: allowed
Maps: U.S.G.S. Beverly Hills and Van Nuys
Trails Illustrated Santa Monica Mountains Nat'l Rec Area

map page 87

Fryman Canyon Park, which encompasses more than 120 acres, sits on a north-facing hillside bordering Mulholland Drive. At the trailhead, the Nancy Hoover Pohl Overlook (formerly known as the Fryman Canyon Overlook) provides views across the wooded canyon to the San Fernando Valley, Santa Susana Mountains, and the San Gabriel Mountains. This hike on the Dearing Mountain Trail descends into the canyon from the overlook, connecting Fryman Canyon Park with Coldwater Canyon Park and Wilacre Park.

To the trailhead

From Sunset Boulevard in Beverly Hills, head north on Beverly Drive for 0.6 miles. At the fork, go right onto Coldwater Canyon Drive. Continue 3 miles to an intersection with Mulholland Drive. Turn right on Mulholland Drive, and go 2 miles to the posted Fryman Canyon Park entrance on the left. Turn left into the parking lot.

From the Ventura Freeway/Highway 101 in Studio City, exit on Laurel Canyon Boulevard. Head 2.8 miles south to the intersection with Mulholland Drive. Turn right on Mulholland Drive, and drive 0.8 miles to the posted Fryman Canyon Park entrance on the right.

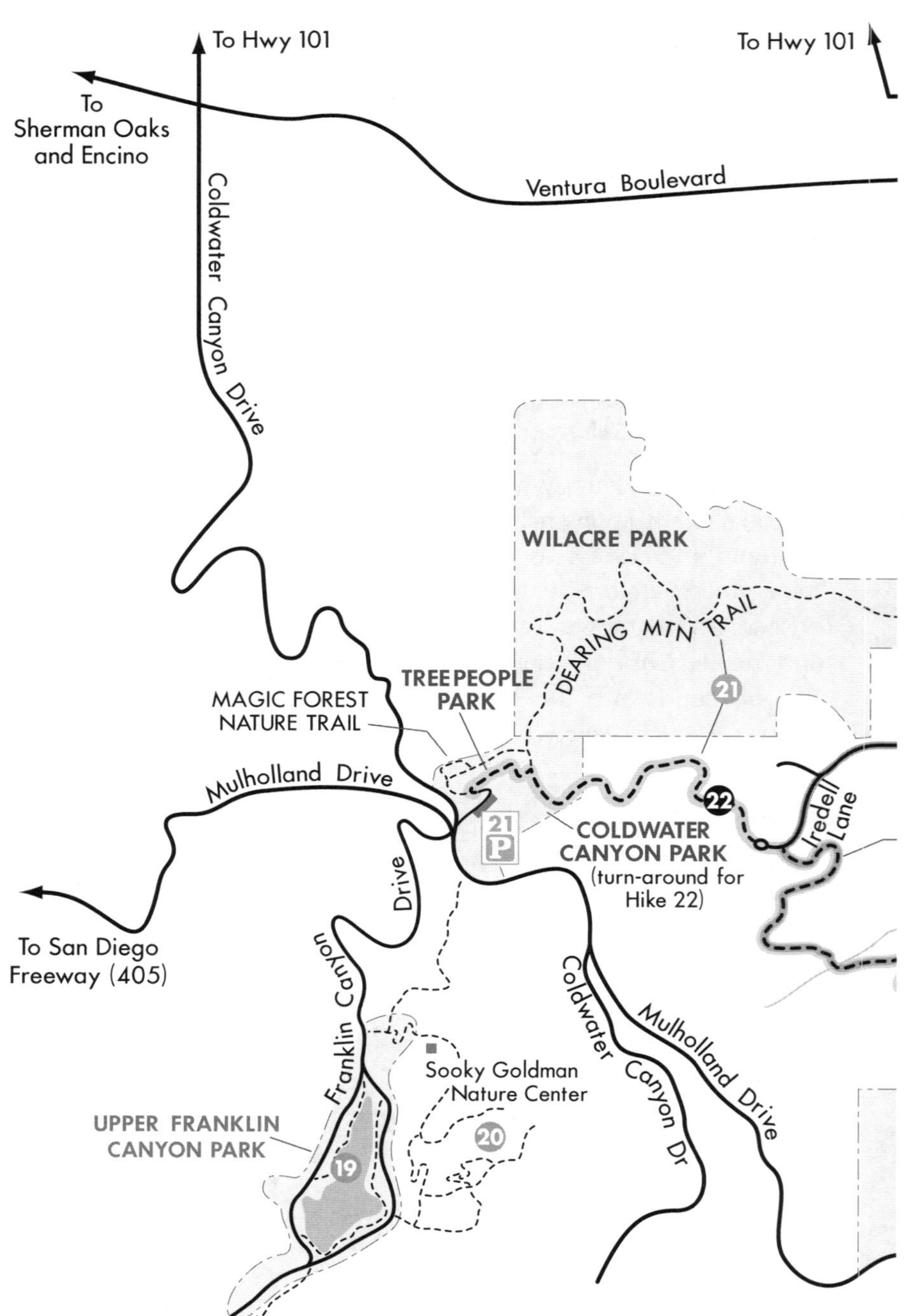

To Hwy 101
To Hwy 101
To
Sherman Oaks
and Encino
Ventura Boulevard
Coldwater Canyon Drive
WILACRE PARK
DEARING MTN TRAIL
21
TREEPEOPLE
PARK
MAGIC FOREST
NATURE TRAIL
Mulholland Drive
22
Iredell
Lane
21
P
COLDWATER
CANYON PARK
(turn-around for
Hike 22)
Drive
Franklin Canyon
To San Diego
Freeway (405)
Coldwater Canyon Dr
Mulholland Drive
Sooky Goldman
Nature Center
20
UPPER FRANKLIN
CANYON PARK
19

22. Dearing Mountain Trail

Fryman Canyon Park to TreePeople Park

23. Fryman Canyon Loop

FRYMAN CANYON PARK

CROSS MOUNTAIN PARK SYSTEM

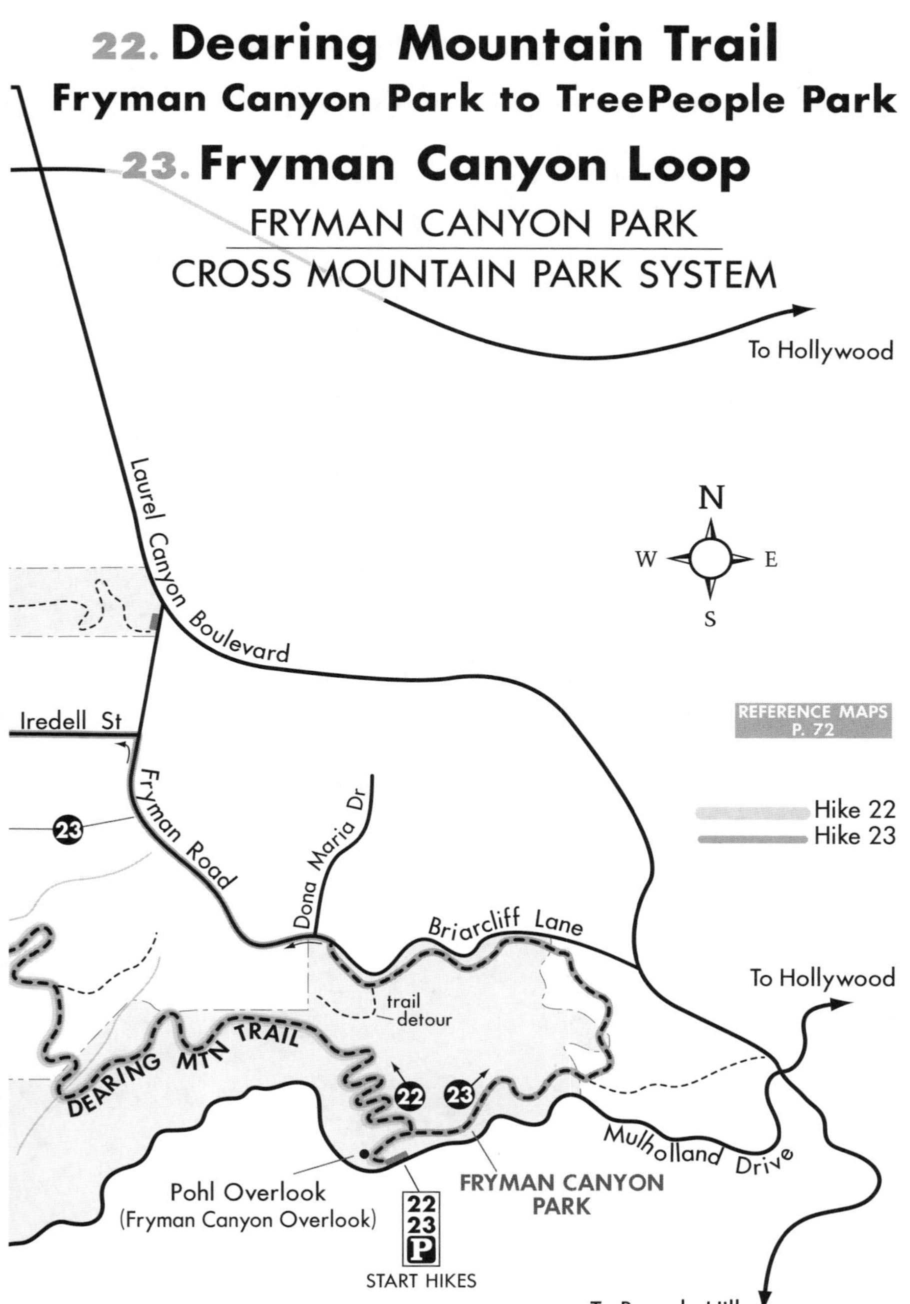

The hike

To the left of the trailhead, steps lead up to the Pohl (Fryman Canyon) Overlook. The posted Dearing Mountain Trail descends to a junction a short distance ahead (also known as the Betty B. Dearing Trail). Bear left and zigzag down seven switchbacks into Fryman Canyon. Follow the contours of the hillside, and make a horseshoe right bend across a spring-fed drainage. Pass remnants of a few old cars, and continue on the canyon wall to a T-junction. Take the left fork and stroll through a mature grove of oak and eucalyptus trees. Cross a stream in a ravine and bear left. Cross another drainage by a huge sandstone outcrop, and pass an overlook of a few showcase homes. Curve right on a footpath and traverse the sloping hillside. Descend steps and emerge on Iredell Lane at 2 miles. Bear left for 0.1 mile to the cul-de-sac. Pick up the posted Dearing Mountain Trail, and ascend the hillside for a half mile to a junction. Bear left and stroll through the Magic Forest Nature Trail, or ascend the steps to the park headquarters and an educational facility at TreePeople Park.

To return to the trailhead, there are three hiking options. Return along the same route for the shortest option. Continue with Hike 21 for a loop through Wilacre Park. Or loop back through residential areas utilizing Iredell Street and Fryman Road—Hike 23. ■

23. Fryman Canyon Loop

FRYMAN CANYON PARK

CROSS MOUNTAIN PARK SYSTEM

8401 Mulholland Drive • Studio City

Hiking distance: 4 miles round trip
Hiking time: 2 hours
Configuration: loop (partially on residential streets)
Elevation gain: 500 feet
Difficulty: easy to moderate
Exposure: exposed slopes and shaded canyon
Dogs: allowed
Maps: U.S.G.S. Beverly Hills and Van Nuys
Trails Illustrated Santa Monica Mountains Nat'l Rec Area

map page 87

The Fryman Canyon Loop passes through Fryman Canyon Park and a quiet residential area along the park border, forming a loop hike. Several parks in this area are collectively referred to as Cross Mountain Park: Fryman Canyon Park (Hikes 22 and 23), Coldwater Canyon Park (Hike 21), Wilacre Park (Hike 21), and Franklin Canyon Park (Hikes 18—20). The mountain paths through this 1,000-acre park system cross ridges, wind through chaparral-covered hillsides, and meander up stream-fed canyons. All of the parks are connected with hiking paths, offering many opportunities for extending your hike.

To the trailhead

From Sunset Boulevard in Beverly Hills, head north on Beverly Drive for 0.6 miles. At the fork, go right onto Coldwater Canyon Drive. Continue 3 miles to an intersection with Mulholland Drive. Turn right on Mulholland Drive, and go 2 miles to the posted Fryman Canyon Park entrance on the left. Turn left into the parking lot.

From the Ventura Freeway/Highway 101 in Studio City, exit on Laurel Canyon Boulevard. Head 2.8 miles south to the intersection with Mulholland Drive. Turn right on Mulholland Drive, and drive 0.8 miles to the posted Fryman Canyon Park entrance on the right.

The hike

To the left of the trailhead, steps lead up to the Nancy Hoover Pohl Overlook (formerly the Fryman Canyon Overlook). The posted Dearing Mountain Trail gradually descends on the chaparral-covered slope. A short distance ahead is a junction on the left, our return route. Stay straight, following the contours of the hillside on a near-level grade that overlooks Fryman Canyon. Pass oak groves to a trail split at 0.4 miles. The right (upper trail) dead-ends in a quarter mile near Laurel Canyon Boulevard. Take the lower (left) fork, dropping down into the canyon to a T-junction with an unpaved road behind a row of homes fronted on Briarcliff Lane. Follow the road downhill to the left for 0.3 miles along the park boundary to the base of Fryman Canyon, where the road becomes paved. Detour left for 100 yards up the canyon on the footpath. Cross a ravine and meander up the canyon floor on the tree-shaded path. Curving right is a narrow, stream-fed canyon where the trail fades and becomes hard to follow.

Return to the road. Bear left 0.1 mile to the south end of Fryman Road. Follow Fryman Road to the left 0.4 miles to Iredell Street. Bear left and walk up the residential road, curving left on Iredell Lane. One hundred yards before the cul-de-sac, pick up the Dearing Mountain Trail on the left. Climb the steps and wind through Fryman Canyon under the shade of eucalyptus and oak groves. Cross a spring-fed drainage, and steadily climb seven switchbacks to the head of Fryman Canyon, completing the loop at the T-junction. Return to the trailhead on the right. ■

24. Dixie Canyon Park

Barbara Asa—Dorian Trail

South end of Dixie Canyon Place • Sherman Oaks

Hiking distance: 0.7-mile loop
Hiking time: 30 minutes
Configuration: loop
Elevation gain: 300 feet
Difficulty: very easy
Exposure: shaded canyon
Dogs: allowed
Maps: U.S.G.S. Van Nuys
Santa Monica Mountains Recreational Topo Map

map page 93

Dixie Canyon Park is a small, twenty-acre, heavily wooded canyon overlooking the San Fernando Valley in Sherman Oaks. The open space was donated to the Santa Monica Mountains Conservancy by actor/director Warren Beatty in 1986. Tucked into the north slope of the Santa Monica Mountains, the shaded canyon is rich with California black walnut and coast live oak, with an understory of mushrooms, ferns, fungus, and poison oak. A perennial stream flows through the heart of the parkland. A short hiking-only loop trail winds through the canyon along both sides of the stream.

To the trailhead

From the Ventura Freeway/Highway 101 in Sherman Oaks, exit on Woodman Avenue. Drive a half mile south to Ventura Boulevard. Turn left and continue 0.4 miles to Dixie Canyon Avenue. Turn right and go 0.7 miles south to Dixie Canyon Place. Veer left on Dixie Canyon Place and go 0.2 miles up the narrow road to the signed trailhead at the end of the cul-de-sac. Park along the side of the road.

The hike

Walk to the end of the cul-de-sac, and pass the trailhead sign. Climb the concrete steps and cross to the east side of the stream. Follow the lush, narrow canyon upstream. Recross the drainage on the second bridge. At the third crossing is a bridge and a junction. Begin the loop on the right fork and head up the hillside. Traverse the west canyon wall on the serpentine path. At 0.3 miles, cross the waterway and loop back on the east side of the canyon. Weave down the hillside with the aid of four switchbacks, completing the loop at the third bridge. ■

25. Getty View Trail

405 Freeway in Bel Air

Hiking distance: 3.6 miles round trip
Hiking time: 2 hours
Configuration: out-and-back
Elevation gain: 600 feet
Difficulty: moderate
Exposure: exposed slopes and ridge
Dogs: allowed
Maps: U.S.G.S. Beverly Hills
Santa Monica Mountains Conservancy map

map page 95

The Getty View Trail in Bel Air ascends the steep hillside from Sepulveda Pass to Casiano Fire Road, an unpaved road on the ridgeline. A three-quarter mile trail climbs through chaparral and pockets of live oak and toyon, providing access to a section of the 376-acre Sepulveda Pass Open Space. The ridge-top trail overlooks Hoag Canyon, with sweeping vistas of the Getty Center Museum, West Los Angeles, Santa Monica, and the Pacific Ocean.

To the trailhead

Heading northbound from Los Angeles on the San Diego Freeway/Interstate 405, take the Getty Center Drive exit. Turn left (north) 0.1 mile to the trailhead parking lot on the right, just before crossing under the freeway.

Heading southbound from the San Fernando Valley on the San Diego Freeway/Interstate 405, take the Getty Center Drive exit. Turn left (south) and cross under the freeway to the trailhead parking lot, immediately on the left.

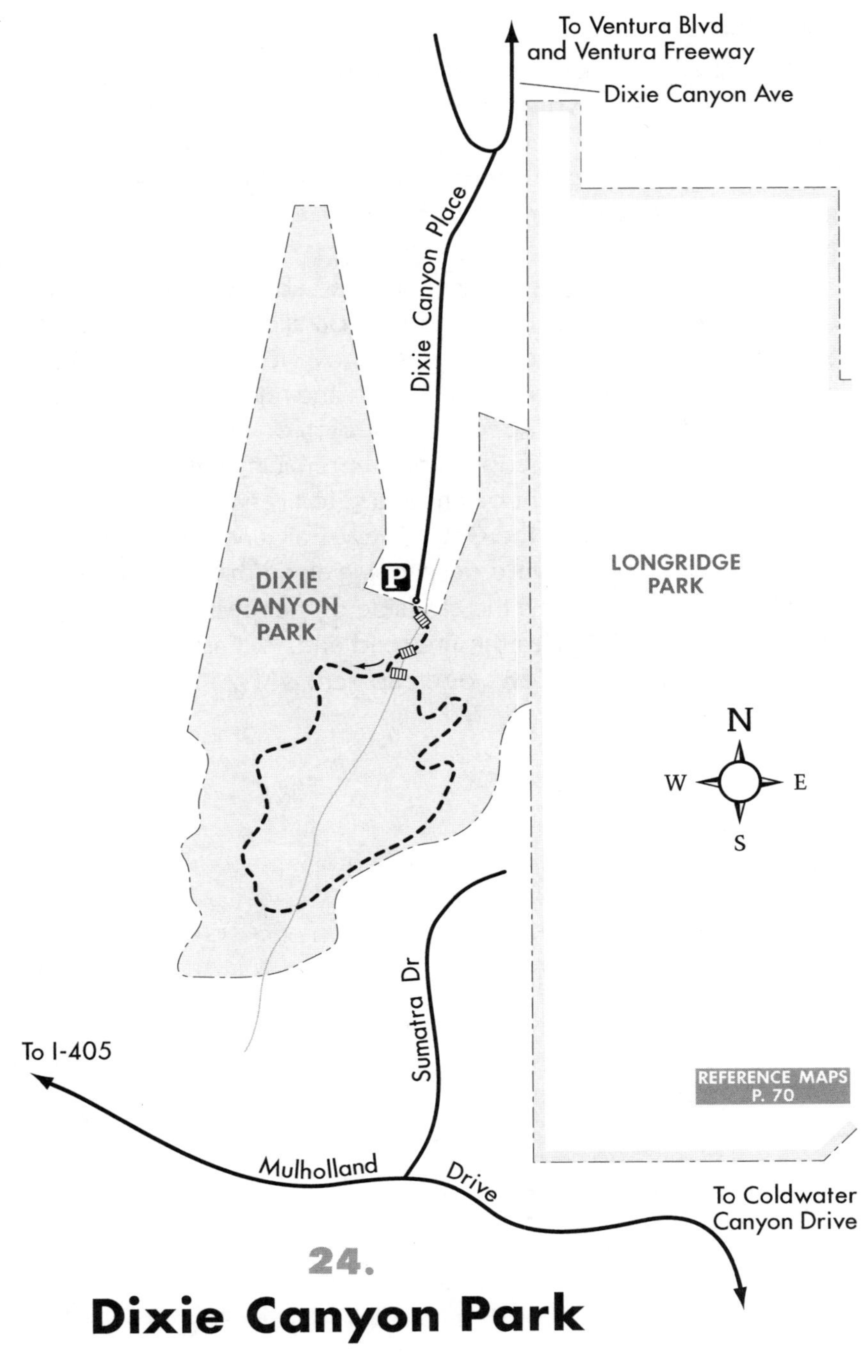

24. Dixie Canyon Park

The hike

From the trailhead map, bear left (north) on the signed trail, and head up the side canyon past sycamore trees. Switchbacks lead up the chaparral-covered hillside east of Sepulveda Pass. The views improve with every step. Switchbacks make the elevation gain very easy. At 0.6 miles, the trail reaches the ridge and a T-junction with the Casiano Fire Road.

Bear left on the ridge-hugging dirt road above the deep and undeveloped Hoag Canyon. A footpath parallels the road on the west, gaining elevation to an incredible overlook by an isolated oak tree. The footpath parallels the cliffs and rejoins the fire road. A short distance ahead, a second side path on the left parallels the road to additional overlooks before rejoining the road again. At 0.4 miles, the pavement begins at a gated residential area.

Return south, back to the Getty View Trail junction. Continue south on the fire road while descending along the ridge. An undulating footpath parallels the east side of the road, overlooking Hoag Canyon. At 0.7 miles the fire road ends at Casiano Road in Bel Air Estates, where views open up across West Los Angeles. Return along the same route. ■

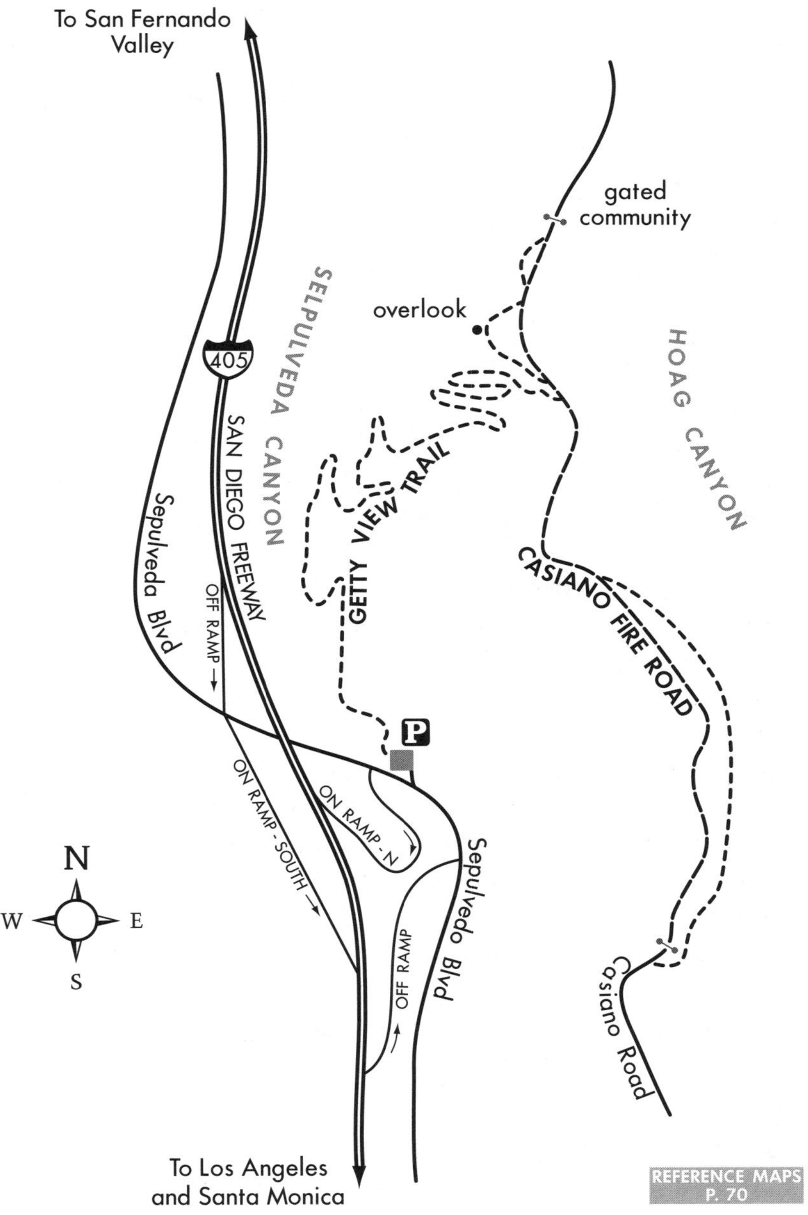

25. Getty View Trail

26. San Vicente Mountain Park and Nike site

from Mulholland Scenic Overlook and Dirt Mulholland

17500 Mulholland Drive • Encino

Hiking distance: 2 miles round trip
Hiking time: 1 hour
Configuration: out-and-back
Elevation gain: 300 feet
Difficulty: easy
Exposure: exposed ridge
Dogs: allowed
Maps: U.S.G.S. Conoga Park • Topanga State Park map
Tom Harrison Maps: Topanga State Park Trail map

map page 98

San Vicente Mountain Park was a former Nike Missile Control Site. From 1956 through 1968, this Cold War sentry post was utilized to guard Los Angeles from Soviet attacks. The site contained radar towers atop the 1,950-foot peak to neutralize Soviet planes. The radar would guide missiles launched from the Sepulveda Basin below to destroy any invading aircraft.

The 10-acre mountaintop park sits at the head of Mandeville Canyon nearly 2,000 feet above the city. It is now home to a self-guided interpretive center with information panels, a radar tower, guard shack, picnic areas, and a variety of overlooks. This hike follows Dirt Mulholland, an unpaved portion of the famous ridge road, to San Vicente Mountain Park. The scenic parkway corridor, constructed in 1924, offers spectacular panoramic vistas across the San Fernando Valley and the Los Angeles Basin to the ocean.

San Vicente Mountain Park can also be accessed from the west via Dirt Mulholland (Hike 45) and from the south via the Westridge Fire Road (Hike 28).

To the trailhead

Heading northbound from Los Angeles on the San Diego Freeway/ Interstate 405, exit on Mulholland Drive. Turn right and drive 0.3 miles to Mulholland Drive. Turn left and follow the scenic winding road 2 miles to the end of the paved road by Encino Hills Drive on the right. Curve left on Dirt Mulholland and park.

Heading southbound from the San Fernando Valley on the San Diego Freeway/Interstate 405, exit on Mulholland Drive. Turn left and drive 0.4 miles to Mulholland Drive. Turn left and follow the winding road 2 miles to the end of the paved road by Encino Hills Drive on the right. Curve left on Dirt Mulholland and park.

The hike

From the overlook of the San Fernando Valley, walk up unpaved Dirt Mulholland. Curve to the southern slope and a view towards Los Angeles, then return to the sweeping valley vistas that span to the San Gabriel Mountains and the Santa Susana Mountains. Continue on a gentle incline above the Encino Reservoir to a fork at the top of Mandeville Canyon at 1 mile. Dirt Mulholland continues straight ahead for one mile to Sullivan Canyon (Hike 28). Tarzana Fire Road and Caballero Canyon are 3.1 miles ahead (Hike 46).

For this hike, bear left into San Vicente Mountain Park, the former Cold War sentry post. At the 1,950-foot rim above Mandeville Canyon, stairs lead up to an overlook platform with

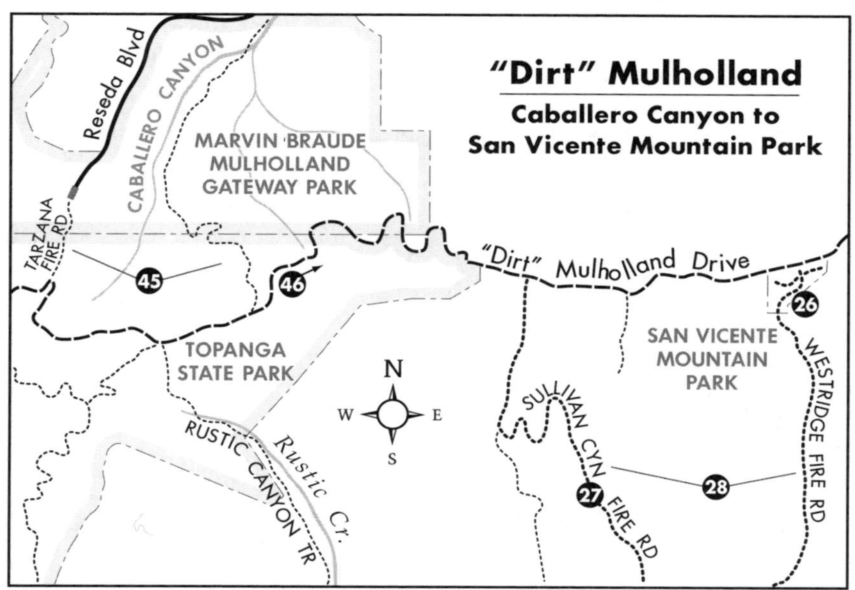

expansive views. The 360-degree vistas stretch from the San Gabriel Mountains and Burbank, across the Los Angeles Basin to the sea, and across the San Fernando Valley from the Santa Susana Mountains to the Santa Monica Mountains. Explore the former helicopter platform and tower platform while savoring the views from the overlooks. Return by retracing your steps. ■

Encino Hills Dr
Mulholland Scenic Overlook
P
Dirt Mulholland Drive
To Sullivan Canyon and Caballero Canyon
46
1,960'
San Vicente Mountain Park
To San Diego Freeway
Mulholland Dr
SULLIVAN CANYON
WESTRIDGE FIRE RD
MANDEVILLE CANYON
N
W
E
S
28
To Rustic Canyon and Will Rogers State Park
REFERENCE MAPS P. 70

26.

San Vicente Mountain Park

from MULHOLLAND SCENIC OVERLOOK

27. Sullivan Canyon

Brentwood

Hiking distance: 8.6 miles round trip
Hiking time: 4 hours
Configuration: out-and-back
Elevation gain: 1,200 feet
Difficulty: moderate to strenuous
Exposure: shaded canyon
Dogs: allowed
Maps: U.S.G.S. Topanga · Topanga State Park map
Tom Harrison Maps: Topanga State Park Trail map

map page 101

Sullivan Canyon is a secluded steam-fed canyon with huge stands of sycamore, oak, willow, and walnut trees. The trail follows the intermittent stream through the steep-walled canyon beneath a rich canopy of green foliage. After meandering up the long, pristine canyon, the trail climbs the chaparral-covered slopes to Sullivan Ridge and magnificent canyon views. This hike can be combined with Hike 28 for a 10-mile loop.

To the trailhead

From Santa Monica, drive 1.6 miles northbound on the Pacific Coast Highway/Highway 1 to Chautauqua Boulevard and turn right. Continue 0.9 miles to Sunset Boulevard and turn right. Drive 2.8 miles and turn left on Mandeville Canyon Road. Turn left again at the first street—Westridge Road—and drive 1.2 miles to Bayliss Road. Turn left on Bayliss Road, and go 0.3 miles to Queensferry Road. Turn left and park near the trailhead gate.

The hike

Step around the vehicle-restricting gate. Walk 0.2 miles down the paved service road to the floor of Sullivan Canyon. Head to the right up the serene, sylvan canyon floor under a lush forest canopy. At 1 mile, cross a seasonal stream and pass sandstone outcroppings amidst high and narrow canyon walls. At 3.5 miles, Sullivan Canyon curves right (northeast) while the trail curves left (northwest) up a narrow side canyon. Climb the west canyon wall overlooking Sullivan Canyon. Follow the contours of the mountain up to the ridge and a T-junction with the Sullivan Ridge Fire Road at 4.3 miles. This is the turn-around spot. Return back down Sullivan Canyon along the same route.

To hike a 10-mile loop, bear right (north) up to Dirt Mulholland, and continue with Hike 28. ■

28. Sullivan Canyon— Westridge Fire Road Loop

Brentwood

Hiking distance: 10-mile loop
Hiking time: 5 hours
Configuration: loop
Elevation gain: 1,300 feet
Difficulty: moderate to strenuous
Exposure: shaded canyon and exposed ridge
Dogs: allowed
Maps: U.S.G.S. Topanga and Conoga Park • Topanga State Park map
Tom Harrison Maps: Topanga State Park Trail map

map page 103

This canyon-to-ridge loop hike follows the forested canyon floor of Sullivan Canyon, climbs the chaparral-covered slopes to Sullivan Ridge, then returns back on the ridge along the Westridge Fire Road. En route, the trail follows Dirt Mulholland Drive a short distance, an unimproved road along the ridge overlooking the west end of Los Angeles, the San Fernando Valley, and the Encino Reservoir. (Dirt Mulholland is the unpaved portion of Mulholland Drive.) At the top end of the loop is San Vicente Mountain Park, formerly a Nike Missile Control Site. The old military outpost was active from 1956 through 1968. The 10-acre park includes a self-guided interpretive center with descriptions of its former life. (Also see Hike 26.) From the park, the trail descends on the Westridge Fire Road, a hiking and biking route straddling the ridge-line between Sullivan Canyon and Mandeville Canyon.

To the trailhead

From Santa Monica, drive 1.6 miles northbound on the Pacific Coast Highway/Highway 1 to Chautauqua Boulevard and turn

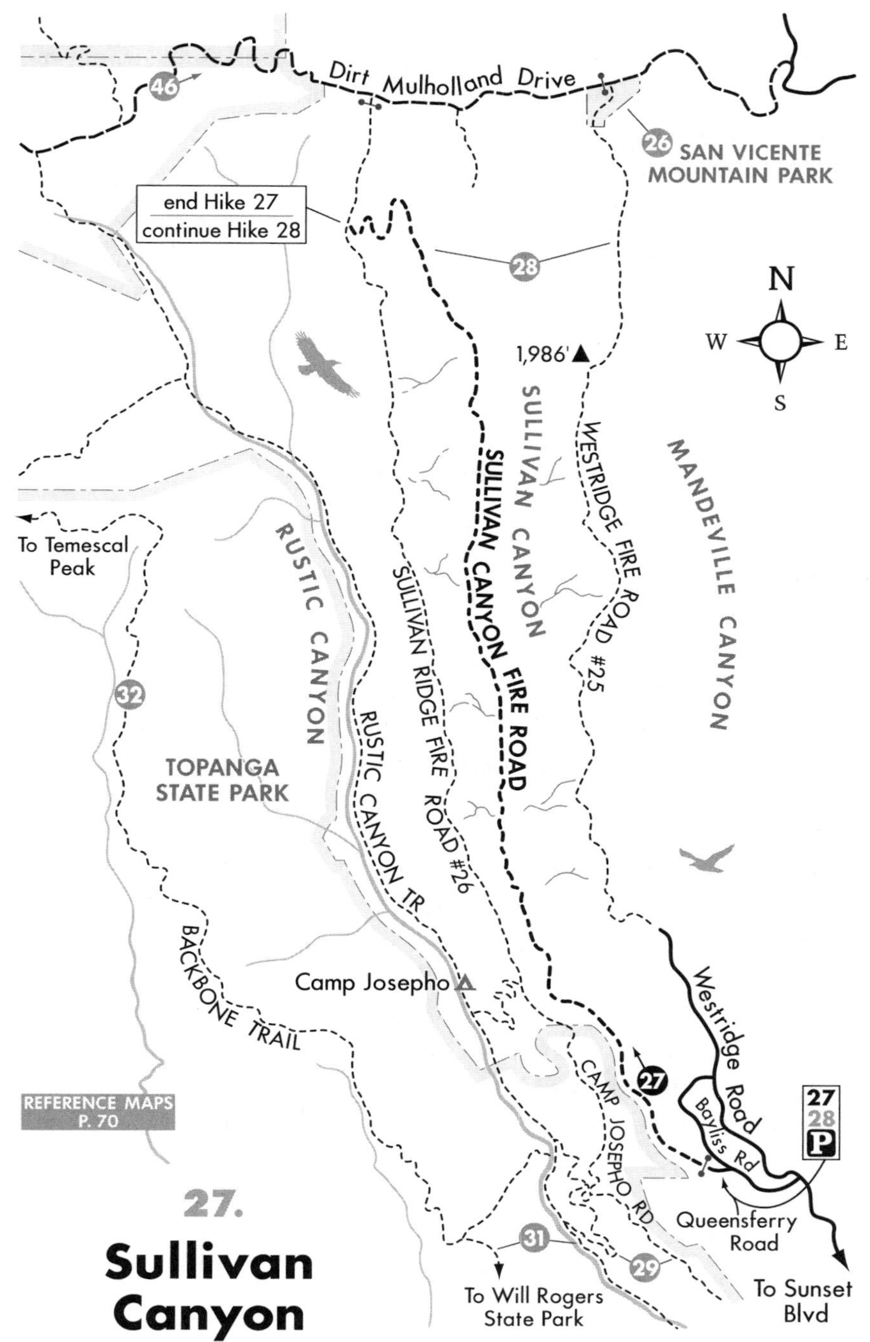

27. Sullivan Canyon

right. Continue 0.9 miles to Sunset Boulevard and turn right. Drive 2.8 miles and turn left on Mandeville Canyon Road. Turn left again at the first street—Westridge Road—and drive 1.2 miles to Bayliss Road. Turn left on Bayliss Road, and go 0.3 miles to Queensferry Road. Turn left and park near the trailhead gate.

The hike

Step around the vehicle-restricting gate. Walk 0.2 miles down the paved service road to the floor of Sullivan Canyon. Head to the right up the serene, sylvan canyon floor under a lush forest canopy. At 1 mile, cross a seasonal stream and pass sandstone outcroppings amidst high and narrow canyon walls. At 3.5 miles, Sullivan Canyon curves right (northeast) while the trail curves left (northwest) up a narrow side canyon. Climb the west canyon wall overlooking Sullivan Canyon. Follow the contours of the mountain up to the ridge and a T-junction with the Sullivan Ridge Fire Road, the turn-around point for Hike 27.

Bear right and head north on the ridge between Rustic Canyon and Sullivan Canyon, reaching Dirt Mulholland at a half mile. Walk around the gate and follow Dirt Mulholland to the right for 0.8 miles, overlooking the Encino Reservoir and the San Fernando Valley. Pass another gate and bear right into San Vicente Mountain Park, the defunct missile silo site. Walk up the paved road and through the park, passing picnic areas and vista overlooks. Take the Westridge Fire Road (also known as Sullivan Ridge East) along the narrow ridge that divides Sullivan and Mandeville Canyons. Follow the ridge south to the high point of the hike at 1,986 feet. Gradually descend along the contours of the ridge, overlooking Sullivan Canyon, Rustic Canyon, the west ridge of Temescal Canyon, and the Los Angeles basin. The fire road continues along the ridge until exiting at Westridge Road. Walk a half mile down Westridge Road, and turn right on Bayliss Road. Walk another half mile to Queensferry Road and turn right, returning to the trailhead. ■

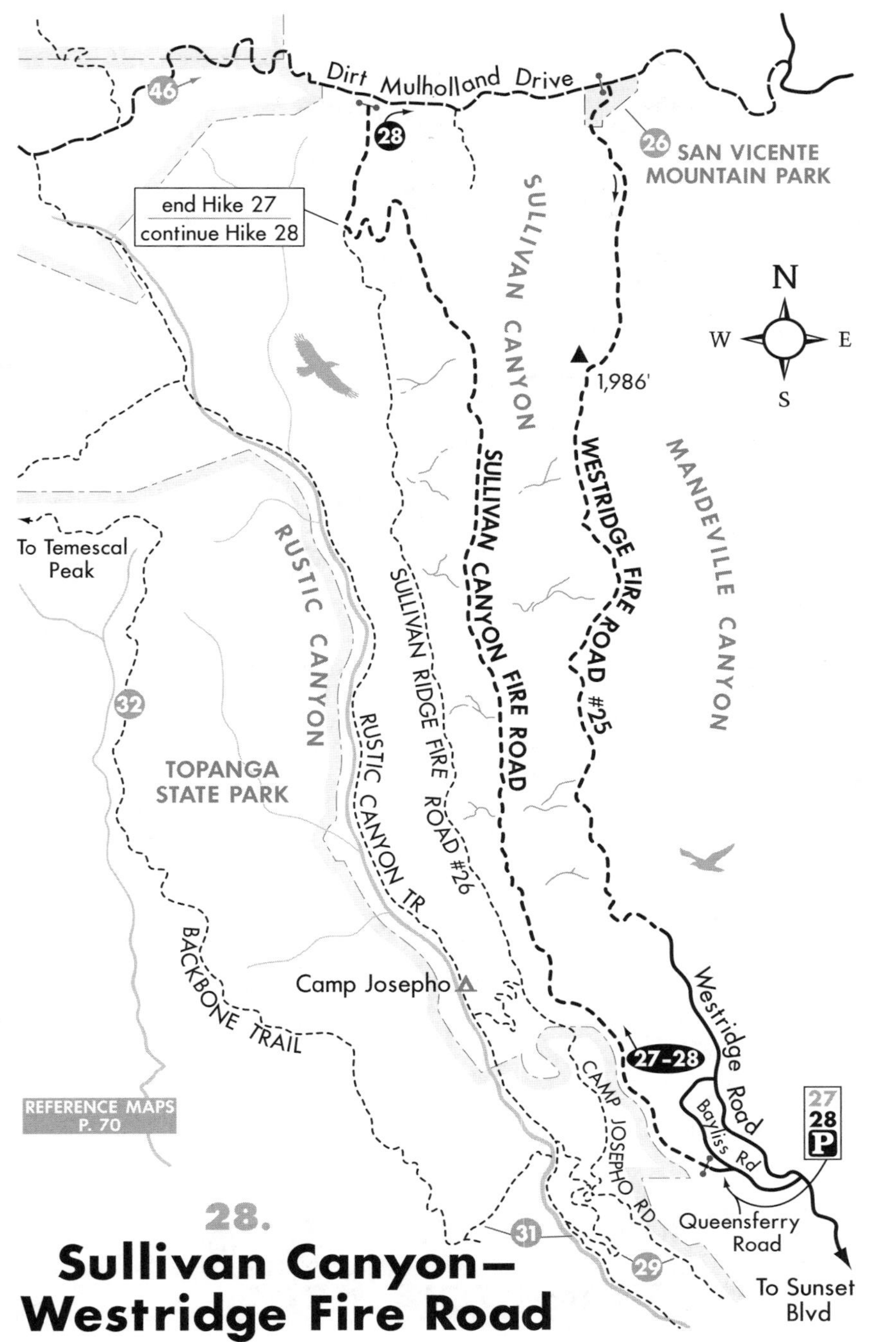

28. Sullivan Canyon— Westridge Fire Road

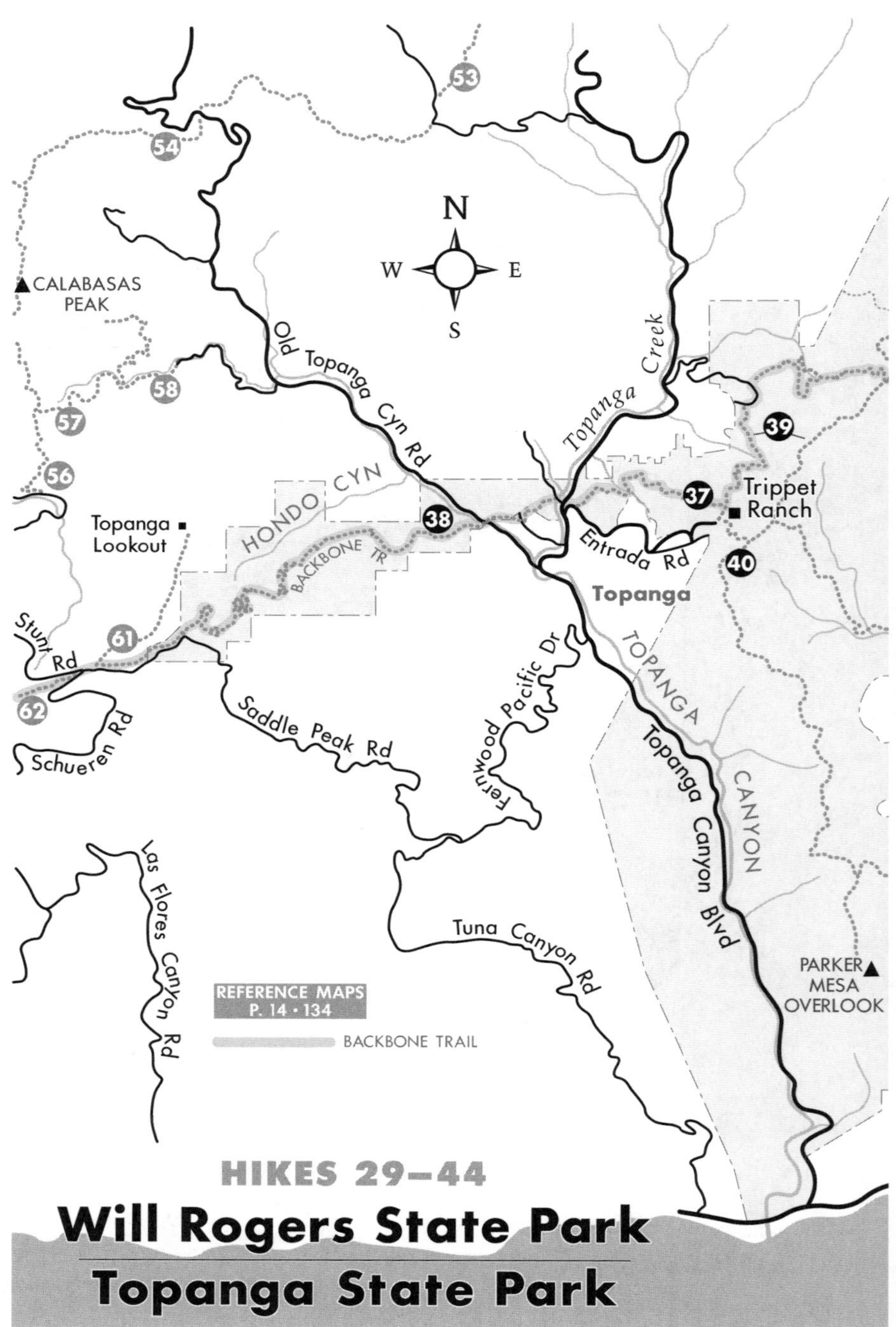
N
W
E
S
CALABASAS PEAK
Old Topanga Cyn Rd
Topanga Creek
HONDO CYN
BACKBONE TR
Trippet Ranch
Entrada Rd
Topanga
Topanga Lookout
Stunt Rd
Schueren Rd
Saddle Peak Rd
Fernwood Pacific Dr
TOPANGA CANYON
Topanga Canyon Blvd
Las Flores Canyon Rd
Tuna Canyon Rd
PARKER MESA OVERLOOK
REFERENCE MAPS P. 14 • 134
BACKBONE TRAIL
53
54
58
57
56
61
62
38
37
39
40
HIKES 29–44
Will Rogers State Park
Topanga State Park

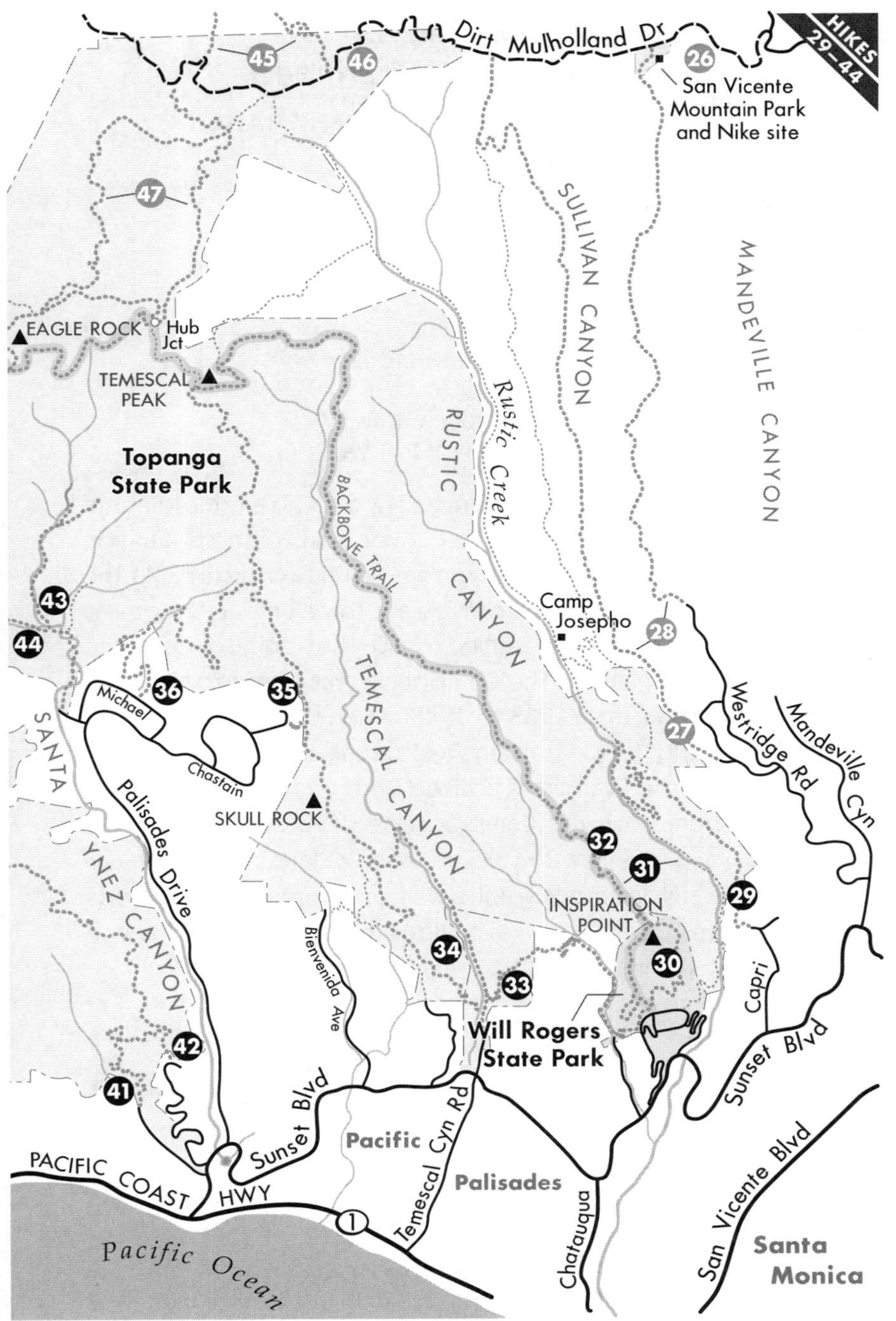

Dirt Mulholland Dr
HIKES 29–44
45
46
26
San Vicente Mountain Park and Nike site
47
SULLIVAN CANYON
MANDEVILLE CANYON
EAGLE ROCK
Hub Jct
TEMESCAL PEAK
Rustic Creek
RUSTIC CANYON
Topanga State Park
BACKBONE TRAIL
CANYON
Camp Josepho
43
44
28
TEMESCAL CANYON
36
35
Michael
SANTA YNEZ CANYON
Westridge Rd
Mandeville Cyn
27
Chastain
Palisades Drive
SKULL ROCK
32
31
29
INSPIRATION POINT
Bienvenida Ave
34
30
33
Capri
42
Will Rogers State Park
41
Sunset Blvd
Temescal Cyn Rd
Pacific
Palisades
Sunset Blvd
San Vicente Blvd
PACIFIC COAST HWY
1
Pacific Ocean
Chatauqua
Santa Monica

29. Rustic Canyon from the Capri Trailhead

CAMP JOSEPHO ROAD to MURPHY RANCH

Pacific Palisades

Hiking distance: 3.4 miles round trip
Hiking time: 2 hours
Configuration: out-and-back with loop
Elevation gain: 400 feet
Difficulty: easy to slightly moderate
Exposure: exposed fire road and shaded forest
Dogs: allowed
Maps: U.S.G.S. Topanga • Topanga State Park map
Tom Harrison Maps: Topanga State Park Trail Map

Rustic Canyon is a deep, stream-fed canyon with a remote atmosphere that lies between Sullivan Canyon and Temescal Canyon above Pacific Palisades. The canyon has an unusual history. At the bottom of the narrow, steep canyon are three unique structures built in the 1930s within a secluded 50-acre compound, once known as Murphy Ranch. The compound was home to a clan of Nazi sympathizers from 1933 to 1945, when they were arrested. In the 1950s and 1960s, the enclave became an artists' colony. The partially burned buildings scarred with graffiti still remain.

This hike begins on the Camp Josepho Fire Road (which becomes Sullivan Ridge Fire Road). The trail descends into the heavily wooded canyon among giant oaks, sycamores, cottonwoods, and eucalyptus trees. The hike includes a loop along the canyon floor, passing the historic structures near the stream.

To the trailhead

From Santa Monica, drive 3 miles northbound on the Pacific Coast Highway/Highway 1 to Sunset Boulevard. Turn right and drive 5 miles to Capri Drive. (Capri Drive is located 1.3 miles past the Will Rogers State Park turnoff.) Turn left and continue 0.6 miles to Casale Road. The trail begins to the left on Casale Road, but this section of the road is a no-parking zone. Instead, turn right and park along the right side or park on Capri Drive.

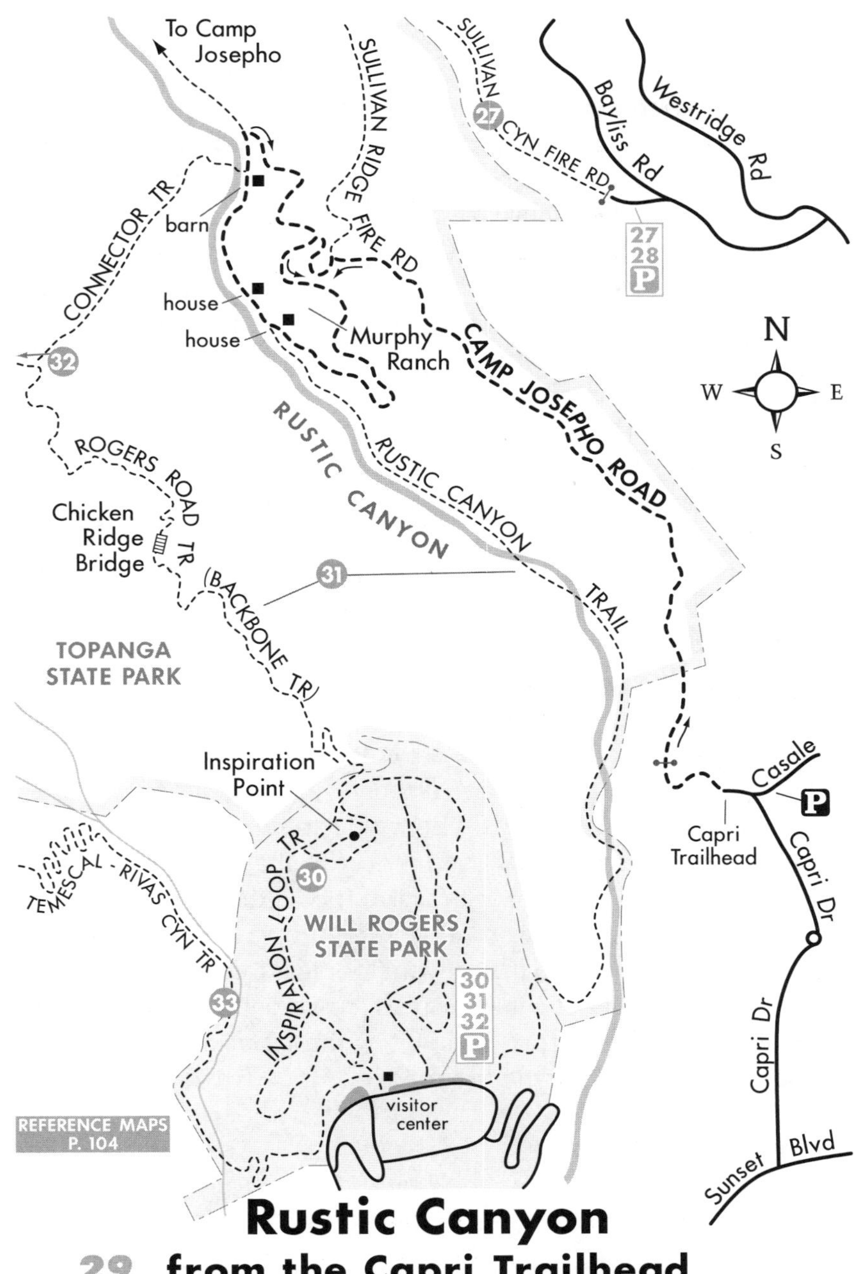

Rustic Canyon

29. from the Capri Trailhead

Camp Josepho Road to Murphy Ranch

The hike

Walk 0.1 mile west on Casale Road and veer to the right. Continue up the Sullivan Ridge Fire Road (also known as Camp Josepho Road), a partially paved road high above forested Rustic Canyon. Pass through a vehicle gate by a map kiosk. Meander up and down the paved mountain road to a rusted version of the Pearly Gates on the left at 1.3 miles. (You can't miss it.)

Leave the paved road and cross through an opening in the rock wall. Descend 0.1 mile on the abandoned road into the shade of the mixed forest to a distinct Y-fork. Begin the loop to the left and gently wend into the canyon. At a half mile from the junction, near the canyon floor, is an abandoned concrete house with pillared arches, originally used as a power-generator building. The entire house is covered inside and out with colorful graffiti and murals. A hundred yards ahead is an equally amazing two-story metal compound with large rusted metal parts scattered about, apparently used as the garage. Both buildings were part of the Murphy Ranch complex. From here, the road turns into a footpath and continues up canyon. Stroll through the dense forest among pine, eucalyptus, oak, bay laurel, spruce, and towering sycamore trees. A short distance ahead is a fence-enclosed wooden barn, once part of Anatol Josepho's ranch. At the abandoned barn is a posted junction. To the left, a connector path leads up the west canyon wall to the Rogers Road Trail atop the ridge, part of the Backbone Trail (Hike 31). For this hike, follow the canyon bottom straight ahead 200 yards to a right bend by a rock wall. To the left, a trail continues up the canyon floor less than a mile to Camp Josepho, a Boy Scout camp. Instead, curve right up the partially paved road to the Y-fork, completing the 1.2-mile loop. Retrace your steps back along the fire road. ■

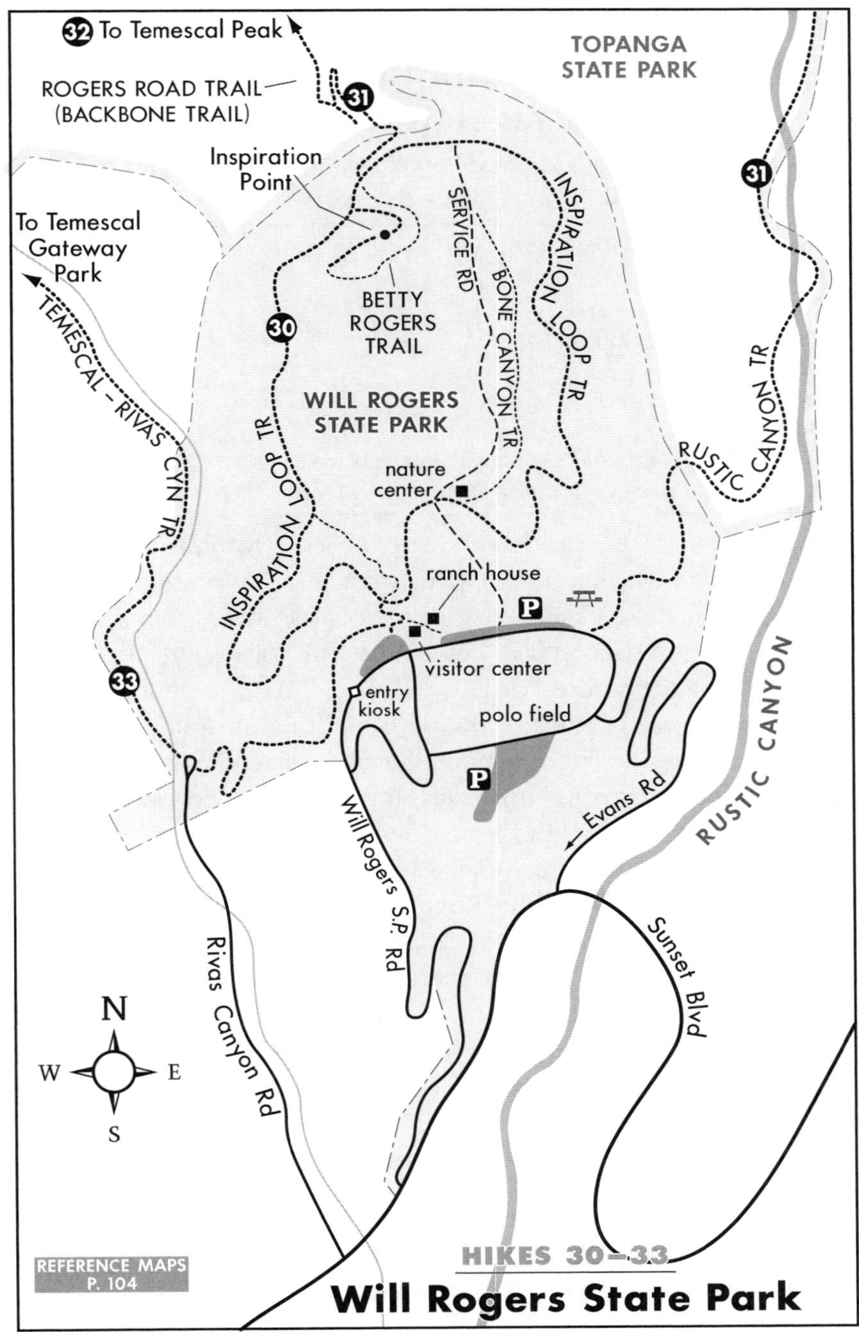

HIKES 30–33

Will Rogers State Park

30. Inspiration Loop Trail to Inspiration Point

WILL ROGERS STATE HISTORIC PARK

1501 Will Rogers State Park Road • Pacific Palisades
Open 8 a.m.—5 p.m. daily

Hiking distance: 2-mile loop
Hiking time: 1 hour
Configuration: loop
Elevation gain: 300 feet
Difficulty: easy
Exposure: exposed
Dogs: allowed
Maps: U.S.G.S. Topanga • Topanga State Park map
Tom Harrison Maps: Topanga State Park Trail Map

Will Rogers State Historic Park is a 186-acre retreat in the hills above Santa Monica. The land was set aside as a state park in 1944. Within the parkland are picnic grounds, horse riding stables, and trails with spectacular views. Tours of Will Rogers' 31-room ranch home are offered daily.

At the upper reaches of the park is Inspiration Point, a broad, flat knoll overlooking the beautiful park grounds and the rugged mountain canyons and ridges. The expansive views from the 751-foot overlook extend from downtown Los Angeles to Santa Monica and across Santa Monica Bay to Palos Verdes. Inspiration Point Loop Trail, designed by Rogers himself, is a two-mile trail that climbs the undeveloped hillside behind the ranch to Inspiration Point. The top of the loop connects with the eastern terminus of the Backbone Trail, which crosses the spine of the Santa Monica Mountains for 64 miles to Point Mugu State Park. For longer hiking options, take the Backbone Trail to Rustic Canyon (Hike 31) or Temescal Peak (Hike 32).

To the trailhead

From Santa Monica, drive 1.6 miles northbound on the Pacific Coast Highway/Highway 1 to Chautauqua Boulevard. Turn right and continue 0.9 miles to Sunset Boulevard. Turn right again. Drive

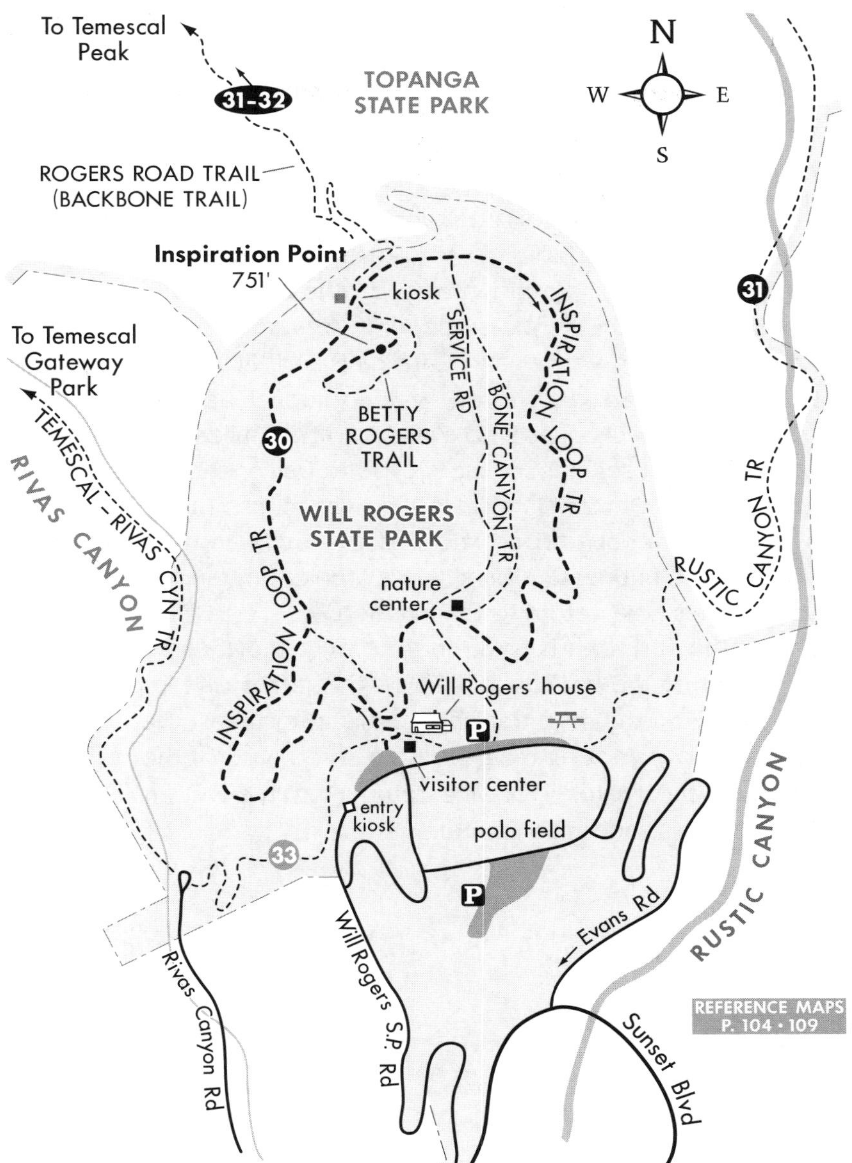

30. Inspiration Loop Trail to Inspiration Point

WILL ROGERS STATE HISTORIC PARK

0.5 miles and turn left at Will Rogers State Park Road. The parking area is 0.7 miles ahead on the left, just past the entrance station. Another parking lot is a short distance farther, on the left by the visitor center. A parking fee is required.

The hike

Begin the hike from the visitor center and Will Rogers' home, built in 1928. Head west (left) past the tennis courts and the Temescal-Rivas Canyon Trail to a dirt fire road—the Inspiration Loop Trail. Head uphill on the gentle slope, with views across coastal Los Angeles to Palos Verdes and Catalina Island. Climb the ridge to the north above Rivas Canyon, with additional views across the mountainous backcountry, to a junction at 0.8 miles. The left fork begins the first segment of the Backbone Trail on the Rogers Road Trail (Hike 31). Detour 0.1 mile to the right to Inspiration Point, an overlook on a flat-topped knoll. After resting and savoring the views of the entire state park, Santa Monica Bay, and the greater Los Angeles area, return to the junction.

Take the fork that is now on your right (northeast). Pass the beginning of the Backbone Trail on the left by an information kiosk. Stay on the main trail and continue northeast. Descend to the south, overlooking the polo field at the base of the hill. Walk through a eucalyptus-lined lane, returning to the well-maintained park grounds and visitor center. ■

31. Rustic Canyon Loop from Will Rogers State Historic Park

WILL ROGERS STATE HISTORIC PARK

TOPANGA STATE PARK

1501 Will Rogers State Park Road • Pacific Palisades

Hiking distance: 5-mile loop
Hiking time: 3 hours
Configuration: loop
Elevation gain: 1,000 feet
Difficulty: moderate to somewhat strenuous
Exposure: exposed ridge and forested canyon
Dogs: allowed on Inspiration Loop Trail only
Maps: U.S.G.S. Topanga • Topanga State Park map
Tom Harrison Maps: Topanga State Park Trail Map

map page 115

Rustic Canyon is a lush, stream-fed canyon to the northeast of Will Rogers State Historic Park. This hike begins in the state park on the Inspiration Loop Trail, then returns back through secluded Rustic Canyon. En route, the hike connects with the Rogers Road Trail, the easternmost segment of the Backbone Trail. The trail straddles the razor-point ridge between Rustic and Rivas Canyons. From the ridge, the canyon and ocean views are spectacular.

The return trail along the narrow floor of steep-walled Rustic Canyon passes three old abandoned structures. The dilapidated, graffiti-covered buildings are the remnants of a 50-acre pro-Nazi compound known as Murphy Ranch. The colony of Nazi sympathizers occupied the canyon from 1933 to 1945. The enclave later became an artists' colony in the 1950s and 1960s. After passing the structures, the trail parallels the year-round watercourse of Rustic Creek through a narrow canyon before looping back to Will Rogers State Park.

To the trailhead

From Santa Monica, drive 1.6 miles northbound on the Pacific Coast Highway/Highway 1 to Chautauqua Boulevard. Turn right and continue 0.9 miles to Sunset Boulevard. Turn right again. Drive 0.5 miles and turn left at Will Rogers State Park Road. The parking area is 0.7 miles ahead on the left, just past the entrance station.

Another parking lot is a short distance farther, on the left by the visitor center. A parking fee is required.

The hike

Begin the hike from the visitor center and Will Rogers' home, built in 1928. Head west (left) past the tennis courts and the Temescal-Rivas Canyon Trail to a dirt fire road—the Inspiration Loop Trail. Head uphill on the gentle uphill grade with views across coastal Los Angeles to Palos Verdes and Catalina Island. At 0.8 miles is a junction and additional views across the mountainous backcountry. Detour 0.1 mile straight ahead to Inspiration Point, with sweeping vistas across Los Angeles.

Return to the junction and head 70 yards north to Rogers Road Trail, the beginning of the Backbone Trail. Head up the footpath, entering Topanga State Park. (Dogs are not allowed on the trail after this point.) Climb north on the ridge between Rivas Canyon and Rustic Canyon. At 1.5 miles, cross Chicken Ridge Bridge and follow the steep, knife-edged slope at an elevation of 1,125 feet. At just under 2 miles is a junction on a saddle. The main trail continues along the ridge and leads to Temescal Peak (Hike 32).

For this hike, leave the Backbone Trail and steeply descend into Rustic Canyon on the right, dropping nearly 700 feet in a half mile. At the canyon floor, cross Rustic Creek to the Rustic Canyon Trail by a fenced barn, once part of Anatol Josepho's ranch. The left fork leads up canyon to Camp Josepho, a Boy Scout camp (named after Anatol Josepho, a friend of Will Rogers). Head down canyon to the right, and stroll through the dense forest among pine, eucalyptus, oak, bay laurel, spruce, and towering sycamore trees. Pass an amazing two-story metal building with rusted metal parts scattered around it and an abandoned concrete house with arches, used as a power-generator building. The entire house is covered inside and out with colorful graffiti and murals. Both buildings were part of the Murphy Ranch complex.

The vertical rock-walled canyon narrows, and the path crisscrosses Rustic Creek in the dense forest. Pass an old flood-control dam built in the early 1900s. The canyon widens and curves uphill to the polo field across from Will Rogers' home, completing the loop. ■

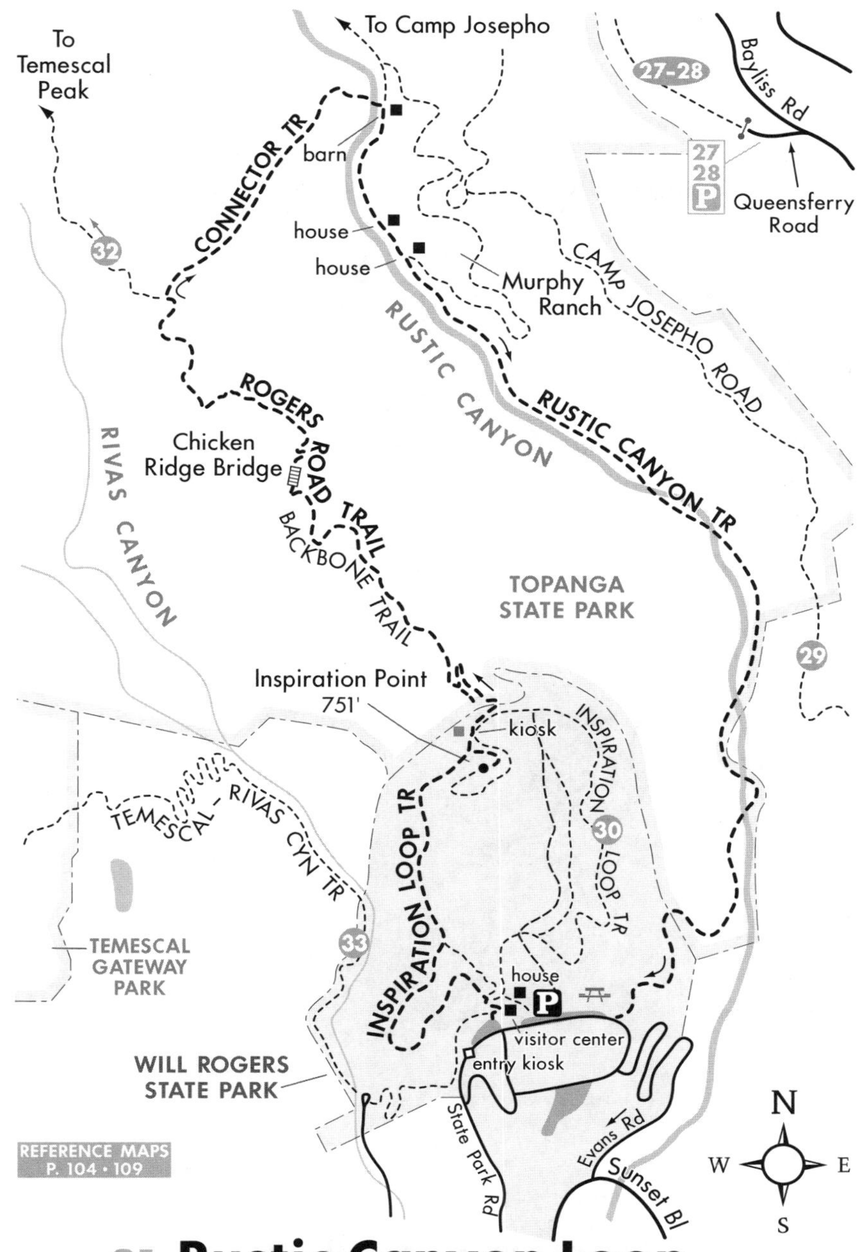

31. Rustic Canyon Loop

WILL ROGERS S.P. • TOPANGA STATE PARK

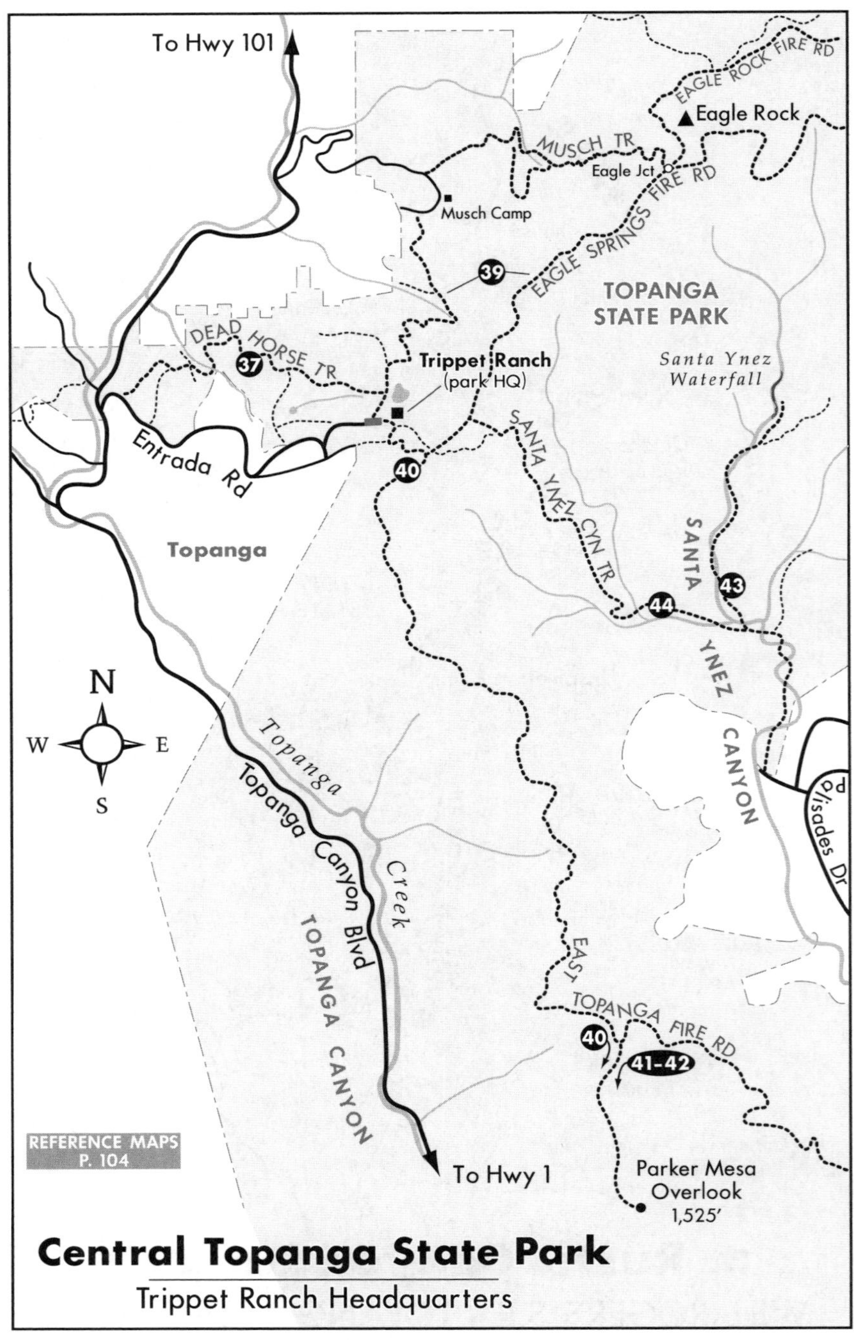

Central Topanga State Park

Trippet Ranch Headquarters

Topanga State Park

Topanga State Park is located adjacent to the unincorporated town of Topanga in western Los Angeles County. The state park is entirely within the city of Los Angeles, making it the world's largest municipal wildland. The 11,525-acre park is bordered by Topanga Canyon on the west and the rugged Rustic Canyon on the east. Between Topanga Canyon and Rustic Canyon are two other major drainages—Temescal Canyon and Santa Ynez Canyon. At the head of Temescal Canyon lies Temescal Peak, the highest peak in the park at 2,126 feet.

The park contains a wide variety of habitats, including open grasslands; stream-fed canyons with riparian forests; live oak woodlands; bay laurel, walnut, and sycamore groves; and coastal sage scrub. Scattered throughout the landscape are boulder-studded ridges, dramatic sandstone cliffs, caves, waterfalls, earthquake faults, marine fossils, and volcanic intrusions. Overlooks, such as Parker Mesa Overlook and Eagle Rock, offer spectacular ocean-to-mountain vistas.

Trippet Ranch, the park headquarters, is located on an old homestead from the 1890s. The 80-acre homestead is currently the main entrance into Topanga State Park and a popular staging area for accessing the trails. At the ranch is a nature center, pond, shaded picnic areas, and trailheads. Another popular access point into the park is the Reseda Boulevard trailhead, northwest of Trippet Ranch at the north boundary.

The sprawling state park wildland has a complex network of more than 36 miles of hiking, mountain biking, and equestrian trails. The trail system is a combination of wide fire roads, single-track trails, and informal footpaths. An unpaved portion of Mulholland Drive runs through the north end of the park. Nearly 15 miles of the Backbone Trail traverse through the heart of the park, beginning at the trail's easternmost trailhead at Will Rogers State Park.

Note: Dogs are not allowed in the state park.

32. Temescal Peak from Will Rogers State Historic Park

WILL ROGERS STATE HISTORIC PARK

TOPANGA STATE PARK

1501 Will Rogers State Park Road • Pacific Palisades

Hiking distance: 14 miles round trip
Hiking time: 7.5 hours
Configuration: out-and-back
Elevation gain: 1,650 feet
Difficulty: strenuous
Exposure: exposed with shady pockets
Dogs: not allowed after first mile
Maps: U.S.G.S. Topanga • Topanga State Park map
Tom Harrison Maps: Topanga State Park Trail Map
Will Rogers State Historic Park map

map page 120

Temescal Peak, rising to a height of 2,126 feet, is the highest peak in Topanga State Park. The peak separates the watersheds of Rustic Canyon, Santa Ynez Canyon, and Temescal Canyon. Atop the peak is a small mound of rocks, a survey benchmark, and a metal post. From the unadorned peak, the sweeping vistas extend north to the Los Padres National Forest, east to the San Gabriel Mountains, south to the Pacific Ocean and Catalina Island, and west across the seemingly endless ridges of the Santa Monica Mountains.

Temescal Peak is accessible from several approaches. This route begins from Will Rogers State Historic Park and follows a ridge northwest between Temescal Canyon and Rustic Canyon, two stream-fed drainages. From Will Rogers State Park, the trail heads into Topanga State Park on the Rogers Road Trail, the easternmost segment of the 69-mile-long Backbone Trail. The trail follows the steep ridge nearly all the way to Temescal Peak. Throughout the hike are wide-angle panoramas of the Santa Monica Mountains stretching across Los Angeles and the San Fernando Valley.

Other accesses to the peak are from the south in Pacific Palisades (Temescal Ridge Trail—Hikes 35 and 36), from the west at Trippet Ranch (Hike 38), and from the north off of Dirt Mulholland (Hike 46).

To the trailhead

From Santa Monica, drive 1.6 miles northbound on the Pacific Coast Highway/Highway 1 to Chautauqua Boulevard. Turn right and continue 0.9 miles to Sunset Boulevard. Turn right again. Drive 0.5 miles and turn left at Will Rogers State Park Road. The parking area is 0.7 miles ahead on the left, just past the entrance station. Another parking lot is a short distance farther, on the left by the visitor center. A parking fee is required.

The hike

Begin the hike from the visitor center and Will Rogers' home, built in 1928. Head west (left) past the tennis courts and the Temescal-Rivas Canyon Trail to a dirt fire road—the Inspiration Loop Trail. Head uphill on the gentle uphill grade with views across coastal Los Angeles to Palos Verdes and Catalina Island. At 0.8 miles is a junction and additional views across the mountainous back-country. Detour 0.1 mile straight ahead to Inspiration Point, with sweeping vistas across Los Angeles.

Return to the junction and head 70 yards north to Rogers Road Trail, the beginning of the Backbone Trail. Head up the footpath, leaving Will Rogers State Park, and enter Topanga State Park. (Dogs are not allowed on the trail after this point.) Climb north on the ridge between Rivas Canyon and Rustic Canyon. At 1.5 miles, cross Chicken Ridge Bridge and follow the steep, knife-edged slope at an elevation of 1,125 feet. Climb to additional views into forested Rustic Canyon and Sullivan Canyon to the right. At just under 2 miles is a junction on a saddle. To the right is the connector trail into Rustic Canyon—Hike 31.

Stay on the main Rogers Road Trail to the left. Descend along the east wall of Temescal Canyon to Lone Oak, a massive coast live oak tree with five trunks. The tree sits on a flat with northern views to the Los Padres National Forest. Veer left and meander through a corridor under a tree-shaded canopy. Weave through the quiet of the backcountry as the trail dips and rises. From 1,900 feet above the city, the views extend across Tarzana, Woodland Hills, and the entire San Fernando Valley. Bear left and cross the head of the canyon. Traverse the north-facing slope to a posted junction with the Bay Tree Trail at 6.3 miles. Stay to the left towards the signed Hub Junction. Wind along the mountainous contours 0.6 miles to the Temescal Ridge Trail. Just shy of this junction, a side path climbs the hill up to Temescal Peak, the 2,126-foot summit of the hike. After enjoying the 360-degree vistas, return along the same trail.

From Temescal Peak, the Backbone Trail connects to the Temescal Ridge Trail, which heads south to Temescal Gateway Park and Sunset Boulevard (Hike 34) and north to Hub Junction and Eagle Rock (Hikes 38 & 46). ■

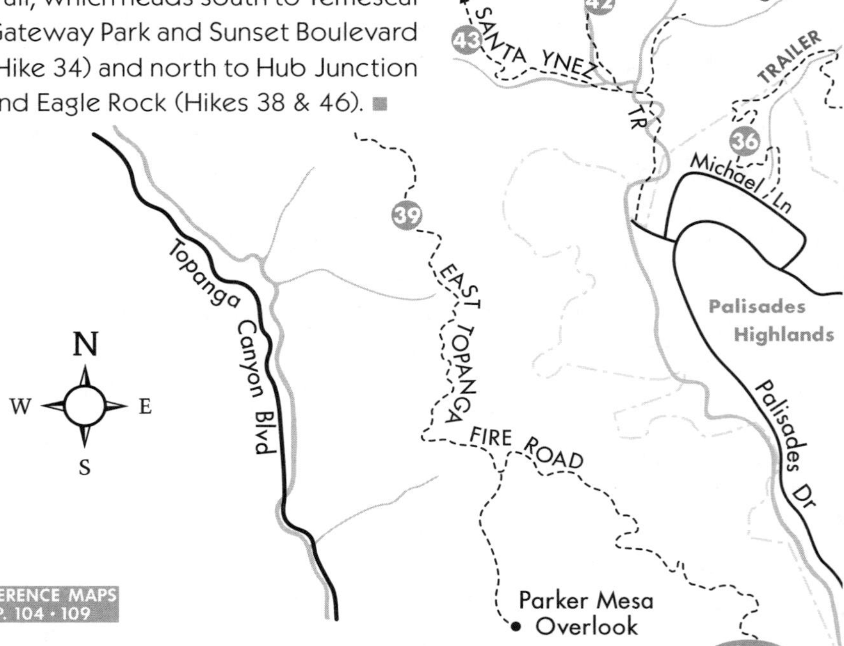

32. Temescal Peak

from Will Rogers State Historic Park

WILL ROGERS STATE HISTORIC PARK

TOPANGA STATE PARK

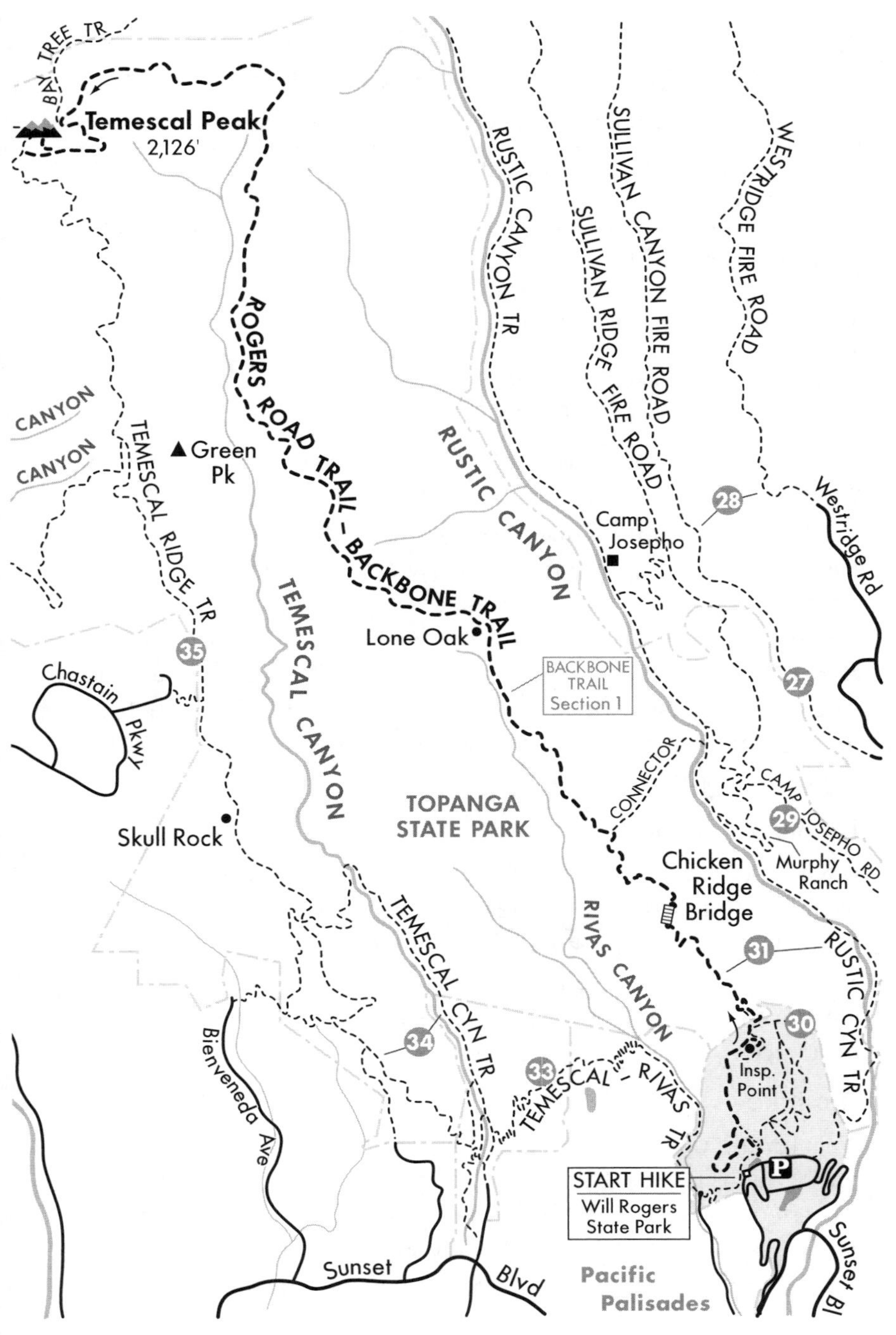
BAY TREE TR
Temescal Peak
2,126'
ROGERS ROAD TRAIL - BACKBONE TRAIL
RUSTIC CANYON TR
SULLIVAN CANYON FIRE ROAD
SULLIVAN RIDGE FIRE ROAD
WESTRIDGE FIRE ROAD
CANYON
CANYON
TEMESCAL RIDGE TR
Green Pk
RUSTIC CANYON
Camp Josepho
28
Westridge Rd
TEMESCAL CANYON
Lone Oak
BACKBONE TRAIL Section 1
35
Chastain Pkwy
27
CONNECTOR
CAMP JOSEPHO RD
TOPANGA STATE PARK
29
Murphy Ranch
Skull Rock
Chicken Ridge Bridge
RIVAS CANYON
TEMESCAL CYN TR
31
RUSTIC CYN TR
30
34
33
TEMESCAL - RIVAS TR
Insp. Point
Bienveneda Ave
START HIKE
Will Rogers State Park
P
Sunset Blvd
Sunset Bl
Pacific Palisades

33. Temescal—Rivas Trail
Temescal Canyon to Will Rogers State Park

15601 Sunset Boulevard • Pacific Palisades

Hiking distance: 4.4 miles round trip
Hiking time: 2.5 hours
Configuration: out-and-back
Elevation gain: 500 feet
Difficulty: moderate
Exposure: mostly forested
Dogs: allowed
Maps: U.S.G.S. Topanga • Topanga State Park map
Tom Harrison Maps: Topanga State Park Trail Map

map page 124

Temescal Canyon and Rivas Canyon are adjacent drainages within Topanga State Park. This connector trail in the hills above Pacific Palisades links Temescal Gateway Park with Will Rogers State Historic Park. The forested trail, which emanates from both popular parks, is a quiet path that avoids the crowds. This hike begins at 141-acre Temescal Gateway Park in Temescal Canyon. The trail climbs through groves of oaks to open, chaparral-clad slopes with coastal views across Santa Monica Bay. The path then weaves into a lush canopy on the floor of Rivas Canyon, offering a shaded respite.

To the trailhead

From Santa Monica, drive 2 miles northbound on the Pacific Coast Highway/Highway 1 to Temescal Canyon Road. Turn right and drive 1.3 miles to the end of Temescal Canyon Road, crossing Sunset Boulevard en route. Park in the Temescal Gateway parking lot at the conference and retreat center. A parking fee is required.

The hike

Walk up the paved road, staying to the right. The posted trail is on the right, just past the first group of cabins. Climb steps into a shaded oak grove. Wind up the hillside along the switchbacks on the east slope of Temescal Canyon. The landscape alternates from chaparral on the sunny slopes to tree-shaded glens. Steadily climb the canyon wall to views of Pacific Palisades and the ocean south to Palos Verdes. At 0.8 miles, the trail reaches an overlook north of the reservoir, with interior views across layers of mountain ridges. Begin the descent on a series of ten switchbacks into Rivas Canyon. Drop into the riparian forest with ferns and vines enveloping the towering sycamore trees. Stroll down the canyon floor under beautiful oak, sycamore, and eucalyptus trees. The footpath crosses an old road at a cul-de-sac, then climbs steps and weaves over the hill. Pass through a gate and into Will Rogers State Park. Cross a grassy flat to the Inspiration Loop Trail, a dirt fire road at 2.2 miles. The visitor center and Will Rogers' home are a short distance to the right. Return by retracing your steps.

To extend the hike, the trail goes left and leads 0.9 miles to Inspiration Point (Hike 29). ■

34. Temescal Canyon Loop

TEMESCAL GATEWAY PARK • TOPANGA STATE PARK

15601 Sunset Boulevard • Pacific Palisades

Hiking distance: 4.2-mile loop
Hiking time: 2 hours
Configuration: loop with half-mile spur to Skull Rock
Elevation gain: 1,000 feet
Difficulty: moderate to somewhat strenuous
Exposure: exposed ridge and forested canyon
Dogs: not allowed
Maps: U.S.G.S. Topanga • Topanga State Park map
Tom Harrison Maps: Topanga State Park Trail map

map page 127

Temescal Canyon is a creek-fed canyon within Topanga State Park that is shaded by oaks, maples, and sycamores. This canyon-to-ridgetop loop hike climbs the hillside cliffs on the west side of the canyon and follows the ridge, offering far-reaching views of Los Angeles and the Pacific coastline. The return route drops into the tree-shaded canyon to a footbridge at the seasonal Temescal Canyon Falls, framed by huge volcanic rocks. The trail begins at Temescal Gateway Park, a 141-acre oasis in the hills

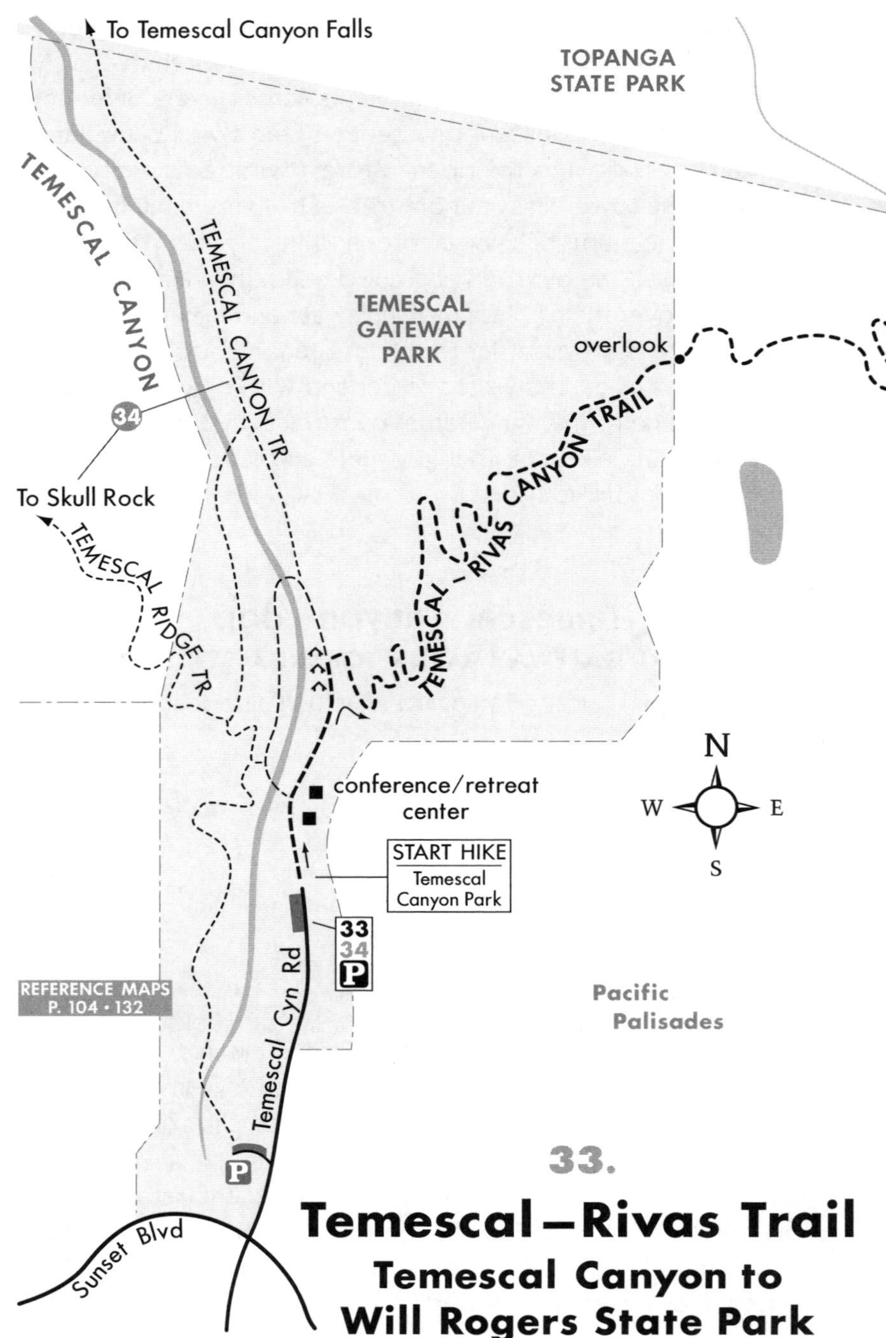

33. Temescal–Rivas Trail

Temescal Canyon to Will Rogers State Park

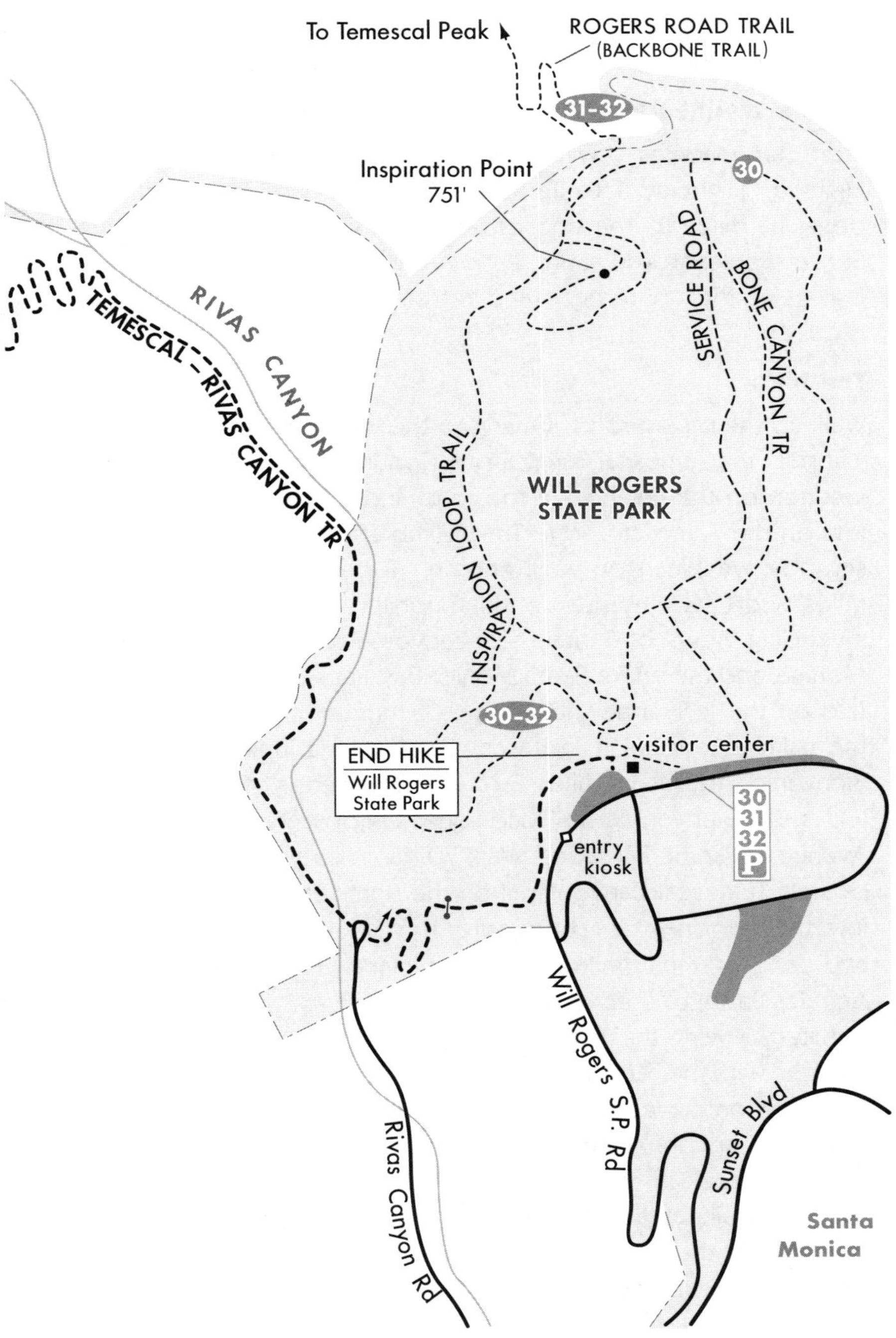
To Temescal Peak
ROGERS ROAD TRAIL
(BACKBONE TRAIL)
31-32
Inspiration Point
751'
30
SERVICE ROAD
BONE CANYON TR
RIVAS CANYON
TEMESCAL - RIVAS CANYON TR
INSPIRATION LOOP TRAIL
WILL ROGERS
STATE PARK
30-32
END HIKE
Will Rogers
State Park
visitor center
30
31
32
P
entry
kiosk
Will Rogers S.P. Rd
Sunset Blvd
Rivas Canyon Rd
Santa
Monica

above Pacific Palisades. En route, a short spur trail leads to Skull Rock, a weather-carved formation resembling a human skull.

To the trailhead

From Santa Monica, drive 2 miles northbound on the Pacific Coast Highway/Highway 1 to Temescal Canyon Road. Turn right and drive 1.3 miles to the end of Temescal Canyon Road, crossing Sunset Boulevard en route. Park in the Temescal Gateway parking lot at the conference and retreat center. A parking fee is required.

The hike

Walk up the paved road, staying to the left at a road split that is just past the Temescal Camp Store. Continue 25 yards to a signed junction on the left. Leave the road and begin the loop to the left on the Temescal Ridge Trail. Climb steps and zigzag up the scrubby west canyon wall, entering Topanga State Park at 0.3 miles. Short switchbacks continue uphill to the open ridge, with sweeping views of Santa Ynez Canyon, Pacific Palisades, Santa Monica, and the entire Santa Monica Bay. Pass the signed Leacock Trail on the left, a neighborhood connector path. Continue up the ridge overlooking Temescal Canyon to a junction with the Bienvenida Trail at 1.6 miles. En route are a series of coastal overlooks. The Bienvenida Trail leads one mile downhill to Bienvenida Avenue in Pacific Palisades. Walk 70 yards straight ahead to the posted Temescal Canyon Trail on the right. The right fork drops into the canyon—the return route. To visit Skull Rock, detour left and continue a half mile uphill, with inland vistas across the Los Angeles Basin, to the wind-sculpted rock.

After viewing the carved sandstone formation, return to the junction with the Temescal Canyon Trail. Take the Temescal Canyon Trail (now on the left/east) and steeply descend into the densely wooded canyon. At the canyon floor is a wooden footbridge over the creek in the rock grotto just below Temescal Canyon Falls. The trail parallels the creek downstream along the east canyon wall. At the canyon floor, wind through the parklands under groves of eucalyptus, sycamore, willow, and coastal oak, back to the trailhead. ■

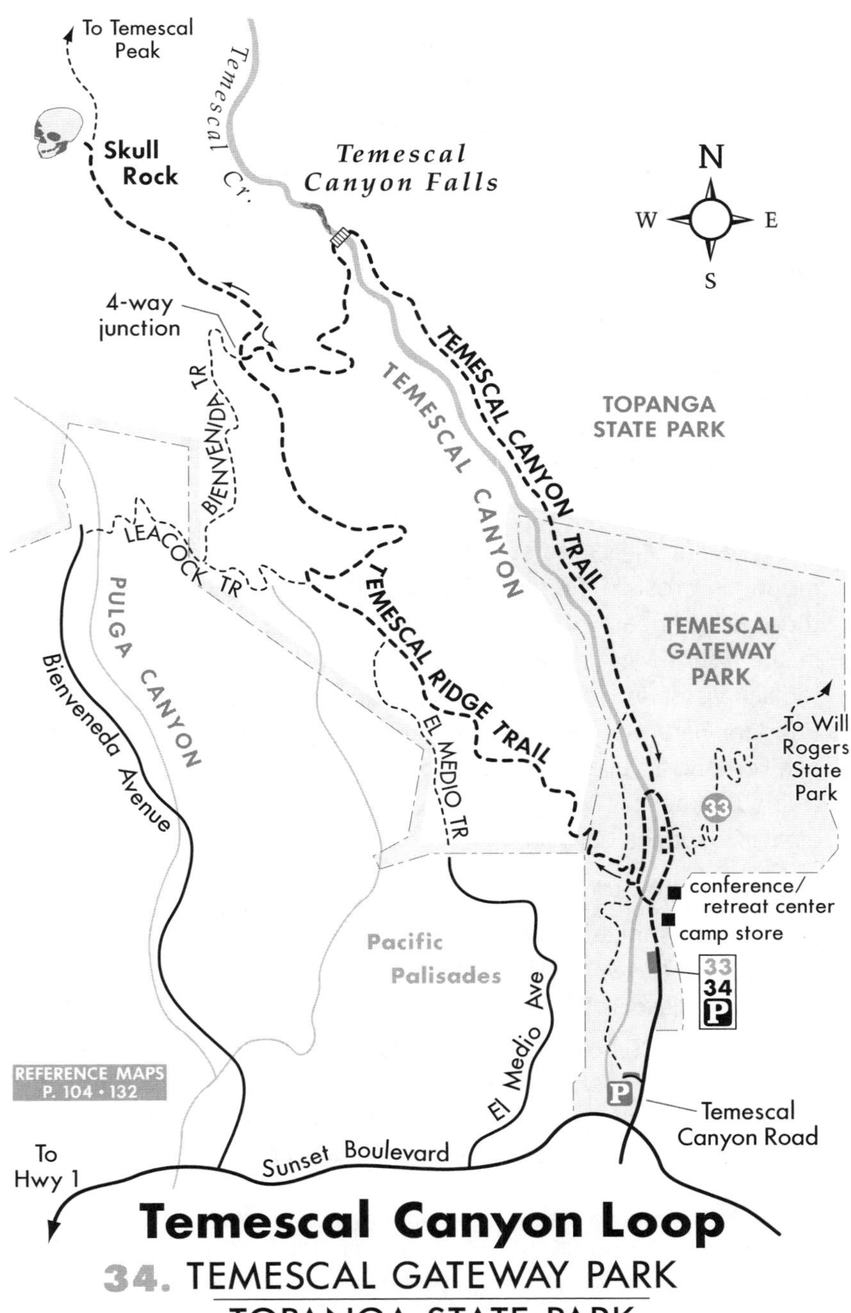

Temescal Canyon Loop

34. TEMESCAL GATEWAY PARK
TOPANGA STATE PARK

35. Temescal Ridge Trail to Temescal Peak

TOPANGA STATE PARK

Pacific Palisades trailhead

Hiking distance: 6 miles round trip
Hiking time: 3 hours
Configuration: up-and-back
Elevation gain: 550 feet
Difficulty: moderate
Exposure: shadeless ridge
Dogs: not allowed
Maps: U.S.G.S. Topanga · Topanga State Park map
Tom Harrison Maps: Topanga State Park Trail Map

The Temescal Ridge Trail is a 7.7-mile-long fire road that connects Pacific Palisades at the coast with Dirt Mulholland on the mountain crest in Tarzana. The undulating ridgetop trail climbs through the heart of Topanga State Park, the largest state park in the Santa Monica Mountains. Throughout the hike are spectacular vistas into Santa Ynez Canyon, Temescal Canyon, Rustic Canyon, Garapito Canyon, and across the Los Angeles Basin and San Fernando Valley. This hike follows the middle section of the trail to Temescal Peak, the highest peak in the mountain range east of Topanga Canyon.

To the trailhead

From Santa Monica, drive 3 miles northbound on the Pacific Coast Highway/Highway 1 to Sunset Boulevard. Turn right and drive 0.4 miles to Palisades Drive. Turn left and continue 3.9 miles to Via Las Palmas, a private road on the right. (En route, Palisades Drive becomes Chastain Parkway.) Turn right and drive 0.1 mile to the trailhead parking spaces on the left. If parking spaces are not available, park along the curb on Chastain Parkway.

The hike

Instead of walking up the road to the north, which seems like the natural route, walk south on the paved walkway. Follow the landscaped corridor along a concrete drainage. Zigzag up three

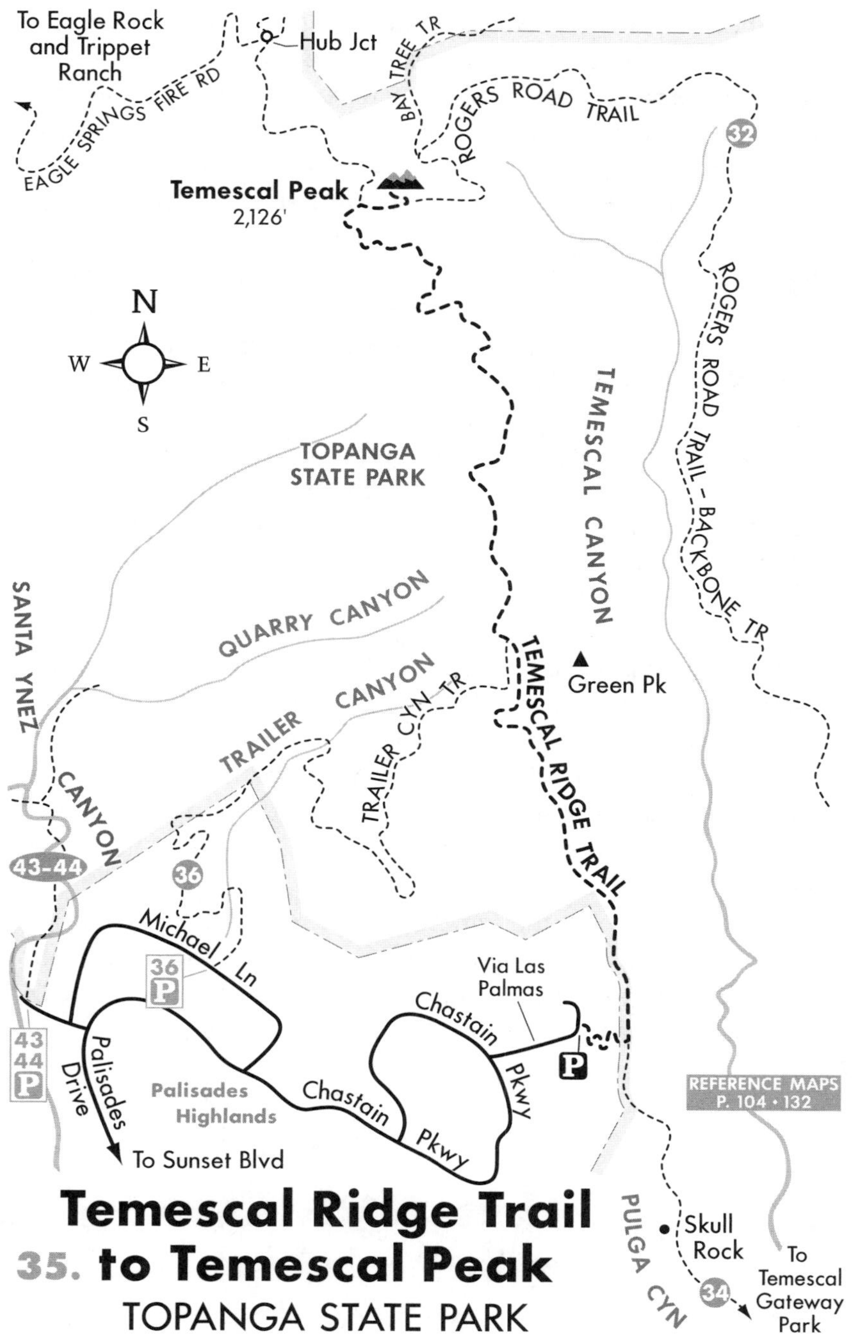

35. Temescal Ridge Trail to Temescal Peak

TOPANGA STATE PARK

switchbacks with sweeping coastal views to where the pavement ends. Climb the dirt footpath above Pulga Canyon, and enter the no-dog zone of Topanga State Park. At a quarter mile is a T-junction on Temescal Ridge. The right fork descends a half mile to Skull Rock and 2.4 miles to Temescal Gateway Park (Hike 34).

Bear left/north on the Temescal Ridge Trail. Head up the 1,800-foot ridge that runs high above Temescal Canyon on the right and the Palisades Highlands on the left. The expansive 360-degree vistas extend from the Pacific Ocean, across the interior of the Santa Monica Mountains, and into the Los Padres National Forest. Cross a saddle and continue up the ridge. The Rogers Road Trail—part of the Backbone Trail (Hike 32)—can be seen on the ridge across Temescal Canyon. Skirt the west/left side of Green Peak, distinguishable by its communication tower atop the summit. Descend and cross another saddle at the head of Trailer Canyon (Hike 36), then Quarry Canyon at 1.4 miles. The serpentine trail follows the ridge, with steady views into Santa Ynez Canyon and Temescal Canyon on opposite sides of the trail.

At 2.9 miles is a junction with the Rogers Road Trail. Go to the right a short distance on the Rogers Road Trail to a side path on the left. Bear left and climb up the hill to Temescal Peak, the 2,126-foot summit of the hike. Atop the peak is a metal pole, a survey benchmark, a small rock pile, a register, and 360-degree vistas. After enjoying the spectacular views, return along the same route.

To extend the hike, the Temescal Ridge Trail continues 0.6 miles north to Hub Junction, a 4-way crossroads by a map kiosk. From Hub Junction, trails to the left access Trippet Ranch (Hike 38); straight ahead leads to Dirt Mulholland (Hike 47). ■

36. Trailer Canyon to Temescal Peak

TOPANGA STATE PARK

Pacific Palisades trailhead

Hiking distance: 7.8 miles round trip
Hiking time: 4 hours
Configuration: up-and-back
Elevation gain: 1,300 feet
Difficulty: moderate to strenuous
Exposure: exposed ridge with random shaded pockets
Dogs: not allowed after first mile (in Topanga State Park)
Maps: U.S.G.S. Topanga • Topanga State Park map
Tom Harrison Maps: Topanga State Park Trail Map

map page 133

Trailer Canyon is a side canyon on the west side of Temescal Ridge in the Palisades Highlands. The Trailer Canyon Trail is a connector route to Temescal Ridge and into Topanga State Park. The trail weaves up the canyon, with views into Quarry Canyon, Santa Ynez Canyon, and the Pacific Ocean. From the ridge, the hike continues north to Temescal Peak, the highest peak in the state park. From the 2,126-foot summit are sweeping vistas across the mountain range and from the Los Angeles Basin to the San Fernando Valley.

To the trailhead

From Santa Monica, drive 3 miles northbound on the Pacific Coast Highway/Highway 1 to Sunset Boulevard. Turn right and drive 0.4 miles to Palisades Drive. Turn left and continue 2.4 miles to Vereda de la Montura. Turn left and go one block to Michael Lane. Turn right and drive a half mile to the posted trailhead on the left. Park alongside the curb.

The hike

Walk 40 yards up the paved alleyway to the gated trailhead. Follow the dirt fire road and wind up the mountain. Views quickly open up to the ocean, Santa Ynez Canyon, and the interior of the mountain range. Traverse the south rim of Quarry Canyon among sandstone outcrops. At 0.9 miles, pass the open gate and enter the no-dog zone of Topanga State Park. Briefly descend, then wend through the rolling hills. The Trailer Canyon Trail ends at 2.2 miles atop Temescal Ridge at the head of Quarry Canyon. The right fork descends 3.5 miles to Temescal Gateway Park.

To reach Temescal Peak, bear left on the Temescal Ridge Trail. The serpentine trail follows the ridge, with ongoing views into Santa Ynez Canyon, Temescal Canyon, and the backcountry of the Santa Monica Mountains. At 3.8 miles is a junction with the Rogers Road Trail, the easternmost segment of the Backbone Trail. Go to the right a short distance on the Rogers Road Trail to a side path on the left. Bear left and climb up the hill up to Temescal Peak, the 2,126-foot summit of the hike. After enjoying the 360-degree vistas, return along the same route.

To extend the hike, the Temescal Ridge Trail continues 0.6 miles north to Hub Junction, a 4-way crossroads by a map kiosk. From Hub Junction, trails to the left access Trippet Ranch (Hike 39); straight ahead leads to Dirt Mulholland (Hike 47). ■

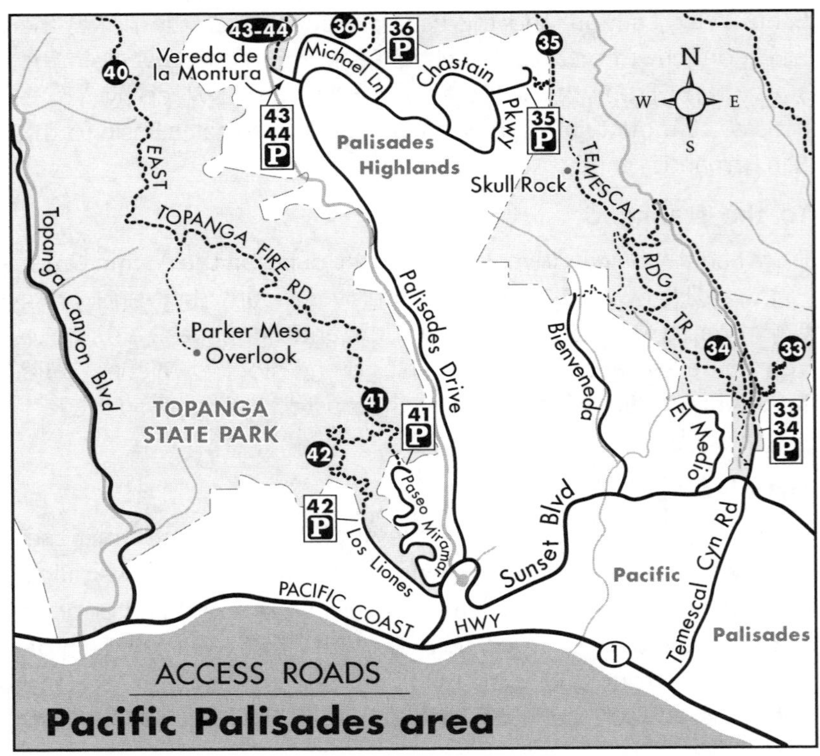

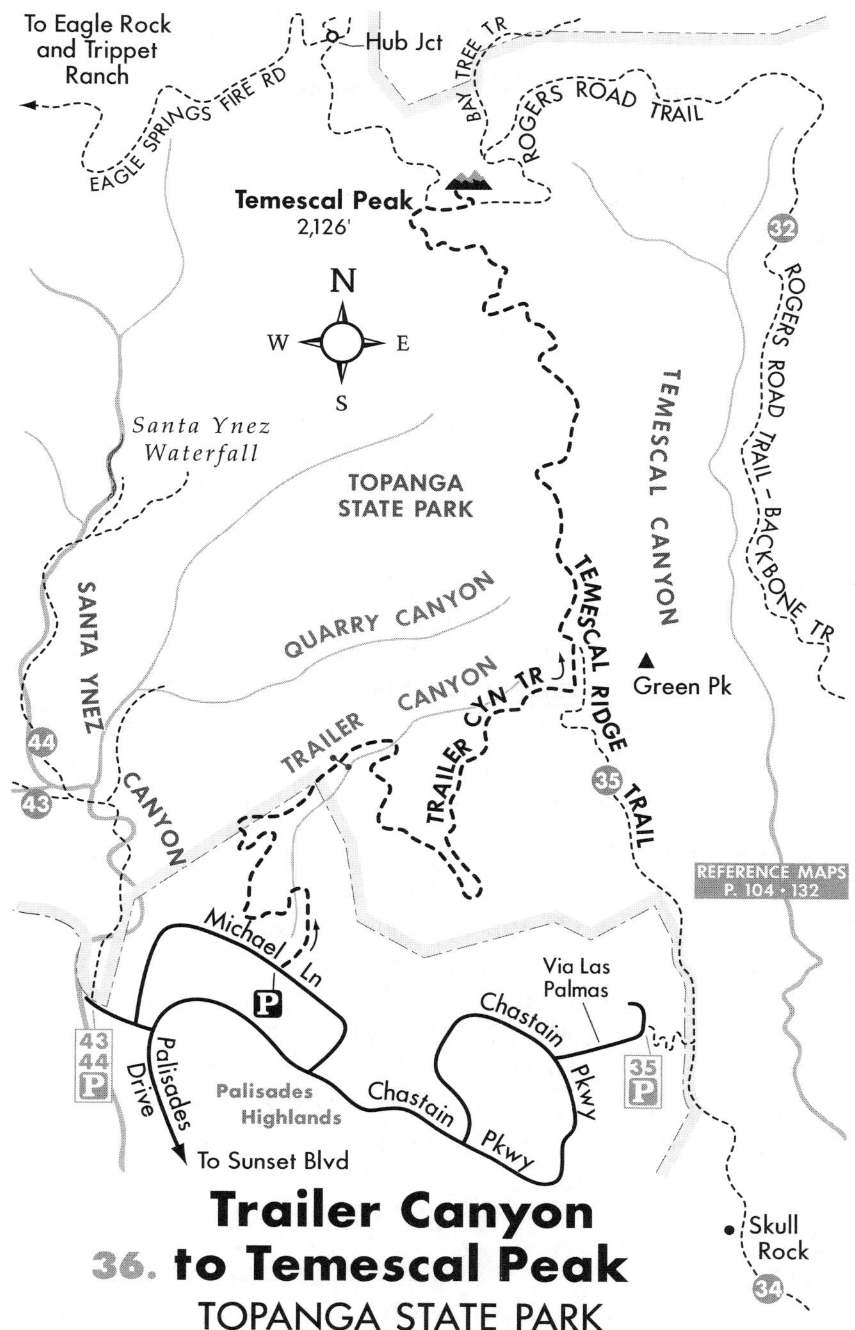

36. Trailer Canyon to Temescal Peak

TOPANGA STATE PARK

37. Dead Horse Trail from Trippet Ranch

TOPANGA STATE PARK

20825 Entrada Road • Topanga

Hiking distance: 2.5 miles round trip
Hiking time: 1.5 hours
Configuration: out-and-back
Elevation gain: 400 feet
Difficulty: easy
Exposure: mixed sun and shade
Dogs: not allowed
Maps: U.S.G.S. Topanga • Topanga State Park map
Tom Harrison Maps: Topanga State Park Trail map

Topanga State Park covers more than 11,500 acres at the west end of Los Angeles County. It has been designated as the world's largest wildland within the boundaries of a major city. Within the park are 36 miles of trails through open grasslands, chaparral, and oak woodlands. The Dead Horse Trail begins at Trippet Ranch, the park headquarters and visitor center. The diverse trail crosses rolling grasslands, enters a riparian forest, and descends into a streamside oak forest. The path crosses a rustic wooden bridge over Trippet Creek in a rocky grotto. The Dead Horse Trail is a segment of the 69-mile-long Backbone Trail.

To the trailhead

From Santa Monica, drive 4 miles northbound on the Pacific Coast Highway/Highway 1 to Topanga Canyon Boulevard and turn right. Continue 4.6 miles to Entrada Road on the right and turn right again. Drive 0.7 miles and turn left, following the state park signs. Turn left again in 0.3 miles into the parking lot.

From the Ventura Freeway/Highway 101 in Woodland Hills, exit on Topanga Canyon Boulevard, and drive 7.6 miles south to Entrada Road. Turn left and follow the posted state park signs to the Trippet Ranch parking lot.

The hike

Take the signed Musch Trail for 50 yards, heading north to a pond on the right. The Dead Horse Trail heads left (west) across from the pond. The footpath parallels a wood rail fence, rolling grasslands, and an oak woodland. At a half mile is a trail split. Take the right fork along the contours of the ridge. Descend into a shady riparian forest of bay and sycamore trees. A wooden bridge crosses the rocky streambed of Trippet Creek in a narrow draw. After crossing, steps lead up to a junction. Take the middle fork downhill to a trail split. Bear right and loop around to the lower parking lot near Topanga Canyon Boulevard. Return by retracing your steps.

The Backbone Trail continues west across from Topanga Canyon Boulevard along Section 3. This short, 0.7-mile section of trail connects to the Hondo Canyon Trail—Hike 38. ■

REFERENCE MAPS P. 104

37. Dead Horse Trail

from Trippet Ranch

TOPANGA STATE PARK

38. Hondo Canyon Trail

Old Topanga Canyon Road to Lois Ewen Overlook

TOPANGA STATE PARK

20825 Entrada Road · Topanga

Hiking distance: 8.6 miles round trip (plus optional 2-mile side trip)
Hiking time: 5 hours
Configuration: out-and-back
Elevation gain: 1,450 feet
Difficulty: moderate to strenuous
Exposure: an equal mix of tree-shaded areas and open slopes
Dogs: not allowed (but many 4-legged friends have been known to enjoy this trail)
Maps: U.S.G.S. Topanga and Malibu Beach · Topanga State Park map
Tom Harrison Maps: Topanga State Park Trail Map

map page 138

The Hondo Canyon Trail, a section of the Backbone Trail, climbs from the stream-fed canyon floor of Old Topanga Canyon to the Lois Ewen Overlook atop the Santa Monica Mountains at Stunt Road. From the summit are northern views across Cold Creek Canyon Preserve and Calabasas Peak to the San Fernando Valley. The sweeping southern views overlook Las Flores Canyon to the expansive Santa Monica Bay. The trail climbs the south wall of Hondo Canyon through majestic live oaks, California bays, and tall chaparral while passing massive sedimentary rock formations. At the top, the Fossil Ridge Trail passes an exceptional display of sea shell fossils embedded in the exposed rock, including clams, snails, and sand dollars.

This hike can also be started from the Lois Ewen Overlook, but it is more pleasant to first walk up from Old Topanga Canyon, then make the descent on the return.

To the trailhead

From Santa Monica, drive 4 miles northbound on the Pacific Coast Highway/Highway 1 to Topanga Canyon Boulevard and turn right. Continue 4.2 miles to Old Topanga Canyon Road on the left (west), just north of the town of Topanga. Turn left and drive 0.4 miles to the posted trailhead and a narrow dirt pullout on the left.

From the Ventura Freeway/Highway 101 in Woodland Hills, exit on Topanga Canyon Boulevard. Drive 8 miles south to Old Topanga Canyon Road on the right (west). Turn right and continue 0.4 miles to the posted trailhead and a narrow dirt pullout on the left.

The hike

Pass the trailhead sign and descend to Old Topanga Creek. Rock-hop over the creek, ascend steps, and walk through a meadow. Enter the lush, live oak forest in a side drainage, and follow the left side of the watercourse. Cross to the north side of the stream, passing through meadows with sandstone outcroppings. Climb up the rolling meadow to a rocky perch with sweeping views. Weave along the contour of the hills, overlooking layers of mountains and canyons. Climb the south wall of Hondo Canyon, zigzagging past conglomerate rock formations. The views span across the Santa Monica Mountains to the San Fernando Valley and Los Padres National Forest. At 3.7 miles, the path reaches a junction by Saddle Peak Road at the head of Hondo Canyon.

Bear right on the Fossil Ridge Trail, and head up to coastal views that span down Las Flores Canyon to Santa Monica Bay and Catalina Island. Parallel Saddle Peak Road, passing an endless display of sea shell fossils embedded in the sedimentary rock. Reach the Topanga Ridge Motorway at 4.3 miles. The right fork leads 0.9 miles to the Topanga Lookout (Hike 61). The left fork ends at a three-way road junction with Saddle Peak Road, Schueren Road, and Stunt Road at the Lois Ewen Overlook. The Saddle Peak Trail (the next section of the Backbone Trail) begins across the road—Hike 62. Return by retracing your steps.

To continue up to the Topanga Fire Lookout, take the paved Topanga Ridge Motorway northeast, following the ridge high above Cold Creek Canyon. At the road split, the paved right fork leads to a radar tower. Stay to the left on the wide, unpaved path to the graffiti-covered concrete foundation, which is all that remains of the lookout tower. It is one mile to the lookout tower, with an additional 200 feet in elevation. ■

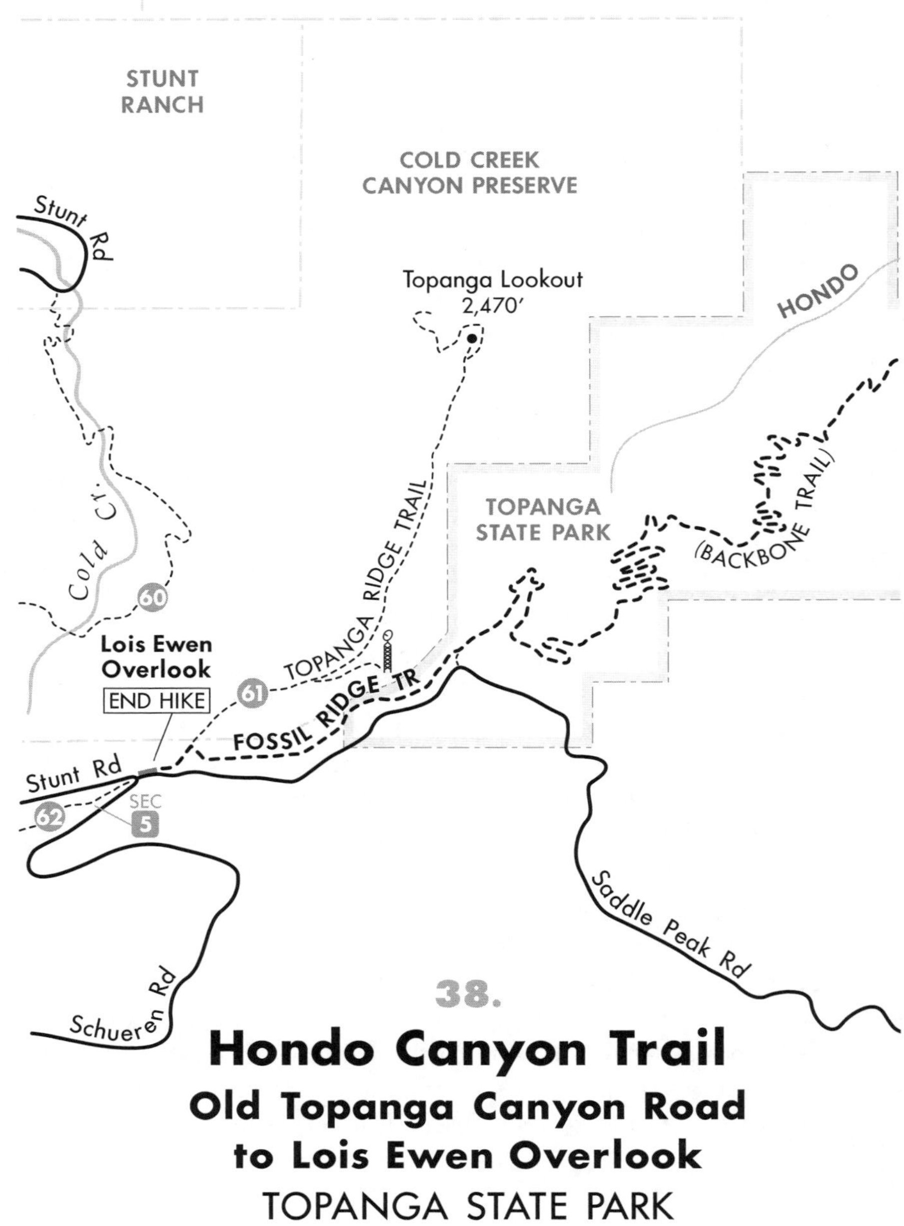

38. Hondo Canyon Trail

Old Topanga Canyon Road to Lois Ewen Overlook

TOPANGA STATE PARK

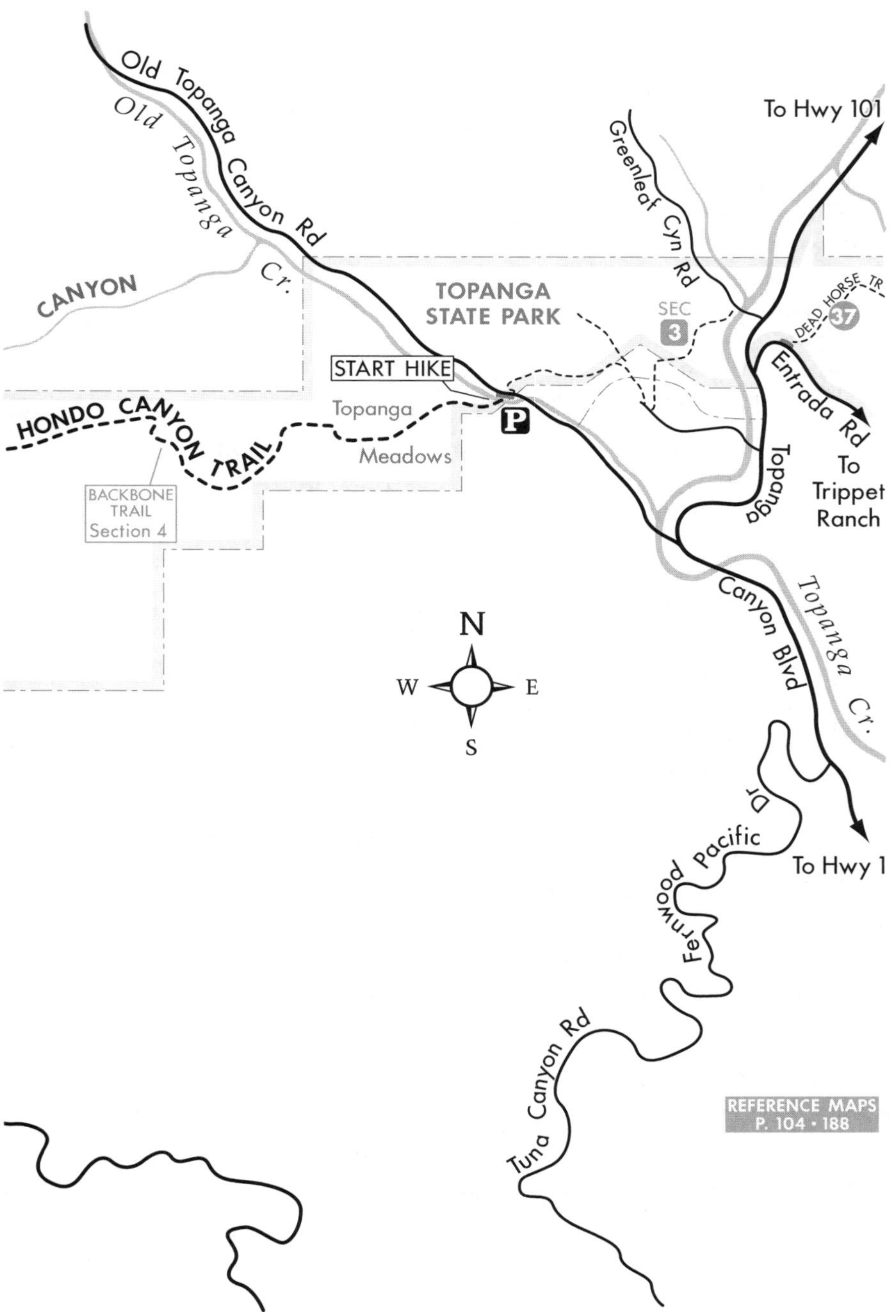
Old Topanga Canyon Rd
Old Topanga Cr.
CANYON
To Hwy 101
Greenleaf Cyn Rd
TOPANGA
STATE PARK
SEC
3
DEAD HORSE TR
37
START HIKE
Entrada Rd
To
Trippet
Ranch
HONDO CANYON TRAIL
Topanga
Meadows
BACKBONE
TRAIL
Section 4
Topanga
Canyon Blvd
Topanga Cr.
N
W
E
S
Dr
Fernwood Pacific
To Hwy 1
Tuna Canyon Rd
REFERENCE MAPS
P. 104 • 188

39. Eagle Rock Loop from Trippet Ranch

TOPANGA STATE PARK

20825 Entrada Road · Topanga

Hiking distance: 8-mile loop
Hiking time: 4 hours
Configuration: figure-eight double loop with short spur to Eagle Rock
Elevation gain: 800 feet
Difficulty: moderate to somewhat strenuous
Exposure: exposed hills and forested pockets
Dogs: not allowed
Maps: U.S.G.S. Topanga · Topanga State Park map
Tom Harrison Maps: Topanga State Park Trail Map

map page 142

Eagle Rock is a massive sandstone outcrop towering over the landscape at the head of Santa Ynez Canyon. The layered crag, pocked with small caves from water erosion, is a popular destination for its unobstructed views. From a perch on the 1,957-foot rock are vistas of the mountains, valleys, and a superb view down Santa Ynez Canyon to the ocean.

This hike begins at Trippet Ranch in Topanga State Park by a bucolic picnic area with a pond and a one-mile nature trail. The hike follows the Eagle Springs Fire Road through grasslands and oak groves up to Eagle Rock. After a short scramble up to the summit, the hike circles around the formation past Hub Junction (a 4-way junction by Temescal Peak) and Eagle Springs (a natural spring seeping out of the sandstone). The hike returns on the Musch Trail. The footpath meanders through lush vegetation that includes ferns, moss-covered rocks, and sycamore, oak and bay trees, making a couple of stream crossings back to Trippet Ranch.

To the trailhead

From Santa Monica, drive 4 miles northbound on the Pacific Coast Highway/Highway 1 to Topanga Canyon Boulevard and turn right. Continue 4.6 miles to Entrada Road on the right and turn right again. Drive 0.7 miles and turn left, following the state park signs. Turn left again and go 0.3 miles into the Topanga State Park parking lot. A parking fee is required.

From the Ventura Freeway/Highway 101 in Woodland Hills, exit on Topanga Canyon Boulevard. Drive 7.6 miles south to Entrada Road. Turn left and follow the posted state park signs to the Trippet Ranch parking lot.

The hike

Walk to the end of the parking lot by the grassy picnic area and weathered live oaks. Follow the trail uphill a short distance to a posted junction. The East Topanga Fire Road (Hike 40) bends right. Bear left on the Eagle Springs Fire Road, and pass the Santa Ynez Canyon Trail (Hike 44) on the right at a half mile. Continue uphill on the ridge road to the Musch Trail on the left—the return route—and a road split at 1.5 miles. Veer left on the Eagle Rock Fire Road, reaching the north slope of prominent Eagle Rock as the road crests. Leave the trail to the right to explore the tilted formation with sculptured caves and hollows. Scramble up the gorgeous monolith for great views down Santa Ynez Canyon to the Pacific.

Back on the Eagle Rock Fire Road, continue east, passing the Garapito Trail on the left (Hike 47). Climb the slope with views across the San Fernando Valley. Top the hill to westward views across Los Angeles to the ocean. Descend to Hub Junction, a 4-way crossroads with a map kiosk at 3 miles. The Temescal Ridge Fire Road, the middle right trail, leads 0.7 miles to Temescal Peak and 4.8 miles to Temescal Gateway Park at the mouth of the canyon (Hikes 34 and 35). To the left, the Temescal Ridge Fire Road leads to Dirt Mulholland and Reseda Boulevard in Tarzana. (South of Hub Junction, the Temescal Ridge Fire Road is called the Temescal Ridge Trail.)

For this hike, make a sharp right back onto the Eagle Springs Fire Road. Descend 1.3 miles, now skirting under the south side of Eagle Rock, to a posted fork with the Musch Trail on the right. (En route, a short side path on the right leads to Eagle Springs, a trickling spring in the sandstone bedrock under a sycamore and oak glen.)

Take the Musch Trail, leaving the fire road, and wind down into a verdant valley. Cross a couple of ravines through lush riparian vegetation and woodlands of oak, sycamore, and bay laurel. One mile down is a junction with Musch Camp at the former Musch Ranch. Follow the trail sign, crossing a meadow. Wind down to a junction with the Dead Horse Trail (Hike 37). Continue straight, passing a pond on the left and crossing an earthen dam to the main Topanga State Park parking lot at Trippet Ranch. ■

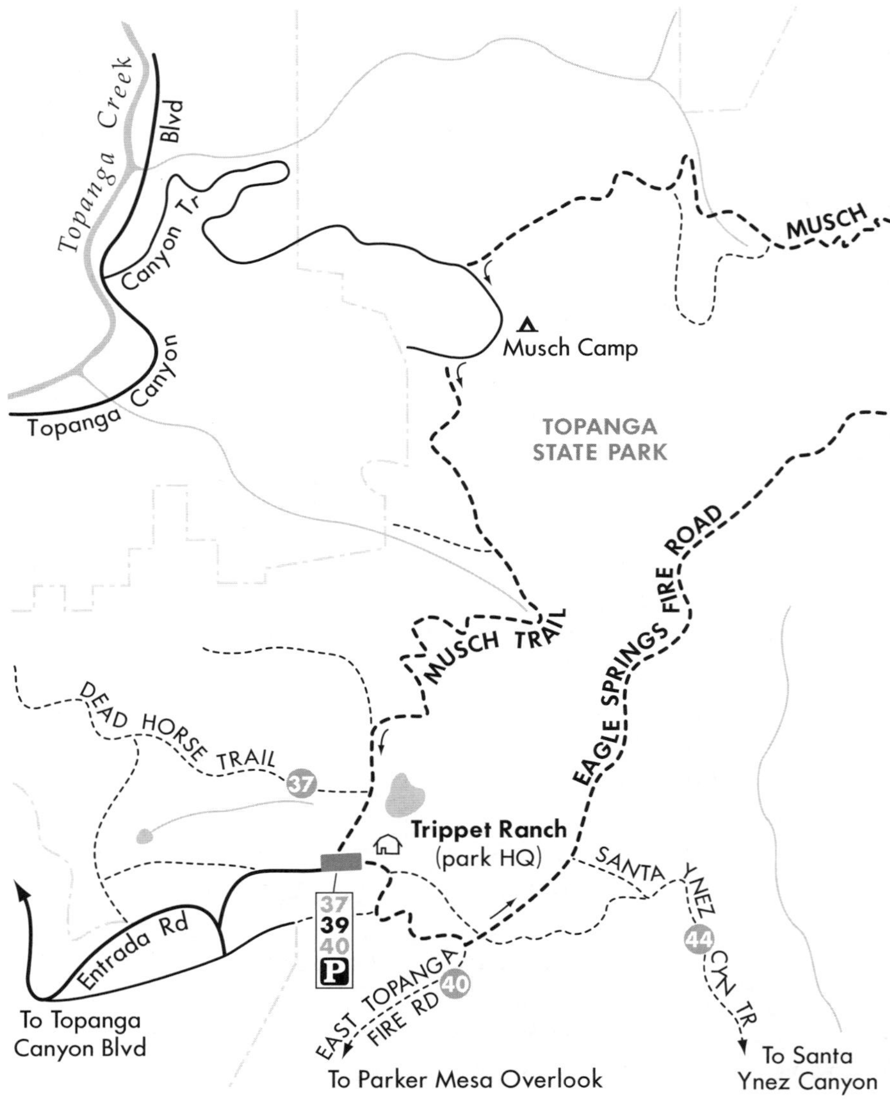

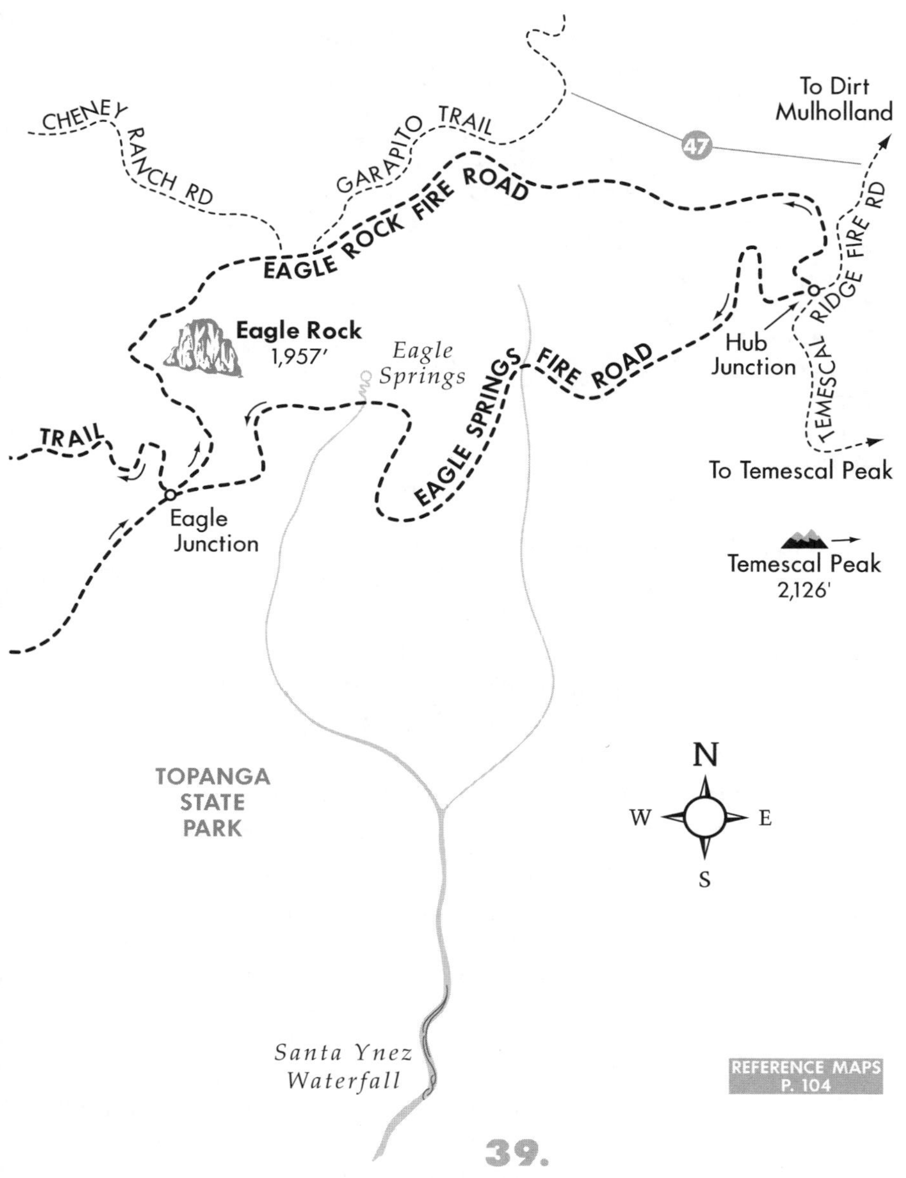

39.
Eagle Rock Loop from Trippet Ranch

TOPANGA STATE PARK

40. Parker Mesa Overlook from Trippet Ranch

EAST TOPANGA FIRE ROAD

TOPANGA STATE PARK

20825 Entrada Road · Topanga

Hiking distance: 6 miles round trip
Hiking time: 3 hours
Configuration: out-and-back
Elevation gain: 800 feet
Difficulty: moderate
Exposure: exposed ridge
Dogs: not allowed
Maps: U.S.G.S. Topanga · Topanga State Park map
Tom Harrison Maps: Topanga State Park Trail map

Parker Mesa Overlook (also referred to as the Topanga Overlook, or simply *the overlook*) is an oceanfront lookout perched 1,525 feet above the Pacific Ocean. East Topanga Fire Road, the access route to the overlook, is a restricted road that travels north and south through Topanga State Park from Trippet Ranch (the park's headquarters) to Paseo Miramar off Sunset Boulevard.

Parker Mesa Overlook can be accessed from three trailheads: from the north via this trailhead at Trippet Ranch, and from the south via the Paseo Miramar trailhead and the Los Liones trailhead (Hikes 41—42). The fire road follows the ridge high above Topanga Canyon and Santa Ynez Canyon, passing enormous slabs of sandstone and numerous ravines that drop into the canyons along both sides of the ridge. Throughout the hike are spectacular vistas in every direction.

To the trailhead

From Santa Monica, drive 4 miles northbound on the Pacific Coast Highway/Highway 1 to Topanga Canyon Boulevard and turn right. Continue 4.6 miles to Entrada Road on the right and turn right again. Drive 0.7 miles and turn left, following the posted state park signs. Turn left again at 0.3 miles into the Topanga State Park parking lot.

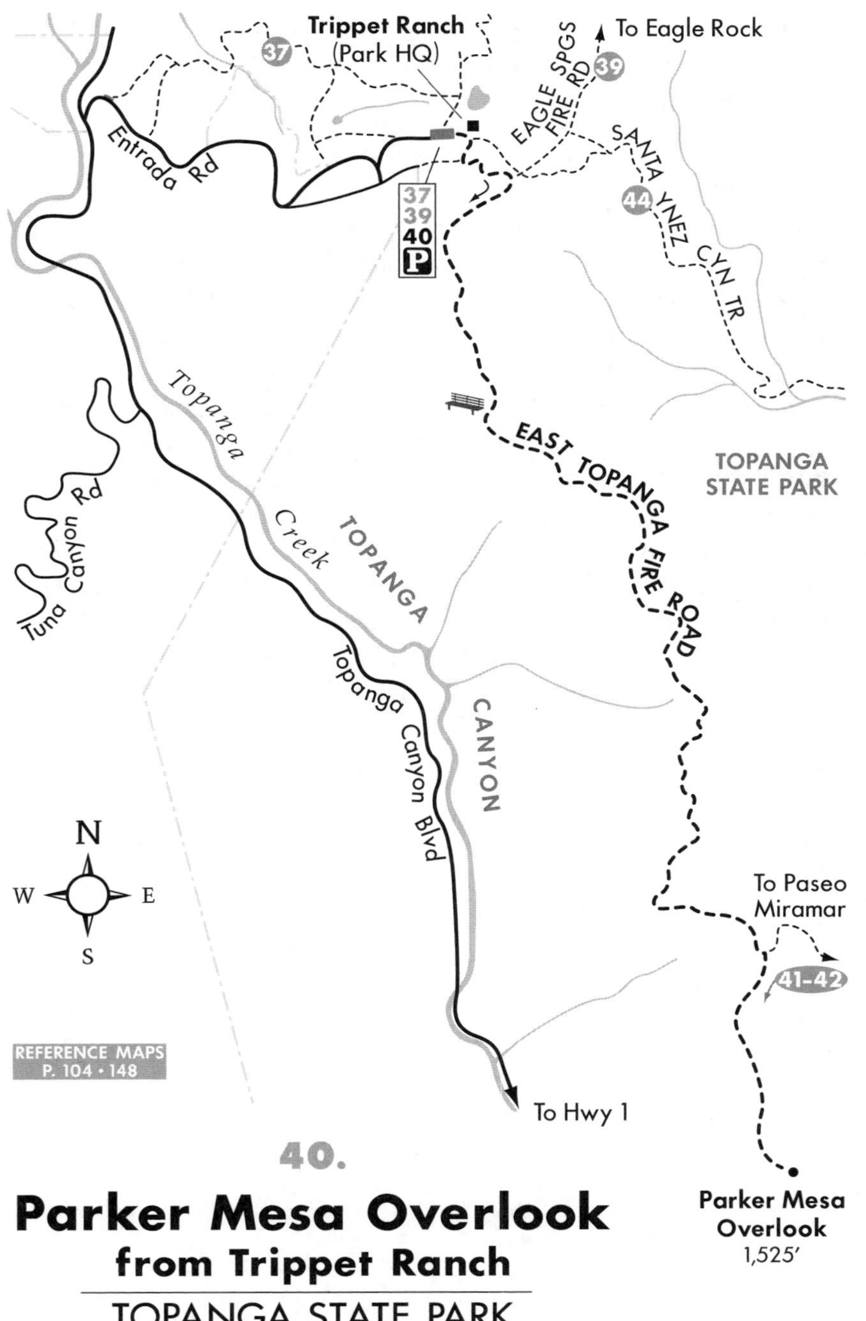

40.

Parker Mesa Overlook
from Trippet Ranch

TOPANGA STATE PARK

From the Ventura Freeway/Highway 101 in Woodland Hills, exit on Topanga Canyon Boulevard, and drive 7.6 miles south to Entrada Road. Turn left and follow the posted state park signs to the parking lot.

The hike

Head southeast on the signed trail towards Eagle Rock to a fire road. Bear left up the road to a junction at 0.2 miles. The left fork leads to Eagle Rock (Hike 39). Take the right fork on the East Topanga Fire Road past a grove of coastal oaks. Continue uphill to a ridge and a bench with panoramic views from Topanga Canyon to the Pacific Ocean. A short distance ahead, the trail crosses a narrow ridge overlooking Santa Ynez Canyon and its tilted sandstone slabs. Follow the ridge south, with alternating views of both canyons. At 2.5 miles is a junction with a trail on the right. The main trail on the left (east) leads to the trailheads at Paseo Miramar and Los Liones Drive (Hikes 41—42). Leave the fire road, and take the right trail a half mile south to the Parker Mesa Overlook at the trail's end. After enjoying the fantastic views, return to Trippet Ranch along the same route. ■

41. Parker Mesa Overlook

from PASEO MIRAMAR

TOPANGA STATE PARK

Paseo Miramar trailhead • Pacific Palisades

Hiking distance: 5.5 miles round trip
Hiking time: 2.5 hours
Configuration: out-and-back
Elevation gain: 1,200 feet
Difficulty: moderate to somewhat strenuous
Exposure: exposed ridge
Dogs: not allowed
Maps: U.S.G.S. Topanga • Topanga State Park map
Tom Harrison Maps: Topanga State Park Trail map

map page 149

Parker Mesa Overlook sits on a wide ridge overlooking the Santa Monica Bay from an elevation of 1,525 feet. From the ocean-front knoll are expansive 360-degree views, extending from the bay to Palos Verdes. The East Topanga Fire Road is a 4.6-mile vehicle-restricted road that connects the community of Pacific Palisades with Trippet Ranch in Topanga State Park. The unpaved road climbs northeast on the high ridge between Santa Ynez Canyon and Los Liones Canyon, all within Topanga State Park. This hike begins from the upper end of Paseo Miramar in Pacific Palisades and follows the lower two miles of the fire road to the Parker Mesa Overlook. Throughout the hike are amazing panoramas of the ocean, city, and mountains.

To the trailhead

From Santa Monica, drive 3 miles northbound on the Pacific Coast Highway/Highway 1 to Sunset Boulevard. Turn right and drive 0.3 miles to Paseo Miramar. Turn left on Paseo Miramar, and drive 1.2 miles to the trailhead at the end of the road. Park alongside the curb on the west side of the street.

The hike

From the north end of Paseo Miramar, pass the trailhead gate and enter Topanga State Park. Hike north on the dirt fire road along the ridge, overlooking Santa Ynez Canyon, Pacific Palisades, and Santa Monica. Bend left to a junction with the Los Liones Trail on the left at 0.2 miles. (The trail leads 1.6 miles downhill to the trailhead at the north end of Los Liones Drive—Hike 42.) Continue straight ahead, staying on the East Topanga Fire Road. Traverse the hillside above Santa Ynez Canyon to a junction at 2 miles. The main road leads 2.7 miles to Trippet Ranch (Hike 40) and 4 miles to Eagle Rock (Hike 39). Instead, leave the fire road and take the trail to the left. Walk a half mile south to the Parker Mesa Overlook at the end of the trail. From the bald knoll are great vistas overlooking the ocean and coastline. After savoring the views, return along the same route. ■

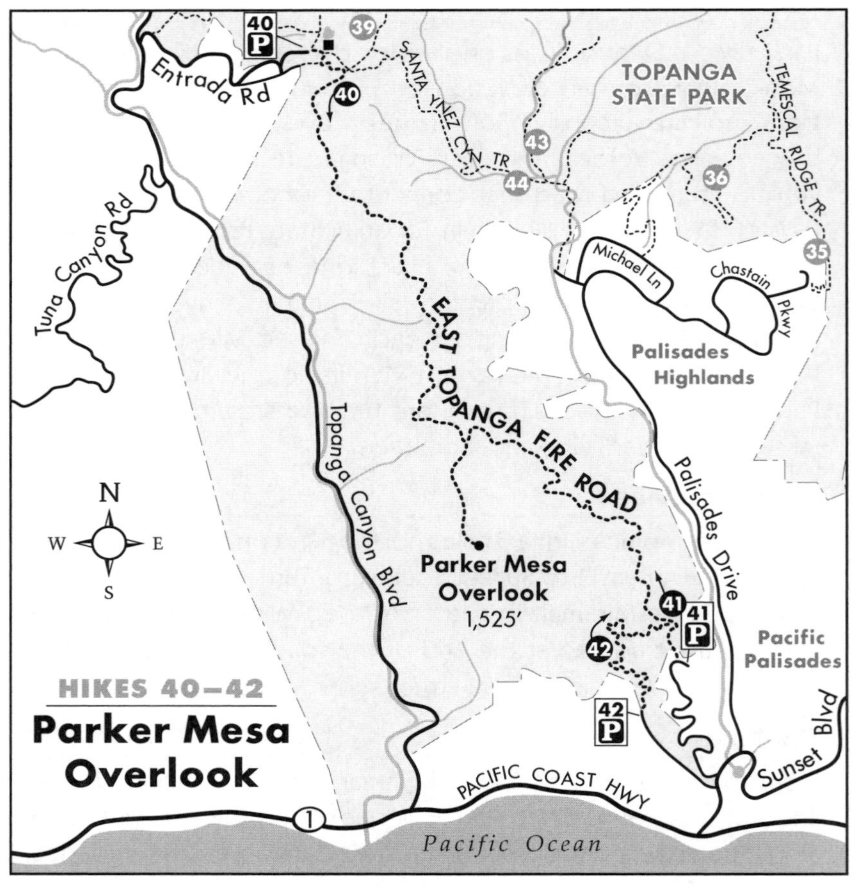

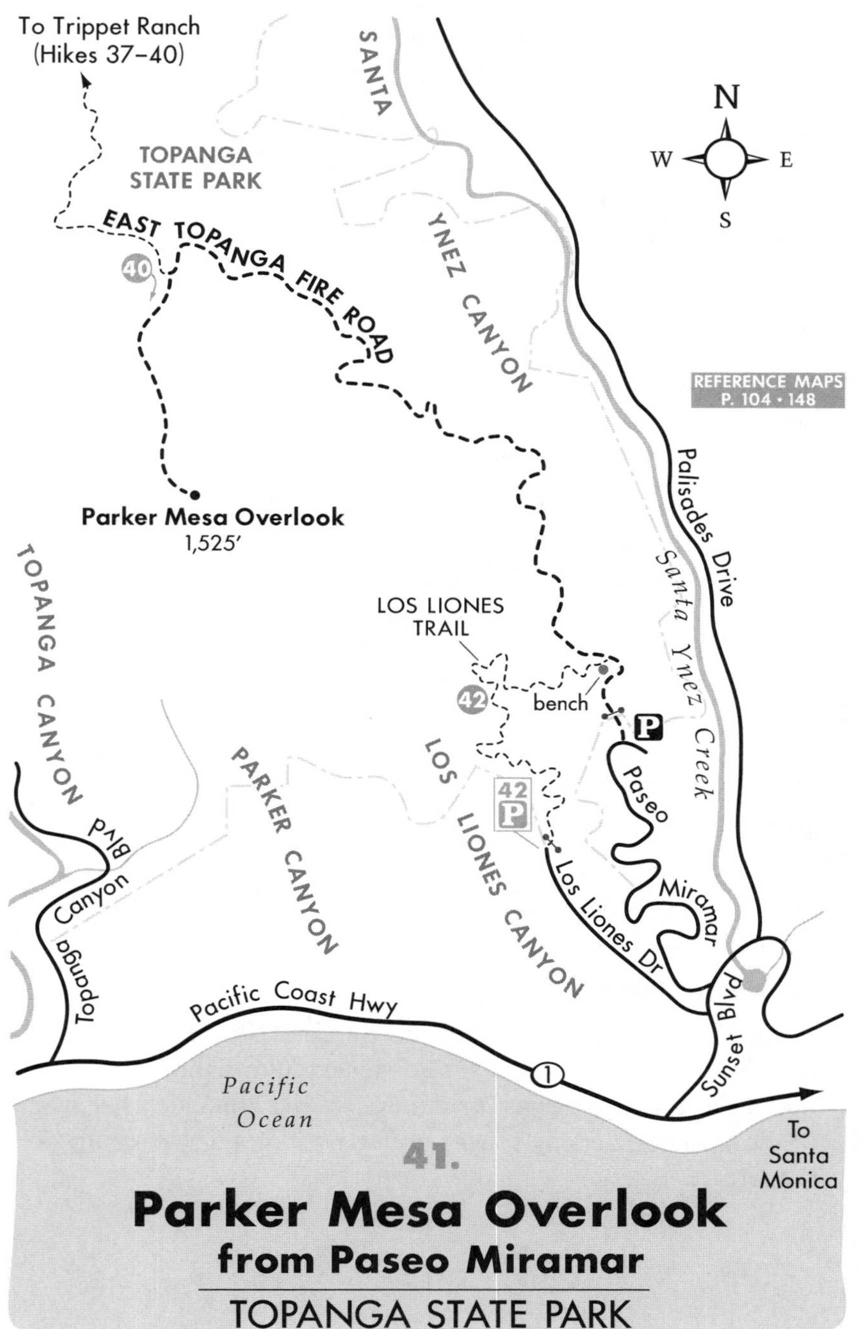

41.

Parker Mesa Overlook

from Paseo Miramar

TOPANGA STATE PARK

42. Parker Mesa Overlook from Los Liones Trail

TOPANGA STATE PARK

Los Liones Drive trailhead • Pacific Palisades

Hiking distance: 8.2 miles round trip
Hiking time: 4 hours
Configuration: out-and-back
Elevation gain: 1,300 feet
Difficulty: moderate to somewhat strenuous
Exposure: exposed ridge and hillsides
Dogs: not allowed
Maps: U.S.G.S. Topanga • Topanga State Park map
Tom Harrison Maps: Topanga State Park Trail Map

The Los Liones Trail is a 1.6-mile-long footpath on the southwest corner of Topanga State Park. The serpentine course climbs a steep-sloped, chaparral-covered side canyon, then connects with the East Topanga Fire Road. The fire road continues along the ridge to Trippet Ranch, the park's headquarters to the north. This hike follows a portion of the ridge road en route to the Parker Mesa Overlook, a 1,525-foot oceanfront perch on a wide ridge that overlooks Santa Monica Bay. Throughout the hike are sweeping views of the ocean, cities, and mountains, extending all the way from Point Dume to Long Point in Palos Verdes.

An optional turn-around point is at 1.6 miles, located at an overlook and bench where the Los Liones Trail joins with the East Topanga Fire Road.

To the trailhead

From Santa Monica, drive 3 miles northbound on the Pacific Coast Highway/Highway 1 to Sunset Boulevard. Turn right and drive a quarter mile to Los Liones Drive. Turn left and continue a half mile to the trailhead parking spaces on the right or along the curb on the left.

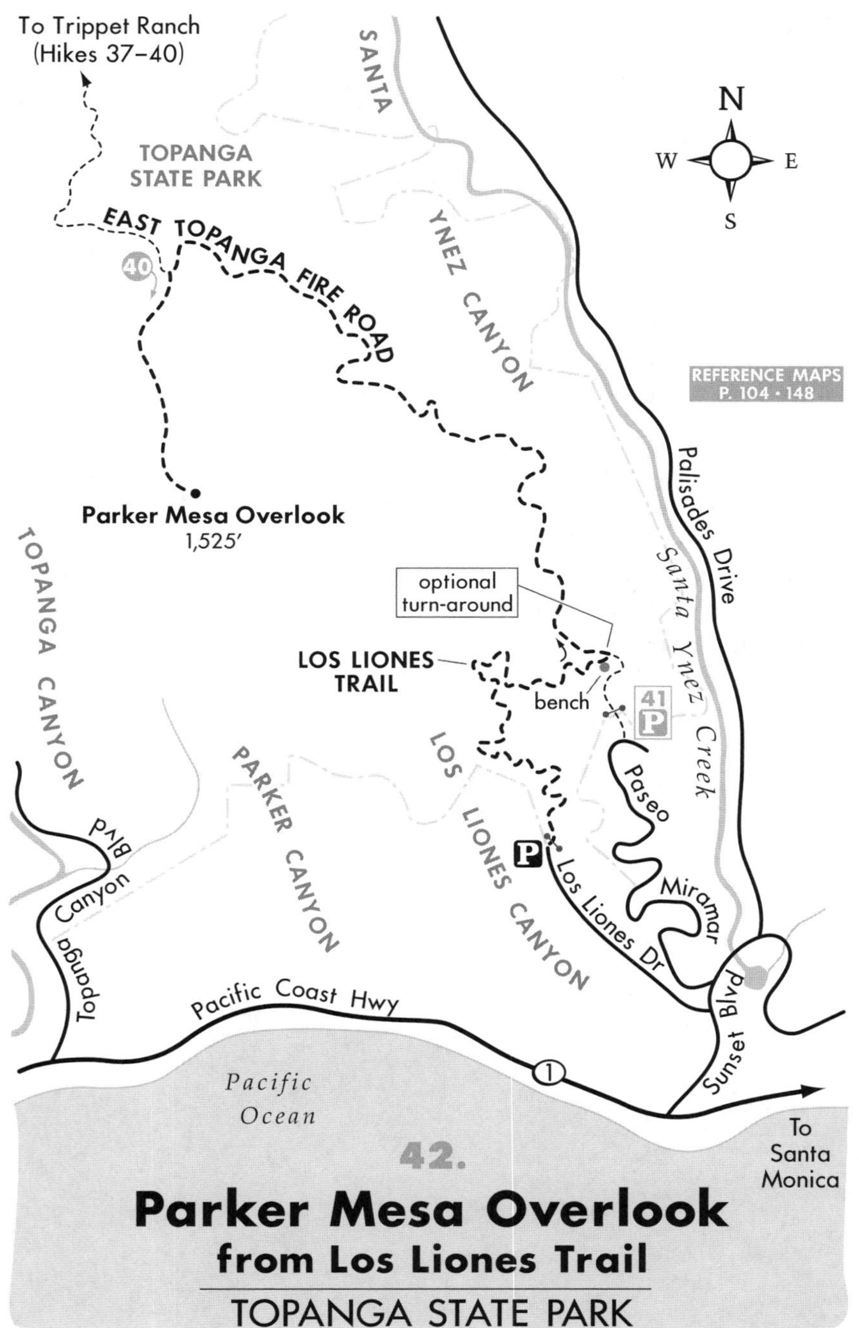

42. Parker Mesa Overlook
from Los Liones Trail

TOPANGA STATE PARK

The hike

Pass through the trailhead gate and enter Topanga State Park. Follow the footpath through dense pockets of oaks and bay laurel. Traverse Los Liones Canyon from the trail perched on the cliffs. Weave through exposed, sunny southern slopes and pockets of shaded forest. Leave the canyon and wind through tall scrub and small side drainages. A little under a mile, ocean vistas come into view and expand with every step. At 1.5 miles, the path levels out, just shy of a T-junction with the East Topanga Fire Road. A bench is located on the right at an overlook that includes southern views down the coastline to Palos Verdes. This is a good turn-around spot for a 3.2-mile hike.

To continue to the Parker Mesa Overlook, climb ninety yards to the fire road. The right fork descends 0.2 miles to the trailhead atop Paseo Miramar (Hike 41). Take the left fork and follow the ridge above Santa Ynez Canyon to a junction at 3.5 miles. The East Topanga Fire Road continues straight ahead, climbing 2.7 miles to Trippet Ranch (Hike 40) and 4 miles to Eagle Rock (Hike 39). Instead, leave the fire road and take the trail to the left. Walk a half mile south to the Parker Mesa Overlook on a bald knoll at the end of the trail. From the 1,525-foot overlook are great vistas overlooking the ocean and coastline. Return by retracing your steps. ■

43. Santa Ynez Canyon Falls

TOPANGA STATE PARK

Pacific Palisades trailhead

Hiking distance: 2.7 miles round trip
Hiking time: 1.5 hours
Configuration: out-and-back
Elevation gain: 300 feet
Difficulty: easy
Exposure: forested
Dogs: not allowed
Maps: U.S.G.S. Topanga • Topanga State Park map
Tom Harrison Maps: Topanga State Park Trail Map

map page 154

Santa Ynez Canyon Falls is a 25-foot cataract within Topanga State Park. The waterfall pours out of a channel in the sandstone rock into a pool. The falls is tucked into a narrow, steep-walled branch of the main canyon in a peaceful grotto surrounded by mossy sandstone cliffs and fern-lined pools. The trail to the falls winds through the natural sanctuary on the forested floor of Santa Ynez Canyon. Along the way are a series of stream crossings, magnificent sandstone formations, and lush riparian vegetation.

To the trailhead

From Santa Monica, drive 3 miles northbound on the Pacific Coast Highway/Highway 1 to Sunset Boulevard. Turn right and drive 0.4 miles to Palisades Drive. Turn left and continue 2.4 miles to Vereda de la Montura on the left. Turn left and park at the end of the road 0.1 mile ahead.

The hike

Pass the trailhead gate and descend steps to Santa Ynez Creek. Follow the east bank of the creek under the shade of sycamore and oak trees. Cross stepping stones over a side stream and continue up canyon. Cross the seasonal creek four consecutive times under a canopy of sycamores, passing sandstone formations with caves. After the fourth crossing is a trail split at Quarry Canyon, named for an abandoned limestone quarry. Stay to the left, crossing to the west side of the creek and a posted trail split at a half mile. The left fork leads 1.5 miles to Trippet Ranch (Hike 44).

Bear right on the Waterfall Trail, and cross to the east side of the creek. Follow the watercourse, crossing four more times as the steep-walled canyon tightly narrows. Work your way up the canyon, passing a jumble of boulders, cave-pocked sandstone formations, and ledges. Boulder-hop up the fern-lined rock grotto to the waterfall at the end of the box canyon. Just before reaching the falls, a path on the right climbs the east canyon wall to an overlook of the canyon. ■

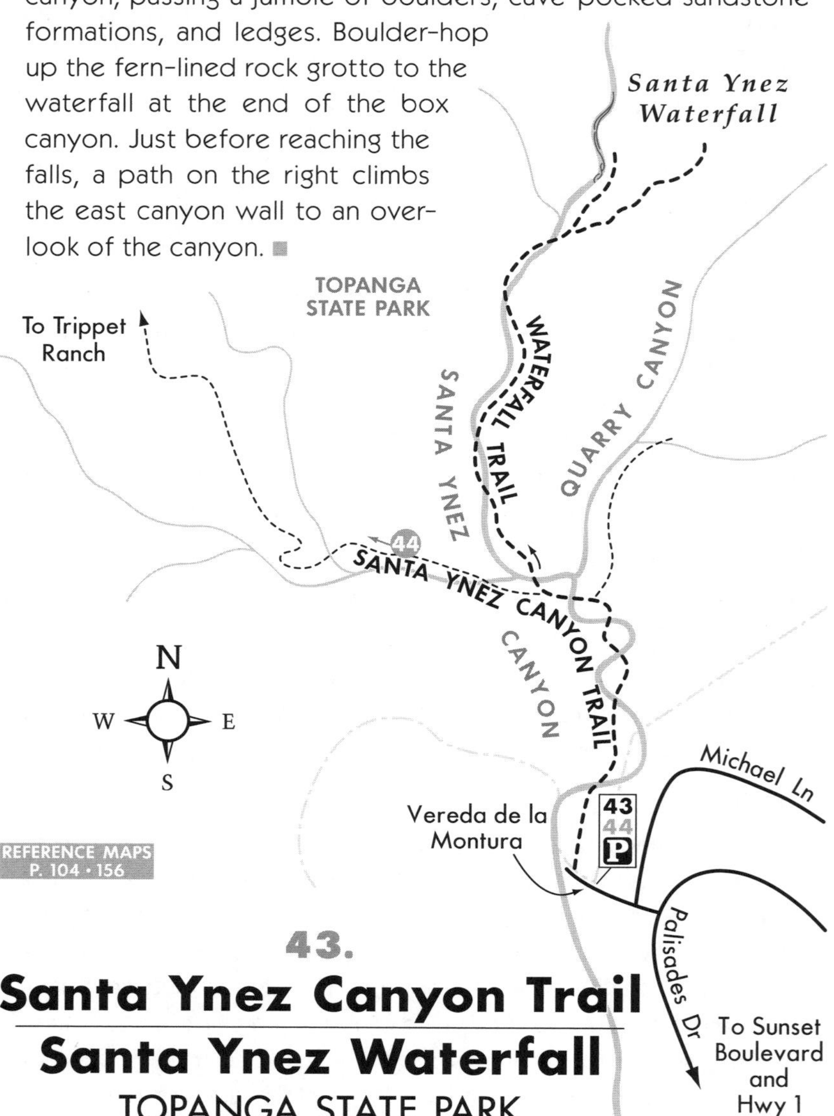

43. Santa Ynez Canyon Trail
Santa Ynez Waterfall
TOPANGA STATE PARK

44. Santa Ynez Canyon to Trippet Ranch

TOPANGA STATE PARK

Pacific Palisades trailhead

Hiking distance: 4 miles round trip
Hiking time: 2 hours
Configuration: out-and-back
Elevation gain: 800 feet
Difficulty: moderate
Exposure: forested and exposed ridge
Dogs: not allowed
Maps: U.S.G.S. Topanga • Topanga State Park map
Tom Harrison Maps: Topanga State Park Trail Map

map page 157

Santa Ynez Canyon runs north and south from the heart of Topanga State Park beneath Eagle Rock and Temescal Peak to the Pacific Highlands. The lush stream-fed canyon and natural sanctuary is filled with oaks, willows, sycamores, bay laurels, and towering sandstone formations. This hike follows the canyon floor with numerous stream crossings, then climbs the canyon wall to spectacular vistas across the Santa Monica Mountains. The trail ends at Trippet Ranch by a tree-shaded picnic area and pond at the park's headquarters.

To the trailhead

From Santa Monica, drive 3 miles northbound on the Pacific Coast Highway/Highway 1 to Sunset Boulevard. Turn right and drive 0.4 miles to Palisades Drive. Turn left and continue 2.4 miles to Vereda de la Montura on the left. Turn left and park at the end of the road 0.1 mile ahead.

The hike

Pass the trailhead gate and descend steps to Santa Ynez Creek. Follow the east bank of the creek under the shade of sycamore and oak trees. Cross stepping stones over a side stream and continue up canyon. Cross the seasonal creek four consecutive times under a canopy of sycamores while passing sandstone boulders with caves. After the fourth crossing is a trail split at Quarry Canyon, named for an abandoned limestone quarry. Stay to the left, crossing to the west side of the creek and a posted trail split at a half mile. The right fork leads 0.8 miles to Santa Ynez Falls (Hike 43).

Stay to the left and wind through the lush riparian habitat, following the ephemeral stream. Cross to the north side of the stream and head up canyon. Ascend the hillside to the exposed, chaparral-covered slopes with dense stands of ceanothus, chamise, sumac, and toyon. From the hillside are 360-degree views of the mountainous backcountry Follow the slab-rock path on the ridge between two canyons feeding Santa Ynez Creek. Continue gaining altitude on the ridge, with a view of Temescal Peak at the head of the canyon to the right. Pass a posted trail on the left that cuts across to the East Topanga Fire Road. Walk straight ahead 150 yards to a junction with the Eagle Springs Fire Road at 2 miles. The left fork leads to Trippet Ranch and a picnic area. The right fork leads to Eagle Rock and Hub Junction (Hike 39). ■

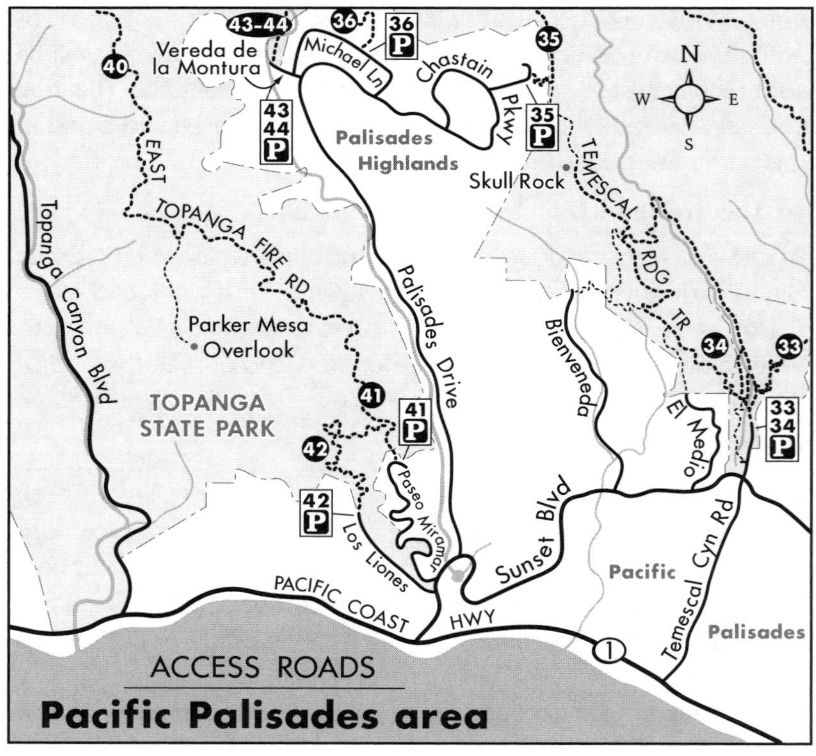

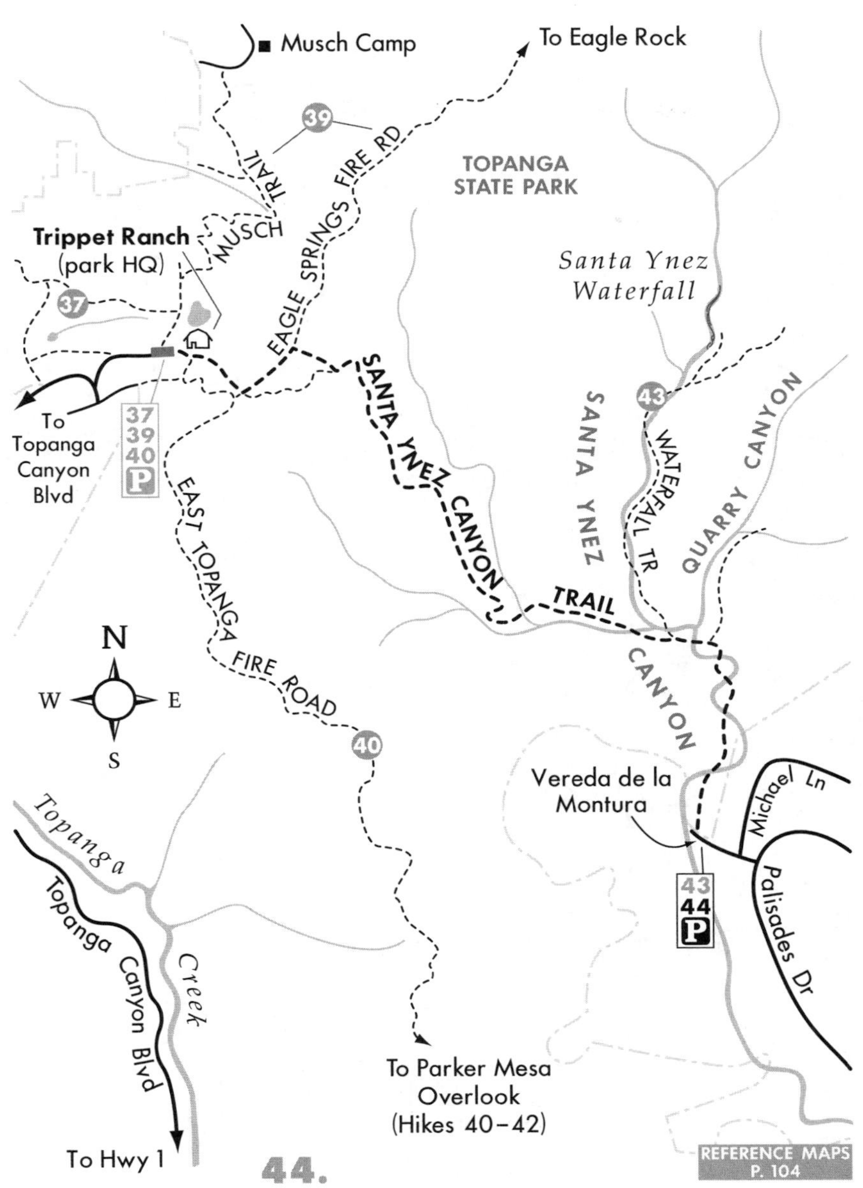

REFERENCE MAPS
P. 104

44. Santa Ynez Canyon to Trippet Ranch

TOPANGA STATE PARK

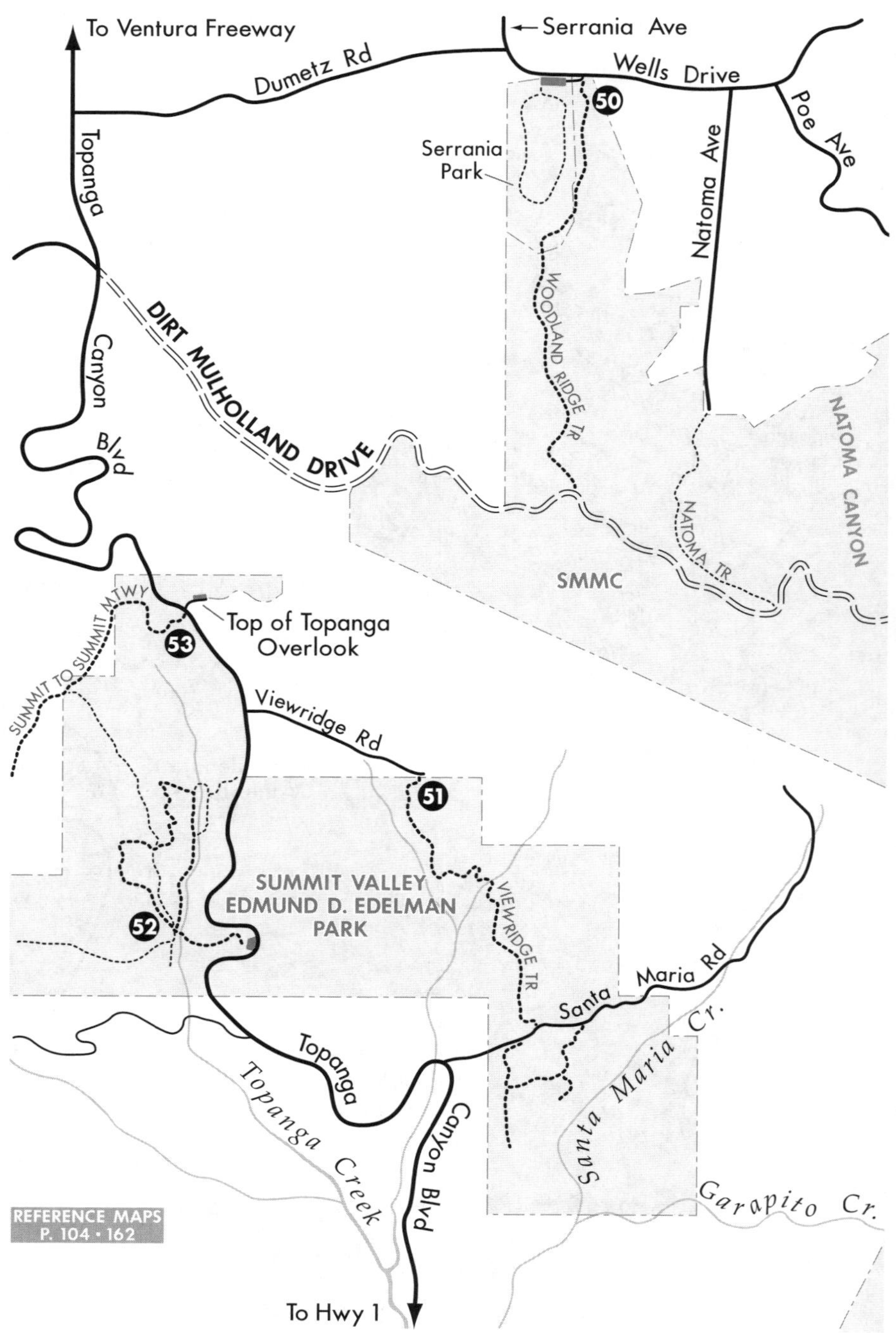

To Ventura Freeway
Serrania Ave
Dumetz Rd
Wells Drive
Topanga
Serrania Park
Poe Ave
Natoma Ave
DIRT MULHOLLAND DRIVE
WOODLAND RIDGE TR
Canyon
Blvd
NATOMA CANYON
NATOMA TR
SMMC
SUMMIT TO SUMMIT MTWY
Top of Topanga Overlook
Viewridge Rd
SUMMIT VALLEY EDMUND D. EDELMAN PARK
VIEWRIDGE TR
Santa Maria Rd
Santa Maria Cr.
Topanga
Topanga Creek
Canyon Blvd
Garapito Cr.
REFERENCE MAPS P. 104 • 162
To Hwy 1
50
51
52
53

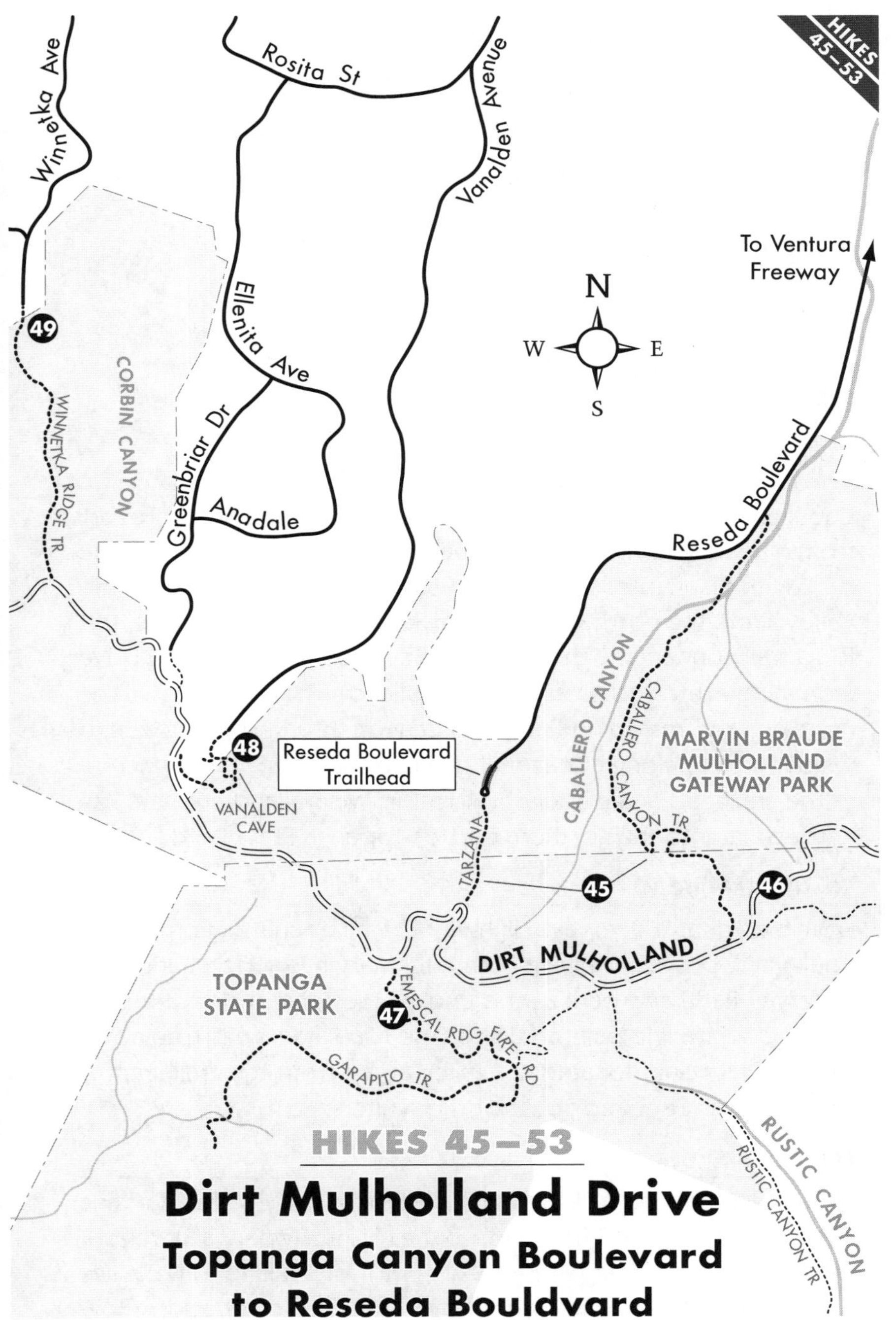

HIKES 45–53

Dirt Mulholland Drive

Topanga Canyon Boulevard to Reseda Bouldvard

45. Caballero Canyon— Dirt Mulholland Loop

MARVIN BRAUDE MULHOLLAND GATEWAY PARK

3600 Reseda Boulevard • Tarzana

Hiking distance: 3.7-mile loop
Hiking time: 2 hours
Configuration: loop (partially on paved road)
Elevation gain: 600 feet
Difficulty: easy to moderate
Exposure: exposed
Dogs: allowed
Maps: U.S.G.S. Conoga Park • Topanga State Park map
Tom Harrison Maps: Topanga State Park Trail map

Caballero Canyon runs into the north border of Topanga State Park from Marvin Braude Mulholland Gateway Park. The grassy hillside park with picnic sites lies adjacent to Tarzana in the San Fernando Valley. From the north slope of the Santa Monica Mountains, this loop trail connects with an unpaved section of Mulholland Drive (commonly referred to as Dirt Mulholland). The hike follows the ridge and returns down Caballero Canyon through sycamore and willow groves along a seasonal streambed.

The trailhead is a popular link to Dirt Mulholland and is a key entry point into the northern part of Topanga State Park.

To the trailhead

From the Ventura Freeway/Highway 101 in Tarzana, exit on Reseda Boulevard. Drive 3.4 miles south into Marvin Braude Mulholland Gateway Park, and park at the end of the road. Inside the park gate is a white line painted across the road. Parking is free north of the white line, located 0.2 miles away from the trailhead. A parking fee is required south of the white line.

The hike

From the south end of Reseda Boulevard, take the gated Tarzana Fire Road, an unpaved fire road, up the hill into Topanga State Park. Pass a second vehicle gate, reaching Dirt Mulholland at 0.2 miles on a U-bend in the road. Bear left on the wide road, and follow

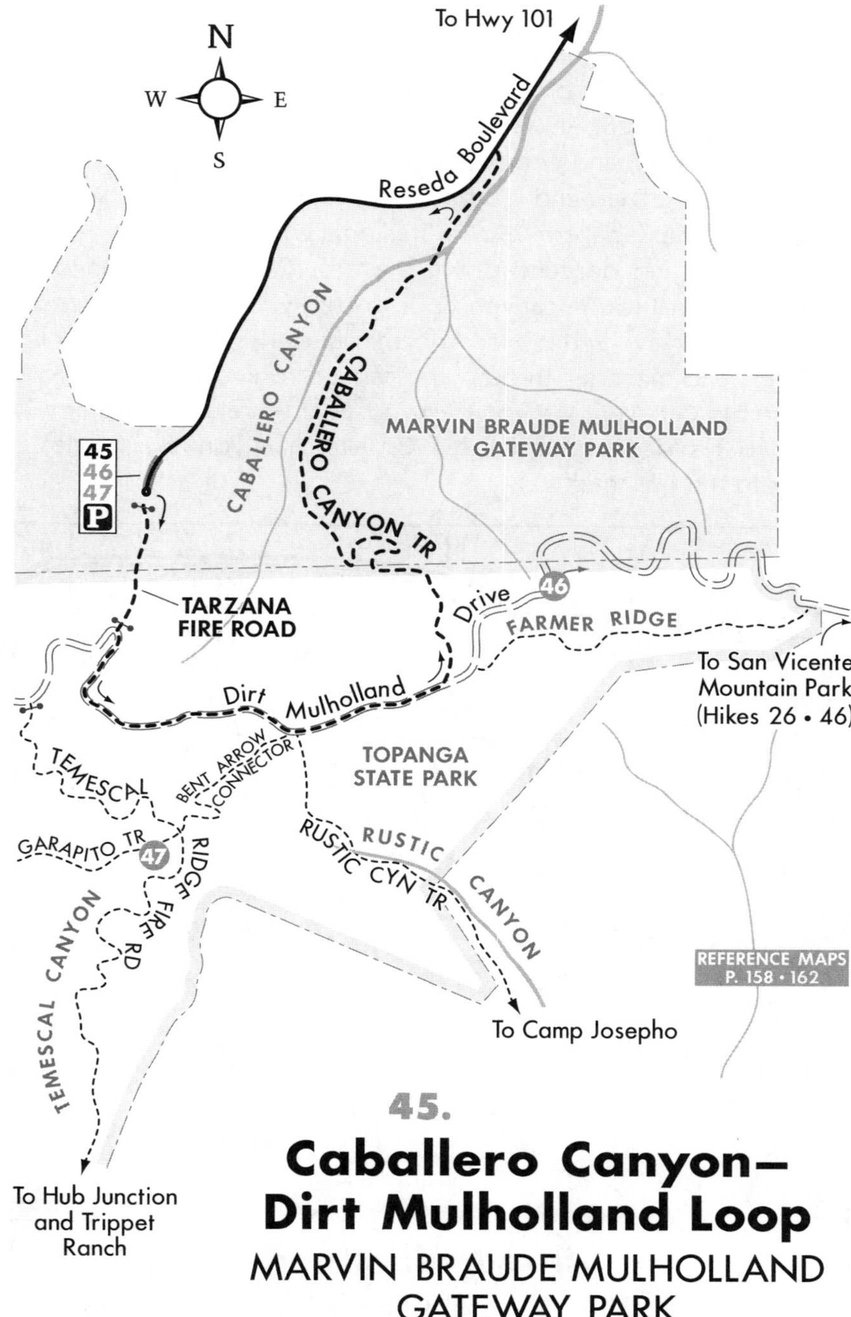

45.

Caballero Canyon— Dirt Mulholland Loop

MARVIN BRAUDE MULHOLLAND GATEWAY PARK

the ridge across the head of Caballero Canyon, curving south then east. From the ridge are southern views into Temescal and Rustic Canyons and northern views into Caballero Canyon. At 0.7 miles, pass the Bent Arrow Trail, a connector trail to the Temescal Ridge Fire Road, and continue along the ridge. Just before the road curves left around a prominent hill known as Farmer Ridge, watch for the Caballero Canyon Trail on the left at 1.1 miles.

Bear left and descend down the east flank of the canyon. Wind downhill to the canyon floor dotted with sycamore trees and coastal sage scrub. Head north, parallel to an intermittent stream, and meander through the canyon to Reseda Boulevard at the old Caballero Canyon trailhead. Bear left and follow landscaped Reseda Boulevard above Caballero Canyon for 1.2 miles, back to the trailhead. ■

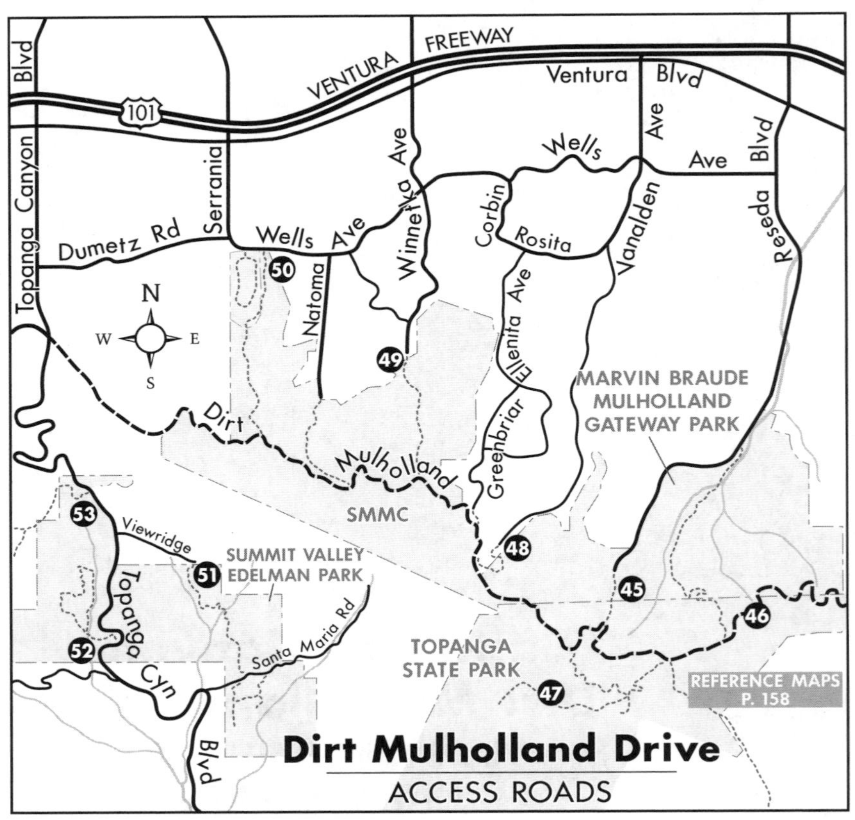

46. Dirt Mulholland to San Vicente Mountain Park and Nike Site

3600 Reseda Boulevard • Tarzana

Hiking distance: 6.8 miles round trip
Hiking time: 3.5 hours
Configuration: out-and-back
Elevation gain: 325 feet
Difficulty: easy to moderate
Exposure: exposed
Dogs: allowed
Maps: U.S.G.S. Conoga Park • Topanga State Park map
Tom Harrison Maps: Topanga State Park Trail Map

map page 165

San Vicente Mountain Park is a 10-acre park at the head of Mandeville Canyon, nearly 2,000 feet above Los Angeles and the San Fernando Valley. The park was one of sixteen Los Angeles area anti-aircraft Nike missile launch sites that were built to protect the skies of Los Angeles from a Soviet nuclear attack during the Cold War. In operation between 1956 and 1968, it is now a mountaintop park managed by the Santa Monica Mountains Conservancy. The current restroom was created from the officers' barracks. The barbed wire fence, radar tower, helicopter pad, and guard shack still remain. Interpretive displays explain the site's military history.

Dirt Mulholland, an unpaved extension of Mulholland Drive, is a vehicle-restricted road that follows the ridge of the Santa Monica Mountains. The gated dirt road stretches 7 miles from the San Diego (405) Freeway in Encino to Conoga Avenue in Woodland Hills. Dirt Mulholland is a popular hiking, biking, equestrian, and dog-friendly route which accesses a large network of trails (including 11,000-acre Topanga State Park). The road winds along the top of the mountain range, connecting with ridgetop fire roads and stream-fed canyon trails.

This hike begins at the 1,500-acre Marvin Braude Mulholland Gateway Park, a popular link to Dirt Mulholland at the southern terminus of Reseda Boulevard in Tarzana. This is also a key entry point into the northern part of Topanga State Park. The route then takes Dirt Mulholland east for nearly the entire hike to San Vicente Mountain Park, following the northern boundary of Topanga State Park.

San Vicente Mountain Park can also be accessed from the east via Dirt Mulholland—Hike 26.

To the trailhead

From the Ventura Freeway/Highway 101 in Tarzana, exit on Reseda Boulevard. Drive 3.4 miles south into Marvin Braude Mulholland Gateway Park, and park at the end of the road. Inside the park gate is a white line painted across the road. Parking is free north of the white line, located 0.2 miles away from the trailhead. A parking fee is required south of the white line.

The hike

From the south end of Reseda Boulevard, take the gated Tarzana Fire Road (the unpaved fire road) up the hill into Topanga State Park. Pass a second vehicle gate, reaching Dirt Mulholland at 0.2 miles on a U-bend in the road. Bear left on the wide road, and follow the ridge across the head of Caballero Canyon, curving south then east. From the ridge are southern views into Temescal Canyon and Rustic Canyon and northern views into Caballero Canyon. At 0.7 miles, pass the Bent Arrow Trail, a connector trail to the Temescal Ridge Fire Road, and continue along the ridge. The vistas stretch across the San Fernando Valley to the left, down primitive Rustic Canyon, and onward to coastal Los Angeles. Pass the Caballero Canyon Trail on the left at 1.1 miles (Hike 45).

Curve left around a prominent hill known as Farmer Ridge, and continue eastward on the serpentine road. At 2.8 miles, pass the posted Sullivan Ridge Fire Road (Hike 28). Stay on Dirt Mulholland, overlooking the Encino Reservoir. Pass through another gate to San Vicente Mountain Park on the right at 3.3 miles, the former Cold War sentry post high above Mandeville Canyon. Bear right and walk through the park, passing picnic areas, vista overlooks and interpretive panels. Stairs lead up the original radar tower to an overlook platform with 360-degree vistas. From the overlook, views stretch from Burbank and Glendale to the San Gabriel

Mountains; across the San Fernando Valley, from the Santa Susana Mountains to the Santa Monica Mountains; and across Los Angeles to the Pacific Ocean. ■

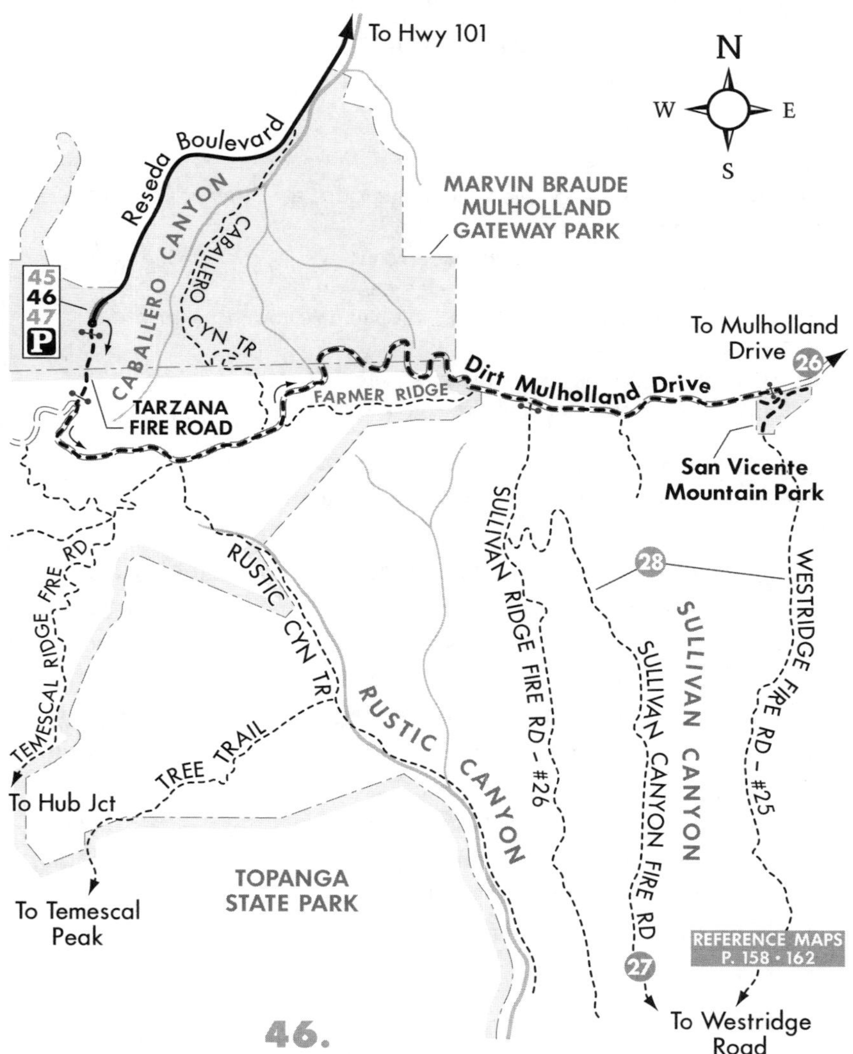

46.

Dirt Mulholland to San Vicente Mountain Park and Nike Site

47. Eagle Rock from Marvin Braude Mulholland Gateway Park

GARAPITO—HUB JUNCTION—TEMESCAL RIDGE LOOP

TOPANGA STATE PARK

3600 Reseda Boulevard • Tarzana

Hiking distance: 7.3 miles
Hiking time: 4 hours
Configuration: out-and-back with large loop; spur trail to Eagle Rock
Elevation gain: 800 feet
Difficulty: moderate to somewhat strenuous
Exposure: exposed ridge and shaded canyon
Dogs: allowed on Dirt Mulholland (first half mile) but not allowed in Topanga State Park
Maps: U.S.G.S. Conoga Park • Topanga State Park map
Tom Harrison Maps: Topanga State Park Trail Map

map page 168

The Garapito Trail is a single track footpath that weaves along the East Fork and South Fork of Garapito Creek, a tributary of Topanga Creek. The trail winds through dense thickets of chaparral, tunnels through tall brush, meanders along the sycamore-shaded canyon bottom, crosses two forks of Garapito Creek, and contours along a west-facing slope. The sinuous course leads to Eagle Rock, a sandstone monolith that dominates the surrounding landscape, and Hub Junction, a major crossroads in Topanga State Park. The return forms a large loop with the Temescal Ridge Fire Road.

The hike begins in Marvin Braude Mulholland Gateway Park, a grassy hillside park with manicured lawns and city-to-mountain views. The park is located at the southern terminus of Reseda Boulevard in Tarzana and links with Dirt Mulholland. The trailhead is a key entry point into the northern part of Topanga State Park.

To the trailhead

From the Ventura Freeway/Highway 101 in Tarzana, exit on Reseda Boulevard. Drive 3.4 miles south into Marvin Braude Mulholland Gateway Park, and park at the end of the road. Inside the park gate is a white line painted across the road. Parking is free north of the white line, located 0.2 miles away from the trailhead. A parking fee is required south of the white line.

The hike

From the south end of Reseda Boulevard, take the gated Tarzana Fire Road (an unpaved fire road) up the hill into Topanga State Park. Pass a second vehicle gate to Dirt Mulholland at 0.2 miles on a U-bend in the road. Bear right on the wide road to a signed junction at a half mile. Leave Dirt Mulholland and bear left on the Temescal Ridge Fire Road. Descend into the mountainous back-country with gorgeous vistas. At one mile, just before crossing a narrow saddle, is the Garapito Trail on the right and the Bent Arrow Trail on the left.

Begin the loop to the right into upper Garapito Canyon. Gently wind downhill into the shade of the forest on the narrow, serpentine footpath. Cross the East Fork of seasonal Garapito Creek under a large oak, and traverse the mountain slope. Drop into the canyon to the south, and cross the transient South Fork Garapito Creek under majestic oaks. Weave up the mountain, and leave the lush canyon bottom to mature chaparral, including ceanothus and mountain mahogany. Near the top, several switchbacks lead to a T-junction with the Eagle Rock Fire Road, a narrow dirt road by Eagle Rock at 3.6 miles.

Take the Eagle Rock Fire Road to the right for a short distance to the northern slope of Eagle Rock. The magnificent sandstone outcrop rises to a height of 1,957 feet and is pitted with water-eroded caves. Leave the trail to explore the tilted formation with caves and hollows. Scramble up the monolith for great views down Santa Ynez Canyon to the Pacific.

After enjoying the views from Eagle Rock, head back to the Garapito-Eagle Rock Fire Road junction. Continue east on the Eagle Rock Fire Road, and climb the east-west ridge to views across the San Fernando Valley. Top the slope to westward views across Los Angeles to the ocean. Descend to Hub Junction, a 4-way crossroads with a map kiosk at 4.4 miles. The Eagle Springs Fire Road goes sharply to the right, leading to Trippet Ranch (Hike 39). The Temescal Ridge Fire Road (also known as the Temescal

Ridge Trail)—the middle right trail—leads 0.7 miles to Temescal Peak and 4.8 miles to Temescal Gateway Park at the mouth of the canyon (Hike 35).

For this hike, bear left on the Temescal Ridge Fire Road. Descend to the north on the meandering dirt road through open grassland, and oak-dotted chaparral slopes. Complete the loop at 5.8 miles by the posted Garapito Trail. Return a half mile to Dirt Mulholland and retrace your steps to the right. ■

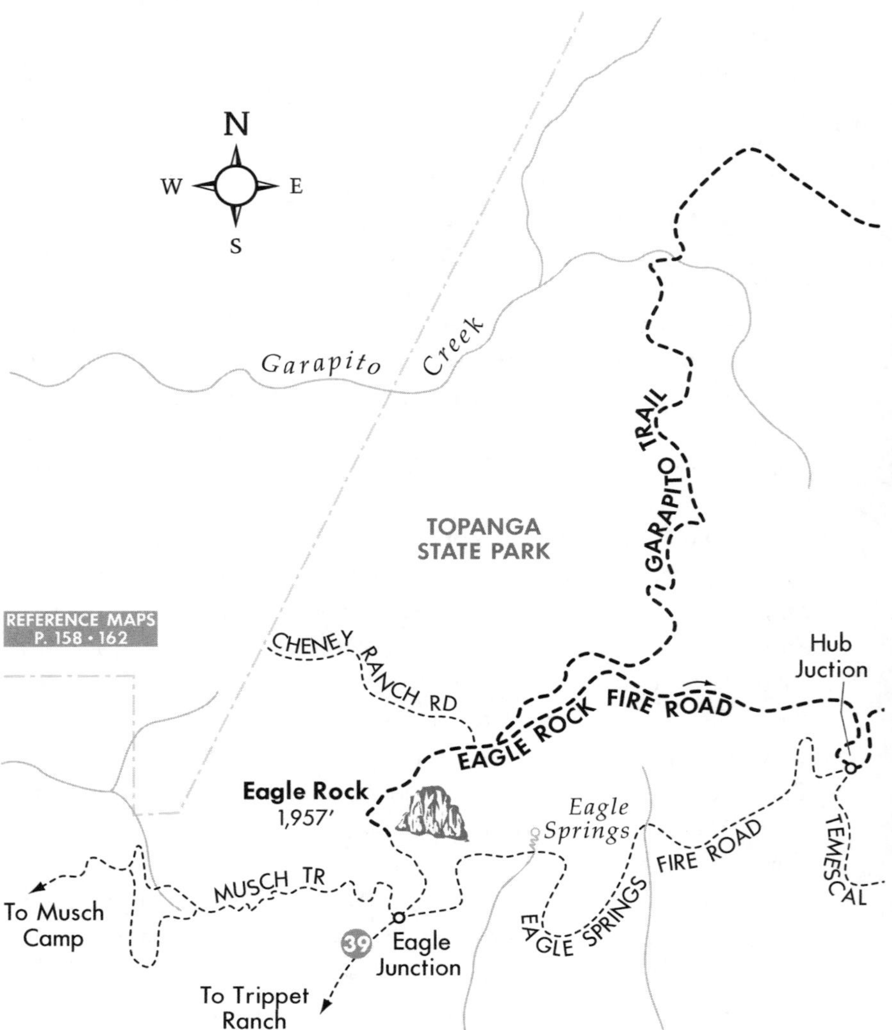

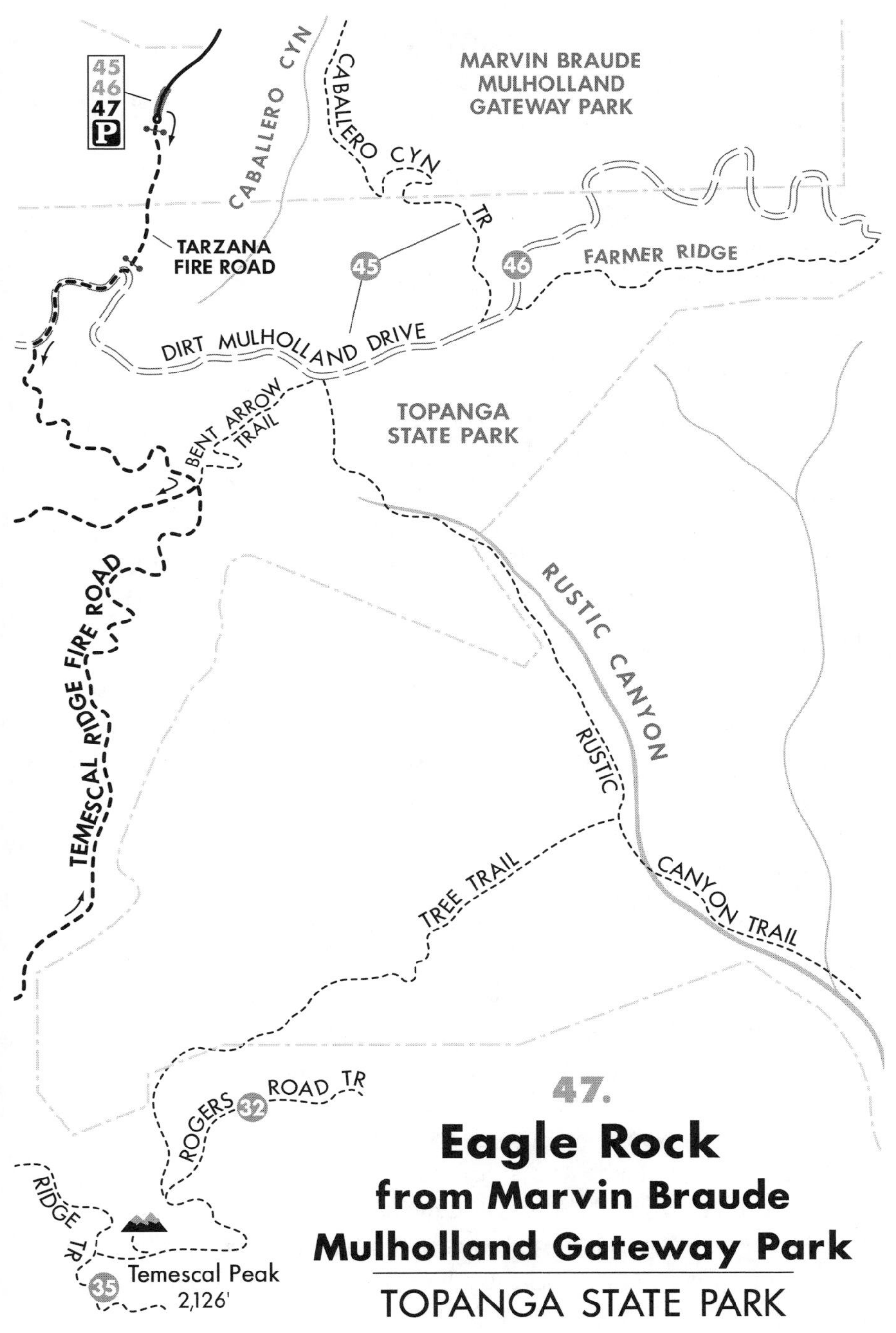

47.

Eagle Rock
from Marvin Braude Mulholland Gateway Park

TOPANGA STATE PARK

48. Vanalden Cave

Tarzana

Hiking distance: 0.8 miles round trip
Hiking time: 30 minutes
Configuration: out-and-back
Elevation gain: 100 feet
Difficulty: easy
Exposure: tall brush
Dogs: allowed
Maps: U.S.G.S. Conoga Park
Tom Harrison Maps: Topanga State Park Trail Map

Vanalden Cave is a massive sandstone cave in the mountain slope above Tarzana. The living-room-size cave is etched with modern-day hieroglyphics and colorful graffiti. The hike is a short but scenic neighborhood trail with vistas across the San Fernando Valley to the Los Padres National Forest. Beyond the cave, the unmaintained trail leads to Dirt Mulholland.

To the trailhead

From the Ventura Freeway (Highway 101) in Tarzana, exit on Tampa Avenue. Drive one block south to Ventura Boulevard. Turn left (east) and go 3 blocks to Vanalden Avenue. Turn right (south) and continue 2.9 miles south to the trailhead at the end of the road.

The hike

From the end of the street, walk over the berms and head south. Wind through the tall brush, gently climbing into the foothills. Drop into a shaded oak grove in a seasonal drainage. A side path on the right leads 30 yards into a box canyon with moss-covered sandstone cliffs. Twenty yards ahead on the main trail is a trail split, forming a loop. Take the left fork 100 yards along the drainage floor to the base of Vanalden Cave. After exploring in and around the cave, climb the slope to the top of the sandstone caves. To hike beyond the cave, carefully cross the roof of the cave, avoiding the four large holes that open into the space below. Veer right and head up the hill on the footpath. The narrow, overgrown path connects with Dirt Mulholland.

To extend the hike along Dirt Mulholland, heading to the right leads a half mile to the Greenbriar Drive connector path and 0.7 miles to the Winnetka Ridge Trail (Hike 49). To the left leads 0.9 miles to the Temescal Ridge Fire Road and 1.2 miles to Tarzana Fire Road at Reseda Boulevard (Hikes 45—47). ■

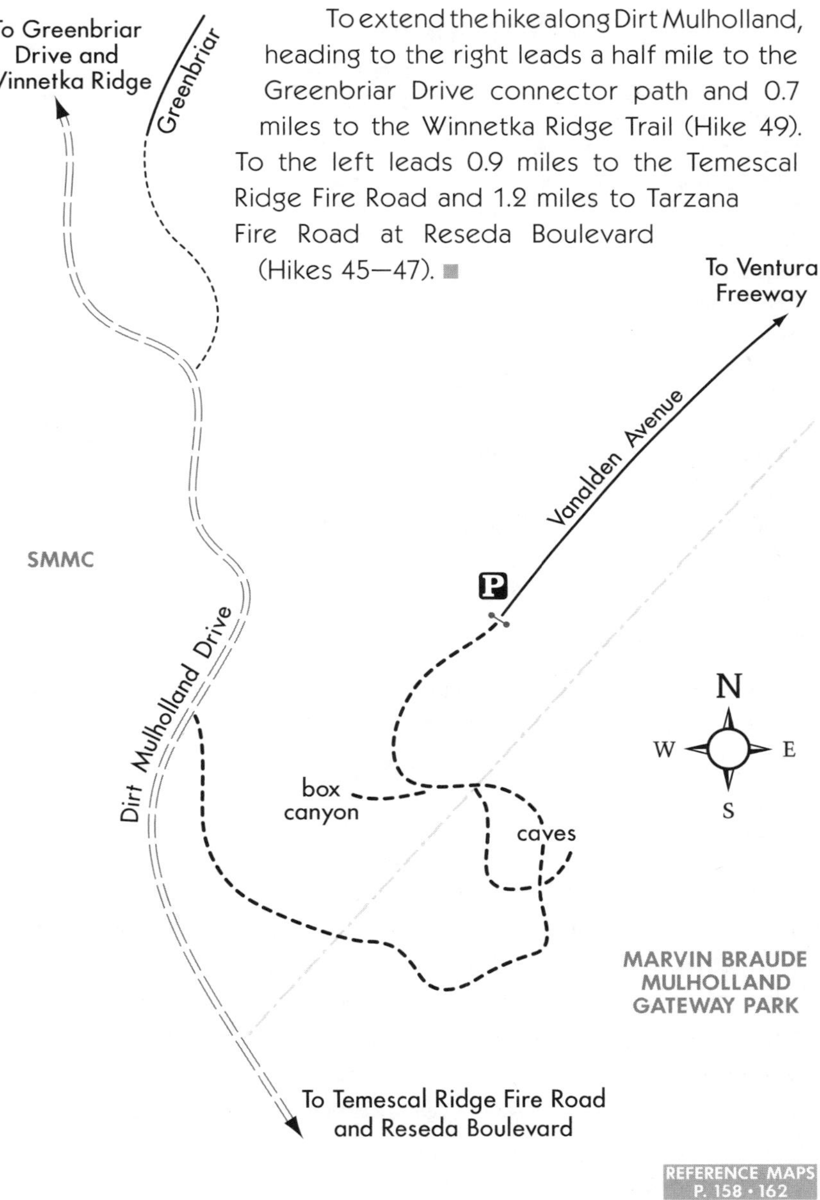

REFERENCE MAPS
P. 158 • 162

48.
Vanalden Cave

49. Winnetka Ridge Trail

Woodland Hills

Hiking distance: 1.6 miles round trip
Configuration: out-and-back
Hiking time: 50 minutes
Elevation gain: 150 feet
Difficulty: easy
Exposure: exposed ridge
Dogs: allowed
Maps: U.S.G.S. Conoga Park
Tom Harrison Maps: Topanga State Park Trail Map

The Winnetka Ridge Trail is an easy, 0.8-mile access trail to Dirt Mulholland. The undulating path heads south, connecting the residential neighborhood in Woodland Hills with the vehicle-restricted road. The Winnetka Ridge Trail follows a minor ridge between Natoma Canyon and Corbin Canyon. The views extend across Woodland Hills and the San Fernando Valley.

To the trailhead

From the Ventura Freeway/Highway 101 in Woodland Hills, exit on Winnetka Avenue. Drive 1.6 miles south to the south end of Winnetka Avenue. Park alongside the curb.

The hike

Walk around the metal barrier, and head up the slope on the Winnetka Ridge Trail. Follow the ridge on the footpath, overlooking Corbin Canyon on the left and Natoma Canyon on the right. Drop down and cross a saddle, then climb up a second hill. Stay atop the ridge, with great views across Woodland Hills and Tarzana. At 0.8 miles, the trail ends at a T-junction with Dirt Mulholland.

There are several options for extending the hike. To the right (west) is a junction with the Natoma Trail at a half mile. This 0.8-mile trail is similar to the Winnetka Ridge Trail and leads to the southern terminus of Natoma Avenue. Farther along, at 1.2 miles, is the junction with the Woodland Ridge Trail (Hike 50). This footpath leads 1.1 miles into Serrania Park off of Serrania Avenue.

To the left (east) on Dirt Mulholland leads 1.6 miles to Temescal Ridge Fire Road (Hike 47) and 2.1 miles to Marvin Braude Mulholland Gateway Park at the southern terminus of Reseda Boulevard. The Reseda Boulevard trailhead is a key entry point into the northern end of Topanga State Park. ■

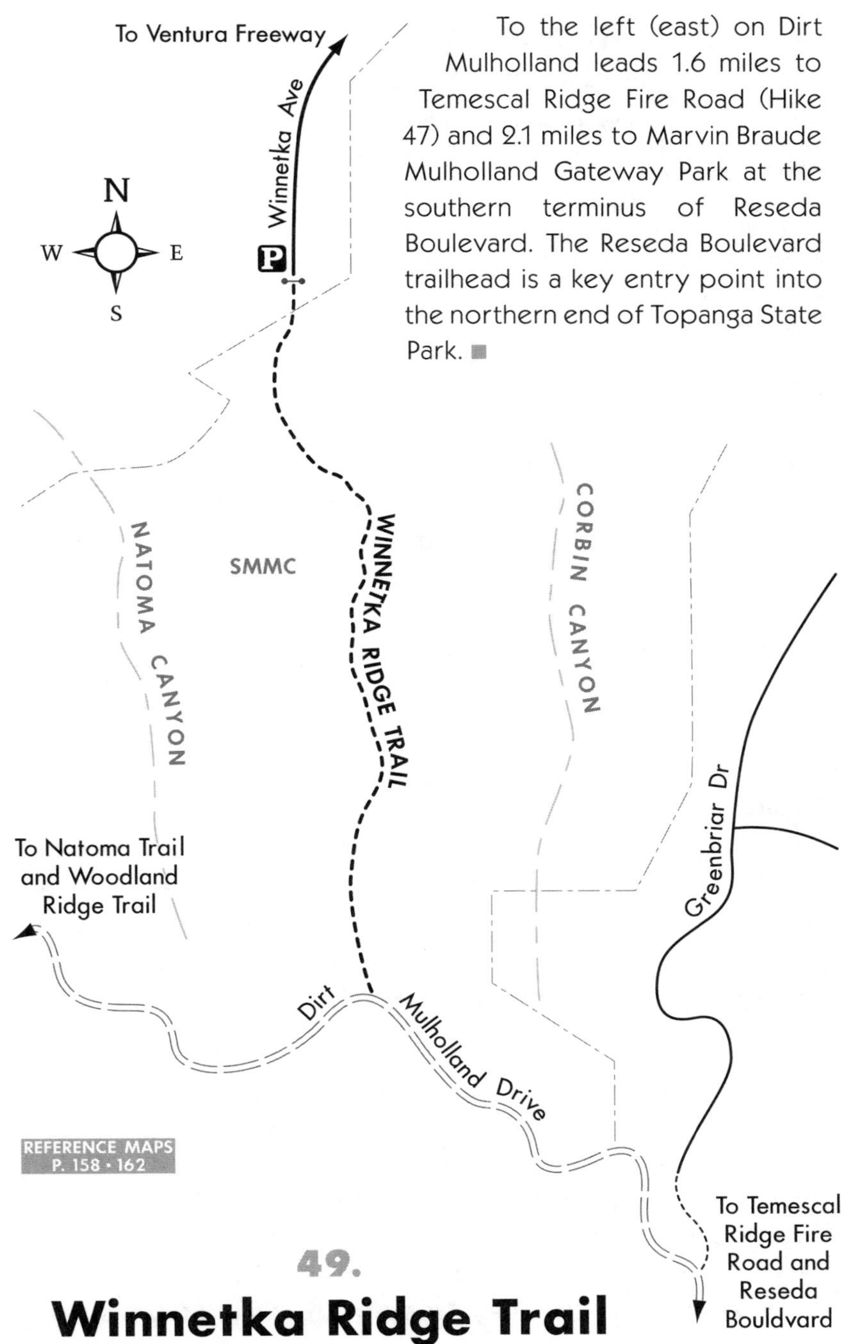

49. Winnetka Ridge Trail

50. Woodland Ridge Trail

Serrania Park to Dirt Mulholland

20864 Wells Drive • Woodland Hills

Hiking distance: 2.3 miles round trip
Hiking time: 1 hour
Configuration: out-and-back
Elevation gain: 500 feet
Difficulty: easy
Exposure: exposed
Dogs: allowed
Maps: U.S.G.S. Conoga Park
Tom Harrison Maps: Topanga State Park Trail map

Serrania Park is a popular neighborhood dog park tucked into a small canyon in Woodland Hills on the San Fernando Valley's south rim. A paved, circular path follows the perimeter of the tree-dotted grassland. On the east edge of the park is the Woodland Ridge Trail, a natural footpath connecting Woodland Hills with Dirt Mulholland just below the crest of the Santa Monica Mountains. (Dirt Mulholland is the unpaved portion of Mulholland Drive.) The trail climbs the hillside, following the rolling ridge across several knolls while offering sweeping views across the valley.

To the trailhead

From the Ventura Freeway/Highway 101 in Woodland Hills, exit on De Soto Avenue. Drive 0.8 miles south on De Soto Avenue (which becomes Serrania Avenue south of Ventura Boulevard) and veer left (east) on Wells Drive. Park alongside the road or turn right into the Serrania Park parking lot.

The hike

From the east edge of Serrania Park, take the footpath, which is set off by a wood railing. Head up the slope through chaparral on the dirt and rock path, with vistas across Woodland Hills and Conoga Park to the Santa Susana Mountains. Follow a narrow ridge above Serrania Park to views of the Santa Monica Mountains backcountry and the San Gabriel Mountains. Continue along the exposed ridge and veer left, just before reaching a steep slope.

Follow the serpentine ridge to a knoll with a survey marker and 360-degree vistas. While staying atop the ridge, descend and climb, reaching Dirt Mulholland at the trail's end.

From Dirt Mulholland, heading left for 1.2 miles leads to the Winnetka Ridge Trail (Hike 49). ■

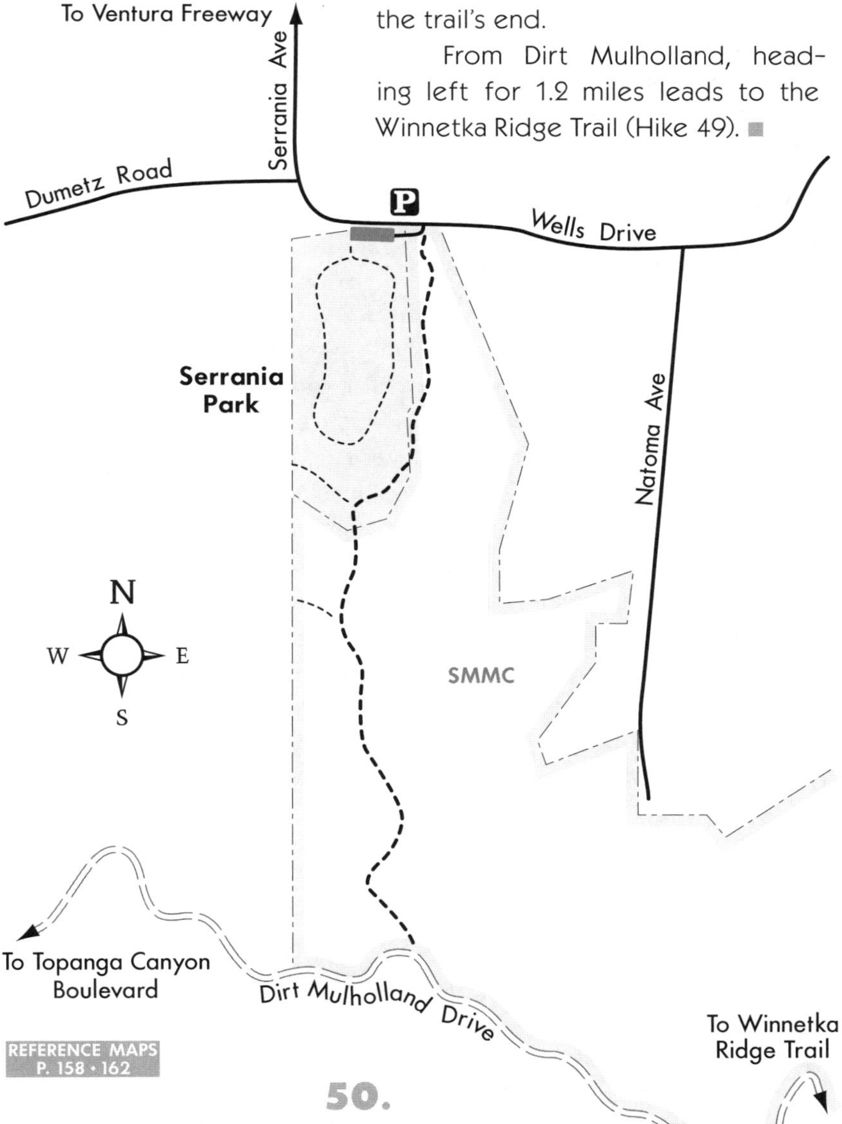

50.

Woodland Ridge Trail

SERRANIA PARK to DIRT MULHOLLAND

51. Viewridge Trail

SUMMIT VALLEY • EDMUND D. EDELMAN PARK

Topanga Canyon Boulevard · Topanga

Hiking distance: 2.5 miles round trip
Hiking time: 1.5 hours
Configuration: out-and-back with small loop
Elevation gain: 200 feet
Difficulty: easy
Exposure: mix of shaded forest and exposed slopes
Dogs: allowed
Maps: U.S.G.S. Conoga Park and Topanga
Tom Harrison Maps: Topanga State Park Trail Map

Edmund D. Edelman Park in Summit Valley covers 652 hillside acres that stretch across both sides of Topanga Canyon Boulevard. Located midway between the town of Topanga and Woodland Hills, the rolling hills of the Summit Valley park are open to hiking, biking, and equestrian use. A network of trails weaves through native grasslands, mixed chaparral communities, and stately oak woodlands. Within the open space is the headwaters of Topanga Creek and the steep cliffs above Santa Maria Canyon. The one-mile Viewridge Trail sits on the lesser-used eastern portion of the park, connecting Viewridge Road with Santa Maria Road. A side loop leads to rock outcroppings with vistas into the Santa Maria Creek drainage and Topanga's rolling hillsides. En route, the 60-foot-long Viewridge Bridge spans a picturesque, 17-foot-deep ravine.

To the trailhead

From Santa Monica, drive 4 miles northbound on the Pacific Coast Highway/Highway 1 to Topanga Canyon Boulevard and turn right. Continue 8.8 miles to the signed Viewridge Road on the right. Turn right and continue 0.4 miles to the trailhead at the end of the road, directly across from Summit Pointe Estates. Park alongside the curb.

From the Ventura Freeway/Highway 101 in Woodland Hills, exit on Topanga Canyon Boulevard. Drive 3.4 miles south to the signed

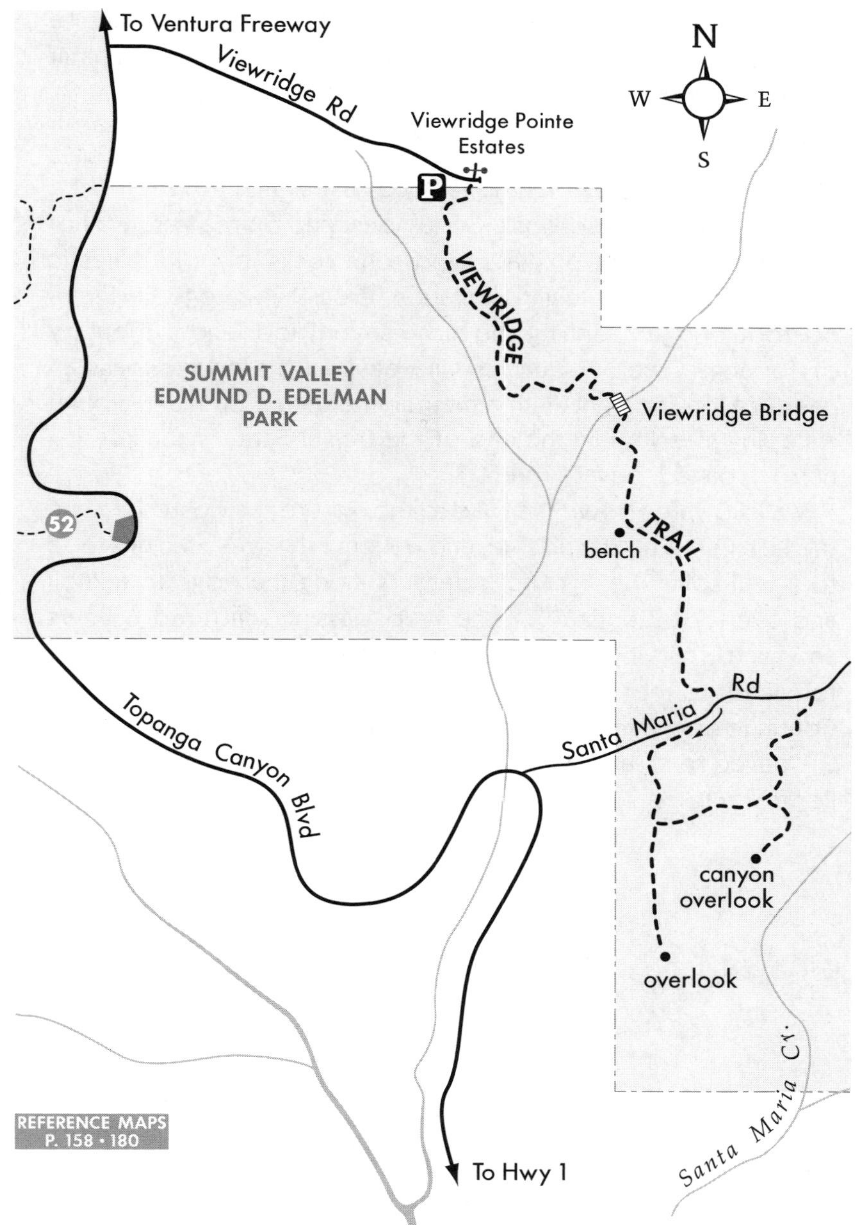

51. Viewridge Trail

SUMMIT VALLEY • EDMUND D. EDELMAN PARK

Viewridge Road on the left. Turn left and continue 0.4 miles to the trailhead at the end of the road, directly across from Summit Pointe Estates. Park alongside the curb.

The hike

On the south side of Viewridge Road, just shy of the end of the street, is the trailhead kiosk. Gently descend on the east wall of the stream-fed canyon. Pass sandstone rocks and old majestic oaks while steadily losing elevation. Cross Viewridge Bridge, a 60-foot bridge spanning the lush canyon floor and a tributary of Topanga Creek. A quarter-mile beyond the bridge, pass an overlook on the right with a memorial bench. Continue through a sloping meadow to the end of the trail at Santa Maria Road, a narrow, paved, private road.

Walk 80 yards down the road to the right to the posted trail on the left. Curve up the hillside, and traverse the west-facing slope to a trail split. The right fork detours along the ridge to a knoll and overlook. Continue on the loop, passing scattered willows and pines, curving to the east and another trail split. The right fork leads to the Canyon Overlook among sandstone formations. Continue on the main path back to Santa Maria Road. Bear left on the paved road, and walk 0.1 mile downhill, completing the loop. Return by retracing your steps to the right. ■

52. Summit Valley Trail

SUMMIT VALLEY • EDMUND D. EDELMAN PARK

Topanga Canyon Boulevard • Topanga

Hiking distance: 2 miles round trip
Hiking time: 1 hour
Configuration: loop
Elevation gain: 300 feet
Difficulty: easy
Exposure: shaded canyon bottom and exposed ridge
Dogs: allowed
Maps: U.S.G.S. Conoga Park • Topanga State Park map
Tom Harrison Maps: Topanga State Park Trail map

map page 181

Edmund D. Edelman Park is located in bowl-shaped Summit Valley at the head of Topanga Canyon. The 1,500-foot ridge at the north end of this 652-acre park separates rural Topanga Canyon from the urban San Fernando Valley. The park's wildlife corridor includes oak woodlands, mixed chaparral communities, native grasslands, and the headwaters of Topanga Creek. The network of trails is open to hikers, bikers, and equestrians. This hike loops through two valleys, crosses the gently rolling hills, and parallels the headwaters of Topanga Creek.

To the trailhead

From Santa Monica, drive 4 miles northbound on the Pacific Coast Highway/Highway 1 to Topanga Canyon Boulevard and turn right. Continue 8.2 miles to the signed Summit Valley/Edmund D. Edelman parking area on the left (west).

From the Ventura Freeway/Highway 101 in Woodland Hills, exit on Topanga Canyon Boulevard, and drive 4 miles south to the parking area on the right (west).

The hike

Head west past the trailhead gate, and descend into the forested stream-fed draw, crossing the headwaters of Topanga Creek. At 0.2 miles is a five-way junction. Take the far right trail—the Summit Valley Canyon Trail—to begin the loop. Head north along the canyon floor, parallel to the seasonal Topanga Creek on the right. At one mile, just before descending into a eucalyptus grove, the unsigned Summit Valley Loop Trail bears left. Take this trail as it zigzags up the hillside towards the south. Traverse the edge of the hill to a ridge and a junction. (For a shorter hike, the left fork returns to the five-way junction along the ridge.) Take the middle fork straight ahead, and descend into the next drainage. The trail curves south, returning down the draw to the five-way junction. ■

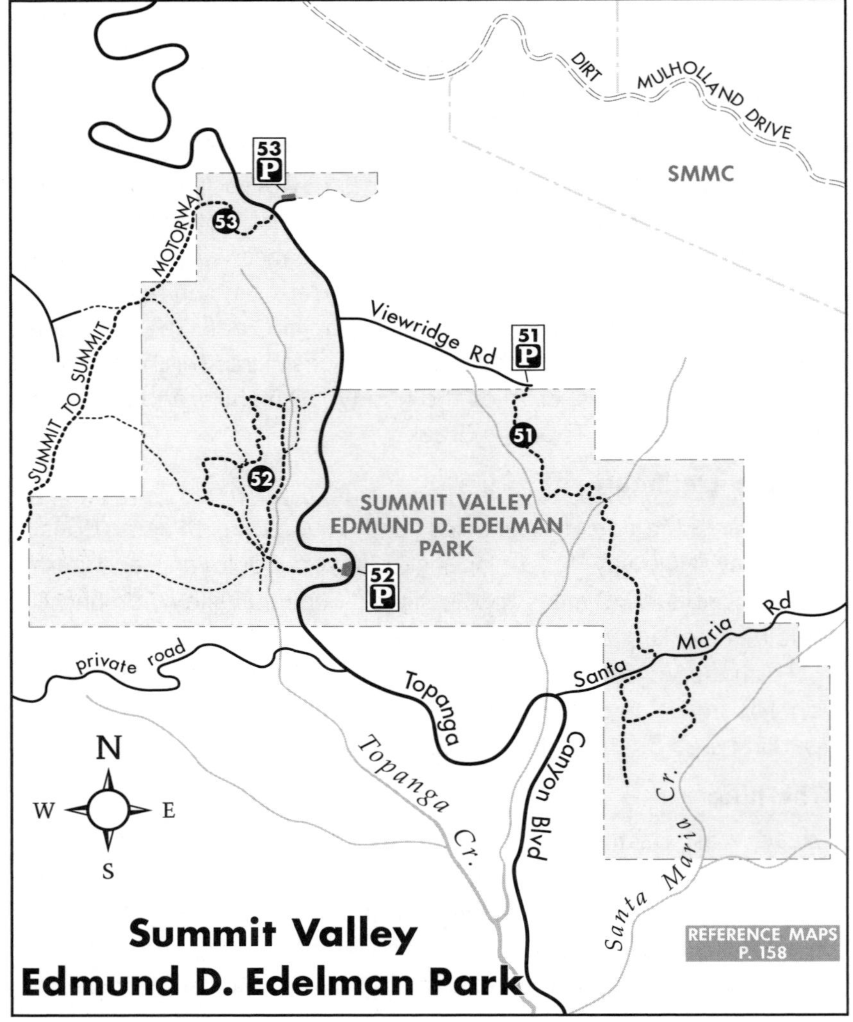

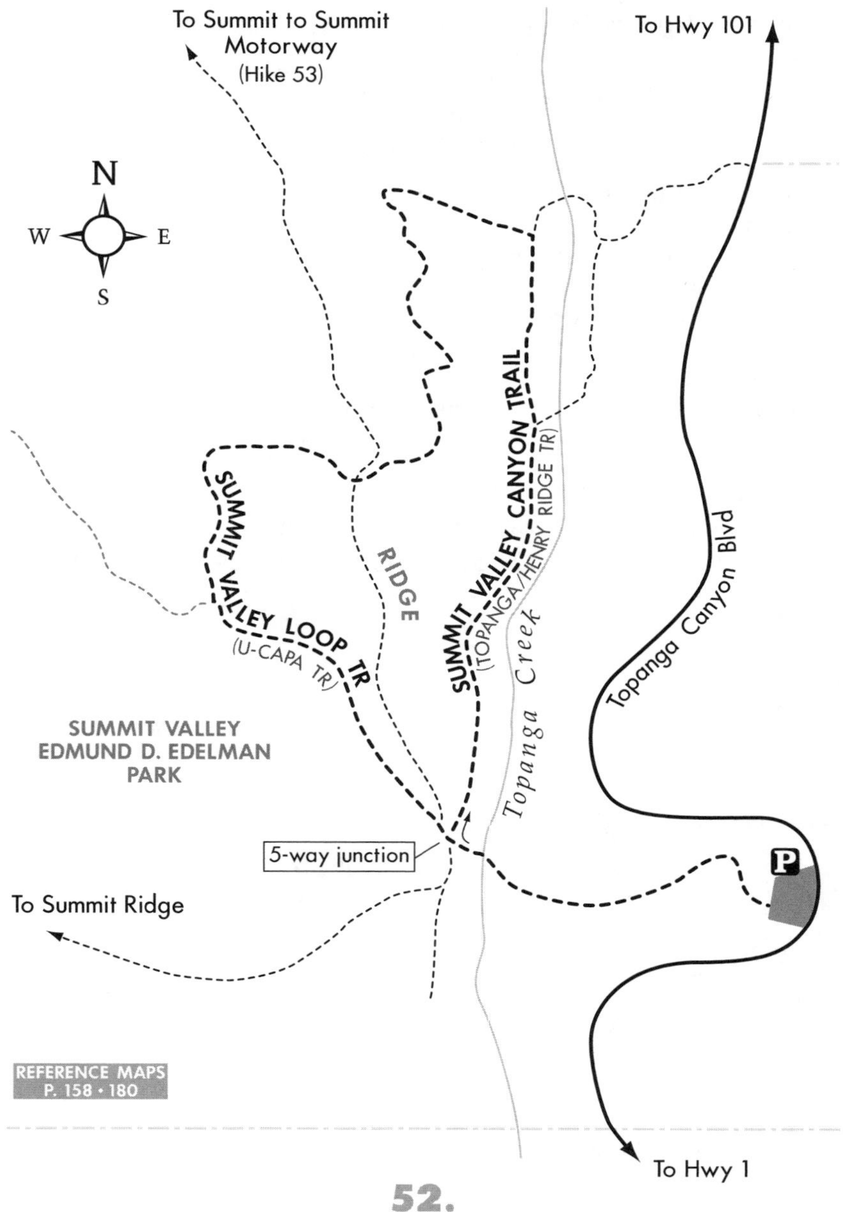

52.
Summit Valley
SUMMIT VALLEY • EDMUND D. EDELMAN PARK

53. Summit to Summit Motorway

Top of Topanga Overlook to Old Topanga Canyon Road

Topanga Canyon Boulevard · Topanga

Hiking distance: 6.6 miles round trip
Hiking time: 3.5 hours
Configuration: out-and-back
Elevation gain: 300 feet
Difficulty: easy to moderate
Exposure: exposed hills
Dogs: allowed
Maps: U.S.G.S. Conoga Park, Topanga, Malibu Beach and Calabasas
Tom Harrison Maps: Topanga State Park Trail Map

The Summit to Summit Motorway is an unpaved fire road perched high above Calabasas and Topanga Canyon. The gated dirt road follows a 1,500-foot ridge that straddles the Topanga

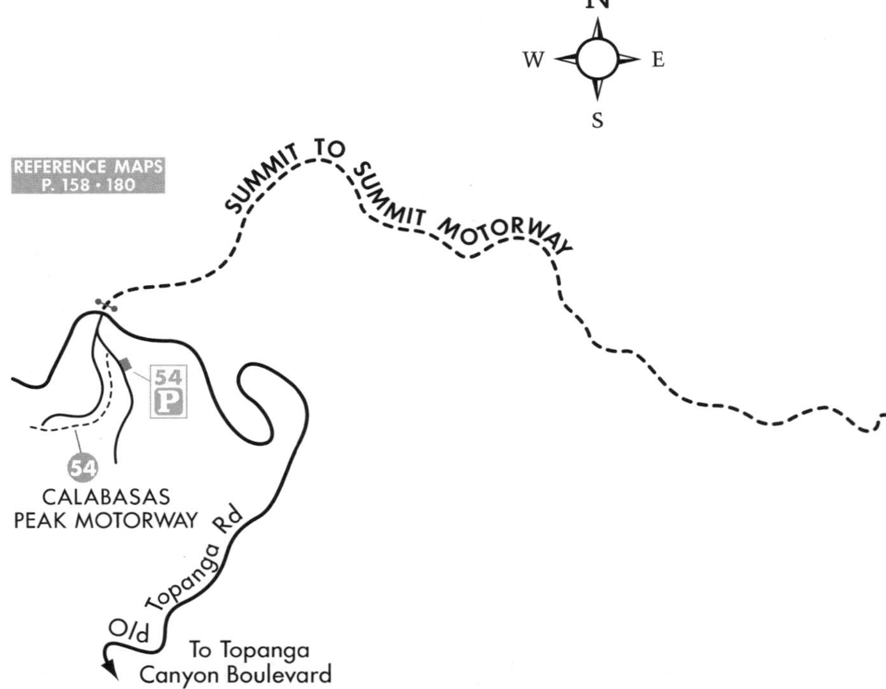

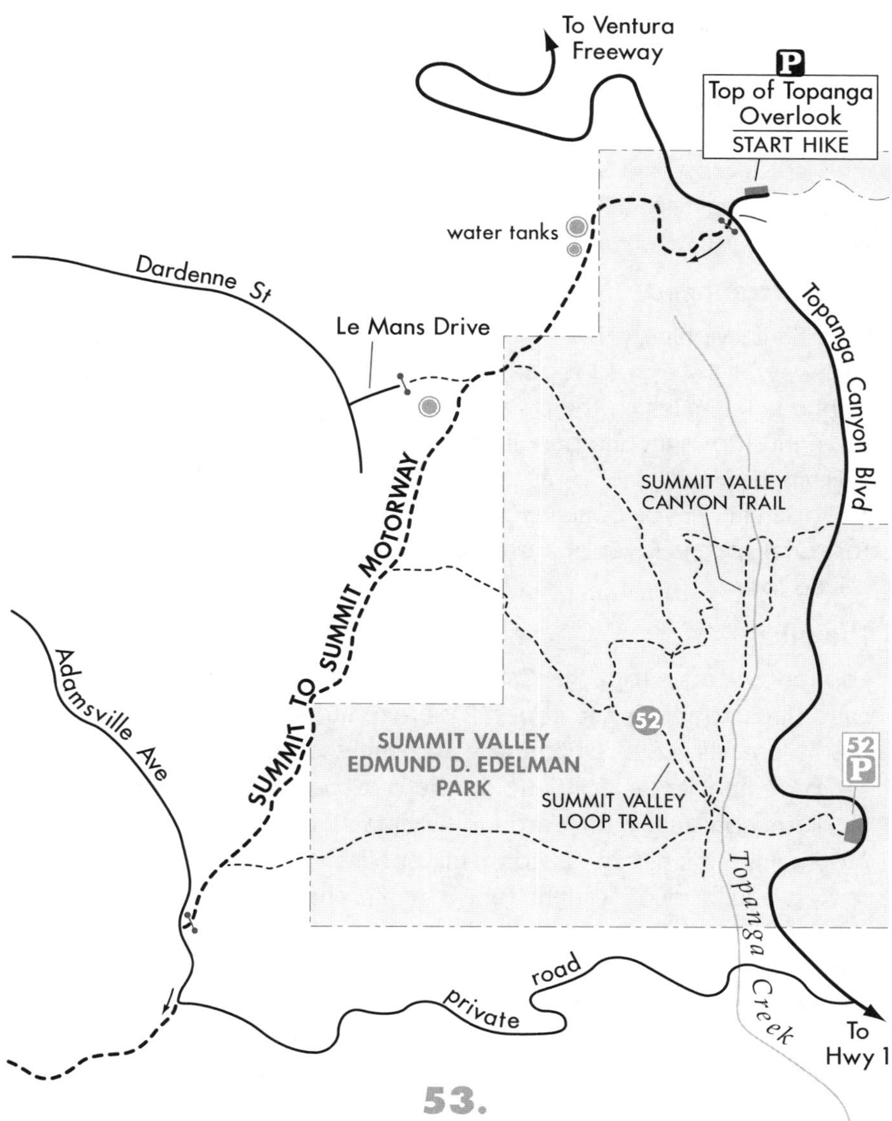

53.

Summit to Summit Motorway

Top of Topanga Overlook to Old Topanga Canyon Road

SUMMIT VALLEY • EDMUND D. EDELMAN PARK

Canyon and San Fernando Valley watershed divide. The historic ridgeline road connects the Top Of Topanga Overlook (just off Topanga Canyon Boulevard) with Old Topanga Canyon Road and the Calabasas Peak Motorway. Throughout the hike are sweeping vistas across the Santa Monica Mountains and San Fernando Valley to the San Gabriel Mountains. The trail offers fantastic views with relatively little elevation gain.

To the trailhead

From Santa Monica, drive 4 miles northbound on the Pacific Coast Highway/Highway 1 to Topanga Canyon Boulevard and turn right. Continue 9.2 miles to the posted Top Of Topanga Overlook on the right. Turn right and park in the paved lot.

From the Ventura Freeway/Highway 101 in Woodland Hills, exit on Topanga Canyon Boulevard. Drive 3 miles south to the posted Top Of Topanga Overlook on the left. Turn left and park in the paved lot.

The hike

Cautiously cross Topanga Canyon Boulevard to the gated fire road directly across the street. Pass the gate and snake through the mountains 0.2 miles to the water tanks on the right, where the pavement ends. Continue on the dirt road, overlooking the San Fernando Valley, the Verdugo Mountains, and the San Gabriel Mountains. At a half mile, atop a minor hill and by another water tank, is a junction. The right fork (straight ahead) descends 150 yards to Dardenne Street by Le Mans Drive. Bear left, just shy of the tanks, and weave down the slope. Head back up the undulating trail roughly following the ridge. Cross a saddle with canyons on both sides of the trail and far-reaching vistas to the ocean. At 1.5 miles, pass a gate onto paved Adamsville Avenue. Bear left on the road and walk 200 yards, returning to the unpaved road.

Continue west on the Summit to Summit Motorway. Wind through the hills on a gradual, 1.4-mile-long downward slope. At 3.3 miles, the trail ends at Old Topanga Canyon Road, directly across the road from the Calabasas Peak Motorway (Hike 54). Return along the same route. ■

54. Calabasas Peak

Calabasas Peak Motorway from Old Topanga Canyon Road

Calabasas • Malibu

Hiking distance: 5 miles round trip
Hiking time: 2.5 hours
Configuration: out-and-back
Elevation gain: 700 feet
Difficulty: moderate
Exposure: exposed
Dogs: allowed
Maps: U.S.G.S. Malibu Beach
Tom Harrison Maps: Topanga State Park Trail Map
Tom Harrison Maps: Malibu Creek State Park Trail Map

map page 187

Calabasas Peak is perched high above the city of Calabasas at an elevation of 2,163 feet. From the summit are views into Red Rock Canyon to the east, Cold Creek Canyon to the south, and the San Fernando Valley to the north. Access to the peak is via the Calabasas Peak Motorway, an unpaved fire road. The gated dirt road follows a ridge between Old Topanga Canyon Road and Stunt Road by Cold Creek Canyon Preserve.

Three routes lead to the rounded peak. This hike ascends to the peak along the fire road from Old Topanga Canyon Road from the northeast. (The next two hikes climb to the peak from its other access routes.) Throughout the hike are weather-carved sandstone outcroppings and sweeping vistas across the Santa Monica Mountains and the San Fernando Valley.

To the trailhead

From Santa Monica, drive 4 miles northbound on the Pacific Coast Highway/Highway 1 to Topanga Canyon Boulevard and turn right. Continue 4.2 miles to Old Topanga Canyon Road on the left. Turn left and drive 4.1 miles up Old Topanga Canyon Road to Calabasas Peak Motorway on the left, across from the Summit to Summit Motorway. Turn left and continue 140 yards to a wide parking area on the left. (En route, the road passes the posted trailhead on the right.) Limited parking is also available in narrow pullouts on the left (southwest) side of Old Topanga Canyon Road.

From the Ventura Freeway/Highway 101 in Woodland Hills, exit on Topanga Canyon Boulevard. Drive 1.3 miles south to Mulholland Drive. Turn right and continue 2.2 miles to Old Topanga Canyon Road on the left. (En route, veer left onto Mulholland Highway.) Turn left on Old Topanga Canyon Road, and drive 1.5 miles to Calabasas Peak Motorway on the right, across from the Summit to Summit Motorway. Turn right and go 140 yards to a wide parking area on the left, passing the signed trailhead on the right. Limited parking is also available in narrow pullouts on the left (southwest) side of Old Topanga Canyon Road.

The hike

From the parking area, walk 60 yards down the paved road to the signed access trail on the left. From Old Topanga Canyon Road, walk 80 yards up the paved road to the signed access trail on the right.

Walk up the slope on the footpath 0.1 mile to a T-junction with the Calabasas Peak Motorway, a dirt fire road. The right fork leads a short distance to a home on private land. Bear left and head west. From the trail are exceptional views of the San Fernando Valley and the interior of the Santa Monica Mountains. Climb the first hill, then descend on the rolling ridge. Steadily climb the second slope, with continuing vistas across the valley to the Los Padres National Forest and the San Gabriel Mountains. At the top of the slope, Calabasas Peak comes into full view. Curve left and head south towards the peak.

At 1.6 miles, pass the signed Calabasas-Cold Creek (Secret) Trail (Hike 55) on the right. Continue up the road 0.9 miles, with alternating east and west views. Just before the crest of the road, a footpath to the summit veers sharply to the right. The main Calabasas Peak Motorway continues straight, leading 1.7 miles down to Stunt Road (Hike 56). Leave the fire road and switchback to the right. Follow the ridge 0.2 miles, bending left to the 2,163-foot summit on a small, exposed knoll. At the peak is a rock cairn, survey pin, and 360-degree vistas. ■

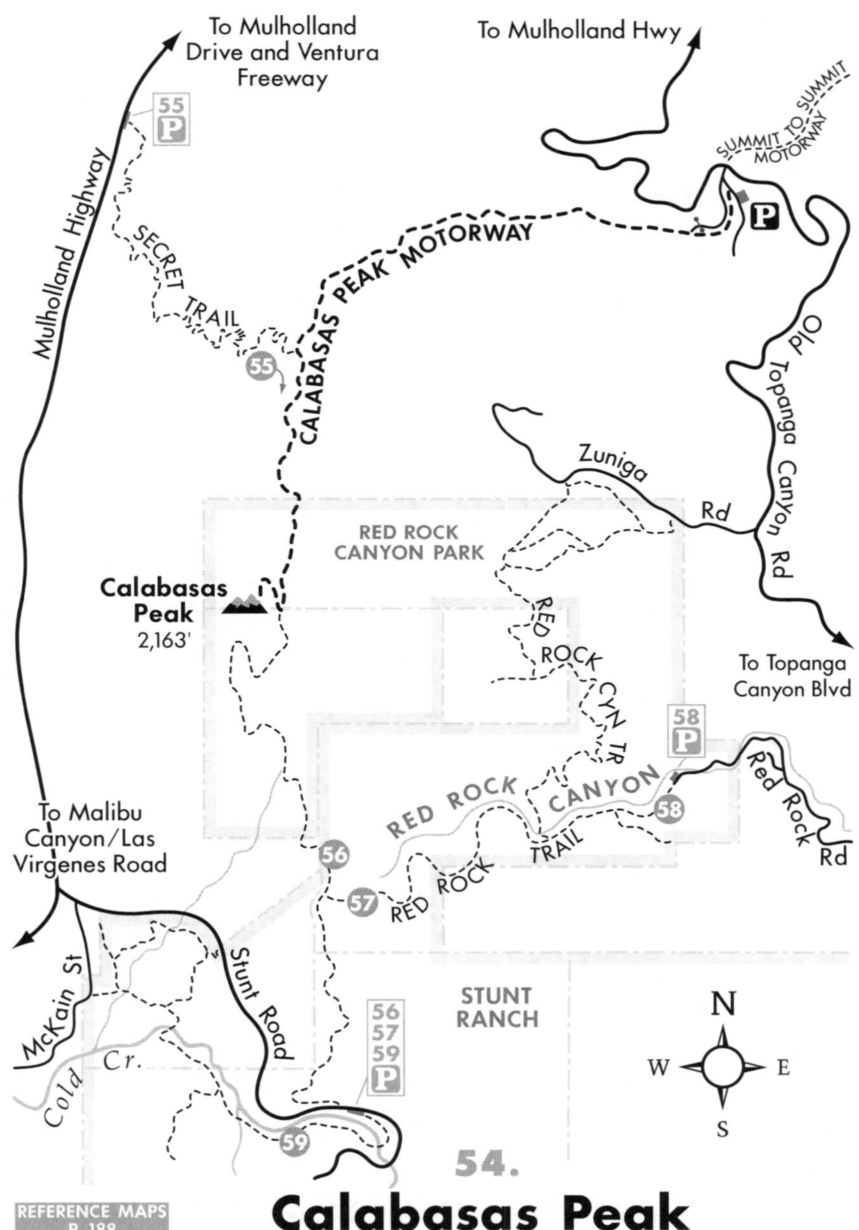

54.

REFERENCE MAPS P. 188

Calabasas Peak

Calabasas Peak Motorway from Old Topanga Canyon Road

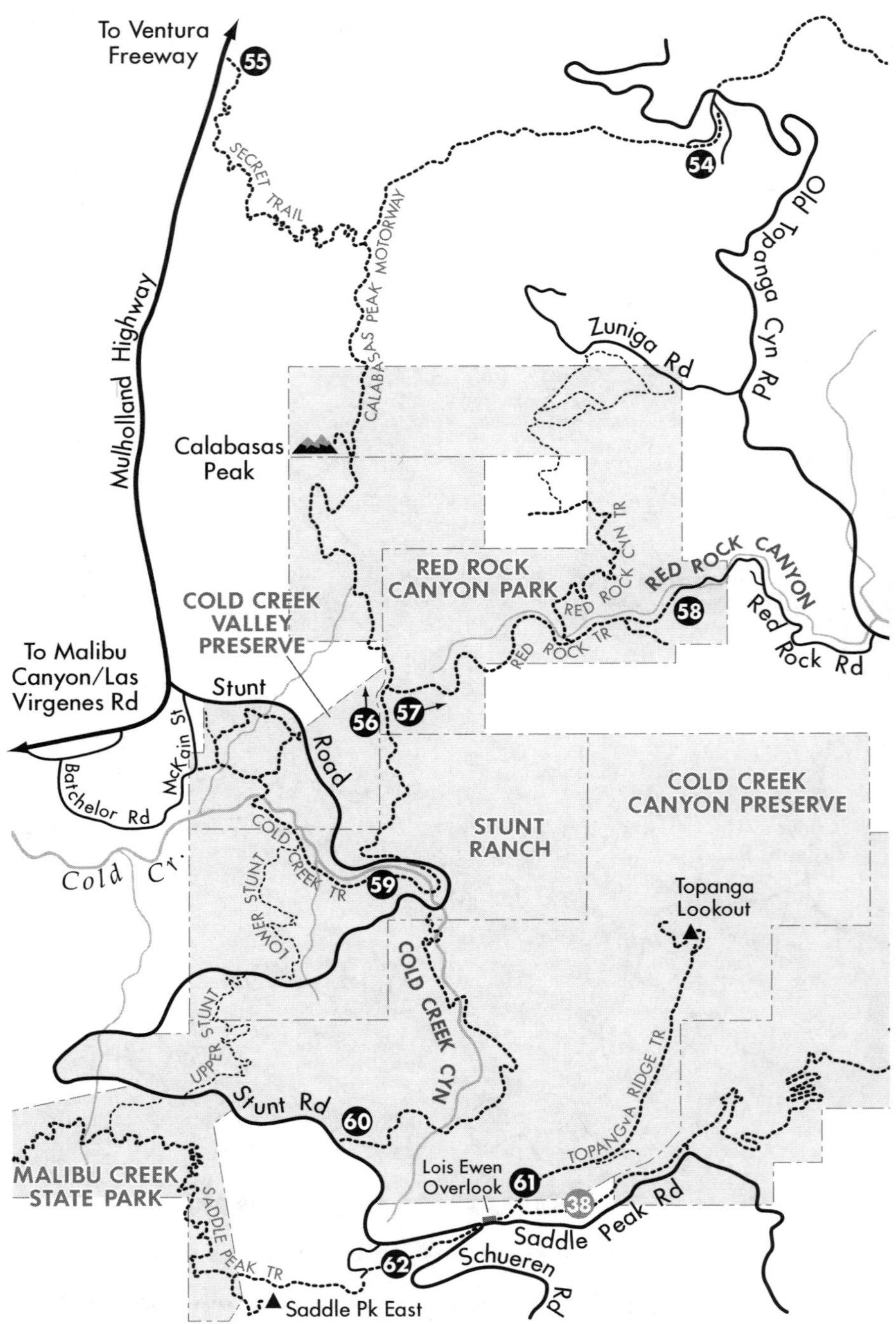
To Ventura Freeway
55
54
Old Topanga Cyn Rd
SECRET TRAIL
CALABASAS PEAK MOTORWAY
Mulholland Highway
Zuniga Rd
Calabasas Peak
RED ROCK CANYON PARK
RED ROCK CYN TR
RED ROCK CANYON
RED ROCK TR
58
Red Rock Rd
COLD CREEK VALLEY PRESERVE
To Malibu Canyon/Las Virgenes Rd
Stunt Road
56
57
McKain St
Batchelor Rd
COLD CREEK CANYON PRESERVE
STUNT RANCH
COLD CREEK TR
Cold Cr.
59
LOWER STUNT
Topanga Lookout
COLD CREEK CYN
UPPER STUNT
TOPANGA RIDGE TR
Stunt Rd
60
MALIBU CREEK STATE PARK
Lois Ewen Overlook
61
38
SADDLE PEAK TR
Saddle Peak Rd
Schueren Rd
62
Saddle Pk East

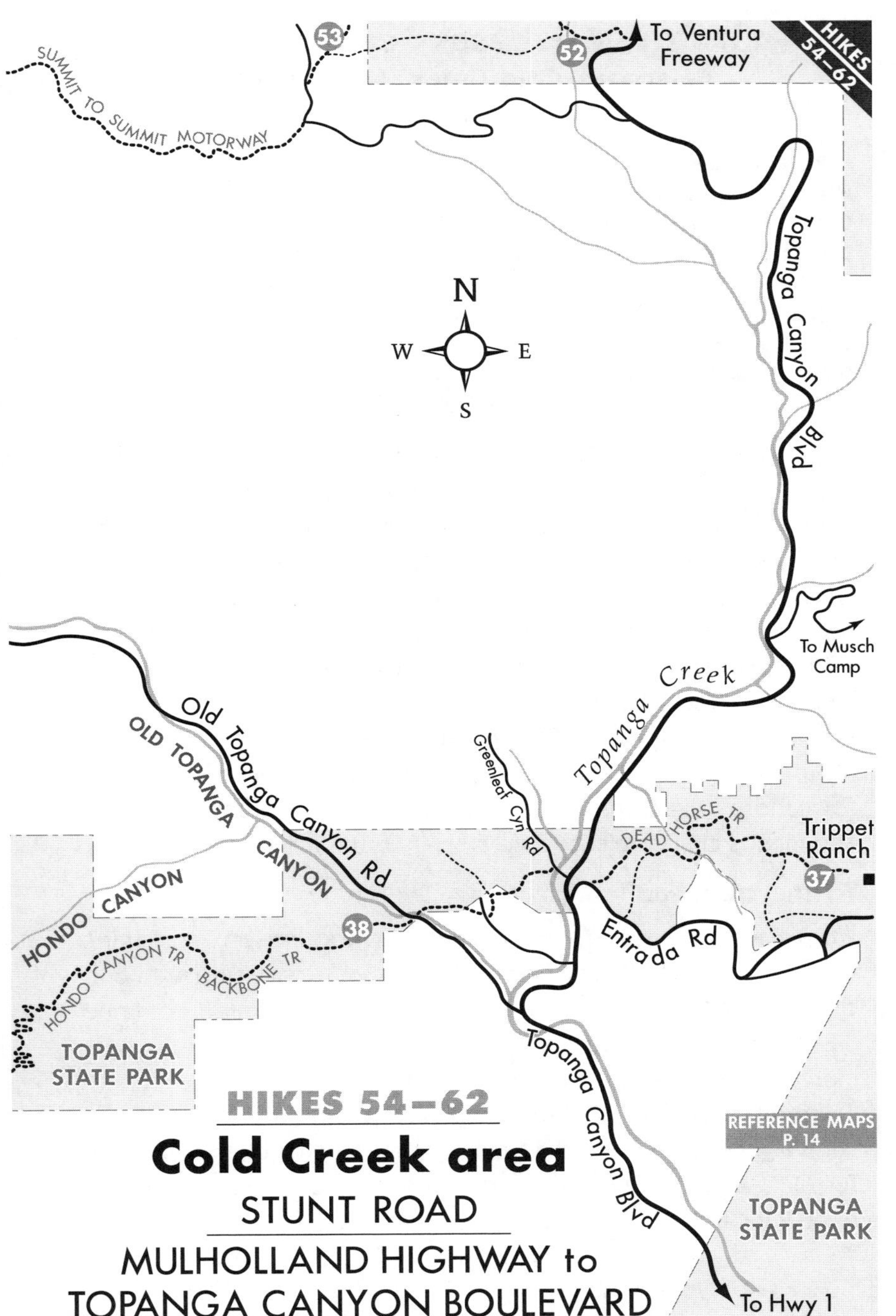

HIKES 54–62

Cold Creek area

STUNT ROAD

MULHOLLAND HIGHWAY to TOPANGA CANYON BOULEVARD

55. Calabasas Peak

Calabasas-Cold Creek (Secret) Trail

Calabasas • Malibu

Hiking distance: 4.6 miles round trip
Hiking time: 2.5 hours
Configuration: out-and-back
Elevation gain: 700 feet
Difficulty: moderate
Exposure: exposed with shaded pockets
Dogs: allowed
Maps: U.S.G.S. Malibu Beach
Tom Harrison Maps: Malibu Creek State Park Trail Map

The Calabasas-Cold Creek Trail (also known as the Secret Trail) is a multi-use trail that winds up the mountain from Mulholland Highway to the Calabasas Peak Motorway. Ascending from the northwest, the 1.5-mile connector path weaves through grasslands, chaparral, oak woodland, riparian willow, and volcanic rock formations. This hike leads through this diverse area to the 2,163-foot summit of Calabasas Peak. The trail offers outstanding vistas into Red Rock Canyon, Cold Creek Canyon, Old Topanga Canyon, and across the San Fernando Valley to the San Gabriel Mountains. En route, the trail passes multi-colored sandstone formations, winds through shaded ravines with scrub oak groves, and climbs chaparral-covered slopes to the ridge.

To the trailhead

From Santa Monica, drive 12 miles northbound on the Pacific Coast Highway/Highway 1 to Malibu Canyon Road. Turn right and drive 6.5 miles to Mulholland Highway. Turn right and continue 5.8 miles to the signed trailhead on the right. Park in the pullouts alongside the road.

From the Ventura Freeway/Highway 101 in Calabasas, exit on Las Virgenes Road. Head 3.1 miles south to Mulholland Highway. Turn left and continue 5.8 miles to the signed trailhead on the right. Park in the pullouts alongside the road.

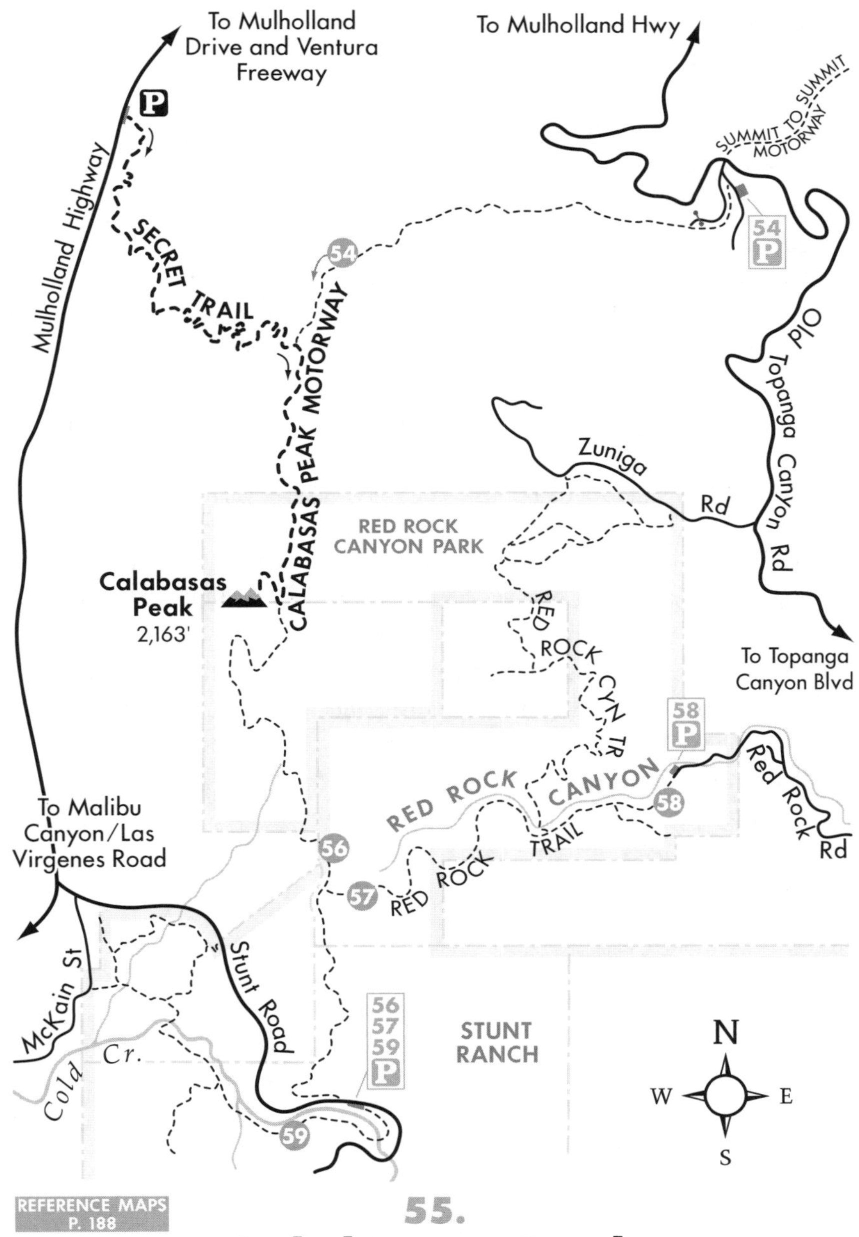

REFERENCE MAPS P. 188

55.

Calabasas Peak

Calabasas–Cold Creek (Secret) Trail

The hike

Pass the trailhead sign and climb the mountain slope. Enter a forest of mature oak trees, then return to the open grassy hillside. Weave along the foothills and enter an oak forest again. Cross a stream and continue above and parallel to Mulholland Highway. Curve left, away from the road, and leave the forest. Steadily head upward to great mountain views. Top a ridge to a close-up view of Calabasas Peak. Drop down into a canyon with eroded sandstone outcroppings. Walk over slab rock and cross the canyon. Climb the south canyon wall, walking among additional weather-carved rock formations. At 1.5 miles, the trail ends at a T-junction with the Calabasas Peak Motorway. The left fork leads 1.4 miles to Old Topanga Canyon Road (Hike 54).

To ascend Calabasas Peak, bear right on the dirt fire road and head south. From the trail are expansive views across the mountains to the ocean. Follow the serpentine path uphill, with alternating east and west views. Just before the crest of the road, a footpath to the summit veers sharply to the right. The Calabasas Peak Motorway continues straight, leading 1.7 miles down to Stunt Road (Hike 56). Leave the fire road and switchback to the right. Follow the ridge 0.2 miles, bending left to the 2,163-foot summit in a low thicket of chaparral. At the peak is a rock cairn, survey pin, and 360-degree vistas. ■

56. Calabasas Peak

Calabasas Peak Motorway from Stunt Road

Calabasas • Malibu

Hiking distance: 4 miles round trip
Hiking time: 2 hours
Configuration: out-and-back
Elevation gain: 900 feet
Difficulty: easy to moderate
Exposure: exposed
Dogs: allowed
Maps: U.S.G.S. Malibu Beach • Topanga State Park map
Tom Harrison Maps: Malibu Creek State Park Trail map

map page 194

Calabasas Peak towers over Red Rock Canyon, Old Topanga Canyon, and bowl-shaped Cold Creek Canyon. The route to the 2,163-foot peak follows the Calabasas Peak Motorway, a graded fire road. The vehicle-restricted road crosses the head of Red Rock Canyon past magnificent geological formations, including large, weathered sandstone outcroppings and tilted sandstone slabs with long ribs. Along the trail are spectacular 360-degree vistas into the surrounding canyons and the San Fernando Valley.

To the trailhead

From Santa Monica, drive 12 miles northbound on the Pacific Coast Highway/Highway 1 to Malibu Canyon Road. Turn right and drive 6.5 miles to Mulholland Highway. Turn right and continue 4 miles to Stunt Road. Turn right again and drive one mile to the pullout on the right.

From the Ventura Freeway/Highway 101 in Calabasas, exit on Las Virgenes Road. Head 3 miles south to Mulholland Highway. Turn left and go 4 miles to Stunt Road. Turn right and drive one mile to the pullout on the right.

The hike

Cross Stunt Road and walk 20 yards downhill to the trailhead on the right. Walk up the unpaved fire road past the gate. The trail zigzags up the mountain to a junction at 0.7 miles on a saddle at the head of Red Rock Canyon. The right fork heads into Red Rock

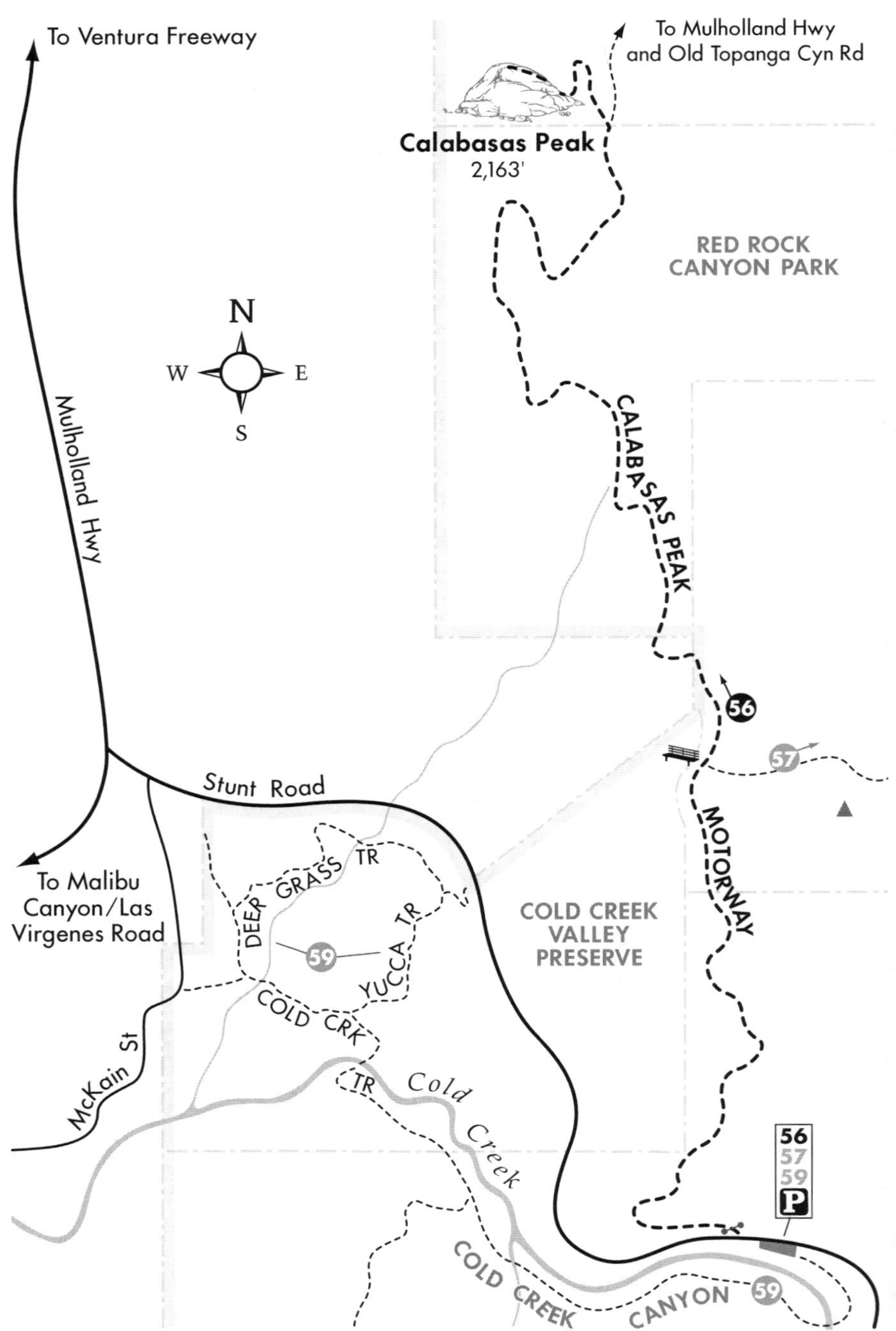
To Ventura Freeway
To Mulholland Hwy
and Old Topanga Cyn Rd
Calabasas Peak
2,163'
RED ROCK
CANYON PARK
N
W
E
S
Mulholland Hwy
CALABASAS PEAK
56
57
Stunt Road
MOTORWAY
To Malibu
Canyon/Las
Virgenes Road
DEER GRASS TR
YUCCA TR
59
COLD CREEK
VALLEY
PRESERVE
COLD CRK
TR
McKain St
Cold
Creek
56
57
59
P
COLD CREEK CANYON
59

Canyon (Hike 57). Continue straight ahead to the north along the cliff's edge, passing large eroded sandstone slabs while overlooking Red Rock Canyon. As Calabasas Peak comes into view, the trail curves sharply to the right, circling the peak along an eastern ridge. From the ridge are views into Old Topanga Canyon to the northeast. Just past the crest of the road, a narrow footpath veers off to the left. Follow the ridge 0.2 miles, bending left to the rounded 2,163-foot summit. At the chaparral-covered peak is a rock cairn, survey pin, and 360-degree vistas.

The Calabasas Peak Motorway continues 2.5 miles north to Old Topanga Canyon Road (Hike 54) and Mulholland Highway (Hike 55). ■

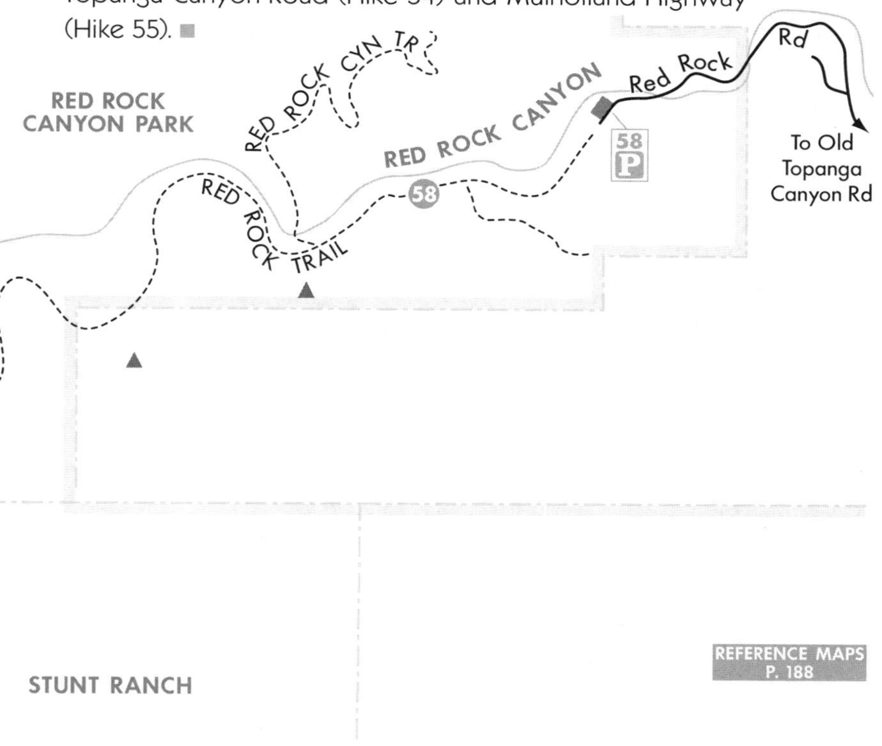

56.
Calabasas Peak
Calabasas Peak Motorway from Stunt Road

57. Red Rock Canyon

COLD CREEK—RED ROCK CANYON

Calabasas • Malibu

Hiking distance: 4 miles round trip
Hiking time: 2 hours
Configuration: out-and-back
Elevation gain: 700 feet
Difficulty: easy
Exposure: exposed
Dogs: allowed
Maps: U.S.G.S. Malibu Beach
Tom Harrison Maps: Malibu Creek State Park Trail map
Tom Harrison Maps: Topanga State Park Trail map

map page 198

Red Rock Canyon is a beautiful, multicolored canyon that looks similar to the canyons in the southwest. Huge weather-sculpted red sandstone formations and conglomerate rocks dominate a landscape that is dotted with oaks and sycamores. Shell fossils can be spotted in the eroded rocks, shallow caves, overhangs, and arches. The riparian canyon is a wildlife corridor connecting Topanga State Park and Malibu Creek State Park. The trail follows the first portion of the Calabasas Peak Motorway—a graded fire road—to the head of Red Rock Canyon.

To the trailhead

From Santa Monica, drive 12 miles northbound on the Pacific Coast Highway/Highway 1 to Malibu Canyon Road. Turn right and drive 6.5 miles to Mulholland Highway. Turn right and continue 4 miles to Stunt Road. Turn right again and drive one mile to the pullout on the right.

From the Ventura Freeway/Highway 101 in Calabasas, exit on Las Virgenes Road. Head 3 miles south to Mulholland Highway. Turn left and go 4 miles to Stunt Road. Turn right and drive one mile to the pullout on the right.

The hike

Cross Stunt Road and walk 20 yards downhill to the trailhead on the right. Walk up the unpaved fire road past the gate. The trail zigzags up the mountain to a junction at 0.7 miles on a saddle at the head of Red Rock Canyon. The trail straight ahead to the north leads to Calabasas Peak (Hike 56).

Take the right fork to the east, and descend into Red Rock Canyon. Continue downhill, skirting the base of the imposing rock walls. At 1.4 miles, the dirt road reaches a posted junction in an oak grove beneath towering sandstone rock. The road continues a half mile straight ahead to Red Rock Road (Hike 58). For this hike, take the footpath to the left. Cross a small stream and walk up wooden steps to the base of additional formations. Curve up the draw, crossing a seasonal stream to 360-degree vistas of the rock formations and surrounding mountains. With every step, new formations and different angles of the gorgeous rocks come into view. Climb the spine of the mountain while being frequently distracted by the visuals. The maintained trail ends among sandstone rocks that sit atop a 1,500-foot knoll on the north rim. Fifty yards beyond the knoll is a fork. The left branch climbs to another knoll, then the path narrows and is overgrown with vegetation. The right fork descends into an adjoining canyon to the north, with an additional display of red rock outcrops. The path to the north ends at Zuniga Road. ■

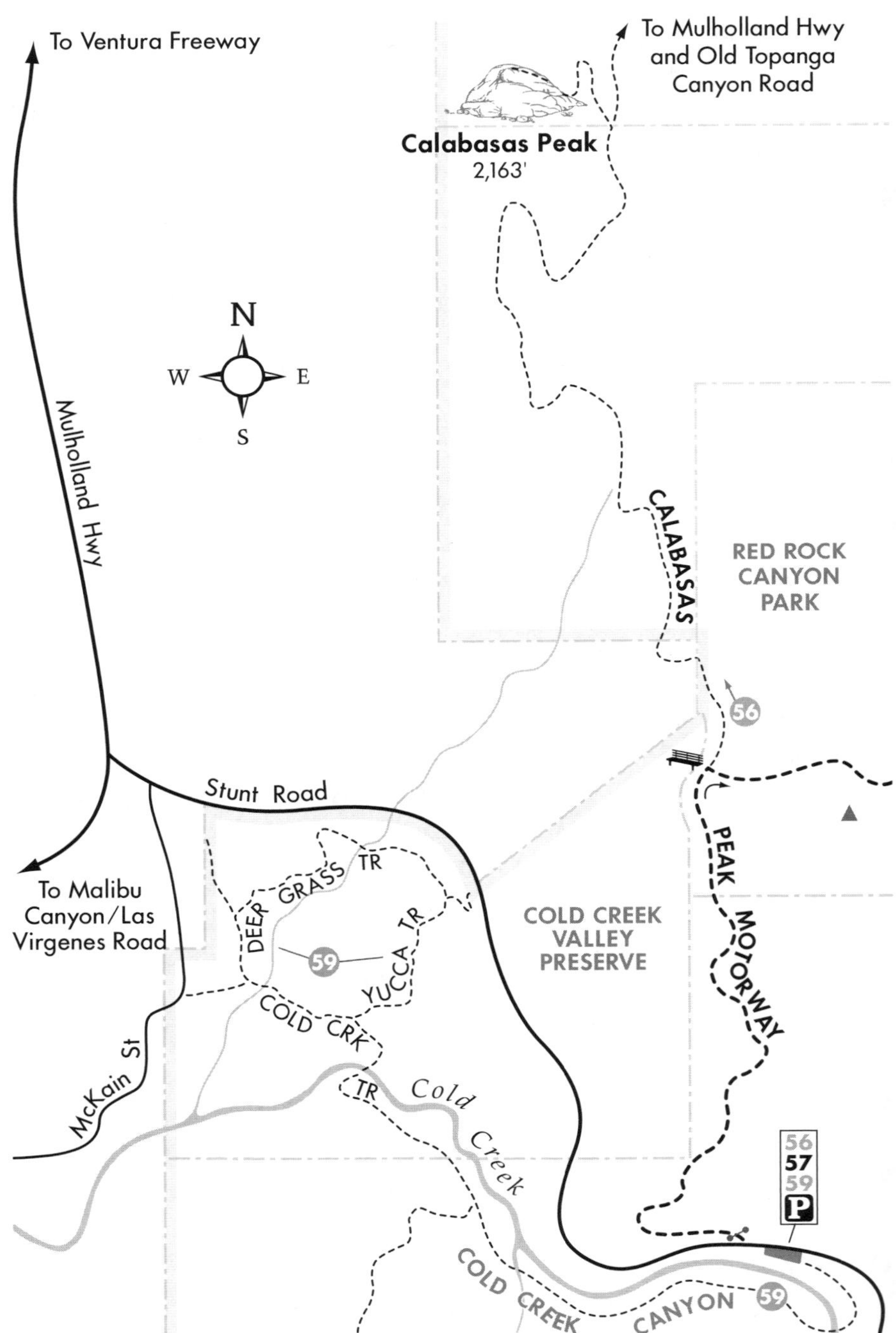
To Ventura Freeway
To Mulholland Hwy
and Old Topanga
Canyon Road
Calabasas Peak
2,163'
N
W
E
S
Mulholland Hwy
CALABASAS
RED ROCK
CANYON
PARK
56
Stunt Road
PEAK
MOTORWAY
To Malibu
Canyon/Las
Virgenes Road
DEER GRASS TR
YUCCA TR
59
COLD CREEK
VALLEY
PRESERVE
COLD CRK
TR
McKain St
Cold
Creek
56
57
59
P
COLD CREEK CANYON
59

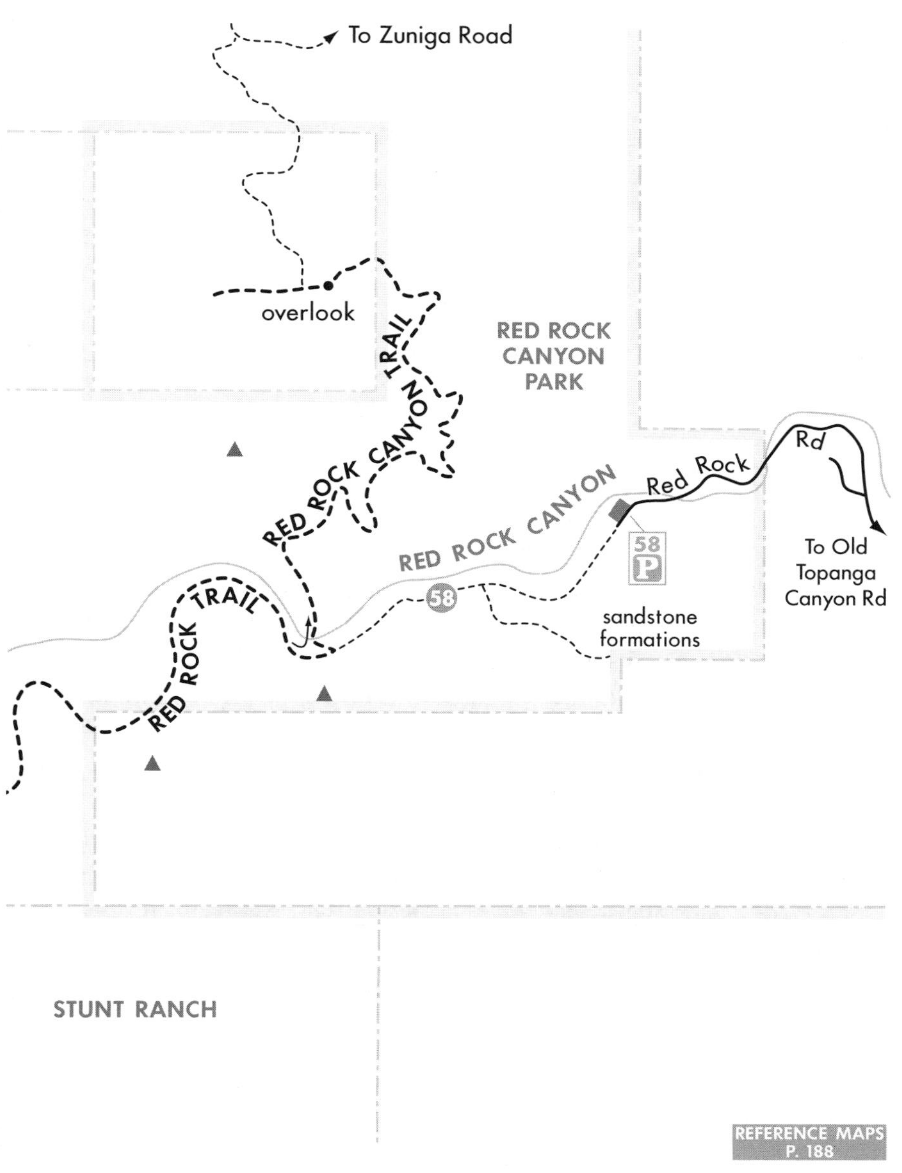

57.

Red Rock Canyon

COLD CREEK–RED ROCK CANYON

58. Red Rock Canyon from Red Rock Road

RED ROCK CANYON PARK

Calabasas • Malibu

Hiking distance: 2.4 miles round trip
Hiking time: 1.5 hours
Configuration: out-and-back
Elevation gain: 500 feet
Difficulty: easy to moderate
Exposure: shaded canyon bottom and exposed hillside
Dogs: allowed
Maps: U.S.G.S. Malibu Beach
Tom Harrison Maps: Malibu Creek State Park Trail map
Tom Harrison Maps: Topanga State Park Trail map

Red Rock Canyon is a picturesque, riparian gorge with sculptured red sandstone formations and conglomerate rocks. The uplifted and tilted outcroppings are a visual treat. The narrow canyon bottom is rich with sycamore and oak trees, creating a stunning contrast of red rocks rising out of the lush green surroundings. The canyon, adjacent to Calabasas Peak, is a wildlife corridor linking Topanga State Park with Malibu Creek State Park.

Red Rock Canyon can be accessed from the west via the Calabasas Peak Motorway off of Stunt Road (Hike 57) and from the east via Red Rock Road off of Old Topanga Canyon Road (this hike). The trail begins on a fire road along the cool canyon floor beneath the towering weather-carved monoliths. The hike climbs the north canyon wall to additional formations and overlooks.

To the trailhead

From Santa Monica, drive 4 miles northbound on the Pacific Coast Highway/Highway 1 to Topanga Canyon Boulevard and turn right. Continue 4.2 miles to Old Topanga Canyon Road on the left. Turn left and drive 1.8 miles up Old Topanga Canyon Road to Red Rock Road on the left. Turn left and drive 0.8 miles on the narrow, winding road to the trailhead and parking area at the end of the road. A parking fee is required.

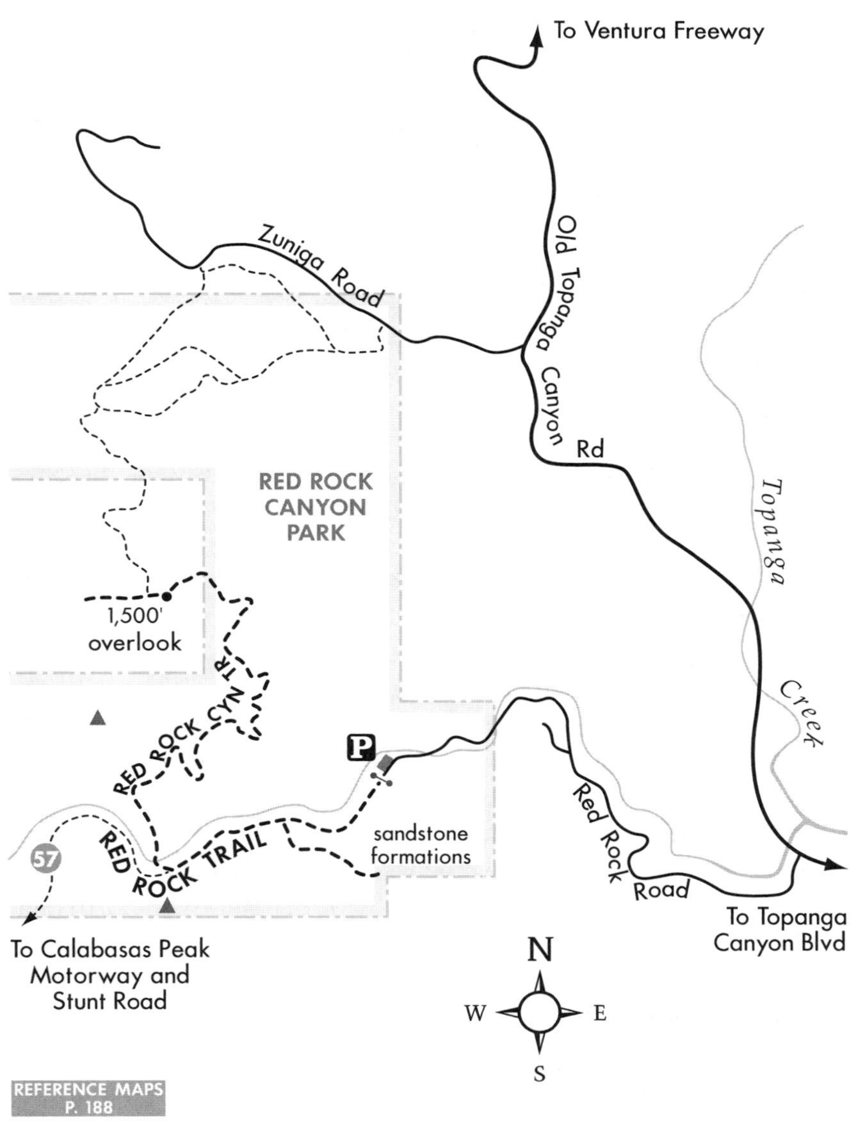

58. Red Rock Canyon from Red Rock Road

RED ROCK CANYON

From the Ventura Freeway/Highway 101 in Woodland Hills, exit on Topanga Canyon Boulevard. Drive 8 miles south to Old Topanga Canyon Road on the right. Turn right and continue 1.8 miles up Old Topanga Canyon Road to Red Rock Road on the left. Turn left and drive 0.8 miles on the narrow, winding road to the trailhead and parking area at the end of the road. A parking fee is required.

The hike

Walk past the trailhead gate and follow the south side of Red Rock Canyon. Wind along the old dirt road besides chaparral, oaks, and sycamores among a magnificent display of cavernous red rock formations and walls of weather-sculpted conglomerates. A short side path on the left detours to massive sandstone formations with weather-carved caves and overhangs. At a half mile, the dirt road reaches a posted junction in an oak grove beneath towering sandstone rock. The road continues 0.8 miles straight ahead to the Calabasas Peak Motorway (Hike 57).

For this hike, take the footpath to the right. Cross a small stream and walk up wooden steps to the base of additional formations. Curve up the draw, crossing a seasonal stream to 360-degree vistas of the rock formations and surrounding mountains. With every step, new formations and different angles of the gorgeous rocks come into view. Climb the spine of the mountain while being frequently distracted by the visuals. The maintained trail ends among sandstone rock atop a 1,500-foot knoll on the north rim. Fifty yards beyond the knoll is a fork. The left branch climbs to another knoll, then the path narrows and is overgrown with vegetation. The right fork descends into an adjoining canyon to the north with an additional display of red rock outcrops. The path to the north ends at Zuniga Road. ■

59. Cold Creek Trail

STUNT RANCH—COLD CREEK VALLEY PRESERVES

Calabasas • Malibu

Hiking distance: 2.5 miles round trip
Hiking time: 1.5 hours
Configuration: out-and-back with loop
Elevation gain: 300 feet
Difficulty: easy
Exposure: exposed
Dogs: allowed
Maps: U.S.G.S. Malibu Beach
Tom Harrison Maps: Malibu Creek State Park Trail map

map page 205

The Cold Creek Valley Preserve sits in a shallow bowl among craggy sandstone peaks. It is home to a wide assortment of flowers and plant communities. Perennial Cold Creek flows through the valley preserve and Cold Creek Canyon. It is one of the few year-round streams in the Santa Monica Mountains. The Cold Creek Trail leads to the 57-acre preserve, parallel to the creek. The trail meanders through riparian woodlands and a gently rolling grass meadow. En route, the trail crosses the creek three times and traverses the hillside under the shade of oaks and sycamores.

To the trailhead

From Santa Monica, drive 12 miles northbound on the Pacific Coast Highway/Highway 1 to Malibu Canyon Road. Turn right and drive 6.5 miles to Mulholland Highway. Turn right and continue 4 miles to Stunt Road. Turn right again and drive one mile to the pullout on the right.

From the Ventura Freeway/Highway 101 in Calabasas, exit on Las Virgenes Road. Head 3 miles south to Mulholland Highway. Turn left and go 4 miles to Stunt Road. Turn right and drive one mile to the pullout on the right.

The hike

Take the trail southeast for a short distance, parallel to Stunt Road. Curve right and cross Cold Creek. Just after crossing, watch for Native American mortar holes ground into the sandstone rocks on the right. Chumash Indians originally lived in this area and formed these holes while grinding acorns. Follow the creek downstream on the Cold Creek Trail, and head into the oak-shaded corridor. Cross a tributary stream to a junction with the Lower Stunt High Trail on the left. Additional ancient mortar holes can be spotted on the sandstone boulder to the left. The left fork leaves the riparian canopy and climbs up the hillside to Stunt Road. Continue straight—staying on the Cold Creek Trail—and follow the creek. Walk northwest as the path rises and returns to Cold Creek. Cross the creek to a junction at one mile.

Begin the half-mile Yucca-Deer Grass Trail loop within the Cold Creek Valley Preserve. Take the Yucca Trail to the right and stroll through the chaparral. Cross a small drainage to a fork. The right fork leads 30 yards to Stunt Road. Bear left on the Deer Grass Trail, and parallel Stunt Road through a meadow. Cross a tributary of Cold Creek and curve left. Climb up and over a hill to a junction with the Cold Creek Trail. The right fork leads to McKain Street. Go left and complete the loop at 1.5 miles. Stay to the right and retrace your steps. ■

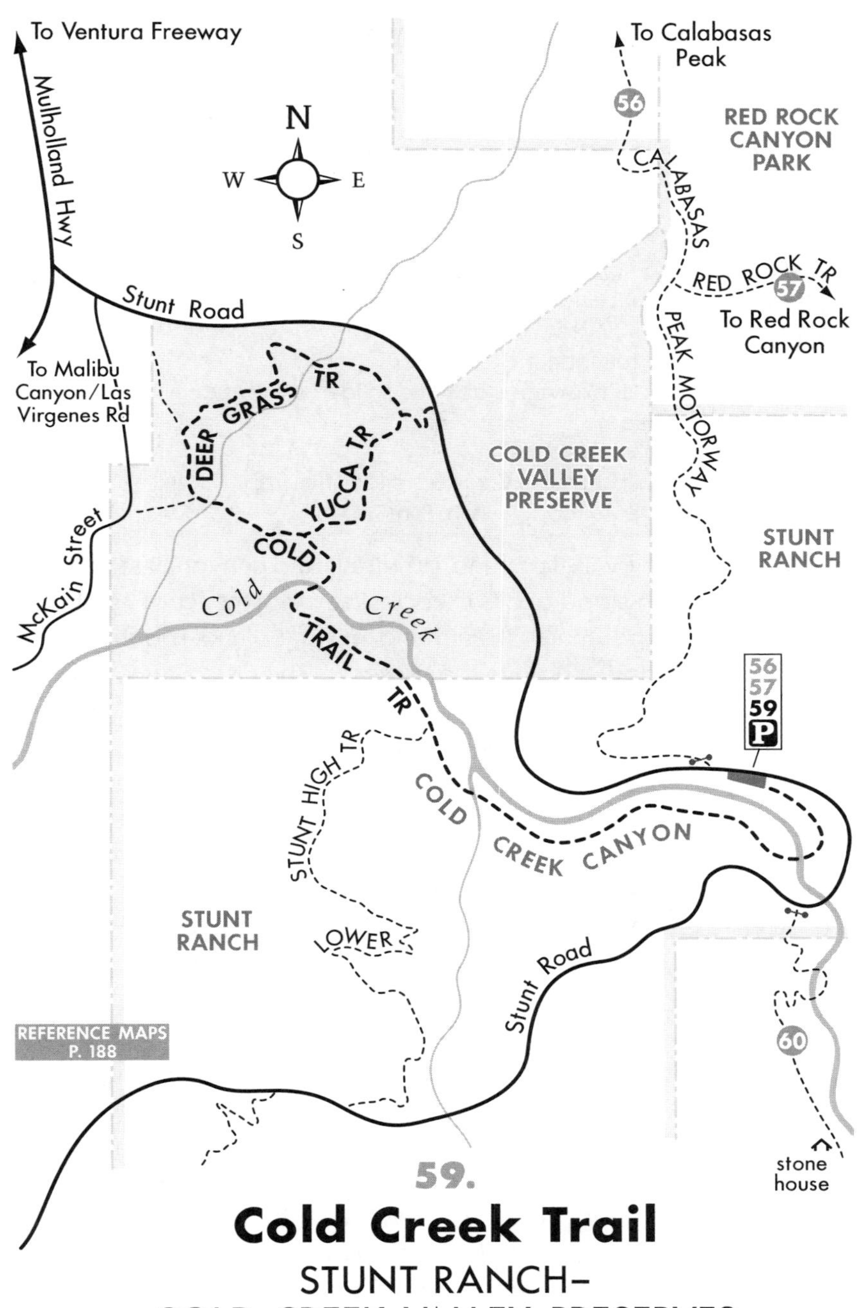

59. Cold Creek Trail

STUNT RANCH– COLD CREEK VALLEY PRESERVES

60. Cold Creek Canyon Preserve

Calabasas • Malibu

A free access permit is required from
The Mountains Restoration Trust: (818) 591-1701
www.mountainstrust.org

Hiking distance: 3.3 miles round trip
Hiking time: 1.5 hours
Configuration: out-and-back
Elevation gain: 800 feet
Difficulty: easy to moderate
Exposure: a mix of exposed slope and shaded streamside habitat
Dogs: not allowed
Maps: U.S.G.S. Malibu Beach
Tom Harrison Maps: Malibu Creek State Park Trail map
Tom Harrison Maps: Topanga State Park Trail map

Cold Creek Canyon is a pristine, bowl-shaped canyon nestled on the steep north slope behind Saddle Peak (northeast of Malibu). Cold Creek, a perennial stream and major upland tributary of Malibu Creek, flows through the preserve. The Cold Creek watershed is among the most biologically diverse ecosystems in the Santa Monica Mountains. It supports manzanita, chaparral, coast live oak, sycamore woodlands, riparian streamside habitats (including orchids), a variety of ferns, phacelia, cattails, red shank, and Humboldt lily. The 1,100-acre nature preserve is owned by the Mountains Restoration Trust, a non-profit land trust created to protect and enhance the natural resources of the Santa Monica Mountains. To protect the fragile resources of the preserve, a free access permit is requested (see contact information above).

Cold Creek Canyon has high ridges, a steep slope, magnificent sandstone formations, rocky grottos, waterfalls, and canyon views. The headwaters of Cold Creek originate within the preserve, rising from springs and cascading down canyon. This hike winds down the north-facing watershed through lush streamside vegetation and jungle-like ferns, passing cascades and small waterfalls. The trail weaves through the natural basin in an idyllic

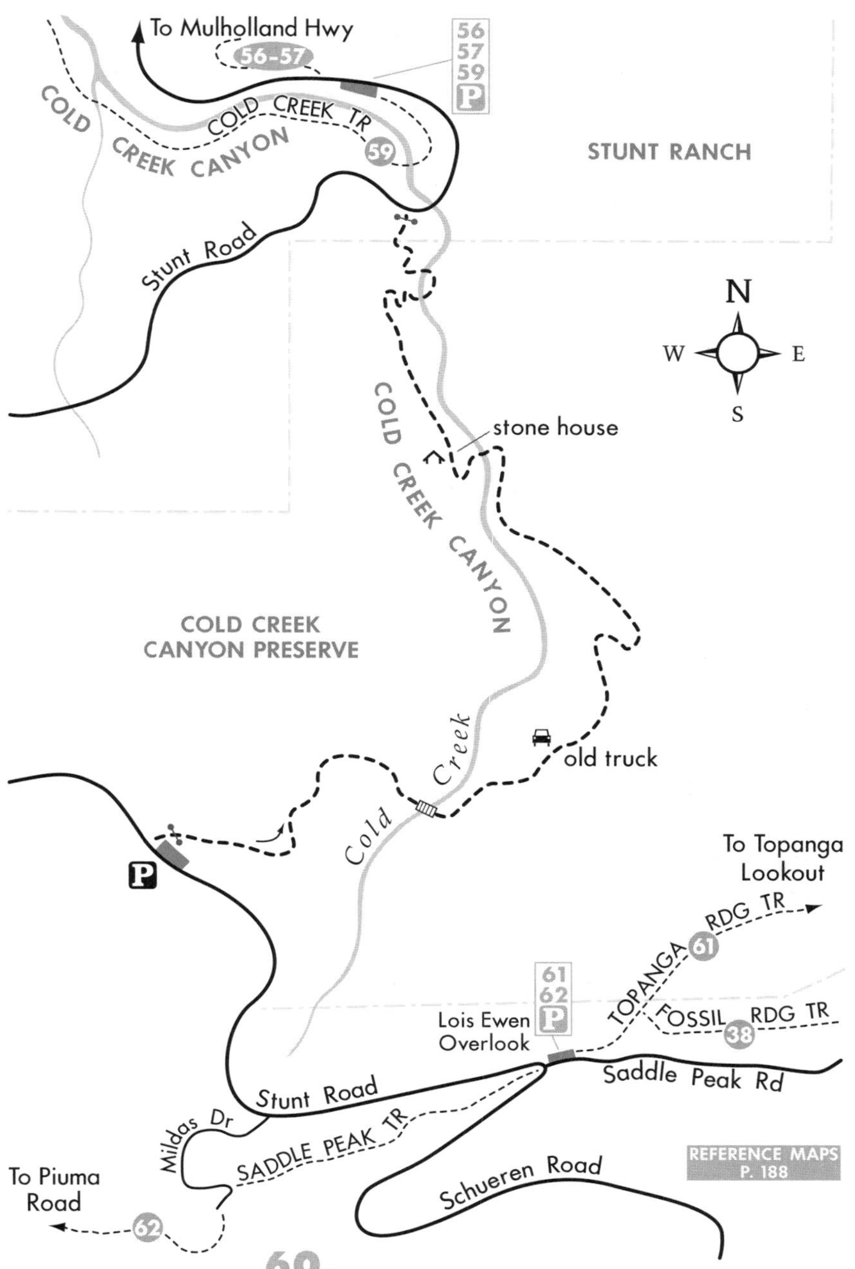

60. Cold Creek Canyon Preserve

setting under oak, maple, sycamore, and bay woodlands. Watch for the remains of a 1900s-era homesteader house, hand-carved into the giant split sandstone boulders.

To the trailhead

From Santa Monica, drive 12 northbound on the Pacific Coast Highway/Highway 1 to Malibu Canyon Road and turn right. Drive 6.5 miles to Mulholland Highway. Turn right and continue 4 miles to Stunt Road. Turn right and drive 3.3 miles to the Cold Creek parking pullout on the left by a chain-link fence. Park off road on the shoulder.

From the Ventura Freeway/Highway 101 in Calabasas, exit on Las Virgenes Road. Head 3 miles south to Mulholland Highway. Turn left and continue 4 miles to Stunt Road. Turn right and drive 3.3 miles to the Cold Creek parking pullout on the left.

The hike

Walk through the gate in the chain-link fence, and head east through the tall chaparral. The trail leads gradually downhill along the contours of the hillside and across a wooden bridge over Cold Creek at 0.6 miles. Pass moss-covered rocks and a rusty classic Dodge truck as you make your way into the lush vegetation and open oak woodland of the canyon floor. Cross Cold Creek again and continue past large sandstone boulders to the remains of gold miner Herman Hethke's stone house. Several switchbacks lead downhill across side streams and past small waterfalls. At 1.6 miles, the path reaches the locked lower gate at Stunt Road. Return by retracing your steps up canyon. ■

61. Topanga Fire Lookout

COLD CREEK CANYON PRESERVE

Calabasas • Malibu

Hiking distance: 2 miles round trip
Hiking time: 1 hour
Configuration: out-and-back
Elevation gain: 150 feet
Difficulty: easy
Exposure: exposed
Dogs: allowed
Maps: U.S.G.S. Malibu Beach
Tom Harrison Maps: Topanga State Park Trail map

map page 210

The Topanga Fire Lookout, destroyed in a 1970 fire, was, ironically, used by the fire department to spot fires. All that remains is a large multi-level concrete foundation perched at the edge of the 2,470-foot mountain. This one-mile trail follows a relatively easy grade along the Topanga Ridge Trail, a fire road along the east ridge of the Cold Creek Canyon Preserve. From the lookout are spectacular views into Old Topanga Canyon, Cold Creek Canyon Preserve, Red Rock Canyon, the expansive San Fernando Valley to Los Angeles, and Santa Monica Bay.

To the trailhead

From Santa Monica, drive 12 miles northbound on the Pacific Coast Highway/Highway 1 to Malibu Canyon Road. Turn right and drive 6.5 miles to Mulholland Highway. Turn right and continue 4 miles to Stunt Road. Turn right and drive 4 miles up the winding road to the end of Stunt Road. Turn left on Saddle Peak Road, and park in the pullout on the left.

From the Ventura Freeway/Highway 101 in Calabasas, exit on Las Virgenes Road. Head 3.1 miles south to Mulholland Highway. Turn left and go 4 miles to Stunt Road. Turn right and drive 4 miles up the road to the end of Stunt Road. Turn left on Saddle Peak Road, and park in the pullout on the left.

The hike

From the parking pullout (the Lois Ewen Overlook), walk to the gated service road. Head northeast on the paved road, following the ridge high above Cold Creek Canyon. Calabasas Peak (Hike 54—56) can be seen to the north. Pass the Fossil Ridge Trail on the right (a section of the Backbone Trail) to a road split at a quarter mile. The paved right fork leads to a radar tower. Stay to the left on the wide, unpaved path and continue gradually uphill. At one mile is a graffiti-covered concrete foundation on a buttress, the site of the abandoned fire lookout. From the old lookout foundation on the mountain's edge is a view into Hondo Canyon, Red Rock Canyon, Old Topanga Canyon, the Cold Creek drainage, and across sections of Los Angeles. Miles beyond, the views span across the San Fernando Valley to the Santa Susana Mountains. ■

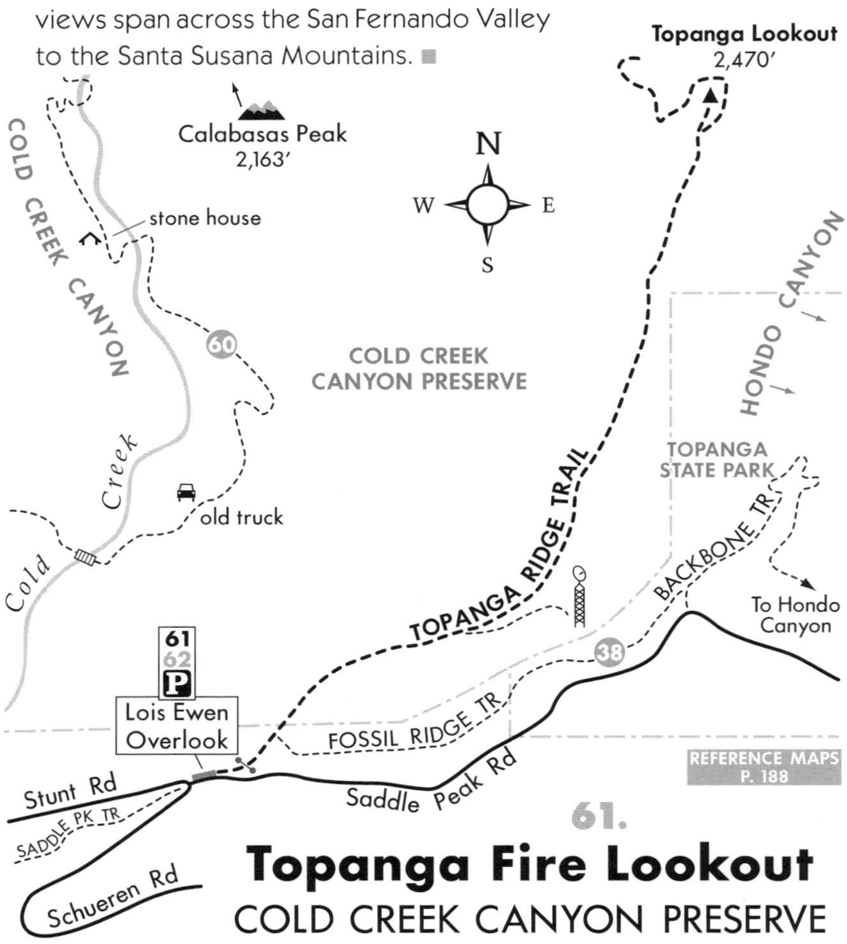

61. Topanga Fire Lookout

COLD CREEK CANYON PRESERVE

62. Saddle Peak Trail to Saddle Peak East Overlook

FROM STUNT ROAD

Calabasas • Malibu

Hiking distance: 2.3 miles round trip
Hiking time: 1.5 hours
Configuration: out-and-back
Elevation gain: 450 feet
Difficulty: easy
Exposure: exposed
Dogs: allowed
Maps: U.S.G.S. Malibu Beach • Malibu Creek State Park Map
Tom Harrison Maps: Malibu Creek State Park Trail Map

map page 212

Saddle Peak is a double-peaked mountain with a connecting saddle sloping between the two peaks. Saddle Peak West, the highest of the two peaks, is covered with communication towers. It is fenced and prohibits hikers. Saddle Peak East, however, just to its northeast, is an easy-to-reach 2,765-foot oceanfront perch with phenomenal vistas. The overlook is strewn with sandstone outcrops. The peak, located between Topanga Canyon and Malibu Canyon, offers panoramic coastal views across Santa Monica Bay, the Santa Monica Mountains, Los Angeles, and the San Gabriel Mountains. This hike follows a section of the Backbone Trail from the Lois Ewen Overlook, a 2,365-foot saddle above Cold Creek Canyon Preserve. The trail follows a ridge among beautiful sandstone formations to the boulder-studded peak.

To the trailhead

From Santa Monica, drive 12 miles northbound on the Pacific Coast Highway/Highway 1 to Malibu Canyon Road. Turn right and drive 6.5 miles to Mulholland Highway. Turn right and continue 4 miles to Stunt Road. Turn right and drive 4 miles up the winding road to the end of Stunt Road. Turn left on Saddle Peak Road, and park in the pullout on the left at the Lois Ewen Overlook.

From the Ventura Freeway/Highway 101 in Calabasas, exit on Las Virgenes Road. Head 3.1 miles south to Mulholland Highway. Turn left and go 4 miles to Stunt Road. Turn right and drive 4 miles up the road to the end of Stunt Road. Turn left on Saddle Peak Road, and park in the pullout on the left.

The hike

After enjoying the views from the Lois Ewen Overlook, scramble up the narrow, V-shaped wedge of land between Stunt Road and Schueren Road. Head west on the ridge, and cross an old concrete foundation. Pick up an asphalt road by a water tower, and curve left up the road one hundred yards. Walk around the left (south) side of the water tank to the trail on the back side. Continue up the spine and north-facing slope,

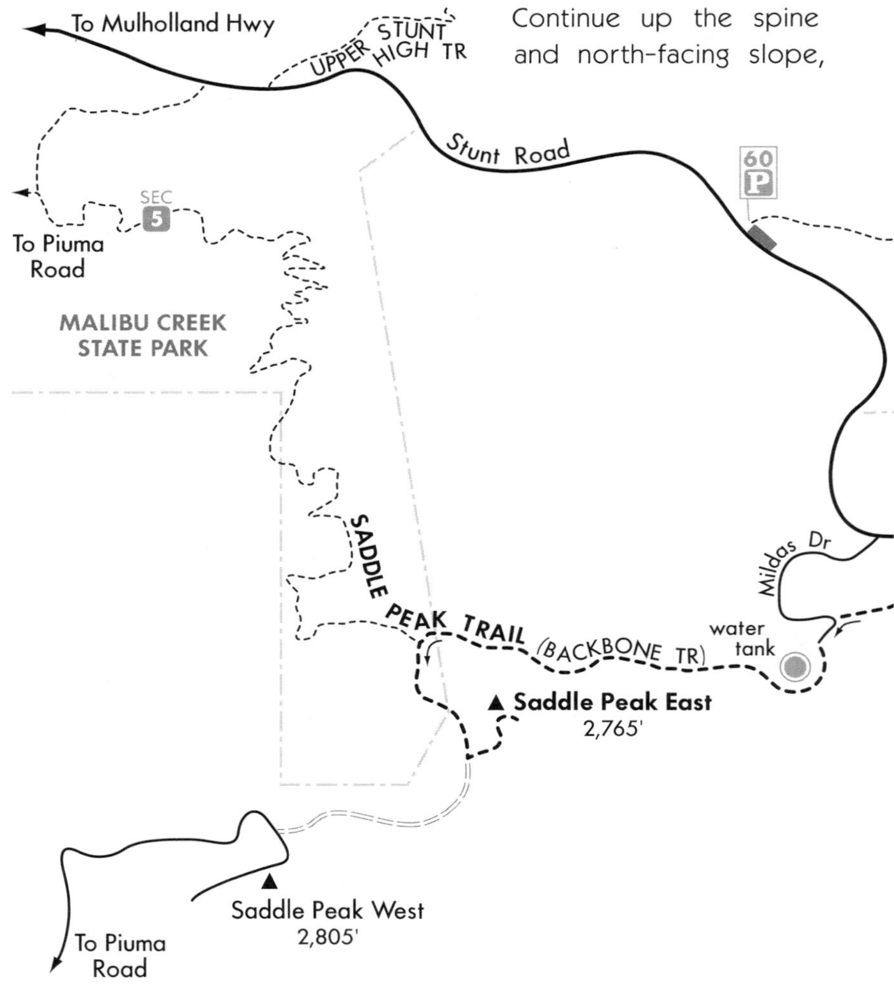

with views of the Cold Creek Canyon Preserve. Reach a junction at 0.8 miles. The Backbone Trail continues straight ahead to Piuma Road (Backbone Trail—Section 5). For this hike, bear left and walk among the massive sandstone formations to a view of the "sci-fi" looking communications towers atop Saddle Peak West. Follow the dirt path to an overlook atop Saddle Peak East. From the lookout are vast coastal vistas; views across Malibu, Santa Monica, and the Los Angeles basin; and the mountainous backcountry. Return by retracing your route.

To continue hiking the trail to Piuma Road, see Section 5 of the Backbone Trail. ■

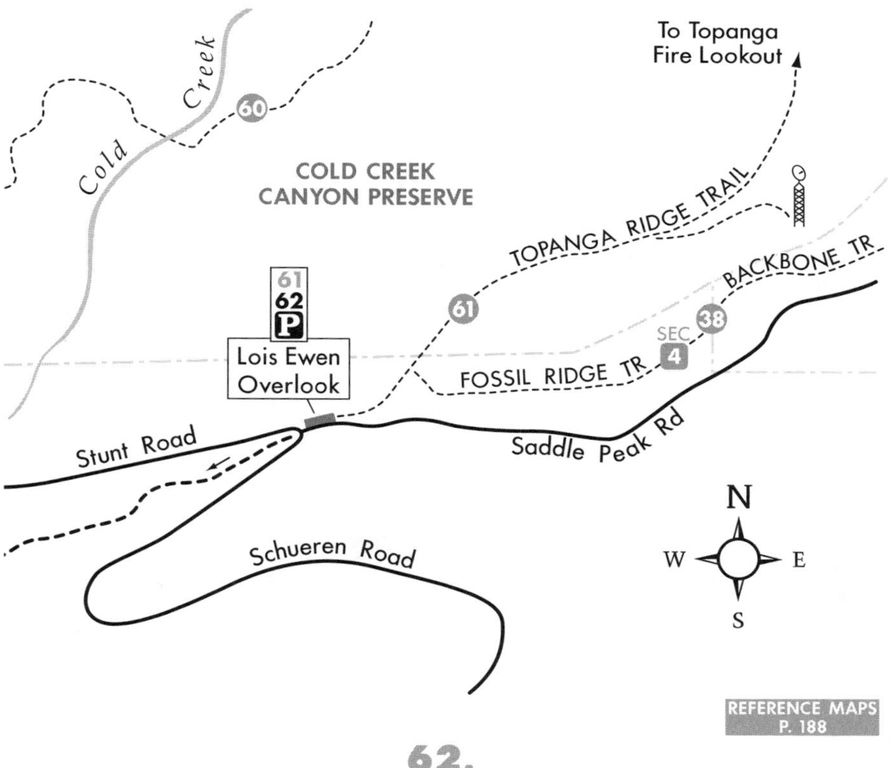

REFERENCE MAPS P. 188

62.

Saddle Peak Trail to Saddle Peak East Overlook

from STUNT ROAD

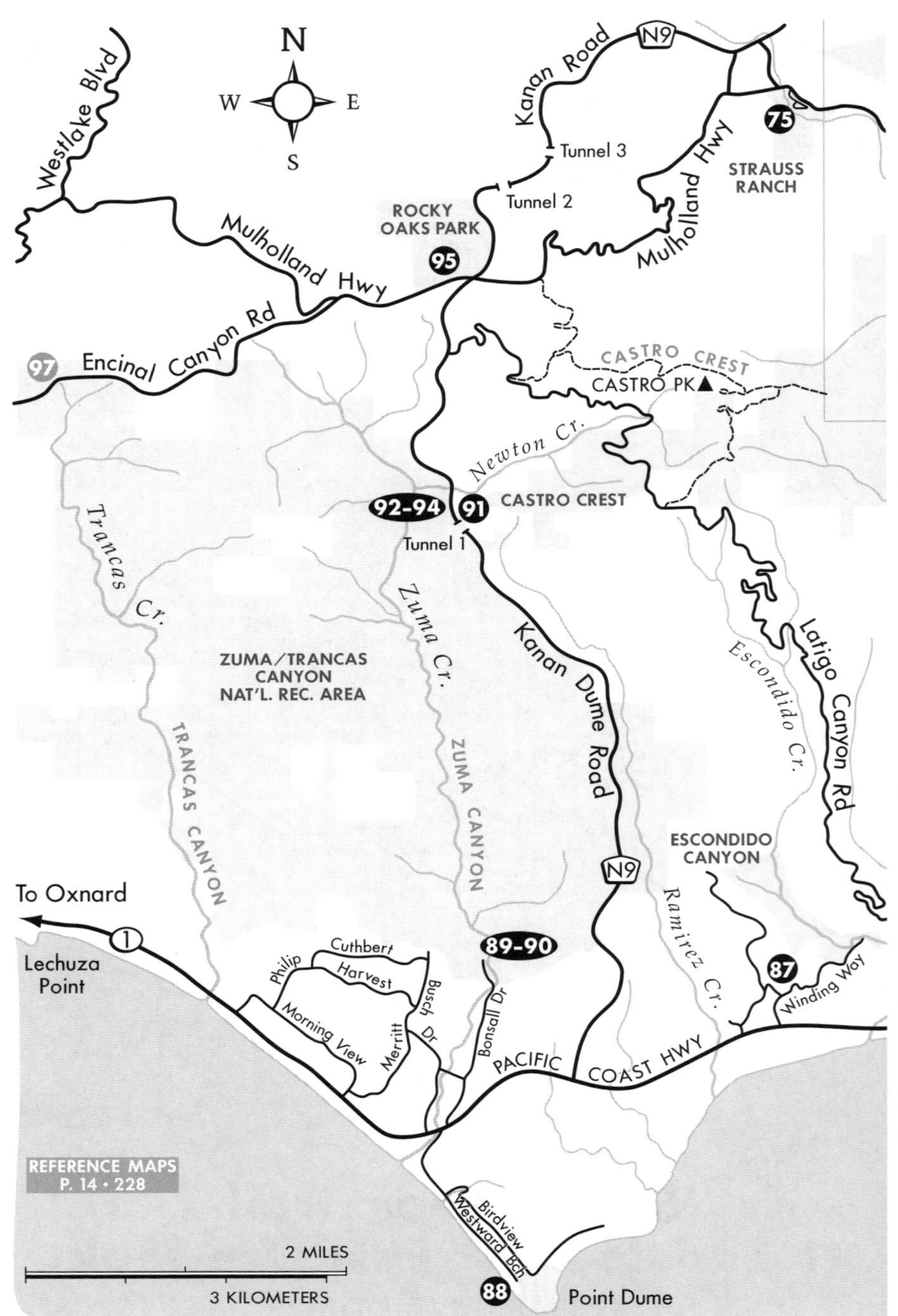
N
W
E
S
Westlake Blvd
Kanan Road
N9
Tunnel 3
Tunnel 2
Mulholland Hwy
75
STRAUSS RANCH
ROCKY OAKS PARK
95
Mulholland Hwy
Encinal Canyon Rd
97
CASTRO CREST
CASTRO PK
Newton Cr.
92-94
91
CASTRO CREST
Tunnel 1
Trancas Cr.
Zuma Cr.
Kanan Dume Road
Latigo Canyon Rd
Escondido Cr.
ZUMA/TRANCAS CANYON NAT'L. REC. AREA
TRANCAS CANYON
ZUMA CANYON
ESCONDIDO CANYON
N9
Ramirez Cr.
To Oxnard
1
Lechuza Point
Cuthbert
Philip
Harvest
Busch Dr
89-90
87
Winding Way
Morning View
Merritt
Bonsall Dr
PACIFIC COAST HWY
REFERENCE MAPS P. 14 • 228
Birdview
Westward Bch
2 MILES
3 KILOMETERS
88
Point Dume

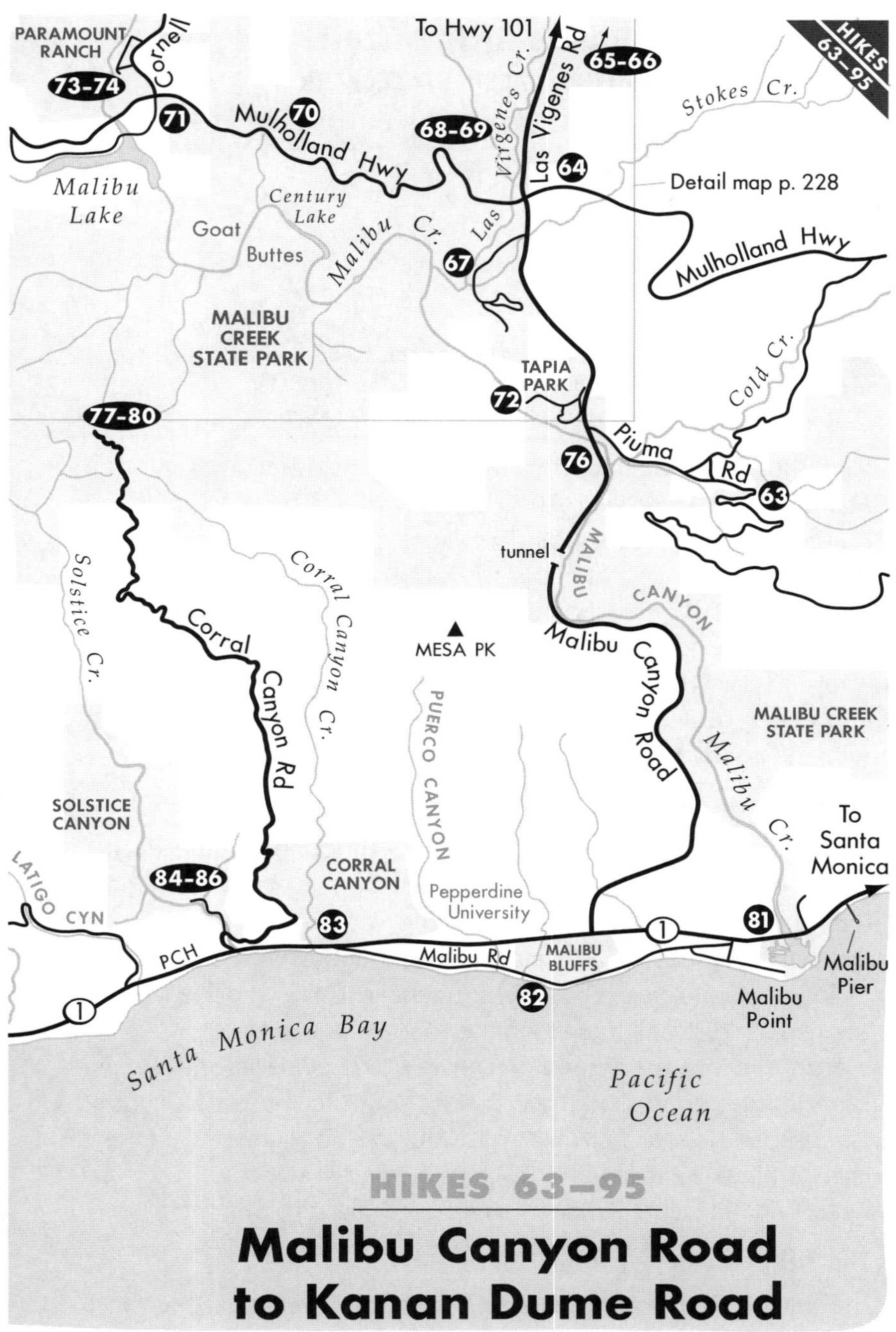

HIKES 63–95

Malibu Canyon Road to Kanan Dume Road

63. Piuma Ridge Trail

MALIBU CREEK STATE PARK

Malibu

Hiking distance: 3.8 miles round trip
Hiking time: 2 hours
Configuration: out-and-back
Elevation gain: 200 feet
Difficulty: easy
Exposure: forested
Dogs: not allowed (but many dogs enjoy this forested trail)
Maps: U.S.G.S. Malibu Beach • Malibu Creek State Park Map
Tom Harrison Maps: Malibu Creek State Park Trail Map

Piuma Ridge is located on the east side of Malibu Canyon in Malibu Creek State Park. The ridge divides the Cold Creek and Malibu Canyon watersheds. The Piuma Ridge Trail is part of the Backbone Trail that connects to the Saddle Peak Trail and Stunt Road. This sections winds along the east-west ridge above the Malibu Creek gorge, traversing the hillside through a mix of chaparral and oak woodlands. The trail then descends into the canyon and down to Piuma Creek in a shady oak and bay laurel forest with moss-covered boulders.

To the trailhead

From Santa Monica, drive 12 miles northbound on the Pacific Coast Highway/Highway 1 to Malibu Canyon Road. Turn right (north) and continue 4.8 miles up the winding canyon road to the traffic light at Piuma Road. Turn right and drive 1.2 miles to a U-shaped bend in the road. The trailhead is in the bend. Park in the narrow dirt pullouts along the road.

From the Ventura Freeway/Highway 101 in Calabasas, take the Las Virgenes Road exit. Drive 5 miles south to the traffic light at Piuma Road (located 1.8 miles past Mulholland Highway). Turn left and continue 1.2 miles to a U-shaped bend in the road. The trailhead is in the bend. Park in the narrow pullouts along the road.

The hike

The Saddle Peak Trail heads east from the trailhead (Section 5 of the Backbone Trail). This hike heads west on the down slope side of the road. Enter the shaded forest and follow the stream on the right. Traverse the hillside slope on a gentle uphill grade. Cross a seasonal drainage and continue west, weaving along the mountain contours. Cross two more drainages while steadily gaining elevation to expanded views across the layers of mountains. Zigzag downhill under a canopy of oak and bay trees. Weave through the forest to a paved driveway. Cross the pavement and follow the path along a wood fence. Return to the forest and rock-hop over Piuma Creek. At 1.9 miles, the path ends on Piuma Road, a half mile shy of Malibu Canyon Road.

Return along the same route. ■

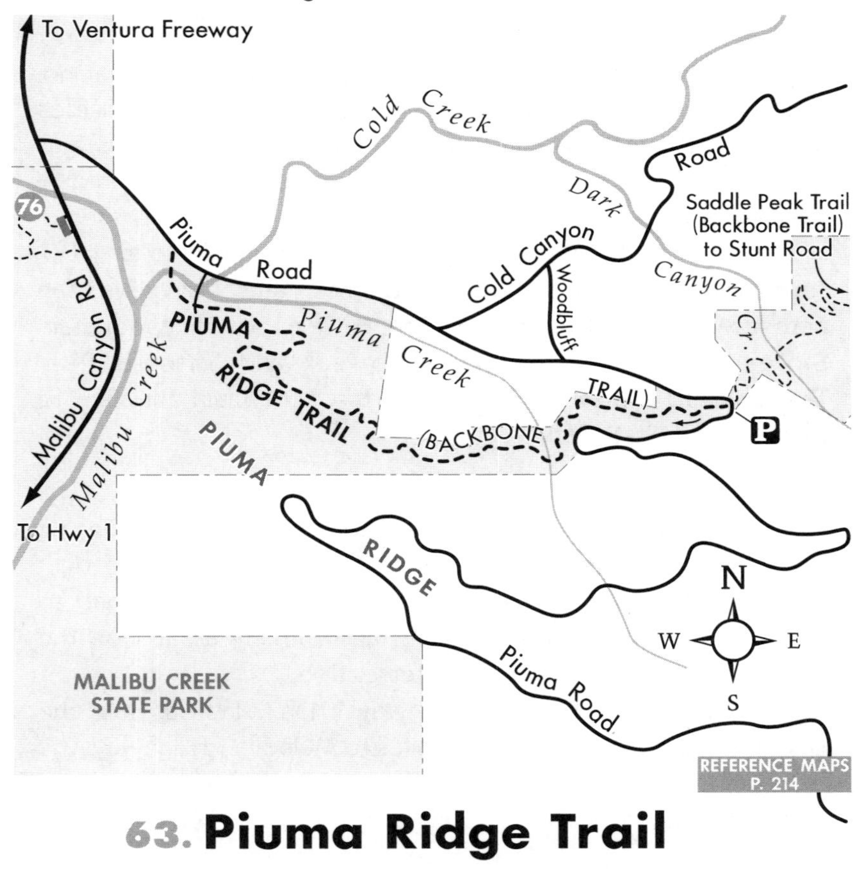

63. Piuma Ridge Trail

MALIBU CREEK STATE PARK

64. Las Virgenes View Trail

LAS VIRGENES VIEW PARK

Calabasas

Hiking distance: 4.8 miles round trip
Hiking time: 2.5 hours
Configuration: out-and-back with small loop at summit
Elevation gain: 450 feet
Difficulty: easy to moderate
Exposure: exposed hillside with shaded pockets of oak
Dogs: allowed
Maps: U.S.G.S. Malibu Beach • Malibu Creek State Park Map
Tom Harrison Maps: Malibu Creek State Park Trail Map

The Las Virgenes View Park stretches across almost 700 acres adjacent to Malibu Creek State Park. Within the park's varied landscape are oak woodlands, rolling grasslands, chaparral hillsides, and a riparian zone with sycamores, willows, cottonwoods, and bays. The undeveloped multi-use park is open to hikers, mountain bikers, equestrians, and dogs.

The Las Virgenes View Trail climbs the rolling hills to an 1,100-foot overlook with sweeping 360-degree vistas. The views span across Malibu Creek State Park, Goat Buttes, Lady Face Mountain, Stokes Canyon, Saddle Peak, Castro Peak, and Calabasas Peak. The trailhead is a short distance north of the main entrance to Malibu Creek State Park.

To the trailhead

From Santa Monica, drive 12 miles northbound on the Pacific Coast Highway/Highway 1 to Malibu Canyon Road. Turn right (north) and continue 6.7 miles up the winding canyon road to Mulholland Highway. The trailhead and parking area is on the northeast (right) corner of the intersection.

From the Ventura Freeway/Highway 101 in Calabasas, take the Las Virgenes Road exit. Drive 3.1 miles to Mulholland Highway. The trailhead and parking area is on the northeast (left) corner of the intersection.

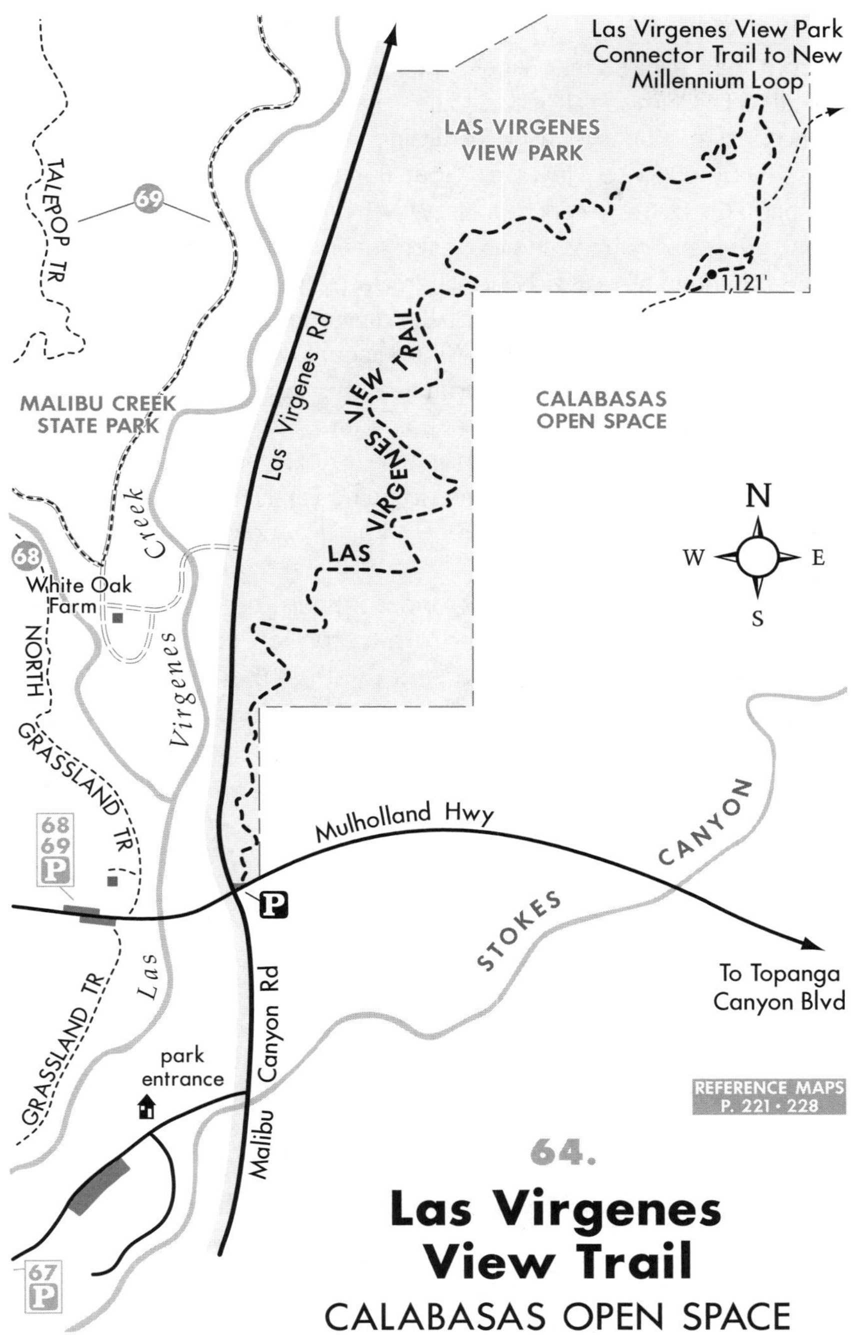

64.

Las Virgenes View Trail

CALABASAS OPEN SPACE

The hike

From the trailhead map kiosk, head up the slope, above and parallel to Las Virgenes Road. Zigzag up the hill on four switchbacks and descend on two more, returning to Las Virgenes Road. Again ascend the hill to views of Goat Buttes and Phantom Ridge in Malibu Creek State Park. Curve away from the road. Walk through oak groves and cross the exposed, chaparral-clad hills. Traverse the mountain at a steady uphill grade through pockets of scrub oak and oak woodlands. Gradually descend again, losing most of the elevation gained. Begin the third ascent, weaving up the south wall of a side canyon. At two miles, the serpentine path makes a horseshoe right bend and heads south. Pass the Las Virgenes View Park Connector Trail, which heads north on an old dirt road. The connector trail follows the ridgeline for 1.5 miles to the New Millennium Loop Trail (Hike 65). A short distance ahead, atop the ridge, is a trail split.

Begin the loop to the right, and continue to a T-junction. The right fork ends at private land. Go to the left to the 1,121-foot peak with sweeping 360-degree vistas. The views include Saddle Peak, Calabasas Peak, Castro Peak, and Goat Buttes. From the summit, descend and complete the loop. Return along the same trail. ■

65. New Millennium Loop Trail

LAS VIRGENES VIEW PARK

Calabasas

Hiking distance: 12.2-mile loop
Hiking time: 7 hours
Configuration: loop
Elevation gain: 1,000 feet
Difficulty: strenuous
Exposure: exposed with forested sections
Dogs: allowed
Maps: U.S.G.S. Calabasas and Malibu Beach
Tom Harrison Maps: Malibu Creek State Park Trail Map

map page 223

The New Millennium Loop Trail is a magnificent, dog-friendly, multi-use trail that is open to hikers, bikers, and equestrians. The trail is located in Las Virgenes View Park in the mountains east

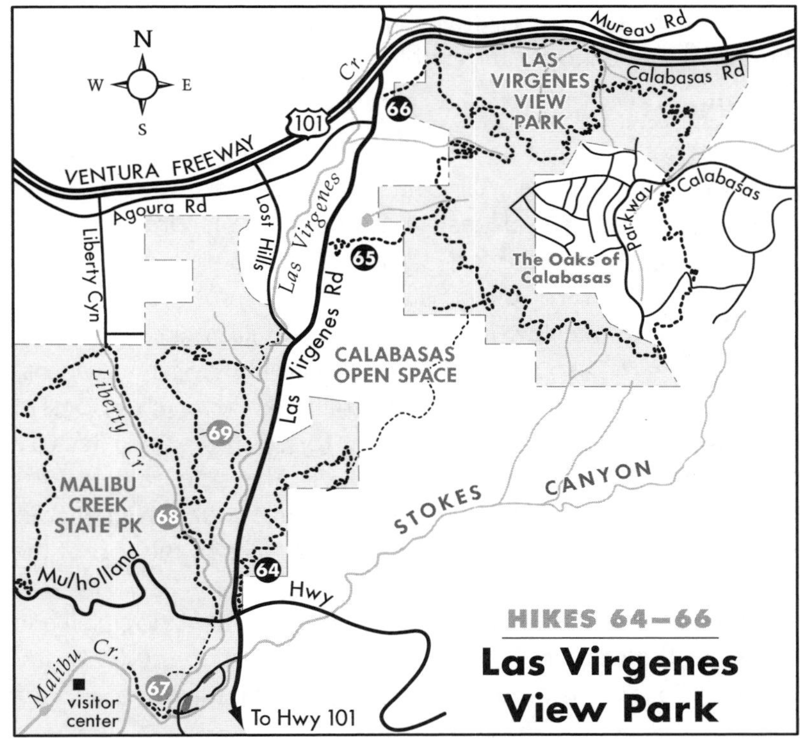

of Las Virgenes Road and south of the Ventura Freeway. This 9.8-mile loop, part of the extensive Calabasas-Cold Creek Trail System, follows chaparral-covered ridges, forested canyons, riparian waterways, rolling grasslands, oak woodlands, and scenic overlooks. The trail also traverses the perimeter of "The Oaks of Calabasas" subdivision, an affluent hillside neighborhood. This hike begins on the Bark Park Trail, a 1.2-mile connector path off of Las Virgenes Road.

To the trailhead

From the Ventura Freeway/Highway 101 in Calabasas, exit on Las Virgenes Road. Drive 0.9 miles south to Bark Park on the left. (It is directly across from Arthur Wright Middle School.) Turn left into the parking lot and park.

From Santa Monica, drive 12 miles northbound on the Pacific Coast Highway/Highway 1 to Malibu Canyon Road. Turn right (north) and continue 9.1 miles to Bark Park on the right. (It is 2.4 miles past Mulholland Highway and directly across from Arthur Wright Middle School.) Turn right into the parking lot and park.

The hike

From the north end of Bark Park, by the trailhead kiosk, head up the signed Bark Park Trail. Skirt the fenced off-leash dog area, and weave up the slope at an easy grade. Pass the Las Virgenes Water District reservoir on the left. Continue up the side canyon to a bowl of tree-dotted rolling hills. At 1.2 miles, the trail ends at a T-junction with the New Millennium Loop Trail. Begin the loop to the right, heading southeast. Views immediately open up across the Santa Monica Mountain Range. Traverse the open slopes to an unsigned fork by a fence. The right fork detours 0.2 miles to a 1,300-foot knoll with 360-degree vistas. This side path, the Las Virgenes View Park Connector Trail continues south on an old dirt road. The trail follows the ridgeline for 1.5 miles to the top of the Las Virgenes View Trail (Hike 64).

Continue on the main loop trail. Follow the ridge downhill and wind into the canyon. Cross a stream and head up the west canyon wall. Follow the mountain contours, dropping in and out of a

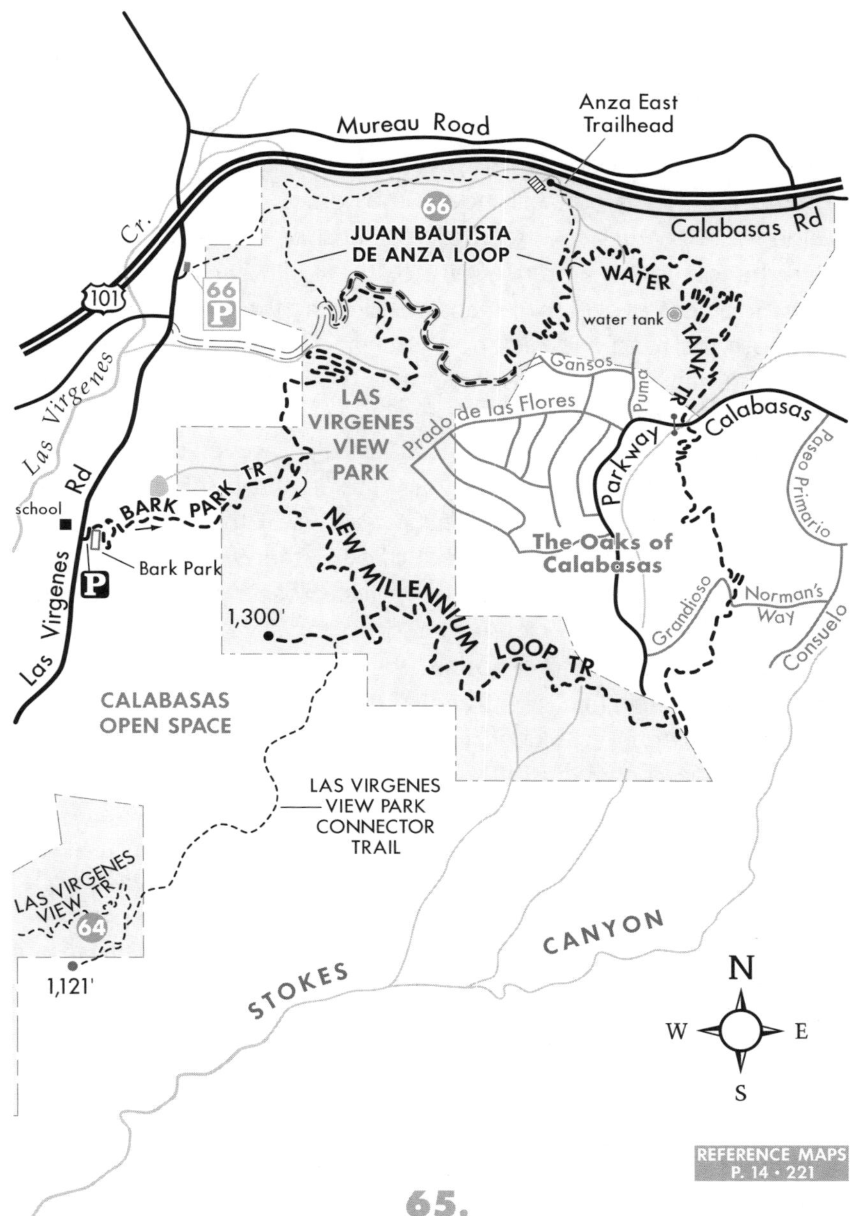

REFERENCE MAPS
P. 14 • 221

65.

New Millennium Loop Trail

LAS VIRGENES VIEW PARK

few drainages. A series of short switchbacks lead up to a ridge that overlooks some mega-size homes. Traverse the ridge and descend into the canyon to the east. The footpath crosses a couple of wood footbridges over drainages descending from the steep hillside. Cross a road within "The Oaks of Calabasas" subdivision, then wind through the hills above the homes. Gradually descend along five switchbacks to the west end of Parkway Calabasas. On the left is the entrance gate of the exclusive subdivision, a development of 550 mini-mansions dotting the Calabasas Hills.

Cross the road and pick up the signed Water Tank Trail. Drop into the canyon and cross over the drainage. Traverse the exposed canyon slope, steadily gaining elevation. Pass a perpetually dripping rock grotto on the left. Zigzag up seven switchbacks to the top of the mountain by a water tank on the left. Curve right and descend, with far-reaching views of the Santa Monica Mountains. Walk through a pocket of oaks, then zipper down the hill to the canyon floor in an oak grove. Cross a wooden bridge over the seasonal creek, and head up the west canyon slope. Climb over the hill and drop into the next drainage to the west. Continue downhill to the stream-fed canyon bottom. Rock-hop across the stream to a junction at 6 miles. The right fork leads 0.2 miles to the Juan Bautista De Anza East Trailhead at the end of Calabasas Road.

Bear left on the Juan Bautista De Anza Loop Trail, and wind up to the ridge. Head downhill into the canyon to the west, and traverse the east canyon wall to a utility road. Go to the right on the old dirt road. Cross the head of the canyon, and descend to a signed junction at 9 miles. The right fork leads 0.8 miles to the Juan Bautista De Anza West Trailhead (Hike 66). Bear left on the New Millennium Loop Trail. Weave along the mountain contours to a stream in a picturesque grotto. Follow the willow-lined stream past an old man-made rock fountain and pool. Continue downhill through a forested canopy. Ascend the hill with the aid of four switchbacks, and meander through the rolling hills to a signed junction, completing the loop at 11.2 miles. Bear right on the Bark Park Trail, and return to the trailhead. ■

66. Juan Bautista De Anza Loop

LAS VIRGENES VIEW PARK

Calabasas

Hiking distance: 4.4-mile loop
Hiking time: 2.5 hours
Configuration: loop
Elevation gain: 500 feet
Difficulty: easy to moderate
Exposure: open slopes with forested pockets
Dogs: allowed
Maps: U.S.G.S. Calabasas
Tom Harrison Maps: Malibu Creek State Park Trail Map

map page 227

The Anza Trail is a portion of the Juan Bautista De Anza National Historic Trail, an old missionary trail from San Diego to San Francisco. The trail represents the route taken in 1775—76, when Anza led approximately 200 colonists, 100 soldiers, and 1,000 head of livestock from what is now Mexico to form a colony in what is now San Francisco. Most of the historic route is on private property, but some segments of the trail are still located on public parklands. The 1.4-mile multi-use trail runs between the western end of Calabasas Road and Las Virgenes Road near the Ventura Freeway. Information panels along the way describe the history and significance. This hike begins on the historic trail and forms a loop with a mixture of single-track and dirt roads. The loop crosses through wetlands, lush canyons, oak woodlands, rolling hills, and open ridges with great mountain views.

To the trailhead

From the Ventura Freeway/Highway 101 in Calabasas, exit on Las Virgenes Road. Drive 0.1 mile south to the turnoff on the left. Turn left and continue 0.1 mile uphill to the posted trailhead and parking area at the end of the dirt road.

The hike

Pass the trailhead kiosk and walk up the canyon to the east. At 0.3 miles is a posted junction. Begin the loop straight ahead on the left fork, hiking clockwise. Traverse the hillside past mature oaks, then curve left and descend. Parallel the south side of Highway 101, dropping into a lush draw. Pass through the slightly swampy area among willows and bay laurel as the path fades in and out. Cross the north side of the stream and return to the distinct trail. Continue east to The Old Road, a small segment of the original El Camino Real, dating back to the early 20th century. Walk 30 yards to the left on the 100-year-old section of pavement, and pick up the footpath again on the right. Rock-hop over the stream and follow the undulating grassy path to a trail on the right at 1.4 miles. The junction is just shy of the Anza East trailhead by a rock pillar commemorating Juan Bautista De Anza. His expedition camped here on February 22, 1776, en route to what is now San Francisco. Bear right and cross the creek on a wooden bridge. Recross the creek to an asphalt road. To the left is Calabasas Road and the Juan Bautista De Anza East Trailhead.

Take the right fork and enter the oak-dotted canyon. Traverse the west canyon slope 0.2 miles on the footpath to a junction with the Water Tank Trail on the left. Continue straight on the Anza Loop Trail, and wind up to the ridge. Head downhill into the canyon to the west, and traverse the east canyon wall to a utility road. Go to the right and take the old dirt road. Cross the head of the canyon, and descend to a signed junction with the New Millennium Trail on the left at 3.4 miles. Stay on the Anza Loop Trail straight ahead. Descend on the serpentine dirt road 300 yards to the "trail" sign on the right in a horseshoe left bend. Bear right and go to the north through the rolling, oak-dotted hills, completing the loop at the head of the canyon. Return to the trailhead 0.3 miles to the left. ■

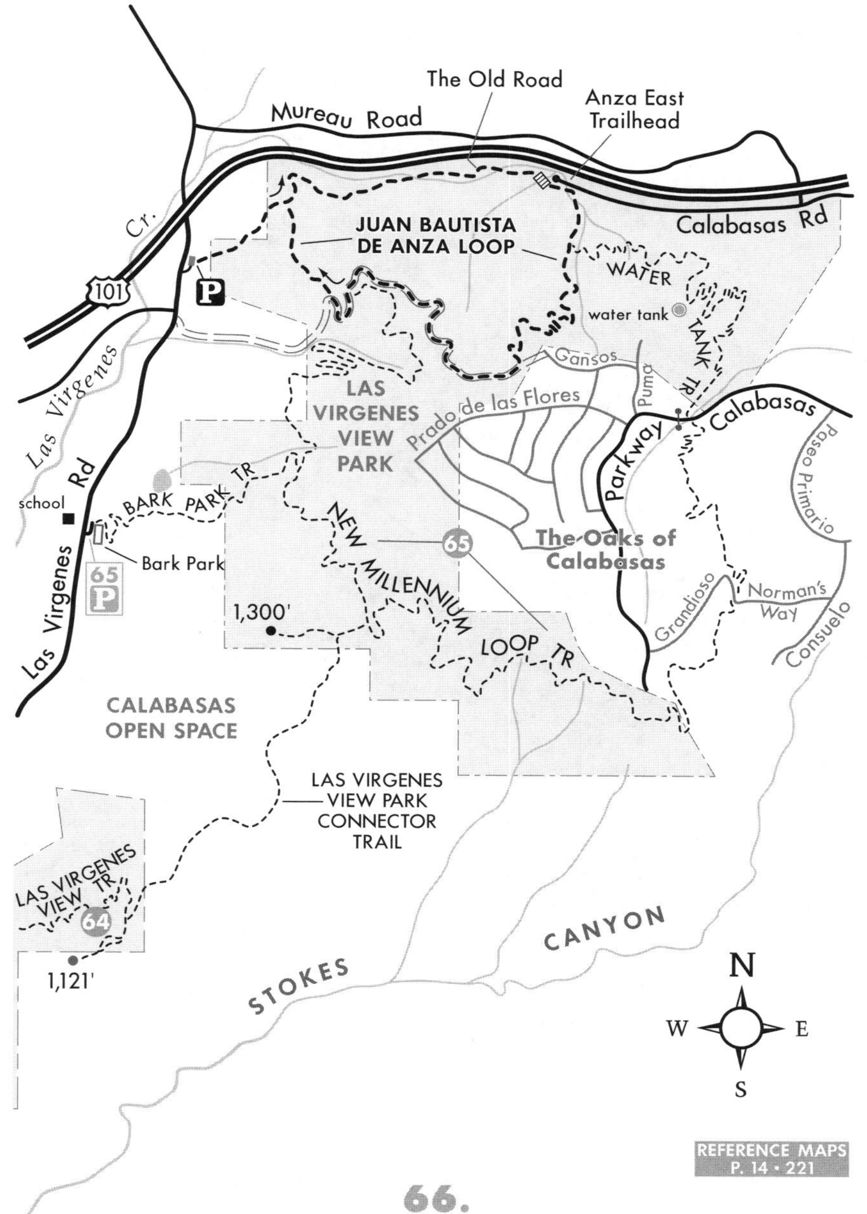

REFERENCE MAPS
P. 14 • 221

66.

Juan Bautista De Anza Loop

LAS VIRGENES VIEW PARK

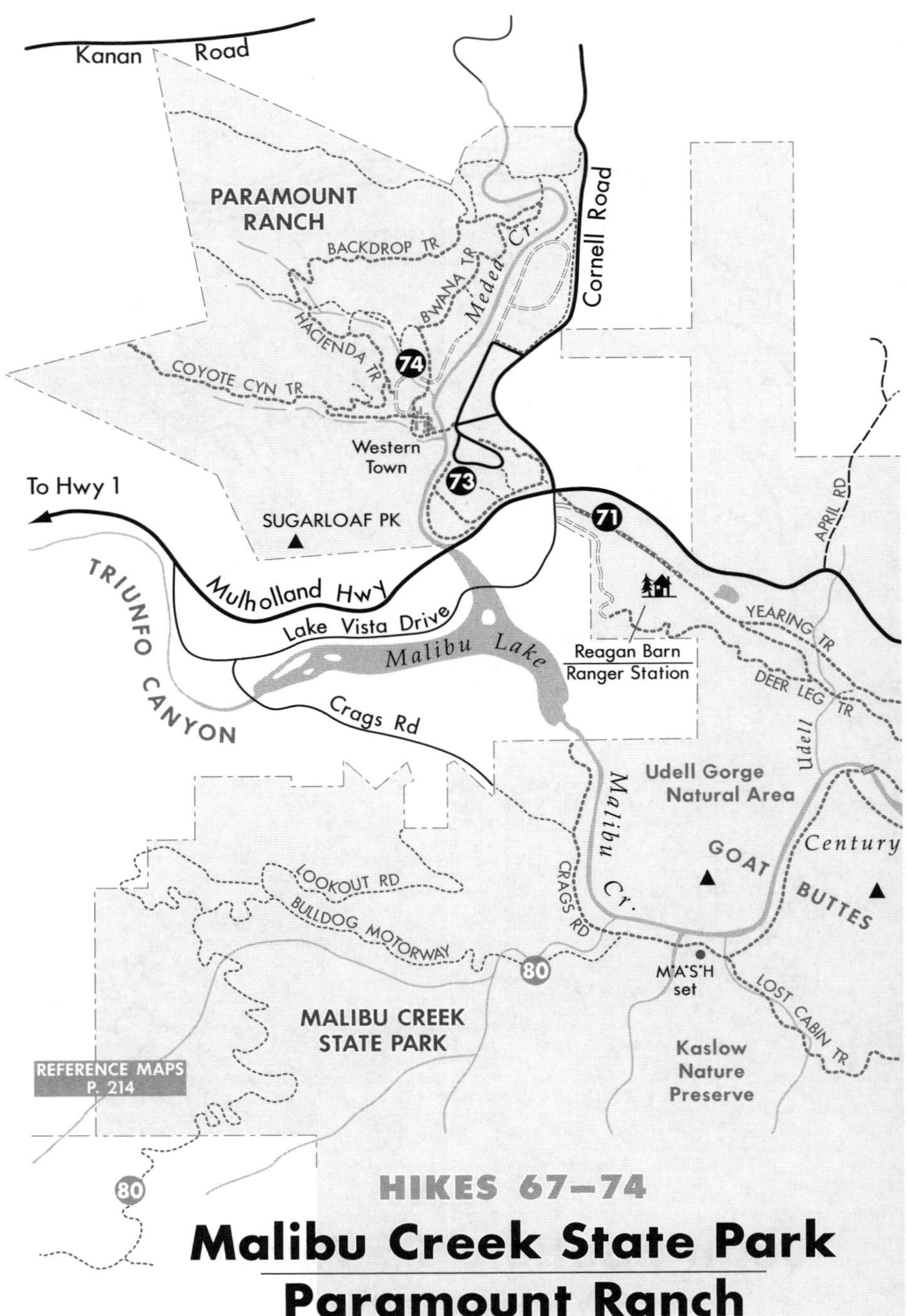

HIKES 67–74

Malibu Creek State Park
Paramount Ranch

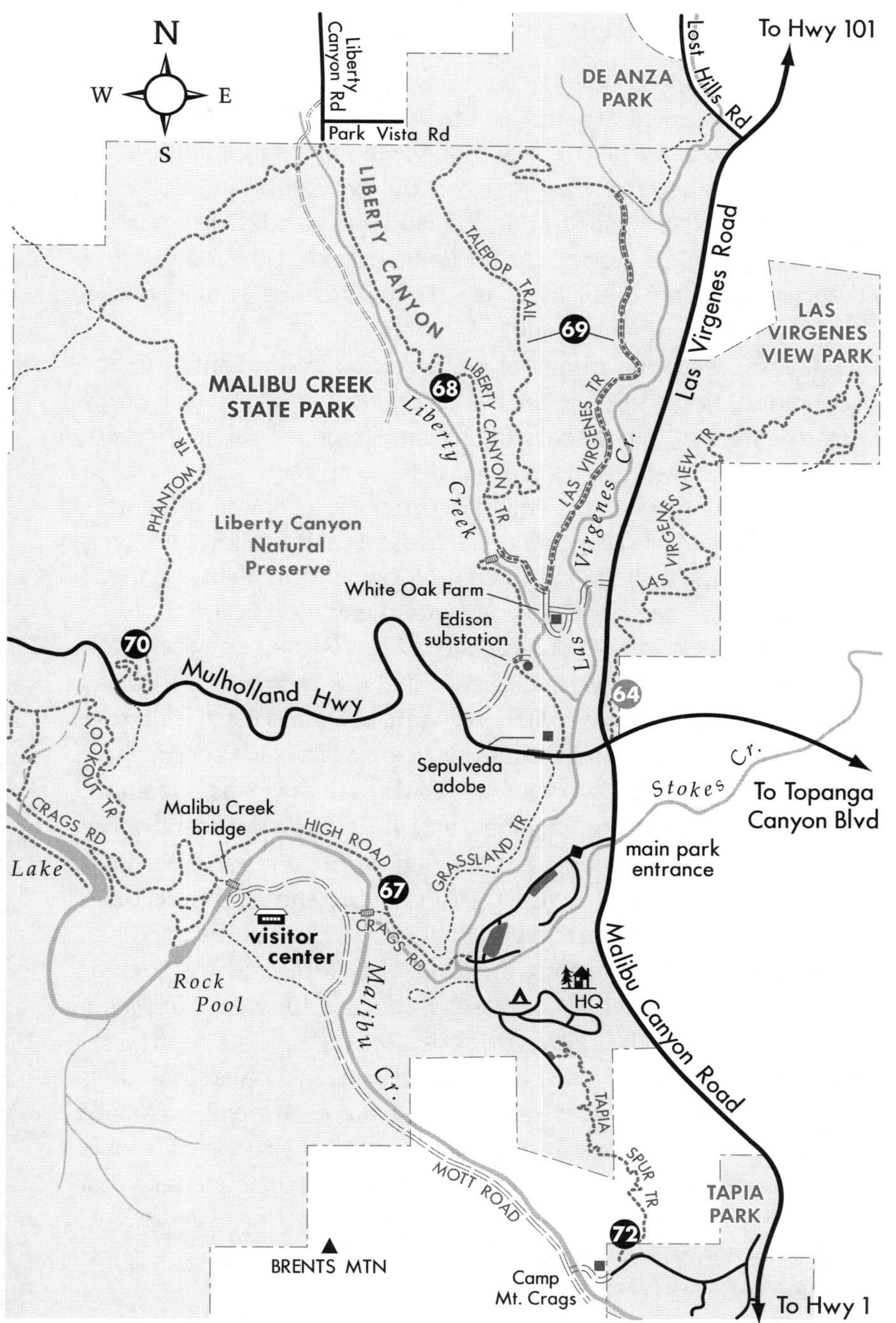
N
W
E
S
Liberty Canyon Rd
Park Vista Rd
Lost Hills Rd
To Hwy 101
DE ANZA PARK
LIBERTY CANYON
TALEPOP TRAIL
69
LAS VIRGENES VIEW PARK
Las Virgenes Road
MALIBU CREEK STATE PARK
68
LIBERTY CANYON TR
Liberty Creek
LAS VIRGENES TR
Virgenes Cr.
Las
LAS VIRGENES VIEW TR
PHANTOM TR
Liberty Canyon Natural Preserve
White Oak Farm
Edison substation
70
Mulholland Hwy
64
LOOKOUT TR
Sepulveda adobe
Stokes Cr.
To Topanga Canyon Blvd
CRAGS RD
Malibu Creek bridge
HIGH ROAD
GRASSLAND TR
main park entrance
Lake
67
visitor center
CRAGS RD
Malibu Cr.
Rock Pool
HQ
Malibu Canyon Road
TAPIA
SPUR TR
MOTT ROAD
TAPIA PARK
72
BRENTS MTN
Camp Mt. Crags
To Hwy 1

Malibu Creek State Park

Malibu Creek State Park, located in the central portion of the Santa Monica Mountains, stretches over 10,000 acres of rugged, diverse terrain. It is one of the mountain range's premier state parks. The land was acquired by the California state park system in 1974. Previous to this, the land was divided into parcels belonging to Bob Hope, Ronald Reagan, and 20th Century Fox. Although the park is still used as a filming site, it is primarily used for day-hiking and picnicking.

Malibu Creek, the principal watercourse in the Santa Monica Mountains, flows through the park from Malibu Lake. It is the only stream-channel that bisects the mountain range. Within the park, Malibu Creek was dammed around 1900 to form Century Lake. The river continues over 13 miles down Malibu Canyon and enters the ocean at Malibu Lagoon at Surfrider Beach. Malibu Canyon is the chief pass-through in the Santa Monica Mountains, connecting the inland valley at Calabasas with the Malibu Coast.

Malibu Creek State Park has a mix of sandstone, conglomerate, and volcanic rock formations that include picturesque buttes, deep gorges, prominent cliffs, vertical peaks, and rocky outcroppings. The diverse plant habitats include coastal sage scrub, chaparral, rolling grasslands, broad meadows, oak savannas, sycamore woodlands, freshwater marshes, and streamside vegetation. The state park is also home to three natural preserves: 1,920-acre Kaslow Preserve, 730-acre Liberty Canyon, and 300-acre Udell Gorge. Amenities include a visitor center and a campground.

The park was the filming location of notable movies such as *Butch Cassidy and the Sundance Kid*, *Daniel Boone*, *Tarzan*, *Planet of the Apes*, and the television series *M*A*S*H*.

More than twenty miles of hiking, biking, and equestrian trails criss-cross the park. The trail system includes streamside strolls, paths through canyons and valleys to natural preserves, movie and historic sites, and high ridges with spectacular scenery that spans from the ocean to the mountains,.

The main entrance into the park is on Malibu Canyon Road, just south of Mulholland Highway.

67. Rock Pool, Century Lake, Udell Gorge Preserve and M*A*S*H Site

MALIBU CREEK STATE PARK

1925 Las Virgenes Road • Calabasas

Hiking distance: 8.3 miles round trip
Hiking time: 4.5 hours
Configuration: out-and-back plus three spur trails
Elevation gain: 400 feet
Difficulty: moderate
Exposure: a mix of exposed hills and shaded forest
Dogs: not allowed
Maps: U.S.G.S. Malibu Beach and Point Dume
Tom Harrison Maps: Malibu Creek State Park Trail Map
Malibu Creek State Park Map

map page 232

The Santa Monica Mountains are bisected near their center by Malibu Creek. It is the only creek that cuts entirely through the mountain range from north to south. The year-round stream flows more than 13 miles, beginning from its headwaters in Westlake Village to the Santa Monica Bay at the Malibu Lagoon. Along the way, it meanders through Malibu Creek State Park and down Malibu Canyon to the ocean. The Malibu Creek watershed, the largest in the range, drains over 100 miles of land from the southern Simi Hills and western San Fernando Valley.

This premier hike begins from the main entrance road to Malibu Creek State Park and follows Malibu Creek through the heart of the state park to Malibu Lake, passing a series of scenic landmarks and man-made features. The creek and trail weave along Goat Buttes, the two picturesque volcanic peaks rising from the center of the park (cover photo). At the base of the buttes are Century Lake and Rock Pool. Century Lake was formed in 1901 when a dam was built at the mouth of a gorge by members of the Crags Country Club. The 20-acre, man-made lake was used for fishing, sailing, and duck hunting. Since that time, the reservoir has silted up and become a pastoral, 7-acre freshwater marsh. Rock Pool is a natural lake dammed by volcanic boulders. The pool sits in a deep gorge in Triunfo Canyon and is framed by

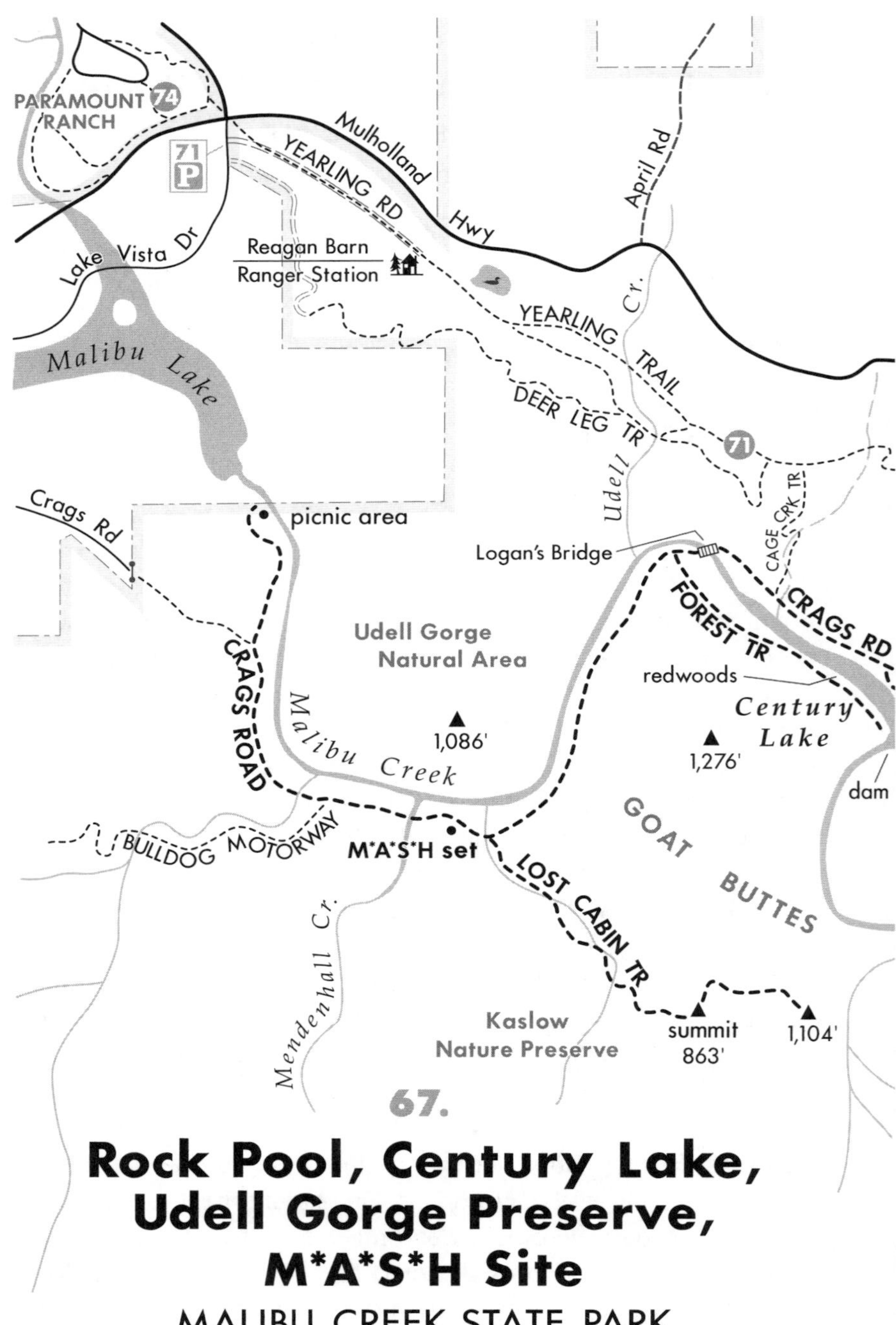

67. Rock Pool, Century Lake, Udell Gorge Preserve, M*A*S*H Site

MALIBU CREEK STATE PARK

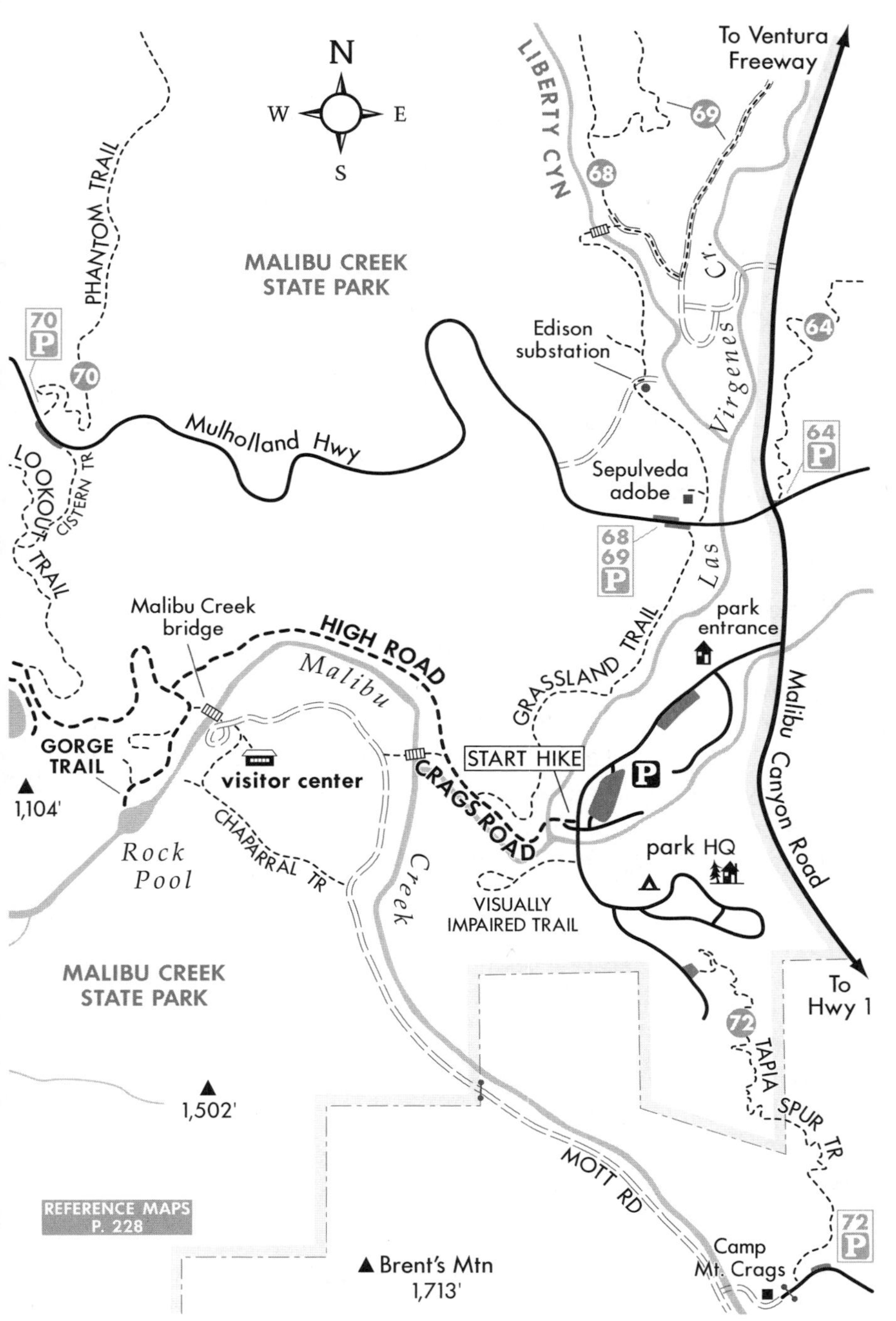
N
W
E
S
To Ventura Freeway
LIBERTY CYN
69
68
MALIBU CREEK STATE PARK
PHANTOM TRAIL
Cr.
70
P
70
64
Edison substation
Virgenes
64
P
Mulholland Hwy
LOOKOUT TRAIL
CISTERN TR
Sepulveda adobe
68
69
P
Las
Malibu Creek bridge
HIGH ROAD
park entrance
Malibu
GRASSLAND TRAIL
Malibu Canyon Road
GORGE TRAIL
START HIKE
visitor center
P
1,104'
CRAGS ROAD
Rock Pool
CHAPARRAL TR
park HQ
Creek
VISUALLY IMPAIRED TRAIL
MALIBU CREEK STATE PARK
To Hwy 1
72
TAPIA SPUR TR
1,502'
MOTT RD
REFERENCE MAPS P. 228
72
P
Camp Mt. Crags
Brent's Mtn 1,713'

massive vertical cliffs and groves of bays and sycamores. The *Tarzan* movies and *South Pacific* were filmed at this site.

The well-known *M*A*S*H* television series was filmed in the park from 1972 to 1983. The *M*A*S*H* site sits in a gorgeous meadow in Triunfo Canyon beneath Goat Buttes. The area was used in the opening sequence of each *M*A*S*H* episode. The production sets are gone, but a rusted jeep and ambulance still remain. The film site is very recognizable from the series.

The trail passes through two of the park's three natural preserves. The Udell Gorge Natural Preserve (300 acres) and Kaslow Natural Preserve (1,920 acres) protects rare plants and volcanic formations. The Kaslow Preserve is also a protected nesting ground for golden eagles. En route, the hike detours to an overlook on the Lost Cabin Trail at the southern edge of Goat Buttes and strolls through a redwood grove on the banks of Century Lake.

To the trailhead

From Santa Monica, drive 12 miles northbound on the Pacific Coast Highway/Highway 1 to Malibu Canyon Road. Turn right (north) and continue 6 miles up the winding canyon road to the signed Malibu Creek State Park entrance on the left. (It is located 0.2 miles shy of Mulholland Highway.) Turn left and drive 0.35 miles to the second parking lot on the left. A parking fee is required.

From the Ventura Freeway/Highway 101 in Calabasas, take the Las Virgenes Road exit. Drive 3.1 miles south to Mulholland Highway. Continue 0.2 miles straight ahead to the signed Malibu Creek State Park entrance on the right. Turn right and drive 0.35 miles to the second parking lot on the left. A parking fee is required.

FREE ROADSIDE PARKING ALTERNATIVE: Park west of the intersection of Malibu Canyon Road/Las Virgenes Road and Mulholland Highway in the pullouts along Mulholland Highway. Take the posted Grassland Trail (a footpath) south 0.7 miles to Crags Road.

The hike

Cross the park road to the posted trailhead. Take Crags Road, crossing over Las Virgenes Creek. The paved road turns to a narrower dirt road. Pass the signed Grassland Trail on the right, a 0.7-mile connector trail from Mulholland Highway. Continue straight, following the north bank of Malibu Creek while enjoying the great views of Goat Buttes. Stroll through overhanging oak groves with picture-perfect views to a posted junction. Detour left towards the visitor center. Walk 60 yards to a trail on the right, just before the Malibu Creek Bridge (which leads to the visitor center).

Veer right on the Gorge Trail and go another 100 yards to a picnic area. The dirt road bends to the right and climbs to the top of the rock formations. Continue straight, staying on the canyon bottom among the deeply eroded rock formations with caves. Follow the west (right) side of the canyon to Rock Pool by a massive, rock-walled gorge.

Return to Crags Road and continue a half mile west to a footpath on the left. Take the path into a lush, shaded canopy with ferns and moss-covered boulders. The short path ends at the dam overlooking Century Lake by another steep-walled gorge.

Return to Crags Road and head northwest along the narrow lake, passing the Lookout Trail and Cage Creek Trail on the right. Stroll through the meadow surrounded by mountains. Cross Logan's Bridge over Malibu Creek. (The bridge was named after the 1998 film *Logan's Run*, which was filmed here.) Walk 75 yards to the signed Forest Trail on the left, where Crags Road becomes a footpath. Detour to the left on the half-mile-long trail along the backside of Century Lake. Walk east through the oak-rimmed meadow. Enter the forest, skirting the south edge of the meadow. The shaded path passes towering redwood trees planted in the 1920s by Crag's Country Club members, and a series of weather-etched volcanic boulders. Follow the south edge of Century Lake, passing more redwoods, to the end of the fern-lined trail at the concrete dam and another view into the vertical-walled gorge beneath Goat Buttes.

Return to Crags Road and continue up the forested canyon. Follow the perimeter of the Udell Gorge Natural Preserve between Malibu Creek and the steep rock wall of Goat Buttes on the left and a dense isolated forest on the right. At the southeast corner of the wetland, where the canyon widens, is a posted junction with the Lost Cabin Trail on the left, just shy of the *M*A*S*H** site. For now, detour left and head south into the Kaslow Natural Preserve, a nesting area for golden eagles. Cross a stream and meander up the isolated side valley along the southern base of Goat Buttes. Cross the stream two more times while walking beneath the gorgeous rock cliffs and pock-marked outcrops. Climb to a 700-foot saddle at the head of the canyon. Curve left and go downhill to the posted end of the trail and the site of the lost cabin, although no remnants remain. The spot is located just before a branch of Malibu Creek in a deep gorge between Century Lake and Rock Pool.

Return to Crags Road. Bear left and enter the *M*A*S*H* site in a meadow framed by the prominent Goat Buttes. Walk around the famous flat surrounded by mountains. Meander among the vehicle props abandoned after filming and an unlocked shed with artifacts and photographs from the TV series. Detour left up the slope to the old helicopter landing area on a perch overlooking the site. After perusing the area, cross Mendenhall Creek and continue through oak-filled Triunfo Canyon to a posted junction with the Bulldog Motorway on the left (Hike 80). This dirt road leads 3.4 miles to Castro Crest, high above Solstice Canyon. Continue straight on Crags Road, and cross another stream to a fork 0.2 miles ahead. Crags Road veers left and leads 0.3 miles to the park boundary and onto residential Crags Road, located 0.7 miles from Lake Vista Drive. Instead, veer right and pass rock-lined pools and massive outcrops to the park boundary, just short of the Malibu Lake Dam. The fenced private land halts access. On the right is a quiet picnic area. Return along the same route. ■

68. Liberty Canyon Natural Preserve

MALIBU CREEK STATE PARK

Calabasas

Hiking distance: 4 miles round trip
Hiking time: 2 hours
Configuration: out-and-back
Elevation gain: 100 feet
Difficulty: easy
Exposure: exposed
Dogs: not allowed
Maps: U.S.G.S. Malibu Beach and Calabasas • Malibu Creek State Park map
Tom Harrison Maps: Malibu Creek State Park Trail map

map page 239

Liberty Canyon Natural Preserve is one of three natural preserves in Malibu Creek State Park. The preserve is home to a rare stand of California valley oaks. This hike begins just north of the main park entrance. The path crosses the rolling grassland at the V-shaped merging of Liberty Canyon and Las Virgenes Canyon. After crossing a bridge that spans Liberty Creek, the route follows the Liberty Canyon Trail, a fire road that parallels the east side of the creek. The trail gently climbs through oak woodlands to the head of the canyon, where there are views of the surrounding hills. En route, the trail connects with the Talepop Trail (Hike 69) and the Phantom Trail (Hike 70).

To the trailhead

From Santa Monica, drive 12 miles northbound on the Pacific Coast Highway/Highway 1 to Malibu Canyon Road. Turn right (north) and continue 6.5 miles up the winding canyon road to Mulholland Highway. Turn left and park 0.1 mile ahead in the parking pullouts on either side of the road.

From the Ventura Freeway/Highway 101, take the Las Virgenes Road exit. Drive 3.1 miles south to Mulholland Highway. Turn right and park 0.1 mile ahead in the parking pullouts.

The hike

Take the signed North Grassland Trail and head north. Pass the Sepulveda Adobe, a historic white adobe house built by pioneer homesteader Pedro Sepulveda in 1863. Cross the rolling grasslands at the convergence of Liberty Canyon and Las Virgenes Canyon. Loop around the west side of the Edison substation. Continue north past oak trees, bearing right at a trail split. Cross a footbridge over Liberty Creek by a small waterfall and pools to a signed T-junction. Head left on the Liberty Canyon Trail, passing a junction at one mile with the Talepop Trail (Hike 69). Continue straight ahead, climbing the hillside through an oak grove overlooking the canyon, then return to the canyon bottom. The trail ends at the head of the canyon by Park Vista Road and Liberty Canyon Road. The Phantom Trail heads southwest through the meadow to the left (Hike 70). Return along the same trail. ■

69. Talepop Trail—Las Virgenes Loop

MALIBU CREEK STATE PARK

Calabasas

Hiking distance: 4.8-mile loop
Hiking time: 2.5 hours
Configuration: loop
Elevation gain: 450 feet
Difficulty: moderate
Exposure: exposed hills and open canyon bottom
Dogs: not allowed
Maps: U.S.G.S. Malibu Beach and Calabasas • Malibu Creek State Park map
Tom Harrison Maps: Malibu Creek State Park Trail map

map page 241

The Talepop-Las Virgenes Loop is on the north end of Malibu Creek State Park in the 730-acre Liberty Canyon Natural Preserve. This loop climbs a grassy ridge between two stream-fed canyons—Liberty Canyon and Las Virgenes Canyon. Both creeks are tributaries of Malibu Creek, the largest watershed in the Santa Monica Mountains. The hike climbs up the ridge on the Talepop Trail, named for a Chumash Indian village that once inhabited the area. From the ridgeline are views into Liberty Canyon and Malibu Canyon. The return route descends into Las Virgenes Canyon along the Las Virgenes Trail. The trail parallels the creek, passing through open meadows surrounded by the oak-studded hills.

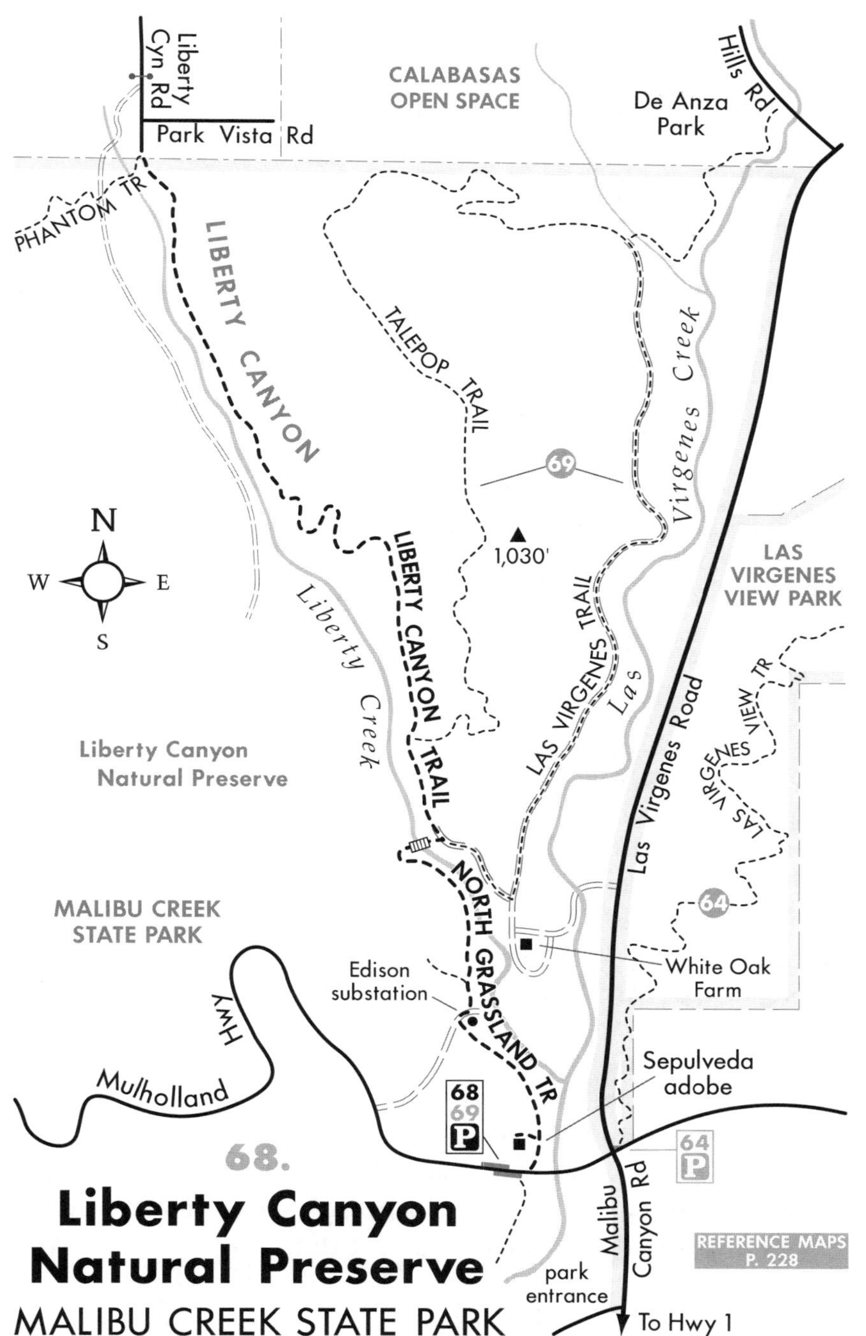

Liberty Canyon Natural Preserve

MALIBU CREEK STATE PARK

To the trailhead

From Santa Monica, drive 12 miles northbound on the Pacific Coast Highway/Highway 1 to Malibu Canyon Road. Turn right and continue 6.5 miles up this beautiful, winding canyon road to Mulholland Highway. Turn left and park 0.1 mile ahead in the parking pullouts on either side of the road.

From the Ventura Freeway/Highway 101, take the Las Virgenes Road exit. Drive 3.1 miles south to Mulholland Highway. Turn right and park 0.1 mile ahead in the parking pullouts.

The hike

Take the signed North Grassland Trail, and head north across the rolling meadow. Pass the Sepulveda Adobe, a historic white adobe house built by pioneer homesteader Pedro Sepulveda in 1863. Loop around an Edison substation as Liberty Canyon and Las Virgenes Canyon separate into a V-shape. Continue north past oak trees, bearing right at a trail split. Cross a footbridge over Liberty Creek by a small waterfall and pools to a signed T-junction.

Take the left fork on the Liberty Canyon Trail, beginning the loop. At one mile is a posted junction with the Talepop Trail on the right. Head right (east) on the Talepop Trail, winding up the west canyon wall a half mile to the ridge. Follow the grassy ridge north to the 1,030-foot summit, overlooking Liberty Canyon on the west and Las Virgenes Canyon on the east. At the northern park boundary, bear right and descend down the hillside. Switchbacks lead to the Las Virgenes Canyon floor by Las Virgenes Creek and a junction at 2.75 miles. The left fork crosses the creek and leads 0.3 miles to De Anza Park.

Take the right fork—the Las Virgenes Trail—along the west side of the creek. As you approach White Oak Farm at the lower end of the loop (a private residence), take the signed Liberty Canyon Trail to the right. A short distance ahead is the junction by the bridge, completing the loop. Bear left on the North Grassland Trail, cross the bridge, and retrace your steps. ■

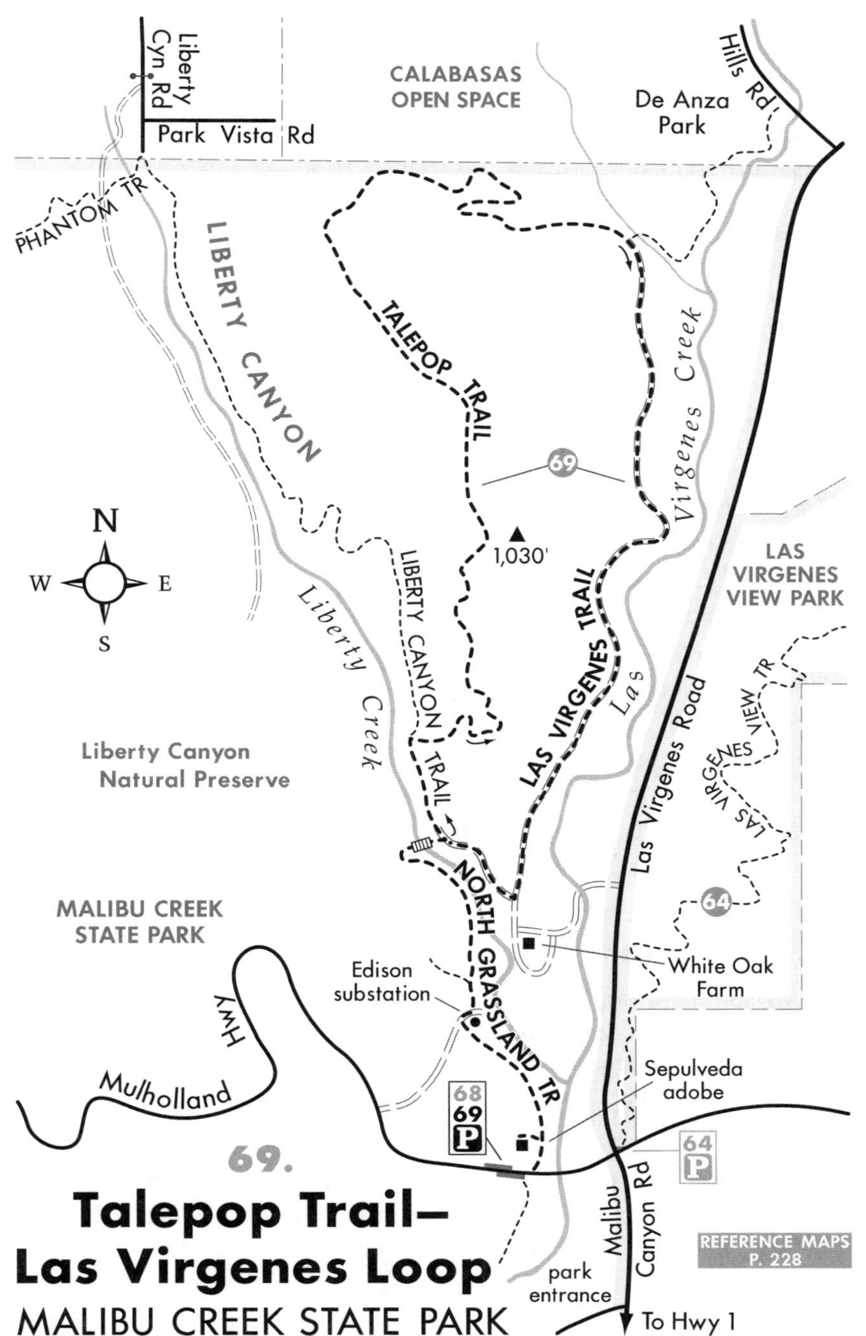

69. Talepop Trail— Las Virgenes Loop

MALIBU CREEK STATE PARK

70. Phantom Trail

MALIBU CREEK STATE PARK

Calabasas

Hiking distance: 5 miles out-and-back or 7-mile loop
Hiking time: 2.5 hours out-and-back or 3.5-hour loop
Configuration: out-and-back or loop
Elevation gain: 400 feet for out-and-back or 900 feet for loop
Difficulty: moderate to somewhat strenuous
Exposure: mostly exposed
Dogs: not allowed
Maps: U.S.G.S. Malibu Beach and Calabasas • Malibu Creek State Park Map
Tom Harrison Maps: Malibu Creek State Park Trail Map

The Phantom Trail follows an undulating ridge in the Liberty Canyon Natural Preserve at the north end of Malibu Creek State Park. The trail follows the west ridge of the Liberty Canyon drainage, alternating from the exposed ridgetop to forested pockets of sage, elderberry, scrub oak, and manzanita. The loop returns via the Liberty Canyon Trail (a fire road) through rolling grasslands, parallel to the east side of Liberty Creek. Throughout the hike are great views of the surrounding hills and Goat Buttes, the two picturesque volcanic peaks rising from the heart of Malibu Creek State Park (cover photo). This hike is configured as a 5-mile, out-and-back route, turning around at Liberty Canyon Road, or as a 7-mile loop, returning down through Liberty Canyon and back to the trailhead along Malibu Creek.

To the trailhead

From Santa Monica, drive 12 miles northbound on the Pacific Coast Highway/Highway 1 to Malibu Canyon Road. Turn right (north) and continue 6.5 miles up the winding canyon road to Mulholland Highway. Turn left and drive 1.9 miles on Mulholland Highway to a long dirt pullout on the left. On the south (left) side of the road, at the east end of the pullout, is the signed Cistern Trail. 150 yards ahead on the right is the Phantom Trailhead. From the Cornell Road intersection, the trailhead pullout is located 1.3 miles west on Mulholland Highway.

From the Ventura Freeway/Highway 101 in Calabasas, take

the Las Virgenes Road exit. Drive 3.1 miles south to Mulholland Highway. Turn right and follow the directions above.

The hike

Cross to the north side of Mulholland Highway to the Phantom Trail sign. Wind up the mountain through scrub oak to a spectacular overlook of Malibu Creek State Park and the Goat Buttes. Follow the ridge uphill, steadily climbing to the first peak atop a 1,150-foot knoll with 360-degree views.

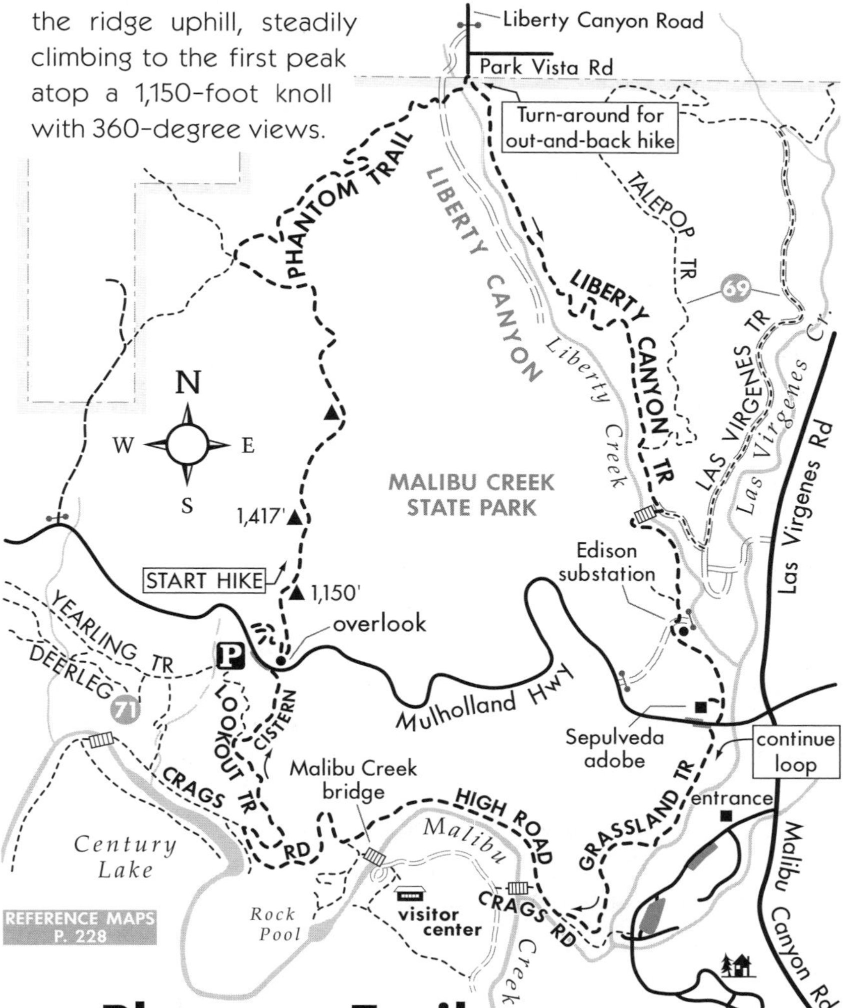

REFERENCE MAPS P. 228

70. Phantom Trail

MALIBU CREEK STATE PARK

Skirt along the east side of the next peak at 0.7 miles, and traverse the upper west slope of Liberty Canyon. Continue along the ridge to another knoll with panoramic vistas of the surrounding mountains and valleys. Make a short but steep descent, and veer left at an arrow sign. Head down a side canyon, then return to a saddle and an unsigned trail fork. The left fork follows the roller-coaster ridge for a mile, then dramatically drops to Agoura Road by the Ventura Freeway. For this hike, cross the saddle straight ahead, staying on the Phantom Trail. Drop into Liberty Canyon on a narrow footpath through the shade of the lush vegetation. Descend to the valley floor, and walk through the open grassland along the south edge of the wetland meadow. Pass through a grove of towering eucalyptus trees to Liberty Canyon Road at the end of the Phantom Trail. For a 5-mile hike, return by retracing your steps.

To form a 7-mile loop, bear right on vehicle-restricted Liberty Canyon Trail/fire road. Head down canyon on the unpaved road, passing through an oak grove and canyon overlooks to a junction with the North Grassland Trail on the right at 3.8 miles. Go right and cross a footbridge over Liberty Creek by a small waterfall and pools. Continue south past oak trees, and loop around the west side of an electrical substation. Cross the rolling grasslands and pass Sepulveda Adobe, a historic structure built by homesteader Pedro Sepulveda in 1863.

At 4.5 miles, the trail reaches Mulholland Highway, just west of Malibu Canyon Road. Carefully cross Mulholland Highway (or cross at the intersection), and pick up the posted Grassland Trail located 50 yards to the right. Continue south, weaving down the open grassland to High Road. Bear right on High Road, curving east, and follow the watercourse of Malibu Creek. At 5.2 miles is a junction with Crags Road. The left fork crosses Malibu Creek Bridge to the visitor center. Take the right fork and head uphill to a junction at the crest of the hill by an overlook of Century Lake and Goat Buttes. Just beyond this junction is the Lookout Trail on the right. Bear right and climb the hillside 0.4 miles to a junction with the Cistern Trail on the right. Veer right and climb up the low ridge to Mulholland Highway at the trailhead parking pullout. ■

71. Reagan Ranch

MALIBU CREEK STATE PARK

Calabasas

Hiking distance: 5.2 miles round trip
Hiking time: 3.5 hours
Configuration: double loop with optional spur trail
Elevation gain: 700 feet
Difficulty: easy to somewhat moderate
Exposure: exposed meadow with forested hillsides
Dogs: not allowed
Maps: U.S.G.S. Malibu Beach • Malibu Creek State Park map
Tom Harrison Maps: Malibu Creek State Park Trail map

map page 247

Reagan Ranch encompasses 305 acres on the northwest corner of Malibu Creek State Park. From 1951 through 1966, it was a second home to former President Ronald Reagan, who raised thoroughbred horses on the ranch. Originally named Yearling Row Ranch, it was sold by the Reagans to pay his campaign debts from the 1966 California governor's campaign. The original barn and stables, currently used as a park maintenance facility, are located in an open meadow at the junction of Mulholland Highway and Cornell Road. A network of trails, once used as horse riding trails by the Reagans, connects the ranch to the heart of Malibu Creek State Park.

This hike, the Yearling-Deer Leg Loop, leads to a duck pond, a large rolling meadow, an oak woodland, stream crossings, and the Reagan barn. There are vistas of the surrounding tree-dotted hills and jagged mountains. The Lake Vista Trail, an optional spur trail, leads to an 1,102-foot overlook of Malibu Lake, Sugarloaf Mountain (in Paramount Ranch), and Medea Valley.

To the trailhead

From Santa Monica, drive 12 miles northbound on the Pacific Coast Highway/Highway 1 to Malibu Canyon Road. Turn right (north) and continue 6.5 miles up this beautiful winding canyon road to Mulholland Highway. Turn left and drive 3.2 miles to Cornell Road. Turn left again and immediately park along the road wherever you find a spot.

From the Ventura Freeway/Highway 101 in Agoura Hills, exit on Kanan Road. Drive south 0.4 miles to Cornell Road. Turn left and continue 2.2 miles to the intersection of Mulholland Highway. Cross and park along the road.

The hike

Enter the ranch at a gateway through the white rail fence on the southeast corner of Mulholland Highway and Cornell Road. Walk a quarter mile east on the paved Yearling Road, lined with stately eucalyptus and oak trees, to the old Reagan Barn. Pass the barn, corral, and ranch buildings, now used by the park service, to the posted Yearling Trail. Take the footpath down the open meadow, passing a pond on the left. Continue to a Y-fork with the Deer Leg Trail, our return route. Stay to the left on the Yearling Trail, continuing through the valley floor. Pass a side path on the right that drops down to Udell Creek and the Deer Leg Trail. Continue straight to a trail split on a minor ridge at the east end of both the Yearling Trail and Deer Leg Trail.

Veer left and descend on the Lookout Trail to a fork with the Cage Creek Trail. Begin what will be another loop on the left fork and climb the hill, staying on the Lookout Trail. Drop into another stream-fed drainage. Weave through the forested side canyon to a fork with the Cistern Trail, a connector trail to Mulholland Highway. Stay to the right on the Lookout Trail. Descend to a T-junction with Crags Road while overlooking Century Lake and the volcanic Goat Buttes. Bear right on the dirt road 100 yards to a side road on the left that leads a short distance to the dam and overlook of Century Lake. The site is in a shaded canopy with ferns and mossy boulders by a steep-walled gorge. After enjoying the area, return to Crags Road and head northwest to the Cage Creek Trail on the right. Bear right on the footpath, crossing Cage Creek twice. Head up the narrow canyon and climb the west canyon wall, completing the 1.4-mile loop at the Lookout Trail.

Bear left and return to the junction on the ridge with the Yearling Trail and Deer Leg Trail. Now take the Deer leg Trail to

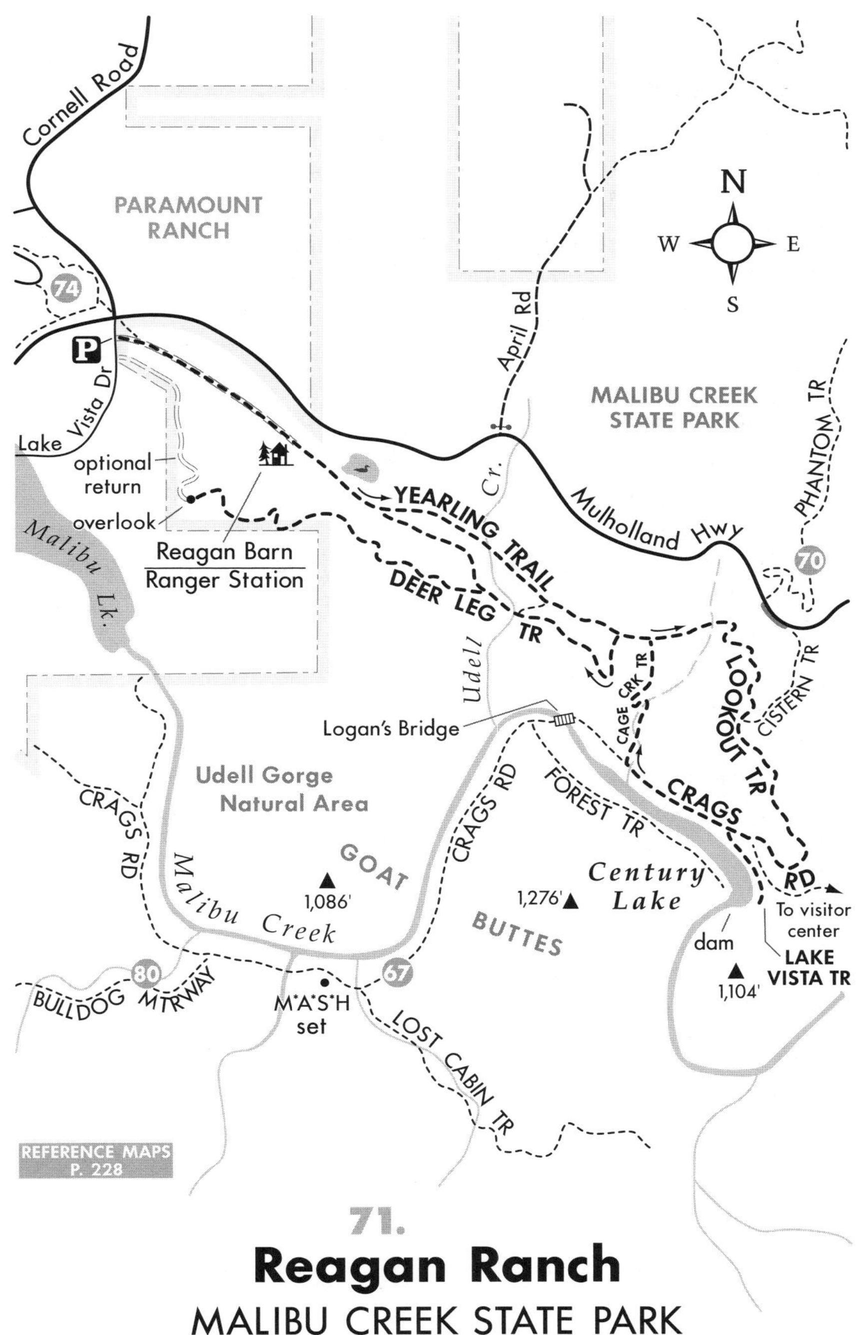

71. Reagan Ranch

MALIBU CREEK STATE PARK

the left and top the slope. Make a U-bend and descend into the forest. Cross a small stream, and pass the Yearling connector path on the right to Udell Creek, a tributary of Malibu Creek. Hop over ephemeral Udell Creek to a picnic area with stone fire pits. In the early 1960s, these barbecue pits were used by the Reagans for entertaining friends, actors, and political figures.

Watch for the unsigned Lake Vista Trail, a distinct footpath on the left by a picnic site. To overlook Malibu Lake, detour left on the footpath. Climb through the shade of oak trees, oak scrub, and tall brush while overlooking Reagan ranch through the foliage. At 0.7 miles, the trail reaches a ridge with a brush-obscured view of Malibu Lake. Veer right and drop down 0.1 mile to a clearing and overlook by a power pole, where there is a great view of Malibu Lake, Sugarloaf Mountain, and the Medea Valley.

From here are two options. For a quick half-mile return, take the unpaved utility road and wind down the hill into a meadow. Veer left along the park boundary to the trailhead at Mulholland Highway and Cornell Road. Or, to continue on the Deer Leg Trail, returning 0.8 miles down the Lake Vista Trail to the picnic area and the Deer Leg Trail. Go to the left and continue 0.3 miles northwest under a canopy of massive oaks, completing the second loop at the Yearling Trail. Return past the pond and ranch buildings to the trailhead. ■

72. Tapia Park to Rock Pool and Century Lake

TAPIA PARK: sub-unit of MALIBU CREEK STATE PARK

884 N. Las Virgenes Road • Calabasas

Hiking distance: 6.4 miles round trip
Hiking time: 3.5 hours
Configuration: out-and-back with optional 1-mile extension
Elevation gain: 350 feet
Difficulty: moderate
Exposure: a mix of exposed hills and shaded forest
Dogs: allowed in Tapia Park (first 0.6 miles); not allowed in Malibu Creek State Park
Maps: U.S.G.S. Malibu Beach • Malibu Creek State Park Map
Tom Harrison Maps: Malibu Creek State Park Trail Map

map page 250

Tapia Park, a sub-unit of Malibu Creek State Park, is a gorgeous 126-acre park that is filled with giant live oaks, sycamores, willow thickets and grassy meadows with picnic areas. The park is named for Jose Bartolome Tapia, a member of Juan Bautista de Anza's 1775 expedition from Mexico to form a colony in what is now San Francisco. Malibu Creek flows through the lower end of the park. Tapia Park abuts the southeast corner of Malibu Creek State Park. It is a well-used portal into the state park, with hiking, biking and equestrian trails (including access to the Backbone Trail).

This hike climbs the forested slope to a ridge overlooking Malibu Creek State Park, then descends into the idyllic Malibu Creek valley and the vast creek-fed meadow. The route then follows the creek to Rock Pool and Century Lake. Rock Pool is a natural lake dammed by volcanic boulders in a deep gorge in Triunfo Canyon. The pool is framed by massive vertical cliffs among groves of bays and sycamores. It was the film site of *South Pacific*, *Swiss Family Robinson*, and the *Tarzan* movies. A short distance farther lies Century Lake, a man-made lake that was created in 1910 when a dam was built at the mouth of a gorge by members of the Crags Country Club. The 20-acre lake was used for fishing, sailing, and duck hunting. Since that time, the reservoir has filled with silt and become a pastoral, 7-acre freshwater marsh. Throughout the hike are vistas of the surrounding mountains, including Goat Buttes, the two landmark volcanic peaks rising from the heart of the park (cover photo).

To the trailhead

From Santa Monica, drive 12 miles northbound on the Pacific Coast Highway/Highway 1 to Malibu Canyon Road. Turn right (north) and continue 4.9 miles up the winding canyon road to the signed Tapia Park entrance on the left. The entrance is located 0.1 mile past the traffic light at Piuma Road. Turn left and quickly veer right 0.1 mile, passing the fee/entrance station, to the turnoff on the left. Turn left and continue 0.2 miles to the parking spaces on the right. A parking fee is required.

From the Ventura Freeway/Highway 101 in Calabasas, take the Las Virgenes Road exit. Drive 4.9 miles south to the signed Tapia Park entrance on the right. The entrance is located 1.6 miles south of Mulholland Highway. Turn right and quickly veer right again for 0.1 mile, passing the fee/entrance station, to the turnoff on the left. Turn left and continue 0.2 miles to the parking on the right.

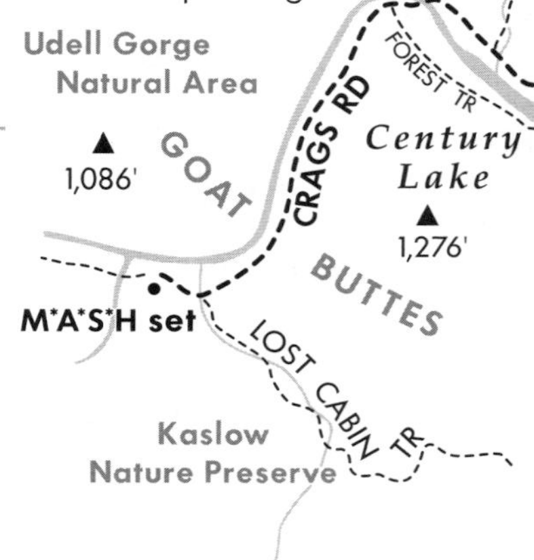

The hike

Walk 100 yards ahead on the park road to the Tapia Spur Trail on the right. The signed path is located just before reaching the Camp Mount Crags entrance. Bear right on the footpath, and walk among beautiful old oaks. Traverse the slope, weaving along the contours of the hills while being surrounded by mountains. Cross a

72.

Tapia Park to Rock Pool and Century Lake

TAPIA PARK: sub-unit of MALIBU CREEK STATE PARK

ridge with a northern view into the heart of Malibu Creek State Park. Wind down the hill to the valley floor, where the Tapia Spur Trail ends at 1.2 miles.

Walk through the campground parking lot, and veer right on the dirt road. Continue to the paved park road and go left. Take the footpath along the left side of the road 300 yards to the "Backcountry Trails" sign, directly across from the main state park parking lot. En route, pass the Malibu Creek Whole Access Trail, a visually impaired trail on the left with interpretive signs in English and Braille.

From the "Backcountry Trails" sign, bear left onto Crags Road. Cross over Las Virgenes Creek as the paved road turns to a narrower dirt road. Pass the signed Grassland Trail on the right, which leads 0.7 miles to Mulholland Highway. Continue straight, parallel

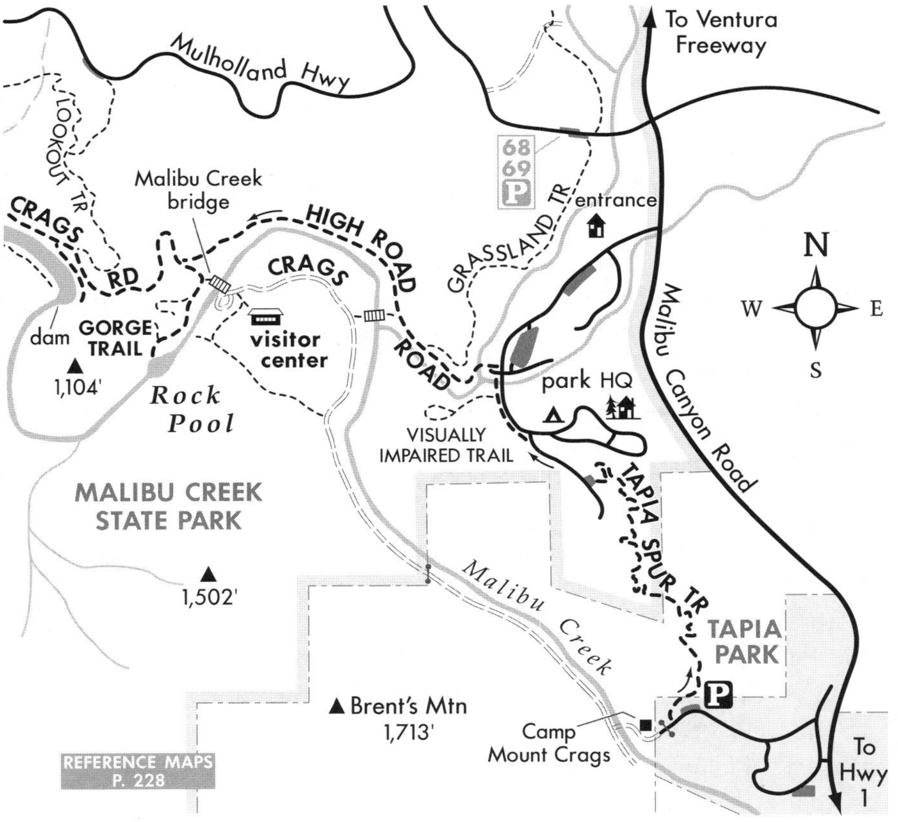

to Malibu Creek, with great views of Goat Buttes and the sloping grassland dotted with valley oak trees. Stroll through oak groves with picture-perfect views (cover photo) to a posted junction.

For a detour to Rock Pool, head left towards the visitor center. Walk 60 yards to a trail on the right, just before the bridge over Malibu Creek that leads to the visitor center. Veer right on the Gorge Trail, and go another 100 yards to a picnic area. The dirt road bends to the right and climbs to the top of the rock formations. Continue straight, staying on the canyon bottom among the deeply eroded rock formations with caves. Follow the west side of the canyon to Rock Pool by a massive, rock-walled gorge.

Return to Crags Road and continue a half mile west to a footpath on the left. Take the path into a lush, shaded canopy with ferns and moss-covered boulders. The short path ends at the dam overlooking Century Lake by another steep-walled gorge. Return again to Crags Road and head northwest, passing the Lookout Trail and Cage Creek Trail on the right. Stroll through the meadow, surrounded by mountains, and cross Logan's Bridge over Malibu Creek (named after the 1998 film *Logan's Run*, which was filmed here). Walk 75 yards to the signed Forest Trail on the left, where Crags Road becomes a footpath.

Bear left on the Forest Trail and head east through an oak-rimmed meadow. Enter the forest, skirting the south edge of the meadow. Pass towering redwood trees planted in the 1920s by Crag's Country Club members, and a series of weather-etched outcrops. Walk along the south edge of Century Lake, passing more redwoods to the end of the half-mile-long trail. At the dam is another view into the vertical-walled gorge beneath Goat Buttes. Return by retracing your steps.

To extend the hike an additional mile to the *M*A*S*H* site, continue on Crags Road. Follow the perimeter of the Udell Gorge Natural Preserve between the steep rock wall of Goat Buttes on the left and a dense isolated forest along Malibu Creek on the right. At the southeast corner of the wetland, the canyon widens to the *M*A*S*H* site, a meadow beneath Goat Buttes with abandoned vehicle props and a shed with artifacts and photographs from the TV series. ■

73. Hacienda—Backdrop—Bwana Loop

PARAMOUNT RANCH

2813 Cornell Road • Agoura Hills

Hiking distance: 2.2 miles round trip
Hiking time: 1 hour
Configuration: loop
Elevation gain: 200 feet
Difficulty: easy
Exposure: shadeless open slopes
Dogs: allowed
Maps: U.S.G.S. Point Dume • N.P.S. Paramount Ranch Site map
Tom Harrison Maps: Malibu Creek State Park Trail Map

map page 255

Paramount Ranch is an old movie ranch once owned by Paramount Studios in the Agoura Hills. The 326-acre parkland is adjacent to the northwest corner of Malibu Creek State Park. The park contains diverse scenery, including movie sets, meadows, grasslands, coast live oaks, valley oak woodlands, eucalyptus groves, creeks, and volcanic Sugarloaf Peak (the dominant mountain to the southwest). The park continues to be used as a working movie site.

This hike forms a loop on a group of trails that weave through the northern half of the park. The trails lead through landscape that has been filmed in countless movies and television shows over the last several decades. The route begins and ends at Western Town. The town, rebuilt over the years, is currently the 1953 version. The movie set contains a couple blocks of western facades used from the 1950s through the 1990s. Heading out of Western Town, the Hacienda Trail passes the site of an old hacienda built by Paramount in the late 1920s. The Medicine Woman Trail passes through Dr. Quinn's fictional Colorado homestead site from the 1990's series *Dr. Quinn, Medicine Woman*. The Backdrop Trail is a hillside path. It is used for open-space shots because of its multi-layered hills that are clear of powerlines and unmarred by any signs of civilization. The hike returns via the Bwana Trail, crossing open grasslands with oak groves. It was used to portray African grasslands in the 1952 film *Bwana Devil* with Robert Stack.

Just north of Western Town is Marco Polo Hill, named for the film set built in the 1930s depicting ancient China in *The Adventures of Marco Polo*.

To the trailhead

From Santa Monica, drive 12 miles northbound on the Pacific Coast Highway/Highway 1 to Malibu Canyon Road. Turn right (north) and continue 6.5 miles up the winding canyon road to Mulholland Highway. Turn left and drive 3.2 miles on Mulholland Highway to Cornell Road. Turn right and go 0.4 miles to the Paramount Ranch entrance on the left. Turn left and continue 0.3 miles to the parking area.

From the Ventura Freeway/Highway 101 in Agoura Hills, exit on Kanan Road. Head 0.4 miles south to Cornell Road and turn left. Drive 1.8 miles to the ranch entrance on the right (west).

The hike

Walk past the trailhead gate, and cross the bridge over Medea Creek. Wander through or curve around the perimeter of Western Town. Pass the Coyote Trail on the left to the second junction, also on the left. Take the trail 100 yards up the slope to a trail split. Continue straight on the Hacienda Trail. Climb the exposed slope, then drop down into an oak grove overlooking the gorgeous valley. Slowly descend to the valley floor and a T-junction with the Medicine Woman Trail. The right fork returns for a short one-mile loop. For this hike, veer left 25 yards to a Y-fork. The left fork leads a 0.4 miles to private property. Take the Backdrop Trail to the right, and follow the wide trail through chaparral, scrub, and oak-dotted grasslands. Stroll along the contour of the hills, weaving in and out of shady glens. Pass the unmaintained Paramount Ridge Trail on the left to a trail split just before reaching Medea Creek. Make a U-shaped right bend on the Bwana Trail, and begin the return portion of the loop. Parallel the Backdrop Trail on the lower slope. Cross the open, rolling terrain above Medea Creek and veer left. Descend down Marco Polo Hill to the park road. Cross the road and take the footpath, completing the loop at Western Town. Walk through the movie set, returning to the trailhead. ■

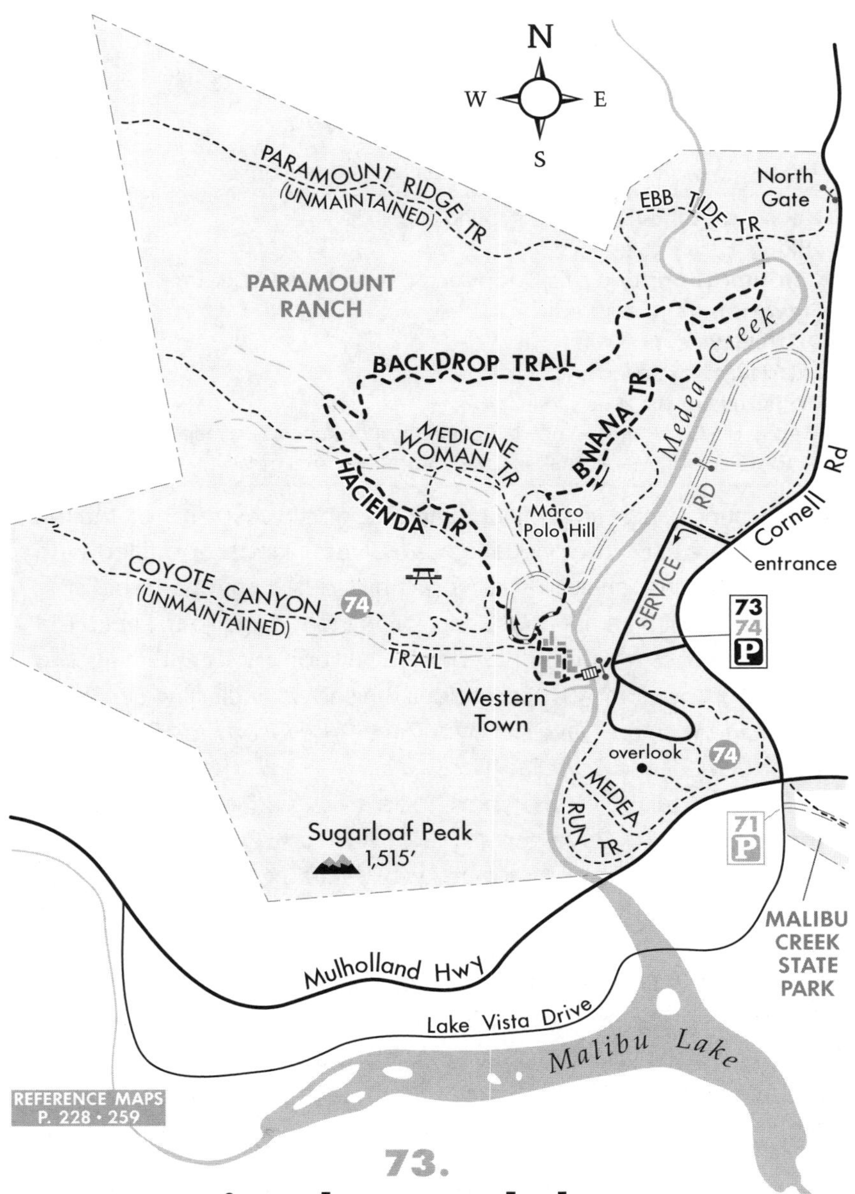

73.
Hacienda–Backdrop–Bwana Loop
PARAMOUNT RANCH

74. Coyote Canyon
Medea Creek—Run Loop

PARAMOUNT RANCH

2813 Cornell Road • Agoura Hills

Hiking distance: 2.75 miles round trip
Hiking time: 1.5 hours
Configuration: two small loops and out-and-back spur trail
Elevation gain: 400 feet
Difficulty: easy
Exposure: exposed
Dogs: allowed
Maps: U.S.G.S. Point Dume • N.P.S. Paramount Ranch Site map
Tom Harrison Maps: Malibu Creek State Park Trail map

Paramount Ranch lies adjacent to the northwest end of Malibu Creek State Park. The parkland has a diverse landscape filled with oak savannahs, chaparral-covered hillsides, canyons, creekside thickets, rolling grasslands, and prominent Sugarloaf Peak. The historic 326-acre ranch has been a motion picture filming site for hundreds of movies and television shows, including *Dr. Quinn, Medicine Woman*; *Have Gun Will Travel*; *The Cisco Kid*; *Gunsmoke*; *The Rifleman*; and *Tom Sawyer.*

This hike takes in two short loop trails within the ranch that represent the diverse terrain. The Medea Creek and Run Trails parallel Medea Creek (a tributary of Malibu Creek) through a riparian zone with willow thickets. The creek flows south through the length of Paramount Ranch into Malibu Lake. The trail loops around an 860-foot hill near Sugarloaf Peak. The second loop follows the Coyote Canyon Trail up a ravine, climbing a chaparral-clad slope to a panorama of the ranch and an overlook of the mountains to the west. To reach the trail, the route leads through the streets of the realistic-looking Western Town movie set with false store fronts, saloons, and hotels.

To the trailhead

From Santa Monica, drive 12 miles northbound on the Pacific Coast Highway/Highway 1 to Malibu Canyon Road. Turn right (north) and continue 6.5 miles to Mulholland Highway. Turn left and drive 3.2 miles to Cornell Road. Turn right and drive 0.4 miles to the Paramount Ranch entrance on the left. Turn left and continue 0.2 miles to the parking area.

From the Ventura Freeway/Highway 101 in Agoura Hills, exit on Kanan Road. Head 0.4 miles south to Cornell Road and turn left. Drive 1.8 miles to the ranch entrance on the right (west).

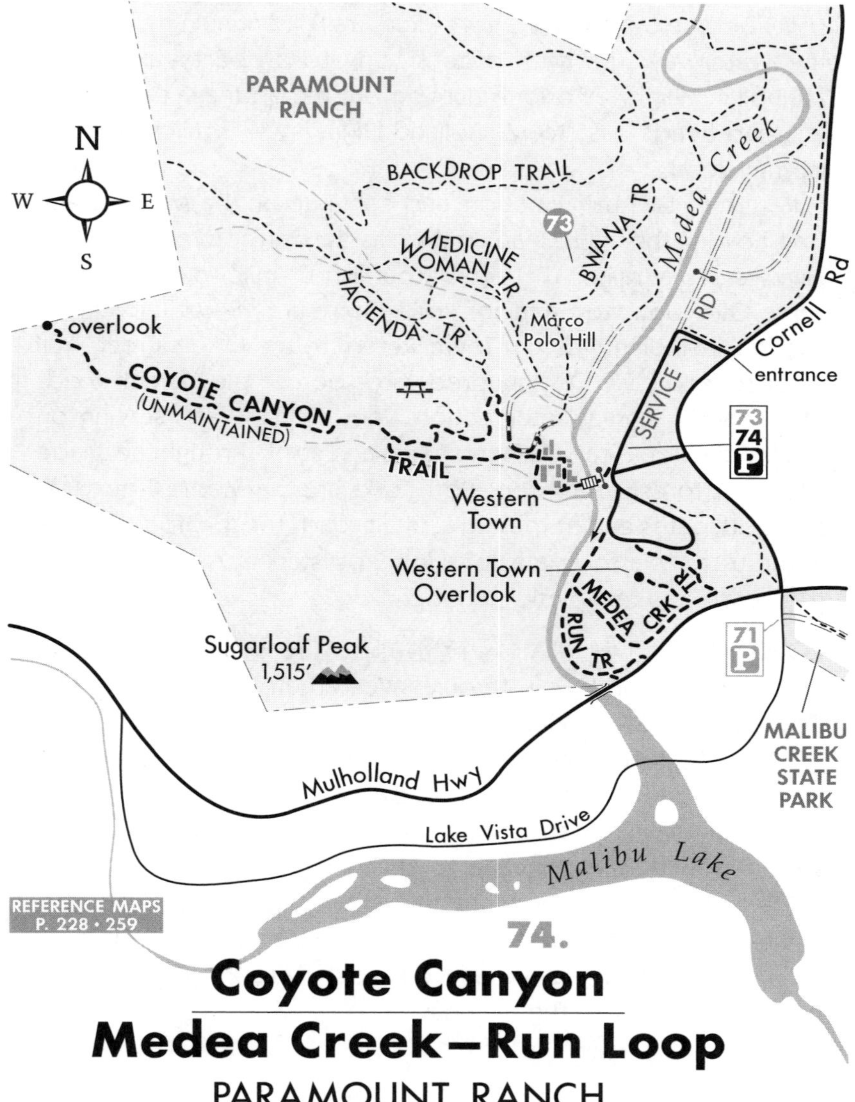

74. Coyote Canyon

Medea Creek—Run Loop

PARAMOUNT RANCH

The hike

MEDIA CREEK AND RUN TRAILS • 1-MILE LOOP: From the parking area, head south on the service road. Parallel Media Creek to a Y-fork. Begin the loop on the right fork, entering an oak and bay laurel forest. Follow Media Creek on the right, with Sugarloaf Peak towering over the trail. A short distance ahead is a trail split. Detour on the right fork (Run Trail), continuing alongside the waterway. The path ends at private property under the Mulholland Highway bridge. Just before the bridge, a trail curves left and heads east to Mulholland Highway, 0.2 miles west of Cornell Road.

Return to the main junction, and continue on the Media Creek Trail, now on the right. Head up the hillside, high above Mulholland Highway, to a trail on the left. Detour left 0.1 mile to the Western Town Overlook atop a minor knoll. There are views in every direction, including Western Town. Return to the Media Creek Trail and proceed east. One hundred yards before the Cornell Road/ Mulholland Highway intersection, veer sharply left, staying on the Media Creek Trail. Descend steps and stroll through the shade of an oak forest to a Y-fork. Both forks are the Media Creek Trail, and both paths end at the old asphalt road. The left fork remains in the trees as a footpath for a longer distance. At the road, go to the left and complete the loop.

COYOTE CANYON TRAIL • 1.75-MILES: Cross the bridge over Medea Creek, and walk through Western Town to the signed Coyote Canyon Trail. Head west up the small ravine to a junction. The left fork leads a half mile on an unmaintained trail to an overlook. The path ends at private property.

Back at the junction, continue on the loop and head northeast, following the ridgeline to another junction. The left fork leads a short distance to a picnic area. Stay to the right, continuing downward to a junction with the Hacienda Trail (Hike 73). Veer right, returning to the paved road by Western Town. Return through the town to the trailhead. ■

75. Peter Strauss Ranch

30000 Mulholland Highway at Troutdale Drive • Agoura Hills

Open Daily: 8 a.m.—5 p.m.

Hiking distance: 1-mile loop
Hiking time: 30 minutes
Configuration: loop
Elevation gain: 200 feet
Difficulty: easy
Exposure: mostly shaded hillside
Dogs: allowed
Maps: U.S.G.S. Point Dume • N.P.S. Peter Strauss Ranch Site map
Tom Harrison Maps: Malibu Creek State Park Trail map

map page 261

Peter Strauss Ranch spreads across 65 acres in Agoura Hills along Mulholland Highway. Triunfo Creek, the main fork of Malibu Creek, flows year around through the ranch. Back in 1926, Harry Miller built a stone ranch house with a white banister, a stone caretaker's

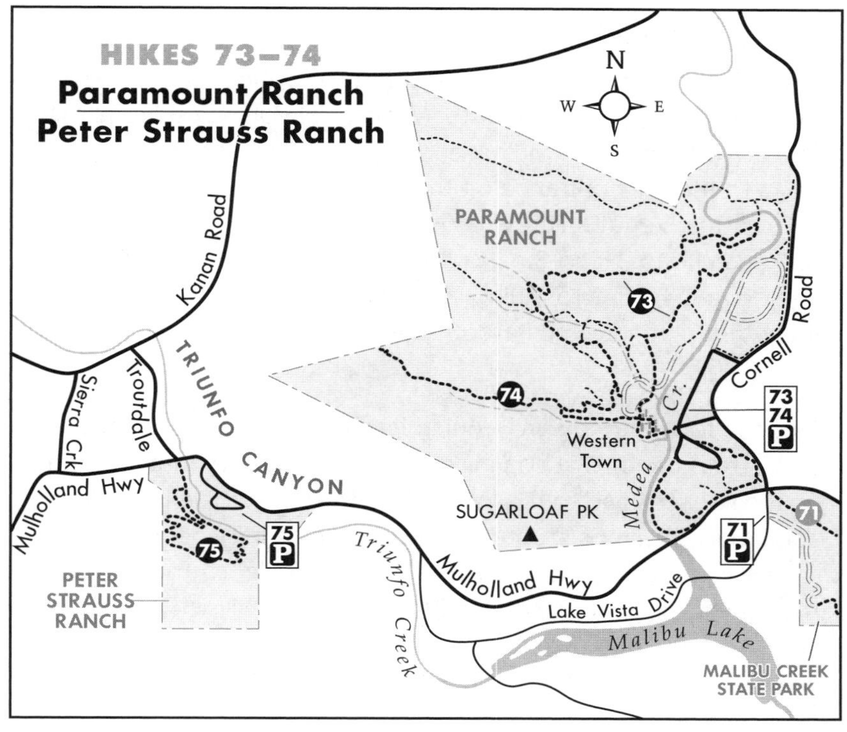

cottage, a giant outdoor aviary, and lookout tower on the property. In the 1930s and 1940s, the ranch became an amusement park and children's summer camp. In the 1940s, a dam was built on Triunfo Creek, forming a lake. The lake was named Lake Enchanto and became a popular swimming, fishing, and boating site. By 1960, the ranch fell into disrepair. The dam washed out in a 1969 flood, and the lake ceased to exist. The ranch was abandoned in the early 1970s. In 1977, actor/producer Peter Strauss purchased the ranch and restored it to a pristine state. He sold it to the Santa Monica Mountains Conservancy in 1983 and the conservancy deeded it to the National Park Service in 1987.

This loop hike explores the stone structures, the outdoor aviary, the tree-shaded lawns along the banks of Triunfo Creek, and the forested hillside terraces. The lush hills are home to diverse habitats with eucalyptus, live oak, scrub oak, California bay, and sycamore groves, with a lush understory of ferns and poison oak.

To the trailhead

From Santa Monica, drive 12 miles northbound on the Pacific Coast Highway/Highway 1 to Malibu Canyon Road. Turn right and drive 6.5 miles to Mulholland Highway. Turn left and drive 5.1 miles to the park entrance on the left.

From the Ventura Freeway/Highway 101 in Agoura Hills, exit on Kanan Road. Head 3 miles south to Troutdale Drive. Turn left and drive 0.4 miles to Mulholland Highway. Turn left and immediately turn right into the Peter Strauss Park entrance.

The hike

Take the footpath towards Mulholland Highway and the entrance arch. Cross the bridge spanning Triunfo Creek, and enter the park on the service road to the left, across from Troutdale Drive. Head south past the amphitheater to the end of the service road by the old Lake Enchanto Dam. Stay to the left, parallel to Triunfo Creek. The forested Peter Strauss Trail traverses the hillside above the creek to a junction. Take the right fork up a series of switchbacks. At the top, the trail levels out and heads west. At the west end, switchbacks zigzag down the slope. Pass small meadows and cross a wooden bridge to a junction. The right fork leads to a picnic area. The left fork completes the loop at the amphitheater and aviary. ■

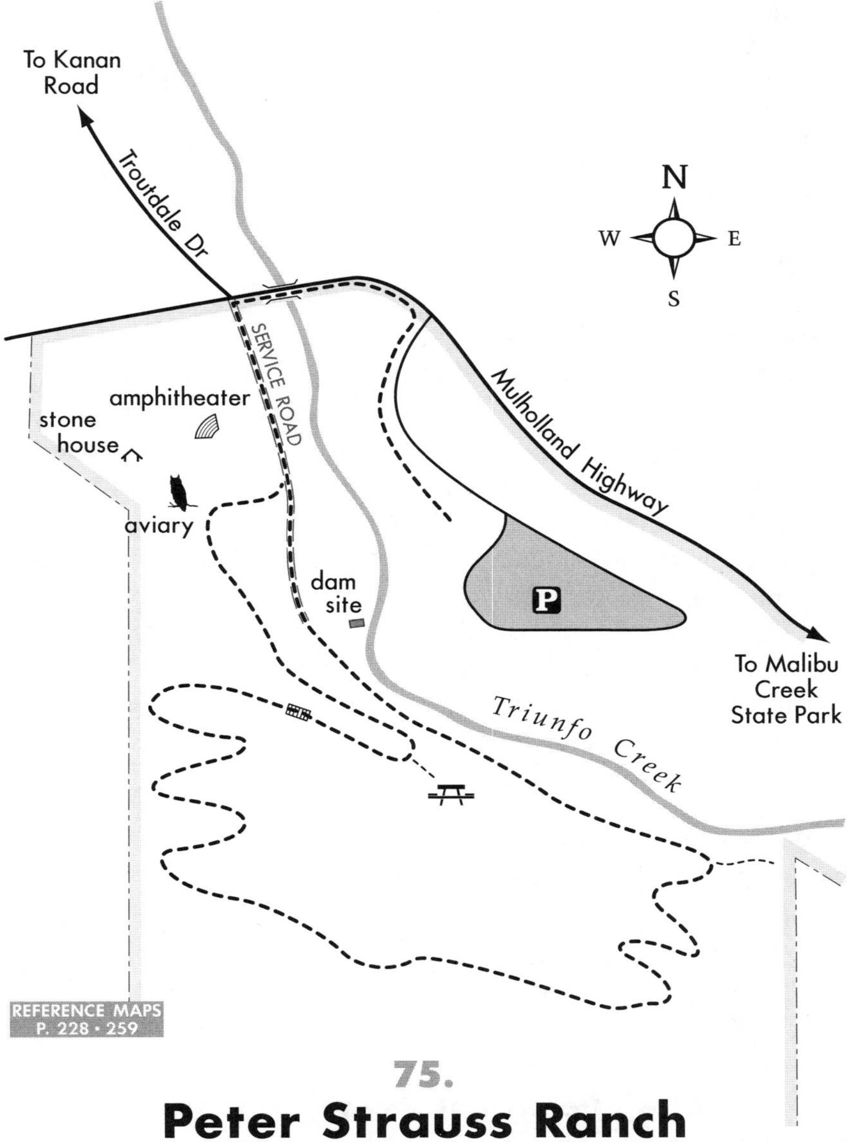

75. Peter Strauss Ranch

76. Mesa Peak

MESA PEAK MOTORWAY from MALIBU CANYON

MALIBU CREEK STATE PARK

Calabasas • Malibu

Hiking distance: 5 miles round trip
Hiking time: 3 hours
Configuration: out-and-back
Elevation gain: 1,400 feet
Difficulty: moderate to strenuous
Exposure: exposed ridge
Dogs: not allowed (but many 4-legged friends have been known to enjoy this trail)
Maps: U.S.G.S. Malibu Beach • Malibu Creek State Park Map
Tom Harrison Maps: Malibu Creek State Park Trail Map

map page 264

Mesa Peak sits on the oceanfront mountains just outside the southern boundary of Malibu Creek State Park. Access to the 1,844-foot peak is via the Mesa Peak Motorway from Corral Canyon (Hike 77) or this hike from Malibu Canyon. Both routes follow the mountain spine along the undeveloped upper, southern portion of Malibu Creek State Park.

This trail from Malibu Canyon follows a forested footpath up to the ridge, connecting with the exposed fire road. From the dramatic ridgetop are spectacular southern views across Santa Monica Bay from Point Dume to Palos Verdes and northern views across Malibu Creek State Park to the San Fernando Valley. The Mesa Peak Motorway is a segment of the Backbone Trail.

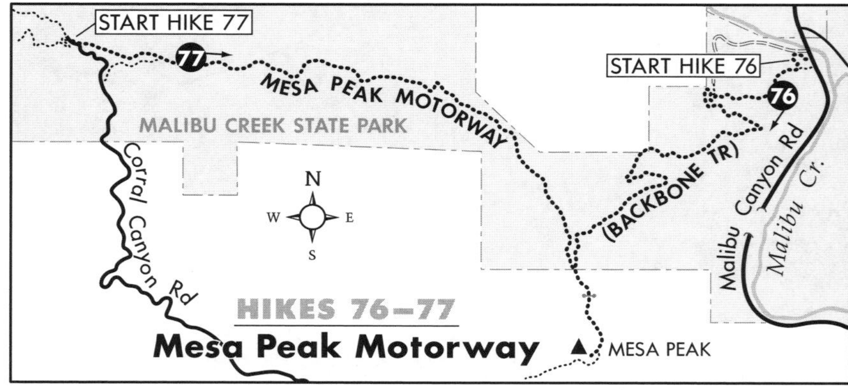

To the trailhead

From Santa Monica, drive 12 miles northbound on the Pacific Coast Highway/Highway 1 to Malibu Canyon Road. Turn right (north) and continue 4.7 miles up the winding canyon road to the paved but unsigned trailhead parking lot on the left. (The parking lot is located 0.1 mile south of the traffic signal at Piuma Road.)

From the Ventura Freeway/Highway 101 in Calabasas, take the Las Virgenes Road exit. Drive 5.1 miles to the Backbone Trail parking lot on the right. (The parking area is located 1.8 miles south of Mulholland Highway.)

The hike

Walk up the slope past the trailhead signs to a posted junction at 100 yards. The trail straight ahead meanders through the hills and dead-ends before reaching the deep gorge at Malibu Creek. Bear left on the Mesa Peak (Backbone) Trail. Wind up the hillside along the wooded canyon wall. At 0.6 miles, the footpath connects with the Mesa Peak Motorway, a dirt fire road. Make a U-shaped left bend around a rock formation. Continue uphill on the serpentine road. There are great views of Brents Mountain, the volcanic Goat Buttes, Malibu Creek State Park to the northwest, and an expanding view of Malibu Canyon. At just under 2 miles, on a sharp right bend, views open up to the Pacific Ocean. Follow the ridge, with 360-degree vistas, to a junction at 2.4 miles by metal posts, located forty yards shy of a sharp right bend. The Mesa Peak Motorway (Backbone Trail) continues straight ahead.

Bear left, leaving the main road on the Puerco Motorway. Drop down and cross a saddle between Malibu Canyon and Corral Canyon. Pass through an open gate at the base of Mesa Peak, leaving Malibu Creek State Park. The dirt road curves around Mesa Peak and descends down Puerco Canyon to the Pacific Coast Highway at Puerco Beach. For this hike, at the base of Mesa Peak, is a short but steep path that climbs to the 1,844-foot summit. From the summit are sweeping coastal views across Santa Monica Bay from the north end at Point Dume to the southern end at Palos Verdes. Inland vistas expand across the layered mountain range. Return by retracing your steps. ■

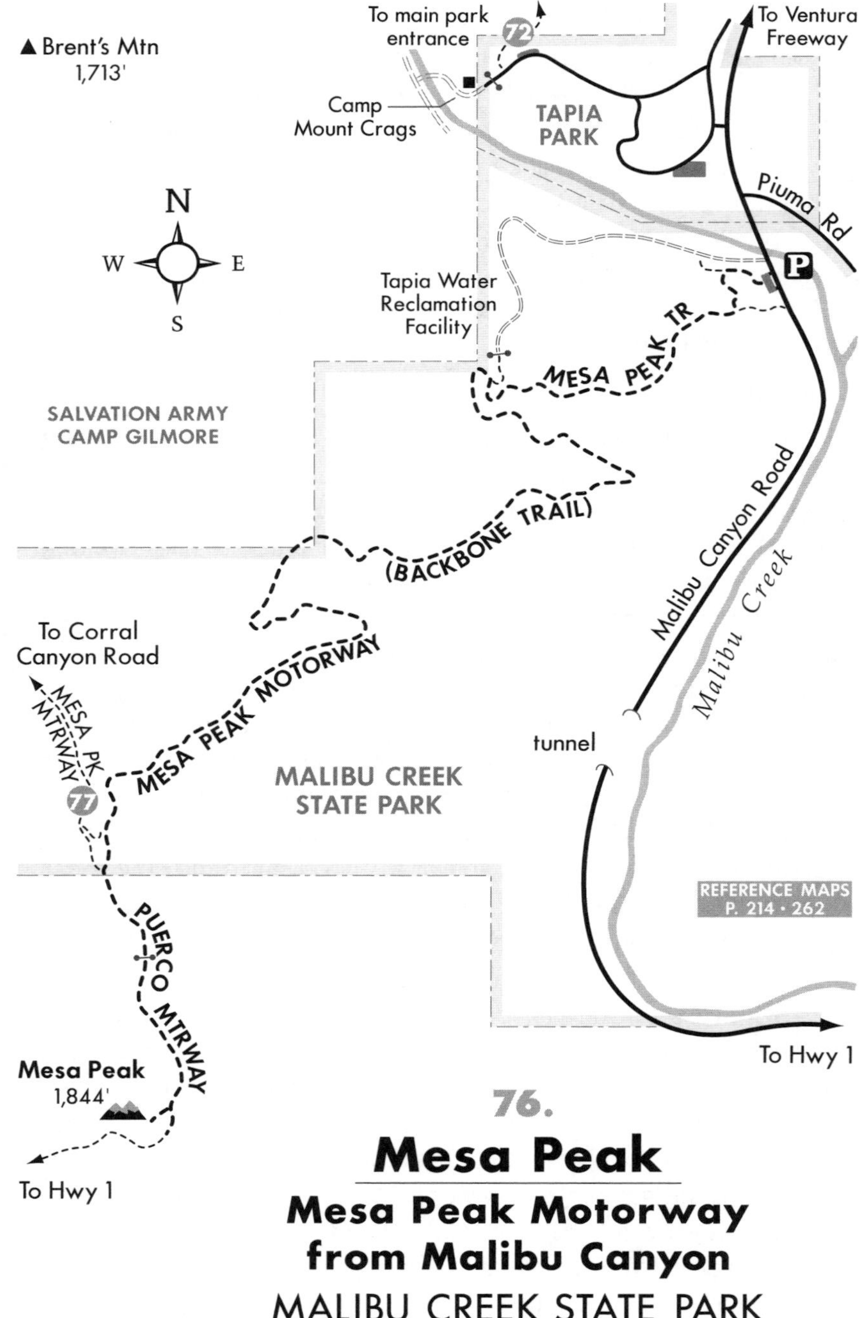

76. Mesa Peak

Mesa Peak Motorway from Malibu Canyon

MALIBU CREEK STATE PARK

77. Mesa Peak

MESA PEAK MOTORWAY from CORRAL CANYON

MALIBU CREEK STATE PARK

Malibu

Hiking distance: 6.6 miles round trip
Hiking time: 3 hours
Configuration: out-and-back
Elevation gain: 250 feet
Difficulty: moderate to somewhat strenuous
Exposure: exposed ridge
Dogs: not allowed (but many 4-legged friends have been known to enjoy this trail)
Maps: U.S.G.S. Point Dume and Malibu Beach
Tom Harrison Maps: Malibu Creek State Park Trail Map
Malibu Creek State Park Map

map page 266

Mesa Peak sits on the oceanfront mountains just outside the southern boundary of Malibu Creek State Park. Access to the 1,844-foot peak is via the Mesa Peak Motorway from Malibu Canyon (Hike 76) or this hike from Corral Canyon by Castro Crest. Both routes follow the mountain spine along the undeveloped upper, southern portion of Malibu Creek State Park.

This hike from Corral Canyon begins in a garden of massive warped and weathered sandstone. Among the wind-eroded sedimentary rock are caves and stone arches that look like windows in the rock. The trail follows the exposed spine of the Santa Monica Mountains. The spectacular views include Santa Monica Bay in the south, from Point Dume to Palos Verdes, and northern views across Malibu Creek State Park to the San Fernando Valley. The Mesa Peak Motorway is a segment of the Backbone Trail.

To the trailhead

From Santa Monica, drive 14.5 miles northbound on the Pacific Coast Highway/Highway 1 to Corral Canyon Road. Turn right and wind 5.2 miles to the end of the paved road. Continue 0.1 mile on the dirt road to the trailhead parking area at the end of the road.

The only access to the trailhead is from the coast. Corral Canyon Road is located 2.5 miles west of Malibu Canyon Road and 3.5 miles east of Kanan Dume Road.

The hike

From the east side of the parking area, take the posted trail east. Follow the dirt and sandstone slab path towards the gorgeous rock formations. Climb the slab rock and weave through the formations to a ridge. Climb the ridge to another amazing group of cave-riddled sandstone formations. Cross over and through the rock sculptures, then descend to the Mesa Peak Motorway at 0.4 miles. Stay to the left on the dirt road, part of the Backbone Trail. The views extend into the Kaslow Natural Preserve (a nesting ground for golden eagles), across

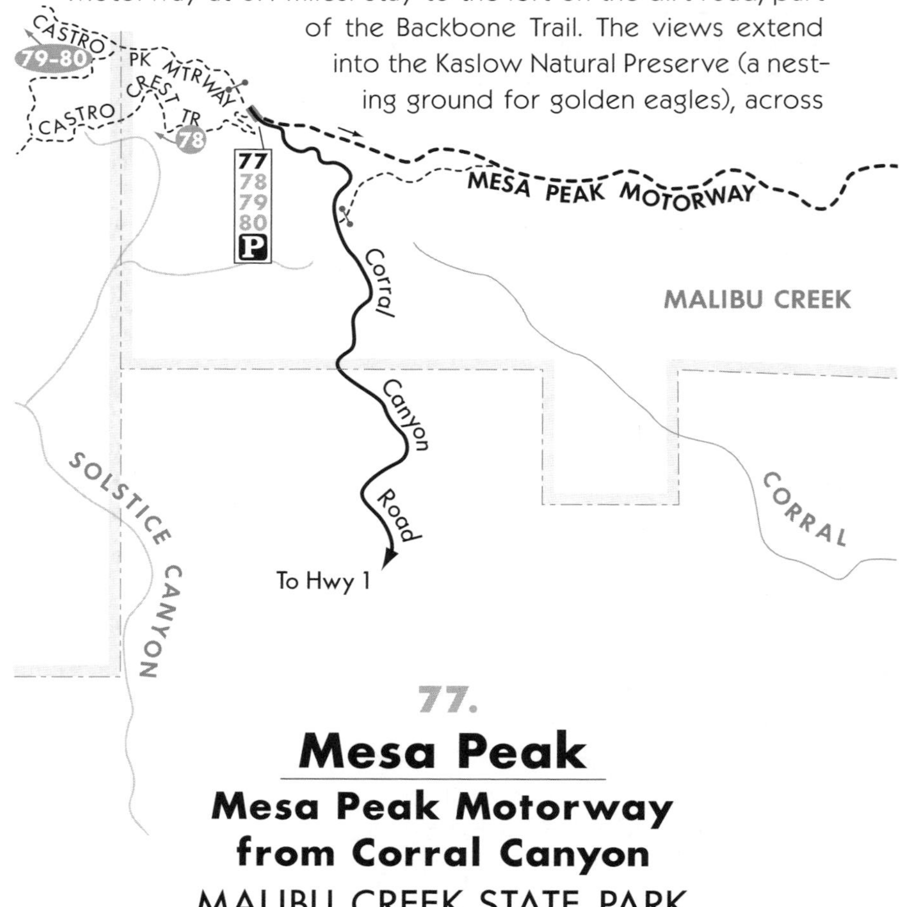

77. Mesa Peak

Mesa Peak Motorway from Corral Canyon

MALIBU CREEK STATE PARK

Malibu Creek State Park on the left and Corral Canyon and the Pacific Ocean on the right. Follow the undulating road, with alternating views of the San Fernando Valley and the coast. Make a long, but easy descent on the open ridge to a saddle while savoring the great views. Cross the saddle and head up the serpentine road. Descend to a trail split at 3 miles. The Mesa Peak Motorway (Backbone Trail) continues east 2.4 miles and ends at Malibu Creek Road (Hike 76).

To ascend Mesa Peak, bear right on the Puerco Motorway. Drop down and cross a saddle between Malibu Canyon and Corral Canyon. Pass through an open gate at the base of Mesa Peak, leaving Malibu Creek State Park. The dirt road curves around Mesa Peak and descends down Puerco Canyon to the Pacific Coast Highway at Puerco Beach. For this hike, at the base of Mesa Peak is a short but steep path that climbs to the 1,844-foot summit. From the summit are sweeping coastal views across Santa Monica Bay, from the northern end at Point Dume to the southern end at Palos Verdes. Inland vistas expand across the layered mountain range. Return by retracing your steps. ■

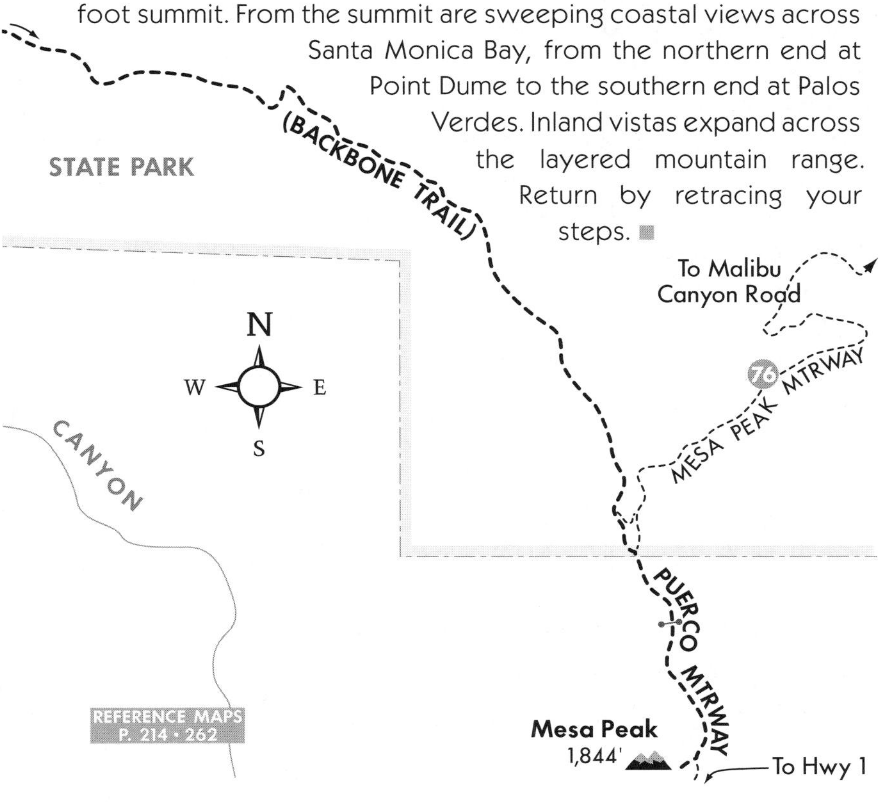

78. Castro Crest Trail from Corral Canyon Road

CASTRO CREST N.P.S.

Malibu

Hiking distance: 8.4 miles round trip
Hiking time: 4.5 hours
Configuration: out-and-back with some exposure
Elevation gain: 600 feet
Difficulty: moderate to strenuous
Exposure: mostly forested
Dogs: allowed
Maps: U.S.G.S. Point Dume · Malibu Creek State Park Map
Tom Harrison Maps: Malibu Creek State Park Trail Map

The Castro Crest Trail, a portion of the Backbone Trail, weaves through upper Solstice Canyon and Newton Canyon to Latigo Canyon Road. This remote and isolated section of trail follows the canyon beneath Castro Crest, a jagged sandstone mountain stretching over two miles. The footpath descends to a lush riparian forest with oak and sycamore woodlands along the waterways in verdant Solstice Canyon. The trail then leads up to the drainage divide with Newton Canyon beneath the shadow of 2,824-foot Castro Peak, the fifth highest peak in the mountain range and easily identified by its radio towers. From the high ridges at both ends of the trail are panoramic views over the Santa Monica Range and across the ocean.

To the trailhead

From Santa Monica, drive 14.5 miles northbound on the Pacific Coast Highway/Highway 1 to Corral Canyon Road. Turn right and wind 5.2 miles to the end of the paved road. Continue 0.1 mile on the dirt road to the trailhead parking area at the end of the road.

The only access is from the coast. Corral Canyon Road is located 2.5 miles west of Malibu Canyon Road and 3.5 miles east of Kanan Dume Road.

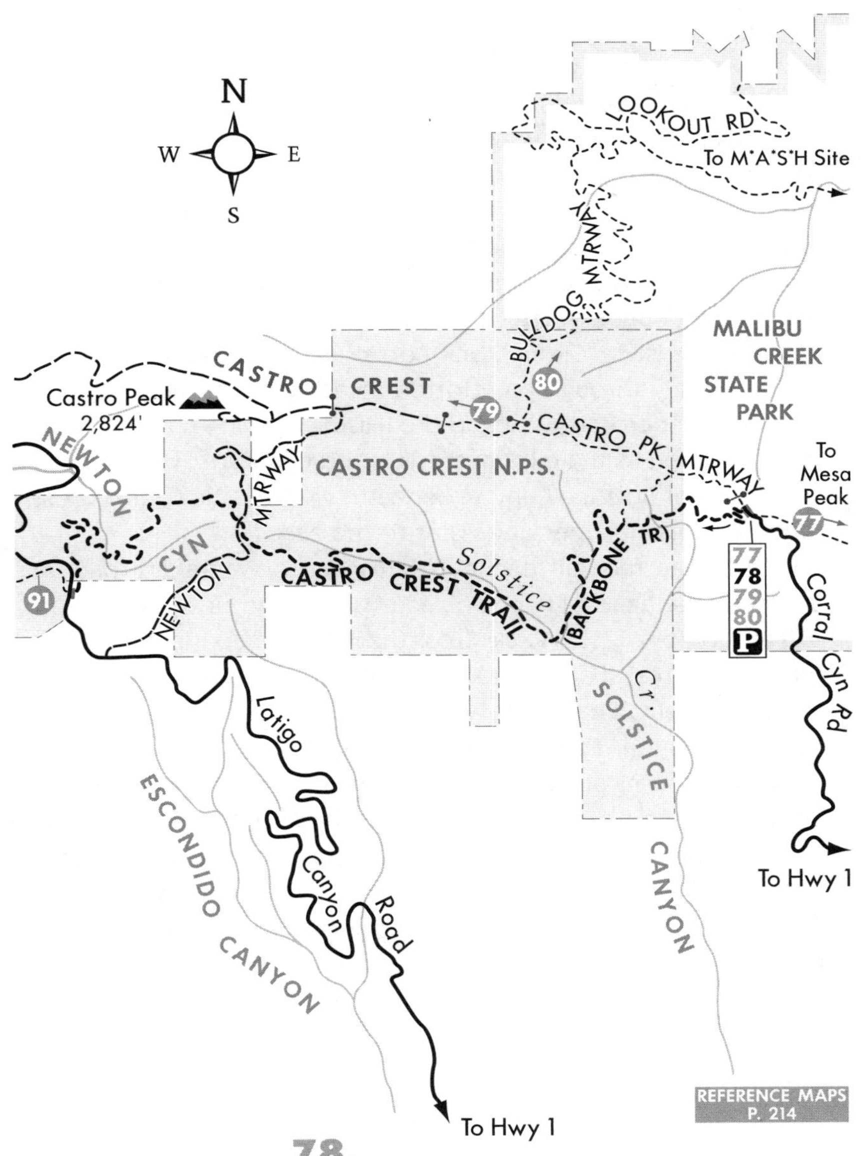

78. Castro Crest Trail

from Corral Canyon Road

CASTRO CREST N.P.S.

The hike

Head west on the posted Castro Crest Trail. Weave down the south-facing mountain slope into Solstice Canyon, overlooking the stream-fed canyons on the left that feed Solstice Creek. Towering above the trail to the north are the magnificent Castro Crest formations. Wind in and out of the shaded drainages while following the mountain contours. Gently descend to the canyon floor, crossing two seasonal streams. At the canyon bottom, veer right and continue west. Walk up canyon along the south side of Upper Solstice Creek. Rock-hop over the creek eight times while strolling through oak-dotted meadows and shaded glens. After the last crossing, ascend the hillside, leaving the lush riparian vegetation to the exposed scrub and chaparral. Traverse the south wall of Solstice Canyon beneath the dramatic Castro Crest mountains and far-reaching vistas to the east.

At 2.8 miles, the trail reaches Newton Motorway, a dirt road on a ridge at the head of both Solstice Canyon and Newton Canyon, 575 feet below Castro Peak. Cross the road and continue west on the Castro Crest (Backbone) Trail, contouring along the southern slope of Castro Peak. Follow the north canyon wall high above Newton Canyon. Top a hill to a coastal vista and a view of the Boney Mountains at Point Mugu State Park. Descend into Newton Canyon on a serpentine course. Enter the shady forest, and cross Newton Creek on the canyon floor. Ascend the slope and climb to Latigo Canyon Road at the trailhead parking area. The Newton Canyon Trail, a section of the Backbone Trail, is directly across Latigo Canyon Road (Hike 89). Return by retracing your route. ■

79. Castro Peak Motorway

CASTRO CREST N.P.S.

Malibu

Hiking distance: 2.2 miles round trip
Hiking time: 1.5 hour
Configuration: out-and-back
Elevation gain: 600 feet
Difficulty: easy to moderate
Exposure: exposed
Dogs: allowed
Maps: U.S.G.S. Point Dume • Malibu Creek State Park Trail Map
Tom Harrison Maps: Malibu Creek State Park Trail Map

map page 273

Castro Peak is a 2,824-foot peak near the geographical center of the Santa Monica Mountains. The peak, covered with radio towers and antennas, stands out on Castro Crest, a massive, two-mile-long wall of grey weathered sandstone that stretches high above Solstice Canyon. This hike on the Castro Peak Motorway follows the east-west ridge along the top of Castro Crest. The trail lies above Malibu Creek State Park to the north and Solstice Canyon to the south. There are fantastic inland views of Triunfo Canyon, Malibu Lake, and the San Fernando Valley to the Santa Susana Mountains. The coastal views extend down Solstice Canyon to the crescent-shaped Santa Monica Bay, from Point Dume to Palos Verdes. The unpaved fire road links to the Bulldog Motorway (Hike 80), a 3.5-mile fire road that connects Castro Crest with Malibu Creek State Park near the M*A*S*H television series filming site.

Unfortunately, the property owner near Castro Peak has a bitter dispute with the park service. Consequently, the Castro Peak Motorway is gated at 1.1 miles, eliminating public access to Castro Peak. The threatening signs near the gate, along with surveillance cameras, are so intense that, beyond the disappointment, it is laughable and a unique oddity to visit.

To the trailhead

From Santa Monica, drive 14.5 miles northbound on the Pacific Coast Highway/Highway 1 to Corral Canyon Road. Turn right and wind 5.2 miles to the end of the paved road. Continue 0.1 mile on the dirt road to the trailhead parking area at the end of the road.

The only access is from the coast. Corral Canyon Road is located 2.5 miles west of Malibu Canyon Road and 3.5 miles east of Kanan Dume Road.

The hike

From the trailhead parking lot, the posted Backbone Trail heads west on the Castro Crest Trail to Latigo Canyon (Hike 78) and east on the Mesa Peak Trail to Mesa Peak and Malibu Canyon (Hike 77). For this hike, walk up the dirt road (the extension of Corral Canyon Road) to the vehicle gate. Pass the gate on the Castro Peak Motorway, and follow the east canyon wall high above Solstice Canyon. Follow the sandstone cliffs to a connector trail with the Castro Crest (Backbone) Trail at 0.2 miles. Staying to the right, continue uphill while enjoying the far-reaching coastal views. Cross over to the north-facing slope with views across the San Fernando Valley, from the Topatopa Mountains at Ojai to the San Gabriel Mountains. Pass through a magnificent display of sandstone outcroppings. At 0.8 miles is a signed junction by a stunning sandstone peak. The Bulldog Motorway (Hike 80) goes right. Stay atop the ridge and continue straight. Pass another awesome display of rock formations. To the right is a view into Malibu Creek State Park, Goat Buttes, and Malibu Lake. Veer left into the shade of an oak grove to the end of the public trail at 1.1 mile. Huge signs that state "No Trespassing," "Stay Out," "Violators Will Be Prosecuted," and "Live Video Surveillance" warmly welcome hikers. Return by retracing your steps. ■

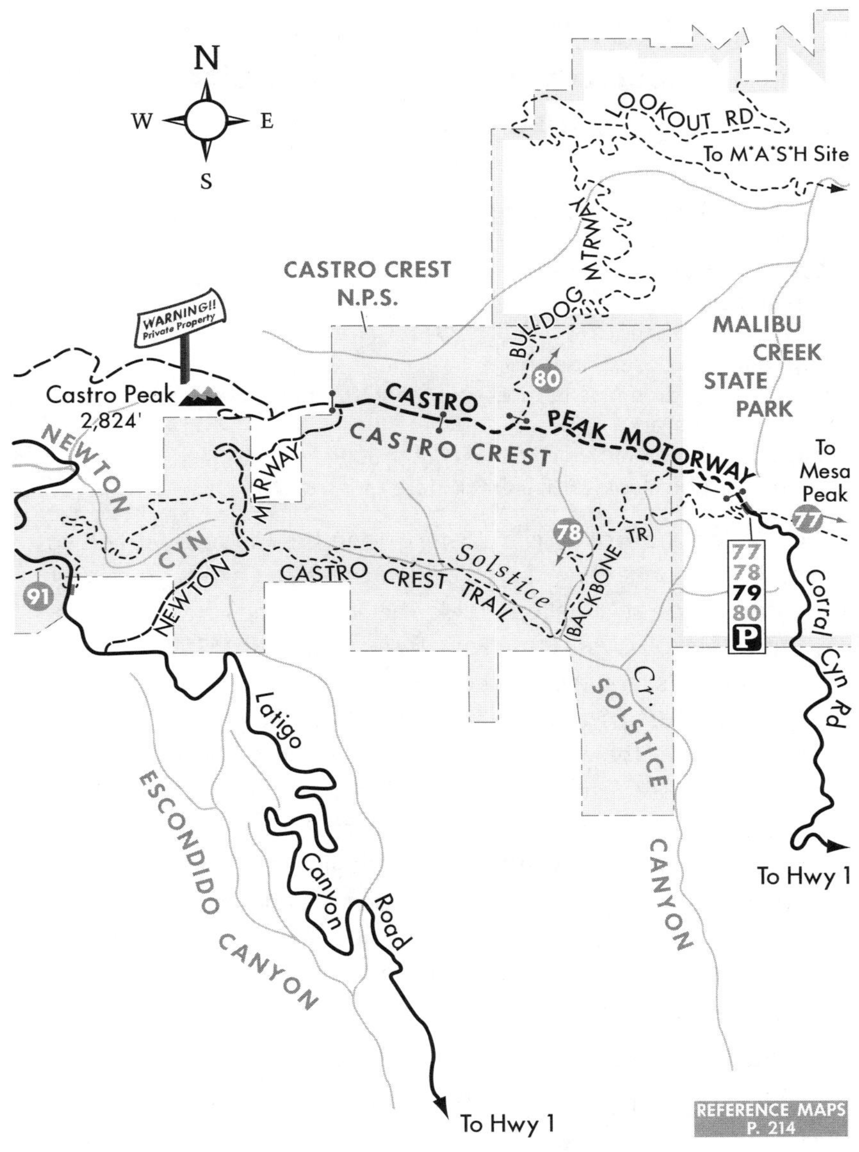

79.

Castro Peak Motorway

CASTRO CREST N.P.S.

80. Bulldog Motorway
Castro Crest to M*A*S*H Site
MALIBU CREEK STATE PARK

Malibu

Hiking distance: 9.4 miles round trip
Hiking time: 5 hours
Configuration: out-and-back
Elevation gain: 1,700 feet
Difficulty: strenuous
Exposure: exposed open ridge
Dogs: allowed on first 1.2 miles, but thereafter not allowed in Malibu Creek State Park
Maps: U.S.G.S. Point Dume • Malibu Creek State Park Trail Map
Tom Harrison Maps: Malibu Creek State Park Trail Map

The Bulldog Motorway is a 3.5-mile-long fire (and powerline access) road connecting the mountain ridge at Castro Crest with Triunfo Canyon and Malibu Creek. The serpentine dirt road, mostly within Malibu Creek State Park, leads to the *M*A*S*H* television series filming site in the heart of the state park. From Castro Crest, just east of Castro Peak, the trail drops 1,800 feet, offering spectacular vistas all the way to the valley floor. The Bulldog Motorway can be accessed from either Triunfo Canyon (via Mulholland Highway) or from this hike via the Castro Peak Motorway at the top of Corral Canyon Road. The hike begins on Castro Crest and follows the spine of the Santa Monica Mountains, overlooking Solstice Canyon, the Pacific Ocean, Malibu Creek State Park, and the inland valleys. The trail then makes a dramatic descent to the floor of Triunfo Canyon.

To the trailhead

From Santa Monica, drive 14.5 miles northbound on the Pacific Coast Highway/Highway 1 to Corral Canyon Road. Turn right and wind 5.2 miles to the end of the paved road. Continue 0.1 mile on the dirt road to the trailhead parking area at the end of the road.

The only access is from the coast. Corral Canyon Road is located 2.5 miles west of Malibu Canyon Road and 3.5 miles east of Kanan Dume Road.

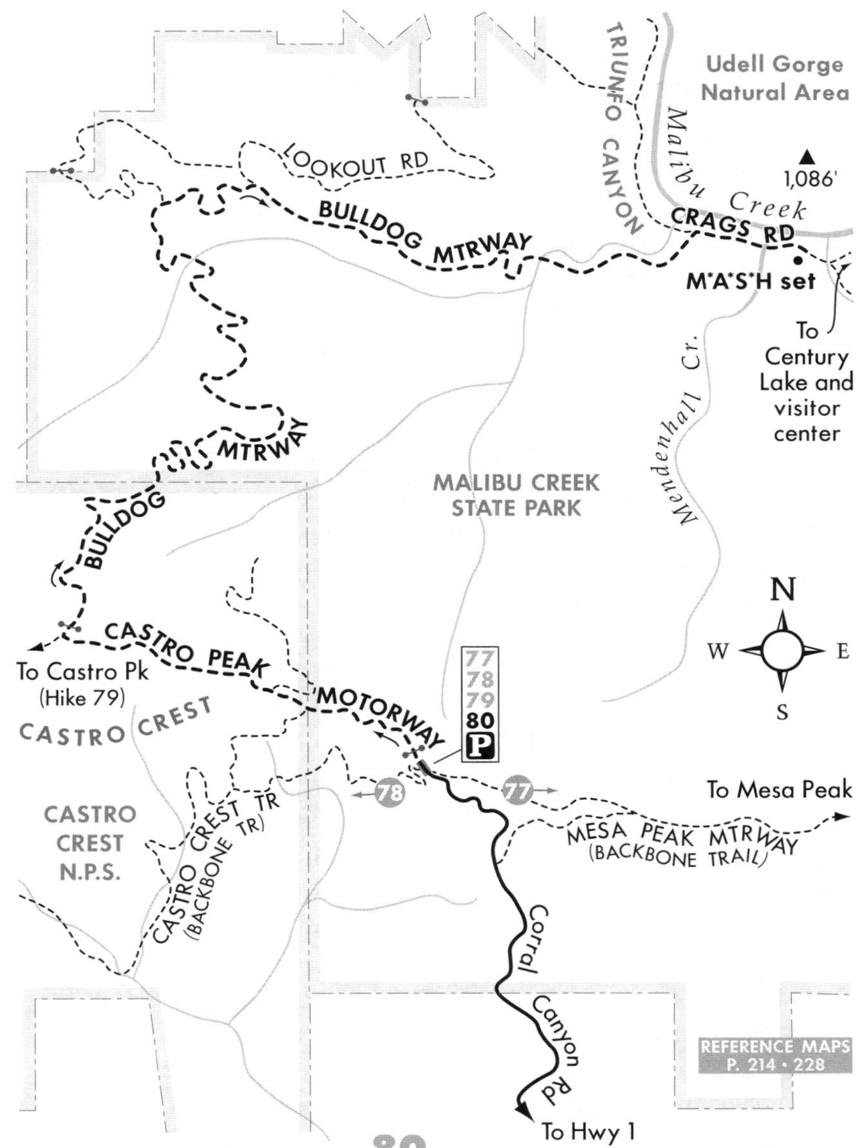

80. Bulldog Motorway Castro Crest to M*A*S*H Site

MALIBU CREEK STATE PARK

The hike

From the trailhead parking lot, the posted Backbone Trail heads west on the Castro Crest Trail to Latigo Canyon (Hike 78) and east on the Mesa Peak Trail to Mesa Peak and Malibu Canyon (Hike 77). For this hike, walk up the dirt road (the extension of Corral Canyon Road) to the vehicle gate. Pass the gate on the Castro Peak Motorway, and follow the east canyon wall high above Solstice Canyon. Follow the sandstone cliffs to a connector trail with the Castro Crest (Backbone) Trail at 0.2 miles. Staying to the right, continue uphill while enjoying the far-reaching coastal views. Cross over to the north-facing slope with views across the San Fernando Valley, from the Topatopa Mountains at Ojai to the San Gabriel Mountains. Pass through a magnificent display of sandstone outcroppings. At 0.8 miles is a signed junction by a stunning sandstone peak. The Castro Peak Motorway (Hike 83) continues straight ahead, passing additional sandstone formations to the gated private land.

For this hike, bear right on the Bulldog Motorway, skirting the east side of the sandstone peak. Pass through a gate and enter the no-dog zone of Malibu Creek State Park. Gently descend among sandstone boulders, with a view into the heart of Malibu Creek State Park, Goat Buttes, and Malibu Lake. The vast northern views extend for miles. Wind down the mountain at an easy grade, losing 1,300 feet over 2.5 miles. Cross a seasonal tributary of Malibu Creek to a trail junction on the valley floor at 3.5 miles.

Bear right, staying on the Bulldog Motorway. Stroll along the scenic oak-dotted valley for a mile, paralleling the stream to a fork on the south edge of the Udell Gorge Natural Preserve. The left branch leads to the dam and picnic area by the east end of Malibu Lake. Go to the right on Crags Road, and walk through the oak-filled meadows and wetland. Cross Mendenhall Creek and enter the *M*A*S*H* site. Walk around the meadow surrounded by mountains, made famous by the opening sequence of the long-running television series. The site contains rusted vehicles abandoned after filming and an unlocked shed with artifacts and photographs from the series. This is our turn-around spot. Return by retracing your steps. ■

81. Malibu Lagoon State Beach

MALIBU POINT

23200 Pacific Coast Highway • Malibu

Hiking distance: 1.5 miles round trip
Hiking time: 1 hour
Configuration: out-and-back
Elevation gain: level
Difficulty: easy
Exposure: exposed beachfront
Dogs: not allowed
Maps: U.S.G.S. Malibu Beach
Tom Harrison Maps: Malibu Creek State Park Trail map

map page 278

Malibu Lagoon State Beach encompasses 167 acres in the heart of Malibu, with 22 acres of wetlands, a brackish lagoon at the mouth of perennial Malibu Creek, and nearly a mile of ocean frontage. The sand-barred lagoon, just off Malibu Point, is a resting and feeding estuary for more than 200 species of migrating and native birds on the Pacific Flyway. The state beach includes a museum; 35-acre Surfrider Beach, popularized by surfing movies in the 1950s and 1960s; and Malibu Pier, a 700-foot long pier in a cove called Kellers Shelter. The historic pier dates back to 1903 and was rebuilt in 1946. To the west of Malibu Point is the exclusive Malibu Colony gated community. Nature trails meander to the beach and around the lagoon.

To the trailhead

From Santa Monica, drive 11 miles northbound on the Pacific Coast Highway/Highway 1 to Cross Creek Road by the posted Malibu Lagoon State Beach turnoff. (The turnoff is 1.1 miles east/southbound of Malibu Canyon Road.) Turn left into the park, passing the entrance station to the parking lot. A parking fee is required.

The hike

Take the paved path from the south (ocean) side of the parking lot, crossing a series of bridges over the wetlands and lagoon. The path ends at the sandy beach on Malibu Point at the north end of Surfrider Beach. From here there are several walking options. Stroll south along Surfrider Beach to the Malibu Pier. Or, head north from Malibu Point along Malibu Beach in front of the Malibu Colony homes. (On this route, stay below the high-tide water line to avoid property owner hassles.) The third choice is to loop around the lagoon on the sandy beach.

Back at the trailhead, on the far end of the parking lot, a bridge crosses an arm of the lagoon on estuary trails to a junction. The right fork leads through tall brush to a small opening at the lagoon. The left fork winds through the brush under the Pacific Coast Highway to the main lagoon channel. ■

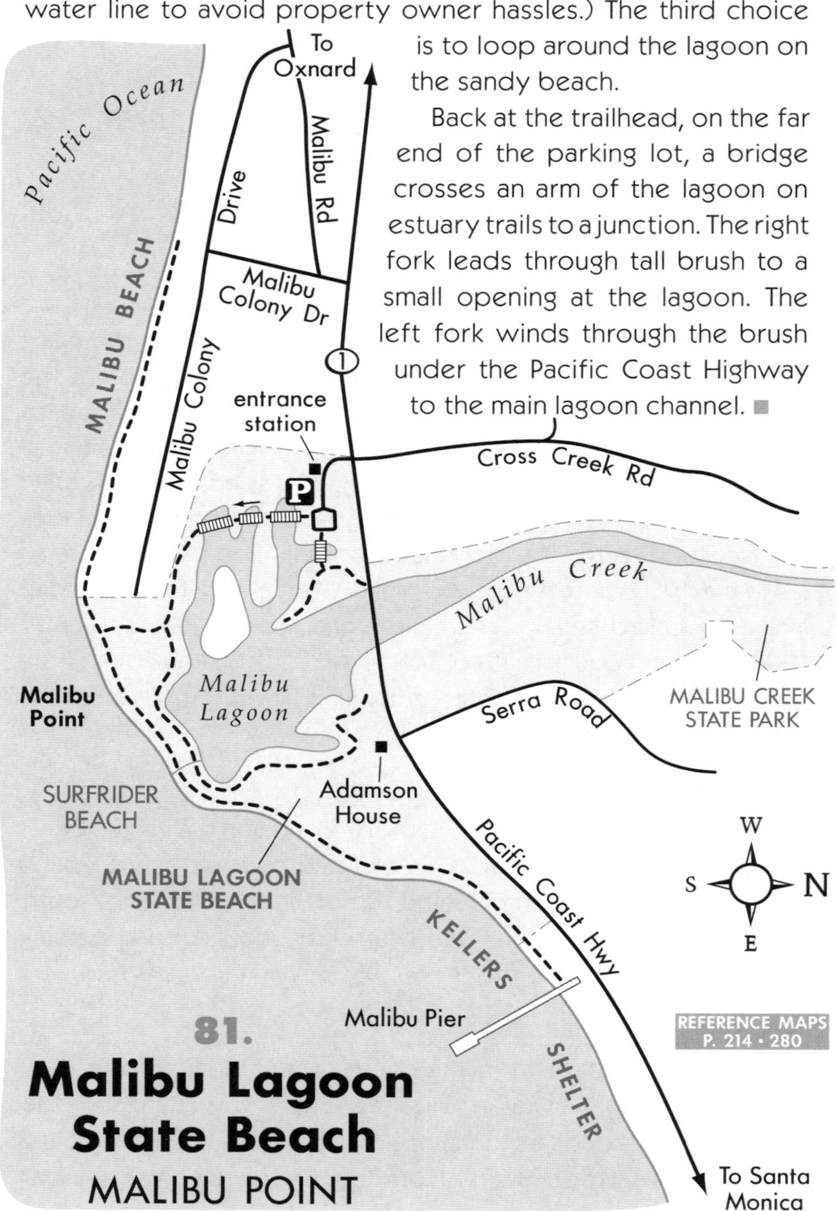

81. Malibu Lagoon State Beach

MALIBU POINT

82. Malibu Bluffs

24250 Pacific Coast Highway • Malibu

Hiking distance: 2-mile loop
Hiking time: 1 hour
Configuration: loop
Elevation gain: 100 feet
Difficulty: easy
Exposure: exposed oceanfront
Dogs: allowed
Maps: U.S.G.S. Malibu Beach
Tom Harrison Maps: Malibu Creek State Park Trail map

map page 281

Malibu Bluffs Open Space comprises 84 acres on the bluffs between the Pacific Coast Highway and Malibu Road, directly opposite of Pepperdine University and Malibu Canyon Road. The 100-foot mountain cliffs rise above Amarillo Beach and Puerco Beach and are covered with coastal sage scrub, willow scrub, and open grasslands. Five public stairways (which adjoin private property) lead down to the shoreline from the base of the bluffs. The open space is adjacent to Malibu Bluffs Community Park, a developed six-acre park with spacious lawns, baseball diamonds, soccer fields, picnic areas, a free parking lot, and a paved walkway lining the park's periphery. This hike begins from the expansive lawns in Malibu Bluffs Community Park. The hike forms an easy loop across the plateau that includes both coastal and mountain views.

To the trailhead

From Santa Monica, drive 12 miles northbound on the Pacific Coast Highway/Highway 1 to Malibu Canyon Road by Pepperdine University. Turn left into the posted Malibu Bluffs Community Park parking lot.

The hike

From the northwest corner of the parking lot, take the path closest to the Pacific Coast Highway and head west. Cross the meadow, passing a pocket of eucalyptus trees on the right, to a T-junction at the edge of deep Marie Canyon. The right fork exits the parkland to the Pacific Coast Highway, just east of John Tyler Drive. Bear left and follow the east rim of the canyon to the bluffs closest to the ocean. Curve left along the edge of the bluffs to a junction. The right fork descends to the oceanfront homes and coastal access stairways at Malibu Road. Bear left and cross the footbridge over a minor drainage to another junction. The right fork gradually climbs to a picnic area at the southwest corner of Malibu Bluffs Community Park. Take the left fork 100 yards, following the east side of the gully. Two switchbacks zigzag up the hillside to great views of Pepperdine University and the Santa Monica Mountains. Continue to a trail fork. The left fork heads straight to the trailhead. Go to the right, climbing to a picnic area and paved path. Follow the blufftop path to the left and circle the park, passing the ball fields while overlooking Malibu Point (Hike 81). The path ends on the park road. Return along the road to the left. ■

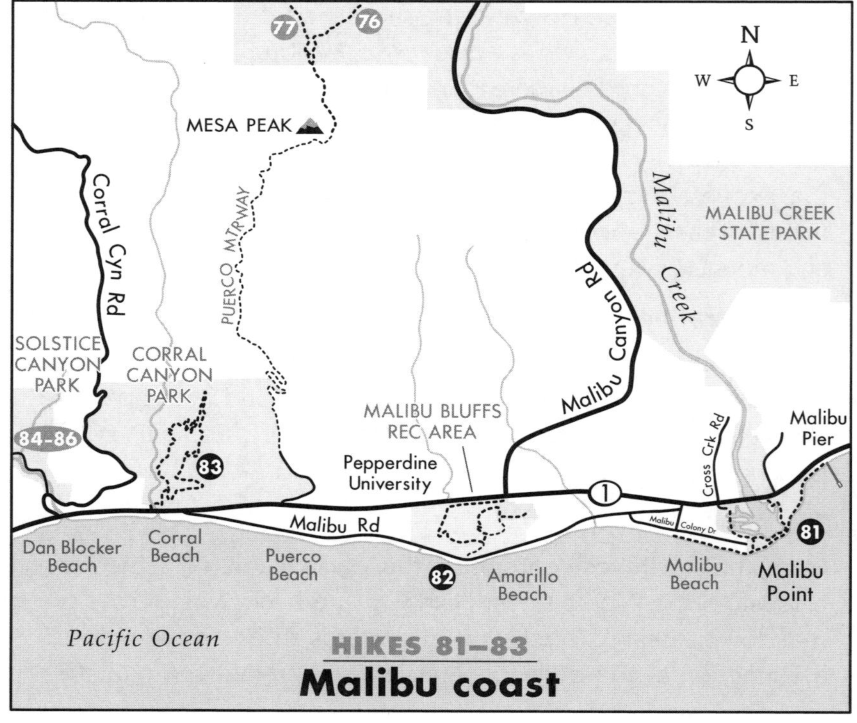

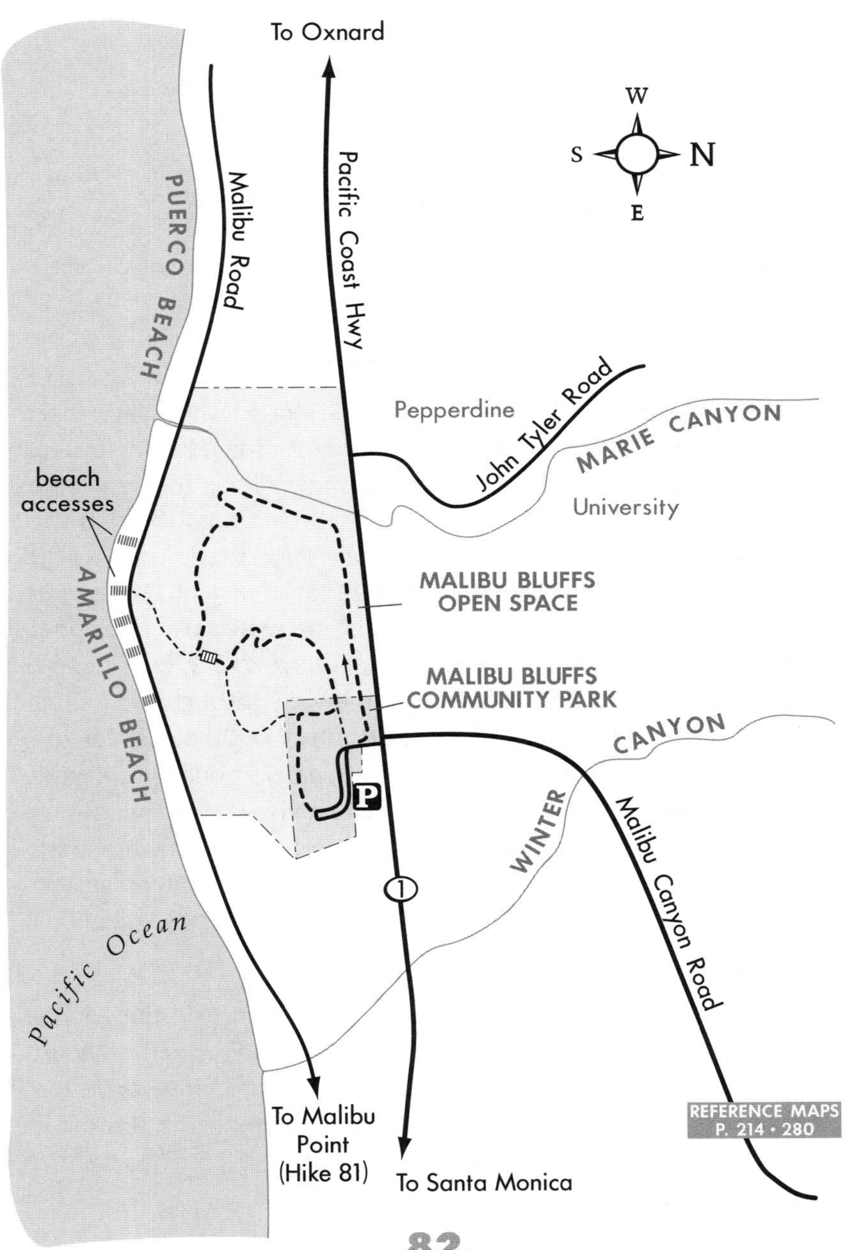

82.

Malibu Bluffs Open Space

83. Corral Canyon Park

25623 Pacific Coast Highway • Malibu

Hiking distance: 2.5-mile loop
Hiking time: 1.5 hours
Configuration: loop
Elevation gain: 400 feet
Difficulty: easy
Exposure: mostly exposed hillside and some shaded canyon bottom
Dogs: allowed
Maps: U.S.G.S. Malibu Beach
Tom Harrison Maps: Malibu Creek State Park Trail map

Corral Canyon is an undeveloped, 2.5-mile-long watershed between Malibu Canyon and Latigo Canyon. The canyon stretches from the crest of the Santa Monica Mountains to the Pacific Ocean. Seasonal Corral Canyon Creek, which runs through the steep draw, forms in Malibu Creek State Park, then drops 2,500 feet through the rugged canyon before emptying into the sea at Dan Blocker State Beach. The area was once owned by entertainer Bob Hope. It has since become Corral Canyon Park, encompassing 340 acres. This 2.5-mile loop trail travels through the center of the park. The well-maintained footpath climbs the east canyon slope on an ancient marine terrace with native bunch grasslands, providing wonderful ocean and mountain views. The trail climbs up through coastal sage scrub to the Puerco Canyon watershed divide. The return descends into the lush riparian canyon among alder, coast live oak, California sycamore, and willow trees.

To the trailhead

From Santa Monica, drive 13.8 miles northbound on the Pacific Coast Highway/Highway 1 to Malibu Seafood Fresh Fish Market on the right. Park along the side of the road for free or in the fee parking lot on the east side of the restaurant. The turnoff is located 1.8 miles past Malibu Canyon Road and 0.5 miles before Corral Canyon Road.

The hike

From the parking lot on the east side of the restaurant, walk to the signed trailhead. Immediately drop into a shaded riparian corridor under oaks, sycamores, and bays. Cross the creek and leave the lush vegetation to the exposed chaparral and veer left. Traverse the east slope of Corral Canyon to an unsigned fork. Begin the loop on the right fork, hiking counter-clockwise. Gently gain elevation to sweeping coastal and canyon views. Weave up the oceanfront hillside, with vistas stretching across Santa Monica Bay from Palos Verdes to Point Dume. Cut back to the left and continue climbing at a moderate grade on the east canyon wall. The path levels out, then begins to descend into the canyon with the aid of five switchbacks. Weave down canyon, passing the remains of an old home on the left with an intact chimney. Return to the creekside vegetation, completing the loop. ■

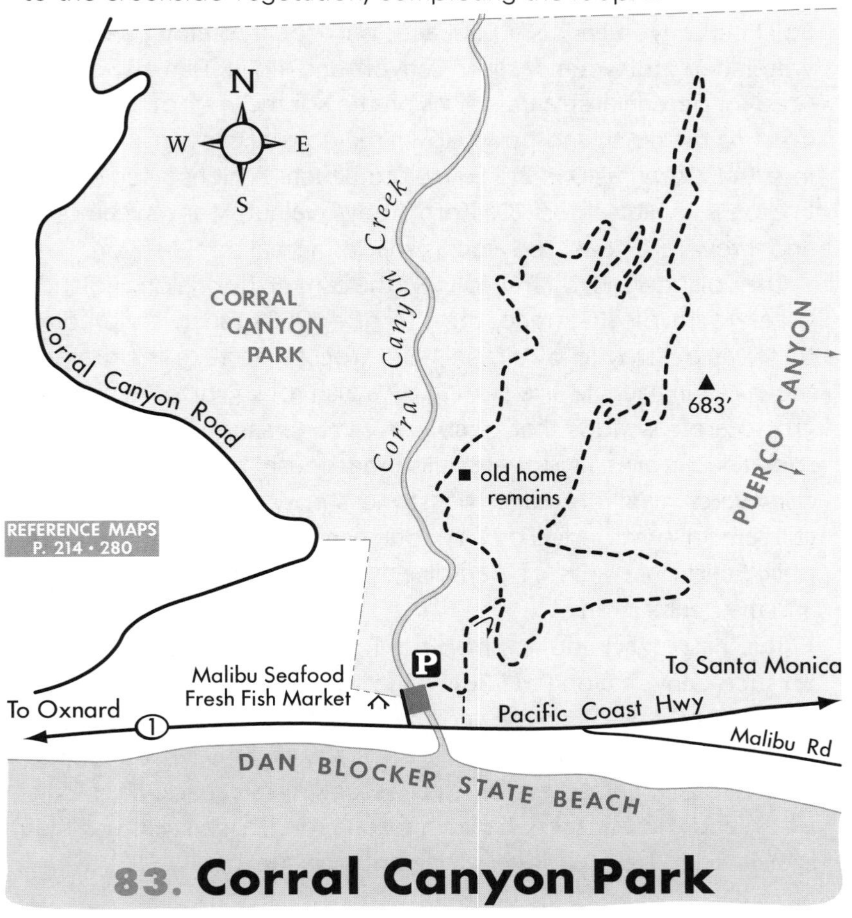

83. Corral Canyon Park

84. Rising Sun—Solstice Canyon Loop

SOLSTICE CANYON PARK

Corral Canyon Road · Malibu

Hiking distance: 3.6-mile loop
Hiking time: 2 hours
Configuration: loop
Elevation gain: 400 feet
Difficulty: easy to moderate
Exposure: exposed hills and shaded canyon
Dogs: allowed
Maps: U.S.G.S. Point Dume and Malibu Beach · N.P.S. Solstice Canyon map
Tom Harrison Maps: Malibu Creek State Park Trail map

map page 286

Solstice Canyon Park is a 550-acre park located along a coastal watershed between Malibu Canyon and Point Dume. Solstice Creek, a perennial stream, forms on the southern slope of Castro Crest to the north and flows down the coastal canyon, emptying into the ocean at Dan Blocker State Beach. A dense canopy of live oaks, white alders, California bay, walnut, giant sycamores, and a few rare coast redwoods shade the pastoral canyon.

The Solstice Canyon Trail follows the canyon floor along Solstice Creek to Tropical Terrace, the site of a 1950s ranch-style home that was destroyed by fire in 1982. Tropical Terrace is set along the creek in a jungle-like setting by a lush rock grotto. Within the grotto are cascades that tumble over huge sandstone boulders, rock-lined pools, and waterfalls. The house foundation, stone courtyard, giant fireplace, flagstone steps, and stone terraces still remain, surrounded by an exotic garden with palms, bamboo, philodendrons, birds-of-paradise, ivy-laced pines, banana trees, and maidenhair ferns.

This hike heads up to Tropical Terrace on the east wall of Solstice Canyon along the Rising Sun Trail, an undulating path that overlooks the lush canyon and the ocean. The hike returns along the canyon floor parallel to Solstice Creek through the shade of the forest. En route, the trail passes grassy meadows, picnic areas, and the Matthew Keller house, a river-rock structure that is claimed to be the oldest stone house in Malibu.

To the trailhead

From Santa Monica, drive 14.3 miles northbound on the Pacific Coast Highway/Highway 1 to Corral Canyon Road and turn right. (Corral Canyon Road is located 2.5 miles west of Malibu Canyon Road and 3.5 miles east of Kanan Dume Road.) Continue 0.2 miles to the gated entrance on the left. Turn left, entering the park, and drive 0.3 miles to the parking lot at road's end.

The hike

Hike north up the steps past the TRW trailhead sign. Wind up the hillside to a service road. Take the road uphill to the right to the TRW buildings, now home of the Santa Monica Mountains Conservancy. The Rising Sun Trail begins to the right of the second building. Long, wide switchbacks lead up to the east ridge of Solstice Canyon. Follow the ridge north towards the back of the canyon, and descend through lush vegetation. At the canyon floor, cross the creek to the ruins. Take the path upstream to the waterfalls and pools that are just past the terrace.

After exploring, return on the service road parallel to Solstice Creek. A half mile down canyon is the Keller House, a stone cottage built in 1865. Bear left at a road split, cross a wooden bridge, and return to the trailhead. ■

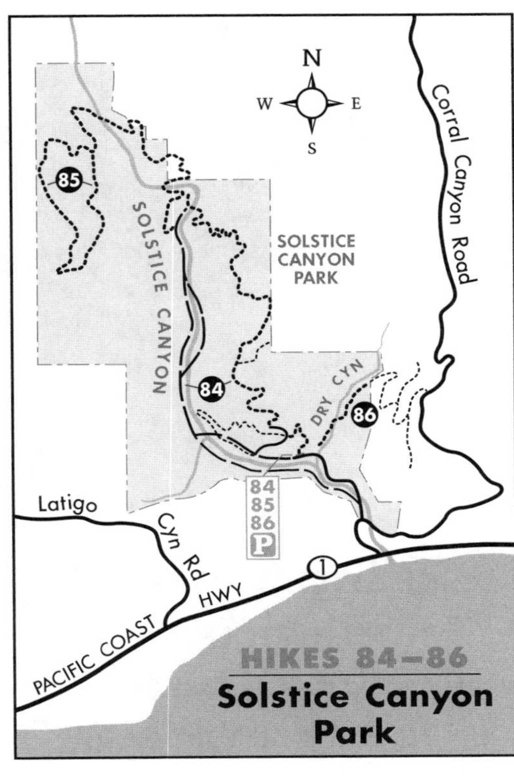

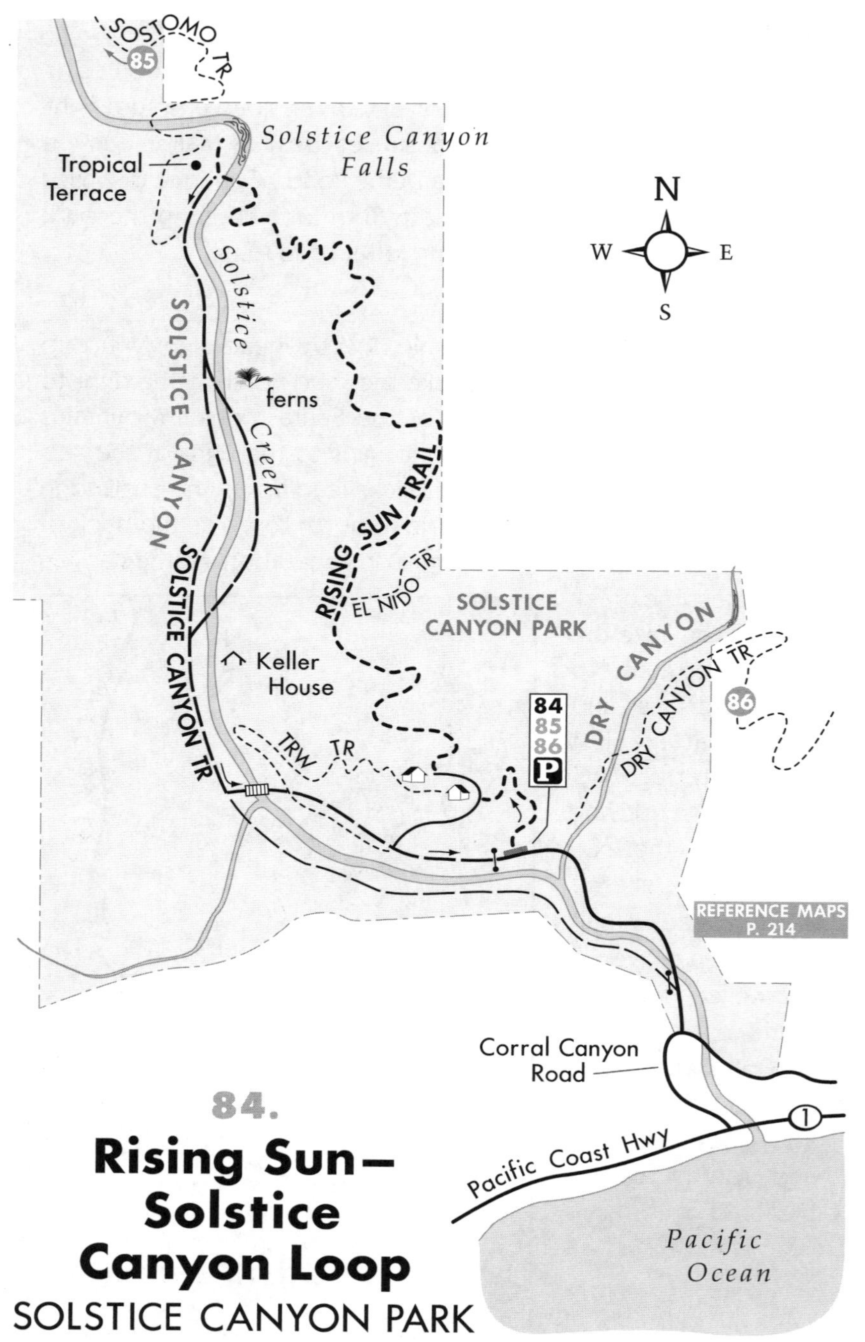

84.

Rising Sun—Solstice Canyon Loop

SOLSTICE CANYON PARK

85. Sostomo—Deer Valley Loop

SOLSTICE CANYON PARK

Corral Canyon Road • Malibu

Hiking distance: 6.2 miles round trip
Hiking time: 3 hours
Configuration: out-and-back with loop
Elevation gain: 1,100 feet
Difficulty: moderate
Exposure: shaded canyon and exposed hills
Dogs: allowed
Maps: U.S.G.S. Point Dume • N.P.S. Solstice Canyon map
Tom Harrison Maps: Malibu Creek State Park Trail map

map page 289

Solstice Canyon Park, formerly the 550-acre Roberts Ranch, was purchased by the Santa Monica Mountains Conservancy and transformed into public parkland. It was opened on June 21, 1988—the summer solstice. Five hiking, biking, and equestrian trails weave through the canyon park. This hike, the Sostomo-Deer Valley Loop, ascends the west wall of Solstice Canyon to a 1,200-foot grassy ridge at the preserve's north end. Sweeping vistas from the grassy flat above Point Dume extend across Santa Monica Bay. En route to the flat, the trail winds through chaparral and coastal sage, with stream crossings, oak woodlands, and grassy meadows. The Sostomo-Deer Valley Loop is accessed by the Solstice Canyon Trail (Hike 84), which follows Solstice Creek along the canyon floor through meadows, picnic areas, and groves of oak and walnut. The trail leads past the historic Keller House, a stone building dating back to 1865.

To the trailhead

From Santa Monica, drive 14.3 miles northbound on the Pacific Coast Highway/Highway 1 to Corral Canyon Road and turn right. (Corral Canyon Road is located 2.5 miles west of Malibu Canyon Road and 3.5 miles east of Kanan Dume Road.) Continue 0.2 miles to the gated entrance on the left. Turn left, entering the park, and drive 0.3 miles to the parking lot at road's end.

The hike

Take the posted Solstice Canyon Trail, and follow the paved road under sycamore trees alongside the creek. Cross a wood bridge to the west side of the creek at 0.2 miles. Continue up canyon past the historic Keller House. Just beyond the house is a trail split. The right fork leaves the main road and meanders through an oak grove, crossing the creek twice before rejoining the road. At 1.2 miles, just shy of Tropical Terrace, is the posted Sostomo Trail.

Bear left on the footpath and begin ascending the west canyon wall. Climb at a moderate grade to magnificent views of Solstice Canyon. Rock hop over the creek in a narrow gorge. Wind up the canyon wall, passing the remnants of a home and chimney. At the head of the canyon is a towering sedimentary rock monolith. The trail skirts the park boundary and curves left before reaching the spectacular outcropping. Cross the creek again, passing the shell of a sturdy rock house. Climb to a junction with the Deer Valley Loop. Begin the loop to the right, leading to an open, grassy flat where the trail levels off. At an unpaved road, bear left for 50 yards and return to the footpath on the left. The sweeping coastal views extend across Santa Monica Bay, including a bird's-eye view of Point Dume. Switchback sharply left at the trail sign, and return on the lower loop. The Rising Sun Trail (Hike 84) can be seen across the canyon. Complete the loop and return by retracing your steps. ■

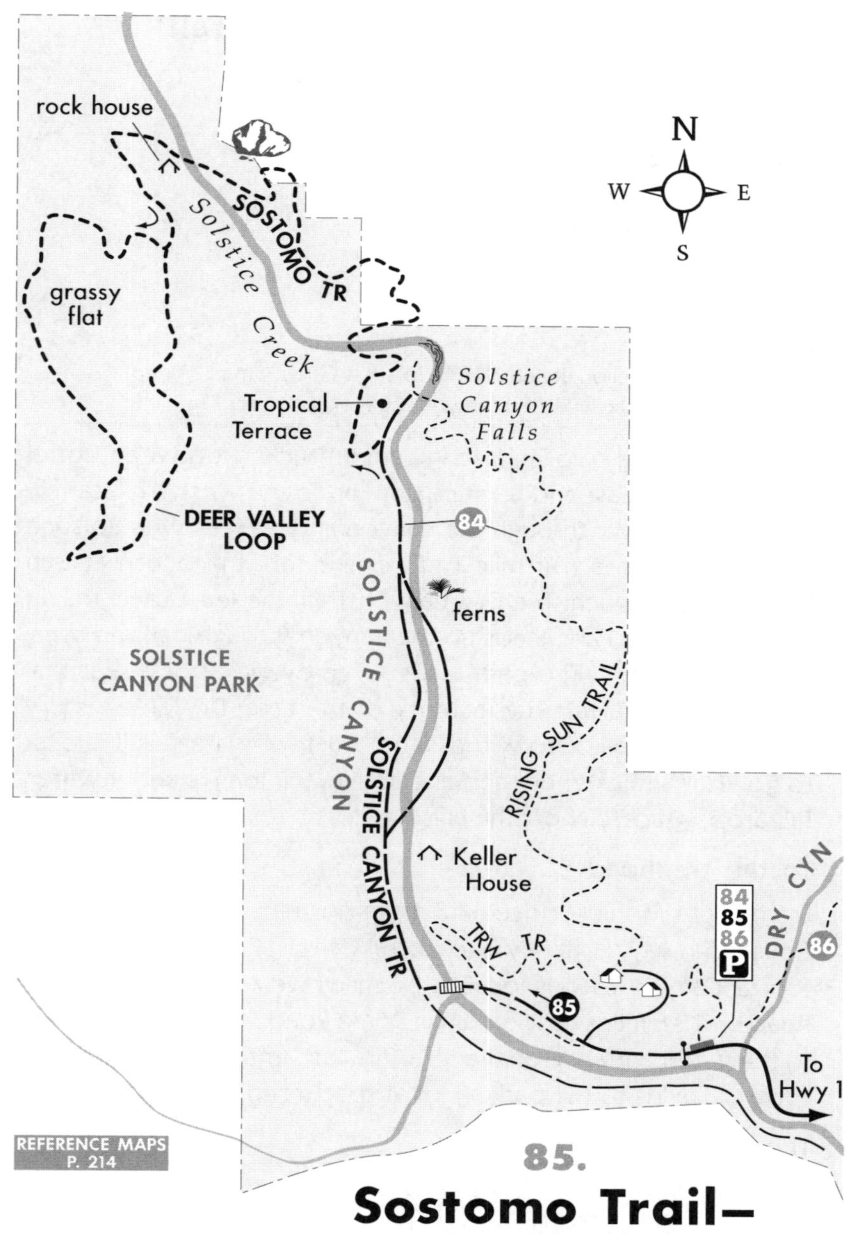

REFERENCE MAPS
P. 214

85.

Sostomo Trail— Deer Valley Loop

SOLSTICE CANYON PARK

86. Dry Canyon Trail to waterfall

SOLSTICE CANYON PARK

Corral Canyon Road • Malibu

Hiking distance: 1.2 miles round trip
Hiking time: 30 minutes
Configuration: out-and-back
Elevation gain: 200 feet
Difficulty: easy
Exposure: shaded
Dogs: allowed
Maps: U.S.G.S. Malibu Beach • N.P.S. Solstice Canyon map
Tom Harrison Maps: Malibu Creek State Park Trail map

Dry Canyon is a two-mile-long canyon tucked between Corral Canyon to the east and Solstice Canyon to the west. An intermittent stream flows through the canyon and merges with Solstice Creek, less than a half mile before it enters the ocean at Dan Blocker State Beach. The Dry Canyon Trail, the least used trail in Solstice Canyon Park, leads up the canyon through oak and sycamore woodlands. The path leads to an overlook of a seasonal, free-falling waterfall. The majority of the time, Dry Creek is dry, as the name implies. To witness the 150-foot waterfall, it is best to go after a rain. When the fall is active, the long, slender waterfall drops gracefully off the hillside cliffs.

To the trailhead

From Santa Monica, drive 14.3 miles northbound on the Pacific Coast Highway/Highway 1 to Corral Canyon Road and turn right. (Corral Canyon Road is located 2.5 miles west of Malibu Canyon Road and 3.5 miles east of Kanan Dume Road.) Continue 0.2 miles to the gated entrance on the left. Turn left, entering the park, and drive 0.3 miles to the parking lot at road's end.

The hike

From the parking area, hike 20 yards back down the road to the signed Dry Creek Trail on the left. Head north into the mouth of the side canyon. Pass through a grassy oak grove on the well-defined trail, parallel to Dry Creek. Cross the creek and gain elevation to the end of the maintained trail at 0.6 miles. Dry Canyon Falls, when active, can be seen across the narrow canyon on the left. This overlook is the turn-around spot.

To hike farther, the trail continues a short distance to the end of the canyon, where switchbacks lead up the canyon wall to Corral Canyon Road. Beyond the overlook, the trail is not maintained and becomes overgrown with brush. ■

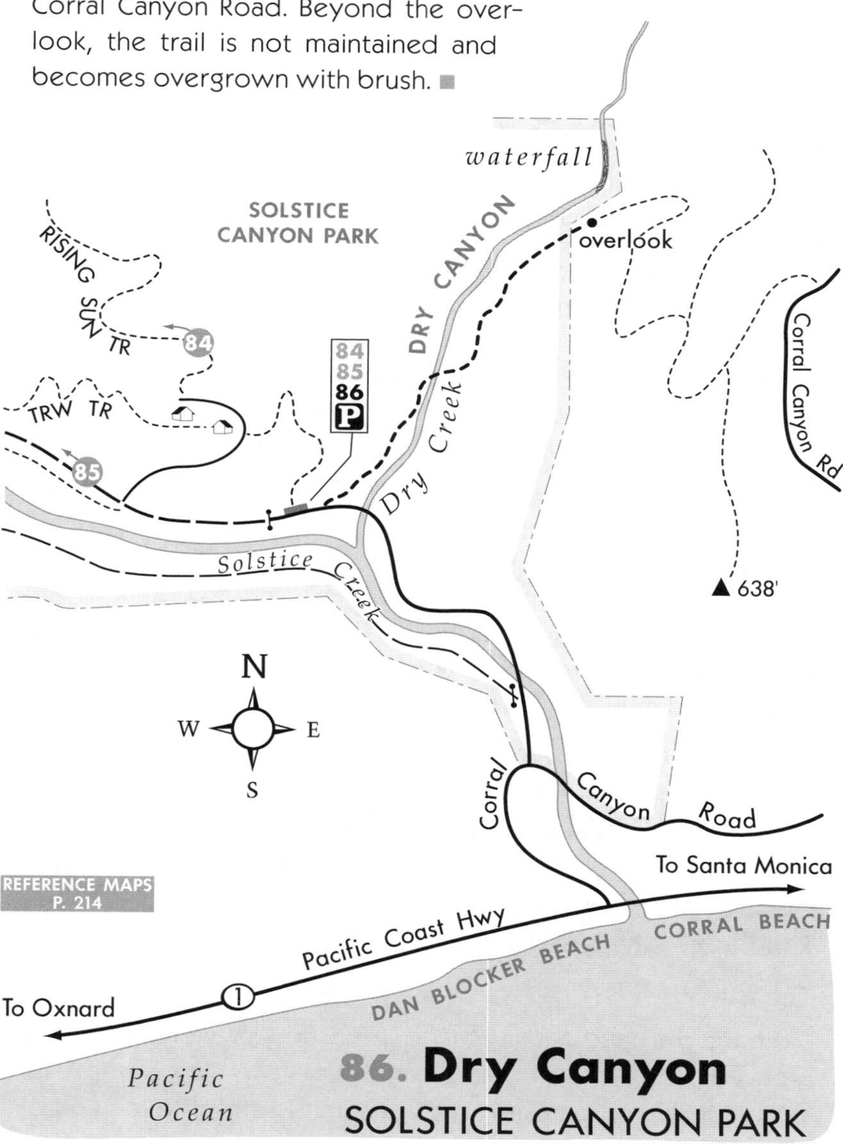

86. Dry Canyon
SOLSTICE CANYON PARK

87. Escondido Falls

ESCONDIDO CANYON NATURAL AREA

27200 Winding Way · Malibu

Hiking distance: 3.4 miles round trip
Hiking time: 2 hours
Configuration: out-and-back
Elevation gain: 300 feet
Difficulty: easy
Exposure: exposed road and shaded canyon
Dogs: allowed
Maps: U.S.G.S. Point Dume
Tom Harrison Maps: Malibu Creek State Park Trail map

Escondido Falls is a multi-tiered 150-foot waterfall, the highest falls in the Santa Monica Mountains. The cataract sits deep in a box canyon within the Escondido Canyon Natural Area. The upper (larger) cascade can be spotted during the hike, but the trail ends at the base of the lower falls, which tumbles 60 feet off limestone cliffs into a shallow pool in a mossy fern grotto. To reach the upper falls requires actual climbing, using hands and feet.

The trail, a multi-use hiking and equestrian trail, winds up the lush canyon floor, criss-crossing the year-round creek. The sylvan path weaves through grassy flats in the shade of riparian woodlands to the waterfall and a pool. The hike begins on a winding, paved residential road.

To the trailhead

From Santa Monica, drive 16.5 miles northbound on the Pacific Coast Highway/Highway 1 to Winding Way East and turn right. The signed trailhead parking lot is on the left side of the road. (Winding Way East is located 4.5 miles west of Malibu Canyon Road and 1.3 miles east of Kanan Dume Road.)

The hike

From the trailhead parking lot, walk north up Winding Way East, a paved public-access road along the ocean-facing slope. Pass beautiful Malibu homes along the residential street to the end of the paved road at 0.8 miles. On the left is the posted Escondido Canyon Trail, a dirt path. Bear left on the well-defined trail, crossing the meadow to the left. Drop down into Escondido Canyon and cross the creek. After crossing, take the left fork upstream. (The right fork leads a half mile towards Latigo Canyon.) Continue up the near-level canyon, following the creek through the forest. Cross the creek a few more times under magnificent coast live oaks and sycamores. At a half mile, the upper falls can be spotted at the back of the towering canyon wall. After the fifth creek crossing, lower Escondido Falls comes into view. Follow the east bank of the stream to the trail's end, located by a shallow pool surrounded by broken travertine rock, ferns, and moss at the base of the waterfall. Return by retracing your steps. ■

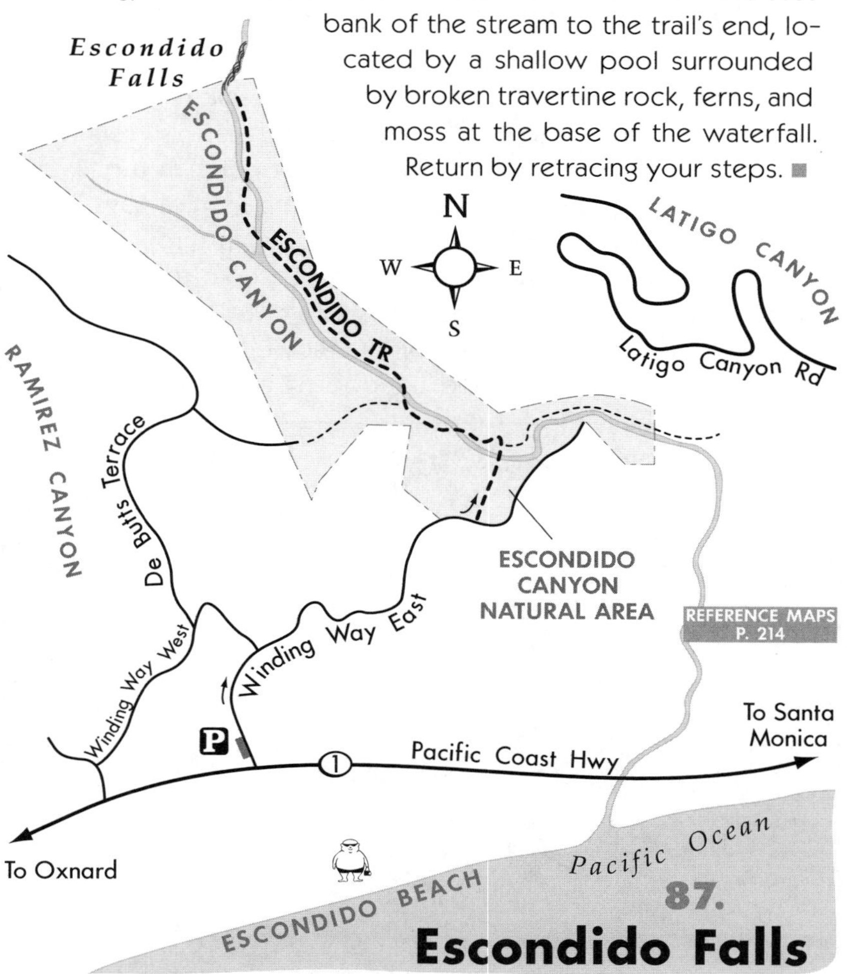

87. Escondido Falls

88. Point Dume Natural Preserve

Malibu

Hiking distance: 1.5 miles round trip
Hiking time: 45 minutes
Configuration: several short out-and-back trails
Elevation gain: 200 feet
Difficulty: easy
Exposure: exposed
Dogs: not allowed
Maps: U.S.G.S. Point Dume
Tom Harrison Maps: Zuma-Trancas Canyons Trail map

Point Dume Natural Preserve is a 35-acre blufftop preserve on the northwest end of Santa Monica Bay. Volcanic rock cliffs jut out to sea along a triangular-shaped headland that is surrounded by water on three sides. From the 203-foot perch at the tip of the promontory, views extend across Santa Monica Bay, from Point Mugu to Palos Verdes. From mid-December through March, the summit is among the finest sites to observe the migrating gray whales en route from the Bering Sea to Baja California. On the west side of the point is Point Dume State Beach, a popular swimming, sunbathing, and tidepooling beach with a rocky

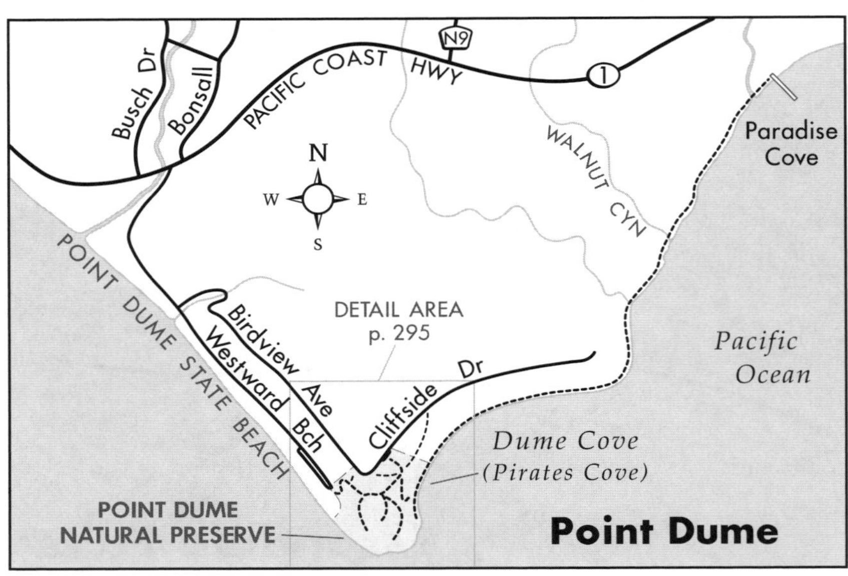

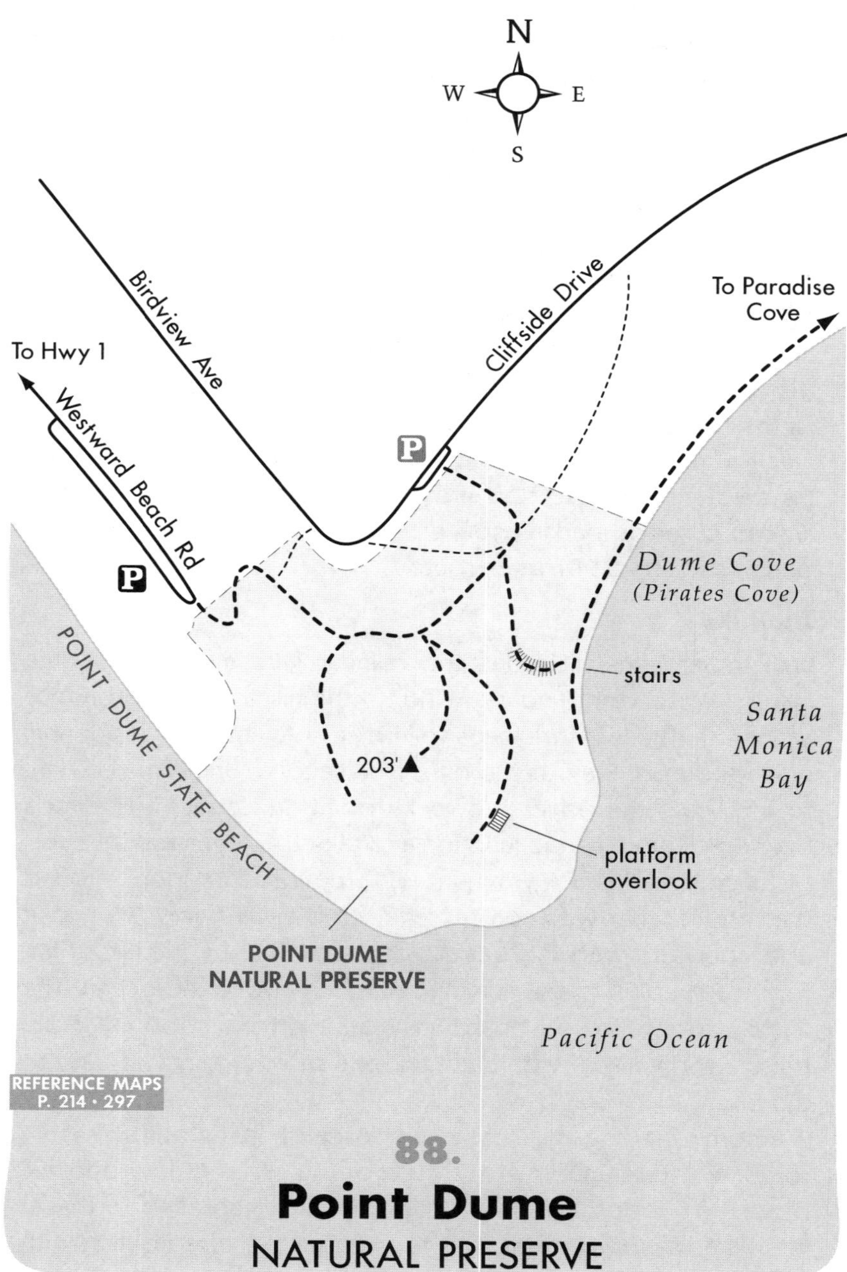
N
W
E
S
Birdview Ave
Cliffside Drive
To Paradise Cove
To Hwy 1
Westward Beach Rd
P
P
Dume Cove
(Pirates Cove)
stairs
Santa Monica Bay
POINT DUME STATE BEACH
203'
platform overlook
POINT DUME NATURAL PRESERVE
Pacific Ocean
REFERENCE MAPS P. 214 · 297
88.
Point Dume
NATURAL PRESERVE

shoreline. To the east, tucked beneath the 200-foot sandstone cliffs, is Dume Cove (locally known as Pirates Cove), a secluded, unofficial clothing-optional beach between two rocky points. This hike climbs the ancient coastal bluffs through coastal scrub, grassland, and dunes to coastal overlooks and an oceanfront viewing platform.

To the trailhead

From Santa Monica, drive 20 miles northbound on the Pacific Coast Highway/Highway 1 to Westward Beach Road by Point Dume and turn left/oceanside. (Westward Beach Road is 0.9 miles west of Kanan Dume Road.) Turn left and drive 0.6 miles to the Point Dume State Beach entrance station. Continue 0.7 miles to the far south end of the parking lot. A parking fee is required.

For a second access point, just before reaching the beach entrance station, turn left on Birdview Avenue, and drive 1 mile to limited curbside parking spaces on the right. (Birdview Avenue becomes Cliffside Drive en route.)

The hike

Walk towards the cliffs, past the trailhead gate, at the Point Dume Natural Preserve boundary. Wind up the hill on the footpath to a junction. The left fork leads to Birdview Avenue in a residential neighborhood. Stay to the right to a second junction. The right fork follows the ridge to a rocky point and ends at a fenced overlook. Return to the junction and take the other fork. A short distance ahead is a 4-way junction. The left fork loops around the terraced flat with coastal sage scrub to Birdview Avenue; it also connects with the beach access to Dume Cove. The right fork leads uphill to the summit, 203 feet above the ocean. The middle fork follows a boardwalk to a platform overlook. From the platform, a sandy path continues a short distance around to the point.

Return to the beach access, and descend on the trail and stairs to Dume (Pirates) Cove at the base of the cliffs. At low tide, explore the tidepools and walk along the rocky shoreline northeast into Paradise Cove, a privately run, crescent-shaped beach with a small pier and concessions. ■

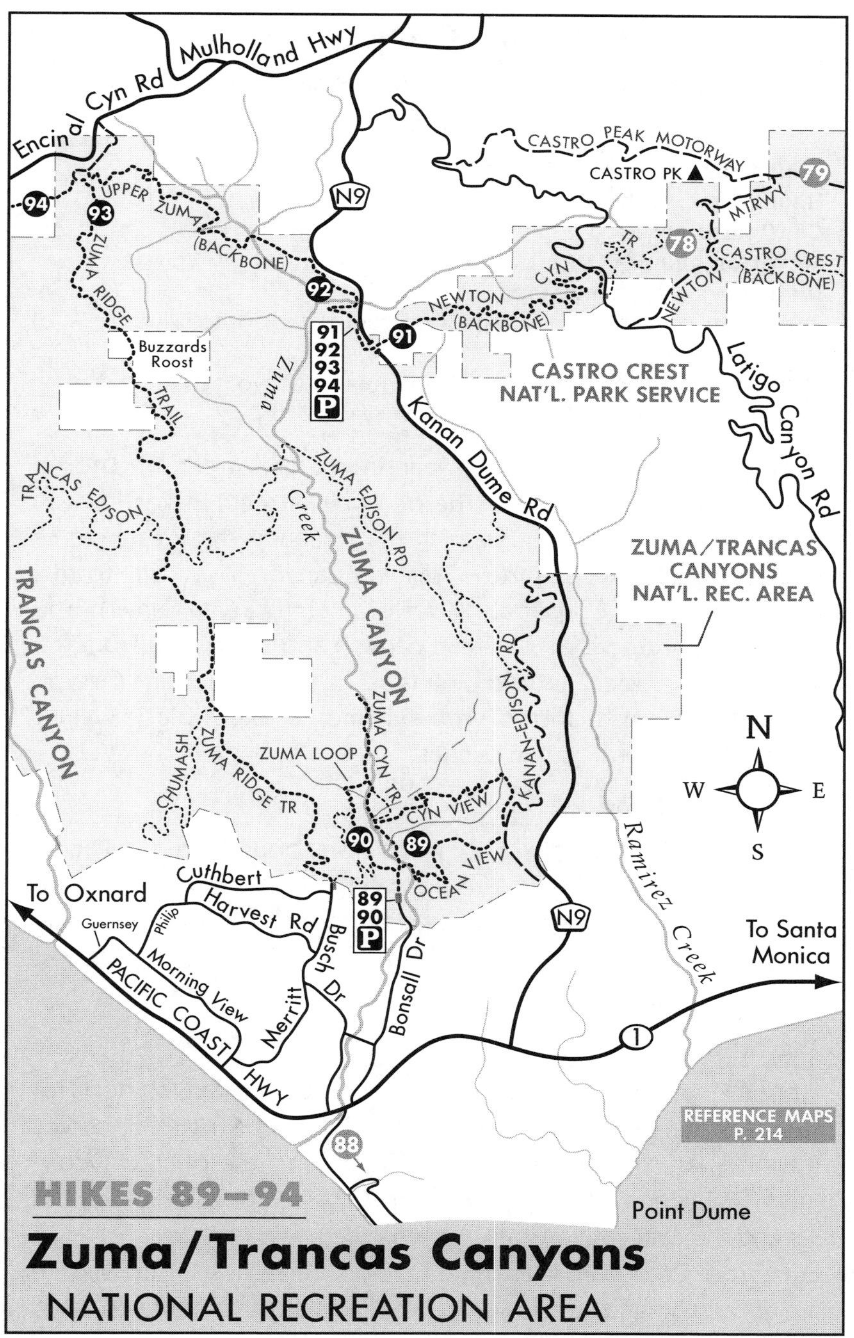
Mulholland Hwy
Encinal Cyn Rd
CASTRO PEAK MOTORWAY
CASTRO PK
UPPER ZUMA (BACKBONE)
ZUMA RIDGE TRAIL
Buzzards Roost
Zuma Creek
NEWTON CYN TR
NEWTON (BACKBONE)
MTRWY
CASTRO CREST (BACKBONE)
NEWTON
CASTRO CREST NAT'L. PARK SERVICE
Kanan Dume Rd
Latigo Canyon Rd
TRANCAS EDISON
ZUMA EDISON RD
ZUMA CANYON
TRANCAS CANYON
ZUMA/TRANCAS CANYONS NAT'L. REC. AREA
KANAN-EDISON RD
ZUMA CYN TR
ZUMA LOOP
CHUMASH
ZUMA RIDGE TR
CYN VIEW
OCEAN VIEW
Ramirez Creek
N
W
E
S
To Oxnard
Cuthbert
Harvest Rd
Guernsey
Philip
Morning View
Merritt
Busch Dr
Bonsall Dr
PACIFIC COAST HWY
To Santa Monica
REFERENCE MAPS P. 214
Point Dume
HIKES 89–94
Zuma/Trancas Canyons
NATIONAL RECREATION AREA

89. Ocean View—Canyon View Loop

ZUMA/TRANCAS CANYONS: Lower Zuma Canyon

Malibu

Hiking distance: 3.1-mile loop
Hiking time: 1.5 hours
Configuration: loop
Elevation gain: 600 feet
Difficulty: easy to moderate
Exposure: partially shaded canyon bottom and exposed hillside
Dogs: allowed
Maps: U.S.G.S. Point Dume • N.P.S. Zuma-Trancas Canyons map
Tom Harrison Maps: Zuma-Trancas Canyons Trail map

Lower Zuma Canyon remains a beautiful, natural stream-fed gorge with minimal development. The perennial stream makes its way down the canyon floor, reaching the ocean at the west end of Point Dume. The Ocean View Trail and Canyon View Trail form a loop through the chaparral-clad hillside along Zuma Canyon. The trail offers great vistas of Zuma Canyon and the ocean from the west-facing slope. This hike begins at the mouth of Zuma Canyon in a riparian wash dotted with sycamores, oaks, black walnut, willows, and laurel sumac bushes.

To the trailhead

From Santa Monica, drive 21 miles northbound on the Pacific Coast Highway/Highway 1 to Bonsall Drive and turn right/north. (The turnoff is one mile west of Kanan Dume Road.) Continue one mile north to the trailhead parking area at road's end. The last 200 yards are on an unpaved lane.

The hike

From the mouth of the canyon, head north up the canyon floor for 0.2 miles to a signed junction. The Zuma Loop Trail (Hike 90) curves left. Stay on the canyon bottom 30 yards to the posted Ocean View Trail. Bear right to begin the loop. Cross a rocky streambed and ascend the east canyon wall. Wind up the hillside to views of Point Dume and the ocean, reaching the ridge at 1.3 miles. At the summit are sweeping coastal views that extend (on clear days) to Palos

Verdes, Point Mugu, and Catalina. The Ocean View Trail ends at a T-junction, but the ocean views continue throughout the hike. Bear left 0.1 mile on the unpaved Kanan Edison Road to a junction with the Canyon View Trail. Curve left and follow the ridge across the head of the small side canyon. Weave down the hillside to the canyon floor and a junction at 2.6 miles. Bear left on the Zuma Canyon Trail and walk down canyon. Parallel the small stream past laurel sumac bushes and sycamore trees. Complete the loop and return to the trailhead. ■

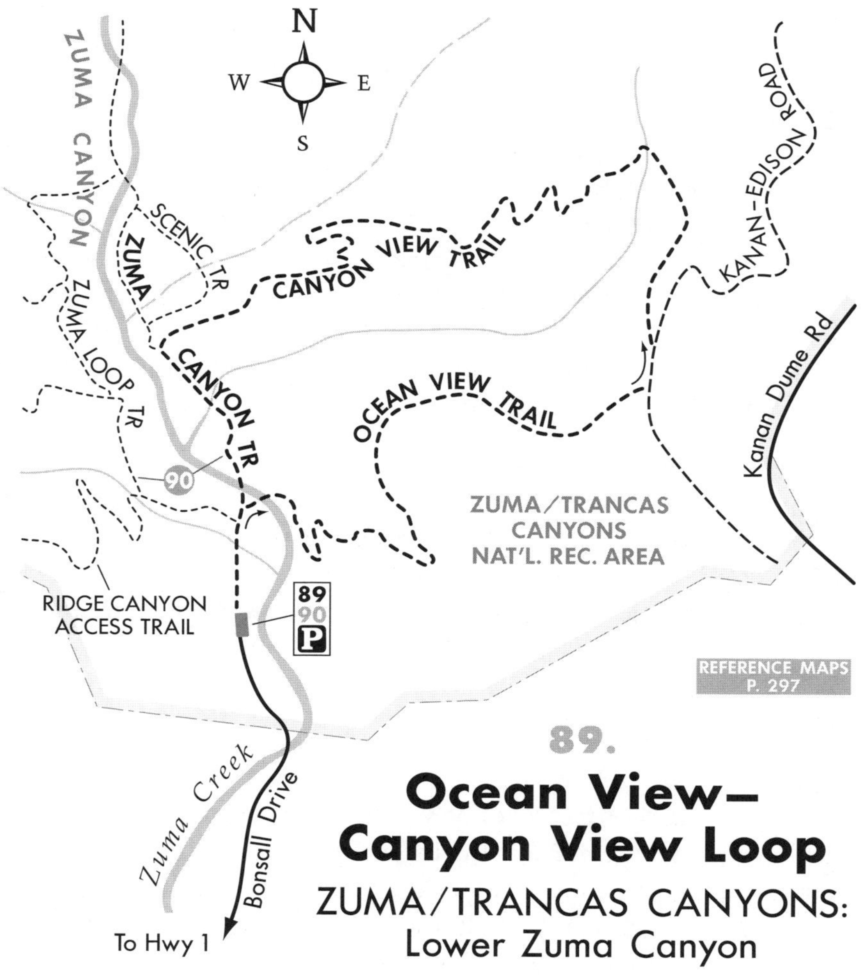

89. Ocean View—Canyon View Loop

ZUMA/TRANCAS CANYONS: Lower Zuma Canyon

90. Zuma Loop Trail

ZUMA/TRANCAS CANYONS: Lower Zuma Canyon

Malibu

Hiking distance: 1.7-mile loop; 1.4-mile spur trail
Hiking time: 1-2 hours
Configuration: loop plus optional spur trail
Elevation gain: 250-450 feet
Difficulty: easy
Exposure: a mix of partially shaded canyon bottom and exposed hillside
Dogs: allowed
Maps: U.S.G.S. Point Dume • N.P.S. Zuma-Trancas Canyons map
Tom Harrison Maps: Zuma-Trancas Canyons Trail map

Zuma Canyon is one of the few canyons in the Santa Monica Mountains that is accessible only to foot and horse traffic. There are no paved roads. This easy loop hike begins on the Zuma Canyon Trail in Lower Zuma Canyon. The trail heads up the drainage parallel to perennial Zuma Creek. The path meanders through lush riparian vegetation that includes oak, willow, black walnut, and sycamore trees. The hike returns on the Zuma Loop Trail above the canyon floor, traversing the east-facing hillside overlooking the canyon and the ocean.

To the trailhead

From Santa Monica, drive 21 miles northbound on the Pacific Coast Highway/Highway 1 to Bonsall Drive and turn right/north. (The turnoff is one mile west of Kanan Dume Road.) Continue one mile north to the trailhead parking area at road's end. The last 200 yards are on an unpaved lane.

The hike

From the end of the road, hike north past the trailhead sign on the Zuma Canyon Trail. Follow the west slope of the wide canyon wash 0.2 miles to a junction with the Zuma Loop Trail on the left, our return route. Begin the loop straight ahead, passing oak and sycamore trees. Continue past a junction with the Ocean View Trail on the right (Hike 89). Rock-hop over Zuma Creek to a junction with the Canyon View Trail at a half mile, also on the

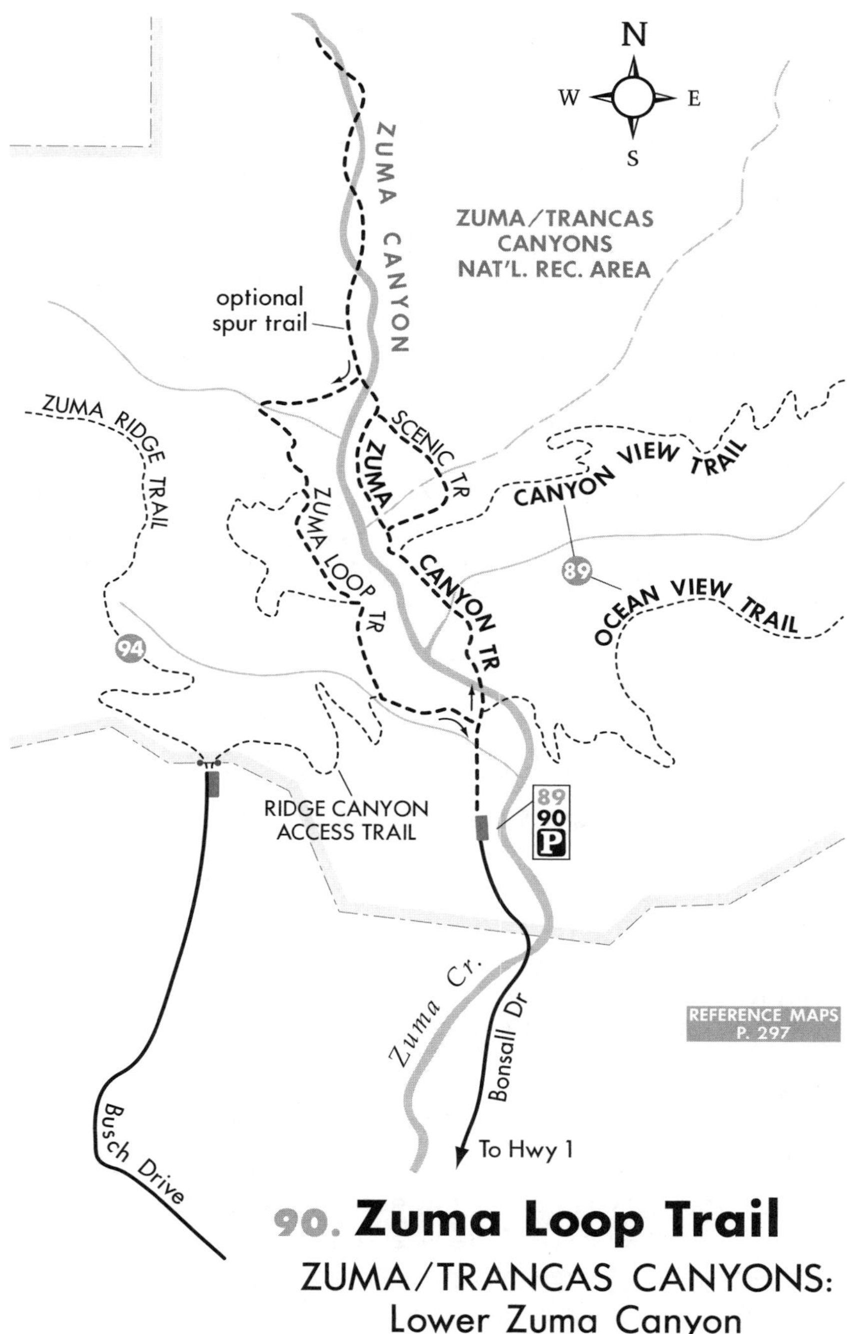

90. Zuma Loop Trail

ZUMA/TRANCAS CANYONS: Lower Zuma Canyon

right. Stay to the left, remaining close to Zuma Creek. Pass the Scenic Trail on the right, a short loop that skirts the east canyon wall. Both paths merge 20 yards before the second creek crossing. Cross the creek and walk another 20 yards to a junction with the Zuma Loop Trail at 0.7 miles. Our return route veers left on the Zuma Loop Trail.

To add 1.4 miles to the hike, detour to the right, staying on the Zuma Canyon Trail. Follow the west side of the drainage. The Zuma Ridge Trail can be seen to the west near the top of the canyon wall (HIke 94). Meander up canyon, crossing Zuma Creek four more times. At the fourth crossing, the path fades. Beyond this point, the trail scrambles up the drainage among the sandstone boulders.

Back at the junction, take the Zuma Loop Trail to the west and traverse the hillside. Follow the ridge south, staying to the left at three separate trail splits. Descend to the canyon floor, completing the loop. ■

91. Newton Canyon

ZUMA/TRANCAS CANYONS • CASTRO CREST N.P.S.

Malibu

Hiking distance: 4.6 miles round trip
Hiking time: 2.5 hours
Configuration: out-and-back
Elevation gain: 300 feet
Difficulty: easy to moderate
Exposure: shaded forest
Dogs: allowed
Maps: U.S.G.S. Point Dume • N.P.S. Zuma-Trancas Canyons map
Tom Harrison Maps: Zuma-Trancas Canyons Trail map

The Newton Canyon Trail is a forested trail that runs through the Castro Crest National Park Service corridor, connecting Zuma/Trancas Canyons Recreation Area to Malibu Creek State Park. This 2.3-mile-long path, part of the Backbone Trail, connects Kanan

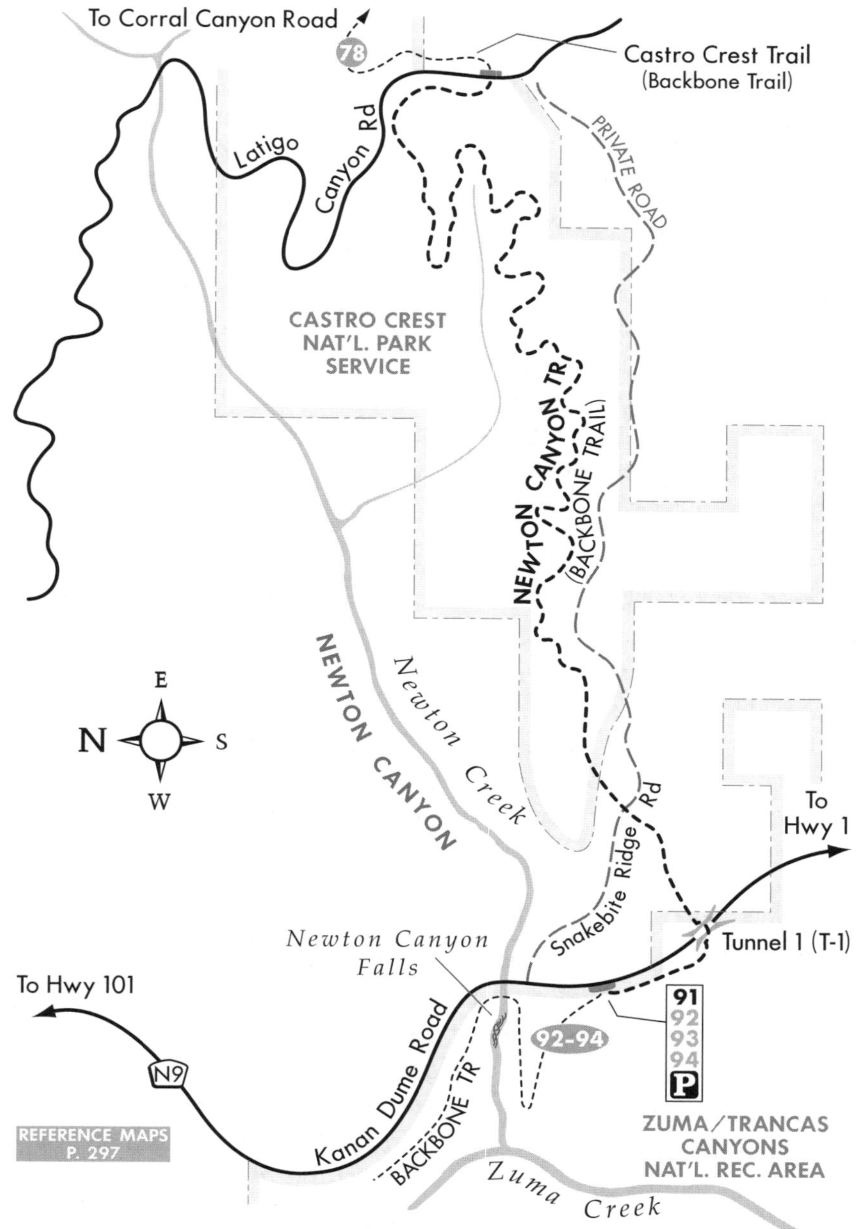

91. Newton Canyon

ZUMA/TRANCAS CANYONS • CASTRO CREST

Dume Road by Tunnel 1 with Latigo Canyon Road beneath Castro Peak. The trail weaves through the oak-filled canyon with ocean views and seasonal stream crossings.

To the trailhead

From Santa Monica, drive 18 miles northbound on the Pacific Coast Highway/Highway 1 to Kanan Dume Road (5.8 miles west of Malibu Canyon Road). Turn right and drive 4.4 miles north to the trailhead parking lot on the left (west). The parking lot is located just after the first tunnel (T-1).

From the Ventura Freeway/Highway 101 in Agoura Hills, exit on Kanan Road. Drive 7.9 miles south to the trailhead parking lot on the right (west). The parking lot is located just before entering the third tunnel (T-1). (Kanan Road becomes Kanan Dume Road south of Mulholland Highway.)

The hike

The signed trail begins alongside Kanan Dume Road. Head south towards the ocean on the old fire road. Climb up to Tunnel 1 and cross over, high above Kanan Dume Road. After crossing, the road narrows to a footpath and enters a forested canopy. Slowly descend into Newton Canyon to Snakebite Ridge Road, a paved private road. Cross the road. Follow the serpentine path under the shade of oak and bay laurel trees, and climb to overlooks of the surrounding mountains. Continue winding along the mountainside and cross over to the north side of the canyon. Stroll through the lush, fern-filled forest. Zigzag up the north slope of Newton Canyon to a great westward view of the jagged ridgeline of the Boney Mountains. The trail exits on Latigo Canyon Road. Across the road is a trailhead parking lot.

To extend the hike, the trail continues on the Castro Crest Trail, a continuation of the Backbone Trail—Hike 78. The trail meanders through Newton Canyon and Solstice Canyon beneath Castro Crest to the north. The jagged sandstone mountain stretches for over two miles. The trail leads 4.2 miles to Corral Canyon Road. ■

92. Newton Canyon Falls

ZUMA/TRANCAS CANYONS: Upper Zuma Canyon

Malibu

Hiking distance: 1.5 miles round trip
Hiking time: 1 hour
Configuration: out-and-back
Elevation gain: 200 feet
Difficulty: easy
Exposure: mostly shaded with some exposed areas
Dogs: allowed
Maps: U.S.G.S. Point Dume • N.P.S. Zuma-Trancas Canyons map
Tom Harrison Maps: Zuma-Trancas Canyons Trail map

map page 306

Newton Canyon Falls is a year-round, 30-foot waterfall in a lush, thickly vegetated, water-worn grotto with mossy rocks, sandstone caves, and a tangle of vines. The hidden cataract on Newton Creek drops off a vertical limestone wall a short distance from the creek's confluence with Zuma Creek. At the base of the falls are large shaded boulders under a canopy of sycamores, bay laurel, and oaks. The hike begins on the first section of the Upper Zuma Canyon Trail—Hike 93—in the Zuma/Trancas Canyons area. The trail is a segment of the Backbone Trail that runs between Kanan Dume Road and Encinal Canyon.

To the trailhead

From Santa Monica, drive 18 miles northbound on the Pacific Coast Highway/Highway 1 to Kanan Dume Road (5.8 miles west of Malibu Canyon Road). Turn right and drive 4.4 miles north to the trailhead parking lot on the left (west). The parking lot is located just after the first tunnel (T-1).

From the Ventura Freeway/Highway 101 in Agoura Hills, exit on Kanan Road. Drive 7.9 miles south to the trailhead parking lot on the right (west). The parking lot is located just before entering the third tunnel (T-1). (Kanan Road becomes Kanan Dume Road south of Mulholland Highway.)

The hike

Hike west, away from Kanan Dume Road, on the signed Backbone Trail (the Upper Zuma Canyon Trail). The trail immediately begins its descent from the open chaparral into the shady canyon. After crossing the trickling Newton Creek, a side trail on the left leads 20 yards to sandstone rocks at the top of the falls. The main trail continues 100 yards downhill to a second cutoff trail on the left. Take this steep side path downhill through a forest of oaks, sycamores, and bay laurels to the creek, bearing to the left on the descent. Once at the creek, hike upstream along the path. Fifty yards up the narrow canyon is a lush grotto at the base of Newton Canyon Falls.

The main trail continues 1.9 miles northwest to the Zuma Ridge Trail, entering the rugged Zuma Canyon with its steep volcanic cliffs (Hikes 93 and 94). Return by retracing your steps. ■

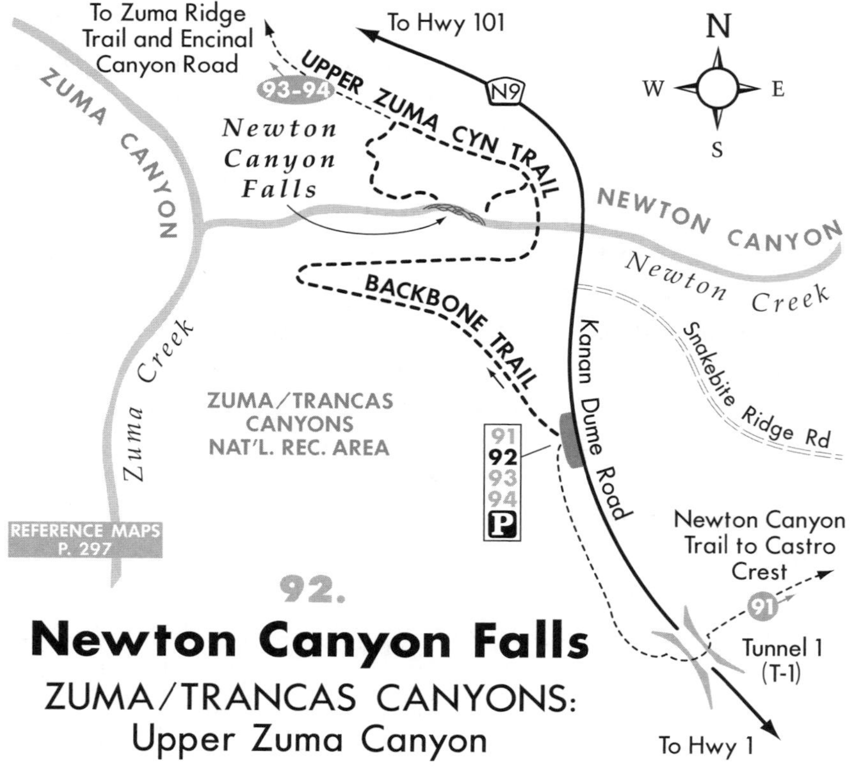

92. Newton Canyon Falls

ZUMA/TRANCAS CANYONS: Upper Zuma Canyon

93. Upper Zuma Canyon— Trancas Canyon

Kanan Dume Road to Encinal Canyon Road

ZUMA/TRANCAS CANYONS: Upper Zuma Canyon

Malibu

Hiking distance: 9.6 miles round trip
Hiking time: 5 hours
Configuration: out-and-back
Elevation gain: 350 feet
Difficulty: moderate
Exposure: exposed hills and forested canyons
Dogs: allowed
Maps: U.S.G.S. Point Dume
Tom Harrison Maps: Zuma-Trancas Canyons Trail Map

map page 308

Zuma Canyon and Trancas Canyon are neighboring V-shaped canyons in the central portion of the Santa Monica Mountains. The steep gorges have perennial streams, weather-carved sandstone boulders, fern-lined pools, and jungle-like forests with oaks, bays, willows, and sycamores. The scenic canyons are located in the Zuma/Trancas Canyons area, managed by the National Park Service, and have remained natural and undisturbed.

This hike traverses the upper slopes of Zuma Canyon, climbs up to Zuma Ridge between the two canyons, and drops into Trancas Canyon. En route, the hike visits Newton Canyon Falls, Upper Zuma Falls, and Trancas Creek. The route utilizes the Upper Zuma Canyon Trail and the Trancas Canyon Trail, both sections of the Backbone Trail that connects Kanan Dume Road with Encinal Canyon Road. The two trails join atop Zuma Ridge.

To the trailhead

From Santa Monica, drive 18 miles northbound on the Pacific Coast Highway/Highway 1 to Kanan Dume Road (5.8 miles west of Malibu Canyon Road). Turn right and drive 4.4 miles north to the trailhead parking lot on the left (west). The parking lot is located just after the first tunnel (T-1).

From the Ventura Freeway/Highway 101 in Agoura Hills, take the Kanan Road exit. Drive 7.9 miles south to the trailhead parking

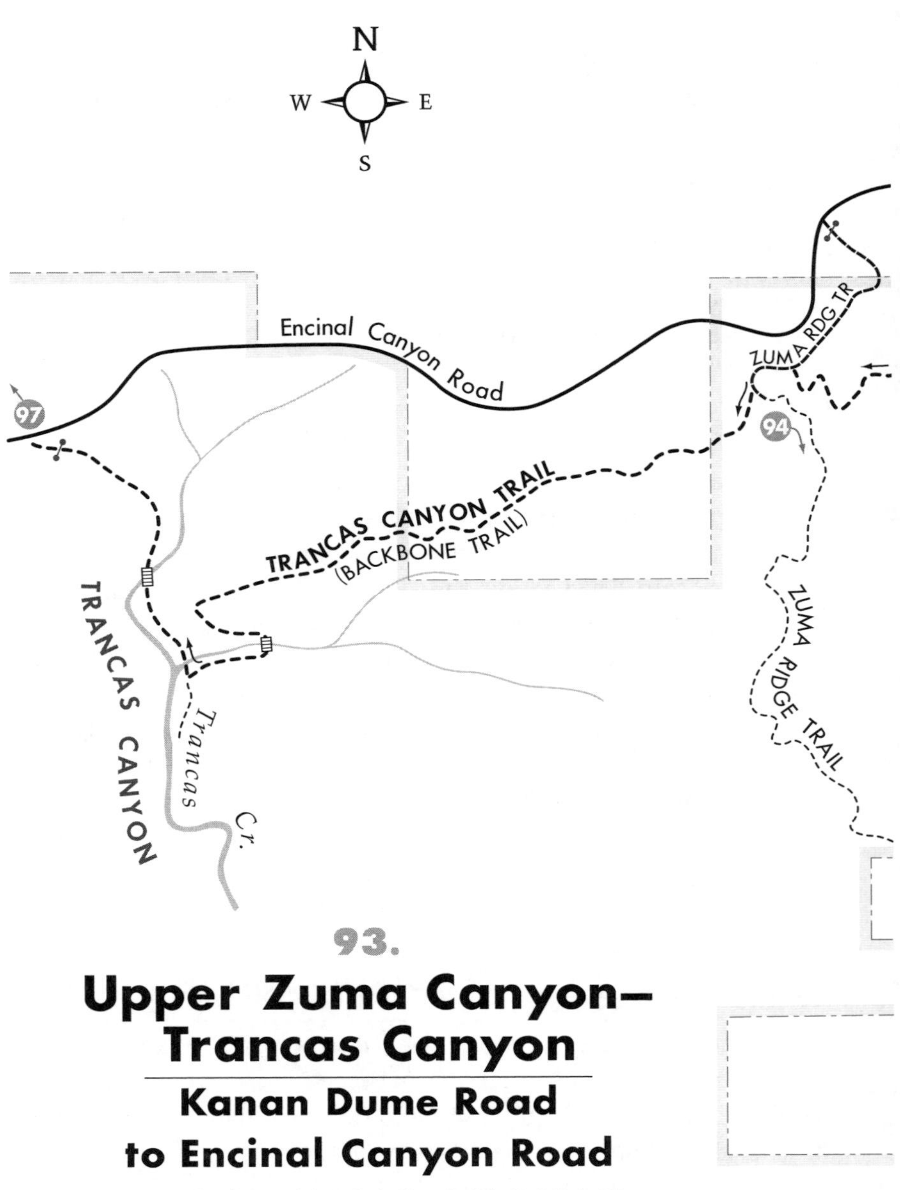

93. Upper Zuma Canyon– Trancas Canyon

Kanan Dume Road to Encinal Canyon Road

ZUMA/TRANCAS CANYONS: Upper Zuma Canyon

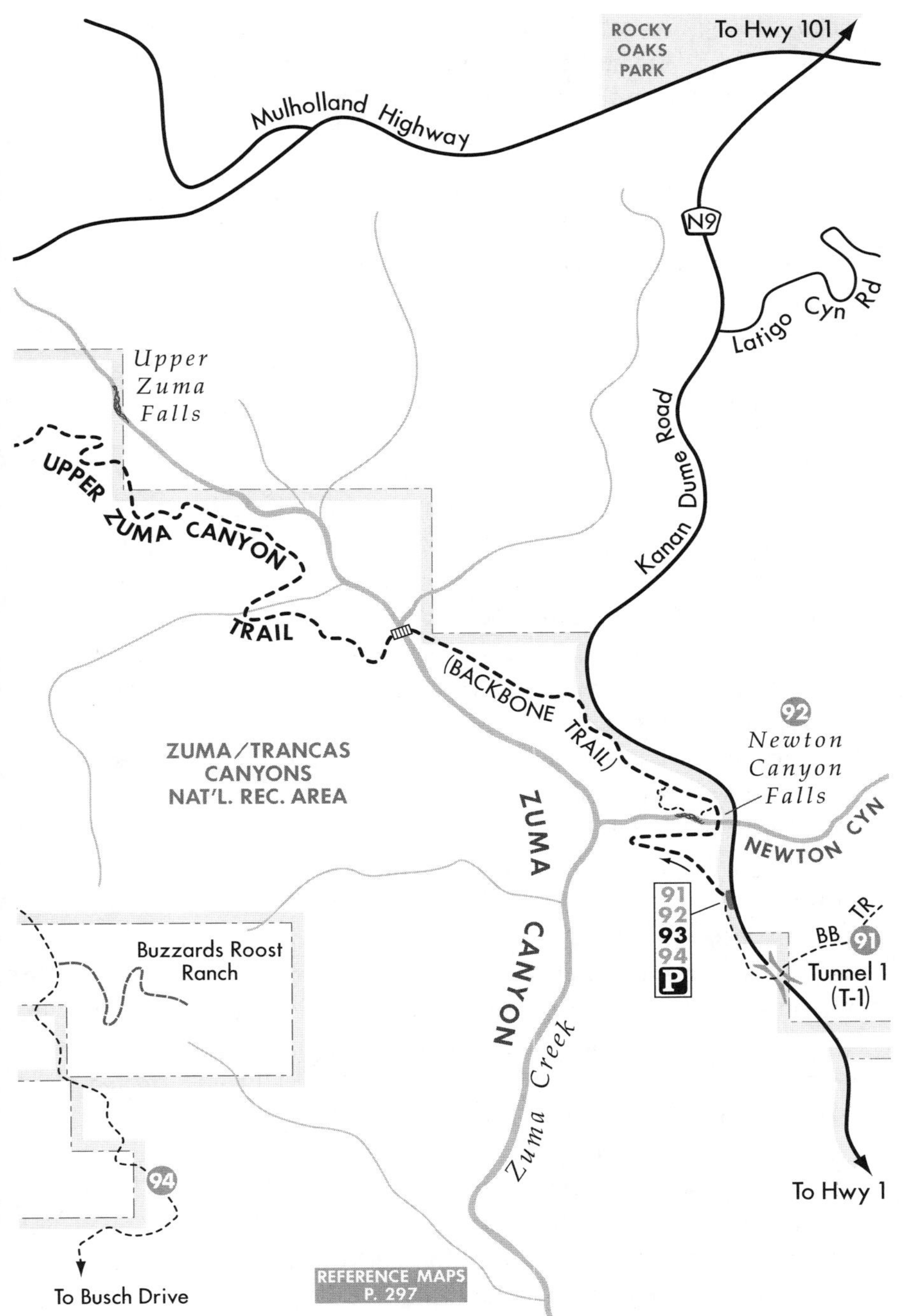
ROCKY
OAKS
PARK
To Hwy 101
Mulholland Highway
N9
Latigo Cyn Rd
Upper
Zuma
Falls
Kanan Dume Road
UPPER ZUMA CANYON
TRAIL
(BACKBONE TRAIL)
ZUMA/TRANCAS
CANYONS
NAT'L. REC. AREA
92
Newton
Canyon
Falls
NEWTON CYN
ZUMA CANYON
91
92
93
94
P
BB TR
91
Tunnel 1
(T-1)
Buzzards Roost
Ranch
Zuma Creek
94
To Busch Drive
REFERENCE MAPS
P. 297
To Hwy 1

lot on the right (west). The parking lot is located just before entering the third tunnel (T-1). (Kanan Road becomes Kanan Dume Road south of Mulholland Highway.)

The hike

Walk past the trailhead kiosk, and head west through the lush vegetation on the Backbone Trail (Upper Zuma Canyon Trail). Descend on the south wall of Upper Zuma Canyon. Switchback to the right and cross over to the north canyon wall. After crossing the trickling Newton Creek, two side paths on the left lead to Newton Canyon Falls. Continue on the rock-embedded path (the main trail) as a coastal view opens up down Zuma Canyon. Descend into the shade of a mixed forest with mature oaks to a bridge spanning Zuma Creek. Cross the bridge and parallel the waterway upstream. Climb to views of the surrounding mountains, then drop back into the forest and cross a feeder stream. Wind through the backcountry on the undulating path to a close-up view of Upper Zuma Falls as it flows down the face of a sandstone wall. Weave along the mountain contours to a posted T-junction with the Zuma Ridge Trail, a gated dirt road at 2.5 miles. The right fork leads 0.4 miles to the trailhead gate on Encinal Canyon Road. Bear left and follow the unpaved road 0.1 mile to a left U-bend. Mid-bend is a junction. The Zuma Ridge Trail (a fire road) continues downhill 5.3 miles to Busch Drive by Zuma Beach—Hike 94.

Bear right on the Trancas Canyon Trail, continuing on another section of the Backbone Trail. Follow the ridge uphill, leaving Zuma Canyon. Descend and traverse the hillside into Trancas Canyon to the posted Backbone Trail sign. Veer left, staying on the Trancas Canyon Trail. Follow the gentle downward slope and switchback to the left, dropping deep into the lush canyon. Continue down to a tributary of Trancas Creek in a shaded forest. Cross a bridge over the tributary, and head down canyon through the oak forest to a fork at Trancas Creek. The left fork follows the creek about 100 feet and ends. Bear right and rock-hop over the creek. Climb the canyon wall, leaving the shade of the forest. Cross a bridge over the creek, and climb out of the canyon to the gated trailhead on Encinal Canyon Road. Return along the same route. ■

94. Zuma Ridge Trail Shuttle

ZUMA/TRANCAS CANYONS: Upper to Lower Zuma Canyon

Malibu

Hiking distance: 8.5-miles one-way (shuttle)
Hiking time: 4.5 hours
Configuration: one-way shuttle
Elevation gain: 900 feet gain and 1,900 feet loss
Difficulty: moderate to strenuous
Exposure: exposed hills
Dogs: allowed
Maps: U.S.G.S. Point Dume
Tom Harrison Maps: Zuma-Trancas Canyons Trail Map

map page 313

The Zuma Ridge Trail follow the ridge between Zuma Canyon and Trancas Canyon—from Encinal Canyon Road, near the crest of the Santa Monica Mountains, to the ocean at Zuma Beach, near Point Dume. Both stream-fed canyons, which run through the Zuma/Trancas Canyons area, have remained natural and undisturbed. The fire road/trail along the ridge offers spectacular non-stop vistas into both of the rugged and undeveloped canyons. The views span for miles across the mountain range, from Boney Mountain in Point Mugu State Park, to Castro Peak and Saddle Peak in the east, and seaward to the vast Pacific Ocean in the south. This one-way shuttle hike follows the fire road south, from the upper reaches of the canyons and downward to the mouth of Zuma Canyon near the ocean. En route are bird's-eye views of the deep water-carved gorges and the sheer rock faces of the sculptured canyon walls.

To the trailhead

From Santa Monica, drive 18 miles northbound on the Pacific Coast Highway/Highway 1 to Kanan Dume Road (5.8 miles west of Malibu Canyon Road). Turn right and drive 4.4 miles north to the trailhead parking lot on the left (west). The parking lot is located just after the first tunnel (T-1).

From the Ventura Freeway/Highway 101 in Agoura Hills, take the Kanan Road exit. Drive 7.9 miles south to the trailhead parking lot on the right (west). The parking lot is located just before entering the third tunnel (T-1). (Kanan Road becomes Kanan Dume Road south of Mulholland Highway.)

Shuttle car

From Santa Monica, drive 19.3 miles northbound on the Pacific Coast Highway/Highway 1 to Busch Drive and turn right. (Busch Drive is one mile west of Kanan Dume Road.) Turn right and drive 1.3 miles up Busch Drive to the trailhead parking lot on the right at the end of the road.

The hike

From the trailhead parking on Kanan Dume Road, walk past the trailhead kiosk, and head west through the lush vegetation on the Backbone Trail (Upper Zuma Canyon Trail). Descend on the south wall of Upper Zuma Canyon. Switchback to the right and cross over to the north canyon wall. Follow the rock-embedded path, with minor dips and rises, as a coastal view opens up down Zuma Canyon. Descend into the shade of a mixed forest with mature oaks to a bridge spanning Zuma Creek. Cross the bridge and parallel the waterway upstream. Climb to views of the surrounding mountains, then drop back into the forest and cross a feeder stream. Wind through the backcountry on the undulating path to a close-up view of Upper Zuma Falls as it flows down the face of a sandstone wall. Weave along the mountain contours to a posted T-junction with the Zuma Ridge Trail, a gated dirt road at 2.5 miles. The right fork leads 0.4 miles to the trailhead gate on Encinal Canyon Road. Bear left and follow the unpaved road 0.1 mile to a left U-bend. On the bend, the Trancas Canyon Trail, another section of the Backbone Trail, continues to the right (Hike 93).

For this hike, continue straight ahead, winding up the mountain to sweeping ocean views. At 3.5 miles, the road reaches the 2,400-foot summit by the signed Buzzard's Roost Ranch on the left. Snake down the oceanfront mountains with spectacular coastal vistas. Leave the easement through the ranch to an overlook high above Zuma Canyon, then a view into Trancas Canyon. Pass a group of conglomerate rock walls to a posted junction with the Zuma Edison Road at 5.8 miles. Continue down the Zuma

Ridge Trail, traversing the east wall of Trancas Canyon to a close-up vista of Zuma Beach and Malibu. Weave down the mountain to the trailhead and shuttle car at the north end of Busch Drive. ■

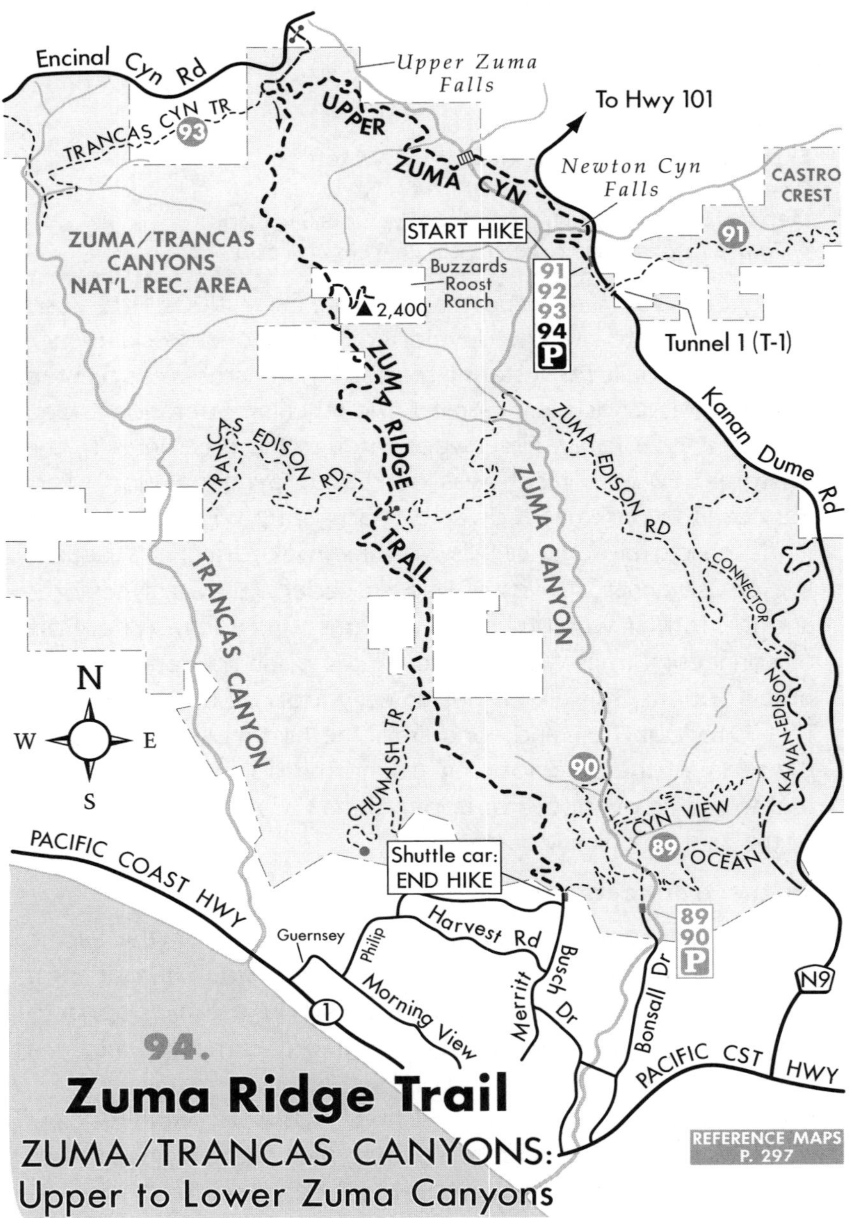

94. Zuma Ridge Trail

ZUMA/TRANCAS CANYONS: Upper to Lower Zuma Canyons

95. Rocky Oaks Park

Malibu

Hiking distance: 2-mile loop
Hiking time: 1 hour
Configuration: loop with optional connecting trails
Elevation gain: 200 feet
Difficulty: easy
Exposure: open slopes and forested pockets
Dogs: allowed
Maps: U.S.G.S. Point Dume • N.P.S. Rocky Oaks Site map
Tom Harrison Maps: Zuma-Trancas Canyons Trail map

Rocky Oaks Park was homesteaded in the early 1900s. Fifty years later, the remote site was developed into a working cattle ranch. A pond was built for watering the cattle, orchards were planted, and the grasslands were farmed. The ranching operation ended after the 1978 Kanan Fire swept through the area. In 1981, the pastoral 200-acre ranch was purchased by the National Park Service. The park has a diverse topography with rolling grasslands, chaparral-covered hills, volcanic rock formations, coastal live oak savannah, groves of Deodar cedar, willows, sycamores, and the former watering pond in a grassy meadow. A network of connecting trails weaves through the open space for several hiking options. This hike forms an easy loop on the Rocky Oaks Trail, Overlook Trail, and Pond Trail. The hike meanders through the heart of the park, looping around the pond to picnic areas and to scenic overlooks of upper Zuma Canyon and the interior of the Santa Monica Mountains.

To the trailhead

From Santa Monica, drive 18 miles northbound on the Pacific Coast Highway/Highway 1 to Kanan Dume Road (5.8 miles west of Malibu Canyon Road). Turn right and drive 6.2 miles north to Mulholland Highway and turn left. Quickly turn right into the Rocky Oaks Park entrance and parking lot.

From the Ventura Freeway/Highway 101 in Agoura Hills, exit on Kanan Road. Drive 6.1 miles south to Mulholland Highway. Turn right and a quick right again into the park entrance.

The hike

Hike north past the rail fence to the Rocky Oaks Loop Trail, which heads in both directions. Take the left fork a short distance, passing old ranch ruins to a 4-way junction. Continue straight ahead on the middle path towards the Overlook Trail. Ascend the hillside overlooking the pond, and make a horseshoe left bend. Beyond the bend is the Overlook Trail. This is a short detour on the left to a scenic overlook with 360-degree panoramic views.

Back on the main trail, continue northeast around the ridge, slowly descending to the valley floor near Kanan Road. Bear sharply to the right, heading south to the Pond Trail junction. Both the left and right forks loop around the pond and rejoin at the south end. At the junction, go south and return to the Rocky Oaks Loop, then retrace your steps back to the trailhead. ■

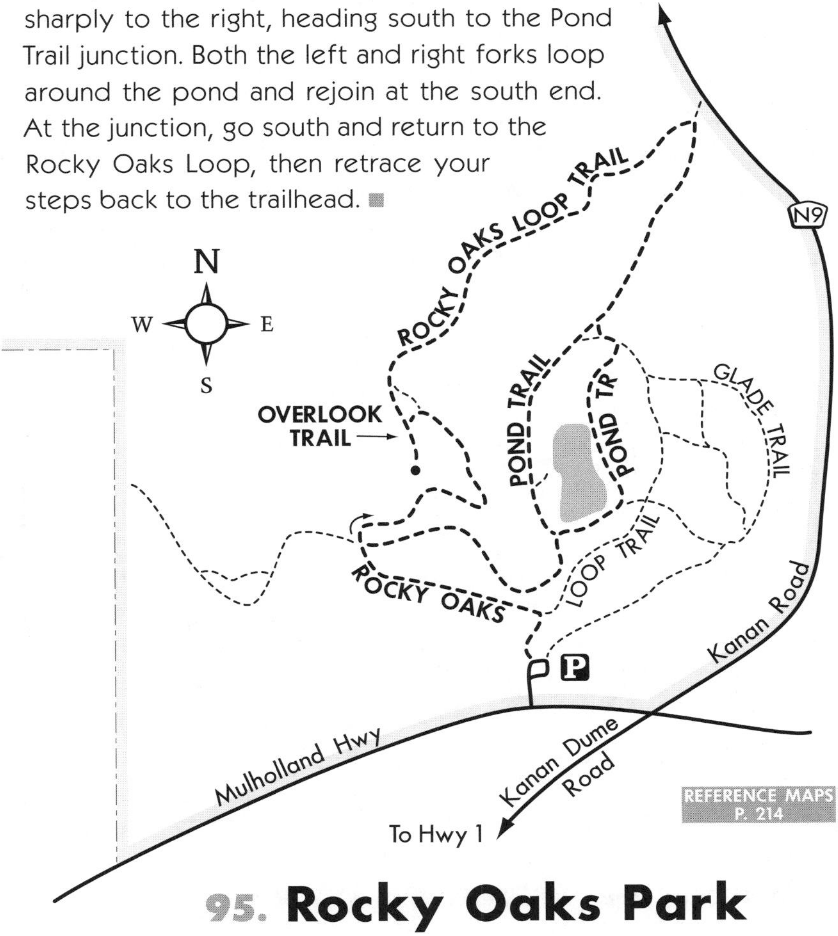

N
W E
S
ROCKY OAKS LOOP TRAIL
OVERLOOK TRAIL
POND TRAIL
POND TR
GLADE TRAIL
LOOP TRAIL
ROCKY OAKS
N9
Kanan Road
Mulholland Hwy
Kanan Dume Road
To Hwy 1

REFERENCE MAPS P. 214

95. Rocky Oaks Park

96. Charmlee Wilderness Park

2577 S. Encinal Canyon Road • Malibu
Open daily 8:00 a.m. to sunset

Hiking distance: 3-mile loop
Hiking time: 1.5 hours
Configuration: loop plus optional connecting trails
Elevation gain: 600 feet
Difficulty: easy
Exposure: exposed with forested pockets
Dogs: allowed
Maps: U.S.G.S. Triunfo Pass • City of Malibu-Charmlee Natural Area map
Tom Harrison Maps: Zuma-Trancas Canyons Trail map

Perched on oceanfront cliffs 1,300 feet above the sea, Charmlee Wilderness Park has a magnificent bird's-eye view of the Malibu coastline. The 532-acre wilderness park, sitting between Encinal Canyon and Lechusa Canyon, was once a cattle ranch. The land was purchased by Los Angeles County in 1968 and opened as

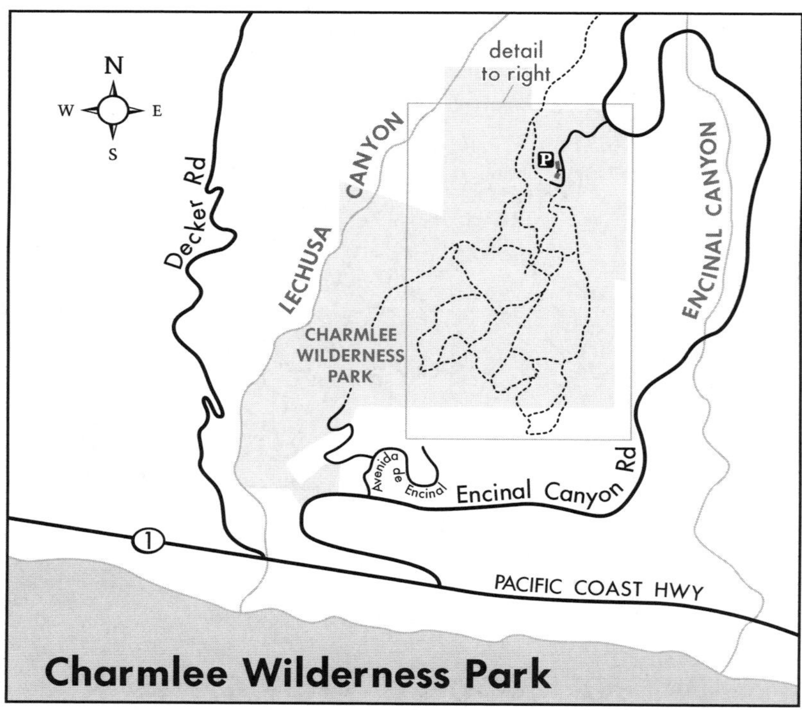

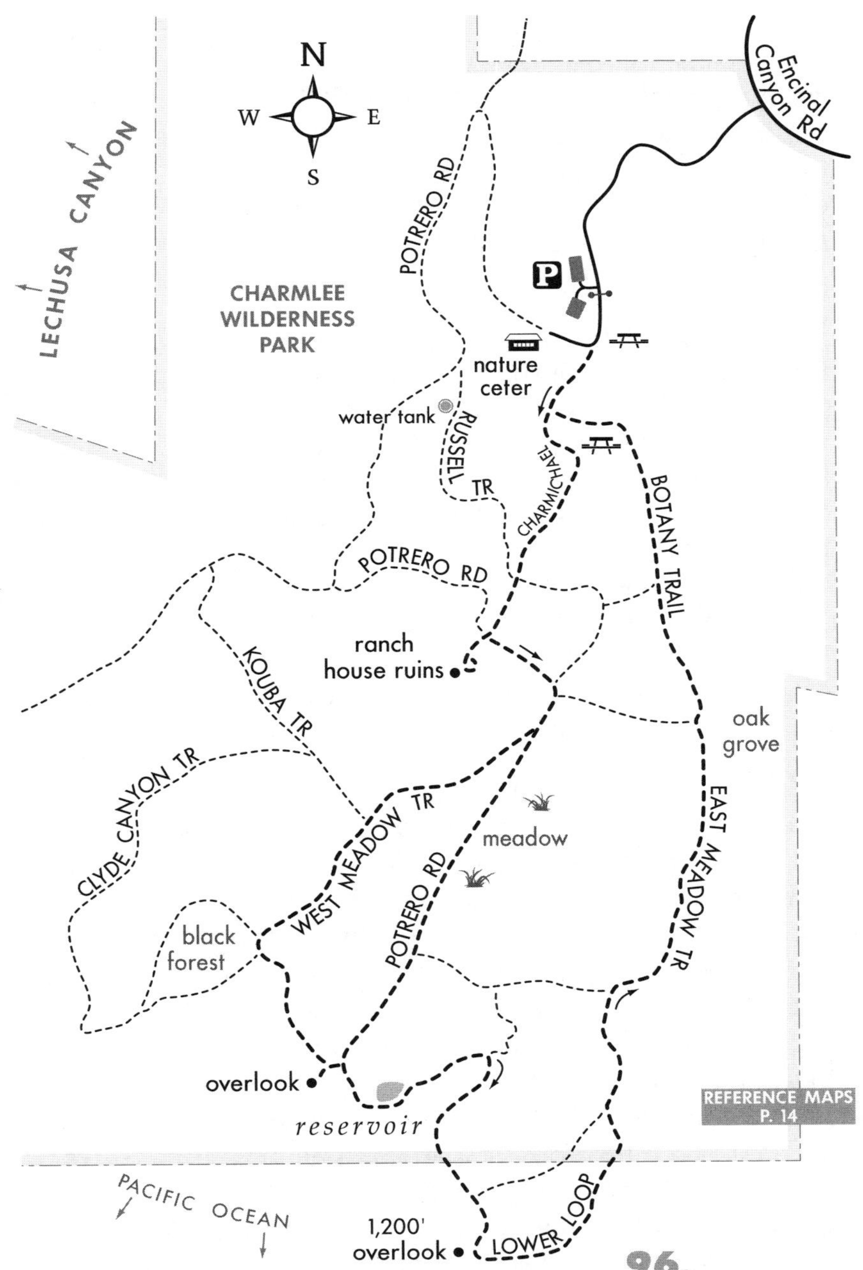

96. Charmlee Wilderness Park

a park in 1981. Eight miles of interconnecting footpaths and old ranch roads weave through expansive mountain terrain with grassy meadows, oak and eucalyptus woodlands, mountain slopes, rocky ridges, sandstone formations, and 1,250-foot bluffs overlooking the sea. The park has picnic areas and a nature center with plant exhibits. This hike crosses the bluffs through meadows and forest groves to the old ranch reservoir and oceanfront overlooks.

To the trailhead

From Santa Monica, drive 23.2 miles northbound on the Pacific Coast Highway/Highway 1 to Encinal Canyon Road and turn right/north. (Encinal Canyon Road is 11.2 miles west of Malibu Canyon Road.) Continue 3.7 miles to the park entrance on the left. Turn left and drive 0.2 miles on the park road to the parking lot. A parking fee is required.

From the Pacific Coast Highway/Highway 1 and Las Posas Road in southeast Oxnard, drive 14 miles southbound on the PCH to Encinal Canyon Road and turn left. Continue 3.7 miles to the Charmlee Park entrance on the left. Follow the park road 0.2 miles to the parking lot.

The hike

Hike past the information board and picnic area on the wide trail. Pass a second picnic area on the left in an oak grove, and continue uphill to a three-way trail split. The middle trail is a short detour leading to an overlook set among rock formations and the old ranch house foundation. Take the main trail to the left into the large grassy meadow. Two trails cross the meadow and rejoin at the south end—the main trail (Potrero Road) heads through the meadow while the right fork (West Meadow Trail) skirts the meadow's western edge. At the far end is an ocean overlook and a trail fork. Bear left past an old ranch reservoir, and pass two junctions to a 1,200-foot overlook on the right. Continue downhill, curving north through an oak grove to the unsigned Botany Trail, a narrow footpath on the right. The Botany Trail winds back to the picnic area and the trailhead. ■

97. Encinal Canyon Road to Etz Meloy Motorway

Malibu

Hiking distance: 7.8 miles round trip
Hiking time: 4 hours
Configuration: out-and-back
Elevation gain: 950 feet
Difficulty: moderate to strenuous
Exposure: exposed with forested pockets
Dogs: allowed
Maps: U.S.G.S. Point Dume and Triunfo Pass
Trails Illustrated: Santa Monica Mountains National Recreation Area
Tom Harrison Maps: Zuma-Trancas Canyons Trail Map

map page 321

This hike follows a section of the Backbone Trail from Encinal Canyon Road, at the upper end of Trancas Canyon, to the Etz Meloy Motorway, an exposed dirt road high on a ridge. The trail weaves up canyon walls to magnificent vistas and an overlook. Throughout the hike are views across the rolling, scalloped mountains to the Pacific Ocean. Mid-way through the hike, the trail crosses Mulholland Highway. Parking is not available along Mulholland Highway, so driving access is only possible from the Encinal Trailhead.

To the trailhead

From Santa Monica, drive 18 miles northbound on the Pacific Coast Highway/Highway 1 to Encinal Canyon Road. (Encinal Canyon Road is 5.5 miles west of Kanan Dume Road.) Drive 5 miles up the mountain to a road split with Lechusa Road. Turn right, staying on Encinal Canyon Road, and continue 1.1 mile to the posted trailhead on the left. Park in the long, narrow pullout on the left. When it is dry, turn a sharp left and descend 130 yards to the circular parking area at the trailhead.

From the Ventura Freeway/Highway 101 in Agoura Hills, exit on Kanan Road. Drive 6.1 miles south to Mulholland Highway. Turn right and continue 0.9 miles to Encinal Canyon Road. Veer left and go 2.3 miles to the posted trailhead on the right. Park in the long, narrow pullout on the right. When it is dry, turn right and descend 130 yards to the circular parking area at the trailhead.

The hike

The Trancas Canyon Trail, an adjoining section of the Backbone Trail, is on the south side of the road (Hike 93). For this hike, head north past the trail sign on the Encinal Trail (Backbone Trail). Descend 130 yards to a parking area. Head up the minor draw, following the curvature of the hills while gaining elevation on an easy grade. Weave up the serpentine path, and traverse the east wall of the stream-fed canyon. At 1.1 mile, the Encinal Trail ends at Mulholland Highway.

Carefully cross the highway and pick up the trail directly across the road, now the Mulholland Trail (but still the Backbone Trail). Walk through the chaparral and grassland. Begin the climb and weave through the forest and up open slopes. The meandering path offers views across the rolling, scalloped mountains and across endless ridges and canyons to the Pacific Ocean. At 3.6 miles, the trail ends at a T-junction with the Etz Meloy Motorway, a dirt road at an elevation of 2,400 feet. To the right, the road descends less than 0.1 mile to signed private land.

Bear left and follow the serpentine road uphill. The views stretch across the green rolling hills to the ocean and the Channel Islands. At a quarter mile is an overlook on the right in a saddle between two ridges. At the overlook, make a U-shaped right bend, and gently climb the east-facing hillside to the summit with 360-degree panoramas. This is a great turn-around spot. Return by retracing your steps.

Public access continues another quarter mile on the Etz Meloy Motorway. At the time of this writing, the final one mile to Yerba Buena Road is on private land. The National Park Service is continuing to seek public access over Etz Meloy Motorway to Yerba Buena Road. Visitors will know when access has been secured when trail signage indicates that the route is open. ■

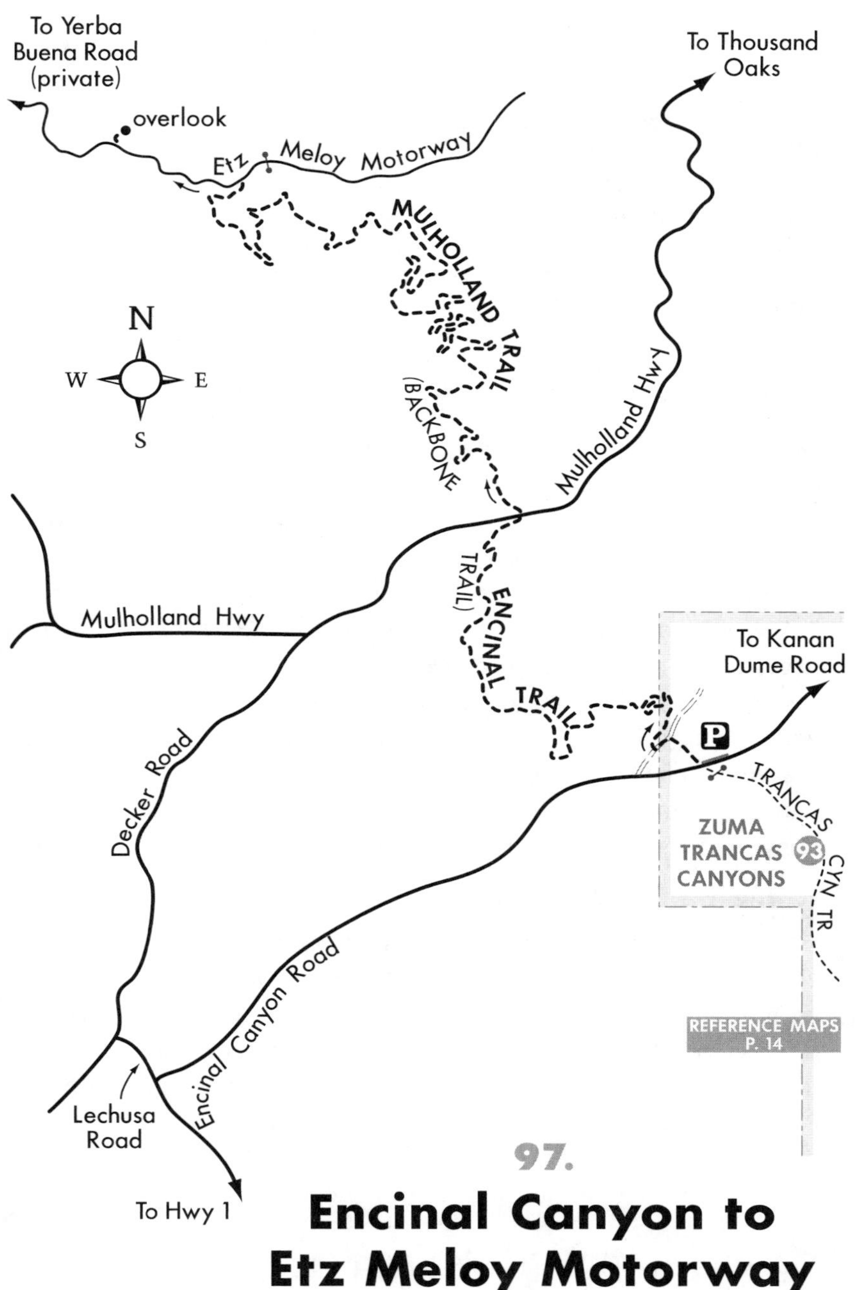

97. Encinal Canyon to Etz Meloy Motorway

98. Pentachaeta Trail

TRIUNFO CREEK PARK

Thousand Oaks

Hiking distance: 3.2 miles round trip
Hiking time: 2 hours
Configuration: out-and-back with loop
Elevation gain: 400 feet
Difficulty: easy to moderate
Exposure: a mix of open slopes and forested canyon
Dogs: allowed
Maps: U.S.G.S. Thousand Oaks
Tom Harrison Maps: Zuma-Trancas Canyons Trail Map
Santa Monica Mountains Conservancy Triunfo Creek Park map

Pentachaeta Trail is located in the 600-acre Triunfo Creek Park, an undeveloped open space in the Westlake Village area at the south end of Thousand Oaks. The protected open space and wildlife habitat is tucked into the foothills of the northern edge of the Santa Monica Mountains. The park contains native grasslands, oak woodlands, and rugged rolling hills. The Pentachaeta Trail is named for a rare, endangered flower found in Triunfo Creek Park. The Pentachaeta lyonii, found only in southern California, has a yellow daisy-like flower that blooms from April through June. The Pentachaeta Trail traverses the mountain slope into Triunfo Canyon, forming a small loop atop the mountain between Triunfo Canyon to the north and Lobo Canyon to the south.

To the trailhead

From the Ventura Freeway/Highway 101 in Westlake Village, exit on Lindero Canyon Road. Drive 1.7 miles south to the junction with Triunfo Canyon Road at the end of the road. Turn left and go 0.1 mile to the signed trailhead on the right, directly across from the Oak Forest Mobile Home Park at 32100 Triunfo Canyon Road. Park alongside the curb.

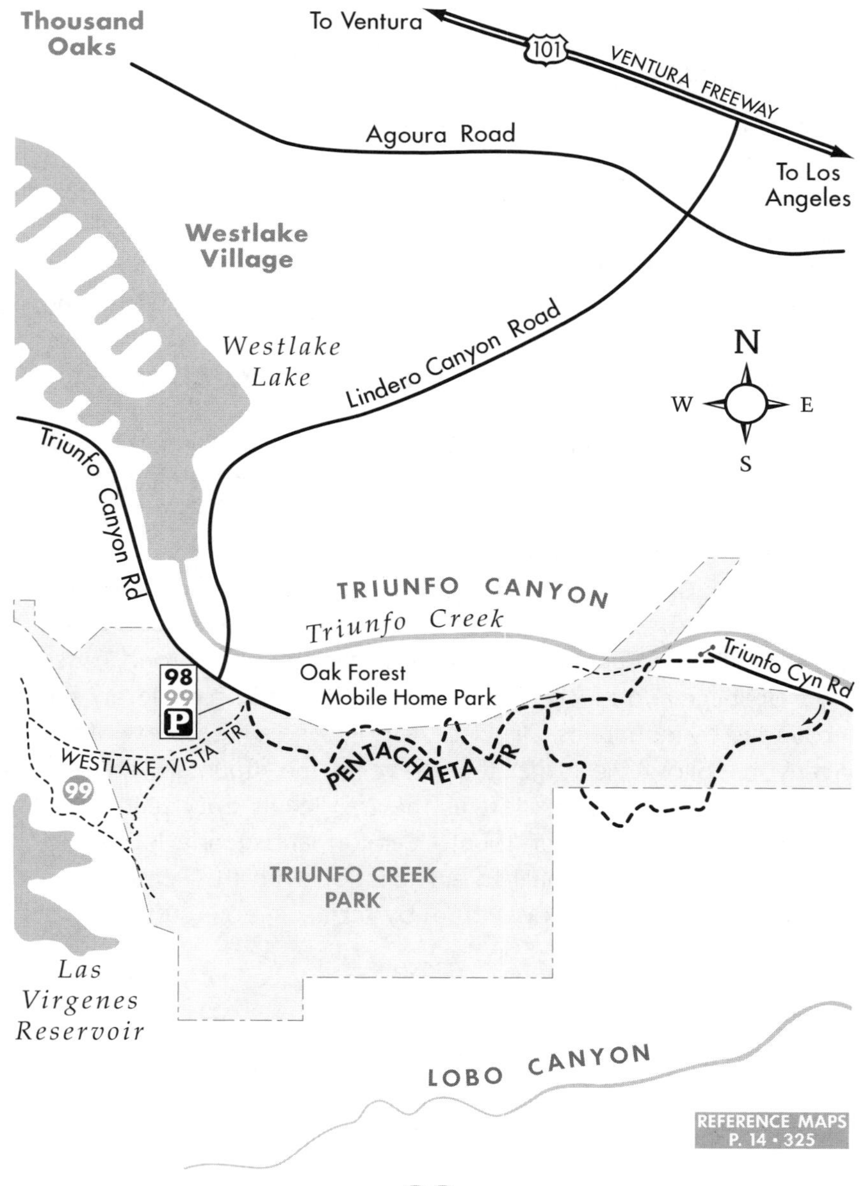

98. Pentachaeta Trail

TRIUNFO CREEK PARK

The hike

At the trailhead is an information kiosk and a signed junction. The Westlake Vista Trail (Hike 99) continues straight ahead on the canyon floor into a bowl surrounded by mountains. Take the Pentachaeta Trail to the left and head into the foothills. Climb the slope through chaparral, passing scattered oaks, then drop into Triunfo Canyon. Traverse the south canyon wall on the dirt road. When the road ends, take the signed footpath on the right. Follow the rolling hills east on the undulating path. Wind along the contours of the canyon wall, passing through a grove of live oaks. Just beyond the shaded grove is an unsigned trail on the right, our return route.

Begin the loop straight ahead, and descend to a T-junction. The left fork parallels Triunfo Creek and ends at the gated Oak Forest Mobile Home Park. Take the right fork to the end of the trail at the western terminus of Triunfo Canyon Road by the Liongate Equestrian Center. Walk a quarter mile to the right on the paved road to a dirt road on the right (located 100 yards shy of a right bend in Triunfo Canyon Road). Walk up the grassy dirt road. Cross the drainage and ascend the hill on the footpath, completely surrounded by mountains. Climb to the ridge and a great view of the canyon. Follow the ridge, then traverse the mountain, steadily gaining elevation. Curve left as the trail levels out. Head west, perched on the wall of Triunfo Canyon, and gently loose elevation. Continue downhill to a T-junction with the Pentachaeta Trail, completing the loop. Return by retracing your steps to the left. ■

99. Westlake Vista Loop to Las Virgenes Reservoir

TRIUNFO CREEK PARK

Thousand Oaks

Hiking distance: 1.2 miles
Hiking time: 40 minutes
Configuration: loop
Elevation gain: 250 feet
Difficulty: easy
Exposure: exposed
Dogs: allowed
Maps: U.S.G.S. Thousand Oaks and Point Dume

map page 327

The Westlake Vista Trail is located on the western portion of Triunfo Creek Park, a 600-acre open space in Westlake Village. From the park, tucked into the foothills, the trail enters an oak and

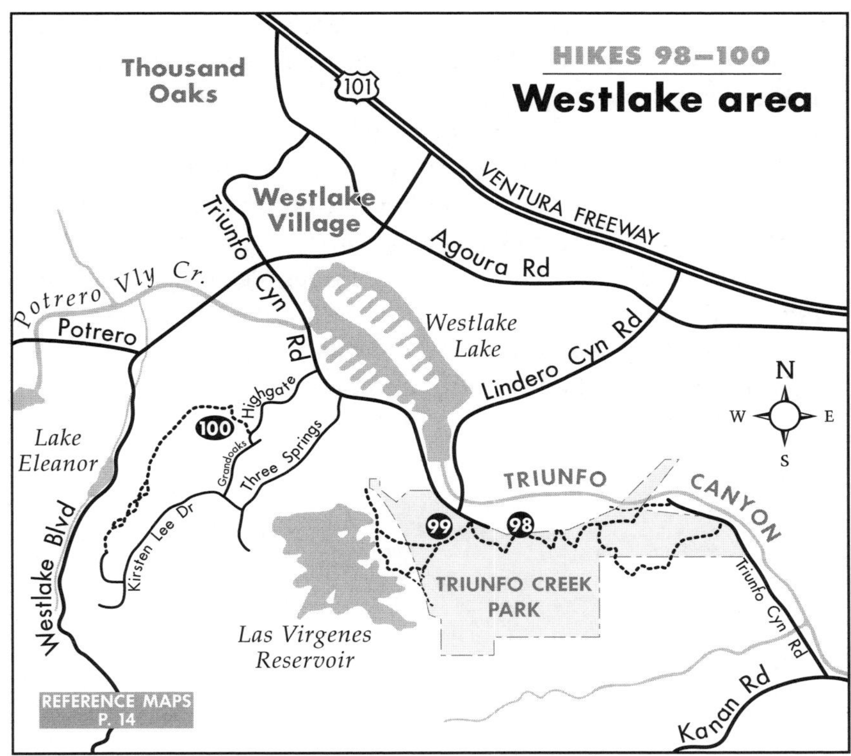

bay-dotted meadow surrounded by mountains. The path climbs the rocky cliffs to a mesa overlooking Las Virgenes Reservoir, a 9,500-acre lake supplying drinking water for the surrounding area. The water, which originates in the high Sierras, is transported more than 400 miles to the reservoir.

To the trailhead

From the Ventura Freeway/Highway 101 in Thousand Oaks, exit on Lindero Canyon Road. Drive 1.7 miles south to the junction with Triunfo Canyon Road at the end of the road. Turn left and go 0.1 mile to the signed trailhead on the right, directly across from the Oak Forest Mobile Home Park at 32100 Triunfo Canyon Road. Park alongside the curb.

The hike

At the trailhead is a signed junction. The Pentachaeta Trail (Hike 98) follows the left fork. Take the right fork—straight ahead on the canyon floor—into a bowl surrounded by mountains. Pass groupings of mature oak and bay trees to an unsigned trail split at 0.2 miles. Begin the loop to the left, hiking clockwise. Head up the slope to the east, and steadily climb on the well-defined path. Near the vertical rock cliffs is a fork. The left fork explores the rock outcroppings and steeply climbs to the plateau by Las Virgenes Reservoir. To make a loop, stay to the right and gently weave up to the plateau at the fenced Las Virgenes Reservoir. Veer to the right, crossing the head of the canyon on the flat mesa. Watch for a trail on the right and bear right. Leave the plateau and descend the hillside to complete the loop. Return 0.2 miles to the trailhead. ■

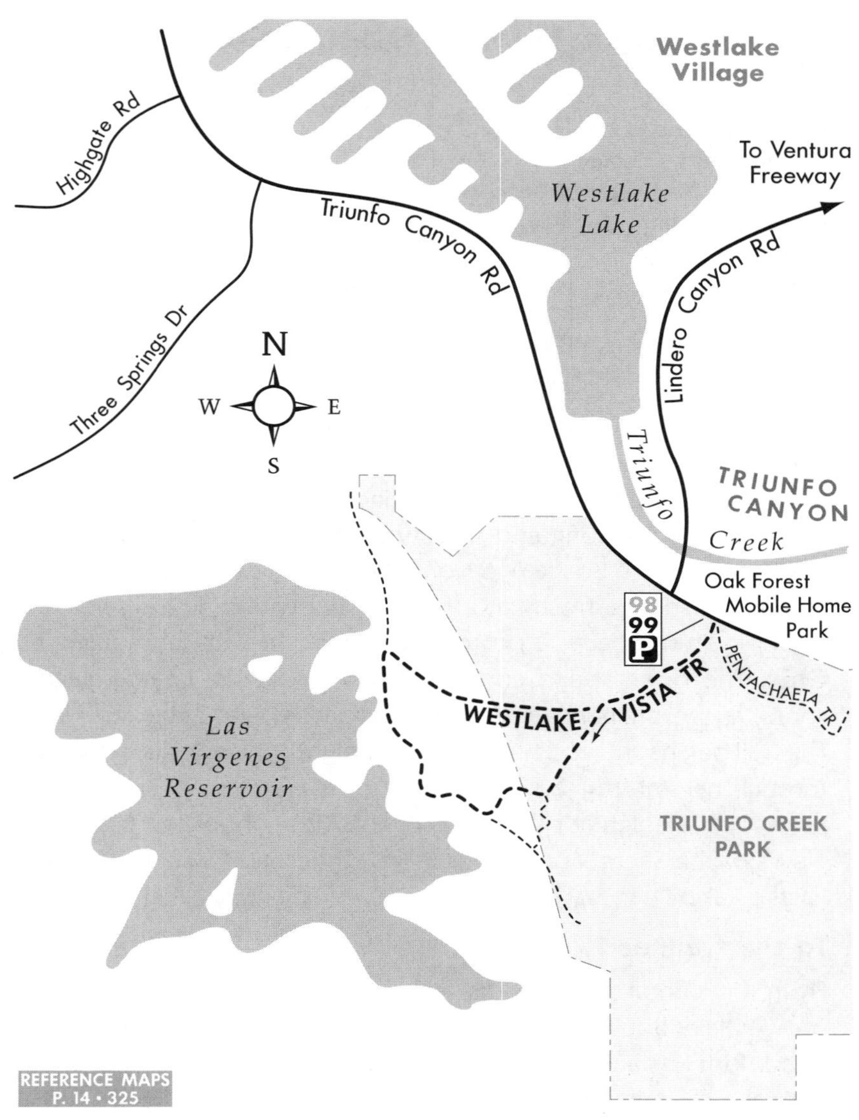

99.

Westlake Vista Loop to Las Virgenes Reservoir

TRIUNFO CREEK PARK

100. Lake Eleanor Open Space

Thousand Oaks

Hiking distance: 2.5 miles round trip
Hiking time: 1.5 hours
Configuration: out-and-back
Elevation gain: 400 feet
Difficulty: easy
Exposure: exposed
Dogs: allowed
Maps: U.S.G.S. Thousand Oaks and Point Dume
Conejo Open Space Foundation Lake Eleanor Open Space map

Lake Eleanor is a small 8-acre lake in a gorge beneath 600-foot vertical rocky cliffs. In 1889, Eleanor Creek was dammed, forming a privately-owned lake for a housing development that never materialized. The long and narrow reservoir is now owned by the Conejo Open Space and Conservation Agency and is closed to public use. The freshwater lake sits within the 529-acre Lake Eleanor Open Space, a protected wildlife habitat in Thousand Oaks. The open space contains oak woodlands, coastal sage scrub, and prominent rocky outcrops amidst undeveloped hills. The trail begins and ends in residential neighborhoods but weaves through natural, rugged terrain. The hike follows an undulating ridgetop trail high above Lake Eleanor. Throughout the hike are views of the Santa Monica Mountains, Thousand Oaks, and three lakes—Lake Eleanor, Las Virgenes Reservoir, and Westlake Lake.

To the trailhead

From the Ventura Freeway/Highway 101 in Thousand Oaks, exit on Westlake Boulevard. Drive one mile south to Triunfo Canyon Road. Turn left and go 0.6 miles to Highgate Road. Turn right and continue 0.5 miles to the trailhead at the end of the road. Park alongside the curb.

The hike

Pass through the gate at the end of the road. Walk 50 yards on the vehicle-restricted road to the footpath on the right. Take the footpath and climb the short hill to an overlook of Thousand

Oaks and the surrounding mountains. Top the slope and follow the rolling ridge. Curve left, staying atop the ridge. The views span in every direction, including Westlake Lake and the Las Virgenes Reservoir. Continue uphill to a knoll at a half mile. Drop down the slope to magnificent sandstone rock formations. Pass a series of three Y-forks. At each one, the left fork stays at a near-level grade, curving around the knolls. The right forks go up and over the knolls, offering views into the canyon and of Lake Eleanor, sitting at the base of the distinct majestic mountain. After each knoll, the two trails rejoin. After the trails reconnect the third time, the path gently descends to the trailhead at the northern terminus of Denver Springs Drive. Return by retracing your route. ■

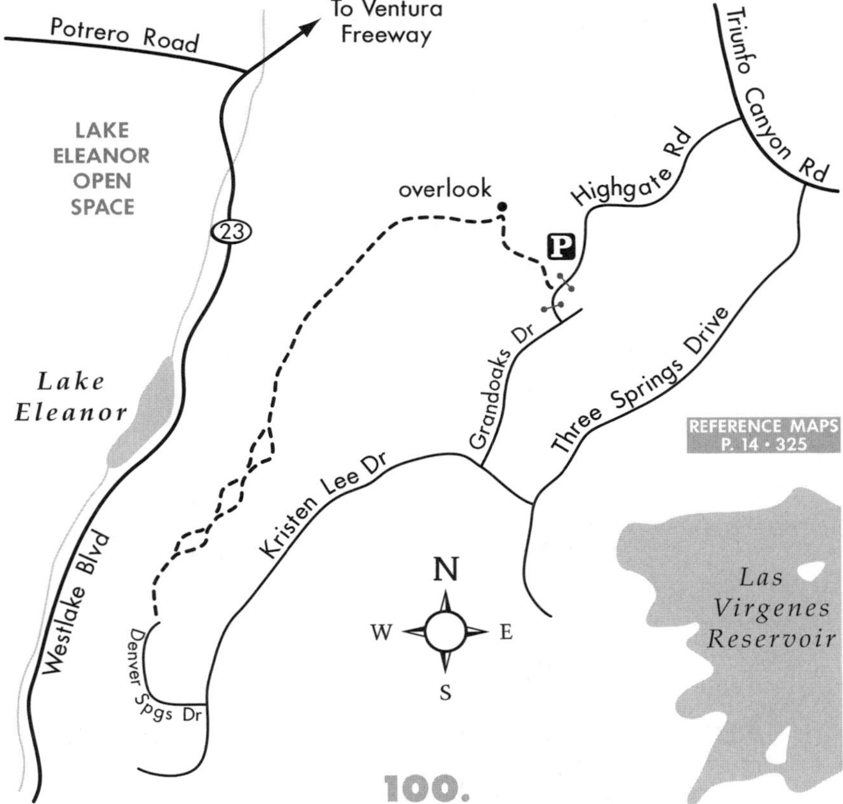

100. Lake Eleanor Open Space

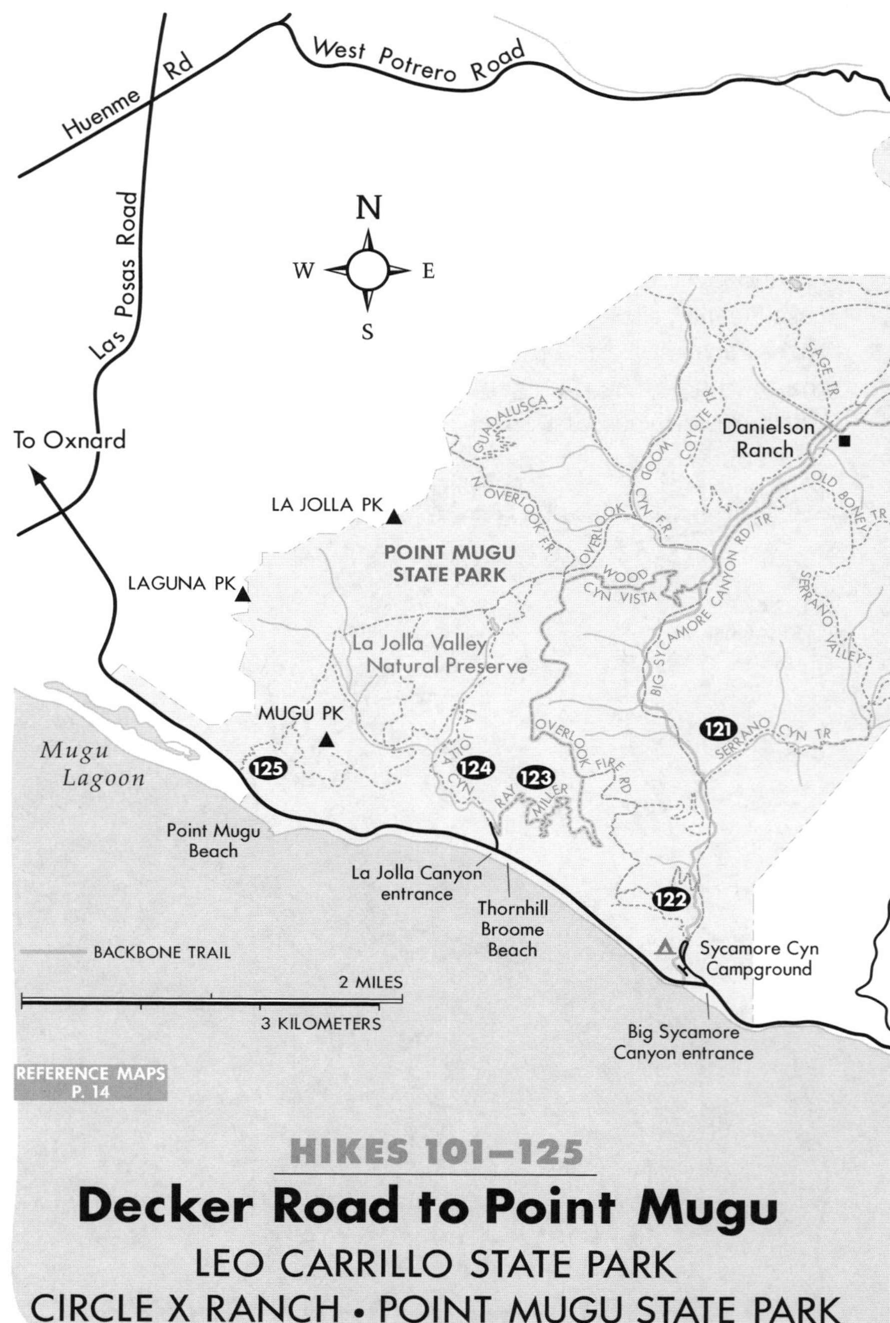

HIKES 101–125

Decker Road to Point Mugu

LEO CARRILLO STATE PARK
CIRCLE X RANCH • POINT MUGU STATE PARK

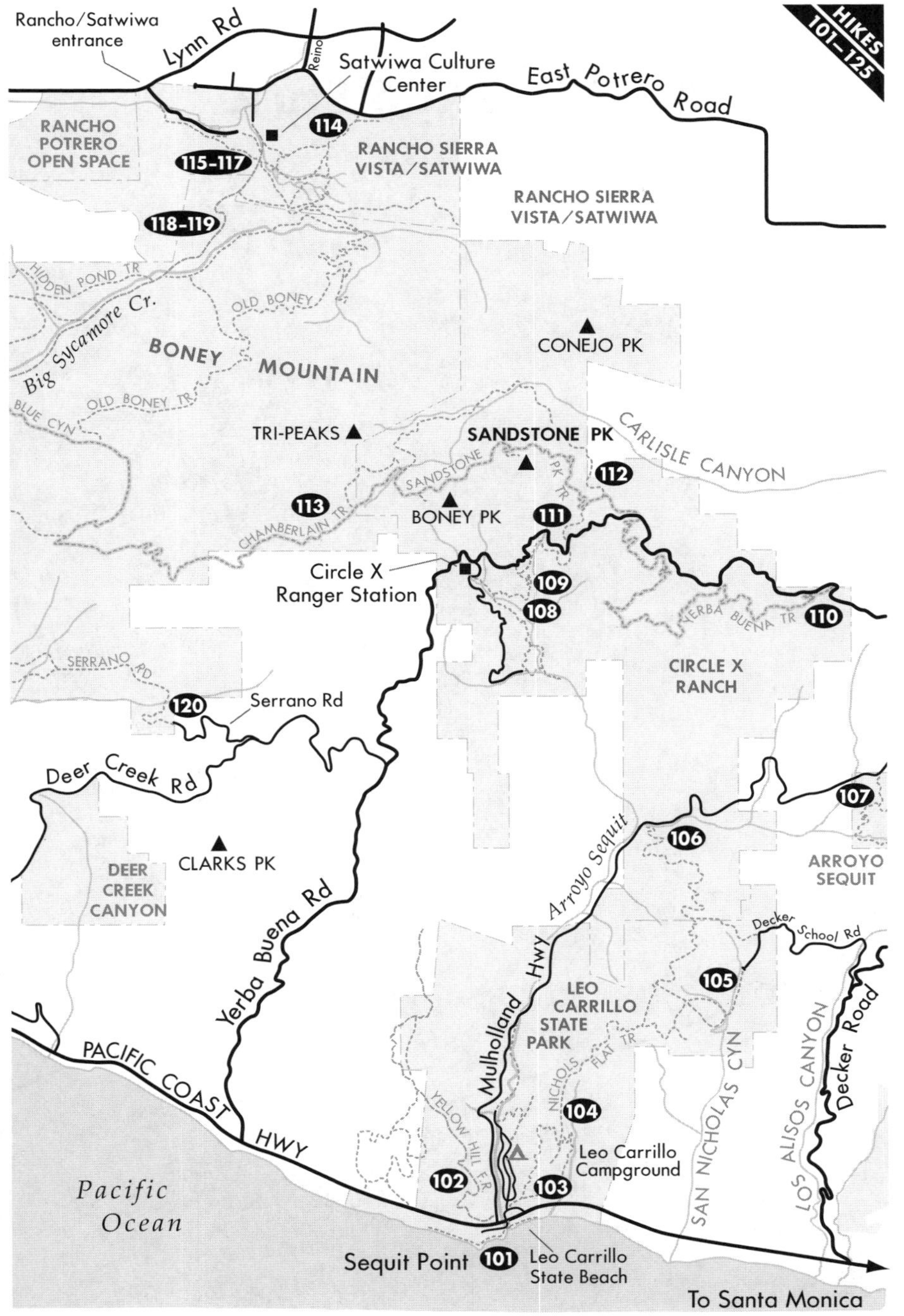
HIKES 101–125
Rancho/Satwiwa entrance
Lynn Rd
Reino
Satwiwa Culture Center
East Potrero Road
RANCHO POTRERO OPEN SPACE
114
115-117
118-119
RANCHO SIERRA VISTA/SATWIWA
RANCHO SIERRA VISTA/SATWIWA
HIDDEN POND TR
OLD BONEY
Big Sycamore Cr.
BONEY MOUNTAIN
CONEJO PK
OLD BONEY TR
BLUE CYN
TRI-PEAKS
SANDSTONE PK
CARLISLE CANYON
SANDSTONE
PK TR
112
113
CHAMBERLAIN TR
BONEY PK
111
Circle X Ranger Station
109
108
YERBA BUENA TR
110
CIRCLE X RANCH
SERRANO RD
120
Serrano Rd
Deer Creek Rd
107
106
Arroyo Sequit
ARROYO SEQUIT
CLARKS PK
DEER CREEK CANYON
Yerba Buena Rd
Decker School Rd
Mulholland Hwy
LEO CARRILLO STATE PARK
105
NICHOLS FLAT TR
SAN NICHOLAS CYN
LOS ALISOS CANYON
Decker Road
PACIFIC COAST HWY
YELLOW HILL F.R.
104
Leo Carrillo Campground
102
103
Pacific Ocean
Sequit Point
101
Leo Carrillo State Beach
To Santa Monica

HIKES 101–106

Leo Carrillo State Park

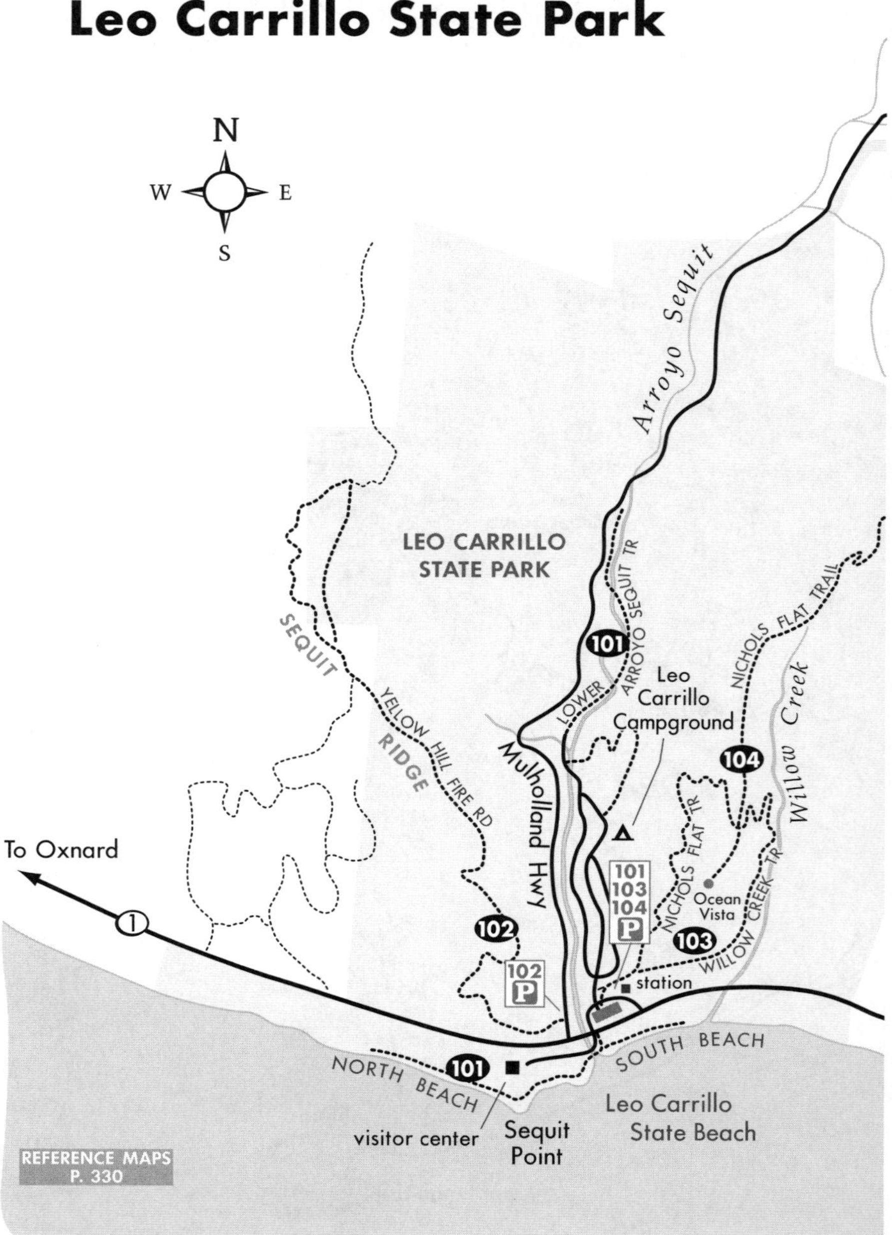

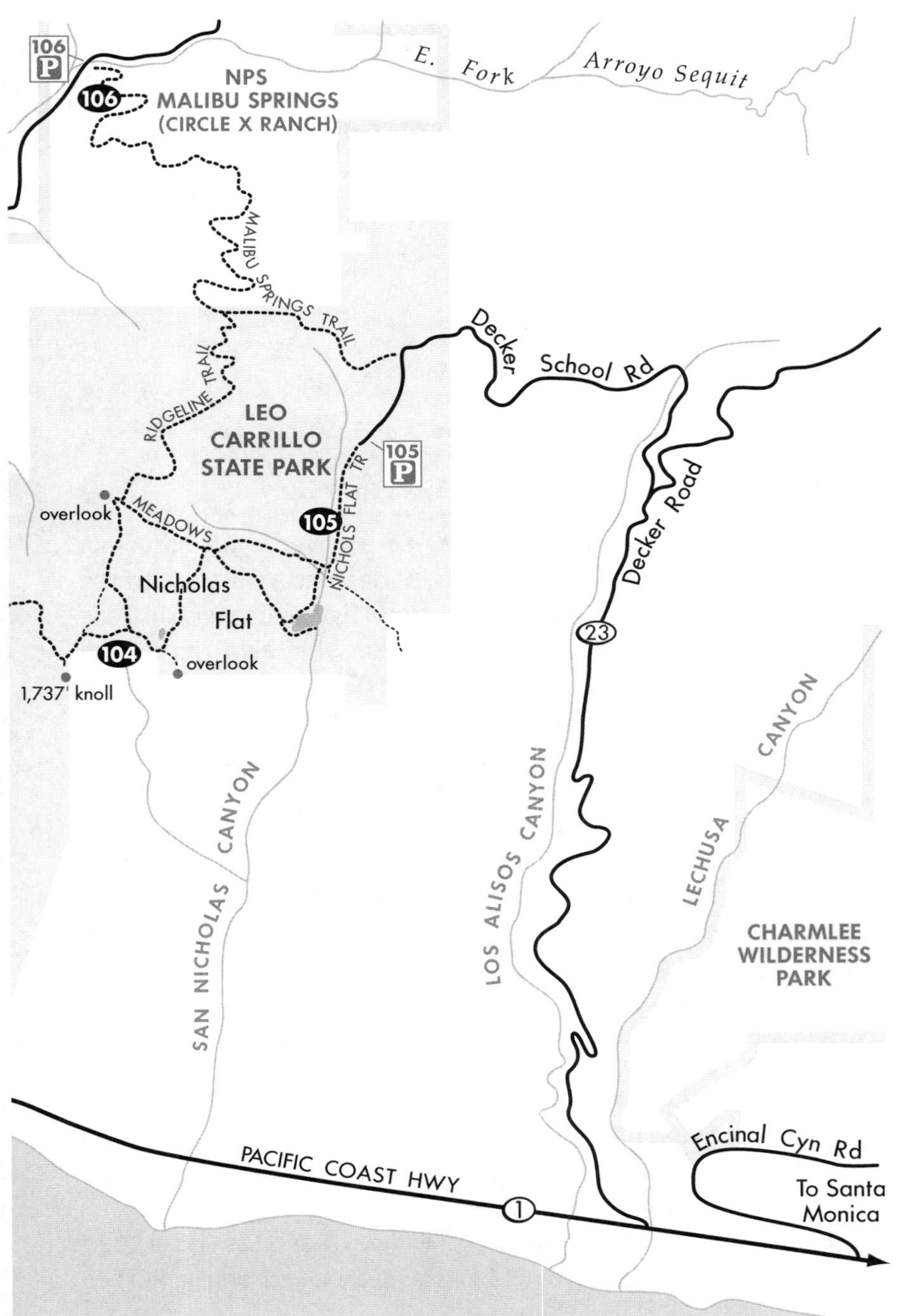
106
P
E. Fork Arroyo Sequit
NPS
106
MALIBU SPRINGS
(CIRCLE X RANCH)
MALIBU SPRINGS TRAIL
RIDGELINE TRAIL
Decker School Rd
LEO
CARRILLO
STATE PARK
105
P
NICHOLS FLAT TR
105
overlook
MEADOWS
Decker Road
Nicholas
Flat
23
104
overlook
1,737' knoll
SAN NICHOLAS CANYON
LOS ALISOS CANYON
LECHUSA CANYON
CHARMLEE
WILDERNESS
PARK
Encinal Cyn Rd
PACIFIC COAST HWY
1
To Santa
Monica

101. Lower Arroyo Sequit Trail and Sequit Point

LEO CARRILLO STATE PARK

35000 W. Pacific Coast Hwy • Malibu

Hiking distance: 3 miles round trip
Hiking time: 1.5 hours
Configuration: two out-and-back trails
Elevation gain: 200 feet
Difficulty: easy
Exposure: shaded canyon; exposed beach
Dogs: not allowed
Maps: U.S.G.S. Triunfo Pass • Leo Carrillo State Beach map
Tom Harrison Maps: Point Mugu State Park Trail map
Tom Harrison Maps: Zuma-Trancas Canyons Trail map

Leo Carrillo State Park is a 2,100-acre haven with mountain canyons, steep chaparral-covered hillsides, and a 1.5-mile stretch of coastline. The area was once inhabited by the Chumash Indians. The Lower Arroyo Sequit Trail leads into a cool, stream-fed canyon shaded with willow, sycamore, oak, and bay trees. The path ends in a deep, rock-walled canyon by large boulders and the trickling stream. At the south end of the park, at the oceanfront, is Sequit Point, a rocky bluff that juts out from the shoreline. The weather-carved point, which divides North Beach from South Beach, has sea caves, coves, ocean-sculpted arches, tidepools, and pocket beaches. A pedestrian tunnel under the Pacific Coast Highway connects South Beach (near the mouth of Arroyo Sequit) with the campground and the tree-shaded canyon.

To the trailhead

From Santa Monica, drive 26 miles northbound on the Pacific Coast Highway/Highway 1 to the posted Leo Carrillo State Beach entrance and turn right. (The state park is 14 miles west of Malibu Canyon Road and 8 miles west of Kanan Dume Road.) Park in the day-use parking lot. A parking fee is required.

From the Pacific Coast Highway/Highway 1 and Las Posas Road in southeast Oxnard, drive 11.1 miles southbound on the PCH to the posted Leo Carrillo State Beach entrance and turn left. Park in the day-use parking lot. A parking fee is required.

The hike

LOWER ARROYO SEQUIT TRAIL: From the parking area, hike north through the campground on the road past mature sycamores and oaks. Pass the amphitheater on the right to a gated road. Continue past the gate, crossing

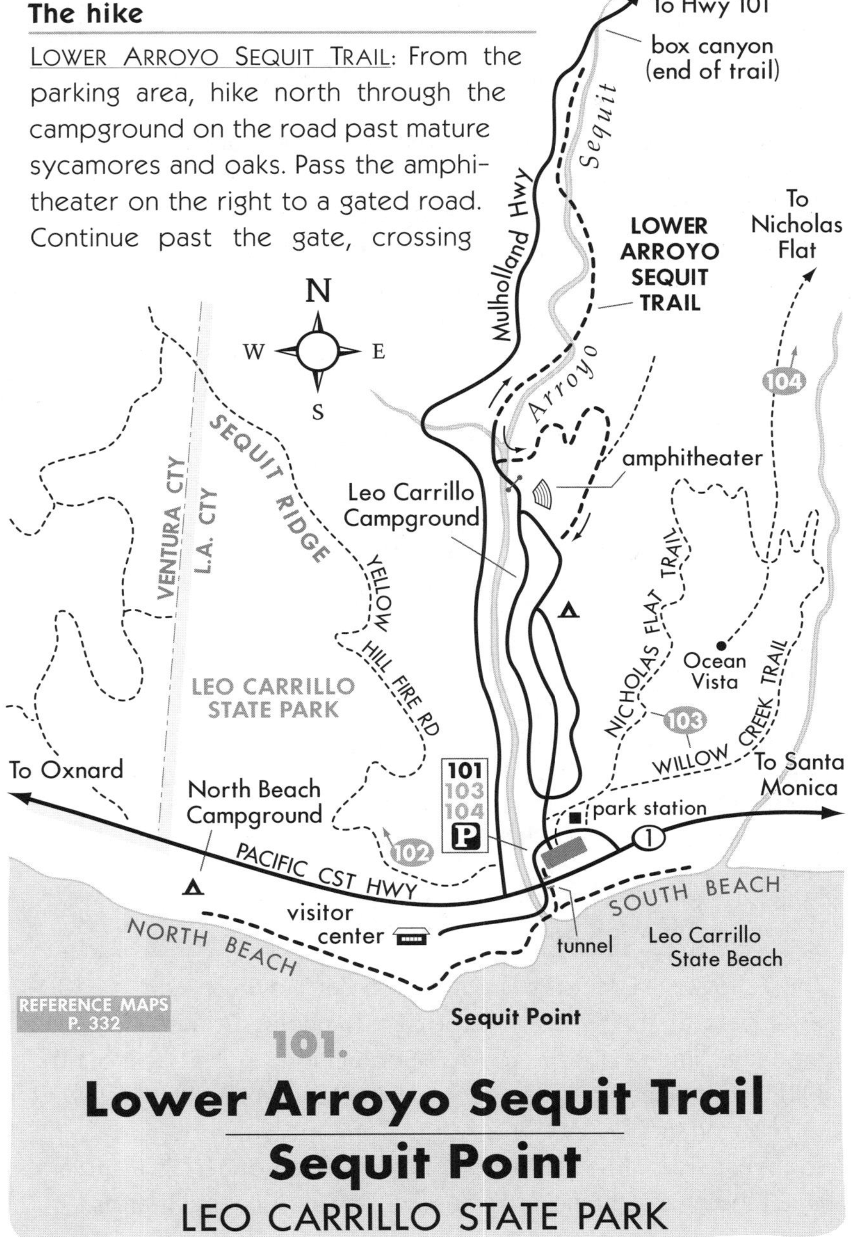

over the seasonal Arroyo Sequit to the end of the paved road. Take the footpath a hundred yards, and rock hop over the creek by a small grotto. Follow the path upstream along the east side of the creek. Recross the creek to the trail's end in a steep-walled box canyon with pools and large boulders.

Retrace your steps to the amphitheater, and now bear left on the footpath. Cross to the east side of the creek and head through the forest canopy. Switchbacks and two sets of wooden steps lead to a flat above the canyon. Descend back to the campground road, and continue back towards the coast.

SEQUIT POINT: To reach Sequit Point, take the paved path and walk through the tunnel under Highway 1 to the sandy beach. To the right (west), by the lifeguard station, are sandstone rock formations with caves, tunnels, a rock arch, tidepools, and a series of beach coves. Many hours can be spent exploring the coastline. ■

102. Yellow Hill Fire Road

LEO CARRILLO STATE PARK

35000 W. Pacific Coast Hwy · Malibu

Hiking distance: 5 miles round trip
Hiking time: 2.5 hours
Configuration: out-and-back with small loop
Elevation gain: 1,300 feet
Difficulty: moderate
Exposure: exposed
Dogs: not allowed
Maps: U.S.G.S. Triunfo Pass · Leo Carrillo State Beach map
Tom Harrison Maps: Point Mugu State Park Trail map

The Yellow Hill Fire Road is within Leo Carrillo State Park, a 2,100-acre park at the western tip of Los Angeles County. The trail steadily climbs a dirt fire road up Sequit Ridge in the backcountry hills. The trailhead begins on the west side of Mulholland Highway in Los Angeles County and follows the mountain ridge, leaving the west side of the state park into Ventura County. En route are outstanding ocean views, including the four Channel Islands.

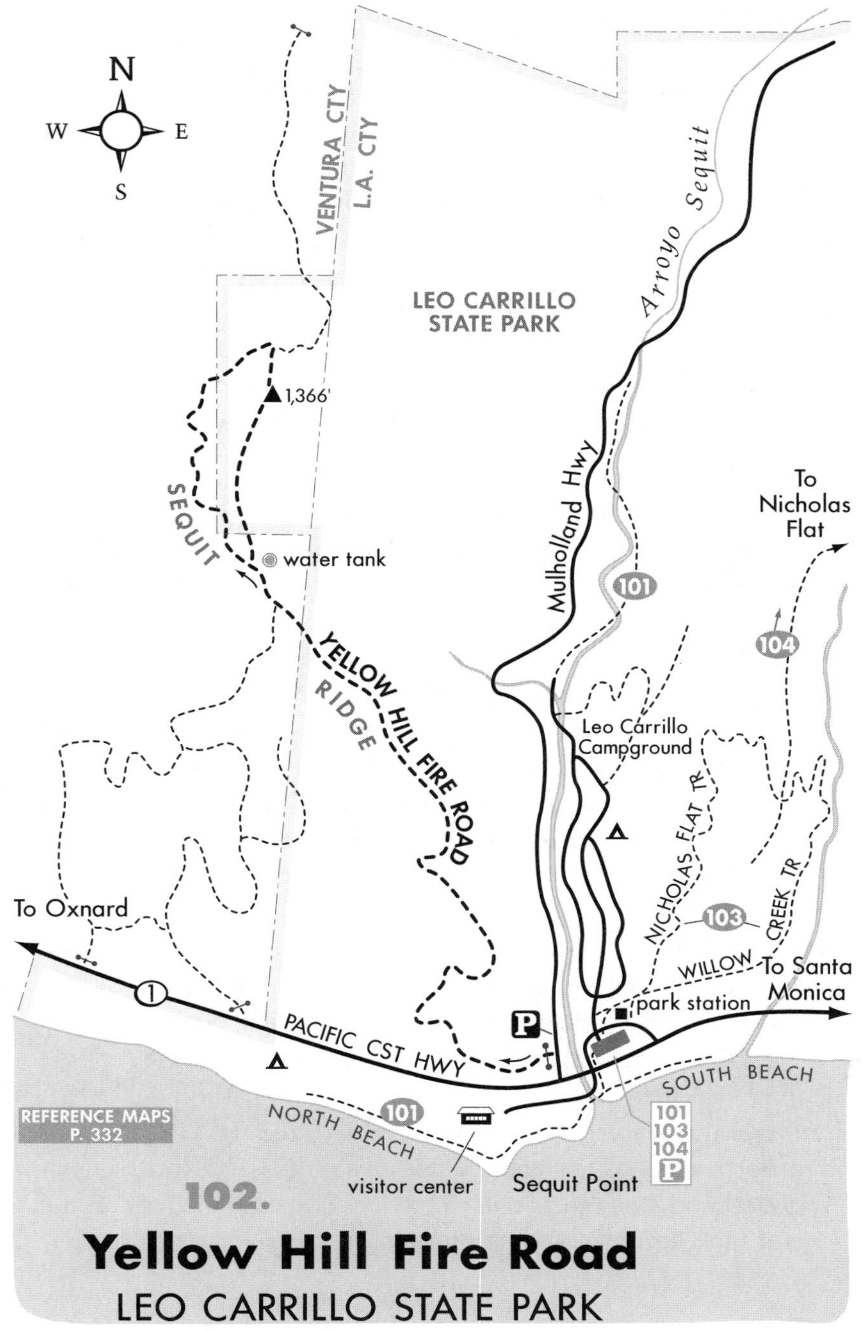

102. Yellow Hill Fire Road

LEO CARRILLO STATE PARK

To the trailhead

Heading northbound on the Pacific Coast Highway/Highway 1 from Santa Monica, drive 14 miles past Malibu Canyon Road and 8 miles past Kanan Dume Road to Mulholland Highway. The highway is located 0.2 miles west of the Leo Carrillo State Beach entrance. Turn right and go 100 yards to the gated fire road on the left. Park along the side of the road. Parking is also available in Leo Carrillo State Park off the PCH.

From the Pacific Coast Highway/Highway 1 and Las Posas Road in southeast Oxnard, drive 10.8 miles southbound on the PCH to Mulholland Highway, just before the posted Leo Carrillo State Beach entrance. Proceed with the directions above.

The hike

Walk around the trailhead gate, and follow the old dirt road, passing prickly pear cactus. Coastal views quickly expand, from Point Dume to Point Mugu and across the ocean to the Channel Islands. The trail parallels the coast for 0.3 miles, then curves inland. Climb steadily up the ridge. Cross over a minor side canyon to a view of the sculptured land forms in the interior of Leo Carrillo State Park and the Arroyo Sequit drainage. At 1.4 miles, the encroaching vegetation narrows the winding road to a single track trail. Cross the county line and walk around a gate, continuing 300 yards ahead to a Y-fork. The left fork descends to the PCH. Stay to the right, below a water tank on the right. At 2 miles the road/trail makes a left bend. On the bend is a footpath veering up the knoll to the right, our return route. Stay on the main trail, curving around the west flank of the knoll. Near the ridge, the uphill grade eases, reaching a trail sign. Continue to the ridge 150 yards ahead, where there is an outstanding view of the Boney Mountain ridgeline.

Leave the road and return on the trail to the right, climbing up the north face of the knoll. Cross over the 1,366-foot summit, and descend along the ridge to the junction with the road at the water tank. Return along the same route. ■

103. Ocean Vista

Willow Creek— Nicholas Flat Loop

LEO CARRILLO STATE PARK

35000 W. Pacific Coast Hwy • Malibu

Hiking distance: 2.5-mile loop
Hiking time: 1.5 hours
Configuration: loop with spur trail to overlook
Elevation gain: 600 feet
Difficulty: easy to moderate
Exposure: mostly exposed with shaded pockets
Dogs: not allowed
Maps: U.S.G.S. Triunfo Pass • Leo Carrillo State Beach map
Tom Harrison Maps: Point Mugu State Park Trail map
Tom Harrison Maps: Zuma-Trancas Canyons Trail map

map page 340

This loop hike in Leo Carrillo State Park leads to Ocean Vista, a 612-foot bald knoll with great views of the Malibu coastline and Point Dume. The Willow Creek Trail traverses the east-facing hill-side up v-shaped Willow Creek Canyon to Ocean Vista at the north end of the loop. En route to the overlook, the trail leads through native grasslands and coastal sage scrub. The hike returns along the Nicholas Flat Trail, one of the few trails connecting the interior Santa Monica Mountains to the Pacific Ocean.

To the trailhead

From Santa Monica, drive 26 miles northbound on the Pacific Coast Highway/Highway 1 to the posted Leo Carrillo State Beach entrance and turn right. (The state park is 14 miles west of Malibu Canyon Road and 8 miles west of Kanan Dume Road.) Park in the day-use parking lot. A parking fee is required.

From the Pacific Coast Highway/Highway 1 and Las Posas Road in southeast Oxnard, drive 11.1 miles southbound on the PCH to the posted Leo Carrillo State Beach entrance and turn left. Park in the day-use parking lot. A parking fee is required.

The hike

The trailhead is 50 yards outside the park entrance station at the posted Camp 13 Trail on the left. Walk 50 yards on the footpath to the information kiosk and junction. The loop begins at this junction. Take the right fork—the Willow Creek Trail—up the hillside and parallel to the ocean, heading east. At a half mile the trail curves north, traversing the hillside while overlooking the arroyo and Willow Creek. Three switchbacks lead aggressively up to a saddle and a signed four-way junction with the Nicholas Flat Trail, which leads north to the upper reaches of the park (Hike 104). The left fork leads a quarter mile to Ocean Vista. After marveling at the views, return to the four-way junction and take the left (west) fork. Head downhill on the lower end of the Nicholas Flat Trail, returning to the trailhead along the grassy slopes above the park campground. ■

104. Nicholas Flat Trail

Nicholas Flat from the coast

LEO CARRILLO STATE PARK

35000 W. Pacific Coast Hwy • Malibu

Hiking distance: 7.4 miles round trip
Hiking time: 4 hours
Configuration: up-and-back with 2 loops
Elevation gain: 1,700 feet
Difficulty: moderate to strenuous
Exposure: exposed hills and shady forest
Dogs: not allowed
Maps: U.S.G.S. Truinfo Pass • Leo Carrillo State Beach map
Tom Harrison Maps: Zuma-Trancas Canyons Trail Map

map page 342

The Nicholas Flat Trail, located entirely within Leo Carrillo State Park, is a 3.8-mile-long footpath that connects the interior mountains with the sea. The trail begins near the Pacific Coast Highway at the south end of the state park and climbs the oceanfront mountain to Nicholas Flat at the upper (north) end of the park. The flat is a large, grassy meadow dotted with oak forests and rock outcrops. A year-round pond lies on the south end of the flat, with mature oaks and picturesque sandstone rocks. From an elevation of 1,700-feet, the flat offers great mountain and coastal views. The trail also leads past Ocean Vista, a 612-foot overlook at the lower end of the park, and Vista Point, a 1,610-foot overlook at Nicholas Flat.

To the trailhead

From Santa Monica, drive 26 miles northbound on the Pacific Coast Highway/Highway 1 to the posted Leo Carrillo State Beach entrance and turn right. (The state park is 14 miles west of Malibu Canyon Road and 8 miles west of Kanan Dume Road.) Park in the day-use parking lot. A parking fee is required.

From the Pacific Coast Highway/Highway 1 and Las Posas Road in southeast Oxnard, drive 11.1 miles southbound on the PCH to the posted Leo Carrillo State Beach entrance and turn left. Park in the day-use parking lot. A parking fee is required.

The hike

The hike begins 50 yards outside the entrance station at the posted Camp 13 Trail on the left. Walk 50 yards on the footpath to the information kiosk and junction. The Willow Creek Trail curves around the hill to the right, our return route. Begin on the Nicholas Flat Trail to the left. Follow the east canyon slope above the campground while ascending through coastal scrub. At one mile, and over 500 feet in elevation, is a saddle and posted 4-way junction on a ridge overlooking Arroyo Sequit Canyon and

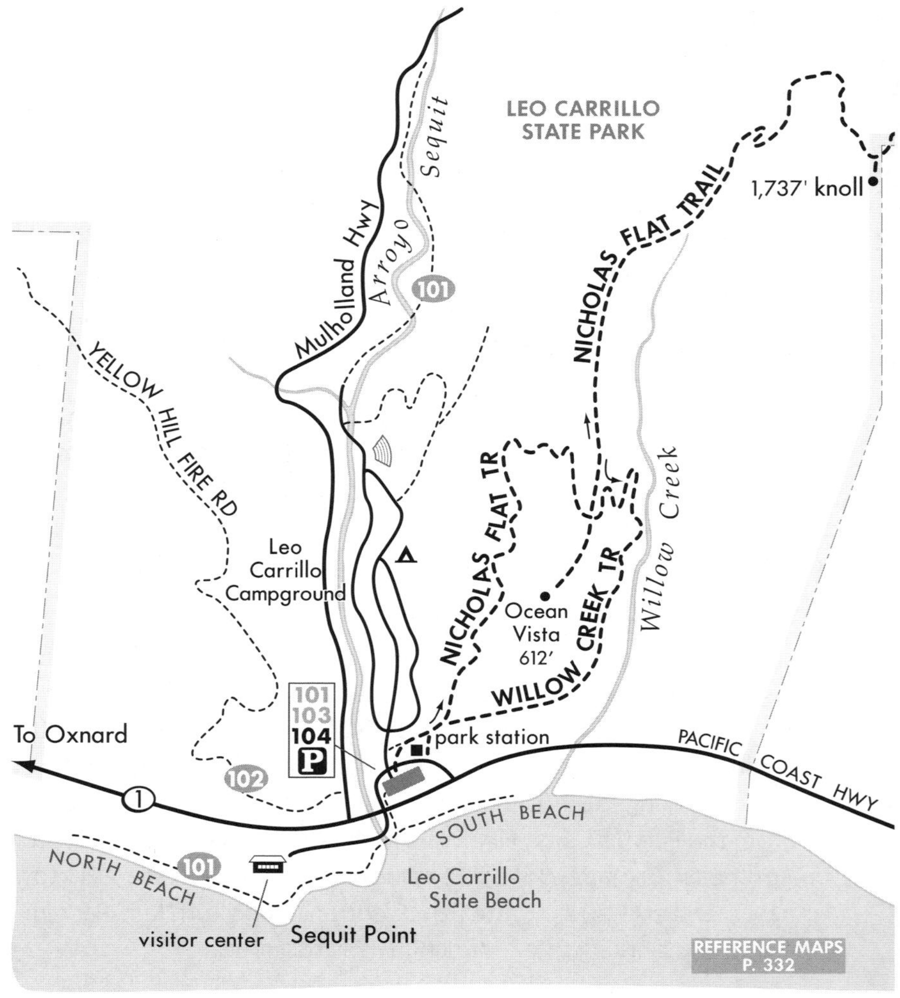

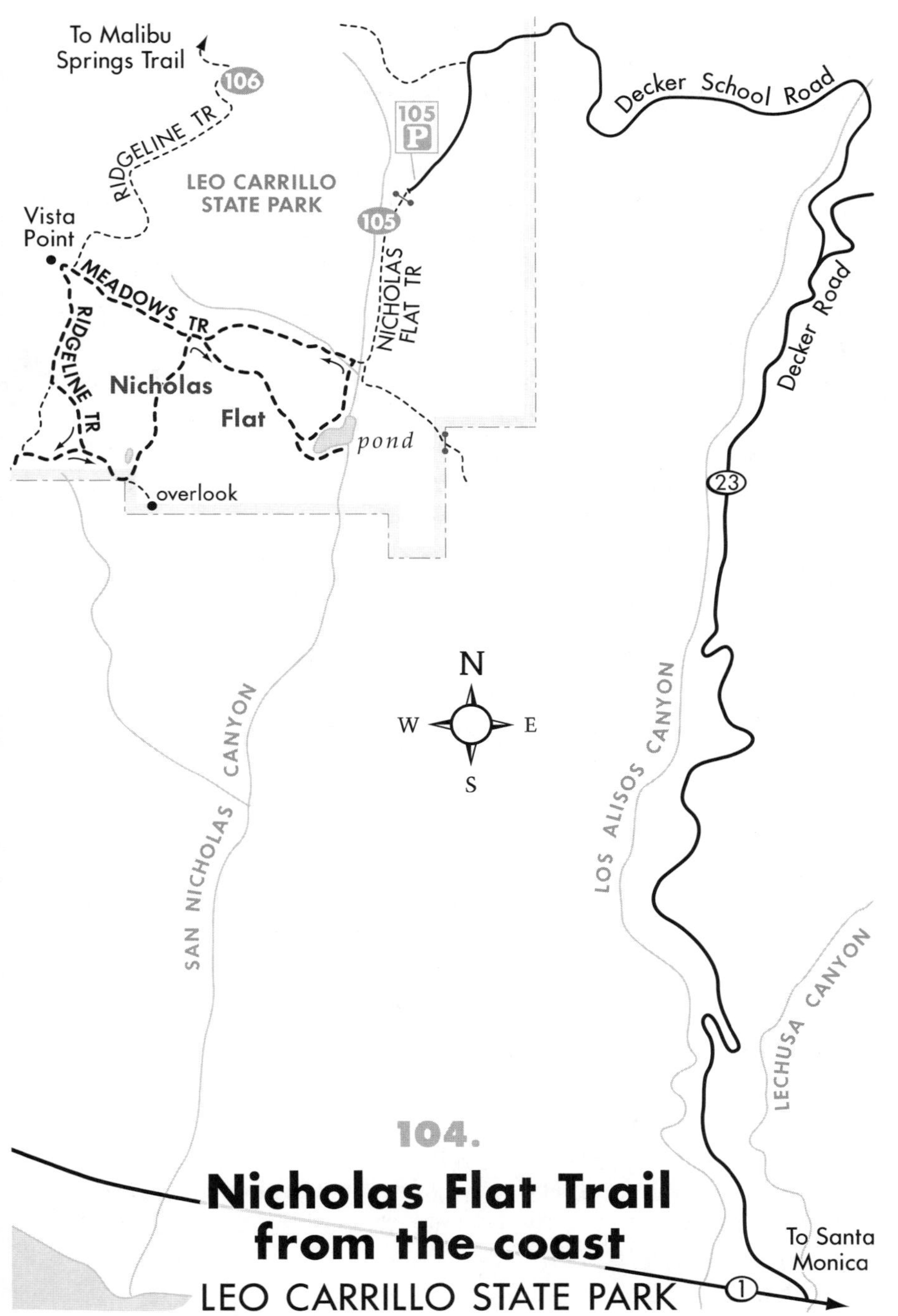

104.

Nicholas Flat Trail from the coast

LEO CARRILLO STATE PARK

Willow Creek Canyon. The trail straight ahead, the Willow Creek Trail, is the return route. To the right, the Ocean Vista Trail climbs a short distance to the 612-foot oceanfront knoll with 360-degree panoramas.

Back at the 4-way junction, continue north on the Nicholas Flat Trail. Follow the ridge inland, with continuous views into both canyons and across the ocean to the Channel Islands. At 2.2 miles, wind through tall, lush foliage in a shaded canopy to an unsigned junction. Detour 100 yards to the right to a 1,737-foot knoll with spectacular views of the Santa Monica Range and the Pacific Ocean. On the main trail, continue about 60 yards and veer right at a trail sign to a junction with the Ridgeline Trail at 2.7 miles.

Begin the loop and continue straight. A trail on the right leads to another overlook. Curve left around a vernal pool and drop into Nicholas Flat, a large grassy plateau dotted with oaks and surrounded by rolling hills. At 3.1 miles is a junction with the Meadow Trail to the left. Bear right and walk 25 yards to a Y-fork. Veer right to the pond. A side path to the right circles the pond to a grove of stately oaks and a beautiful rock formation. Continue on the main trail, walking through the meadow on the northwest side of the pond to a junction. The trail straight ahead leads to the trailhead at the end of Decker School Road (Hike 105). Take the left fork and complete the loop at the junction with the Meadow Trail. Walk straight ahead on the Meadow Trail to a T-junction with the Ridgeline Trail at 4.1 miles. The right fork leads to the Malibu Springs Trail (Hike 106). Bear left and weave through the forest to Vista Point, overlooking Nicholas Flat. Continue to a junction with the Nicholas Flat Trail, completing the double loop at 4.7 miles.

Retrace your steps 1.7 miles (back towards the ocean) to the junction with the Willow Creek Trail at the lower end of the park. Take the Willow Creek Trail to the left. Descend on the west wall of secluded Willow Creek Canyon. Steadily loose elevation down three switchbacks. At the mouth of the canyon curve right. Parallel the Pacific Coast Highway, where there is a great view of Leo Carrillo State Beach. The 0.9-mile Willow Creek Trail ends at the trailhead kiosk. ■

105. Nicholas Flat

LEO CARRILLO STATE PARK

Decker School Road • Malibu

Hiking distance: 2.5-mile double loop
Hiking time: 1.5 hours
Configuration: double loop
Elevation gain: 100 feet
Difficulty: easy
Exposure: a mix of exposed meadows and shaded oak forest
Dogs: not allowed
Maps: U.S.G.S. Triunfo Pass • Leo Carrillo State Beach map
Tom Harrison Maps: Point Mugu State Park Trail map
Tom Harrison Maps: Zuma-Trancas Canyons Trail map

map page 346

Nicholas Flat, in the upper reaches of Leo Carrillo State Park, is a grassy highland meadow with large oak trees, an old cattle pond, and sandstone outcroppings that lie 1,700 feet above the sea. This hike skirts around Nicholas Flat on old ranch roads. The easy hike offers spectacular views of the ocean, San Nicholas Canyon, and the surrounding mountains. The Nicholas Flat Trail may be hiked 3.8 miles downhill to the Pacific Ocean (see Hike 104).

To the trailhead

From Santa Monica, drive 23.8 miles northbound on the Pacific Coast Highway/Highway 1 to Decker Road and turn right. (Decker Road is 11.8 miles west of Malibu Canyon Road.) Continue 2.4 miles north to Decker School Road and turn left. Drive 1.5 miles to the road's end and park alongside the road.

From the Pacific Coast Highway/Highway 1 and Las Posas Road in southeast Oxnard, drive 13.3 miles southbound on the PCH to Decker Road and turn left. Continue 2.4 miles north to Decker School Road and turn left. Drive 1.5 miles to the road's end and park alongside the road.

The hike

Hike south past the gate and kiosk. Stay on the wide, oak-lined trail to a junction at 0.3 miles. Take the right fork, beginning the first loop. At 0.6 miles is another junction. Again take the right fork—the Meadows Trail. Continue to the Ridgeline Trail and an overlook, where there are great views into the canyons. Curve south to a junction with the Nicholas Flat Trail, leading to the coastline at the southern end of Leo Carrillo State Park. Take the Nicholas Flat Trail to the left, following the perimeter of the southern end of the flat. A trail on the right leads to another vista point. Complete the west loop at 1.8 miles. Take the trail to the right at two successive junctions to the pond. A side path to the right circles the pond to a grove of stately oaks and a beautiful rock formation. Return to the main trail and walk through the meadow along the northwest side of the pond to a junction, completing the east loop. Return to the trailhead. ■

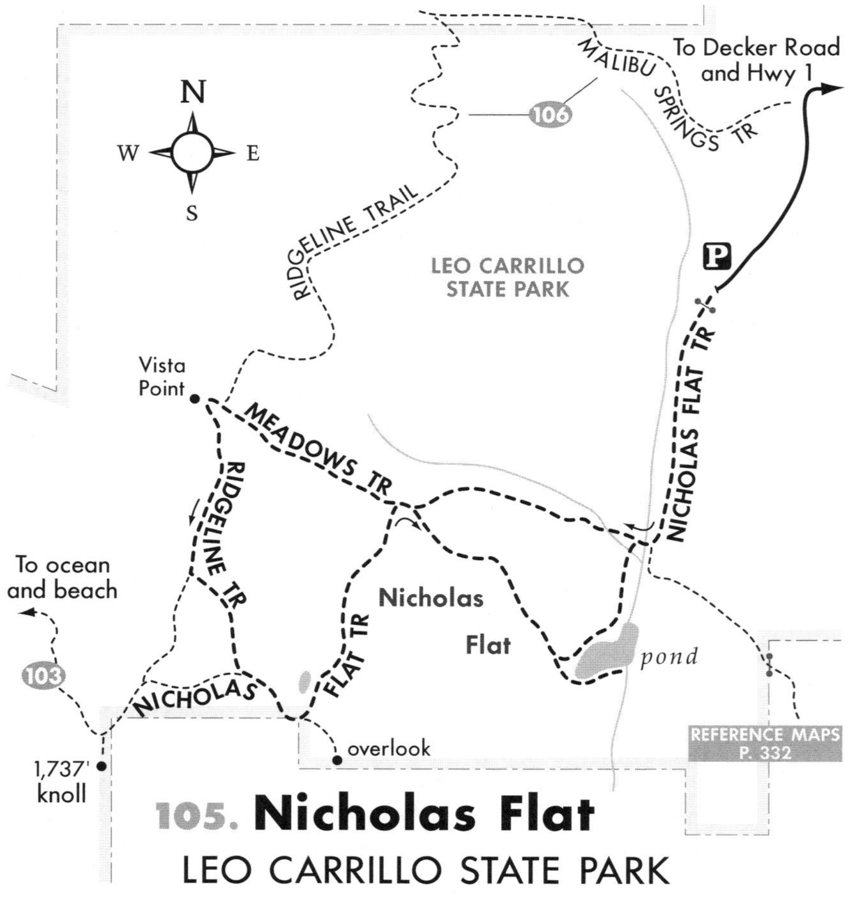

106. Malibu Springs Trail to Nicholas Flat

LEO CARRILLO STATE PARK

Mulholland Highway • Malibu

Hiking distance: 7 miles
Hiking time: 3.5 hours
Configuration: out-and-back with large loop
Elevation gain: 1,300 feet
Difficulty: moderate to strenuous
Exposure: a mix of exposed hills and shady forest
Dogs: allowed on first 1.9 miles; not allowed in Leo Carrillo State Park
Maps: U.S.G.S. Truinfo Pass • Leo Carrillo State Beach map
Tom Harrison Maps: Zuma-Trancas Canyons Trail Map

map page 349

The Malibu Springs Trail enters Leo Carrillo State Park and Nicholas Flat from the north. The trail begins from a pullout on Mulholland Highway by the confluence of the East Fork and West Fork of the Arroyo Sequit. The remote trail climbs the north-facing slope above the east fork through an oak woodland up to the coastal sage scrub and chaparral. The climb offers steady views of the mountainous backcountry, including the jagged ridge of Boney Mountain. The trail connects with the Ridgeline Trail, an extension of the Malibu Springs Trail within Leo Carrillo State Park, then forms a loop around Nicholas Flat. The path curves past an old cattle pond set in a grassy meadow with a grove of oaks and picturesque sandstone outcroppings. En route, the trail leads to overlooks of Nicholas Flat and the Pacific Ocean.

To the trailhead

From Santa Monica, drive 26.2 miles northbound on the Pacific Coast Highway/Highway 1 to Mulholland Highway and turn right. (Mulholland Highway is 8.6 miles west of Kanan Dume Road and 0.2 miles west of Leo Carrillo State Park entrance.) Turn right and drive 3.2 miles up the canyon to the signed trailhead on the right. Park in the pullout by the trailhead.

From the Pacific Coast Highway/Highway 1 and Las Posas Road in southeast Oxnard, drive 10.8 miles southbound on the PCH to

Mulholland Highway. Turn left and drive 3.2 miles up the canyon to the signed trailhead on the right. Park in the pullout by the trailhead.

The hike

Walk 100 yards up the slope and pass through a trail gate. Steadily climb the mountain while enjoying the views of the Arroyo Sequit Canyon. Pass through oak groves to a posted Y-fork at 1.9 miles and an elevation gain of 1,150 feet. Begin the loop to the right on the Ridgeline Trail. Continue up the mountain to an overlook of the Pacific Ocean. Descend through a shaded canopy to an overlook of Nicholas Flat. Steadily descend to a posted T-junction at 2.7 miles. The left fork, the Meadows Trail, goes directly into Nicholas Flat for a shorter loop.

For a longer loop (adding one mile), stay on the Ridgeline Trail to the right. Weave through the forest and up to another overlook of Nicholas Flat. At 3.3 miles is a T-junction with the Nicholas Flat Trail. The right fork leads to the Leo Carrillo Campground and Leo Carrillo State Beach (Hike 104). Bear left and gently descend. Curve left around a vernal pool and drop into Nicholas Flat, a large grassy plateau dotted with oaks and surrounded by green rolling hills. At 3.7 miles is a junction with the Meadows Trail (the shorter loop). Bear right and walk 25 yards to a Y-fork. Veer to the right to the pond. A side path to the right circles the pond to a grove of stately oaks and a beautiful rock formation. Continue on the main trail, walking through the meadow on the northwest side of the pond to a junction. Go to the right, meandering through the oaks to another junction. Veer left, staying on the Nicholas Flat Trail. Weave through the forest on the narrow dirt road to the trailhead at the terminus of Decker School Road. Walk 0.2 miles up the paved road to the signed Malibu Springs Trail on the left as Decker School Road bends to the right. Take the footpath and head west, high above Arroyo Sequit Canyon. A half mile from Decker School Road, complete the loop at the junction with the Ridgeline Trail. Return 1.9 miles straight ahead to the trailhead. ■

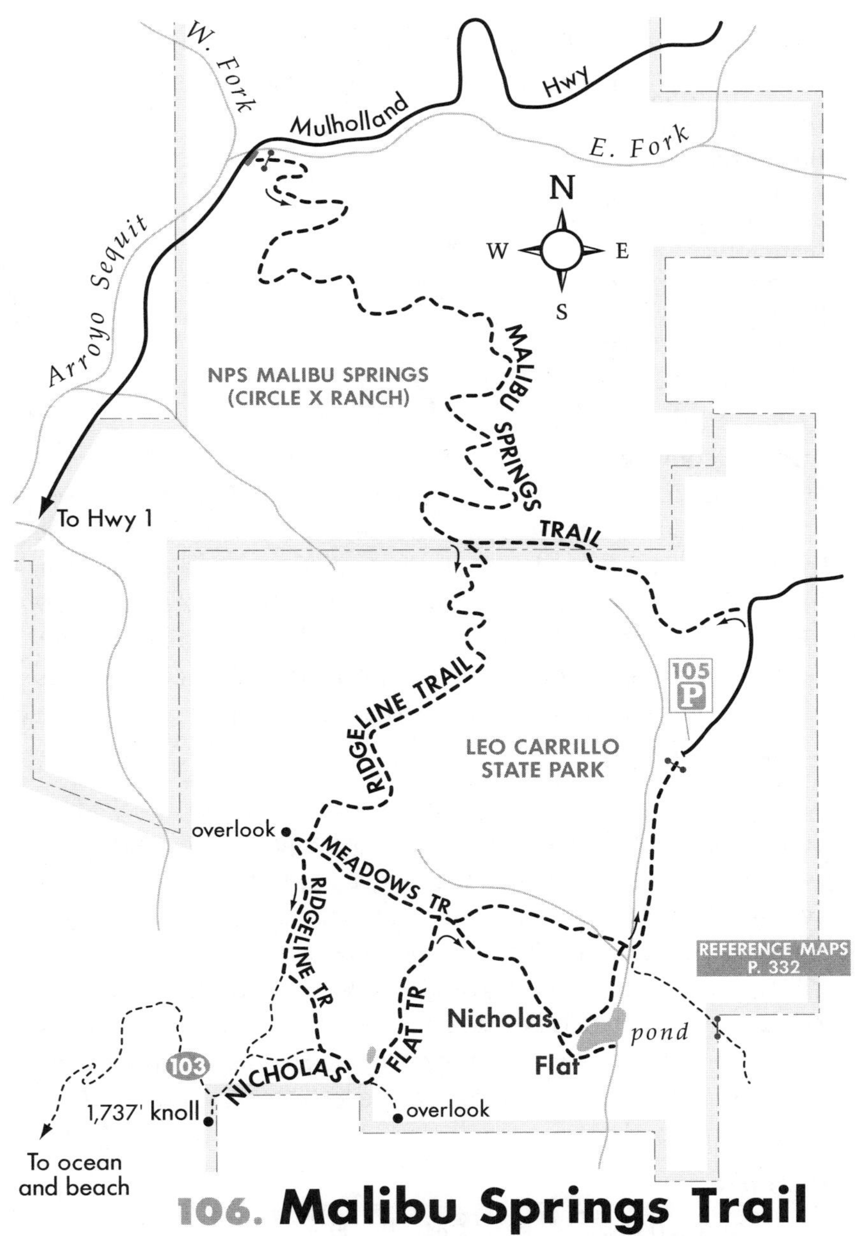

106. Malibu Springs Trail to Nicholas Flat

LEO CARRILLO STATE PARK

107. Arroyo Sequit Park

34138 Mulholland Highway • Malibu

Hiking distance: 2-mile loop
Hiking time: 1 hour
Configuration: loop
Elevation gain: 250 feet
Difficulty: easy
Exposure: mostly exposed with a few shaded areas
Dogs: allowed
Maps: U.S.G.S. Triunfo Pass
Tom Harrison Maps: Point Mugu State Park Trail map
Tom Harrison Maps: Zuma-Trancas Canyons Trail map

Arroyo Sequit Park was a ranch purchased by the Santa Monica Mountains Conservancy in 1985. Within the 155-acre park are open grassland meadows, picnic areas, and a small canyon cut by the East Fork Arroyo Sequit with oak groves and a waterfall. From the meadows are panoramic views of the ocean and surrounding mountains. This easy loop hike visits the diverse park habitats, crossing the meadows and dropping into the gorge that runs parallel to the East Fork Arroyo Sequit.

To the trailhead

From Santa Monica, drive 26.2 miles northbound on the Pacific Coast Highway/Highway 1 to Mulholland Highway and turn right. (Mulholland Highway is 14.2 miles west of Malibu Canyon Road.) Continue 5.5 miles up the canyon to the signed turnoff on the right at mailbox 34138. Turn right into the park entrance and park.

From the Pacific Coast Highway/Highway 1 and Las Posas Road in southeast Oxnard, drive 10.8 miles southbound on the PCH to Mulholland Highway. Turn left and drive 5.5 miles up the canyon to the signed turnoff on the right at mailbox 34138. Turn right into the entrance and park.

The hike

Head south on the park road past the gate, kiosk, and old ranch house. At 0.2 miles take the road to the left—past a barn, the astronomical observing site, a few coast live oaks, and the picnic area—to the footpath on the right. Leave the service road on the nature trail, heading south. Skirt the east edge of the meadow, with a great view of Boney Mountain to the northwest, then descend into a small canyon. Cross several seasonal tributaries of the Arroyo Sequit. Head west along the southern wall of the gorge, passing a waterfall on the left. Cross a wooden footbridge over the stream, and descend to the canyon floor. Continue west, cross the East Fork Arroyo Sequit, and begin the ascent out of the canyon to a junction. Continue on the right fork (straight ahead) up the hill. A series of switchbacks lead up the short but steep hill. Once at the top, cross the meadow to the road. Take the service road back to the parking area. ■

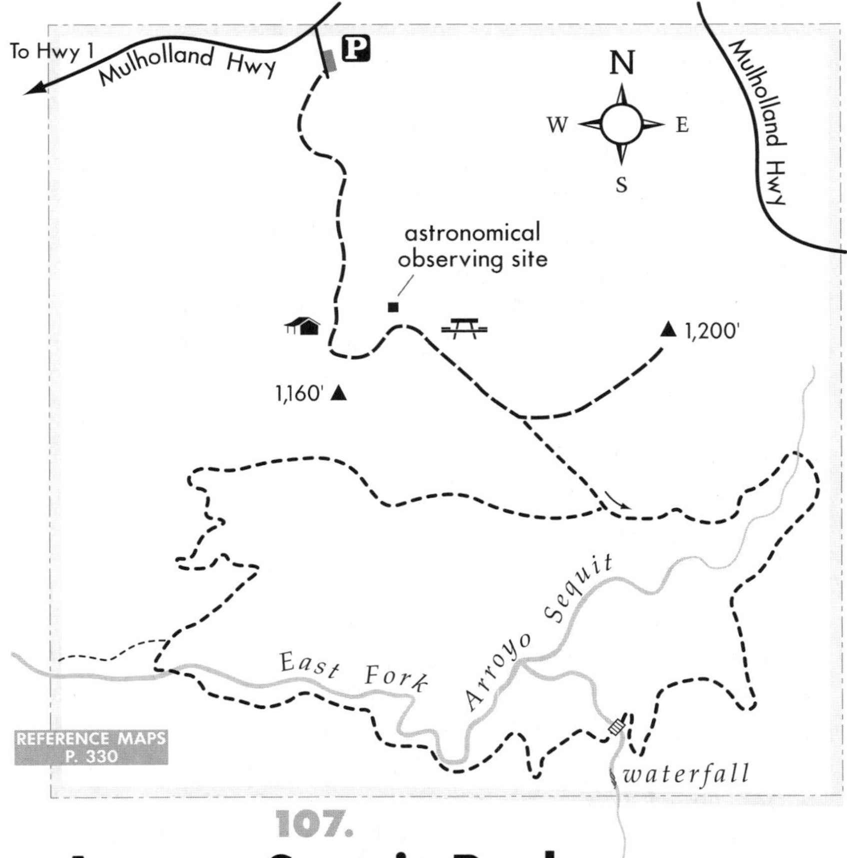

107.
Arroyo Sequit Park

108. Grotto Trail

CIRCLE X RANCH

12896 Yerba Buena Road • Malibu

Hiking distance: 3.5 miles round trip
Hiking time: 2 hours
Configuration: out-and-back with small loop
Elevation gain: 500 feet
Difficulty: easy to moderate
Exposure: mostly shaded canyon with some exposed hills
Dogs: allowed
Maps: U.S.G.S. Triunfo Pass • N.P.S. Circle X Ranch map
Tom Harrison Maps: Zuma-Trancas Canyons Trail map
Tom Harrison Maps: Point Mugu State Park Trail map

The Grotto Trail is located in the 1,655-acre Circle X Ranch, adjacent to the northeast end of Point Mugu State Park. Once a Boy Scout wilderness retreat, the Circle X Ranch is now part of the Santa Monica Mountains National Recreation Area. The scenic trail leads to The Grotto, a maze of large, volcanic boulders in a sheer, narrow gorge formed from landslides. The natural rock garden contains numerous caves, small waterfalls, and pools. The West Fork of the Arroyo Sequit flows through the caves and caverns of The Grotto, creating cascades and pools. En route, the path descends into a stream-cut gorge and passes Botsford Falls. The trail includes close-up vistas of the chiseled pinnacles of Boney Mountain and Sandstone Peak, the highest point in the Santa Monica Mountains at 3,111 feet.

To the trailhead

From the Pacific Coast Highway/Highway 1 in Santa Monica, drive 38 miles northbound to Yerba Buena Road and turn right. (Yerba Buena Road is 10.1 miles west of Kanan Dume Road and 2 miles west of Leo Carrillo State Beach.) Continue 5.3 miles up the winding road to the Circle X Ranger Station on the right. Park by the ranger station, or continue 0.2 miles downhill to the day-use parking area, located just past the posted Grotto Trailhead.

From the Pacific Coast Highway/Highway 1 and Las Posas Road in southeast Oxnard, drive 9 miles southbound to Yerba Buena

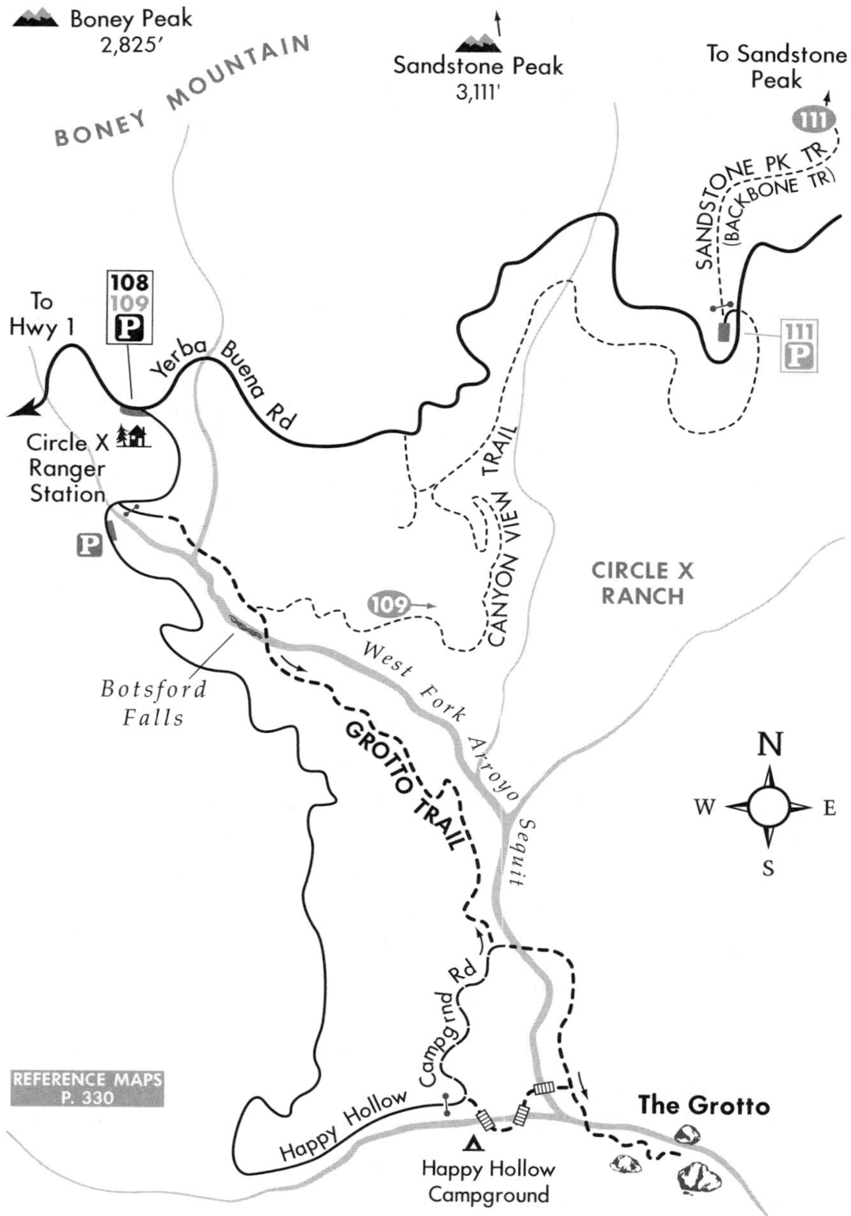

108. Grotto Trail

CIRCLE X RANCH

Road (3.3 miles past Big Sycamore Canyon) and turn left. Continue up Yerba Buena Road, following the directions above.

From the Ventura Freeway/Highway 101 in Thousand Oaks, exit on Westlake Boulevard (Highway 23). Drive 6.9 miles south on Westlake Boulevard, winding up the mountain road to Mulholland Highway at a stop sign. Turn right and go 0.4 miles to Little Sycamore Canyon Road. Turn right and drive 5.7 miles to the Circle X Ranger Station on the left. (At the county line, Little Sycamore Canyon Road becomes Yerba Buena Road.)

The hike

From the ranger station, walk 0.2 miles down the unpaved road to the posted Grotto Trailhead, located just before reaching the lower parking area. Pass the trail gate and follow the dirt road past a picnic area to another trail sign. Take the footpath downhill, heading south into the canyon among oaks, sycamores, and willows. Cross the West Fork Arroyo Sequit, and parallel the east side of the creek to a signed junction with the Canyon View Trail (Hike 109) on the left at 0.4 miles. Continue straight ahead on the left fork and recross the creek at 30-foot Botsford Falls.

After crossing, curve left and traverse the grassy meadow on a ridge. Great views extend down the gorge of volcanic and sandstone rock formations and up to jagged Boney Mountain and Sandstone Peak. Descend to the canyon floor, where the trail joins the gated Happy Hollow Campground Road at 1.2 miles. Follow the road to the left into a primitive campground. Cross the creek and pick up the Grotto Trail again. Head downstream to a bridge that crosses the creek into the Happy Hollow Campground. Instead of crossing the bridge, continue straight ahead, crossing the West Fork Arroyo Sequit by a pump house. Follow the east bank of the creek downstream in an oak woodland. After a few hundred feet, the path enters the sheer volcanic-rock walls of The Grotto, a sycamore-shaded cavern set among a jumble of massive boulders, small caves, cascades, small falls, pools, and ferns.

After exploring The Grotto, return to the bridge that accesses the Happy Hollow Campground. Cross the bridge and walk through the camp to the vehicle-restricted road. Bear right and follow the winding road. Rejoin the Grotto Trail on the left, completing the loop. Retrace your steps to the parking lot. ■

109. Canyon View—Yerba Buena Road Loop

CIRCLE X RANCH

12896 Yerba Buena Road • Malibu

Hiking distance: 3.2-mile loop
Hiking time: 1.5 hours
Configuration: loop
Elevation gain: 500 feet
Difficulty: easy to moderate
Exposure: mostly exposed mountain slope with some shaded areas
Dogs: allowed
Maps: U.S.G.S. Triunfo Pass • N.P.S. Circle X Ranch map
Tom Harrison Maps: Zuma-Trancas Canyons Trail map
Tom Harrison Maps: Point Mugu State Park Trail map

map page 357

Circle X Ranch, a former Boy Scout camp, sits below majestic Boney Mountain in the upper canyons of Arroyo Sequit. The Canyon View Trail traverses the brushy hillside of the deep, east-facing canyon. The panoramic views extend down the canyon to the Pacific Ocean. The northern views reach the jagged Boney Mountain ridge and the 3,111-foot Sandstone Peak, the highest peak in the Santa Monica Mountains. The trail connects the Grotto Trail (Hike 108) with the Sandstone Peak Trail (Hike 111).

To the trailhead

From the Pacific Coast Highway/Highway 1 in Santa Monica, drive 38 miles northbound to Yerba Buena Road and turn right. (Yerba Buena Road is 10.1 miles west of Kanan Dume Road and 2 miles west of Leo Carrillo State Beach.) Continue 5.3 miles up the winding road to the Circle X Ranger Station on the right. Park by the ranger station, or continue 0.2 miles downhill to the day-use parking area, located just past the posted Grotto Trailhead.

From the Pacific Coast Highway/Highway 1 and Las Posas Road in southeast Oxnard, drive 9 miles southbound to Yerba Buena Road (3.3 miles past Big Sycamore Canyon) and turn left. Continue up Yerba Buena Road, following the directions above.

From the Ventura Freeway/Highway 101 in Thousand Oaks, exit on Westlake Boulevard (Highway 23). Drive 6.9 miles south on Westlake Boulevard, winding up the mountain road to Mulholland Highway at a stop sign. Turn right and go 0.4 miles to Little Sycamore Canyon Road. Turn right and drive 5.7 miles to the Circle X Ranger Station on the left. (At the county line, Little Sycamore Canyon Road becomes Yerba Buena Road.)

The hike

From the ranger station, walk 0.2 miles down the unpaved road to the posted Grotto Trailhead, located just before reaching the lower parking area. Pass the trail gate and follow the dirt road past a picnic area to another trail sign. Take the footpath downhill, heading south into the canyon among oaks, sycamores, and willows. Cross the West Fork Arroyo Sequit, and parallel the east side of the creek to a signed junction with the Canyon View Trail on the left at 0.4 miles. (To see 30-foot Botsford Falls, detour 20 yards straight ahead. This trail continues downhill to The Grotto—Hike 108.)

From the junction, take the Canyon View Trail to the left (east). Traverse the canyon wall, following the contours of the mountain. Climb two switchbacks to a junction. For a shorter 1.5-mile loop, take the Connector Trail 100 yards to the left to Yerba Buena Road, and return 0.35 miles to the ranger station.

For this longer hike, stay to the right and cross a rocky wash. Head up the hillside to a south view that spans down canyon to the ocean and the Channel Islands and a north view of the Boney Mountain ridge. Continue to Yerba Buena Road, across from the Sandstone Peak (Backbone) Trail (Hike 111). For a loop hike, return to the left on Yerba Buena Road, and walk 1.1 mile back to the trailhead at the Circle X Ranger Station. ■

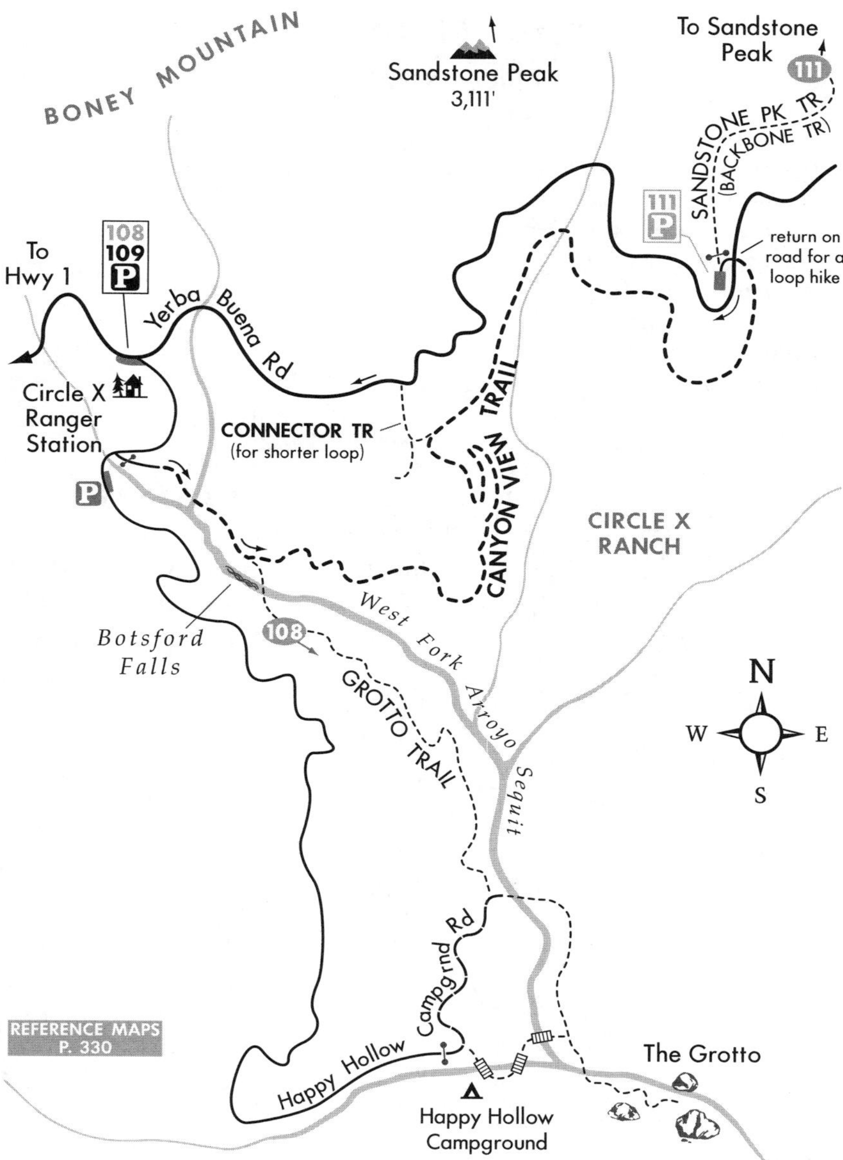

109. Canyon View Trail—Yerba Buena Road

CIRCLE X RANCH

110. Yerba Ridge Trail

CIRCLE X RANCH

Yerba Buena Road · Malibu

Hiking distance: 9 miles round trip
Hiking time: 4.5 hours
Configuration: out-and-back
Elevation gain: 500 feet
Difficulty: moderate
Exposure: exposed
Dogs: allowed
Maps: U.S.G.S. Triunfo Pass
Tom Harrison Maps: Zuma-Trancas Canyons Trail Map
Tom Harrison Maps: Point Mugu State Park Trail Map

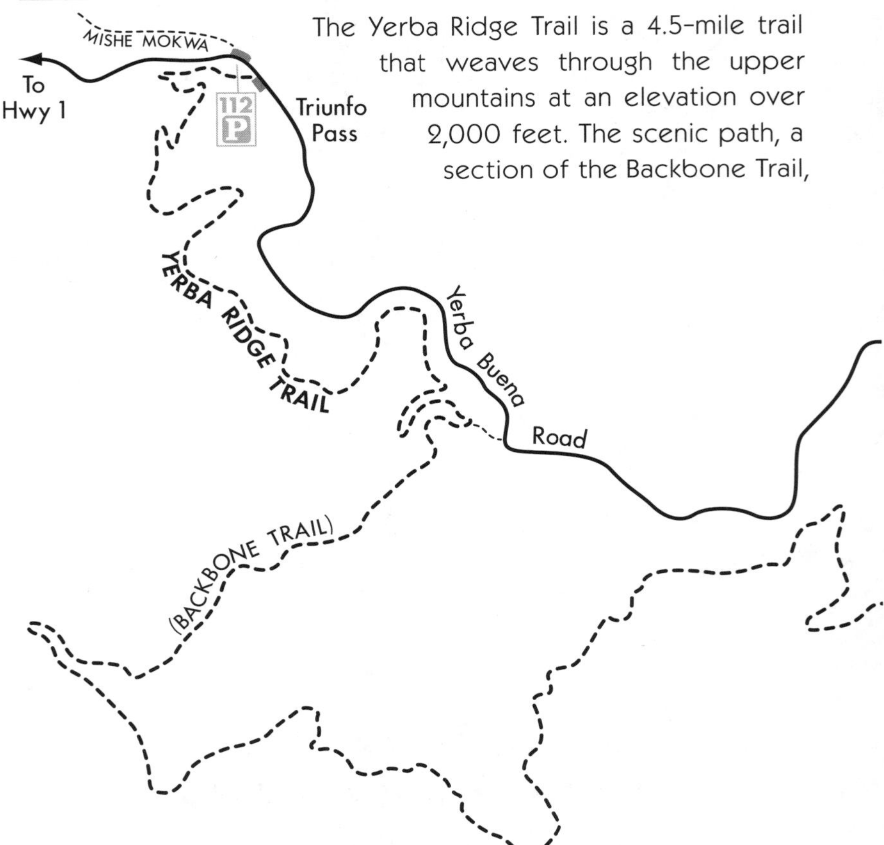

The Yerba Ridge Trail is a 4.5-mile trail that weaves through the upper mountains at an elevation over 2,000 feet. The scenic path, a section of the Backbone Trail, connects with Yerba Buena Road on both ends in Circle X Ranch. Throughout the hike are views of the mountainous backcountry, Boney Mountain (the western sentinel of the Santa Monica Mountains), Conejo Valley, Thousand Oaks, Simi Valley, and the surrounding sandstone formations.

To the trailhead

From Santa Monica, drive 38 miles northbound on the Pacific Coast Highway/Highway 1 to Yerba Buena Road and turn right. (Yerba Buena Road is 10.1 miles west of Kanan Dume Road and 2 miles west of Leo Carrillo State Beach.) Continue 5.3 miles up the winding road to the Circle X Ranger Station on the right. From the ranger station, continue 3.7 miles to a large dirt pullout on the right and park. (The trailhead is located 0.1 mile ahead along the road.)

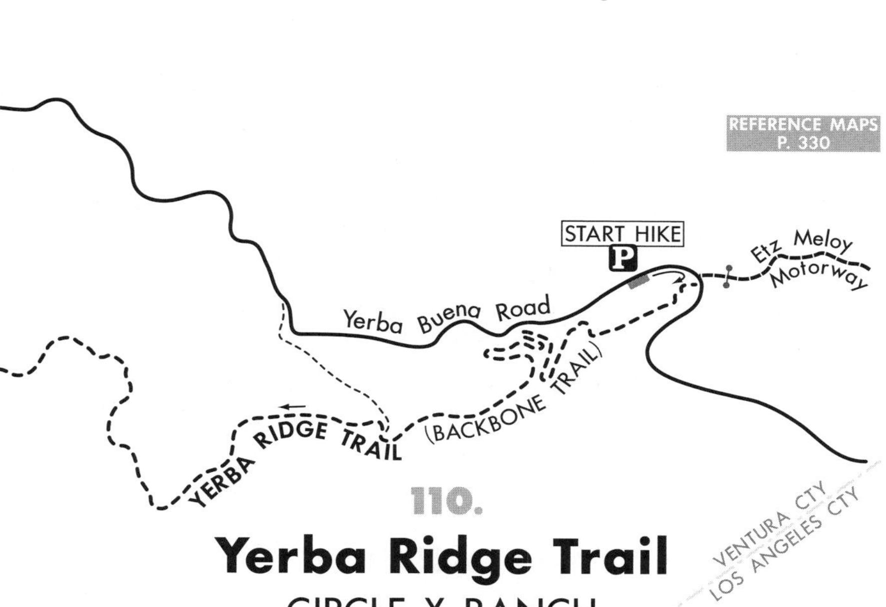

110. Yerba Ridge Trail

CIRCLE X RANCH

From the Pacific Coast Highway/Highway 1 and Las Posas Road in southeast Oxnard, drive 9 miles southbound to Yerba Buena Road and turn left. Continue up Yerba Buena Road, following the directions above.

From the Ventura Freeway/Highway 101 in Thousand Oaks, exit on Westlake Boulevard (Highway 23). Drive 6.9 miles south on Westlake Boulevard, winding up the mountain road to Mulholland Highway at a stop sign. Turn right and go 0.4 miles to Little Sycamore Canyon Road. Turn right and drive 2 miles to a large dirt pullout on the left. (At the county line, Little Sycamore Canyon Road becomes Yerba Buena Road.)

The hike

From the parking pullout, the trailhead is located 0.1 mile ahead along the road. Take the posted Yerba Ridge (Backbone) Trail to the right (east), and descend on the wide path. Weave through tall scrub and chaparral at an easy grade. The views span across the Conejo Valley and Thousand Oaks to the Santa Susana Mountains and the Los Padres National Forest. At 0.6 miles, by a ridge on the left, is an unsigned side path on the right. The path leads 0.2 miles back to Yerba Buena Road. Continue straight (west) and follow the contours of the hills to the south-facing slope overlooking the mountainous backcountry. Walk toward the base of a mountain. At the base, veer left and traverse the slope on a gentle uphill grade. Round a bend to a great view of the scalloped peaks of Boney Ridge. At 3.7 miles is a junction by Yerba Buena Road. Twenty yards straight ahead is a pullout along the road. Take the switchback to the left, staying on the trail, and descend into the canyon. Follow the serpentine path through the canyon, which lies far below the road. Wind up the hillside to the Yerba Buena Trailhead, where Yerba Buena Road goes over the saddle at Triunfo Pass. Directly across the road is the Mishe Mokwa Trail (Hike 112). ■

111. Sandstone Peak and Inspiration Point

CIRCLE X RANCH

12896 Yerba Buena Road • Malibu

Hiking distance: 4.0 miles round trip
Hiking time: 2.5 hours
Configuration: out-and-back
Elevation gain: 1,100 feet
Difficulty: moderate to somewhat strenuous
Exposure: exposed
Dogs: allowed
Maps: U.S.G.S. Triunfo Pass • N.P.S. Circle X Ranch map
Tom Harrison Maps: Point Mugu State Park Trail Map

map page 363

Sandstone Peak, atop Boney Ridge, stands as the highest point in the Santa Monica Mountains. Despite the name, Sandstone Peak is actually a mass of volcanic rock. From the 3,111-foot summit are far-reaching vistas that sprawl out as far as the eye can see, including the sweep of the mountain range, the Oxnard Plain, the Topatopa Mountains at Ojai, and the Pacific Ocean, which dominates the southern view. The Sandstone Peak Trail climbs the east slope of Boney Mountain high above Carlisle Canyon to the summit of Sandstone Peak. Inspiration Point—another overlook along the spine of the mountain—lies a short distance to the west of the peak.

The Sandstone Peak Trail is a segment of the Backbone Trail, which continues west into Big Sycamore Canyon—Hike 113. This trail can also be hiked as a 5.3-mile loop, combined with the Mishe Mokwa Trail—Hike 112.

To the trailhead

From Santa Monica, drive 38 miles northbound on the Pacific Coast Highway/Highway 1 to Yerba Buena Road and turn right. (Yerba Buena Road is 10.1 miles past Kanan Dume Road and 2 miles past Leo Carrillo State Beach.) Turn right and drive 5.3 miles up the winding road to the Circle X Ranger Station on the right. From the ranger station, continue 1 mile to the Sandstone Peak Trailhead parking lot on the left.

From the Pacific Coast Highway/Highway 1 and Las Posas Road in southeast Oxnard, drive 9 miles southbound to Yerba Buena Road and turn left. Continue up Yerba Buena Road, following the directions above.

From the Ventura Freeway/Highway 101 in Thousand Oaks, exit on Westlake Boulevard (Highway 23). Drive 6.9 miles south on Westlake Boulevard, winding up the mountain road to Mulholland Highway at a stop sign. Turn right and go 0.4 miles to Little Sycamore Canyon Road. Turn right and drive 4.7 miles to the Sandstone Peak Trailhead parking lot on the right. (At the county line, Little Sycamore Canyon Road becomes Yerba Buena Road.)

The hike

Pass the trailhead kiosk and take the Sandstone Peak Trail, a fire road. Head north to the posted Mishe Mokwa Connector Trail at 0.3 miles. Continue straight ahead on the rock-embedded Sandstone Peak Trail. Wind along the mountain contours while marveling at the great vistas. After 1.1 mile and a 1,000-foot elevation gain, the trail reaches a signed fork on the left. A short detour on the left leads 150 yards to 3,111-foot Sandstone Peak, the highest peak in the Santa Monica Mountains. The side path climbs steps to the multi-colored outcroppings atop the peak.

After savoring the 360-degree views, return to the Sandstone Peak Trail. Continue west while overlooking stunning sandstone formations to another side path on the left at just under 2 miles. The left fork detours under 100 yards to Inspiration Point, a 2,800-foot overlook. This is our turn-around spot.

To extend the hike, the trail zigzags down the slope, passing a non-ending display of weather-carved outcrops. Drop into a small valley surrounded by eroded rock monoliths to a Y-fork at 2.7 miles. The left fork leads to Tri-Peaks and to Big Sycamore Canyon. The right fork leads 1.3 miles to Split Rock on the Mishe Mokwa Trail for a longer loop trail—Hike 112. Return by retracing your steps. ■

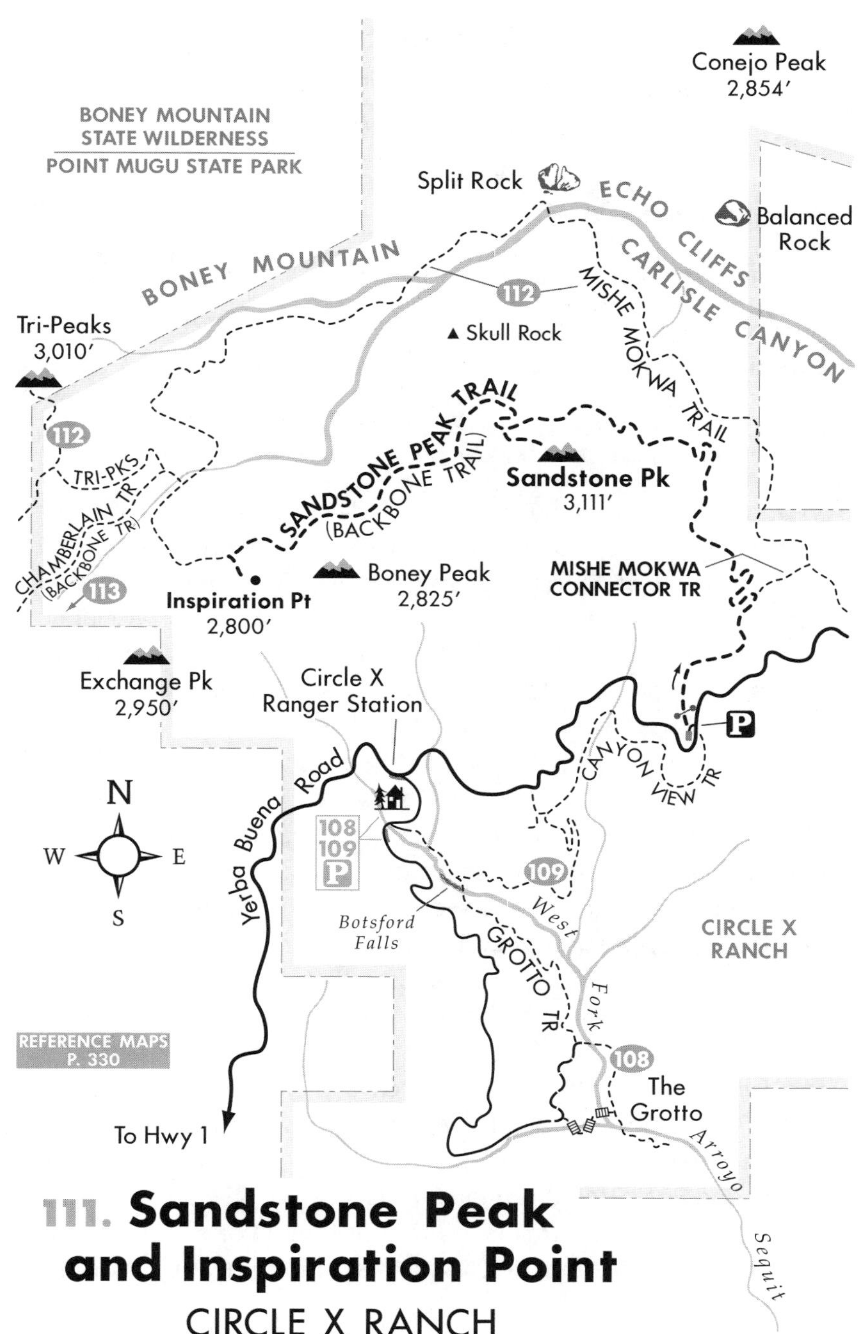

111. Sandstone Peak and Inspiration Point

CIRCLE X RANCH

112. Tri-Peaks

Mishe Mokwa-Sandstone Peak Loop

CIRCLE X RANCH

Yerba Buena Road • Malibu

map page 366

Hiking distance: 7.5 miles
Hiking time: 4 hours
Configuration: double loop with spur trails to summits
Elevation gain: 1,250 feet
Difficulty: moderate to strenuous
Exposure: mix of exposed hillside and shaded forest
Dogs: allowed
Maps: U.S.G.S. Triunfo Pass and Newbury Park • N.P.S. Circle X Ranch map
Tom Harrison Maps: Point Mugu State Park Trail Map

Tri-Peaks is a group of three large boulders atop a jumble of rocks at an elevation of 3,010 feet. The multi-peaked mountain is located one mile west of Sandstone Peak and 100 feet lower. Tri-Peaks lies just outside of Circle X Ranch inside the Boney Mountain State Wilderness. From the rocky summit are 360-degree vistas across the mountains to Thousand Oaks, Camarillo, Simi Valley, Malibu, and the Pacific Ocean to the Channel Islands.

This hike follows the Mishe Mokwa Trail from Yerba Buena Road, the shortest and easiest route to Tri-Peaks. The Mishe Mokwa Trail in Circle X Ranch traverses the southwest wall of Carlisle Canyon, a deep, chiseled canyon along Boney Mountain. The footpath parallels the upper canyon slope past weathered red volcanic formations with far-reaching vistas. There are views of the sculpted caves and crevices of Echo Cliffs and Balanced Rock, an enormous house-sized boulder precariously teetering on a smaller pedestal rock. A short distance past Balanced Rock is a forested streamside picnic area by Split Rock, a fractured volcanic boulder with a pathway through its middle.

After scrambling up the trail to Tri-Peaks, the hike returns via the Sandstone Peak Trail through a garden of countless windswept rock formations. The trail leads to Inspiration Point, perched on an exposed ridge, and Sandstone Peak, the highest point in the

Santa Monica Range. Both points overlook the ocean, the Channel Islands, and the surrounding mountains.

To the trailhead

From Santa Monica, drive 38 miles northbound on the Pacific Coast Highway/Highway 1 to Yerba Buena Road and turn right. (Yerba Buena Road is 10.1 miles west of Kanan Dume Road and 2 miles west of Leo Carrillo State Beach.) Turn right and drive 5.3 miles up the winding road to the Circle X Ranger Station on the right. From the ranger station, continue 1.7 miles to the large parking areas on both sides of the road. Park on either side.

From the Pacific Coast Highway/Highway 1 and Las Posas Road in southeast Oxnard, drive 9 miles southbound to Yerba Buena Road and turn left. Continue up Yerba Buena Road, following the directions above.

From the Ventura Freeway/Highway 101 in Thousand Oaks, exit on Westlake Boulevard (Highway 23). Drive 6.9 miles south on Westlake Boulevard winding up the mountain road to Mulholland Highway at a stop sign. Turn right and go 0.4 miles to Little Sycamore Canyon Road. Turn right and drive 4 miles to the large parking areas on both sides of the road. (At the county line, Little Sycamore Canyon Road becomes Yerba Buena Road.)

The hike

Walk past the posted trailhead, and follow the north-facing slope of Carlisle Canyon. The canyon is rich with magnificent red rock sandstone formations. At 0.6 miles is a posted junction. The left fork (Mishe Mokwa Connector Trail) leads 0.2 miles to the Sandstone Peak Trail, our return route. Begin the loop straight ahead, staying on the Mishe Mokwa Trail. Weave along the contour of the mountain, following the western wall of Carlisle Canyon. Echo Cliffs and Balanced Rock can be seen on the opposite wall of the canyon. At 1.3 miles, descend natural rock steps and cross a stream in a rock grotto. Descend deeper into Carlisle Canyon, shaded by oaks, bay laurel, and sycamores. Cross Carlisle Creek to Split Rock and a streamside picnic area under towering oaks at 1.9 miles. The cabin size volcanic boulder is split in two with a yard-wide access. Continue on the main trail along the floor of

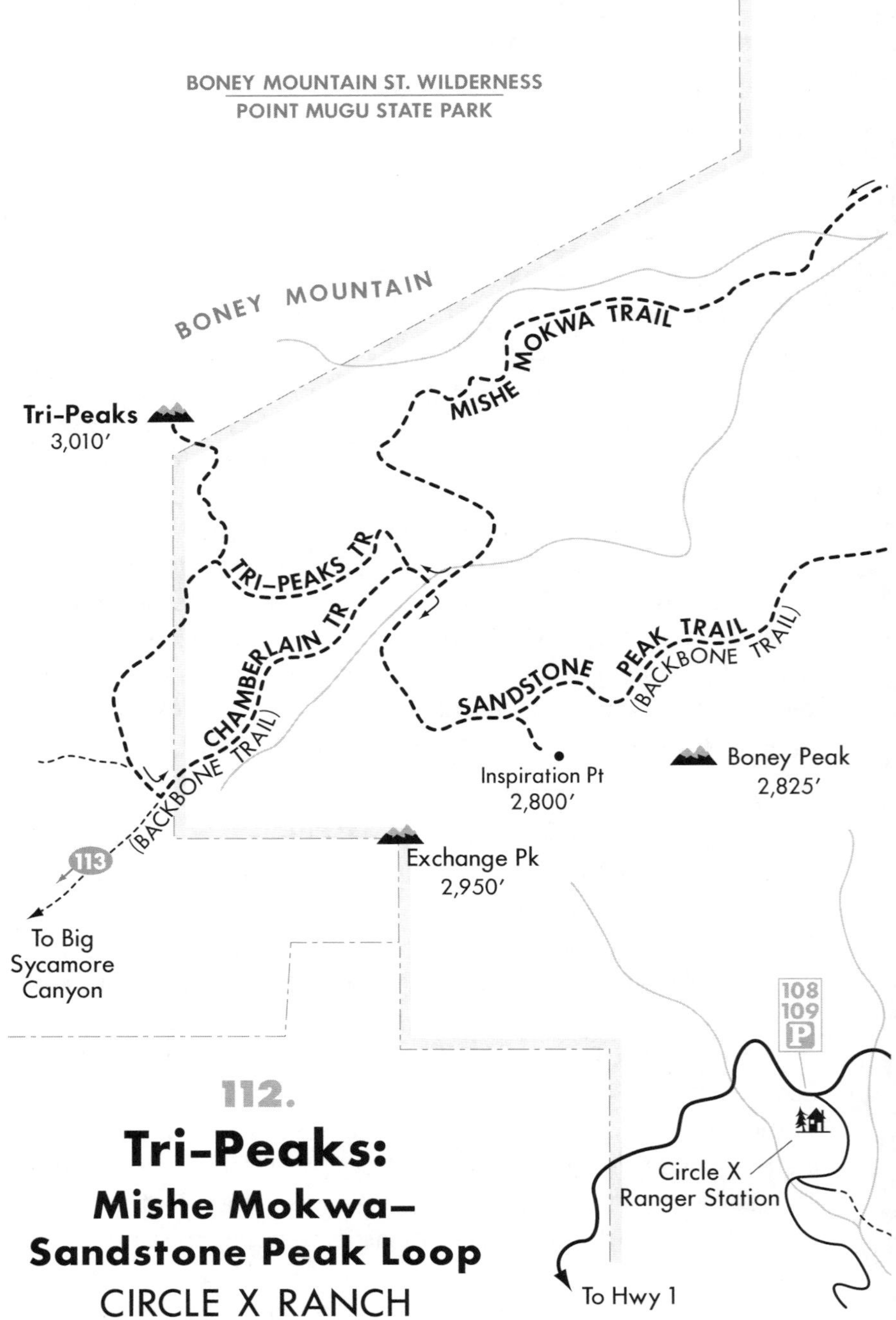

112.

Tri-Peaks:
Mishe Mokwa–Sandstone Peak Loop
CIRCLE X RANCH

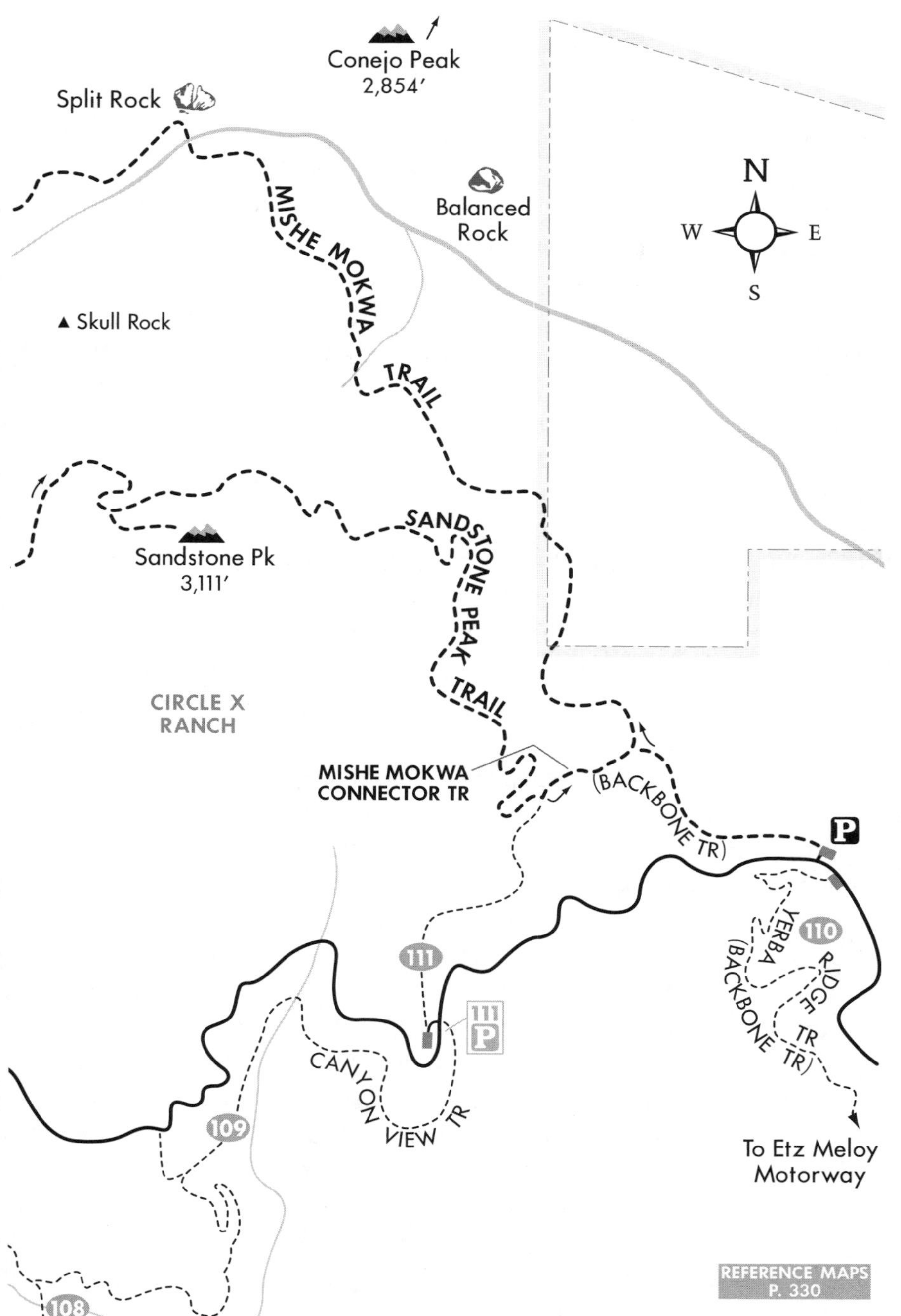
Conejo Peak
2,854′
Split Rock
Balanced
Rock
N
W
E
S
Skull Rock
MISHE MOKWA
TRAIL
SANDSTONE PEAK
TRAIL
Sandstone Pk
3,111′
CIRCLE X
RANCH
MISHE MOKWA
CONNECTOR TR
(BACKBONE TR)
P
110
YERBA
RIDGE
TR
(BACKBONE TR)
111
111
P
CANYON VIEW TR
109
108
To Etz Meloy
Motorway
REFERENCE MAPS
P. 330

Carlisle Canyon on the north flank of Sandstone Peak. Veer left and head west, walking parallel to the stream through the shade of coast live oaks and sycamores. Cross the stream by weather-sculpted volcanic rocks. Gradually ascend out of Carlisle Canyon among a continuing display of outcroppings to a signed junction at 3.2 miles. To the left is the Sandstone Peak Trail, part of the Backbone Trail and our return route.

For now, veer right and walk 30 yards to a Y-fork. The left fork (also the Backbone Trail) descends to Big Sycamore Canyon in Point Mugu State Park. For this hike, go to the right on the Tri-Peaks Trail. Climb up the narrow, rocky path to a signed T-junction. The left fork is the return route. For now, detour right and loop around the hill to the rocky southern base of the massive formation. An unmaintained path weaves among the rocks (and includes some rock-scrambling) to the three-pointed summit. The commanding views range across the surrounding mountains, the Conejo Valley, and Thousand Oaks to the mountains beyond. After taking in the views, return to the junction and continue straight ahead at a near-level grade. Then drop down on the rocky path to a T-junction at 4.3 miles. Bear left and walk a half mile down canyon, parallel to a seasonal drainage to complete the far loop.

Bear right on the Sandstone Peak Trail, zigzagging up the slope towards Inspiration Peak. Pass a non-ending display of weather-carved outcrops to a junction. A short side path on the right leads up to the south-facing rocky overlook atop 2,800-foot Inspiration Peak. Continue east about 0.7 miles to another junction at a spur trail to Sandstone Peak. Detour to the right 150 yards to the 3,111-foot peak. The side path climbs steps and rocks to the multi-colored outcroppings atop the peak.

After savoring the 360-degree views, return to the main trail. Descend over the next 1.3 miles on the rock-embedded path while enjoying the spectacular vistas and losing 1,000 feet in elevation. At a junction with the connector trail, the right fork leads 0.3 miles downhill to the Sandstone Peak Trailhead at Yerba Buena Road. Bear left on the connector path, and go 0.2 miles to the Mishe Mokwa Trail, completing the larger loop. Bear right and return to the trailhead 0.6 miles ahead. ■

113. Sandstone Peak to Big Sycamore Canyon Shuttle

CIRCLE X RANCH • POINT MUGU STATE PARK

Trailhead: Yerba Buena Road · Malibu
Shuttle car: 9000 W. Pacific Coast Hwy · Malibu

Hiking distance: 11.3-mile one-way shuttle
Hiking time: 6-7 hours
Configuration: one-way shuttle
Elevation gain: 900 feet gain and 2,950 feet loss
Difficulty: strenuous
Exposure: a mix of exposed ridges and hillsides; shaded groves and canyon bottoms
Dogs: allowed on first 2.7 miles; not allowed in Point Mugu State Park
Maps: U.S.G.S. Triunfo Pass, Newbury Park and Point Mugu
Tom Harrison Maps: Point Mugu State Park Trail Map
Point Mugu State Park map

map page 372

This mountain-to-coast shuttle hike is among the most spectacular hikes in the Santa Monica Mountains. The hike begins atop the mountain range near Sandstone Peak, the highest peak in the mountain range, and travels over 11 miles to the coastline at Big Sycamore Canyon in Point Mugu State Park. The network of five trails weaves through gardens of weather-carved sandstone outcroppings and leads to a series of spectacular overlooks. The trails follow streams, traverse rugged interior mountains, wind through shaded forests of oaks and sycamores, and descend through several canyons. The most dramatic descent is through Big Sycamore Canyon to the Pacific Ocean at the mouth of the canyon. Over half of the route is along the Backbone Trail.

To the trailhead

From Santa Monica, drive 38 miles northbound on the Pacific Coast Highway/Highway 1 to Yerba Buena Road and turn right. (Yerba Buena Road is 10.1 miles west of Kanan Dume Road and 2 miles west of Leo Carrillo State Beach.) Turn right and drive 5.3 miles up the winding road to the Circle X Ranger Station on the right. From the ranger station, continue 1 mile to the Sandstone Peak Trailhead parking lot on the left.

From the Pacific Coast Highway/Highway 1 and Las Posas Road in southeast Oxnard, drive 9 miles southbound to Yerba Buena Road and turn left. Continue up Yerba Buena Road, following the directions above.

From the Ventura Freeway/Highway 101 in Thousand Oaks, exit on Westlake Boulevard (Highway 23). Drive 6.9 miles south on Westlake Boulevard, winding up the mountain road to Mulholland Highway at a stop sign. Turn right and go 0.4 miles to Little Sycamore Canyon Road. Turn right and drive 4.7 miles to the Sandstone Peak Trailhead parking lot on the right. (At the county line, Little Sycamore Canyon Road becomes Yerba Buena Road.)

Shuttle car

From Santa Monica, drive 31 miles northbound on the Pacific Coast Highway/Highway 1 to the posted Big Sycamore Canyon entrance on the right. (The trailhead entrance is 13.3 miles west of Kanan Dume Road in Malibu and 5.3 miles west of the well-marked Leo Carrillo State Beach.) Turn right and park in the day-use pay parking lot 0.1 mile ahead on the left. (Parking is free in the pullouts along the PCH.)

Heading southbound on the Pacific Coast Highway/Highway 1 from Las Posas Road in southeast Oxnard, drive 5.8 miles to the posted Big Sycamore Canyon entrance on the left.

The hike

Pass the trailhead kiosk and take the Sandstone Peak Trail, a fire road. Head north to the posted Mishe Mokwa Connector Trail at 0.3 miles. Continue straight ahead on the rock-embedded Sandstone Peak Trail. Wind along the mountain contours while marveling at the great vistas. After 1.6 miles and a 1,000-foot elevation gain, the trail reaches a signed fork on the left. A short detour on the left leads 150 yards to 3,111-foot Sandstone Peak, the highest peak in the Santa Monica Mountains. The side path climbs steps to the multi-colored outcroppings atop the peak.

After savoring the 360-degree views, return to the Sandstone Peak Trail. Zigzag down the slope while overlooking stunning sandstone formations. Pass a non-ending display of weather-carved outcrops. Drop into a small valley surrounded by eroded rock monoliths to a Y-fork at 2.7 miles. The right fork leads 1.3 miles to Split Rock on the Mishe Mokwa Trail.

Veer left and walk 30 yards to another Y-fork. To the right, the Tri-Peaks Trail leads a half mile to the massive formation (Hike 112). Follow the valley floor a half mile, parallel to a seasonal drainage, to the second junction with the Tri-Peaks Trail and the Boney Mountain State Wilderness boundary at 3.2 miles. Continue straight ahead on the Chamberlain (Backbone) Trail. Weave through the rolling terrain on a generally downward slope interspersed with numerous small rises. Stroll through a canopy of scrub oak and manzanita high above the canyon, with vistas across Thousand Oaks to the Los Padres National Forest. Follow a long, downhill, cliff-hugging stretch. Cross a narrow ridge, with the meadows of Serrano Valley on the left and forested Big Sycamore Canyon on the right. Descend to a T-junction at 6 miles at the Old Boney Trail. The left fork leads to Serrano Valley and is another route to Big Sycamore Canyon.

Bear right on the Old Boney Trail, with close-up views of the towering mountain peaks from which the trail just descended. Walk down to the canyon floor, parallel to Blue Canyon Creek. Cross stream forks three times to a posted junction with the Blue Canyon Trail at 7.1 miles. The Old Boney Trail bears right, leading to the Danielson Monument and Sycamore Canyon Falls (Hike 117). Continue straight on the Blue Canyon Trail on a gentle downward slope through the riparian corridor. Pass conglomerate boulders and cross the stream five more times. After the fifth crossing, walk through the forested grasslands to the Danielson Ranch on the floor of Big Sycamore Canyon. Pass the picnic area and corrals to Big Sycamore Canyon Road by the ranch house at 8.1 miles. The right fork leads up canyon to Hidden Ponds and the Satwiwa Native American Indian Cultural Center (Hike 115).

Bear left on the old paved road, heading down canyon. Pass the Old Boney Trail on the left, the Wood Canyon Fire Road on the right, and the posted Wood Canyon Vista Trail on the right. (The Backbone Trail continues on the Wood Canyon Vista Trail.) Continue down the forested canyon under a canopy of sycamores and coast live oaks, passing the Serrano Canyon Trail on the left, the Overlook Fire Road on the right, and the Scenic Trail on the right. The trailhead gate appears shortly after at 11.2 miles. From the gate, the paved path leads through the campground to the shuttle car at the Big Sycamore Canyon trailhead. ■

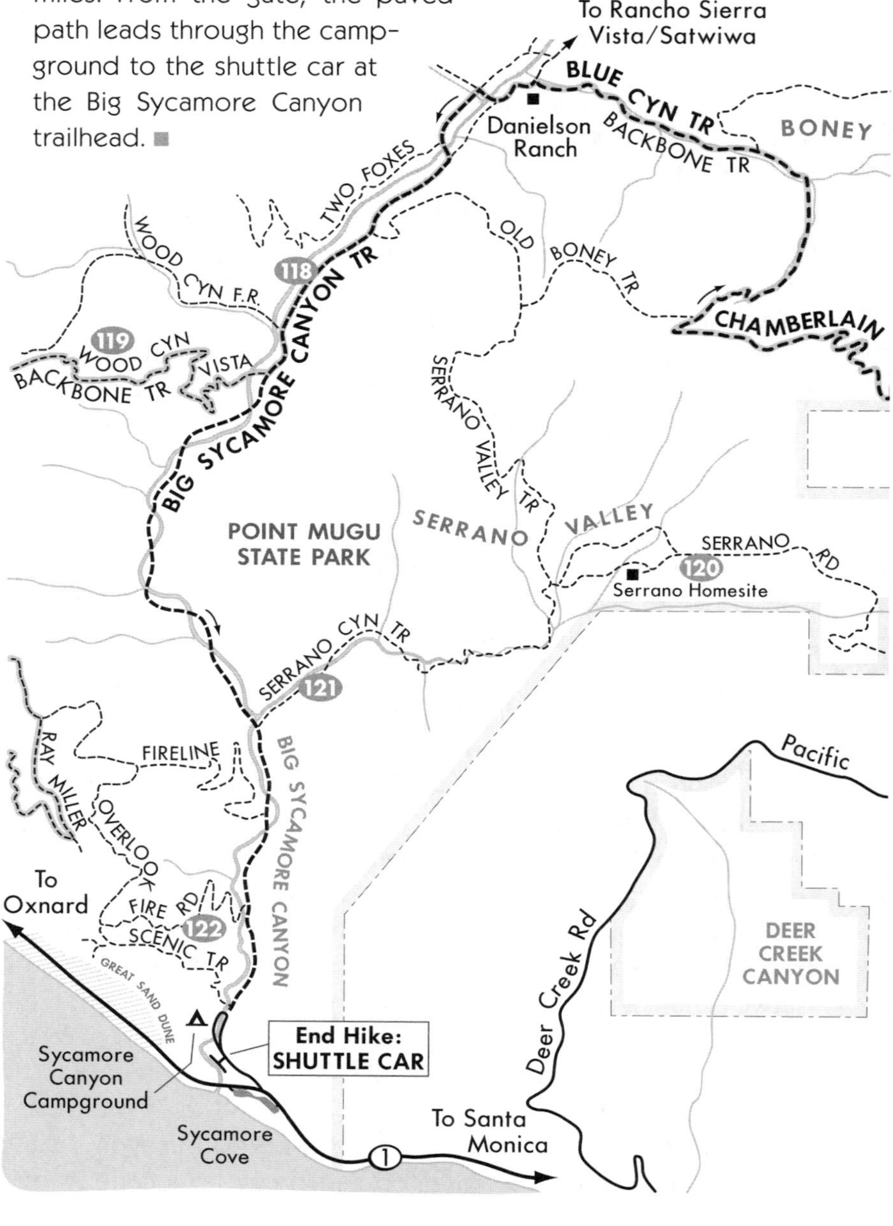

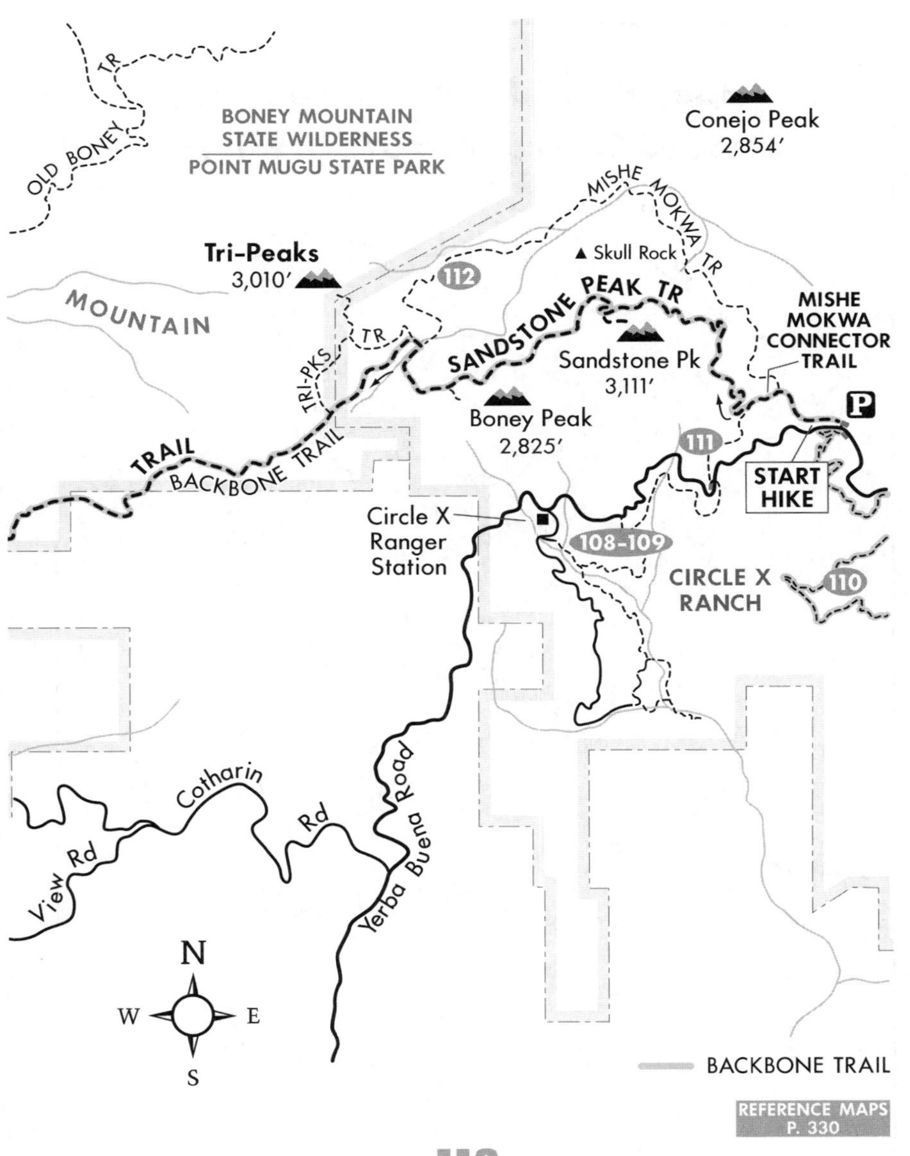

113.

Sandstone Peak to Big Sycamore Canyon shuttle

CIRCLE X RANCH • POINT MUGU STATE PARK

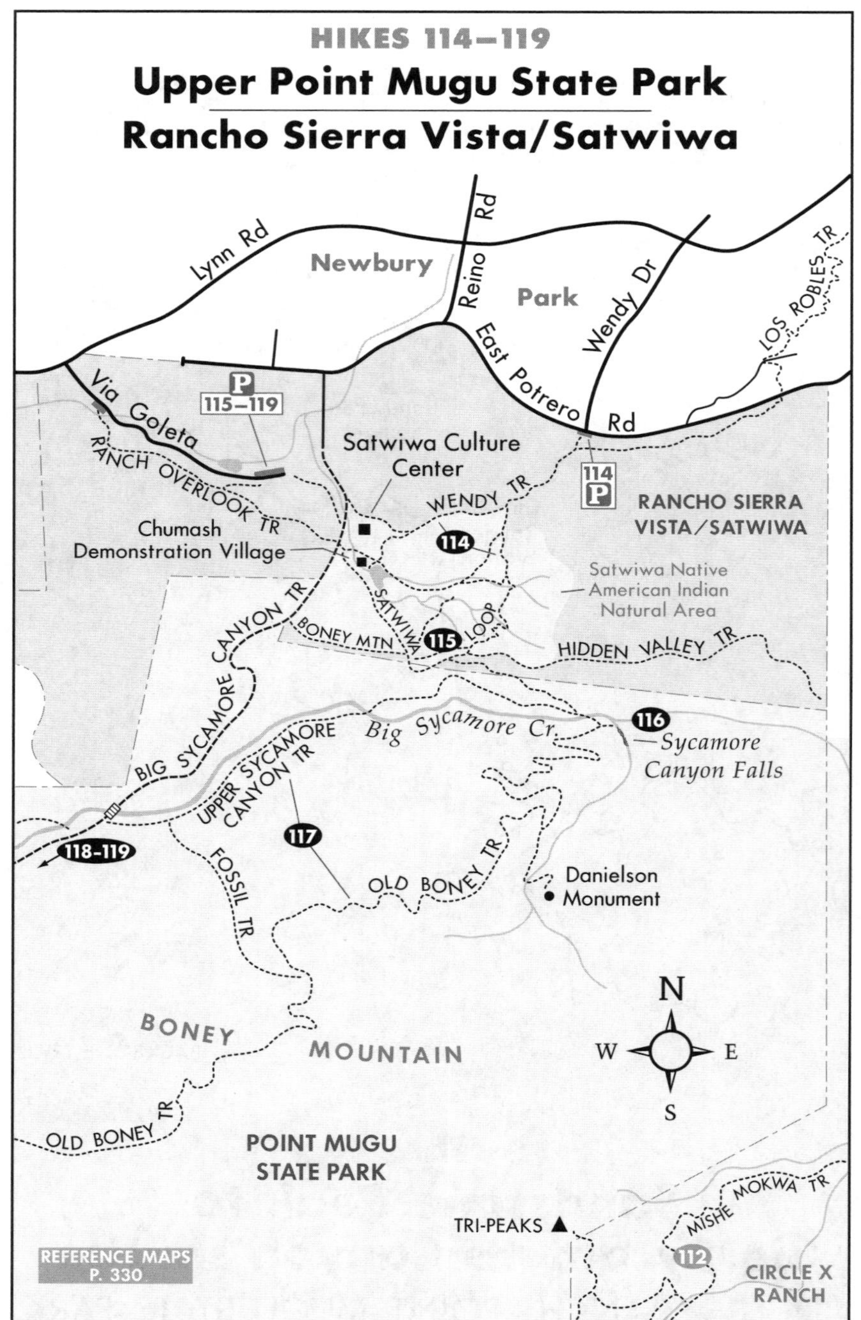
HIKES 114–119
Upper Point Mugu State Park
Rancho Sierra Vista/Satwiwa
Lynn Rd
Reino Rd
Newbury
Park
Wendy Dr
East Potrero Rd
LOS ROBLES TR
Via Goleta
115–119
RANCH OVERLOOK TR
Satwiwa Culture Center
WENDY TR
114
RANCHO SIERRA VISTA/SATWIWA
Chumash Demonstration Village
Satwiwa Native American Indian Natural Area
SATWIWA LOOP
BIG SYCAMORE CANYON TR
BONEY MTN TR
115
HIDDEN VALLEY TR
116
Big Sycamore Cr.
Sycamore Canyon Falls
UPPER SYCAMORE CANYON TR
118-119
117
FOSSIL TR
OLD BONEY TR
Danielson Monument
N
W
E
S
BONEY MOUNTAIN
OLD BONEY TR
POINT MUGU STATE PARK
TRI-PEAKS
MISHE MOKWA TR
112
CIRCLE X RANCH
REFERENCE MAPS P. 330

Point Mugu State Park

Rancho Sierra Vista/Satwiwa

Point Mugu State Park lies at the west end of the Santa Monica Mountains in Ventura County, adjacent to the Pacific Ocean to the south, Newbury Park to the north, and Oxnard to the west. The 16,000-acre state park is the largest and most remote in the mountain range. The state park is accessed from its north end directly through Rancho Sierra Vista/Satwiwa, a preserved parcel of land operated by the National Park Service. Weaving throughout are nearly 75 miles of hiking, biking, and equestrian trails. The trail system combines fire roads, paved service roads, single-track trails, and primitive paths.

The sprawling parkland spans from the Pacific to the upper reaches of the Santa Monica Range. Five miles of ocean shoreline include rocky bluffs, sandy beaches, and sandy dunes. The rugged hills and uplands include two major creek-fed canyons and grass valleys dotted with oaks, walnuts, and sycamores. Big Sycamore Canyon runs the length of the park. It is a deep, tree-shaded, stream-fed canyon. A hiking trail (fire road) follows the canyon bottom for its entire length. Numerous connecting paths lead up to the high ridges to either side of the canyon. The Boney Mountain State Wilderness occupies the eastern portion of the park. The wilderness area, a 6,000-acre preserve, contains the jagged, rocky peaks of Boney Mountain with pinnacles rising above 3,000 feet (the highest promontories of the Santa Monica Range). At the base of Boney Mountain is Serrano Valley, a gorgeous grassland marbled with slow-moving streams. The western side of the park is home to the La Jolla Valley Natural Preserve, a 600-acre upland valley with a rare native bunchgrass prairie.

Rancho Sierra Vista/Satwiwa is located at the northern boundary of Point Mugu State Park and the south edge of Newbury Park. The historical site is named for its two cultural legacies. For thousands of years it was the ancestral land of the Chumash and Gabrielino Indians. It later became a horse and cattle ranch named Rancho Sierra Vista. To reflect the Native American heritage, the Satwiwa Culture Center and Natural Area was established. A hub of hiking trail disperses from the center.

Dogs are not allowed in Point Mugu State Park.

114. Wendy—Satwiwa Loop Trail

RANCHO SIERRA VISTA/SATWIWA

East Potrero Road • Newbury Park

Hiking distance: 2.2-mile loop
Hiking time: 1 hour
Configuration: loop
Elevation gain: 200 feet
Difficulty: easy
Exposure: exposed
Dogs: allowed
Maps: U.S.G.S. Newbury Park • Point Mugu State Park map
N.P.S. Rancho Sierra Vista/Satwiwa map
Tom Harrison Maps: Point Mugu State Park Trail map

Rancho Sierra Vista/Satwiwa sits on the bluffs at the head of Big Sycamore Canyon on the northern boundary of Point Mugu State Park. The land within the Satwiwa Native American Indian Natural Area was occupied for thousands of years by the Chumash and Gabrielino Indians. Big Sycamore Canyon was part of a Chumash trade route to the ocean. Satwiwa, the name of the Chumash village, means *the bluffs*. This easy loop hike through the heart of the preserved land explores the rolling terrain covered with chaparral and grasslands and the forested ravines with oaks and sycamores. The prominent volcanic cliffs of Boney Mountain are in view throughout the hike. The mountain is the highest promontory of the Santa Monica Range.

To the trailhead

From the Ventura Freeway/Highway 101 in Newbury Park, exit on Wendy Drive. Drive 2.7 miles south to Potrero Road. Park in the parking area straight ahead, across the road.

The hike

Head southwest past a signed junction with the Los Robles Connector Trail, and cross the grassy slope dotted with oaks and sycamores. At 0.3 miles is a signed junction, the start of the loop. Leave the Wendy Trail for now, and bear left towards the windmill. Climb a short, steep hill to another junction. Again bear left, reaching the windmill and a junction at a half mile. Both trail forks follow the Satwiwa Loop Trail. The left fork leads to the Boney Mountain Trail. Take the right fork, and descend through a narrow ravine under an oak-shaded canopy. Cross the drainage and follow the open slopes, passing an unsigned path. Curve around the hillside to a 4-way junction by a pond. Straight ahead is the cultural center. The left fork leads to the pond. Bear right and climb to a junction at the crest of the hill. Take the right fork, staying on the Wendy Trail. Traverse the hillside northeast and complete the loop. ■

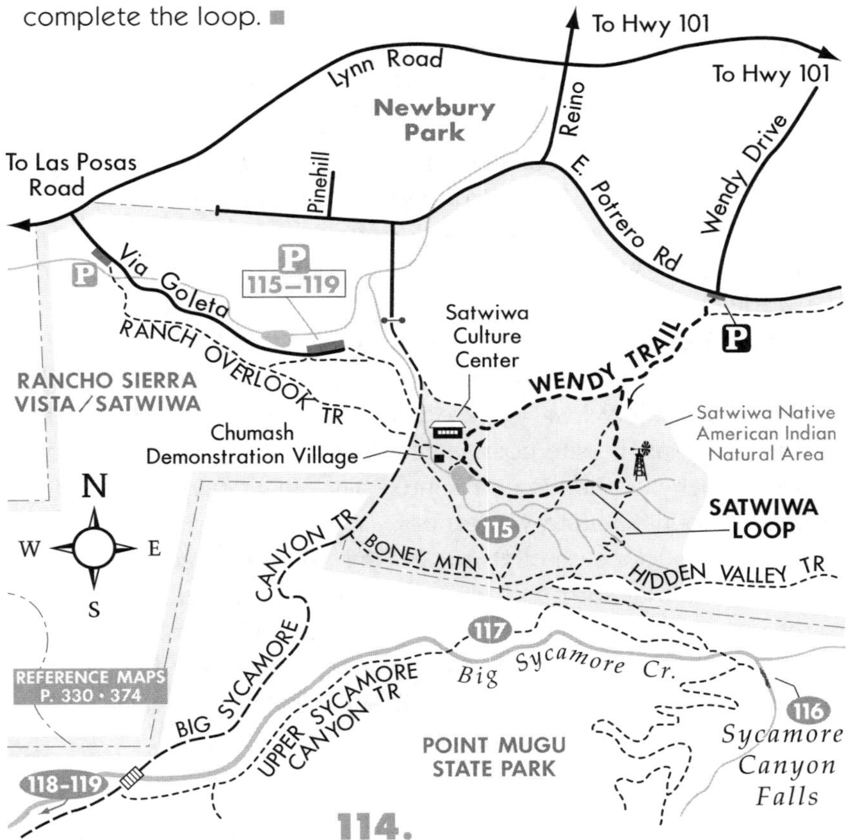

114.
Wendy—Satwiwa Loop Trail

RANCHO SIERRA VISTA/SATWIWA
POINT MUGU STATE PARK

115. Ranch Overlook Trail—Satwiwa Loop

RANCHO SIERRA VISTA/SATWIWA

East Potrero Road • Newbury Park

Hiking distance: 2.5-mile loop
Hiking time: 1.5 hours
Configuration: double loop
Elevation gain: 300 feet
Difficulty: easy
Exposure: exposed
Dogs: allowed
Maps: U.S.G.S. Newbury Park • Point Mugu State Park map
N.P.S. Rancho Sierra Vista/Satwiwa map
Tom Harrison Maps: Point Mugu State Park Trail map

Rancho Sierra Vista/Satwiwa is located at the northern boundary of Point Mugu State Park and the south edge of Newbury Park. The historical site is named for its two cultural legacies. For thousands of years it was the ancestral land of the Chumash and Gabrielino Indians. It was later a horse and cattle ranch named Rancho Sierra Vista. In 1980, an area of the parkland, part of the Santa Monica Mountains National Recreation Area, was designated as the Satwiwa Native American Indian Culture Center and Natural Area. The site hosts a network of hiking trails and is the hub to many connecting trails into Point Mugu State Park and the Boney Mountain State Wilderness.

This hike loops through the rolling grasslands and chaparral to the hills that surround the meadow. The second loop circles through the Satwiwa Native American Indian Natural Area, land that was set aside for the preservation of Native American cultures. Towering over the meadow are the massive, craggy cliffs of Boney Mountain.

To the trailhead

From Highway 101/Ventura Freeway in Newbury Park, exit on Wendy Drive. Drive 2 miles south to Lynn Road and turn right. Continue 1.7 miles to Via Goleta, the park entrance road. (En

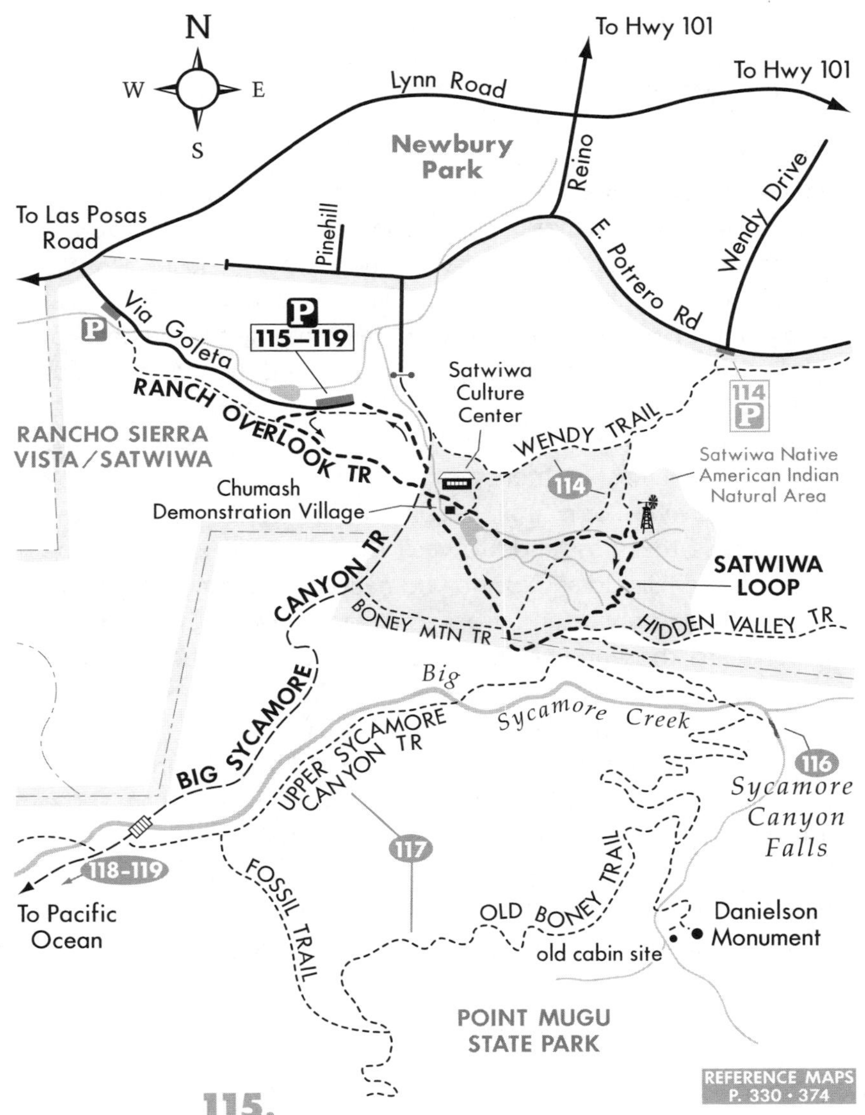

115.

Ranch Overlook Trail—Satwiwa Loop

RANCHO SIERRA VISTA/SATWIWA

POINT MUGU STATE PARK

route, Lynn Road becomes West Potrero Road.) Turn left into the park, and drive 0.7 miles to the main parking lot at the end of the road.

The hike

Walk back up the entrance road 0.1 mile to the posted Ranch Overlook Trail on the left. Bear left and climb the hill overlooking Rancho Sierra Vista, the Satwiwa Natural Area, the jagged Boney Mountain ridge, and Big Sycamore Canyon. Follow the ridge east to a junction with the main park road. To the right is the head of Big Sycamore Canyon (Hikes 118 and 119), and to the left leads to Potrero Road.

Cross the road over two bridges to the cultural center on the left and a Chumash demonstration village on the right. Take the signed Satwiwa Loop Trail, passing an old cattle pond on the right. Cross the grasslands toward the windmill, which can be seen on the hillside ahead. As you near the windmill, drop into an oak-shaded ravine and cross a seasonal stream. Climb a short distance to the windmill and a junction. Bear to the right and traverse the upper slope of the meadow to a Y-fork. Stay to the left on the Hidden Valley Connector Trail. Head 50 yards to a magnificent overlook of Hidden Valley and Big Sycamore Canyon. Go to the right and follow the ridge downhill to a trail split. The left fork leads to Sycamore Canyon Falls (Hike 116). Continue straight to a 3-way trail split at the top of the meadow. Take the middle fork, completing the loop at the cultural center. Cross the road and return to the parking area on the wide gravel path. ■

116. Boney Mountain Trail to Sycamore Canyon Falls

RANCHO SIERRA VISTA/SATWIWA
POINT MUGU STATE PARK

East Potrero Road • Newbury Park

Hiking distance: 3 miles round trip
Hiking time: 1.5 hours
Configuration: out-and-back
Elevation gain: 350 feet
Difficulty: easy
Exposure: a mix of shaded canyon and exposed grassland
Dogs: allowed in Rancho Sierra Vista/Satwiwa but not allowed in Point Mugu State Park
Maps: U.S.G.S. Newbury Park • Point Mugu State Park map
N.P.S. Rancho Sierra Vista/Satwiwa map
Tom Harrison Maps: Point Mugu State Park Trail map

map page 383

The Boney Mountain Trail climbs up the west slope of Boney Mountain at the upper reaches of Point Mugu State Park. This hike follows the lower portion of the trail to Sycamore Canyon Falls (also known as Rancho Sierra Vista Falls), a layered waterfall with a series of cascades set in a shaded, fern-filled grotto. The waterfall is surrounded by deep sandstone walls, lush vegetation, and small pools in the shade of a dense sycamore, bay, maple, and oak forest. The hike begins north of Point Mugu State Park in the Rancho Sierra Vista/Satwiwa area. The area is located at an early ranching site and on former Native American land.

To the trailhead

From Highway 101/Ventura Freeway in Newbury Park, exit on Wendy Drive. Drive 2 miles south to Lynn Road and turn right. Continue 1.7 miles to Via Goleta, the park entrance road. (En route, Lynn Road becomes West Potrero Road.) Turn left into the park and drive 0.7 miles to the main parking lot at the end of the road.

The hike

Take the posted trail past the restrooms a quarter mile to the service road at the Satwiwa Native American Indian Cultural Center. Bear right on the road, entering Point Mugu State Park. As you approach the ridge overlooking Big Sycamore Canyon, take the Boney Mountain Trail to the left along the brink of the canyon. Climb a short hill, passing the Satwiwa Loop Trail on the left, and continue around a ridge to a trail split. Take the right fork, descending down to the forested canyon floor. Stay on the main trail and cross the streambed, where the trail switchbacks sharply to the right. Instead of taking this horseshoe turn to the right (Hike 117), bear to the left, taking the footpath 100 yards to a stream crossing at the base of the waterfall. Return along the same trail, or take one of the many trail options around the culture center. ■

117. Old Boney Trail to Danielson Monument

BONEY MOUNTAIN STATE WILDERNESS and POINT MUGU STATE PARK

East Potrero Road • Newbury Park

Hiking distance: 7.8 miles
Hiking time: 4 hours
Configuration: out-and-back with large loop
Elevation gain: 1,000 feet
Difficulty: moderate to strenuous
Exposure: a mix of shaded canyon and exposed grassland and hillsides
Dogs: allowed in Rancho Sierra Vista/Satwiwa but not allowed in Point Mugu State Park
Maps: U.S.G.S. Newbury Park • Point Mugu State Park map
Tom Harrison Maps: Point Mugu State Park Trail map

map page 385

The Boney Mountain State Wilderness area occupies the eastern portion of Point Mugu State Park. The centerpiece of the preserved area is Boney Mountain, a rocky, jagged formation that rises 1,500 feet above Sycamore Canyon. The scenic mountain

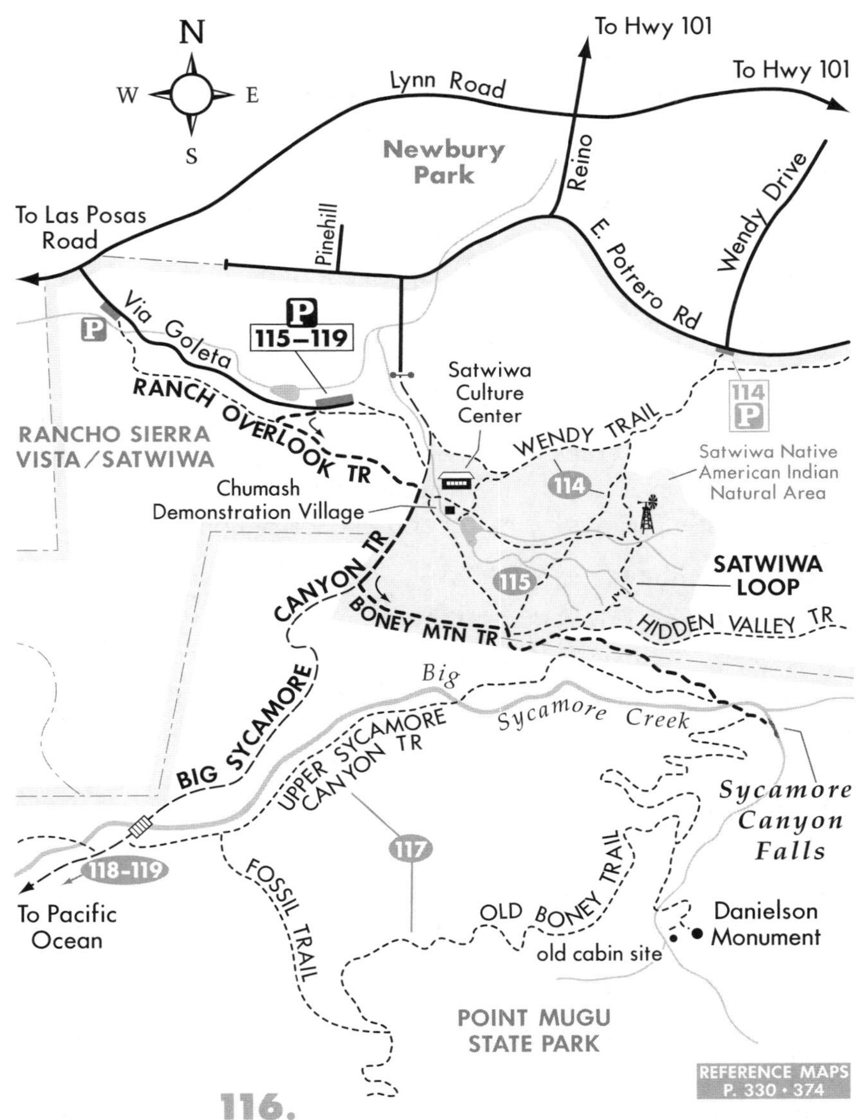

116.

Boney Mountain Trail to Sycamore Canyon Falls

RANCHO SIERRA VISTA/SATWIWA

POINT MUGU STATE PARK

contains four of the highest peaks in the coastal Santa Monica Range, including well-known Sandstone Peak (Hike 111).

This hike begins in Rancho Sierra Vista/Satwiwa and loops through the wilderness area at the northern end of Point Mugu State Park. The route follows the Old Boney Trail in Upper Sycamore Canyon to the Danielson Monument, a stone monument with a metal arch honoring Richard Danielson. Danielson donated the ranch to the National Park Service for preservation as an open space. Near the monument is the old cabin site of Richard Danielson Jr., where a rock fireplace still remains. En route to the monument, the trail passes Sycamore Canyon Falls, a 70-foot cascade in a lush box canyon along the riparian corridor of Big Sycamore Creek. The hike weaves through open grassland, wooded forests, and a stream-fed canyon. Mountain overlooks offer close-up views of the sheer rock face of Boney Mountain.

To the trailhead

From Highway 101/Ventura Freeway in Newbury Park, exit on Wendy Drive. Drive 2 miles south to Lynn Road and turn right. Continue 1.7 miles to Via Goleta, the park entrance road. (En route, Lynn Road becomes West Potrero Road.) Turn left into the park and drive 0.7 miles to the main parking lot at the end of the road.

The hike

Take the posted trail past the restrooms a quarter mile to the service road at the Satwiwa Native American Indian Culture Center. Bear right on the road, entering Point Mugu State Park. As you approach the ridge overlooking Big Sycamore Canyon, take the Boney Mountain Trail to the left along the brink of the canyon. Climb a short hill, passing the Satwiwa Loop Trail on the left, and continue around to a ridge and a trail split. Take the right fork, descending down to the forested canyon floor and a junction with the Upper Sycamore Canyon Trail at 1.3 miles (the return route).

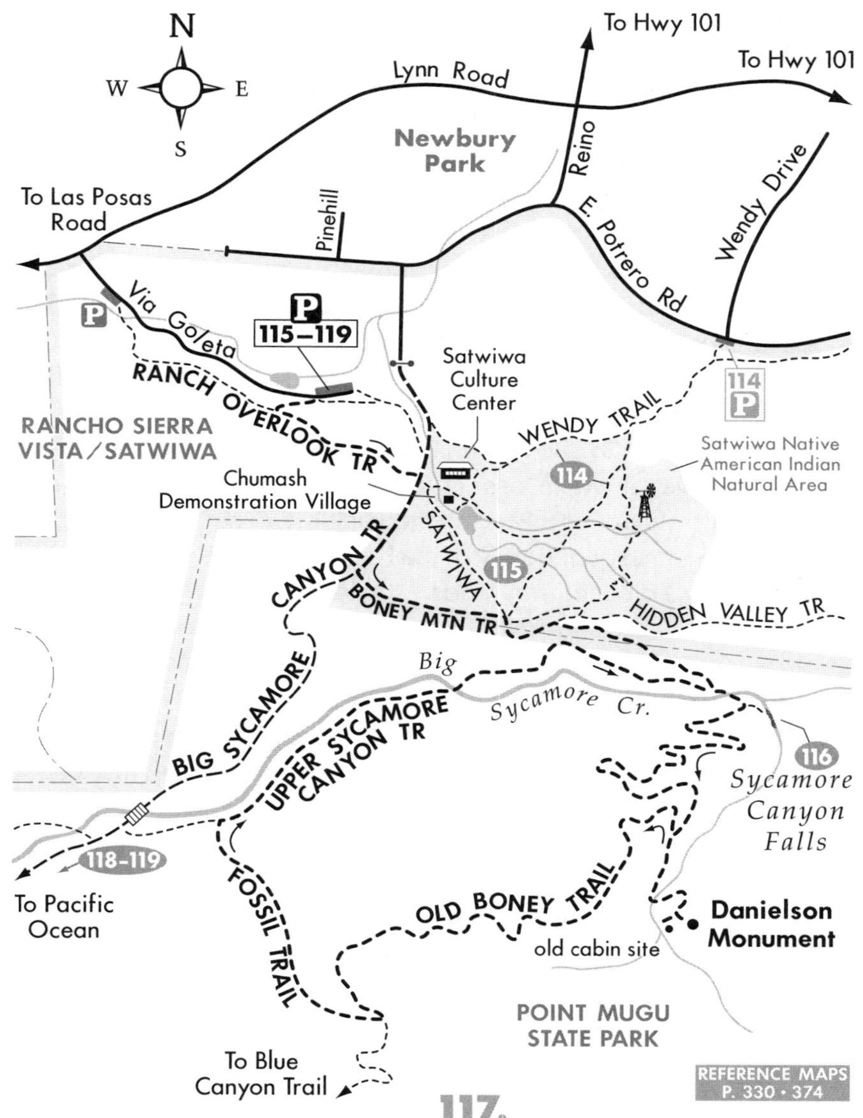

117. Old Boney Trail to Danielson Monument

BONEY MOUNTAIN STATE WILDERNESS
POINT MUGU STATE PARK

Begin the loop straight ahead under a canopy of oaks, sycamores, and bay laurel to a U-shaped right bend. Detour 100 yards to the left to seasonal Sycamore Canyon Falls in a rock-walled box canyon. Return to the Old Boney Trail, and continue up the hillside on the north flank of Boney Mountain to an overlook of Sycamore Canyon, the Oxnard Plain, and the Channel Islands. Inland views extend to the Los Padres National Forest. Steadily climb to a posted junction and views of the rounded rock formations of upper Boney Mountain. Detour 0.3 miles on the left fork, dropping down and crossing a seasonal drainage to the Danielson Monument at the end of the trail. To the right is the old cabin site with the remaining rock chimney and fireplace.

Return to the Old Boney Trail, and walk through the tall brush, gaining elevation while passing occasional overlooks that span from Point Mugu State Park to the Pacific Ocean. Gradually descend to a signed junction with the Fossil Trail at 4.4 miles. Straight ahead, the Old Boney Trail leads 2.1 miles to the Blue Canyon Trail, part of the Backbone Trail. (To the west, the Backbone Trail connects to the Danielson Ranch in Big Sycamore Canyon—Hike 118. To the east, the trail leads to Sandstone Peak—Hike 111.)

For this hike go to the right on the Fossil Trail, and descend into the stream-fed canyon. Follow the east canyon wall downstream, passing dozens of shell fossils embedded in the rock along the path. Near the bottom, enter an oak grove to a T-junction with the Upper Sycamore Canyon Trail. The left fork leads 0.1 mile to the Big Sycamore Canyon Fire Road/Trail. Bear right and head east upstream, following the upper canyon floor. Complete the loop at 6.5 miles, 0.2 miles shy of Sycamore Canyon Falls. Bear left and retrace your steps 1.3 miles back to the trailhead. ■

118. Big Sycamore Canyon shuttle

Rancho Sierra Vista/Satwiwa to Big Sycamore Canyon Trailhead

POINT MUGU STATE PARK

Trailhead: East Potrero Road • Newbury Park
Shuttle car: West Pacific Coast Highway • Malibu

Hiking distance: 8.4-mile one-way shuttle
Hiking time: 4.5 hours
Configuration: one-way shuttle
Elevation loss: 900 feet loss
Difficulty: moderate
Exposure: mostly shaded canyon with some exposed slope
Dogs: not allowed
Maps: U.S.G.S. Newbury Park, Camarillo and Point Mugu
Tom Harrison Maps: Point Mugu State Park Trail map
Point Mugu State Park map

map page 388

With a shuttle car parked at the bottom of the canyon, this hike down the Big Sycamore Canyon Trail is a one-way, mountains-to-the-sea journey. The canyon was originally part of the Chumash Indian trade route. The trail, now a partially paved service road and fire road, connects Newbury Park at the Rancho Sierra Vista/Satwiwa site with the Sycamore Canyon Campground at the Pacific Ocean. The hike parallels Big Sycamore Creek through the heart of 15,000-acre Point Mugu State Park in a deep, wooded canyon under towering sycamores and oaks.

To the trailhead

From Highway 101/Ventura Freeway in Newbury Park, exit on Wendy Drive. Drive 2 miles south to Lynn Road and turn right. Continue 1.7 miles to Via Goleta, the park entrance road. (En route, Lynn Road becomes West Potrero Road.) Turn left into the park and drive 0.7 miles to the main parking lot at the end of the road.

Shuttle Car

From Santa Monica, drive 31 miles northbound on the Pacific Coast Highway/Highway 1 to the posted Big Sycamore Canyon

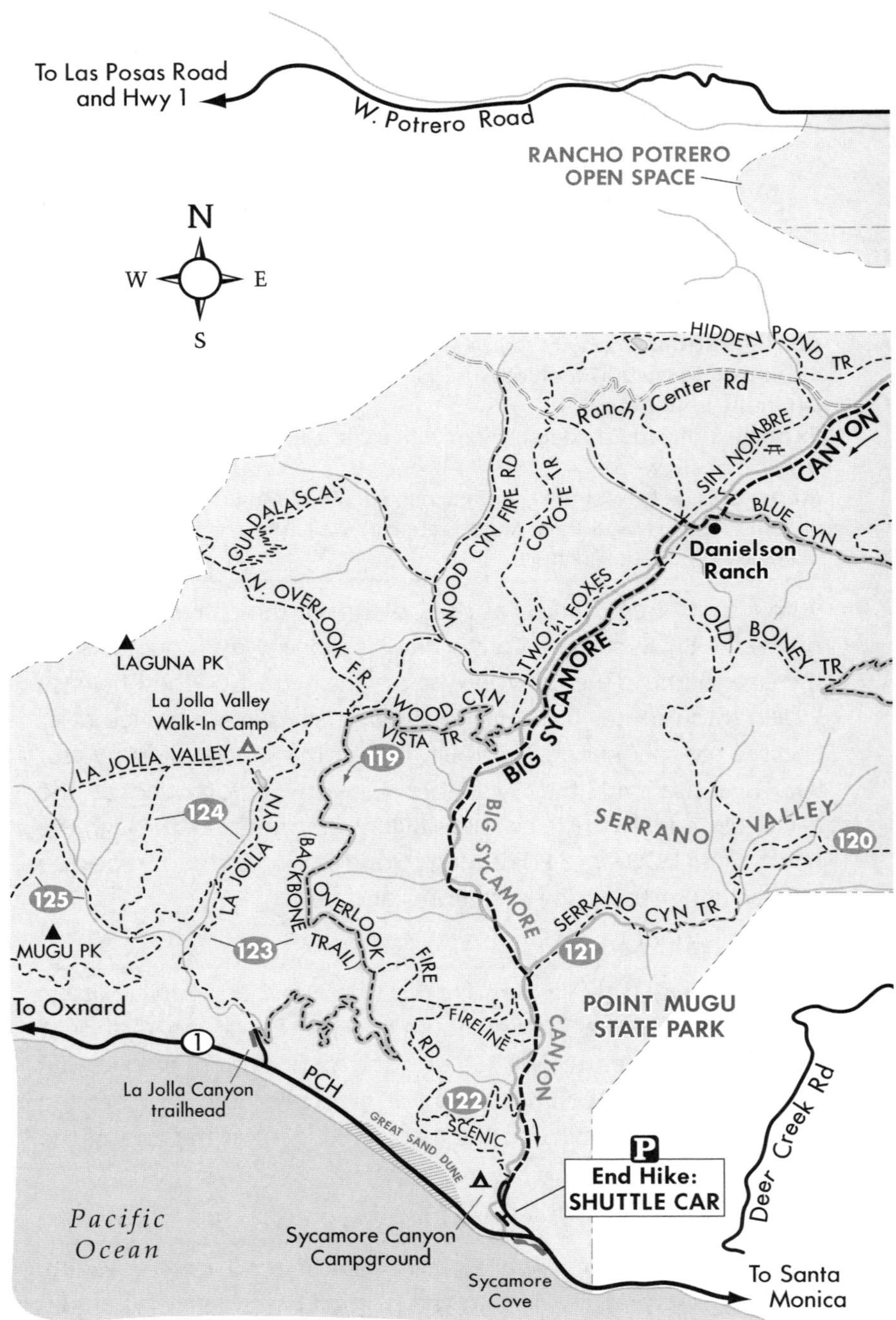
To Las Posas Road and Hwy 1
W. Potrero Road
RANCHO POTRERO OPEN SPACE
N
W
E
S
HIDDEN POND TR
Ranch Center Rd
SIN NOMBRE
CANYON
BLUE CYN
Danielson Ranch
GUADALASCA
WOOD CYN FIRE RD
COYOTE TR
N. OVERLOOK F.R.
TWO FOXES
BIG SYCAMORE
OLD BONEY TR
LAGUNA PK
La Jolla Valley Walk-In Camp
WOOD CYN VISTA TR
LA JOLLA VALLEY
119
124
LA JOLLA CYN
(BACKBONE TRAIL)
OVERLOOK FIRE
BIG SYCAMORE
SERRANO VALLEY
120
125
MUGU PK
123
SERRANO CYN TR
121
To Oxnard
FIRELINE RD
POINT MUGU STATE PARK
CANYON
1
PCH
La Jolla Canyon trailhead
122
SCENIC
GREAT SAND DUNE
Deer Creek Rd
P
End Hike: SHUTTLE CAR
Pacific Ocean
Sycamore Canyon Campground
Sycamore Cove
To Santa Monica

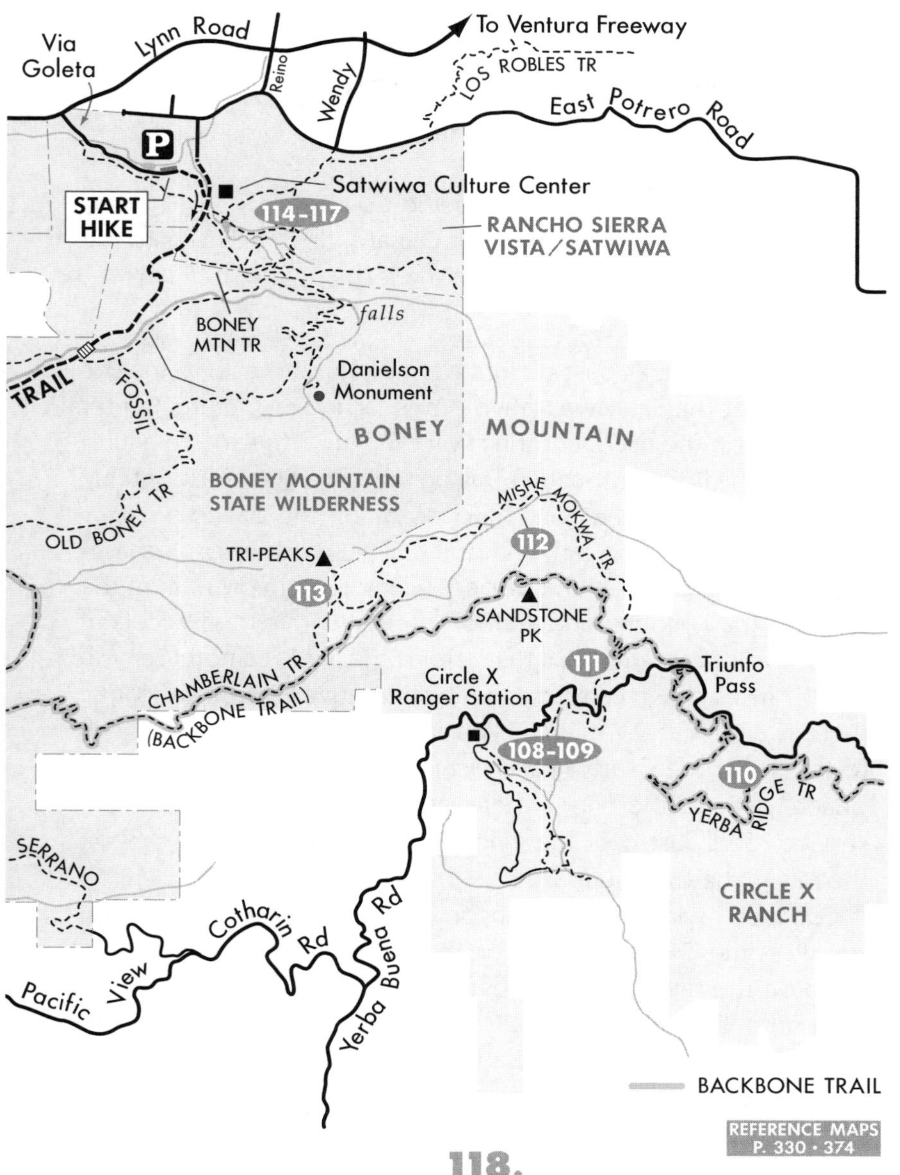

REFERENCE MAPS
P. 330 · 374

118.

Big Sycamore Canyon Trail

POINT MUGU STATE PARK

entrance on the right. (The trailhead entrance is 13.3 miles west of Kanan Dume Road in Malibu and 5.3 miles west of the well-marked Leo Carrillo State Beach.) Turn right and park in the day-use pay parking lot 0.1 mile ahead on the left. (Parking is free in the pullouts along the PCH.)

Heading southbound on the Pacific Coast Highway/ Highway 1 from Las Posas Road in southeast Oxnard, drive 5.8 miles to the Point Mugu State Park entrance on the left.

The hike

Take the posted trail past the restrooms a quarter mile to the service road at the Satwiwa Native American Indian Cultural Center. Bear right on the road, entering Point Mugu State Park, to a junction with the Boney Mountain Trail on the left (Hike 117). Continue straight and begin the winding descent on the paved, vehicle-restricted road to the canyon floor. Cross a wooden bridge over Big Sycamore Creek to the Upper Sycamore Canyon Trail on the left and the Hidden Pond Trail on the right. This is an excellent single track alternative trail that rejoins the Big Sycamore Canyon Trail 1.7 miles down canyon. On the alternative Hidden Pond Trail, there is a split at 2.2 miles. Take the left fork (Sin Nombre Trail) to the Sycamore Camping and Picnic Area. At 3 miles is a signed "beach" path on the right, where the alternative trail rejoins the service road. Just past the junction is the Danielson Ranch. Past the ranch, the trail is unpaved.

Continue heading down canyon on the Big Sycamore Canyon Trail. Pass the Old Boney Trail on the left, the Wood Canyon Fire Road on the right, and the posted Wood Canyon Vista Trail on the right. (The Backbone Trail continues on the Wood Canyon Vista Trail.) Continue down the forested canyon under a canopy of sycamores and coast live oaks, passing the Serrano Canyon Trail on the left, the Overlook Fire Road on the right, and the Scenic Trail on the right. The trailhead gate appears shortly after the Scenic Trail. From the gate, the paved path leads through the campground to the shuttle car at the Big Sycamore Canyon trailhead. ■

119. Big Sycamore Canyon to La Jolla Canyon shuttle

Rancho Sierra Vista/Satwiwa to La Jolla Canyon Trailhead

POINT MUGU STATE PARK

Trailhead: East Potrero Road · Newbury Park
Shuttle car: West Pacific Coast Highway · Malibu

Hiking distance: 11.3-mile one-way shuttle
Hiking time: 6 hours
Configuration: one-way shuttle
Elevation gain: 800 feet gain and 870 feet loss
Difficulty: strenuous
Exposure: a mix of shaded canyons and exposed hills and ridges
Dogs: not allowed
Maps: U.S.G.S. Triunfo Pass, Newbury Park and Point Mugu
Tom Harrison Maps: Point Mugu State Park Trail Map
Point Mugu State Park map

map page 394

Big Sycamore Canyon is a deep stream-fed canyon running through the heart of Point Mugu State Park. The upper reaches of the canyon sit within Rancho Sierra Vista/Satwiwa at nearly 900 feet in elevation. The Big Sycamore Canyon Trail, a fire road, follows the waterway over eight miles through a canopy of sycamores, live oaks, and alders to the ocean at Sycamore Cove. This one-way shuttle hike descends through the upper half of Big Sycamore Canyon, then climbs the west canyon wall to the Overlook Fire Road atop the ridge (following the Backbone Trail). The Overlook Fire Road threads along the undulating mountain crest between Big Sycamore Canyon and La Jolla Valley. From the ridge a thousand feet above Big Sycamore Canyon, the views are fantastic. Boney Mountain dominates the eastern horizon, rising above the Serrano Valley. To the west is a view across the tree-dotted grasslands of the La Jolla Valley Natural Preserve, rimmed by the mountain crest of Mugu Peak, Laguna Peak, and La Jolla Peak. To the south is the Pacific Ocean. The hike ends on the Ray Miller Trail, snaking down the oceanfront hillside to the mouth of La Jolla Canyon (the western terminus of the Backbone Trail).

To the trailhead

From Highway 101/Ventura Freeway in Newbury Park, exit on Wendy Drive. Drive 2 miles south to Lynn Road and turn right. Continue 1.7 miles to Via Goleta, the park entrance road. (En route, Lynn Road becomes West Potrero Road.) Turn left into the park and drive 0.7 miles to the main parking lot at the end of the road.

Shuttle car

From Santa Monica, drive 33 miles northbound on the Pacific Coast Highway/Highway 1 to the posted La Jolla Canyon entrance on the right. (The trailhead entrance is 15 miles west of Kanan Dume Road in Malibu and 1.6 miles west of the well-marked Big Sycamore Canyon.) Turn right and park in the day-use pay parking lot 0.1 mile ahead on the left. (Parking is free in the pullouts along PCH.)

Heading southbound on the Pacific Coast Highway/Highway 1 from Las Posas Road in southeast Oxnard, drive 4.2 miles to the entrance on the left.

The hike

Take the posted trail past the restrooms a quarter mile to the service road at the Satwiwa Native American Indian Culture Center. Bear right on the road, entering Point Mugu State Park, to a junction with the Boney Mountain Trail on the left (Hike 117). Continue straight on the Big Sycamore Canyon Road, and wind down the paved, vehicle-restricted road to the canyon floor. Cross a wooden bridge over Big Sycamore Creek to Upper Sycamore Canyon Trail on the left and Hidden Pond Trail on the right. Gently descend, staying on the main road along the canyon bottom to Danielson Ranch, a multi-use recreation area at 3.2 miles.

At the ranch, the Blue Canyon Trail, part of the Backbone Trail, heads up the east canyon wall to Tri-Peaks and Sandstone Peak (Hike 111). Continue past the Danielson Ranch, where the fire road turns to dirt. Pass the Old Boney Trail on the left and Wood Canyon Fire Road on the right. Walk 0.2 miles farther to the posted Wood Canyon Vista Trail on the right (the Backbone Trail).

Leave the Big Sycamore Canyon Trail, and take the footpath to the right, weaving up the west canyon wall. Steadily climb to magnificent views of the canyon and mountains. After gaining 750 feet in elevation, follow a ridge between two canyons. Cross the level ridge to a T-junction with the Overlook Fire Road on a saddle overlooking La Jolla Valley at 10.2 miles.

Bear left and head up the slope on the Overlook Fire Road. Traverse the upper west rim of Big Sycamore Canyon, overlooking La Jolla Valley, Serrano Valley, Big Sycamore Canyon, and one of the best views of the jagged Boney Mountains, all in one sweeping panorama. Follow the north/south-running ridge to the top of the hill and expansive ocean vistas. Descend while enjoying the continuous, far-reaching views. After 2 miles on the Overlook Fire Road is the signed Ray Miller Trail on a left bend. This is the final (and westernmost) leg of the Backbone Trail. Bear right on the footpath, and wind along the contours of the ocean-front mountains. The trail, perched on the cliffs, descends at an easy grade. Near the bottom, pass the group camp/upper picnic area, and drop down to the trailhead parking lot. ■

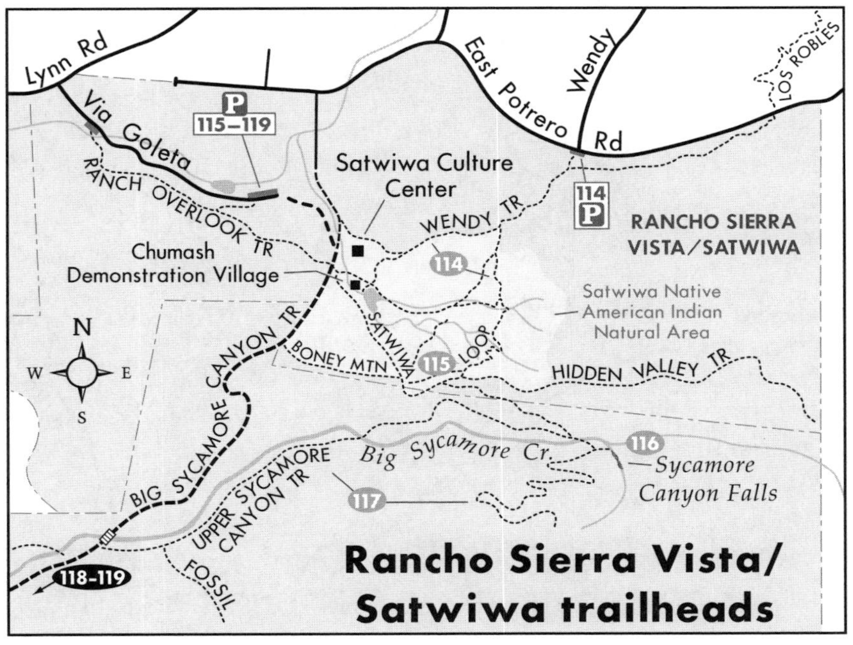

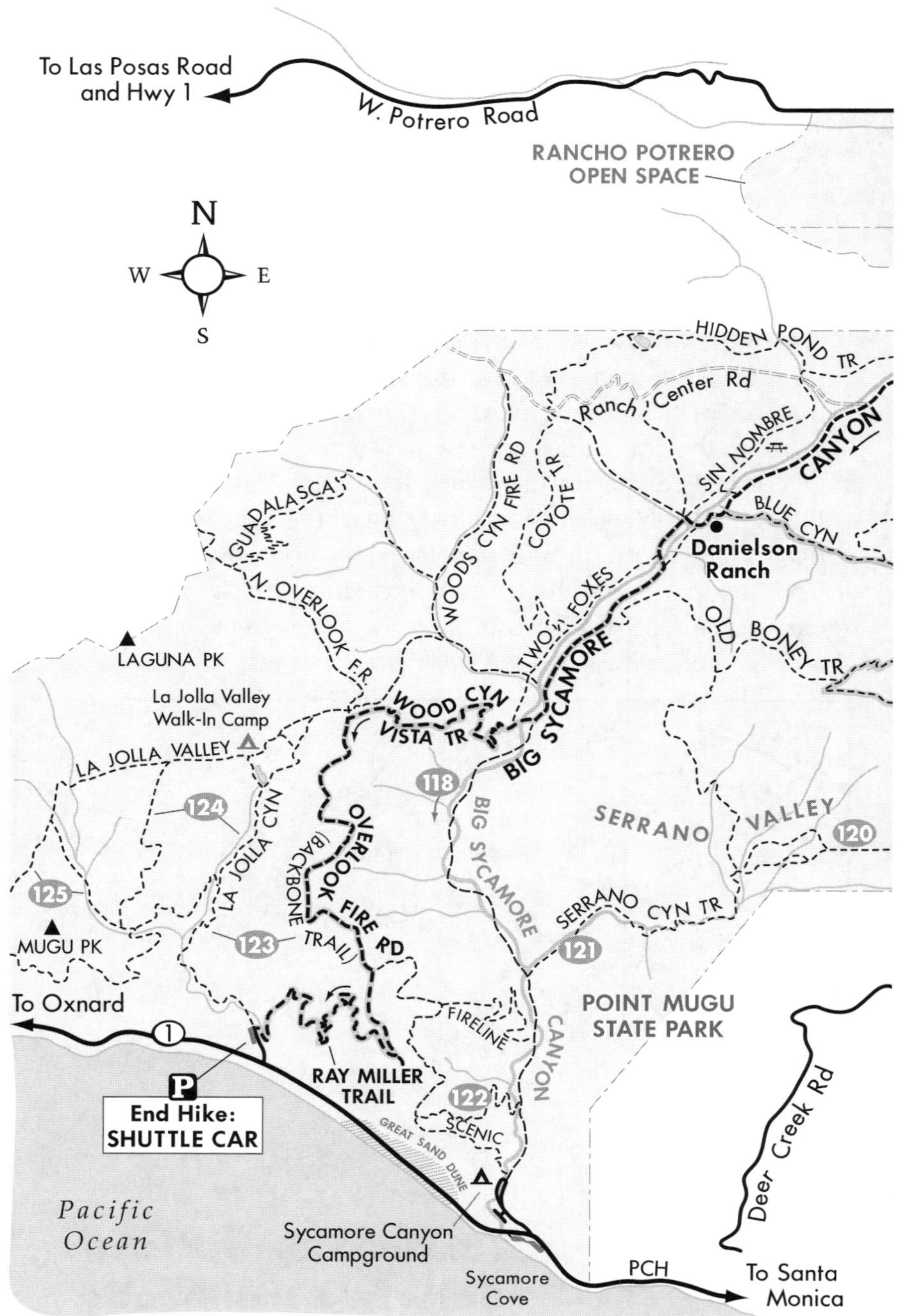
To Las Posas Road and Hwy 1
W. Potrero Road
RANCHO POTRERO OPEN SPACE
N
W
E
S
HIDDEN POND TR
Ranch Center Rd
SIN NOMBRE
CANYON
BLUE CYN
Danielson Ranch
WOODS CYN FIRE RD
COYOTE TR
GUADALASCA
N. OVERLOOK F.R.
TWO FOXES
BIG SYCAMORE
OLD BONEY TR
LAGUNA PK
La Jolla Valley Walk-In Camp
WOOD CYN VISTA TR
LA JOLLA VALLEY
118
124
LA JOLLA CYN
OVERLOOK FIRE RD
(BACKBONE TRAIL)
BIG SYCAMORE
SERRANO VALLEY
120
125
MUGU PK
123
SERRANO CYN TR
121
To Oxnard
1
FIRELINE
CANYON
POINT MUGU STATE PARK
RAY MILLER TRAIL
End Hike: SHUTTLE CAR
122
SCENIC
GREAT SAND DUNE
Deer Creek Rd
Pacific Ocean
Sycamore Canyon Campground
Sycamore Cove
PCH
To Santa Monica

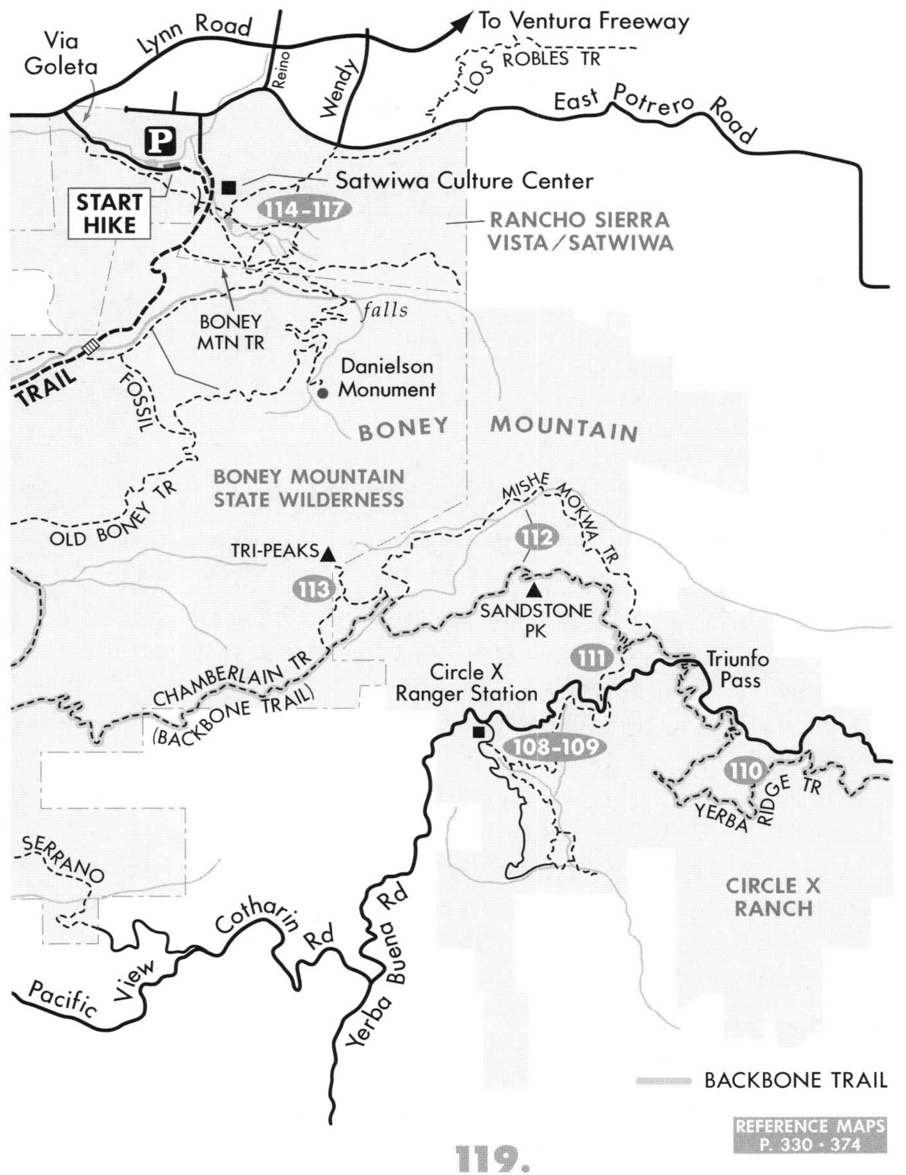

119.

Big Sycamore Canyon to La Jolla Canyon shuttle

POINT MUGU STATE PARK

120. Serrano Valley from Serrano Road

Serrano Homesite to Old Boney Trail

POINT MUGU STATE PARK

Malibu

Hiking distance: 3 miles round trip to homesite; 7 miles round trip to Old Boney Trail
Hiking time: 1.5—3.5 hours
Configuration: out-and-back
Elevation gain: 350 to 900 feet
Difficulty: moderate
Exposure: mostly exposed
Dogs: not allowed
Maps: U.S.G.S. Triunfo Pass and Point Mugu
Tom Harrison Maps: Point Mugu State Park Trail Map

Serrano Valley lies in the southwest corner of Point Mugu State Park in the Boney Mountain State Wilderness. The towering cliffs and jagged peaks of Boney Mountain rise from the north edge of the gorgeous, rolling grasslands. The scenic meadow is marbled with slow-moving streams.

The remote, high-mountain valley can be accessed from three directions. This hike begins at the gated west end of Serrano Road. The hike follows the length of Serrano Valley on the abandoned road to the remains of the old Serrano homestead. From the west end of the valley, the hike climbs the shoulder of Boney Mountain to the 1,000-foot ridge dividing Big Sycamore Canyon and the Serrano Valley, where the trail joins with the Old Boney Trail. Throughout the hike are stunning views of Boney Mountain.

To the trailhead

From Santa Monica, drive 30 miles northbound on the Pacific Coast Highway/Highway 1 to Deer Creek Road on the right. (The turnoff is 11.6 miles west of Kanan Dume Road.) Turn right and drive 4.5 miles up the winding paved road to posted Serrano Road on the left. (En route, Deer Creek Road becomes Pacific View Road, then Cotharin Road.) Turn sharply left on Serrano Road, and drive one mile down the narrow road to the gate at the end of the road. Park along the roadside.

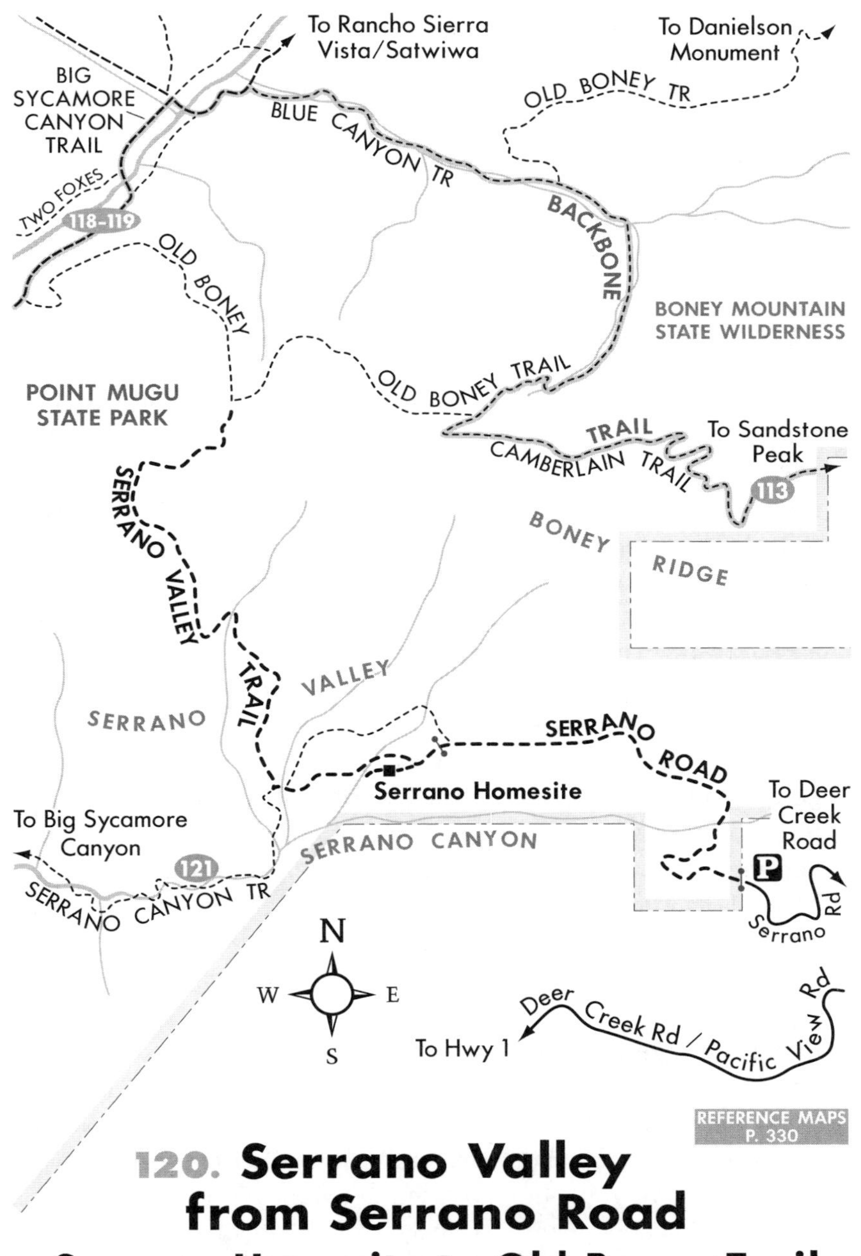

REFERENCE MAPS P. 330

120. Serrano Valley from Serrano Road

Serrano Homesite to Old Boney Trail

POINT MUGU STATE PARK

Heading southbound on the Pacific Coast Highway/Highway 1 from Las Posas Road in southeast Oxnard, drive 7.6 miles to Deer Creek Road on the left. (The turnoff is located 1.2 miles past the well-marked Sycamore Canyon entrance.) Turn left on Deer Creek Road, and follow the directions above.

The hike

Walk past the trailhead gate on the narrow asphalt road. Steadily descend on the road (being reclaimed by the vegetation) while marveling at Boney Mountain, the beautiful mountain ridge directly across Serrano Valley. At 0.6 miles, cross over a fork of Serrano Creek on the valley floor. Curve left and head west through the scenic grassland valley. Walk through the open, rolling terrain to a Y-fork by a wire fence at 1.4 miles. Take the left fork and pass through a rusted gate. The trail continues on Serrano Road (now a single-track path) for a short distance through the heart of the valley. Pass the old entry pillars to the remains of the Serrano Homesite. Past the pillars are the foundation slab, wood corral, and old farm machinery. One hundred yards ahead are two more pillars, more rusted ranch machinery, and remnants of a foundation. Return 20 yards past the first pillars to a signed junction.

For a shorter 3-mile hike, head back to the trailhead. For a longer and steeper hike, bear left (west) on a faint path that follows the fenceline and quickly becomes more distinct. Descend to Serrano Creek in a lush oak grove at 1.9 miles. Hop over the creek and follow it downstream. Weave through the meadow to an unsigned fork on a minor knoll at 2.2 miles. The Serrano Canyon Trail goes to the left and leads 1.7 miles to Big Sycamore Canyon Road (Hike 121). Bear right on the Serrano Valley Trail. Traverse the upper meadow with 360-degree vistas. Top the ridge and descend into the next stream-fed canyon. Cross the stream and climb out of the canyon to the ridge. Steadily climb the west end of Boney Mountain to the upper ridge. Descend a short distance to a 3-way junction with the Old Boney Trail on the ridge between Serrano Valley and Big Sycamore Canyon. The right fork leads 0.9 miles to the Chamberlain Trail and Tri-Peaks (Hike 112). The left fork descends 1.2 miles into the bottom of Big Sycamore Canyon (Hike 121). Return along the same trail. ■

121. Serrano Valley Loop from Big Sycamore Canyon

POINT MUGU STATE PARK

9000 W. Pacific Coast Hwy • Malibu

Hiking distance: 9.5 miles
Hiking time: 5 hours
Configuration: out-and-back with large loop
Elevation gain: 1,000 feet
Difficulty: moderate to strenuous
Exposure: mostly shaded with some exposed areas
Dogs: not allowed
Maps: U.S.G.S. Point Mugu and Triunfo Pass
Tom Harrison Maps: Point Mugu State Park Trail Map

map page 401

This hike begins where Big Sycamore Canyon empties into the Pacific. The hike heads up the canyon along the fire road, then veers east into Serrano Canyon, a deep, water-carved rock gorge that drains into Big Sycamore Canyon from Serrano Valley. The narrow, mile-long canyon is filled with live oaks, sycamores, bay laurel, ferns, and poison oak. The hiking-only footpath winds up the steep-walled canyon, crossing the stream numerous times and passing shallow pools and small waterfalls. The trail emerges to Serrano Valley, a gorgeous, rolling grassland backed by the dramatically rising wall of Boney Mountain, the western sentinel of the Santa Monica Mountains. After crossing the west end of Serrano Valley, with overlooks down into the valley, the hike returns back through Big Sycamore Canyon along the shaded floor.

To the trailhead

From Santa Monica, drive 31 miles northbound on the Pacific Coast Highway/Highway 1 to the posted Big Sycamore Canyon entrance on the right. (The trailhead entrance is 13.3 miles west of Kanan Dume Road in Malibu and 5.3 miles west of the well-marked Leo Carrillo State Beach.) Turn right and park in the day-use pay parking lot 0.1 mile ahead on the left. (Parking is free in the pullouts along PCH.)

Heading southbound on the Pacific Coast Highway/Highway 1 from Las Posas Road in southeast Oxnard, drive 5.8 miles to the posted Big Sycamore Canyon entrance on the left.

The hike

Walk up Big Sycamore Canyon, passing through the campground to the trailhead gate. Head up the dirt road under a canopy of sycamore trees and lush streamside vegetation. Pass the Scenic Trail (Hike 122), Overlook Fire Road, and Fireline Trail, all on the left. At 1.2 miles is the signed Serrano Canyon Trail on the right.

Veer right on the footpath and begin the loop. Enter the mouth of Serrano Canyon, and skirt the south edge of the canyon floor. Meander under the shade of the lush riparian vegetation, including sycamore trees and scrub oak. Rock-hop over the stream, and steadily head up the remote canyon. Cross the creek two more times as the canyon narrows between the vertical rock walls. Climb railroad-tie and rock steps up the north canyon wall. Descend and curve right, following the course of the serpentine canyon. Parallel the stream through the dense forest with a fern ground cover, crossing the creek ten more times. At just under 3 miles, emerge from the canyon to beautiful Serrano Valley. The trail looks out across the open, rolling meadow to scalloped Boney Ridge, which rises dramatically from the north edge of the valley. The footpath quickly reaches an unsigned fork with the Serrano Valley Trail. The right fork (straight ahead) leads to the Serrano Homesite (Hike 120) and on to Serrano Road.

Veer left on the Serrano Valley Trail, and traverse the upper meadow with 360-degree vistas. Top the ridge and descend into the next stream-fed canyon. Cross the stream and climb out of the canyon to the ridge. Steadily climb the west shoulder of Boney Mountain to the upper ridge. Descend a short distance to a 3-way junction with the Old Boney Trail on the ridge between Serrano Valley and Big Sycamore Canyon at 4.7 miles. The right fork leads 0.9 miles to the Chamberlain Trail and Tri-Peaks (Hike 112). Go to the left, descending 770 feet over the next 1.2 miles while overlooking Big Sycamore Canyon. Near the canyon floor,

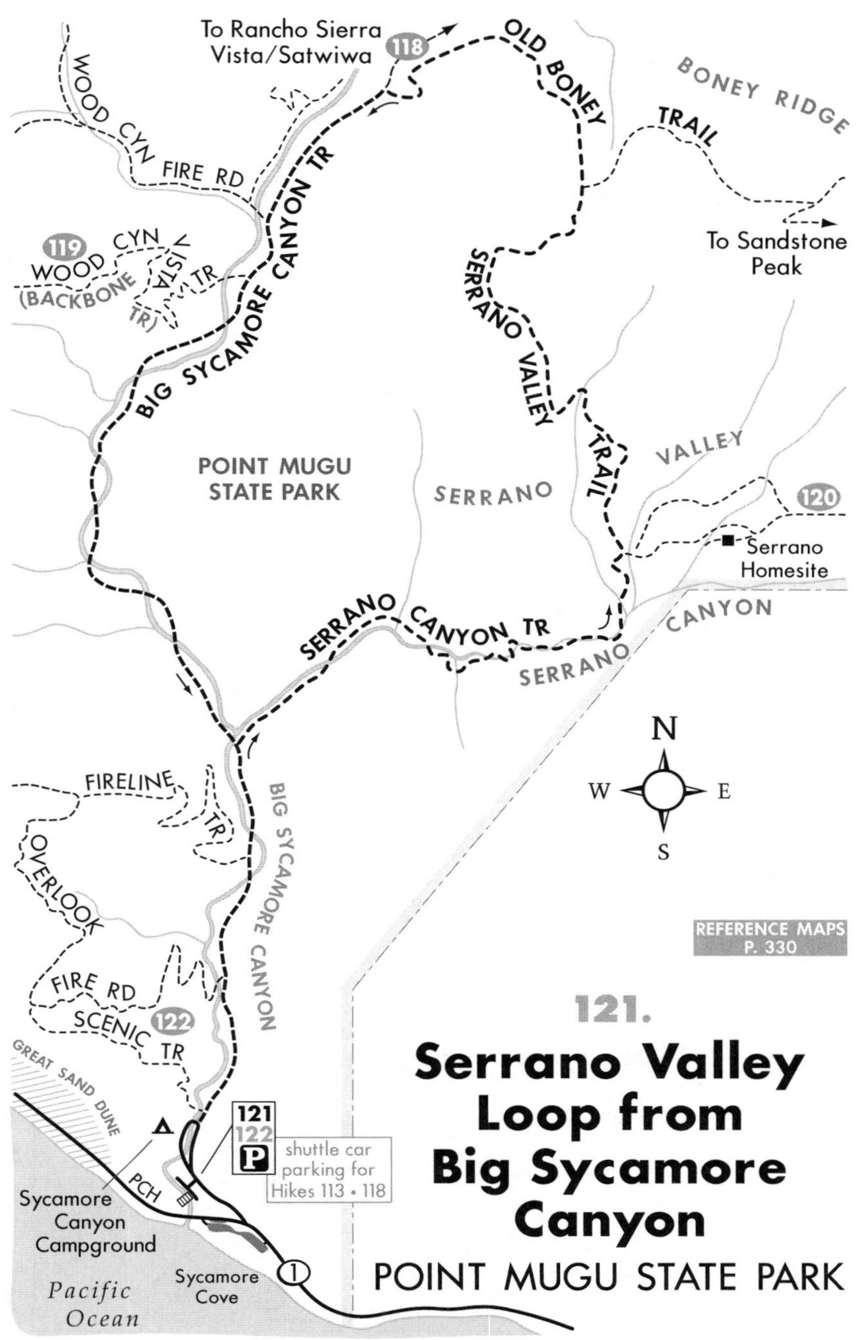
To Rancho Sierra Vista/Satwiwa
118
OLD BONEY
BONEY RIDGE
TRAIL
To Sandstone Peak
WOOD CYN FIRE RD
BIG SYCAMORE CANYON TR
119
WOOD CYN VISTA TR
(BACKBONE TR)
SERRANO VALLEY TRAIL
POINT MUGU STATE PARK
SERRANO
VALLEY
120
Serrano Homesite
SERRANO CANYON TR
CANYON
SERRANO
N
W
E
S
FIRELINE TR
OVERLOOK FIRE RD
BIG SYCAMORE CANYON
REFERENCE MAPS P. 330
SCENIC TR
122
GREAT SAND DUNE
121
122
P
shuttle car parking for Hikes 113 • 118
PCH
Sycamore Canyon Campground
1
Sycamore Cove
Pacific Ocean
121.
Serrano Valley Loop from Big Sycamore Canyon
POINT MUGU STATE PARK

switchback across a stream to a T-junction with the Big Sycamore Canyon Trail at 5.9 miles.

From the large, tree-dotted meadow on the canyon floor, bear left and head down canyon, skirting the edge of the meadow surrounded by hills. Pass the Wood Canyon Fire Road and the Wood Canyon Vista Trail, both on the right. Continue down the forested canyon under a canopy of sycamores to the Serrano Canyon Trail on the left, completing the loop at 8.3 miles. Return 1.2 miles down canyon to the trailhead. ■

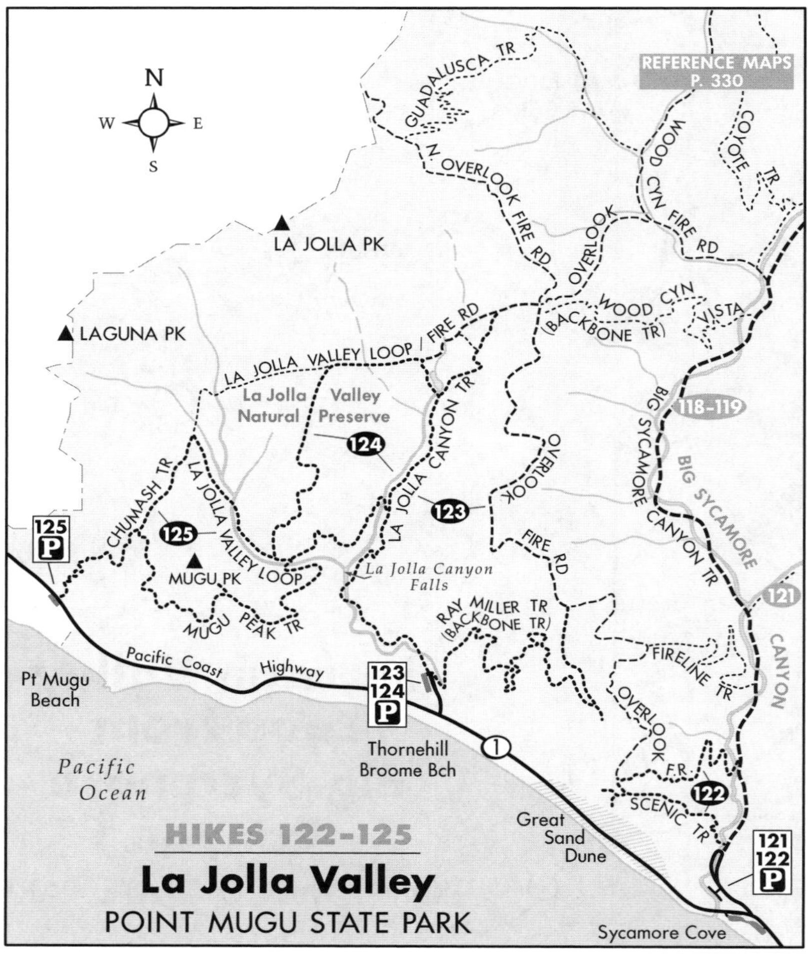

122. Scenic Trail— Overlook Fire Road Loop

POINT MUGU STATE PARK

9000 W. Pacific Coast Hwy • Malibu

Hiking distance: 2-mile loop
Hiking time: 1 hour
Configuration: loop
Elevation gain: 900 feet
Difficulty: easy to moderate
Exposure: mostly exposed
Dogs: not allowed
Maps: U.S.G.S. Point Mugu • Point Mugu State Park map
Tom Harrison Maps: Point Mugu State Park Trail map

map page 404

The Scenic and Overlook Trails are located along the oceanfront mountains of Point Mugu State Park. The Overlook Fire Road, an unpaved, vehicle-restricted road, follows a high north/south-running ridgeline that separates Big Sycamore Canyon from La Jolla Valley. The Scenic Trail is a footpath that contours the oceanfront slope on a chaparral-covered ridge to panoramic overlooks of the Pacific. Both trails begin in the shade of Big Sycamore Canyon and form a loop on the west canyon slope.

To the trailhead

From Santa Monica, drive 31 miles northbound on the Pacific Coast Highway/Highway 1 to the posted Big Sycamore Canyon entrance on the right. (The trailhead entrance is 13.3 miles west of Kanan Dume Road in Malibu and 5.3 miles west of the well-marked Leo Carrillo State Beach.) Turn right and park in the day-use pay parking lot 0.1 mile ahead on the left. (Parking is free in the pullouts along the PCH.)

Heading southbound on the Pacific Coast Highway/ Highway 1 from Las Posas Road in southeast Oxnard, drive 5.8 miles to the Big Sycamore Canyon entrance on the left.

The hike

From the parking area, walk up the road past the campground to the Big Sycamore Canyon trailhead gate. Continue up the unpaved road about 50 yards to the signed junction with the Scenic Trail. Take the trail to the left (west) across Big Sycamore Creek, and head up the wooden steps. Steadily gain elevation up an open, grassy hillside with views of Big Sycamore Canyon. At the saddle near the top of the hill is a trail split. The left fork leads a short distance to an oceanfront overlook. Continue up to several more viewpoints. Return back to the junction, and head north to a junction with the Overlook Fire Road. Take this service road downhill to the right, winding 0.9 miles back to the Big Sycamore Canyon floor. Near the bottom, five gentle switchbacks lead to the junction across the creek. Take the canyon trail to the right, leading 0.4 miles back to the trailhead gate. ■

123. Ray Miller—Overlook Fire Road— La Jolla Canyon Loop

POINT MUGU STATE PARK

W. Pacific Coast Hwy • Malibu

Hiking distance: 7.4-mile loop
Hiking time: 4 hours
Configuration: loop
Elevation gain: 1,200 feet
Difficulty: moderate to strenuous
Exposure: exposed
Dogs: not allowed
Maps: U.S.G.S. Point Mugu
Tom Harrison Maps: Point Mugu State Park Trail Map

map page 407

The Ray Miller Trail begins from the mouth of La Jolla Canyon at Thornhill Broome Beach. It is the westernmost segment of the Backbone Trail, a continuous 69-mile trail, leading to Will Rogers State Park in Pacific Palisades. The Ray Miller Trail snakes up the oceanfront hillsides through coastal sage scrub at an easy grade, ending at the Overlook Fire Road at the mountain crest. The Overlook Fire Road continues threading up the undulating mountain crest between Big Sycamore Canyon and La Jolla Valley. From the ridge, a thousand feet above Big Sycamore Canyon, Boney Mountain can be seen dominating the eastern horizon above Serrano Valley. To the west is a view across the tree-dotted grasslands of the La Jolla Valley Natural Preserve, rimmed by the mountain crest of Mugu Peak, Laguna Peak, and La Jolla Peak. The hike returns through the east end of the 600-acre grassy plain to La Jolla Canyon. The footpath descends down the narrow gorge with a perennial stream and small waterfall.

To the trailhead

From Santa Monica, drive 33 miles northbound on the Pacific Coast Highway/Highway 1 to the posted La Jolla Canyon entrance on the right. (The trailhead entrance is 15 miles west of Kanan Dume Road in Malibu and 1.6 miles west of the well-marked Big Sycamore Canyon.) Turn right and park in the day-use pay parking lot 0.1 mile ahead on the left. (Parking is free in the pullouts along the PCH.)

Heading southbound on the Pacific Coast Highway/Highway 1 from Las Posas Road in southeast Oxnard, drive 4.2 miles to the entrance on the left.

The hike

The trail at the end of the road, by the vehicle gate, is the La Jolla Canyon Trail—the return route. Take the signed Ray Miller (Backbone) Trail, located just shy of the gate on the east (right) side of the road. Weave up the south wall of La Jolla Canyon, and cross over a small rise, leaving La Jolla Canyon. Wind up the side canyon, with great coastal views, while following the contours of the oceanfront mountain. The ascent is steady but never steep. Cross another ridge, then traverse the mountainside, crossing into a third drainage. At 2.2 miles, veer sharply left, high above Big Sycamore Canyon. Ahead is a full panorama of Boney Mountain, including Sandstone Peak, the tallest peak in the Santa Monica Range. Follow the ridge north as the path levels out and drops slightly to a T-junction with the Overlook Fire Road at 2.7 miles. The right fork leads 2.7 miles to Big Sycamore Canyon Fire Road (Hike 118).

Bear left on the narrow dirt road, and walk along the northern ridge of Big Sycamore Canyon, with far-reaching views up the canyon to the Potrero Hills and the Los Padres National Forest. As the path levels out, views open up again to the ocean. Cross an 1,100-foot saddle, following the north/south-running ridge between Big Sycamore Canyon and La Jolla Valley. At 4.7 miles is the posted Wood Canyon Vista Trail on the right, where the Backbone Trail continues to the east. Stay on the road for 120 yards to a 4-way junction. The right fork descends into Big Sycamore Canyon via the Overlook Fire Road. The North Overlook Fire Road goes straight ahead, linking to the Guadalasca Trail.

For this hike, bear left on the La Jolla Valley Fire Road. Descend 0.2 miles to the open valley floor and posted La Jolla Canyon Trail on the left. The right fork leads out across the expansive valley (Hike 124). Instead, go left on the footpath, and stroll through

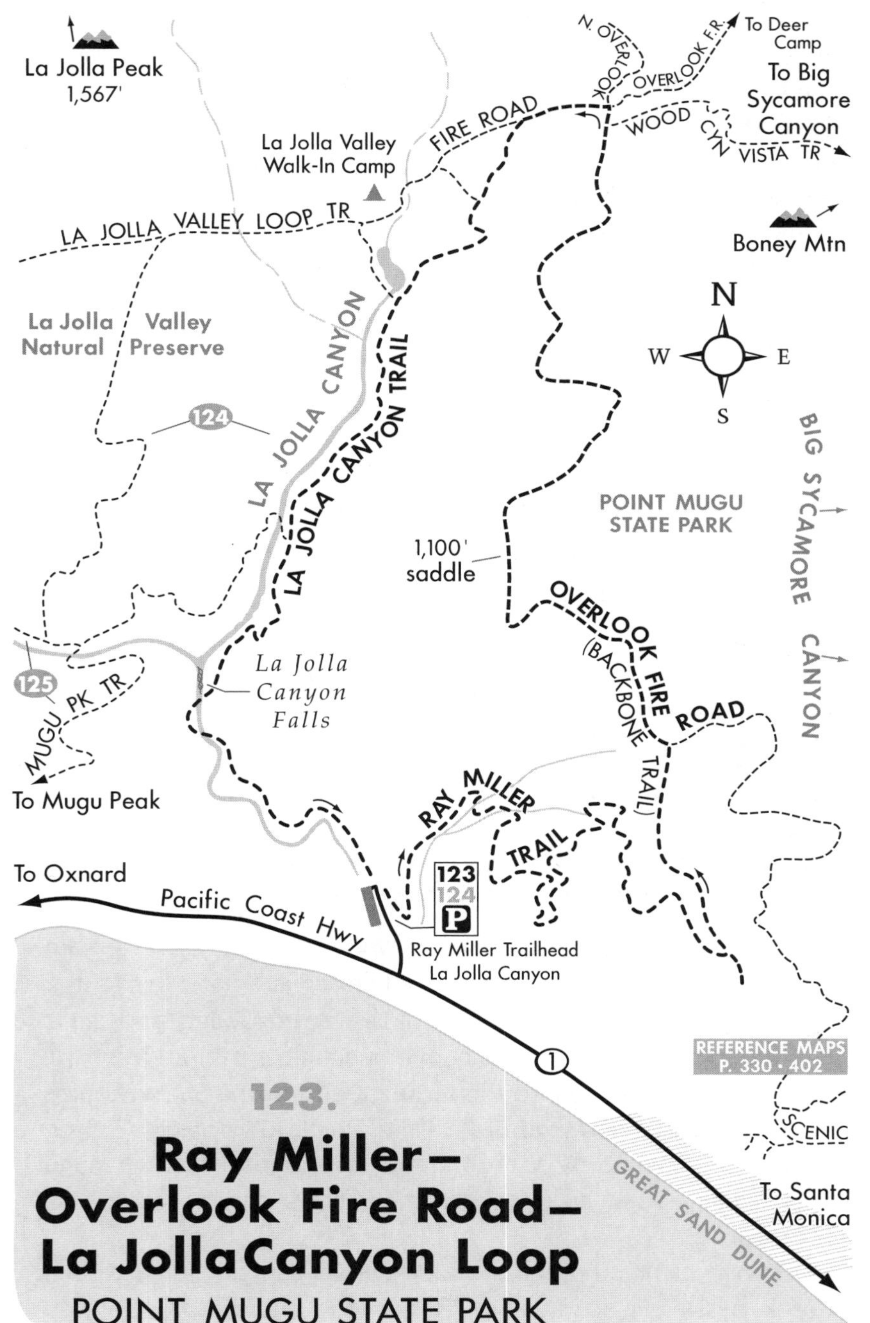

123.

Ray Miller— Overlook Fire Road— La Jolla Canyon Loop

POINT MUGU STATE PARK

the east end of the vast 600-acre meadow. Walk through tall brush to the east edge of a pond at 5.5 miles. Continue down the valley, passing a side path on the right that leads to the pond. Soon the canyon narrows and the footpath traverses the sheer cliff walls on the southeast slope. Zigzag down to the canyon bottom on the rock-embedded path. Pass the 15-foot waterfall and a pool surrounded by large boulders. Descend on natural rock steps, and cross the stream at the base of the falls. After crossing, the canyon widens and the dirt path leads to the trailhead gate, completing the loop. ■

124. La Jolla Valley Loop from La Jolla Canyon

POINT MUGU STATE PARK

W. Pacific Coast Hwy • Malibu

Hiking distance: 6 miles
Hiking time: 3 hours
Configuration: out-and-back with large loop
Elevation gain: 750 feet
Difficulty: moderate to strenuous
Exposure: mostly exposed with some forested pockets
Dogs: not allowed
Maps: U.S.G.S. Point Mugu • Point Mugu State Park map
Tom Harrison Maps: Point Mugu State Park Trail map

La Jolla Canyon is a steep, narrow gorge with a perennial stream and a 15-foot waterfall. The rocky canyon is a gateway to the La Jolla Valley Natural Preserve, a 600-acre unspoiled landscape protecting the rare perennial native bunchgrass prairie. The natural preserve is tucked into the far west end of the Santa Monica Range within Point Mugu State Park. The 800-foot-high rolling grassland is rimmed by an arc of mountain ridges, including Mugu Peak, Laguna Peak, and La Jolla Peak, and is only accessible to foot traffic.

This hike climbs through the rock-walled canyon along La Jolla Creek, passing La Jolla Canyon Falls en route to the broad valley.

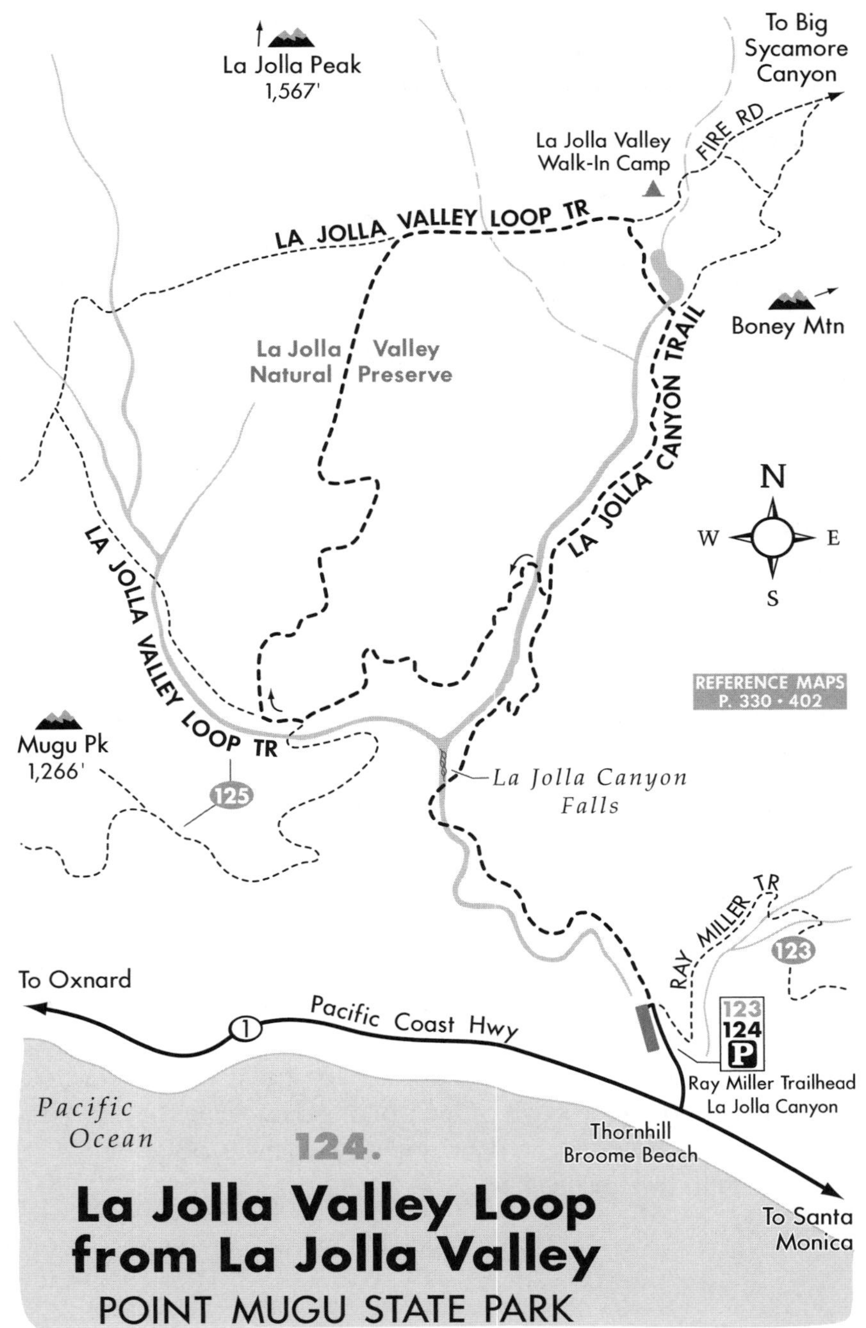

124.

La Jolla Valley Loop from La Jolla Valley

POINT MUGU STATE PARK

The trail loops around the vast meadow, passing a seasonal tule and cattail-fringed pond, a walk-in campground, picnic areas, and coastal and mountain overlooks.

To the trailhead

From Santa Monica, drive 33 miles northbound on the Pacific Coast Highway/Highway 1 to the posted La Jolla Canyon entrance on the right. (The trailhead entrance is 15 miles west of Kanan Dume Road in Malibu and 1.6 miles west of the well-marked Big Sycamore Canyon.)

Heading southbound on the Pacific Coast Highway/Highway 1 from Las Posas Road in southeast Oxnard, drive 4.2 miles to the La Jolla Canyon entrance on the left.

The hike

Take the La Jolla Canyon Trail at the end of the road by the vehicle gate. Follow the wide path up the canyon, crossing the stream several times. The third crossing is just below La Jolla Canyon Falls, a beautiful 15-foot waterfall with a shallow pool surrounded by large boulders. Natural rock steps lead to the top of the falls. Continue along the east side of the canyon, passing large sandstone rocks and caves as the canyon narrows. At a gorge, the trail sharply doubles back to the right, leading up the side of the canyon. At 1.2 miles, take the left fork towards Mugu Peak. Cross the stream and head southwest to a ridge above La Jolla Canyon and the ocean. The trail levels out and passes two trail junctions with the Mugu Peak Trail and the Chumash Trail (Hike 125). Stay to the right both times, heading north across the rolling grassland. At 2.7 miles the trail joins the wide La Jolla Valley Loop Trail/Fire Road—head to the right through upper La Jolla Valley. As you near the mountains of La Jolla Canyon, take the first cutoff trail to the right, skirting the edge of the pond and rejoining the La Jolla Canyon Trail. Head to the right, and go two miles down canyon, returning to the trailhead. ■

125. Chumash Trail—Mugu Peak Loop

POINT MUGU STATE PARK

W. Pacific Coast Hwy • Malibu

Hiking distance: 4.5-mile loop
Hiking time: 2.5 hours
Configuration: loop
Elevation gain: 1,100 feet
Difficulty: moderate to strenuous
Exposure: mostly exposed with some forested pockets
Dogs: not allowed
Maps: U.S.G.S. Point Mugu • Point Mugu State Park map
Tom Harrison Maps: Point Mugu State Park Trail map

map page 413

The Chumash Trail is the westernmost trail in the Santa Monica Mountains. For centuries, this historic trail was a Chumash Indian route connecting their coastal village at Mugu Lagoon with La Jolla Valley atop the mountain. It is the steepest and most direct route to La Jolla Valley, an expansive, high-mountain valley within Point Mugu State Park. The oak-studded grassland rests 800 feet above the ocean at the foot of Mugu Peak. The high ridges of Laguna Peak, La Jolla Peak, and Mugu Peak curve around the west side of the rolling meadow.

This hike steeply ascends the oceanfront mountain on the west flank of Mugu Peak. The path climbs through giant coreopsis, yucca, and prickly pear cactus in full view of the Pacific Ocean, Mugu Lagoon, the adjoining wetlands, and the Oxnard Plain. From atop the mountain, the hike forms a loop on the west side of La Jolla Valley. The elevated Mugu Peak Trail circles the mountain slope below the twin peaks, offering sweeping mountain-to-coast vistas. A side path leads to the rounded, grassy summit of Mugu Peak.

To the trailhead

From Santa Monica, drive 35 miles northbound on the Pacific Coast Highway/Highway 1 to the large parking pullout on the right, across from the Navy Rifle Range and Mugu Lagoon. (The trailhead parking area is 16.8 miles west of Kanan Dume Road in Malibu and 3.5 miles west of the well-marked Big Sycamore Canyon.)

Heading southbound on the Pacific Coast Highway/Highway 1 from Las Posas Road in southeast Oxnard, drive 2.3 miles to the parking area on the left by the posted trailhead.

The hike

Begin climbing up the hillside covered in chaparral and cactus, gaining elevation with every step. At a half mile, the trail temporarily levels out on a plateau, where there are sweeping coastal views that include the Channel Islands. The steadily ascending trail gains 900 feet in 0.7 miles to a T-junction on a saddle. Begin the loop to the left, crossing over the saddle into the vast La Jolla Valley. The valley is surrounded by rounded mountain peaks, the jagged Boney Mountain ridge, and the surrealistic Navy radar towers atop Laguna Peak. Cross the open expanse to a posted junction with the La Jolla Valley Loop Trail at 1.2 miles.

Take the right fork and head southeast across the meadow on a slight downward slope. Drop into an oak woodland and cross a stream. Parallel the stream through a small draw to another junction. Take the right fork 100 yards to a path on the right by an old circular metal tank. Bear right on the Mugu Peak Trail and cross the creek. Traverse the hillside to the west edge of La Jolla Canyon. Follow the ridge south on the oceanfront cliffs. Wind along the south flank of Mugu Peak, following the contours of the mountain to a trail split on a saddle between the mountain's double peaks. The right fork ascends the grassy 1,266-foot summit. Continue hiking on the main trail along the steep hillside to the west side of the peak. Cross another saddle and complete the loop. Return down the mountain to the trailhead. ■

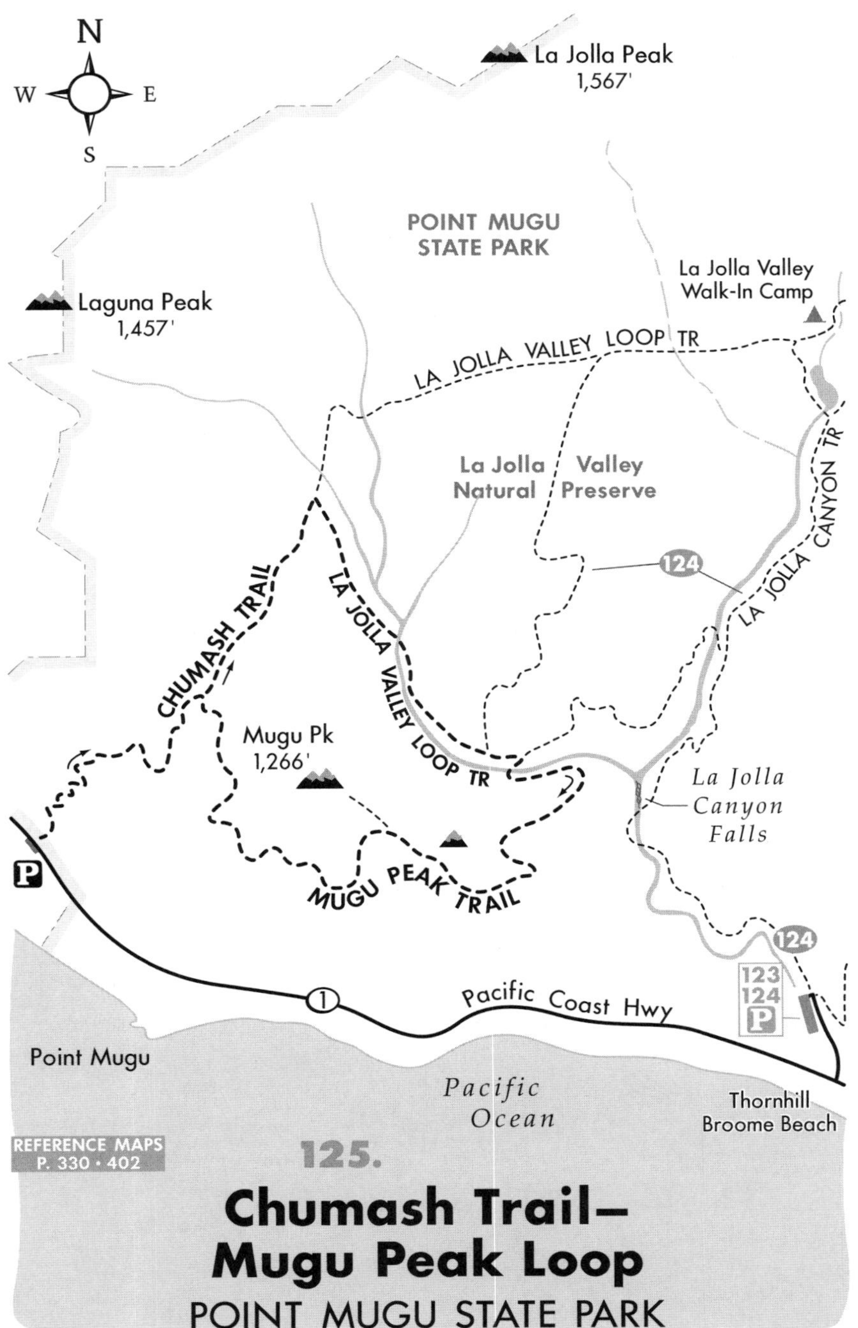

125. Chumash Trail— Mugu Peak Loop

POINT MUGU STATE PARK

The Backbone Trail

Will Rogers State Historic Park in Pacific Palisades to La Jolla Canyon in Point Mugu State Park

One-way Mileage

EAST to WEST: 69.3 miles

Will Rogers State Historic Park in Pacific Palisades
to La Jolla Canyon in Point Mugu State Park

The Backbone Trail

The Backbone Trail is a 69-mile trail that crosses the length of the Santa Monica Mountains as the range runs parallel to the Pacific coast. The route weaves sinuously along the range's open ridgeline and down through verdant canyons, offering spectacular views along the entire length. Numerous trails have been linked together to form the continuous Backbone Trail. From the jagged ridgelines perched thousands of feet above to the water-carved canyons that drain to sandy coastal beaches, the Backbone Trail offers memorable access to more than 65,000 acres of open space and natural parks.

This section of the book includes the entire sequential Backbone Trail divided into 13 segments. Although all sections of the trail can be hiked in either direction, the Backbone Trail—as presented in this guide— is hiked from the east to west. The eastern terminus is located at Will Rogers State Historic Park in Pacific Palisades. The western terminus is located at Thornhill Broome Beach at the mouth of La Jolla Canyon in Point Mugu State Park.

Establishment of the Backbone Trail began in the 1980s and continues to this day. Since the Santa Monica Mountains is a patchwork of private and public ownership, creating an unbroken trail has been a challenging task of acquiring property, establishing easements, and building trails to complete the continuous route. As of 2011, there was only one unresolved gap in the trail (see section 11). The trail links miles of paths, trails, and backcountry roads, from old animal paths developed into single-track trails to fire roads through parklands.

The trail runs through Will Rogers State Historic Park, Topanga State Park, Malibu Creek State Park, and Point Mugu State Park. Linking these major state parks are national park service lands, open spaces, preserves, and public easements. The Backbone Trail crosses a few paved roadways, including Topanga Canyon Boulevard, Stunt Road, Piuma Road, Malibu Canyon Road, Latigo Canyon Road, Encinal Canyon Road, and Yerba Buena Road. These roads offer easy access to the trails and the opportunity to hike the route in shorter day-hike segments.

The Backbone Trail generally winds along the spine of the Santa Monica Mountains, but the route includes a vast array of landscapes and geophysical features. Highlights include forested canyons with hidden creeks, knobby volcanic ridges, wildflower meadows beneath the peaks and steep cliffs, and panoramic views from the mountainous backcountry to the Pacific Ocean. The dramatic trail system winds through tilted sandstone formations;

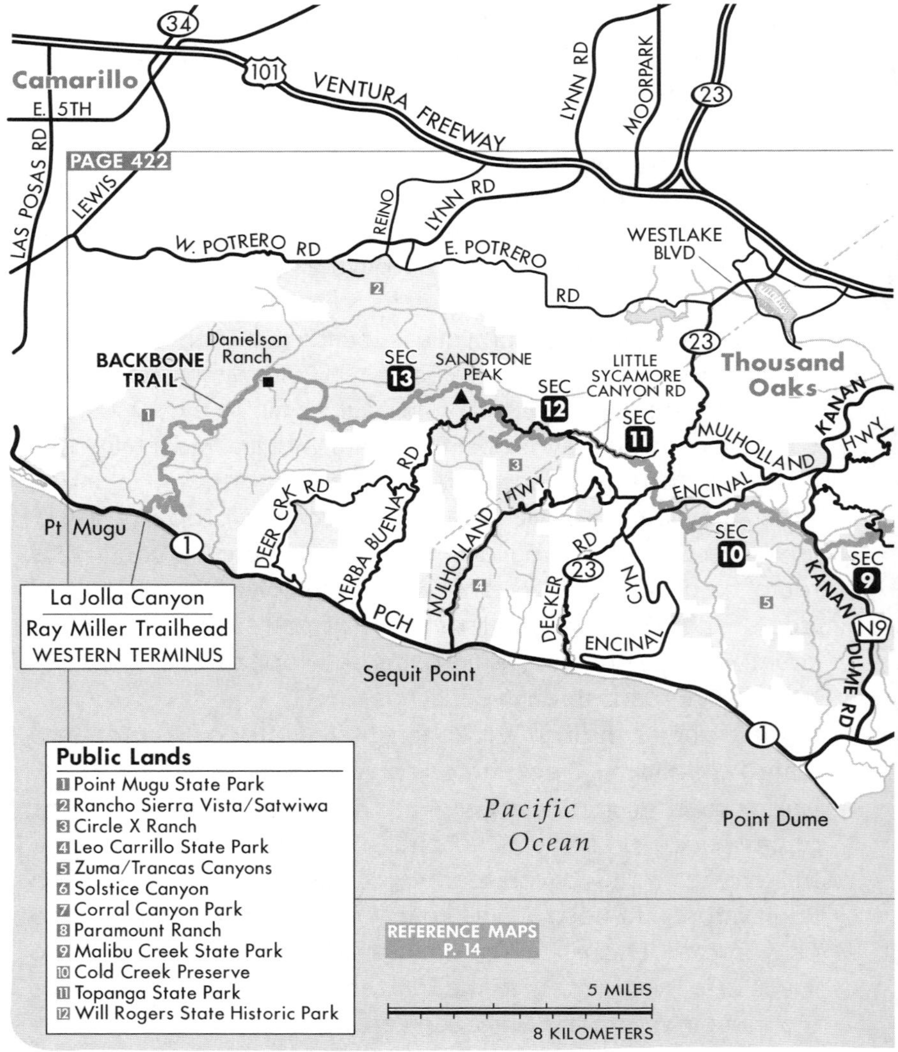

eroded caves and crevices, ruddy volcanic outcroppings; thick, impenetrable chaparral, oak, and riparian woodlands; and perennial streams and waterfalls.

Dogs are allowed on the trails throughout the Santa Monica Mountains except in the Cold Creek Canyon Preserve and these state parks: Topanga, Malibu Creek, and Point Mugu. Dog information is also clarified in the trail statistics for each hike.

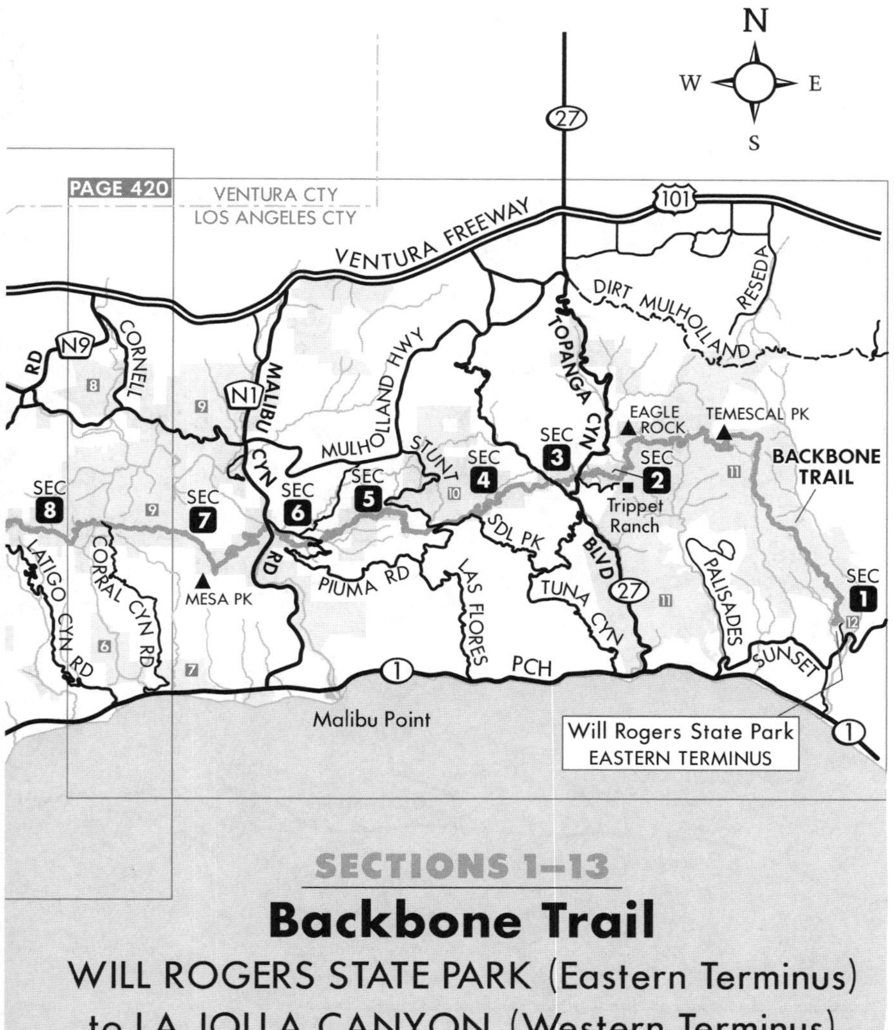

SECTIONS 1–13

Backbone Trail

WILL ROGERS STATE PARK (Eastern Terminus) to LA JOLLA CANYON (Western Terminus)

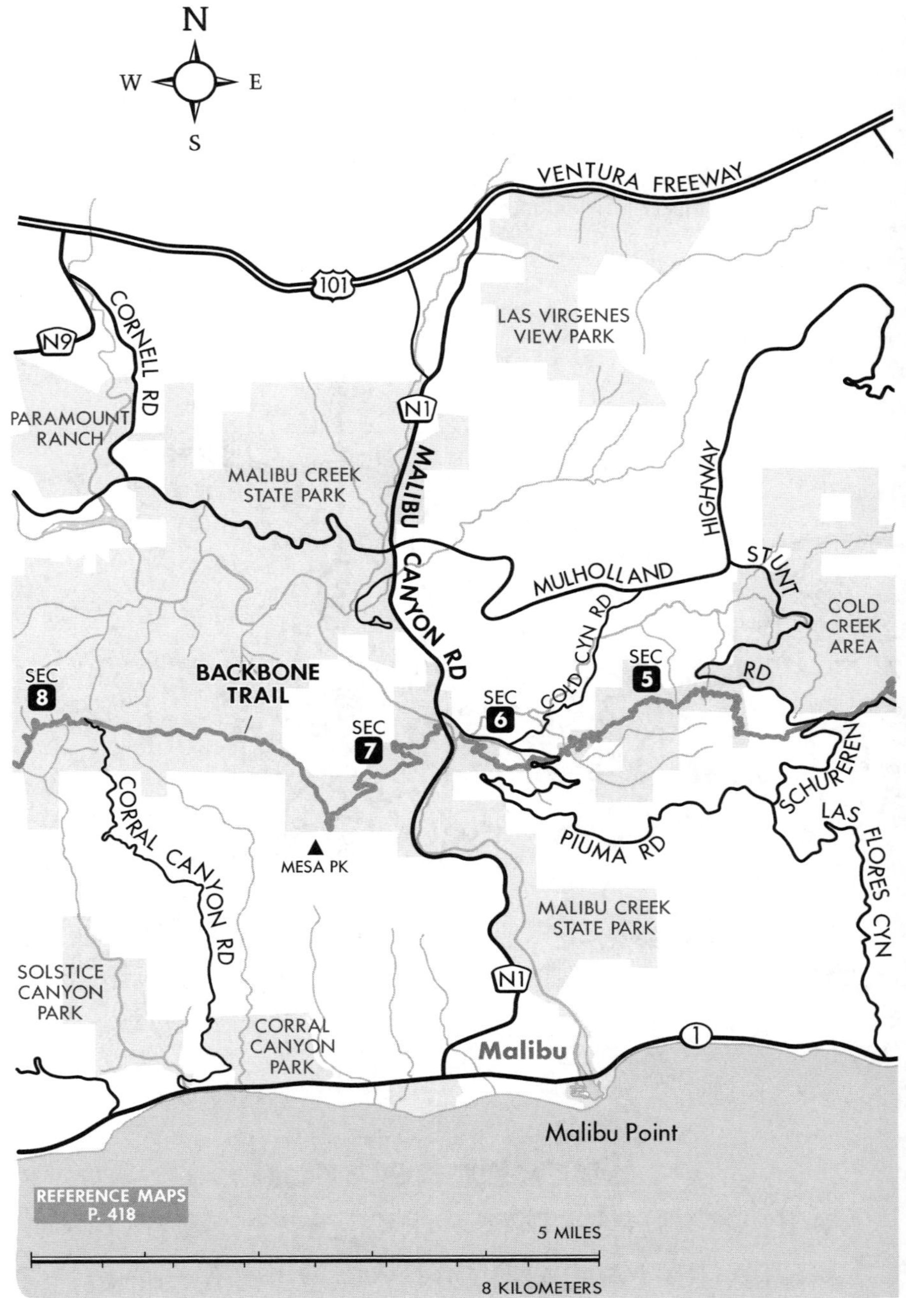
N
W
E
S
VENTURA FREEWAY
101
N9
CORNELL RD
PARAMOUNT RANCH
LAS VIRGENES VIEW PARK
N1
MALIBU CANYON RD
MALIBU CREEK STATE PARK
HIGHWAY
MULHOLLAND
STUNT
RD
COLD CREEK AREA
COLD CYN RD
SEC 5
SEC 6
SEC 7
SEC 8
BACKBONE TRAIL
SCHUREREN
LAS FLORES CYN
PIUMA RD
CORRAL CANYON RD
MESA PK
MALIBU CREEK STATE PARK
SOLSTICE CANYON PARK
N1
CORRAL CANYON PARK
Malibu
1
Malibu Point
REFERENCE MAPS P. 418
5 MILES
8 KILOMETERS

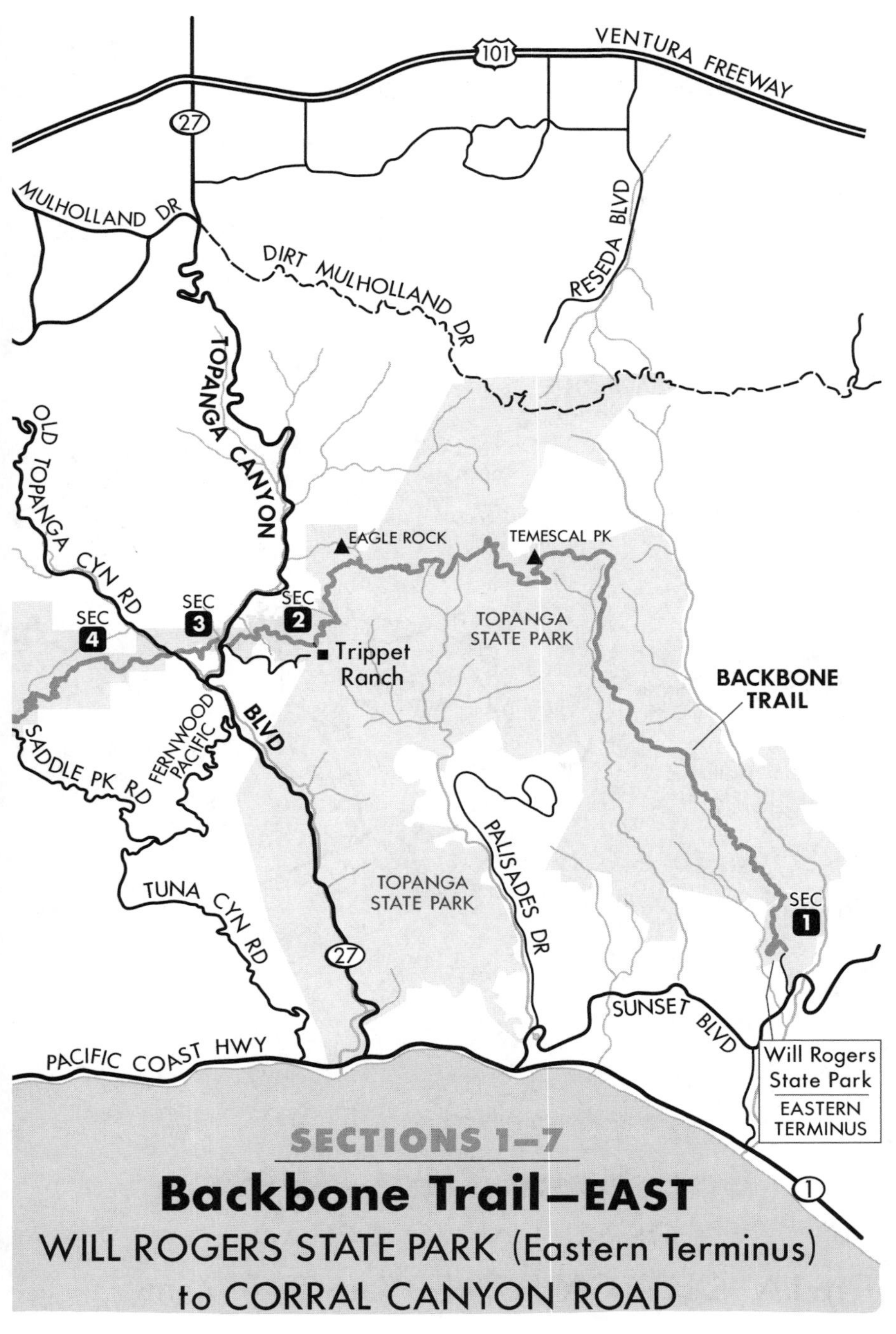
101
VENTURA FREEWAY
27
MULHOLLAND DR
DIRT MULHOLLAND DR
RESEDA BLVD
TOPANGA CANYON
OLD TOPANGA CYN RD
EAGLE ROCK
TEMESCAL PK
SEC 4
SEC 3
SEC 2
Trippet Ranch
TOPANGA STATE PARK
BACKBONE TRAIL
BLVD
FERNWOOD PACIFIC
SADDLE PK RD
PALISADES DR
TOPANGA STATE PARK
TUNA CYN RD
27
SEC 1
SUNSET BLVD
PACIFIC COAST HWY
Will Rogers State Park
EASTERN TERMINUS
1
SECTIONS 1–7
Backbone Trail—EAST
WILL ROGERS STATE PARK (Eastern Terminus)
to CORRAL CANYON ROAD

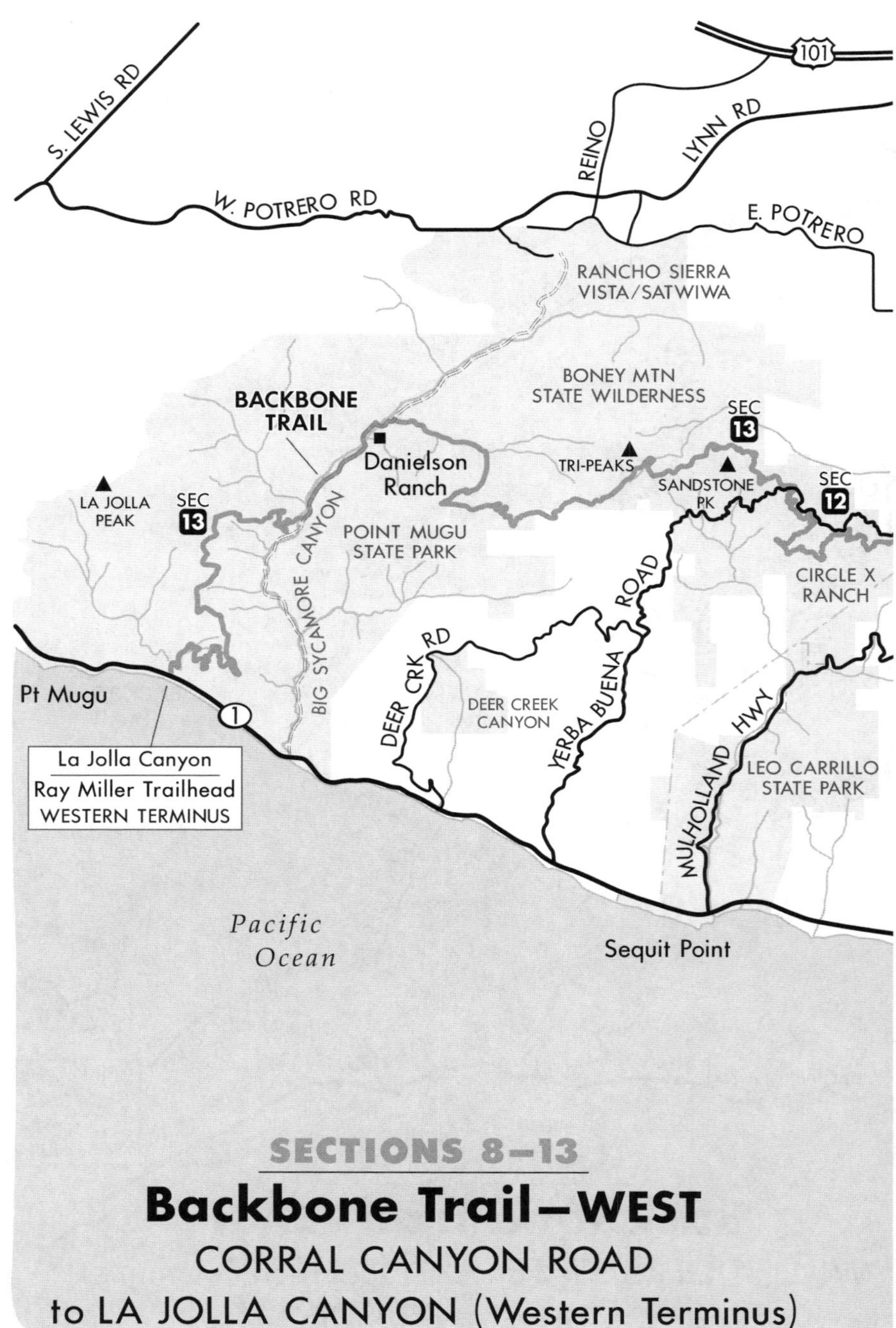

SECTIONS 8–13

Backbone Trail—WEST

CORRAL CANYON ROAD
to LA JOLLA CANYON (Western Terminus)

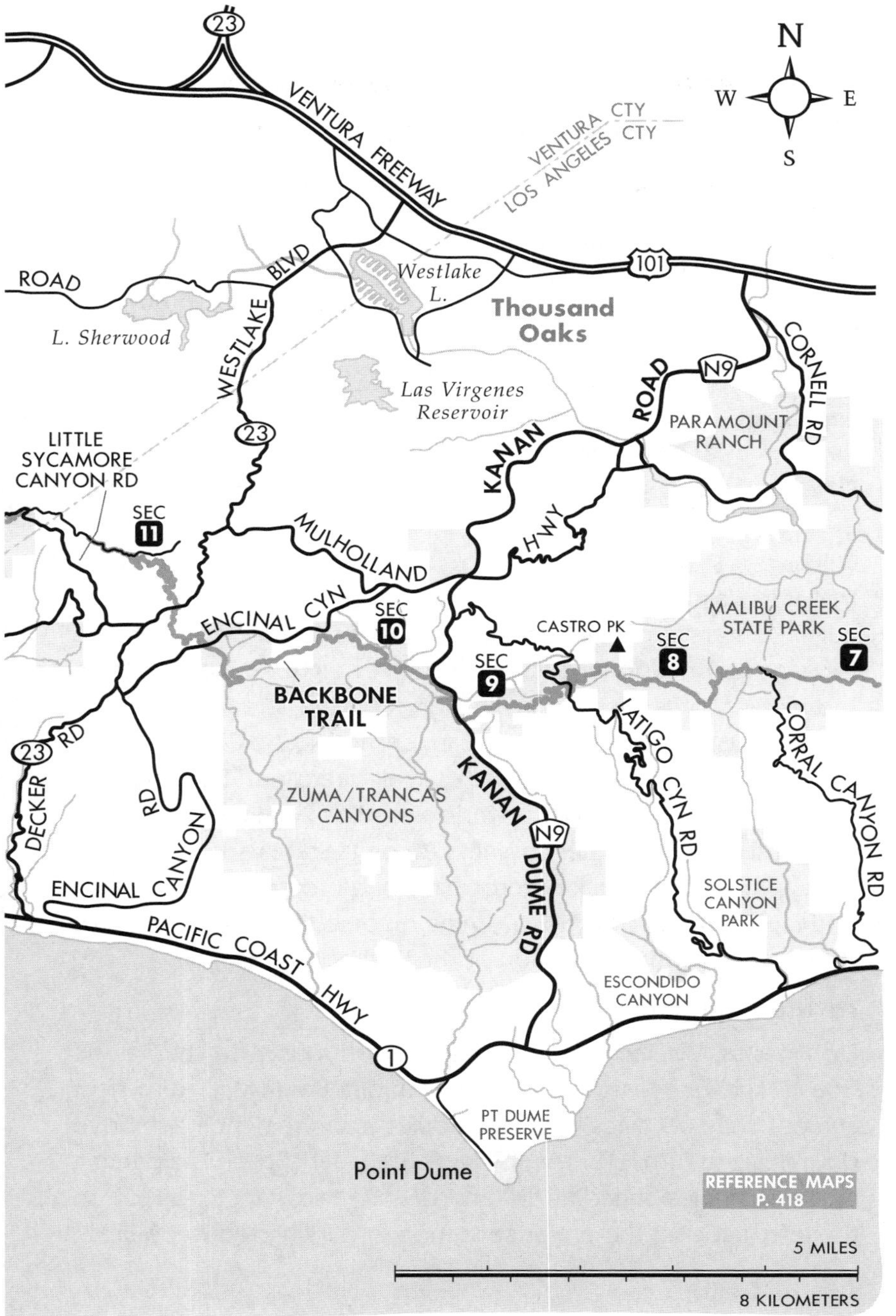
23
VENTURA FREEWAY
VENTURA CTY
LOS ANGELES CTY
N
W
E
S
101
ROAD
BLVD
Westlake L.
Thousand Oaks
L. Sherwood
WESTLAKE
Las Virgenes Reservoir
N9
CORNELL RD
ROAD
KANAN
PARAMOUNT RANCH
LITTLE SYCAMORE CANYON RD
SEC 11
MULHOLLAND
HWY
ENCINAL CYN
SEC 10
CASTRO PK
MALIBU CREEK STATE PARK
SEC 8
SEC 7
SEC 9
BACKBONE TRAIL
LATIGO CYN RD
CORRAL CANYON RD
DECKER RD
RD
ZUMA/TRANCAS CANYONS
KANAN
DUME RD
ENCINAL CANYON
SOLSTICE CANYON PARK
PACIFIC COAST HWY
ESCONDIDO CANYON
1
PT DUME PRESERVE
Point Dume
REFERENCE MAPS P. 418
5 MILES
8 KILOMETERS

Will Rogers State Historic Park to Trippet Ranch in Topanga State Park

Inspiration Loop Trail • Rogers Road Trail • Temescal Ridge Trail • Eagle Springs Fire Road • Musch Trail

Hiking distance: 10.8-mile one-way shuttle
Hiking time: 6 hours
Configuration: one-way shuttle
Elevation gain: 1,650 feet
Difficulty: strenuous
Exposure: exposed with shady pockets
Dogs: allowed on first mile, not allowed after in Topanga State Park
Maps: U.S.G.S. Topanga • Tom Harrison Maps: Topanga State Park Trail Map Topanga State Park map • Will Rogers State Historic Park map

map page 426

Will Rogers State Historic Park marks the beginning of the Backbone Trail at its eastern terminus. This first section of the Backbone Trail quickly enters Topanga State Park and leads to Trippet Ranch, the Topanga Park headquarters, on a series of eight connecting trails. The hike follows a steep ridge between the stream-fed drainages of Rivas Canyon, Temescal Canyon, and Rustic Canyon. There are spectacular far-reaching vistas in all directions. En route, the hike visits Inspiration Point, overlooking Los Angeles; 2,126-foot Temescal Peak, the highest point in Topanga State Park; Eagle Rock, a massive volcanic rock outcropping; and crosses Chicken Ridge Bridge, a narrow footbridge on the razor-edged ridge. This hike is the second longest section of the Backbone Trail.

To the trailhead

From Santa Monica, drive 1.6 miles northbound on the Pacific Coast Highway/Highway 1 to Chautauqua Boulevard. Turn right and continue 0.9 miles to Sunset Boulevard. Turn right again. Drive 0.5 miles and turn left at Will Rogers State Park Road. The parking area is 0.7 miles ahead at the end of the road. Park in the lot on the left, just past the entrance station. A parking fee is required.

Shuttle car

From Santa Monica, drive 4 miles northbound on the Pacific Coast Highway/Highway 1 to Topanga Canyon Boulevard and turn right (north). Continue 4.6 miles to Entrada Road on the right and turn right again. Drive 0.7 miles and turn left, following the state park signs. Turn left again and go 0.3 miles into the Topanga State Park parking lot. A parking fee is required.

From the Ventura Freeway/Highway 101 in Woodland Hills, exit on Topanga Canyon Boulevard. Drive 7.6 miles south to Entrada Road. Turn left and follow the posted state park signs to the Trippet Ranch parking lot.

The hike

Begin the hike from the visitor center and Will Rogers' home, built in 1928. Head west (left) past the tennis courts and the Temescal-Rivas Canyon Trail to a dirt fire road—the Inspiration Loop Trail. Head uphill on the gentle uphill grade, overlooking Rivas Canyon on the left. The views span across coastal Los Angeles and Santa Monica Bay to Palos Verdes and Catalina Island. At 0.8 miles is a junction and additional views across the mountainous back-country. Detour 0.1 mile straight ahead to Inspiration Point, with sweeping vistas across Los Angeles. Return to the junction and head 70 yards north to Rogers Road Trail, the beginning of the Backbone Trail.

Head up the footpath, leaving Will Rogers State Park, and enter Topanga State Park. (Dogs are not allowed on the trail after this point.) Climb north on the ridge between Rivas Canyon and Rustic Canyon. At 1.5 miles, cross Chicken Ridge Bridge, and follow the steep, knife-edged slope at an elevation of 1,125 feet. Climb to additional views into forested Rustic Canyon and Sullivan Canyon to the right. At just under 2 miles is a junction on a saddle. To the right is the connector trail into Rustic Canyon.

Stay on the main Rogers Road Trail to the left. Descend along the east wall of Temescal Canyon to Lone Oak, a massive coast live oak tree with five trunks. The tree sits on a flat with northern views towards the Los Padres National Forest. Veer left and meander through a corridor under a tree-shaded canopy. Weave

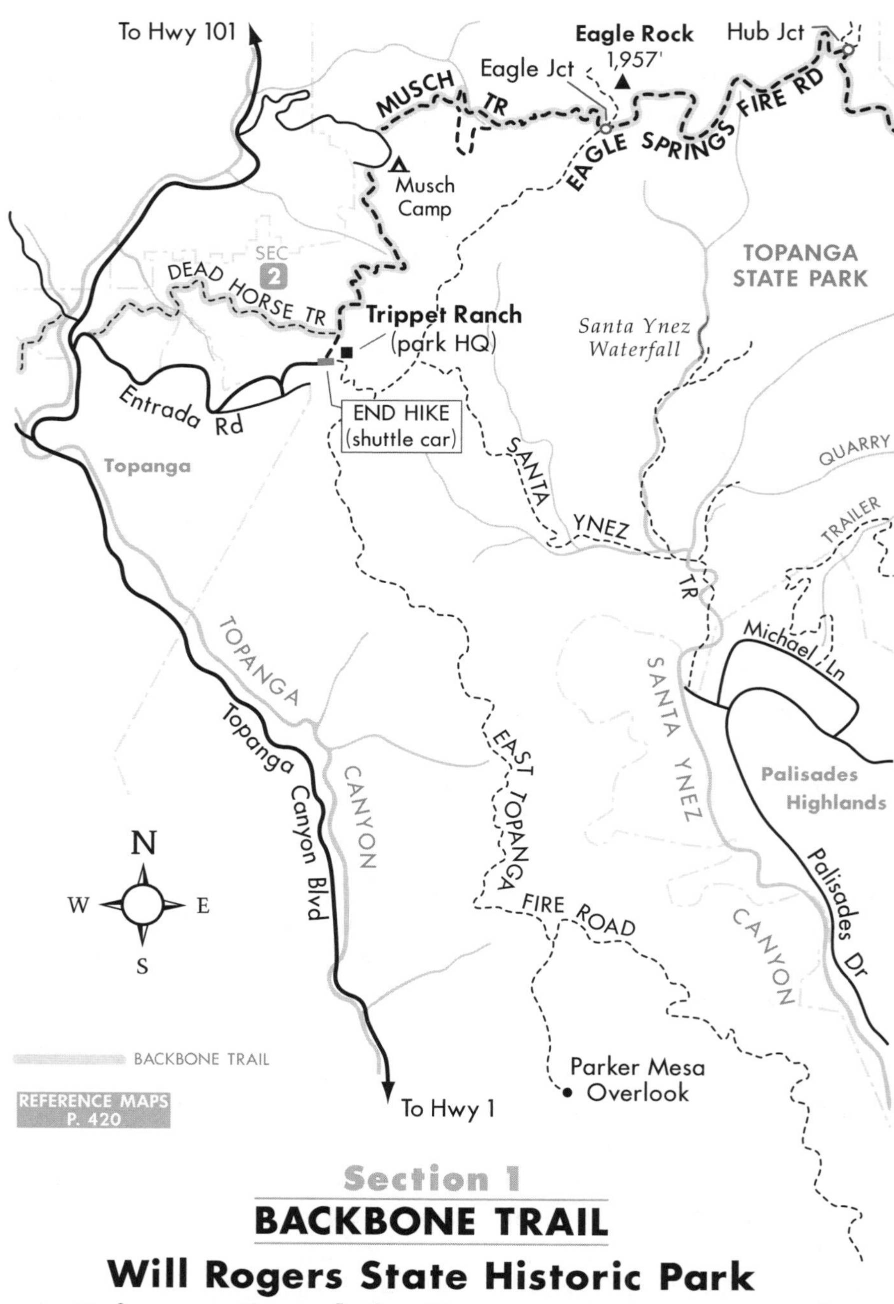

Section 1

BACKBONE TRAIL

Will Rogers State Historic Park to Trippet Ranch in Topanga State Park

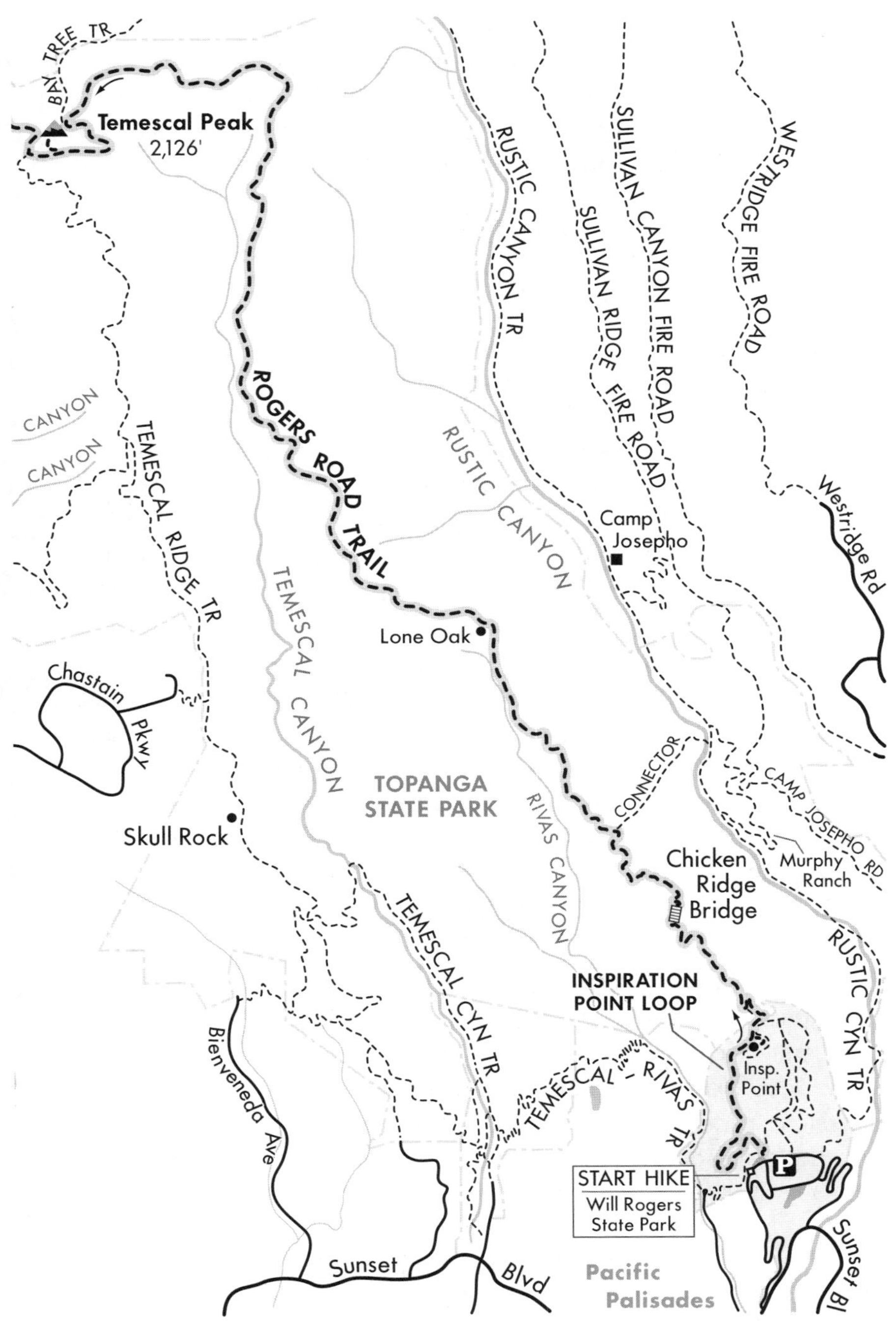
BAY TREE TR
Temescal Peak
2,126'
RUSTIC CANYON TR
SULLIVAN CANYON FIRE ROAD
SULLIVAN RIDGE FIRE ROAD
WESTRIDGE FIRE ROAD
CANYON
CANYON
TEMESCAL RIDGE TR
ROGERS ROAD TRAIL
RUSTIC CANYON
Camp
Josepho
Westridge Rd
TEMESCAL CANYON
Lone Oak
Chastain
Pkwy
CONNECTOR
CAMP JOSEPHO RD
TOPANGA
STATE PARK
RIVAS CANYON
Skull Rock
Chicken
Ridge
Bridge
Murphy
Ranch
TEMESCAL CYN TR
RUSTIC CYN TR
INSPIRATION
POINT LOOP
Insp.
Point
Bienveneda Ave
TEMESCAL - RIVAS TR
START HIKE
Will Rogers
State Park
P
Sunset
Blvd
Pacific
Palisades
Sunset Bl

through the quiet of the backcountry as the trail dips and rises. From 1,900 feet above the city, the views extend across Tarzana, Woodland Hills, and the entire San Fernando Valley. Bear left and cross the head of the canyon. Traverse the north-facing slope to a posted junction with the Bay Tree Trail at 6.3 miles. Stay to the left towards the signed Hub Junction. Wind along the mountainous contours 0.6 miles to the Temescal Ridge Trail. Just shy of this junction, a side path climbs up the hill up to Temescal Peak, the 2,126-foot summit of the hike.

After enjoying the 360-degree vistas, return to the Temescal Ridge Trail, a dirt fire road. Bearing left leads to Trailer Canyon and Temescal Canyon. The Backbone Trail continues to the right (northwest) and steadily descends. Pass Cathedral Rock, a cavernous sandstone formation on the right, and cross a ridge to Hub Junction, an intersection of four fire roads with an information kiosk. Straight ahead leads 1.9 miles to Dirt Mulholland. The middle fork leads to the Garapito Trail and to the upper north slope of Eagle Rock.

Bear left on the Eagle Springs Fire Road (Backbone Trail) and descend 1.3 miles, skirting under the south side of Eagle Rock, beneath the massive sandstone outcrop that towers over the landscape. At 8.8 miles is a posted fork with the Musch Trail on the right. (En route, a short side path on the right leads to Eagle Springs, a trickling spring in the sandstone bedrock under a sycamore and oak glen.)

Take the Musch Trail, leaving the fire road, and wind down into a valley. Cross a couple of ravines through lush riparian vegetation and woodlands of oak, sycamore, and bay laurel. One mile down is a junction with Musch Camp at the former Musch Ranch. Follow the trail sign, crossing a meadow. Wind down to a junction with the Dead Horse Trail (Section 2 of the Backbone Trail). Continue straight, passing a pond on the left and crossing an earthen dam to the main Topanga State Park parking lot at Trippet Ranch. ■

Trippet Ranch to Topanga Canyon Boulevard

Dead Horse Trail

Hiking distance: 1.3 miles one way; 2.6 miles round trip
Hiking time: 1.5 hours each way
Configuration: one-way shuttle or out-and-back
Elevation gain: 400 feet
Difficulty: easy
Exposure: exposed and forested
Dogs: not allowed
Maps: U.S.G.S. Topanga • Topanga State Park map
Tom Harrison Maps: Topanga State Park Trail Map

map page 430

This short section of the Backbone Trail begins at Trippet Ranch, the park headquarters of Topanga State Park, and follows the Dead Horse Trail. The diverse trail crosses grassland meadows, tall and shady chaparral, drops into a streamside oak forest, winds through a riparian canyon, and crosses an old wooden bridge over Trippet Creek in a rocky grotto.

To the trailhead

From Santa Monica, drive 4 miles northbound on the Pacific Coast Highway/Highway 1 to Topanga Canyon Boulevard and turn right (north). Continue 4.6 miles to Entrada Road on the right and turn right again. Drive 0.7 miles and turn left, following the state park signs. Turn left again and go 0.3 miles into the Topanga State Park parking lot. A parking fee is required.

From the Ventura Freeway/Highway 101 in Woodland Hills, exit on Topanga Canyon Boulevard. Drive 7.6 miles south to Entrada Road. Turn left and follow the posted state park signs to the Trippet Ranch parking lot.

Shuttle car (optional)

Use the same driving directions to Entrada Road as above except, after turning onto Entrada Road, only drive 0.1 mile to the Dead Horse Trailhead parking lot on the left. A parking fee is required.

The hike

Take the signed Musch Trail north for 50 yards and cross an earthen dam and a pond on the right to a junction. Bear left on the Dead Horse (Backbone) Trail, parallel to a wood-rail fence. Stroll through the rolling grasslands and an oak woodland. At a half mile is a trail split. Stay to the right, following the contours of the ridge. Descend into the shade of a riparian woodland of bay and sycamore trees. Cross a wooden footbridge over the rocky, fern-lined streambed of Trippet Creek in a narrow draw. After crossing, steps lead up to a junction. Take the middle fork downhill to a trail fork. Bear right and loop around the parking lot near Topanga Canyon Boulevard.

To continue with Section 3 of the Backbone Trail, walk down to Topanga Canyon Boulevard. Go 0.1 mile to the right to Greenleaf Canyon Road on the left. The trailhead is on the left (south) side of Greenleaf Canyon Road. ■

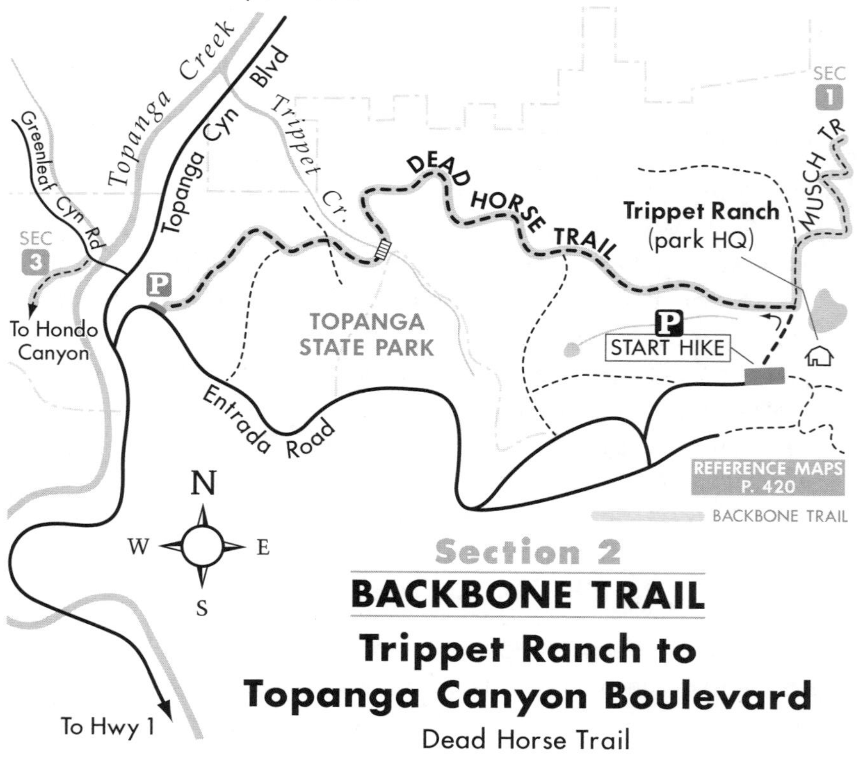

Topanga Canyon Boulevard to Old Topanga Canyon Road

Hiking distance: 0.7 miles one way; 1.4 miles round trip
Hiking time: 20 minutes each way
Configuration: one-way connector or out-and-back
Elevation gain: 150 feet
Difficulty: easy
Exposure: forested
Dogs: allowed
Maps: U.S.G.S. Topanga • Tom Harrison Maps: Topanga State Park Trail Map

map page 432

Section 3 of the Backbone Trail is a short 0.7-mile connector segment. The scenic path connects Section 2 (Dead Horse Trail) with Section 4 (Hondo Canyon Trail), linking Topanga Canyon Boulevard with Old Topanga Canyon Road. The trail gently climbs up and over the southern end of Henry Ridge, a wooded hill rich with atmosphere. The hike weaves under the shade of an old forest with majestic oaks.

To the trailhead

From Santa Monica, drive 4 miles northbound on the Pacific Coast Highway/Highway 1 to Topanga Canyon Boulevard and turn right. Continue 4.7 miles to Greenleaf Canyon Road on the left (west), just north of the town of Topanga. Turn left and park in the dirt pullouts on either side of the road.

From the Ventura Freeway/Highway 101 in Woodland Hills, exit on Topanga Canyon Boulevard. Drive 7.5 miles south to Greenleaf Canyon Road on the right (west). Turn right and park in the dirt pullouts on either side of the road.

Shuttle car (optional)

From Santa Monica, drive 4 miles northbound on the Pacific Coast Highway/Highway 1 to Topanga Canyon Boulevard and turn right. Continue 4.2 miles to Old Topanga Canyon Road on the left (west), just north of the town of Topanga. Turn left and drive 0.4 miles to the posted trailhead and a narrow dirt pullout on the left.

From the Ventura Freeway/Highway 101 in Woodland Hills, exit on Topanga Canyon Boulevard. Drive 8 miles south to Old Topanga Canyon Road on the right (west). Turn right and continue 0.4 miles to the trailhead and a narrow dirt pullout on the left.

The hike

From the west side of Greenleaf Canyon Road, take the distinct but unsigned footpath into the oak and bay laurel forest. Stroll under the forest canopy on an upward slope. At 0.4 miles is a trail split. The right fork steeply climbs Henry Ridge. Stay to the left and follow the path above the Topanga Elementary School under the shade of oaks and pines. Descend wooden steps to the paved road. Follow the asphalt road 60 yards to the right, heading towards the water tank. Skirt past the left side of the water tank on the footpath. Descend through the bucolic forest, reaching Old Topanga Canyon Road at 0.7 miles. Directly across the road is the signed Hondo Canyon Trail, Section 4 of the Backbone Trail. ■

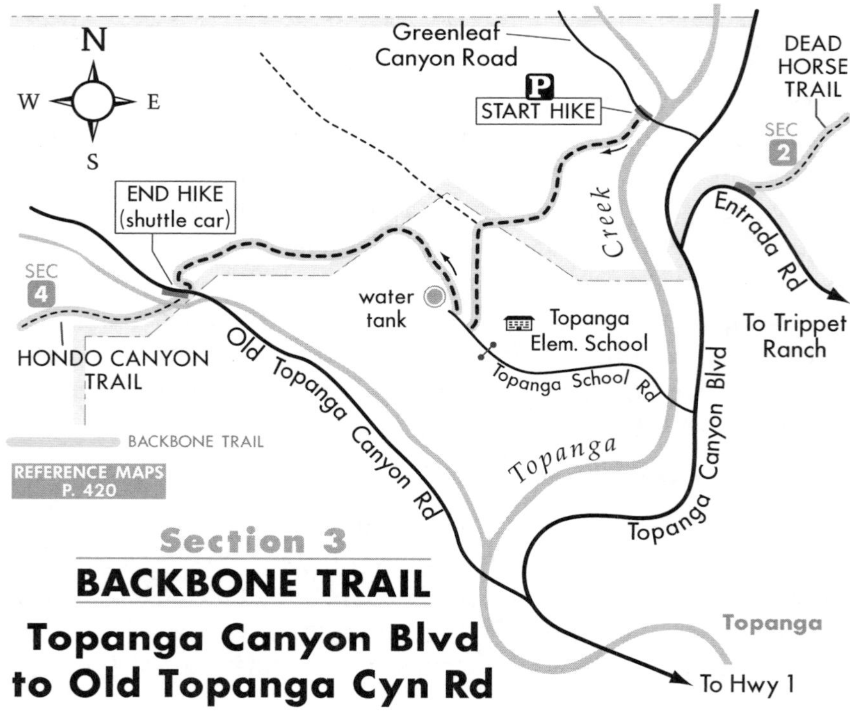

Old Topanga Canyon Road to Stunt Road

Hondo Canyon Trail • Fossil Ridge Trail

Hiking distance: 4.3 miles one way; 8.6 miles round trip
Hiking time: 2.5 hours each way
Configuration: one-way shuttle or out-and-back
Elevation gain: 1,650 feet
Difficulty: moderate to strenuous
Exposure: an equal mix of tree-shaded areas and open slopes
Dogs: not allowed (but many 4-legged friends have been known to enjoy this trail)
Maps: U.S.G.S. Topanga and Malibu Beach • Topanga State Park map
Tom Harrison Maps: Topanga State Park Trail Map

map page 434

Section 4 of the Backbone Trail is on the Hondo Canyon Trail and Fossil Ridge Trail. The trail begins at Old Topanga Canyon Road and climbs the mountain from the canyon floor to the Lois Ewen Overlook atop the Santa Monica Mountains. The northern views span across Cold Creek Canyon Preserve and Calabasas Peak to the San Fernando Valley. The southern views overlook Las Flores Canyon to the sweeping Santa Monica Bay. En route to the overlook, the trail climbs the south wall of Hondo Canyon through majestic live oaks, California bays, and tall chaparral, passing massive sedimentary rock formations. At the top of the climb, the Fossil Ridge Trail passes an exceptional display of sea shell fossils embedded in the rock, including clams, snails, and sand dollars.

To the trailhead

From Santa Monica, drive 4 miles northbound on the Pacific Coast Highway/Highway 1 to Topanga Canyon Boulevard and turn right. Continue 4.2 miles to Old Topanga Canyon Road on the left (west), just north of the town of Topanga. Turn left and drive 0.4 miles to the posted trailhead and a narrow dirt pullout on the left.

From the Ventura Freeway/Highway 101 in Woodland Hills, exit on Topanga Canyon Boulevard. Drive 8 miles south to Old Topanga Canyon Road on the right (west). Turn right and continue 0.4 miles to the posted trailhead and a dirt pullout on the left.

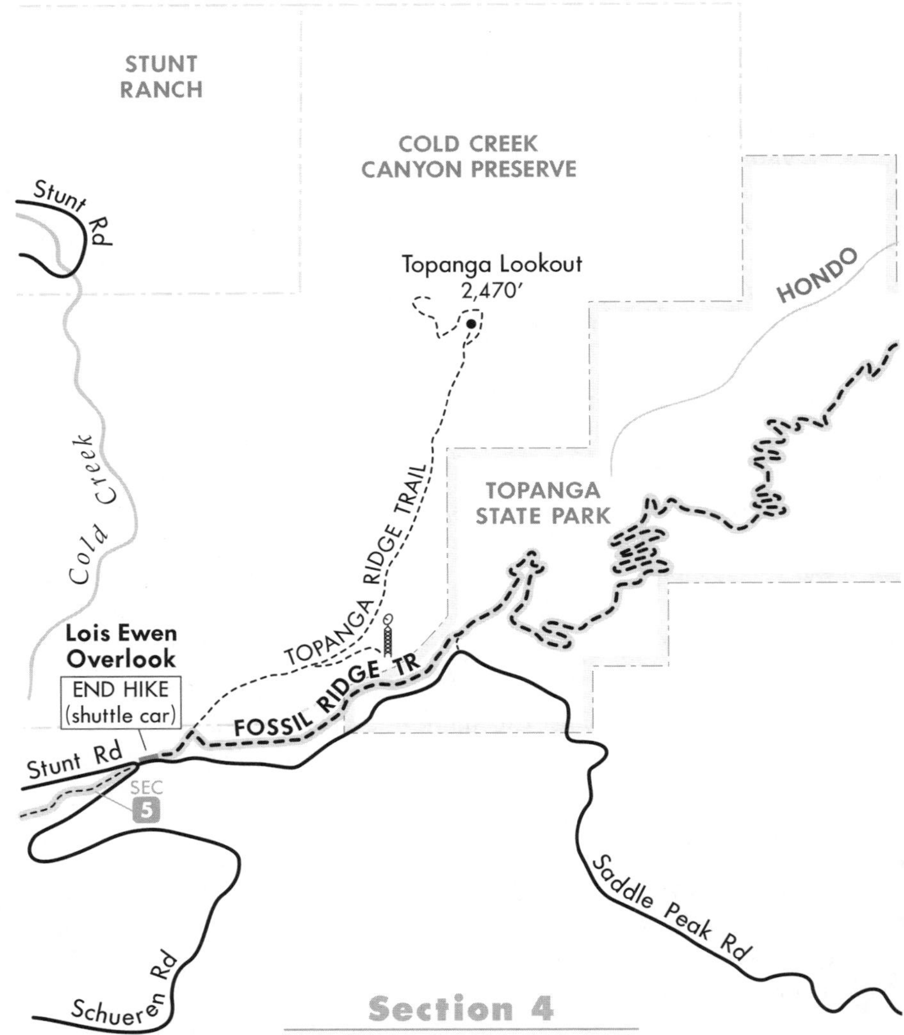

Section 4

BACKBONE TRAIL

Old Topanga Canyon Road to Stunt Road

Honda Canyon Trail • Fossil Ridge Trail

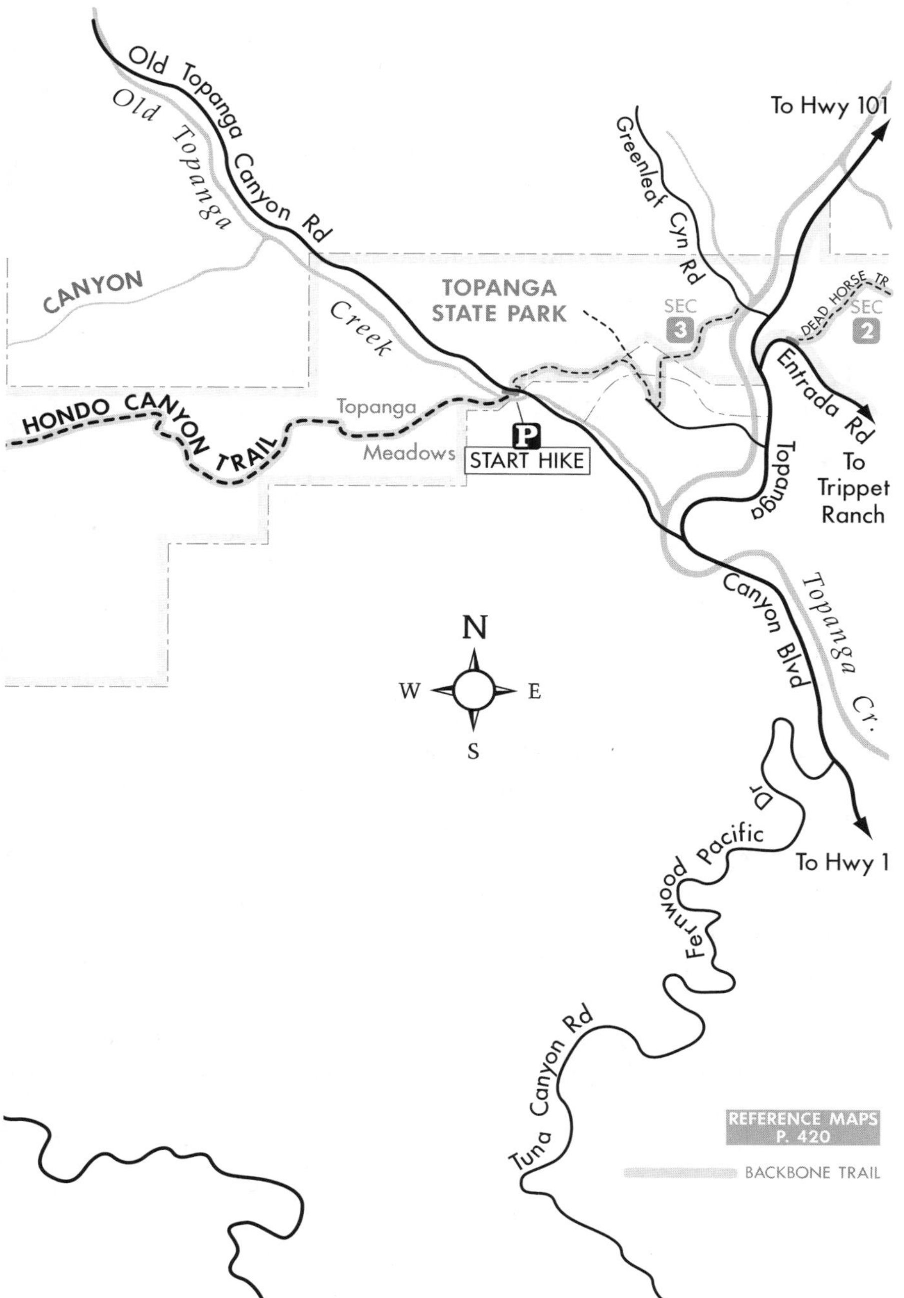
Old Topanga Canyon Rd
Old Topanga
CANYON
Creek
TOPANGA STATE PARK
Greenleaf Cyn Rd
To Hwy 101
SEC 3
DEAD HORSE TR
SEC 2
Entrada Rd
To Trippet Ranch
HONDO CANYON TRAIL
Topanga Meadows
START HIKE
Topanga Canyon Blvd
Topanga Cr.
N
W
E
S
Fernwood Pacific Dr
To Hwy 1
Tuna Canyon Rd
REFERENCE MAPS P. 420
BACKBONE TRAIL

Shuttle car

From Santa Monica, drive 12 miles northbound on the Pacific Coast Highway/Highway 1 to Malibu Canyon Road. Turn right and drive 6.5 miles to Mulholland Highway. Turn right and continue 4 miles to Stunt Road. Turn right and drive 4 miles up the winding road to the end of Stunt Road. Turn left on Saddle Peak Road, and park in the pullout on the left.

From the Ventura Freeway/Highway 101 in Calabasas, exit on Las Virgenes Road. Head 3.1 miles south to Mulholland Highway. Turn left and go 4 miles to Stunt Road. Turn right and drive 4 miles up the road to the end of Stunt Road. Turn left on Saddle Peak Road, and park in the pullout on the left.

The hike

Pass the trailhead sign and descend to Old Topanga Creek. Rock-hop over the creek, ascend steps, and walk through Topanga Meadows. Enter the lush, live oak forest in a side drainage, and follow the left side of the watercourse. Cross to the north side of the stream, passing through meadows with sandstone outcroppings. Climb up the rolling meadow to a rocky perch with sweeping views across Hondo Canyon. Weave along the contour of the hills, overlooking layers of mountains and canyons. Climb the south wall of Hondo Canyon, zigzagging past conglomerate rock formations. The views range across the Santa Monica Mountains to the San Fernando Valley and Los Padres National Forest. At 3.7 miles, the path reaches a junction by Saddle Peak Road at the head of Hondo Canyon.

Bear right on the Fossil Ridge Trail, and head up to coastal views that span down Las Flores Canyon to Santa Monica Bay and Catalina Island. Parallel Saddle Peak Road, passing an endless display of sea shell fossils embedded in the sedimentary rock. Reach the Topanga Ridge Motorway at 4.3 miles. The right fork leads 0.9 miles to the Topanga Lookout. The left fork ends at a three-way junction with Saddle Peak Road, Schueren Road, and Stunt Road at the Lois Ewen Overlook.

The Saddle Peak Trail—the next segment of the Backbone Trail (Section 5)—begins across the road. ■

Stunt Road to Piuma Road

Saddle Peak Trail

Hiking distance: 5.2 miles one way; 10.4 miles round trip
Hiking time: 2.5 hours each way
Configuration: one-way shuttle or out-and-back
Elevation gain: 350 feet gain and 2,000 feet loss
Difficulty: easy one-way (going west); strenuous round trip
Exposure: exposed ridge and forested canyon
Dogs: allowed on first 0.8 miles; not allowed after in Malibu Creek State Park (but many dogs have been known to enjoy the entire trail)
Maps: U.S.G.S. Malibu Beach • Malibu Creek State Park Map
Tom Harrison Maps: Malibu Creek State Park Trail Map

map page 438

Section 5 of the Backbone Trail begins atop Stunt Road at the Lois Ewen Overlook, a 2,365-foot saddle above Cold Creek Canyon Preserve, and descends into the Malibu Creek watershed at Piuma Creek. The hike follows the Saddle Peak Trail from the crest of the mountain along the northwest flank of two-peaked Saddle Peak. The trail weaves through natural gardens of massive sandstone formations and chaparral-cloaked slopes with manzanita (back cover photo). Beyond the peaks, the trail descends into Dark Canyon, a steep-walled, stream-fed canyon in a dense, fern-draped forest with live oaks, alders, and sycamores. En route, the footpath winds in and out of small canyons while traversing the mountainside. Throughout the hike are phenomenal vistas, including the Santa Monica Bay, Los Angeles, Cold Creek Canyon, Malibu Canyon, and Goat Buttes in the heart of Malibu Creek State Park.

To the trailhead

From Santa Monica, drive 12 miles northbound on the Pacific Coast Highway/Highway 1 to Malibu Canyon Road. Turn right and drive 6.5 miles to Mulholland Highway. Turn right and continue 4 miles to Stunt Road. Turn right and drive 5 miles up the winding road to the end of Stunt Road. Turn left on Saddle Peak Road, and park in the pullout on the left.

From the Ventura Freeway/Highway 101 in Calabasas, exit on Las Virgenes Road. Head 3.1 miles south to Mulholland Highway. Turn left and go 4 miles to Stunt Road. Turn right and drive 4 miles up the road to the end of Stunt Road. Turn left on Saddle Peak Road, and park in the pullout on the left.

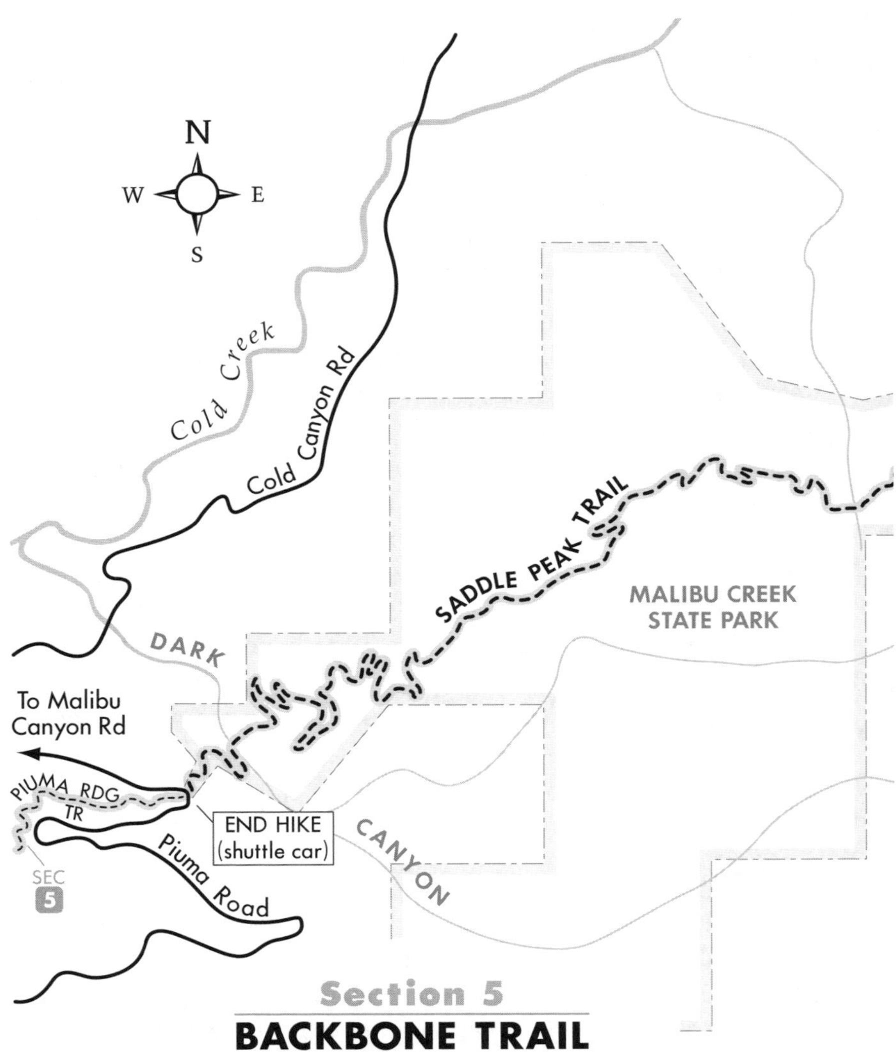

Section 5
BACKBONE TRAIL
Stunt Road to Piuma Road
Saddle Peak Trail

Shuttle car

From Santa Monica, drive 12 miles northbound on the Pacific Coast Highway/Highway 1 to Malibu Canyon Road. Turn right (north) and continue 4.8 miles up the winding canyon road to

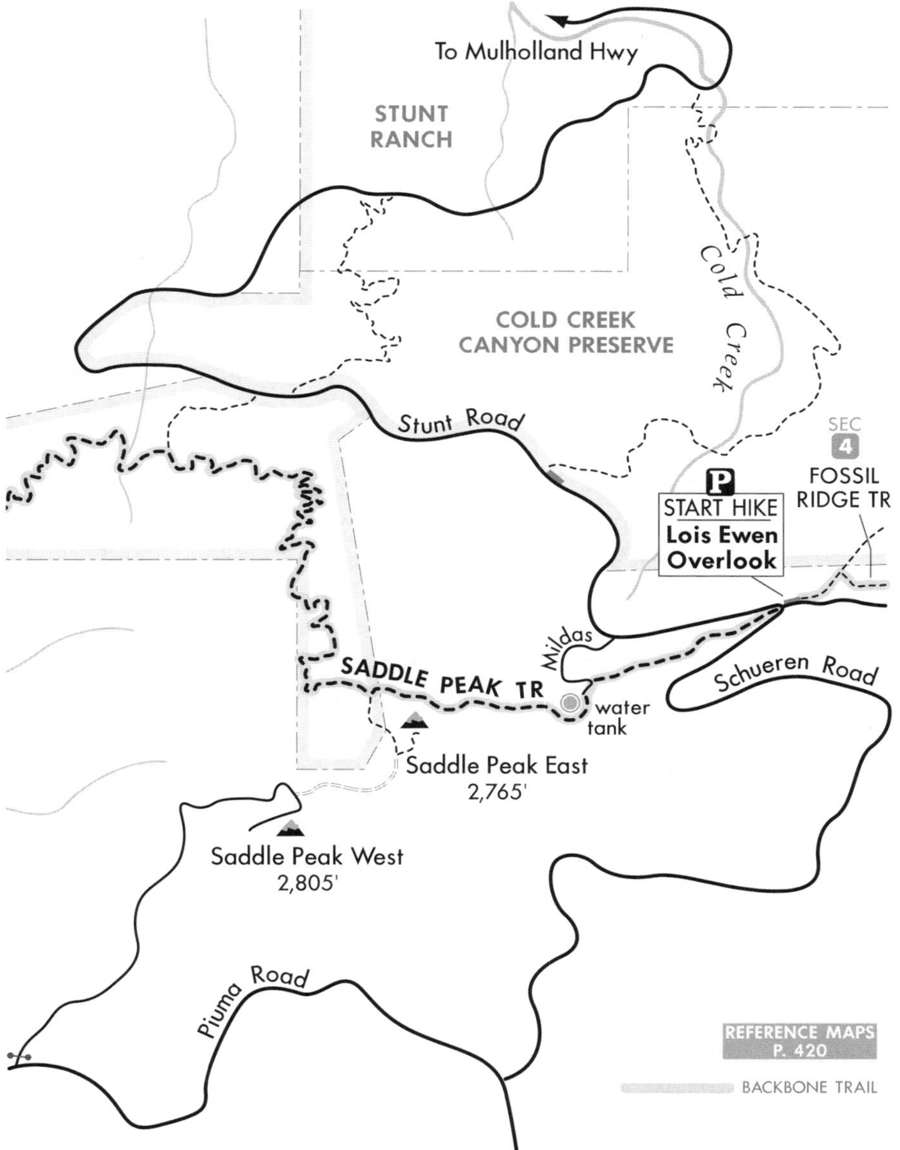

the traffic light at Piuma Road. Turn right and drive 1.2 miles to a U-shaped bend in the road. The parking area is in the bend. Park in the narrow dirt pullouts along the road.

From the Ventura Freeway/Highway 101 in Calabasas, take the Las Virgenes Road exit. Drive 5 miles south to the traffic light at Piuma Road (located 1.8 miles past Mulholland Highway). Turn left and continue 1.2 miles to a U-shaped bend in the road. The parking area is in the bend. Park in the narrow dirt pullouts along the road.

The hike

After enjoying the views from the parking area, walk up the short, steep wedge of land between Stunt Road and Schueren Road. Cross an old concrete foundation, and follow the footpath west along the ridge. Pick up an asphalt road by a water tower, and curve left up the road one hundred yards. Curve around the left (south) side of the water tank to the trail on the back side. Continue up the spine and north-facing slope, with views of the Cold Creek Canyon Preserve. Reach a junction at 0.8 miles. A short detour to the left leads to an overlook atop Saddle Peak East. Saddle Peak West, with the "sci-fi" looking communications towers, is a short distance to the southwest.

Continue straight ahead on the Backbone Trail. Descend through a garden of magnificent sandstone formations with caves. Zipper down the mountain to a junction at 2 miles. The right fork leads 0.2 miles to Stunt Road near the Upper Stunt High Trail. Stay to the left, weaving along the mountainside path. Pass huge boulders and steadily descend into the canyon. Cross the seasonal stream and continue down canyon. Cross a grassy ridge with a view of Mesa Peak and Goat Buttes in the heart of Malibu Creek State Park. Views open up of the winding canyon roads and homes. Head down to Dark Canyon Creek among sycamores, alders, and ferns. Rock-hop over the creek and veer left (upstream). Climb up four switchbacks, then descend to Piuma Road.

Section 6 of the Backbone Trail (Piuma Ridge Trail) is directly across Piuma Road. ■

Piuma Road to Malibu Canyon Road

Piuma Ridge Trail

Hiking distance: 1.9 miles one way; 3.8 miles round trip
Hiking time: 1 hour each way
Configuration: one-way shuttle or out-and-back
Elevation gain: 200 feet
Difficulty: easy
Exposure: forested
Dogs: not allowed (but many dogs have enjoy this forested trail)
Maps: U.S.G.S. Malibu Beach • Malibu Creek State Park Map
Tom Harrison Maps: Malibu Creek State Park Trail Map

map page 443

Piuma Ridge divides the Cold Creek and Malibu Canyon watersheds along the east side of Malibu Canyon. Section 6 of the Backbone Trail follows the Piuma Ridge Trail from Piuma Road to just before Malibu Canyon Road. The trail winds along the ridge perched above the Malibu Creek gorge and descends to Puima Creek in the shade of the forest. The footpath traverses the hillside through a mix of chaparral and oak woodlands, then descends into the canyon to an oak and bay laurel forest with moss-covered boulders.

To the trailhead

From Santa Monica, drive 12 miles northbound on the Pacific Coast Highway/Highway 1 to Malibu Canyon Road. Turn right (north) and continue 4.8 miles up the winding canyon road to the traffic light at Piuma Road. Turn right and drive 1.2 miles to a U-shaped bend in the road. The trailhead is in the bend. Park in the narrow dirt pullouts along the road.

From the Ventura Freeway/Highway 101 in Calabasas, take the Las Virgenes Road exit. Drive 5 miles south to the traffic light at Piuma Road (located 1.8 miles past Mulholland Highway). Turn left and continue 1.2 miles to a U-shaped left bend in the road. The trailhead is in the bend. Park in the narrow dirt pullouts along the road.

Shuttle car (optional)

From Santa Monica, drive 12 miles northbound on the Pacific Coast Highway/Highway 1 to Malibu Canyon Road. Turn right (north) and continue 4.8 miles up the winding canyon road to the traffic light at Piuma Road. Turn right and drive 0.4 miles. Park in the dirt pullouts along the right side of the road.

From the Ventura Freeway/Highway 101 in Calabasas, take the Las Virgenes Road exit. Drive 5 miles south to the traffic light at Piuma Road (located 1.8 miles past Mulholland Highway). Turn left and continue 0.4 miles and park in the dirt pullouts along the right side of the road.

The hike

The Saddle Peak Trail heads east from the trailhead—Section 5 of the Backbone Trail. This hike heads west on the downslope side of the road. Enter the shaded forest and follow the stream on the right. Traverse the hillside slope on a gentle uphill grade. Cross a seasonal drainage and continue west, weaving along the mountain contours. Cross two more drainages while steadily gaining elevation to expanded views across the layers of mountains. Zigzag downhill under a canopy of oak and bay laurel trees. Weave through the forest to a paved driveway. Cross the pavement and follow the path along a wood fence. Return to the forest and rock-hop over Piuma Creek. At 1.9 miles, the path ends on Piuma Road, a half mile shy of Malibu Canyon Road.

Section 7 of the Backbone Trail—the Mesa Peak Motorway—begins across Malibu Canyon Road and 100 yards to the south. ■

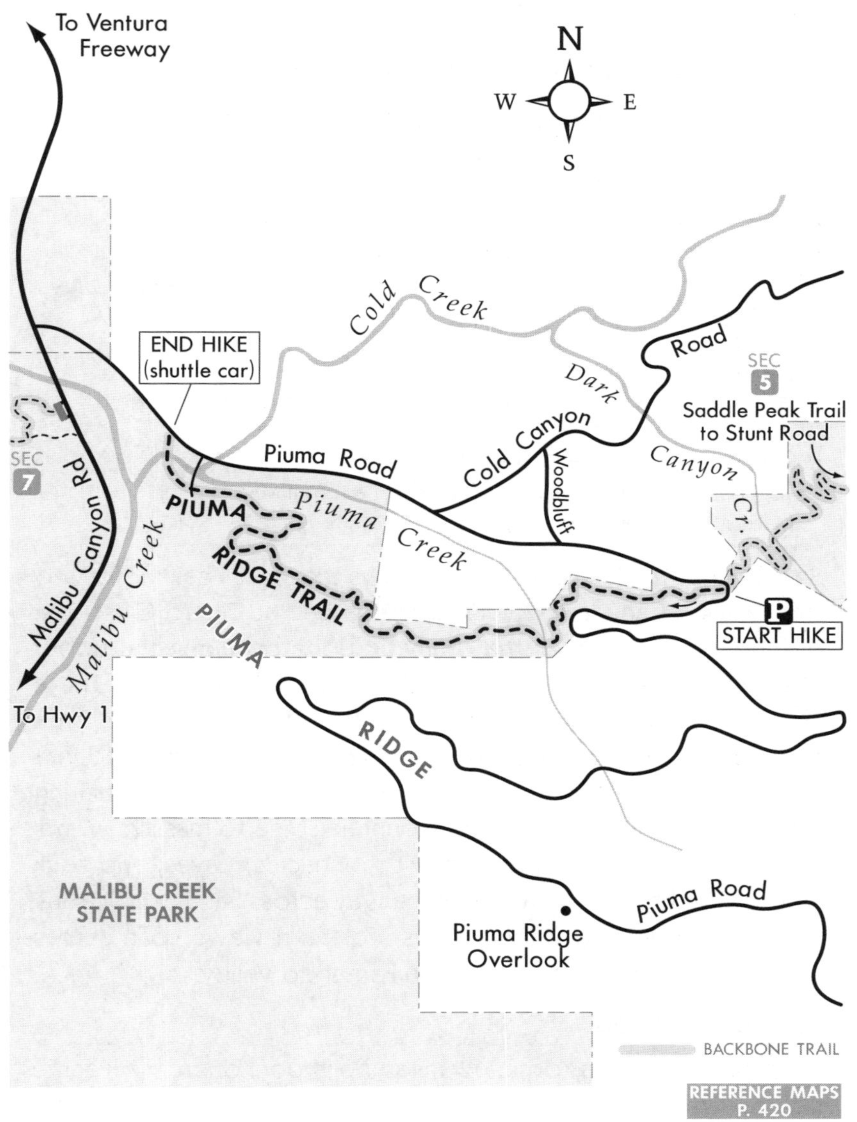

Section 6

BACKBONE TRAIL

Piuma Road to Malibu Canyon Road

Piuma Ridge Trail

Malibu Canyon Road to Corral Canyon Road

Mesa Peak Motorway

Hiking distance: 5.4 miles one way; 10.8 miles round trip
Hiking time: 3 hours each way
Configuration: one-way shuttle or out-and-back
Elevation gain: 1,600 feet
Difficulty: moderate to strenuous
Exposure: exposed ridge
Dogs: not allowed (but many 4-legged friends have been known to enjoy this trail)
Maps: U.S.G.S. Malibu Beach and Point Dume
Tom Harrison Maps: Malibu Creek State Park Trail Map
Malibu Creek State Park Map

map page 446

Section 7 of the Backbone Trail follows the Mesa Peak Motorway from Malibu Canyon to Corral Canyon Road at Castro Crest. The dirt fire road traverses the dramatic ridgetop along the upper reaches of Malibu Creek State Park toward Castro Peak. There are spectacular vistas in every direction. The hike begins on a forested footpath, but soon continues along the exposed fire road, gaining 1,400 feet over the first 2.4 miles. The undulating dirt road follows the exposed mountain spine to massive, wind-eroded sandstone formations with pinnacles, caves, and rock arches. Southern views reach all the way across Santa Monica Bay, from Point Dume to Palos Verdes; northern views span across Malibu Creek State Park to the San Fernando Valley.

To the trailhead

From Santa Monica, drive 12 miles northbound on the Pacific Coast Highway/Highway 1 to Malibu Canyon Road. Turn right (north) and continue 4.7 miles up the winding canyon road to the paved but unsigned trailhead parking lot on the left. (The parking lot is located 0.1 mile south of the traffic signal at Piuma Road.) A parking fee is required.

From the Ventura Freeway/Highway 101 in Calabasas, take the Las Virgenes Road exit. Drive 5.1 miles to the Backbone Trail parking lot on the right. (The parking area is located 1.8 miles south of Mulholland Highway.)

Shuttle car

From Santa Monica, drive 14.5 miles northbound on the Pacific Coast Highway/Highway 1 to Corral Canyon Road. Turn right and wind 5.2 miles to the end of the paved road. Continue 0.1 mile on the dirt road to the parking area at the end of the road.

The only access to the shuttle car parking is from the coast. Corral Canyon Road is located 2.5 miles west of Malibu Canyon Road and 3.5 miles east of Kanan Dume Road.

The hike

Walk up the slope past the trailhead signs to a posted junction at 100 yards. The trail straight ahead meanders through the hills and dead-ends before reaching the deep ravine at Malibu Creek. Bear left on the Mesa Peak (Backbone) Trail. Wind up the hillside along the wooded canyon wall. At 0.6 miles, the footpath connects with the Mesa Peak Motorway, a dirt fire road. Make a U-shaped left bend around a rock formation. Continue uphill on the serpentine road. There are great views of Brents Mountain, Goat Buttes, Malibu Creek State Park to the northwest, and an expanding view of Malibu Canyon. At just under 2 miles, on a sharp right bend, views open to the Pacific Ocean. Follow the ridge, with 360-degree vistas, to a junction at 2.4 miles by metal posts, located forty yards before a sharp right bend. To ascend 1,844-foot Mesa Peak or drop down Puerco Canyon to the ocean via the Puerco Motorway, bear left (south).

For this hike, continue straight ahead on the Mesa Peak Motorway (Backbone Trail). Head up the road, then slowly descend to a saddle while savoring the great views on the exposed ridge. From the saddle, begin a long but easy ascent. Follow the undulating road, with alternating views of the San Fernando Valley and the coast. On the right, the trail overlooks the Kaslow Natural Preserve (a nesting ground for golden eagles) and Malibu Creek

State Park; on the left is Corral Canyon and the Pacific Ocean. At just under 5 miles, the dirt road weaves through magnificent sandstone formations. Just before reaching a massive outcrop, the road splits. The left fork follows the Mesa Peak Motorway 0.3 miles to Corral Canyon Road. Stay to the right on the Backbone Trail. Weave through the stunning, cave-riddled rock outcroppings to the Corral Canyon Trailhead 0.4 miles from the junction.

Across the road is the Castro Crest Trail, Section 8 of the Backbone Trail. ■

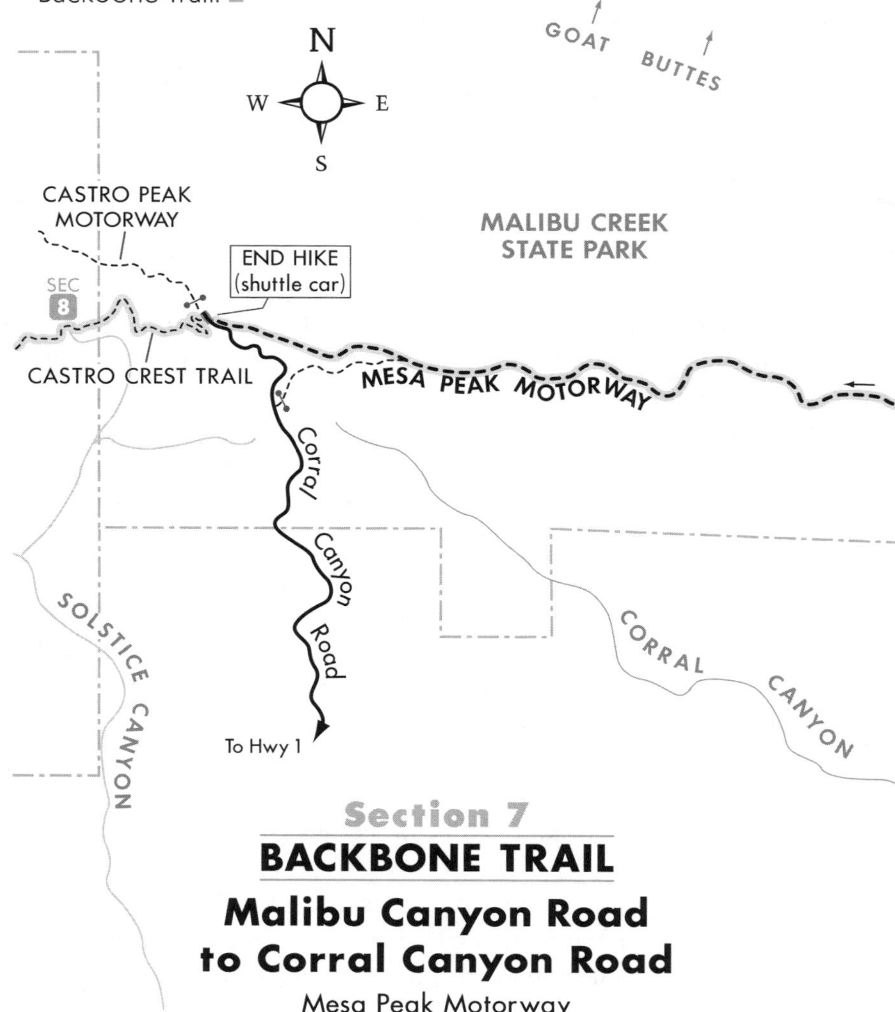

Section 7
BACKBONE TRAIL
Malibu Canyon Road to Corral Canyon Road
Mesa Peak Motorway

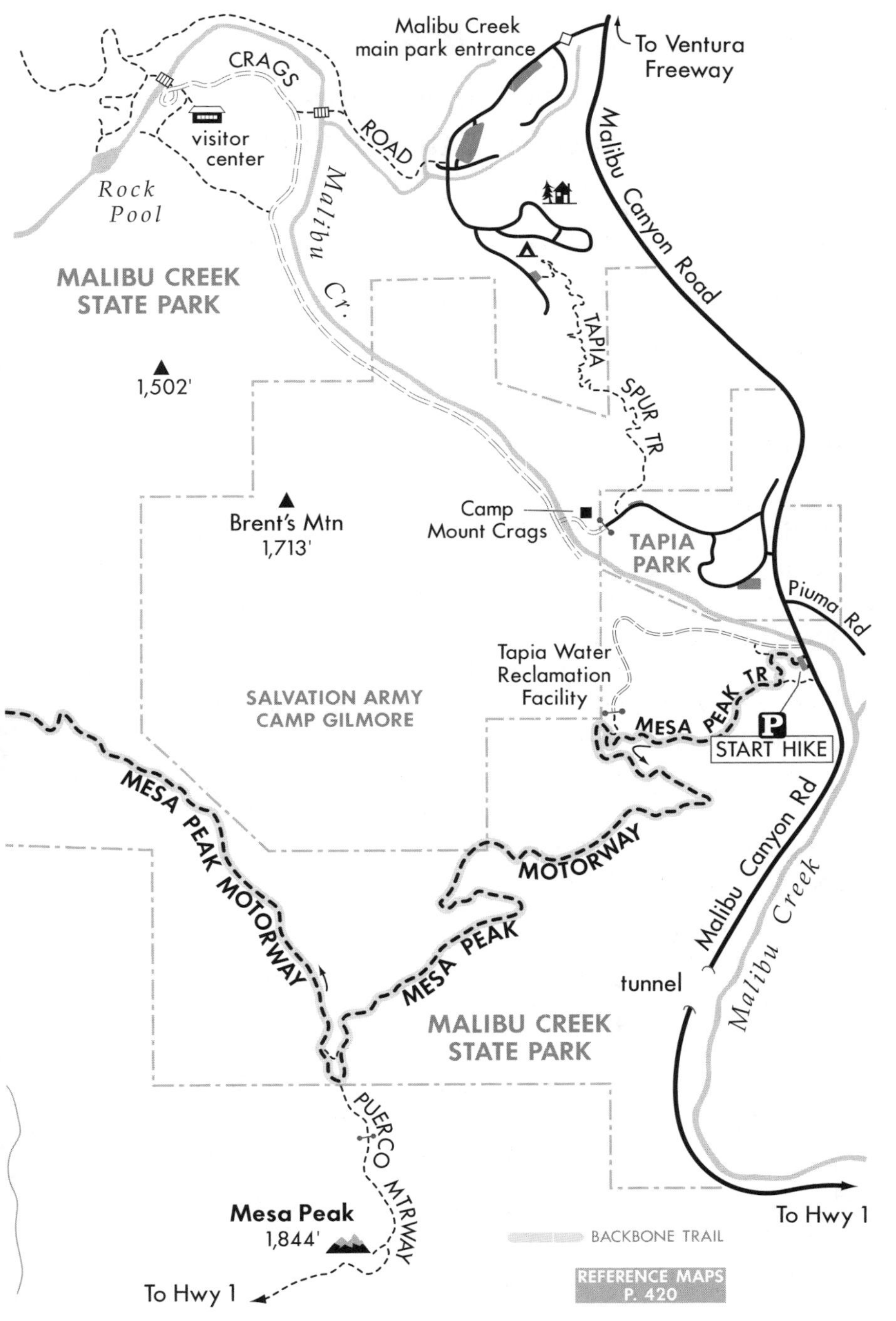
Malibu Creek
main park entrance
To Ventura
Freeway
CRAGS
ROAD
visitor
center
Rock
Pool
Malibu
Cr.
Malibu Canyon Road
MALIBU CREEK
STATE PARK
TAPIA
SPUR TR
1,502'
Brent's Mtn
1,713'
Camp
Mount Crags
TAPIA
PARK
Piuma Rd
Tapia Water
Reclamation
Facility
SALVATION ARMY
CAMP GILMORE
MESA PEAK TR
START HIKE
MESA PEAK MOTORWAY
MOTORWAY
Malibu Canyon Rd
Malibu Creek
MESA PEAK
tunnel
MALIBU CREEK
STATE PARK
PUERCO MTRWAY
Mesa Peak
1,844'
To Hwy 1
BACKBONE TRAIL
REFERENCE MAPS
P. 420
To Hwy 1

Corral Canyon Road to Latigo Canyon Road

Castro Crest Trail

Hiking distance: 4.2 miles one way; 8.4 miles round trip
Hiking time: 2 hours each way
Configuration: one-way shuttle or out-and-back
Elevation gain: 600 feet
Difficulty: moderate
Exposure: mostly forested
Dogs: allowed
Maps: U.S.G.S. Point Dume • Malibu Creek State Park Map
Tom Harrison Maps: Malibu Creek State Park Trail Map

Section 8 of the Backbone Trail follows the Castro Crest Trail from Corral Canyon Road to Latigo Canyon Road. This remote footpath weaves through upper Solstice Canyon and Newton Canyon beneath Castro Crest, a massive east/west-running sandstone wall that stretches over two miles. The hike leads through a lush riparian forest with oak and sycamore woodlands and along the verdant waterways beneath the shadow of 2,824-foot Castro Peak, the fifth highest peak in the mountain range and easily identified by its radio towers. From the high ridges on both ends of the trail are panoramic views over the Santa Monica Range and across Santa Monica Bay.

To the trailhead

From Santa Monica, drive 14.5 miles northbound on the Pacific Coast Highway/Highway 1 to Corral Canyon Road. Turn right and wind 5.2 miles to the end of the paved road. Continue 0.1 mile on the dirt road to the trailhead parking area at the road's end.

The only access to the trailhead is from the coast. Corral Canyon Road is located 2.5 miles west of Malibu Canyon Road and 3.5 miles east of Kanan Dume Road.

Shuttle car

From Santa Monica, drive 15 miles northbound on the Pacific

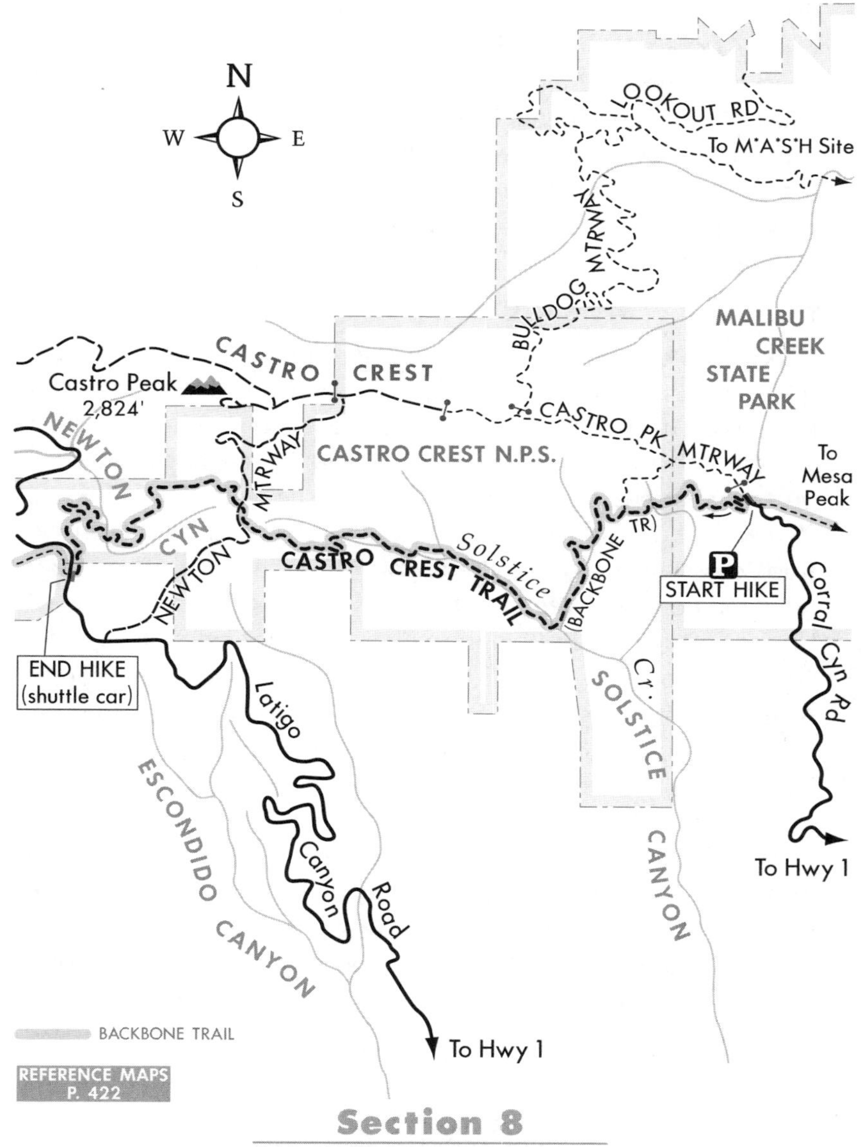

Section 8

BACKBONE TRAIL

Corral Canyon Road to Latigo Canyon Road

Castro Crest Trail

Coast Highway/Highway 1 to Latigo Canyon Road. Turn right and wind 7.3 miles to the parking area on the right. (Latigo Canyon Road is located 3.2 miles west of Malibu Canyon Road and 2.8 miles east of Kanan Dume Road.)

From the Ventura Freeway/Highway 101 in Agoura Hills, take the Kanan Road exit. Drive 6.7 miles south to Latigo Canyon Road (located 0.7 miles south of Mulholland Highway). Turn left and continue 2.9 miles to the parking area on the left.

The hike

Head west on the posted Castro Crest (Backbone) Trail. Weave down the south-facing mountain slope in a bowl overlooking the stream-fed canyons on the left that feed Solstice Creek. Towering above the trail to the north are the magnificent Castro Crest formations. Wind in and out of the shaded drainages while following the mountain contours. Gently descend to the canyon floor, crossing two seasonal streams. At the canyon bottom, veer right and continue west. Walk up canyon along the south side of Upper Solstice Creek. Rock-hop over the creek eight times while strolling through oak-dotted meadows and a shaded oak forest. After the last crossing, ascend the hillside, leaving the lush riparian vegetation to the exposed scrub and chaparral. Traverse the south wall of Solstice Canyon beneath the dramatic Castro Crest mountains while far-reaching vistas stretch to the east.

At 2.8 miles, the trail reaches Newton Motorway, a dirt road on the ridge at the head of both Solstice Canyon and Newton Canyon, 575 feet below Castro Peak. To the right, Newton Motorway leads up to Castro Peak, but it is gated and access is no longer permitted. The Castro Crest (Backbone) Trail continues west, directly across the road. Follow the north canyon slope high above Newton Canyon. Top a slope to a coastal vista and a view of Boney Mountain at Point Mugu State Park. Descend into Newton Canyon on a serpentine course. Enter the shaded forest and cross Newton Creek on the canyon floor. Ascend the slope and climb to Latigo Canyon Road at the trailhead parking area.

Section 9 of the Backbone Trail—Newton Canyon Trail—is directly across Latigo Canyon Road. ■

Latigo Canyon Road to Kanan Dume Road

Newton Canyon Trail

Hiking distance: 2.3 miles one way; 4.6 miles round trip
Hiking time: 1.5 hours each way
Configuration: one-way shuttle or out-and-back
Elevation gain: 600 feet
Difficulty: easy to moderate
Exposure: shaded forest
Dogs: allowed
Maps: U.S.G.S. Point Dume
Tom Harrison Maps: Zuma-Trancas Canyons Trail Map

map page 453

Section 9 of the Backbone Trail follows the Newton Canyon Trail between Latigo Canyon Road and Kanan Dume Road by Tunnel 1. The trail runs beneath Castro Peak through the Castro Crest National Park Service corridor, a section of land that connects Malibu Creek State Park with Zuma/Trancas Canyons Recreation Area. This short, 2.3-mile-long section weaves through the oak-filled canyon along the south canyon wall. The hike includes ocean views and seasonal stream crossings.

To the trailhead

From Santa Monica, drive 15 miles northbound on the Pacific Coast Highway/Highway 1 to Latigo Canyon Road. Turn right and wind 7.3 miles to the trailhead parking area on the right. (Latigo Canyon Road is located 3.2 miles west of Malibu Canyon Road and 2.8 miles east of Kanan Dume Road.)

From the Ventura Freeway/Highway 101 in Agoura Hills, take the Kanan Road exit. Drive 6.7 miles south to Latigo Canyon Road (located 0.7 miles south of Mulholland Highway). Turn left and continue 2.9 miles to the trailhead parking area on the left.

Shuttle car (optional)

From Santa Monica, drive 18 miles northbound on the Pacific Coast Highway/Highway 1 to Kanan Dume Road (5.8 miles west of Malibu Canyon Road). Turn right and drive 4.4 miles north to the parking lot on the left (west), located just after the first tunnel (T-1).

From the Ventura Freeway/Highway 101 in Agoura Hills, take the Kanan Road exit. Drive 7.9 miles south to the trailhead parking lot on the right (west), located just before entering the third tunnel (T-1). (Kanan Road becomes Kanan Dume Road after it crosses Mulholland Highway.)

The hike

Cross Latigo Canyon Road to the signed trailhead, where there is a great westward view of the jagged ridgeline of the Boney Mountains. Descend on the north slope into Newton Canyon. Continue downhill with the aid of switchbacks, deep into the lush, fern-filled forest. Cross to the south canyon wall, and follow the gentle uphill slope to views of the surrounding mountains. Head downhill again on the serpentine path under the shade of oak and bay laurel trees. Cross Snakebite Ridge Road, a paved private road, and continue on the footpath. Cross over Tunnel 1, high above Kanan Dume Road. After crossing, curve right, dropping down to the Kanan Dume Road trailhead parking lot at 2.3 miles.

Section 10 of the Backbone Trail—Upper Zuma Canyon Trail—begins at the parking lot. ■

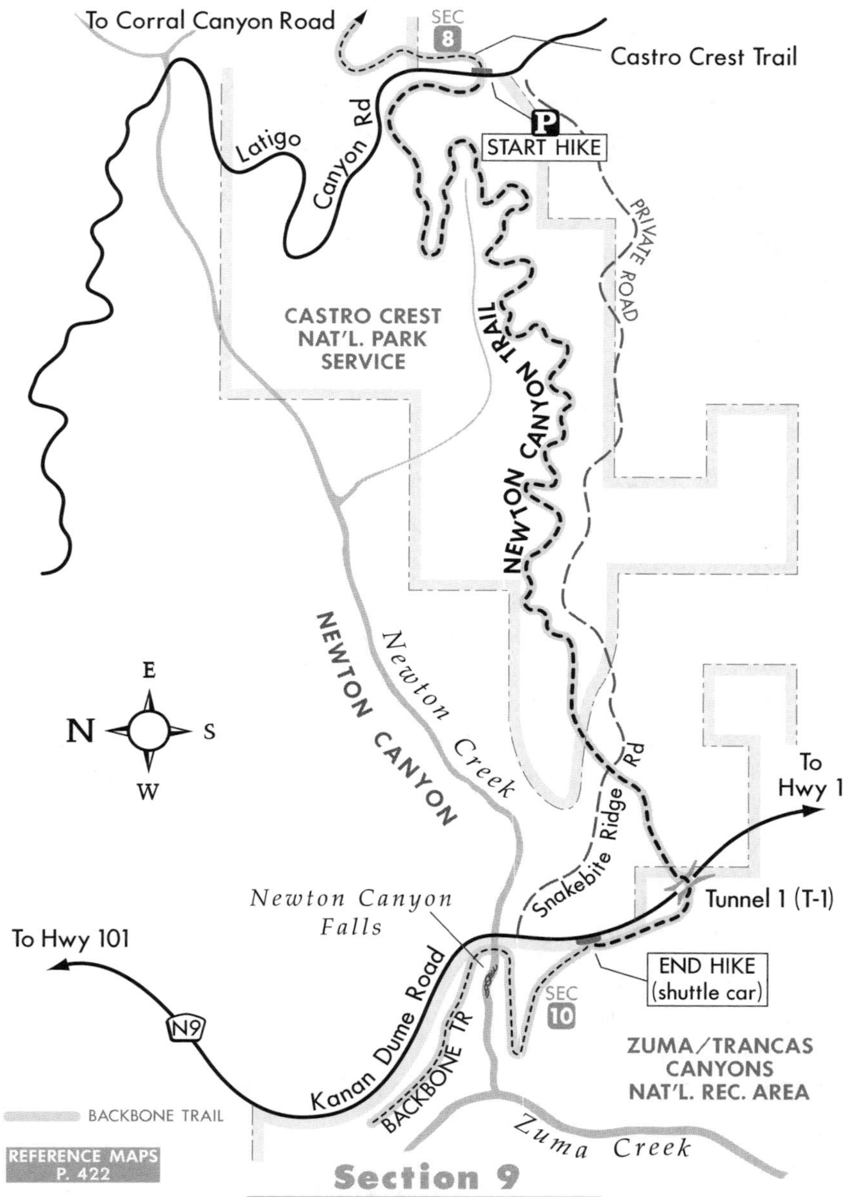

Section 9

BACKBONE TRAIL

Latigo Canyon Road to Kanan Dume Road

Newton Canyon Trail

Kanan Dume Road to Encinal Canyon Road

Upper Zuma Canyon Trail • Trancas Canyon Trail

Hiking distance: 4.8 miles one way; 9.6 mile round trip
Hiking time: 2.5 hours each way
Configuration: one-way shuttle or out-and-back
Elevation gain: 350 feet
Difficulty: moderate
Exposure: exposed hills and forested canyons
Dogs: allowed
Maps: U.S.G.S. Point Dume
Tom Harrison Maps: Zuma-Trancas Canyons Trail Map

map page 456

Section 10 of the Backbone Trail runs through the upper end of Zuma/Trancas Canyons Recreation Area between Kanan Dume Road and Encinal Canyon Road. The trail crosses Zuma Canyon and Trancas Canyon, neighboring V-shaped canyons in the central portion of the Santa Monica Mountains. The steep gorges have perennial streams, weather-carved sandstone boulders, fern-lined pools, and jungle-like forests with oaks, bays, willows, and sycamores. The scenic canyons have remained natural and undisturbed. The hike traverses the upper slopes of Zuma Canyon, climbs up to Zuma Ridge between the two canyons, and drops into Trancas Canyon. En route, the hike visits Newton Canyon Falls, Upper Zuma Falls, and Trancas Creek.

To the trailhead

From Santa Monica, drive 18 miles northbound on the Pacific Coast Highway/Highway 1 to Kanan Dume Road (5.8 miles west of Malibu Canyon Road). Turn right and drive 4.4 miles north to the trailhead parking lot on the left (west). The parking lot is located just after the first tunnel (T-1).

From the Ventura Freeway/Highway 101 in Agoura Hills, take the Kanan Road exit. Drive 7.9 miles south to the trailhead parking lot on the right (west). The parking lot is located just before entering the third tunnel (T-1). (Kanan Road becomes Kanan Dume Road after it crosses Mulholland Highway.)

Shuttle car

From Santa Monica, drive 18 miles northbound on the Pacific Coast Highway/Highway 1 to Encinal Canyon Road. (Encinal Canyon Road is 5.5 miles west of Kanan Dume Road.) Drive 5 miles up the mountain to a road split with Lechusa Road. Turn right, staying on Encinal Canyon Road, and continue 1.1 mile to the posted trailhead on the left. Park in the long, narrow pullout on the left. When it is dry, turn a sharp left and descend 130 yards to the circular parking area at the trailhead.

From the Ventura Freeway/Highway 101 in Agoura Hills, exit on Kanan Road. Drive 6.1 miles south to Mulholland Highway. Turn right and continue 0.9 miles to Encinal Canyon Road. Veer left and go 2.3 miles to the posted trailhead on the right. Park in the long, narrow pullout on the right. When it is dry, turn right and descend 130 yards to the circular parking area at the trailhead.

The hike

Walk past the trailhead kiosk, and head west through the lush vegetation on the Backbone (Upper Zuma Canyon) Trail. Descend on the south wall of Upper Zuma Canyon. Switchback to the right and cross over to the north canyon wall. After crossing trickling Newton Creek, two side paths on the left lead to Newton Canyon Falls. Continue on the rock-embedded path (the main path) as it dips and rises. Coastal view open downwards to Zuma Canyon. Descend into the shade of a mixed forest with mature oaks to a bridge spanning Zuma Creek. Cross the bridge and parallel the waterway upstream. Climb to views of the surrounding mountains, then drop back into the forest and cross a feeder stream. Wind through the backcountry on the undulating path to a close-up view of Upper Zuma Falls as it flows down the face of a sandstone wall. Weave along the mountain contours to a posted T-junction with the Zuma Ridge Trail, a gated dirt road at 2.5 miles. The right fork leads 0.4 miles to the trailhead gate on Encinal Canyon Road. Bear left and follow the unpaved road 0.1 mile to a left U-bend. Mid-bend is a junction. The Zuma Ridge Trail (a fire road) continues downhill 5.3 miles to Busch Drive by Zuma Beach near Point Dume.

Bear right on the Trancas Canyon Trail, continuing on the next section of the Backbone Trail. Follow the ridge uphill, leaving Zuma Canyon. Descend and traverse the hillside into Trancas Canyon to the posted Backbone Trail sign. Veer left on the 1.6-mile-long Trancas Canyon Trail (Backbone Trail). Follow the gentle downward slope and switchback to the left, dropping deep into the lush canyon. Continue down to a tributary of Trancas Creek in a shaded forest. Cross a bridge over the tributary, and head down canyon through the oak forest to a fork at Trancas Creek. The left fork follows the creek about 100 feet. Bear right and rock-hop over the creek. Climb the canyon wall, leaving the shade of the forest. Cross a bridge over the creek, and climb out

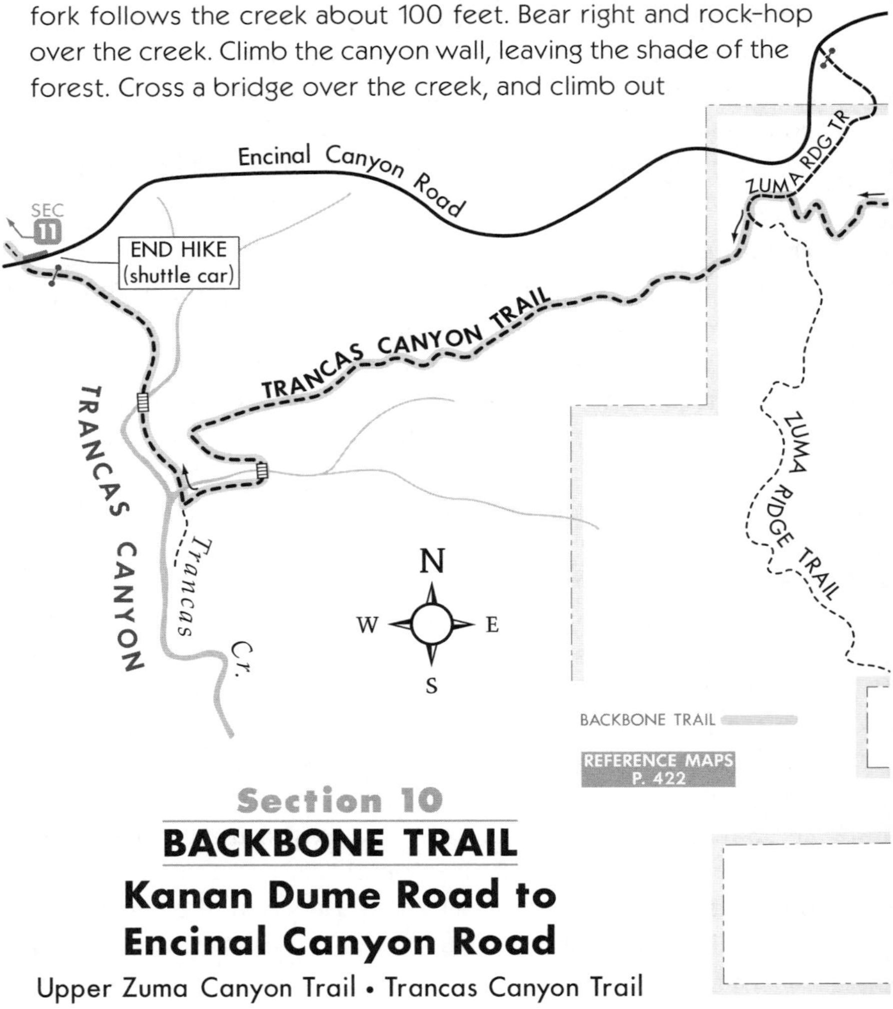

REFERENCE MAPS P. 422

Section 10
BACKBONE TRAIL
Kanan Dume Road to Encinal Canyon Road

Upper Zuma Canyon Trail • Trancas Canyon Trail

of the canyon to the gated trailhead on Encinal Canyon Road.

Section 11 of the Backbone Trail—the Encinal Trail—is directly across Encinal Canyon Road. ■

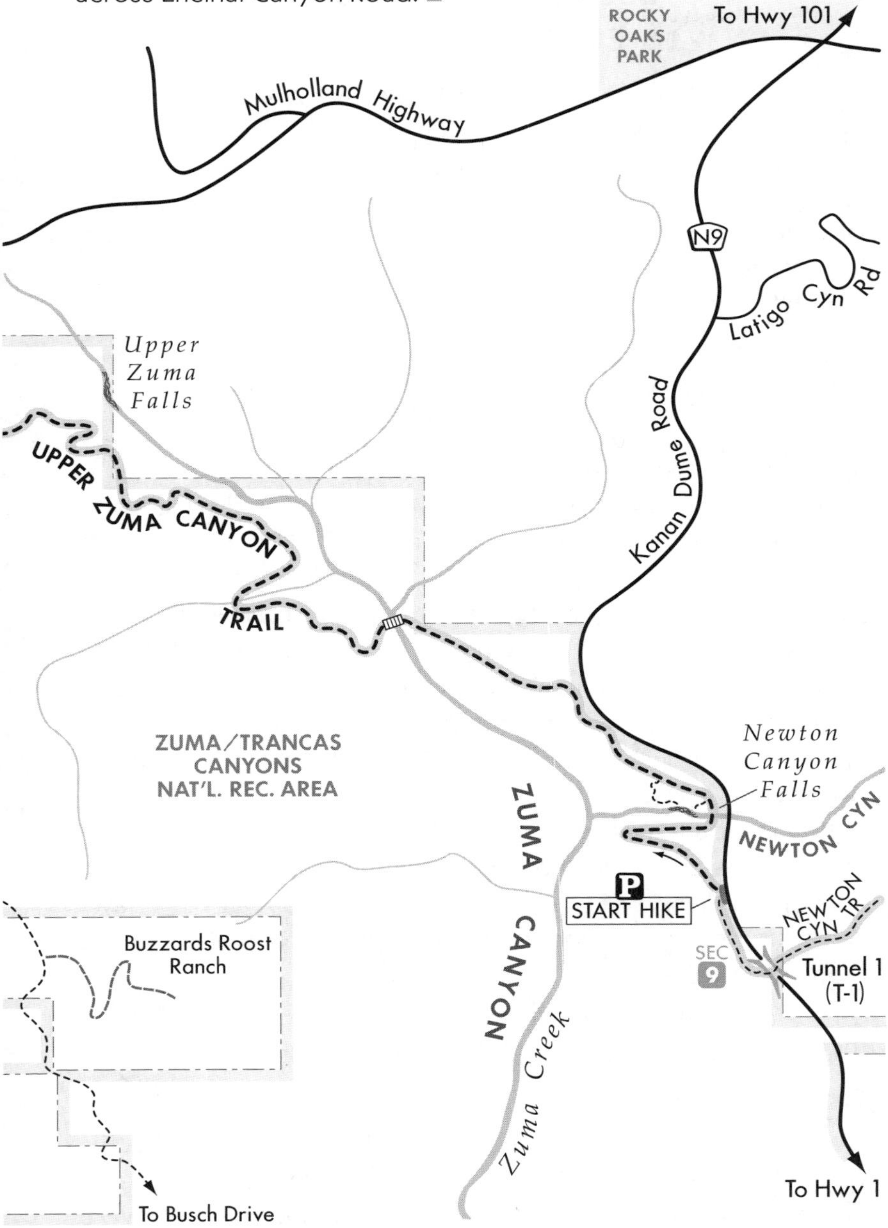

Encinal Canyon Road to Etz Meloy Motorway

Encinal Trail • Mulholland Trail • Etz Meloy Motorway

Hiking distance: 7.8 miles round trip (shuttle not yet available)
Hiking time: 4 hours each way
Configuration: out-and-back
Elevation gain: 950 feet
Difficulty: moderate to strenuous
Exposure: exposed with forested pockets
Dogs: allowed
Maps: U.S.G.S. Point Dume and Triunfo Pass
Trails Illustrated Map: Santa Monica Mountains National Rec. Area
Tom Harrison Maps: Zuma-Trancas Canyons Trail Map

map page 460

Section 11 of the Backbone Trail connects Encinal Canyon Road to the Etz Meloy Motorway, an east/west-running dirt road high on a ridge. This is the only segment of the Backbone Trail which has to be hiked as an out-and-back trail instead of a one-way shuttle. The Etz Meloy Motorway is a private road with limited access. At the time of this writing, a one-mile section of the road is off-limits to the public. The National Park Service is continuing to seek public access over the Etz Meloy Motorway, connecting the high mountain road to Yerba Buena Road, across from the Yerba Ridge Trail (Section 12).

The footpath weaves through the hills on the Encinal Trail, then zigzags up the Mulholland Trail to the motorway, crossing Mulholland Highway. Throughout the hike are far-reaching views across the seemingly endless ridges and canyons of the Santa Monica Mountains to the Pacific Ocean.

Parking is not available along Mulholland Highway, so both of these trail segments must be combined into one section.

To the trailhead

From Santa Monica, drive 18 miles northbound on the Pacific Coast Highway/Highway 1 to Encinal Canyon Road. (Encinal Canyon Road is 5.5 miles west of Kanan Dume Road.) Drive 5 miles up the mountain to a road split with Lechusa Road. Turn right, staying on Encinal Canyon Road, and continue 1.1 mile to the posted trailhead on the left. Park in the long, narrow pullout on the left. When it is dry, turn a sharp left and descend 130 yards to the circular parking area at the trailhead.

From the Ventura Freeway/Highway 101 in Agoura Hills, exit on Kanan Road. Drive 6.1 miles south to Mulholland Highway. Turn right and continue 0.9 miles to Encinal Canyon Road. Veer left and go 2.3 miles to the posted trailhead on the right. Park in the long, narrow pullout on the right. When it is dry, turn right and descend 130 yards to the circular parking area at the trailhead.

The hike

The Trancas Canyon Trail—Section 10 of the Backbone Trail—is on the south side of the road. For this hike, head north past the trail sign on the Encinal (Backbone) Trail. Descend 130 yards to a parking area. Head up the minor draw, following the curvature of the hills while gaining elevation on an easy grade. Weave up the serpentine path, traversing the east wall of the stream-fed canyon. At 1.1 mile, the Encinal Trail ends at Mulholland Highway.

Carefully cross the highway and pick up the Mulholland (Backbone) Trail directly across the road. Walk through the chaparral and grassland. Begin the climb and weave through the forest and up open slopes. The meandering path offers views across the rolling, scalloped mountains and across endless ridges and canyons to the Pacific Ocean. At 3.6 miles, the trail ends at a T-junction with the Etz Meloy Motorway, a dirt road at an elevation of 2,400 feet. To the right, the road descends less than 0.1 mile to signed private land.

Bear left, staying on the Backbone Trail, and follow the serpentine road uphill. The views stretch across the green rolling hills to the ocean and the Channel Islands. At a quarter mile is an overlook on the right in a saddle between two ridges. For a short but rewarding detour, make a U-shaped right bend, and gently climb the east-facing hillside to the summit with 360-degree panoramas. This is a great turn-around spot. Public access continues another quarter mile on the Etz Meloy Motorway. However, the

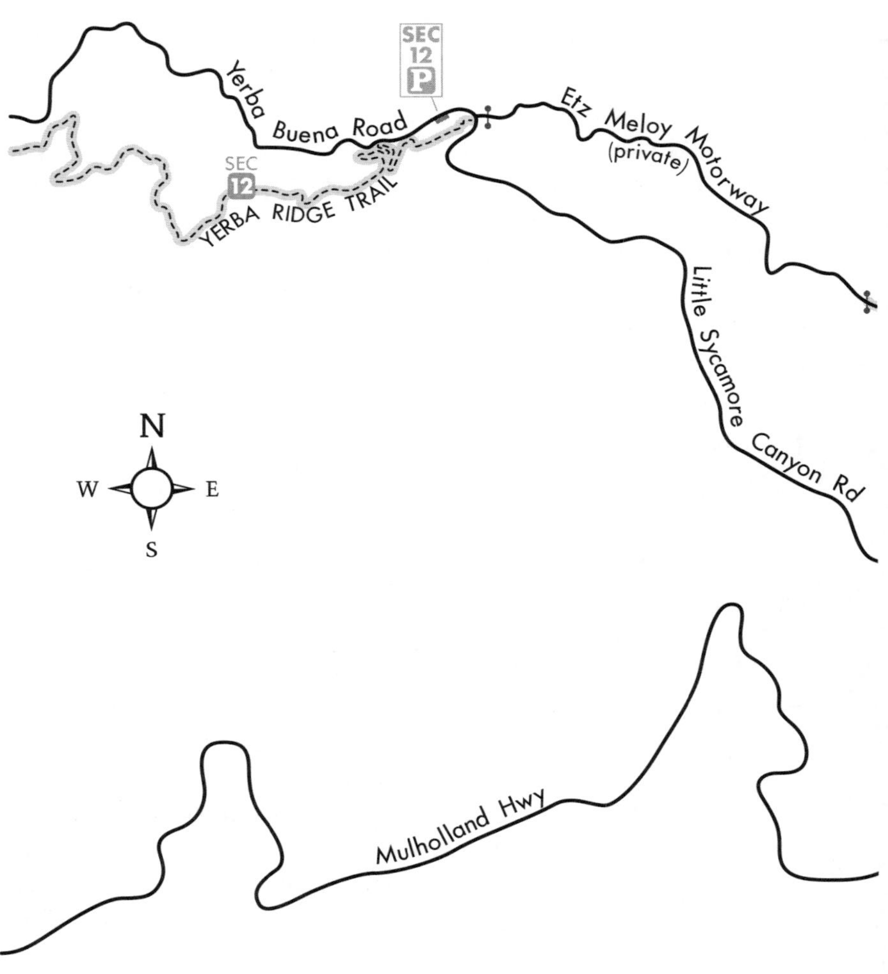

Section 11

BACKBONE TRAIL

Encinal Canyon Road to Etz Meloy Motorway

Encinal Trail • Mulholland Trail • Etz Meloy Motorway

final one mile to Yerba Buena Road is on private land. This is the only unresolved stretch of trail needed to link together the entire Backbone Trail. Visitors will know when access has been secured when trail signage indicates that the route is open. Return by retracing your steps.

Section 12 of the Backbone Trail—Yerba Buena Trail—starts across Yerba Buena Road and about 100 yards south of its junction with the Etz Meloy Motorway. ■

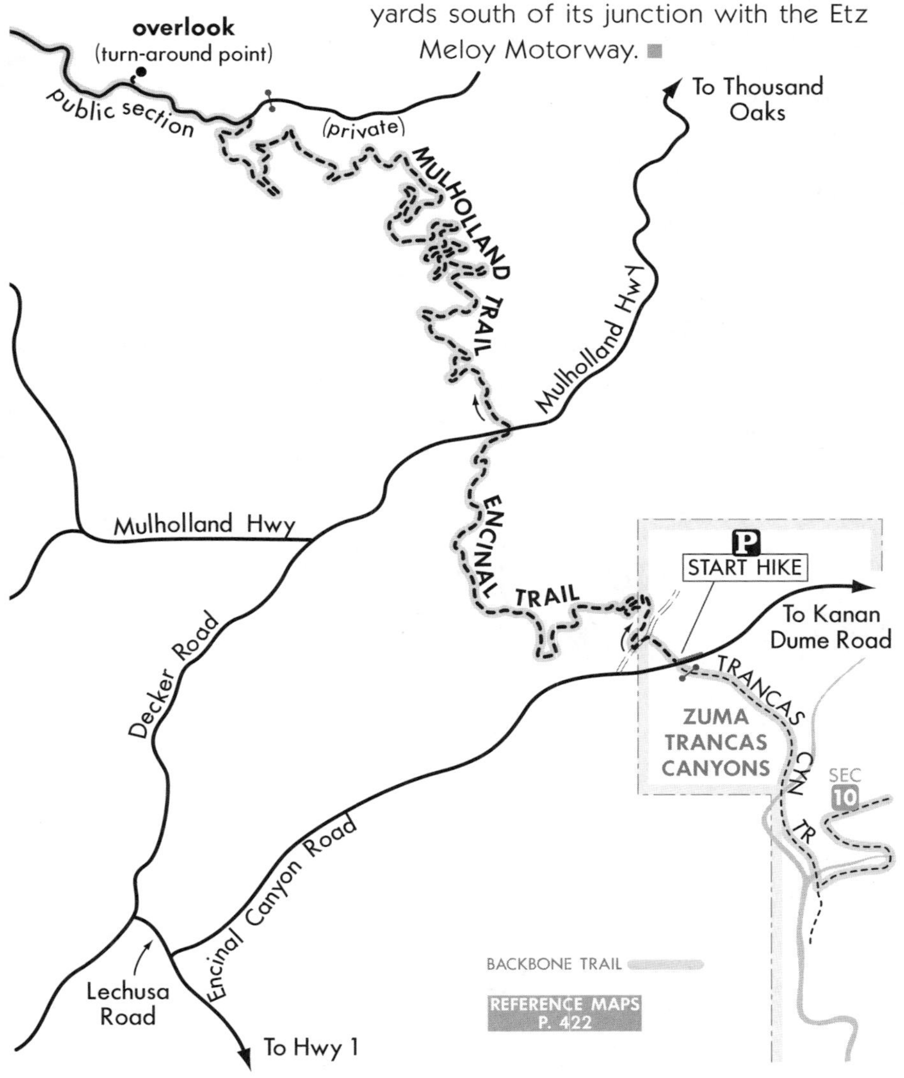

Etz Meloy Motorway to Mishe Mokwa Trailhead

Yerba Ridge Trail

Hiking distance: 4.5 miles one way; 9 miles round trip
Hiking time: 2.5 hours each way
Configuration: one-way shuttle or out-and-back
Elevation gain: 500 feet
Difficulty: moderate
Exposure: exposed
Dogs: allowed
Maps: U.S.G.S. Triunfo Pass
Tom Harrison Maps: Zuma-Trancas Canyons Trail Map
Tom Harrison Maps: Point Mugu State Park Trail Map

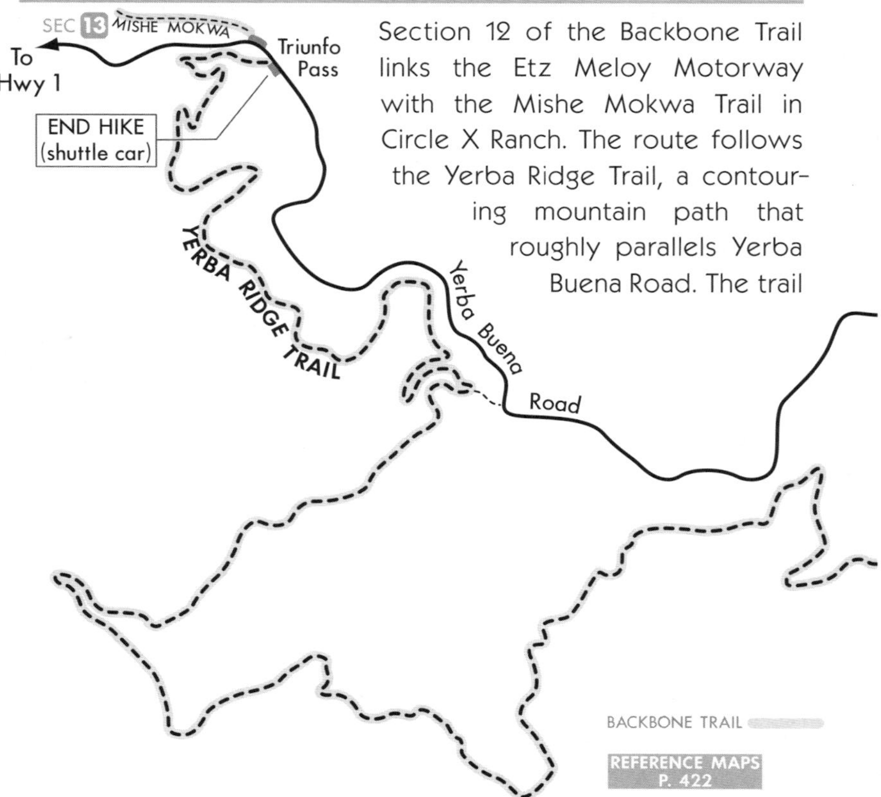

Section 12 of the Backbone Trail links the Etz Meloy Motorway with the Mishe Mokwa Trail in Circle X Ranch. The route follows the Yerba Ridge Trail, a contouring mountain path that roughly parallels Yerba Buena Road. The trail weaves through the upper mountains at an elevation over 2,000 feet. Throughout the hike are sweeping vistas of the mountainous backcountry, Boney Mountain (the western sentinel of the Santa Monica Mountains), the Conejo Valley, Thousand Oaks, Simi Valley, and the surrounding sandstone formations.

To the trailhead

From Santa Monica, drive 38 miles northbound on the Pacific Coast Highway/Highway 1 to Yerba Buena Road and turn right. (Yerba Buena Road is 10.1 miles west of Kanan Dume Road and 2 miles west of Leo Carrillo State Beach.) Continue 5.3 miles up the winding road to the Circle X Ranger Station on the right. From the ranger station, continue 3.7 miles to a large dirt pullout on the right and park. From the parking pullout, the trailhead is located 0.1 mile ahead along the road.

From the Pacific Coast Highway/Highway 1 and Las Posas Road in southeast Oxnard, drive 9 miles southbound to Yerba Buena Road and turn left, following the directions above.

From the Ventura Freeway/Highway 101 in Thousand Oaks, exit on Westlake Boulevard (Highway 23). Drive 6.9 miles south on Westlake Boulevard, winding up the mountain road to Mulholland

Section 12

BACKBONE TRAIL

Etz Meloy Motorway to Mishe Mokwa Trailhead

Yerba Ridge Trail

Highway at a stop sign. Turn right and go 0.4 miles to Little Sycamore Canyon Road. Turn right and drive 2 miles to a large dirt pullout on the left. (At the county line, Little Sycamore Canyon Road becomes Yerba Buena Road.) Turn left and park

Shuttle car

From Santa Monica, the shuttle car parking area is 1.7 miles east of the Circle X Ranger Station on Yerba Buena Road. It is located 2.0 miles before the trailhead, where Yerba Buena Road goes over the saddle at Triunfo Pass. Park in the large parking area on the right (south).

From the Ventura Freeway/Highway 101, the shuttle car parking area is 2.0 miles west of the trailhead on Yerba Buena Road.

The hike

From the parking pullout, the trail is located 0.1 mile ahead along the road. Take the posted Yerba Ridge (Backbone) Trail to the right (east), and descend on the wide path. Weave through tall scrub and chaparral at an easy grade. The views span across the Conejo Valley and Thousand Oaks to the Santa Susana Mountains and the Los Padres National Forest. At 0.6 miles, by a ridge on the left, is an unsigned side path on the right. The path leads 0.2 miles back to Yerba Buena Road. Continue straight (west) and follow the contour of the hills to the south-facing slope overlooking the mountainous backcountry. Walk toward the base of a mountain. At the base, veer left and traverse the slope on a gentle uphill grade. Round a bend to a great view of the scalloped peaks of Boney Ridge. At 3.7 miles is a junction by Yerba Buena Road. Twenty yards straight ahead is a pullout along the road. Take the switchback to the left, staying on the trail, and descend into the canyon. Follow the serpentine path through the canyon, which is far below the road. Wind up the hillside to the Yerba Buena Trailhead, where Yerba Buena Road goes over the saddle at Triunfo Pass.

Directly across the road is the Mishe Mokwa trailhead. Section 13—the final (and longest) segment of the Backbone Trail—begins on the Mishe Mokwa Trail. ■

Yerba Buena Road to La Jolla Canyon Trailhead

Mishe Mokwa Trailhead • Sandstone Peak Trail • Chamberlain Trail
Old Boney Trail • Blue Canyon Trail • Big Sycamore Canyon Trail
Wood Canyon Vista Trail • Overlook Fire Road • Ray Miller Trail

Hiking distance: 16.1 miles one way
Hiking time: 8-9 hours
Configuration: one-way shuttle
Elevation gain: 1,800 feet gain and 2,950 feet loss
Difficulty: very strenuous
Exposure: a mix of exposed hills and shaded canyons
Dogs: allowed on first 3.2 miles; not allowed in Point Mugu State Park
Maps: U.S.G.S. Triunfo Pass, Newbury Park and Point Mugu
Tom Harrison Maps: Point Mugu State Park Trail Map
Point Mugu State Park map

map page 466

Section 13 of the Backbone Trail is the westernmost and longest segment of the 69-mile trail. Nine individual trails make up this section, traveling from the high peaks of Boney Mountain to the Pacific coast at the mouth of La Jolla Canyon. This hike is arguably the most dramatic section of the Backbone Trail, making it the grand culmination of the trail.

The hike begins by Triunfo Pass near Sandstone Peak, the highest peak in the Santa Monica Range. En route to the Pacific Ocean, the trail weaves through gardens of weather-carved sandstone outcroppings, leads to a series of spectacular overlooks, follows streams, traverses rugged interior mountains, winds through shaded forests of oaks and sycamores, descends through several canyons, and traverses oceanfront cliffs to the mouth of La Jolla Canyon and the western terminus of the Backbone Trail.

To the trailhead

From Santa Monica, drive 38 miles northbound on the Pacific Coast Highway/Highway 1 to Yerba Buena Road and turn right. (Yerba Buena Road is 10.1 miles west of Kanan Dume Road and 2 miles west of Leo Carrillo State Beach.) Turn right and drive

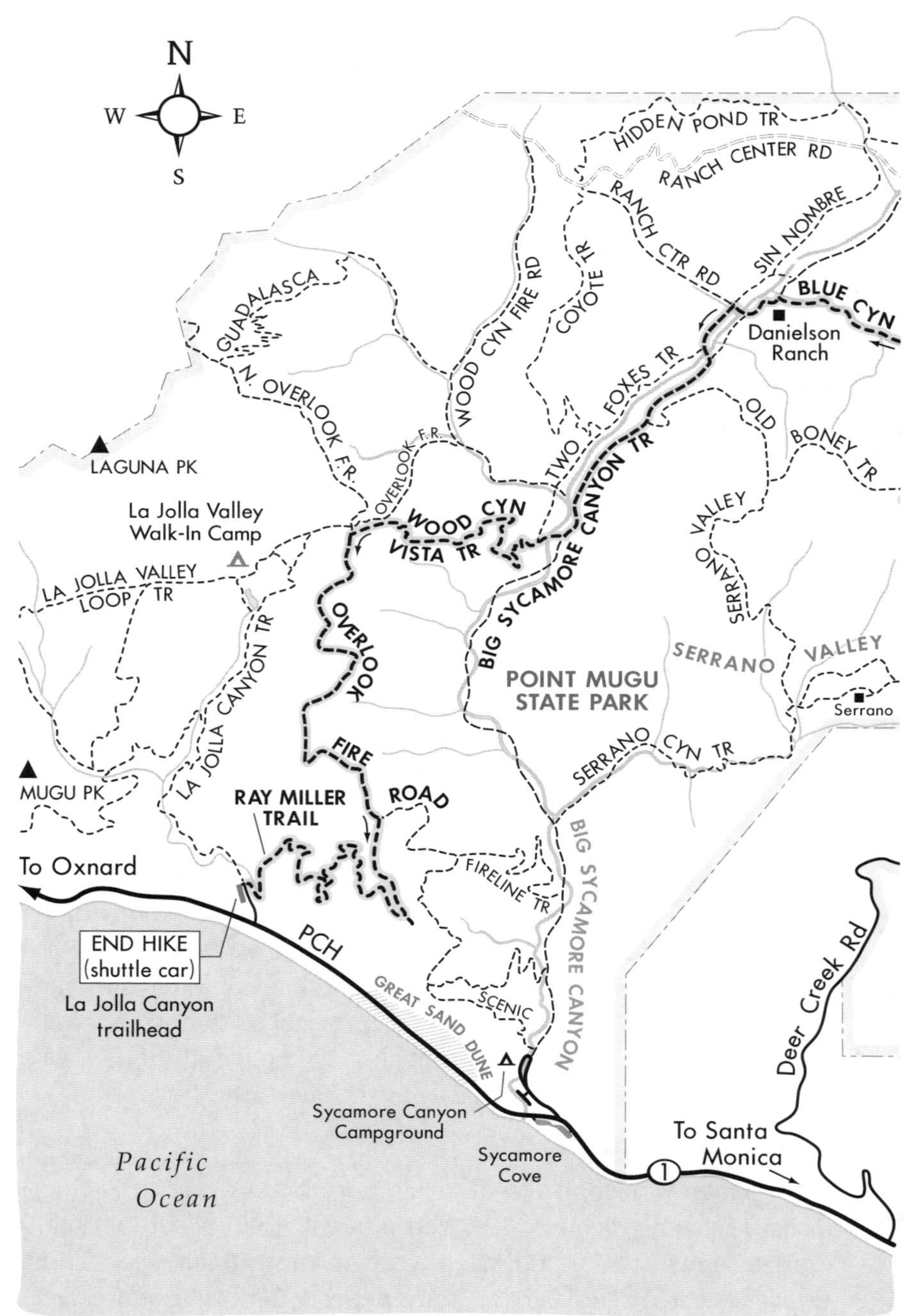
N
W
E
S
HIDDEN POND TR
RANCH CENTER RD
RANCH CTR RD
SIN NOMBRE
BLUE CYN
Danielson Ranch
GUADALASCA
WOOD CYN FIRE RD
COYOTE TR
FOXES TR
N. OVERLOOK F.R.
OVERLOOK F.R.
TWO
BIG SYCAMORE CANYON TR
OLD
BONEY TR
LAGUNA PK
La Jolla Valley Walk-In Camp
WOOD CYN
VISTA TR
VALLEY
SERRANO
LA JOLLA VALLEY LOOP TR
LA JOLLA CANYON TR
OVERLOOK
FIRE
ROAD
POINT MUGU STATE PARK
SERRANO VALLEY
Serrano
SERRANO CYN TR
MUGU PK
RAY MILLER TRAIL
BIG SYCAMORE CANYON
FIRELINE TR
To Oxnard
PCH
END HIKE (shuttle car)
La Jolla Canyon trailhead
GREAT SAND DUNE
SCENIC
Deer Creek Rd
Sycamore Canyon Campground
Sycamore Cove
To Santa Monica
1
Pacific Ocean

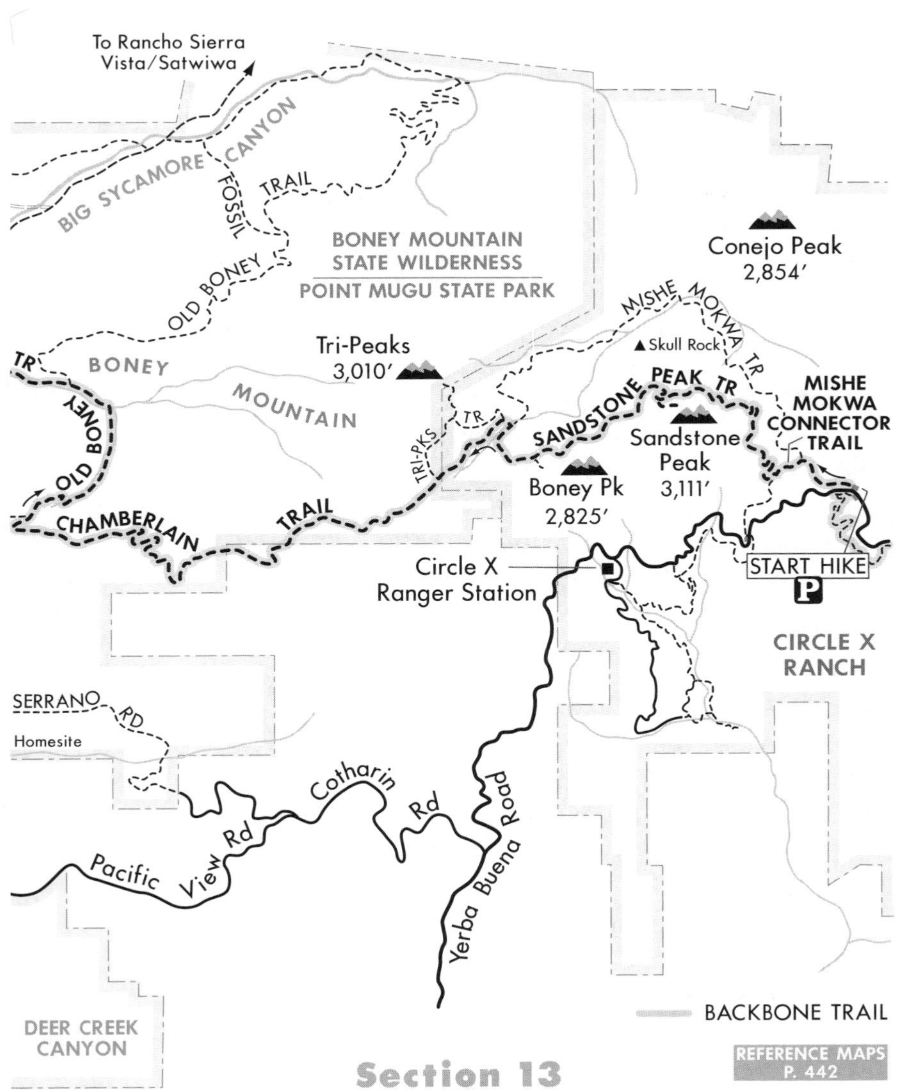

Section 13

BACKBONE TRAIL

Yerba Buena Road to to La Jolla Canyon Trailhead

Mishe Mokwa Trailhead • Sandstone Peak Trail • Chamberlain Trail • Old Boney Trail • Blue Canyon Trail • Big Sycamore Canyon Trail Wood Canyon Vista Trail • Overlook Fire Road • Ray Miller Trail

5.3 miles up the winding road to the Circle X Ranger Station on the right. From the ranger station, continue 1.7 miles to large parking areas on both sides of the road. Turn into either parking area and park.

From the Pacific Coast Highway/Highway 1 and Las Posas Road in southeast Oxnard, drive 9 miles southbound to Yerba Buena Road and turn left. Continue up Yerba Buena Road, following the directions above.

From the Ventura Freeway/Highway 101 in Thousand Oaks, exit on Westlake Boulevard (Highway 23). Drive 6.9 miles south on Westlake Boulevard, winding up the mountain road to Mulholland Highway at a stop sign. Turn right and go 0.4 miles to Little Sycamore Canyon Road. Turn right and drive 4 miles to the large parking areas on both sides of the road. Turn into either parking area and park. (At the county line, Little Sycamore Canyon Road becomes Yerba Buena Road.)

Shuttle car

From Santa Monica, drive 33 miles northbound on the Pacific Coast Highway/Highway 1 to the posted La Jolla Canyon entrance on the right. (The trailhead entrance is 15 miles west of Kanan Dume Road in Malibu and 1.6 miles west of the well-marked Big Sycamore Canyon.) Turn right and park in the day-use pay parking lot 0.1 miles ahead on the left. (Parking is free in the pullouts along the PCH.)

Heading southbound on the Pacific Coast Highway/Highway 1 from Las Posas Road in southeast Oxnard, drive 4.2 miles to the entrance on the left.

The hike

From the north (upper) side of the road, walk past the posted trailhead, and follow the north-facing slope of Carlisle Canyon. The canyon is rich with magnificent red rock sandstone formations. At 0.6 miles is a posted junction. Bear left (Mishe Mokwa Connector Trail), staying on the Backbone Trail. Walk 0.2 miles to the Sandstone Peak Trail. The left fork leads 0.3 miles downhill to the Sandstone Peak Trailhead at Yerba Buena Road. Go to the right

Segment mileage		Total mileage
1.6 miles	to Sandstone Peak	1.6
1.6 miles	to Chamberlain Trail	3.2
2.8 miles	to Old Boney Trail	6.0
2.1 miles	to Big Sycamore Cyn. Tr.	8.1
1.5 miles	on Big Sycamore Cyn. Tr.	9.6
1.8 miles	on Vista Trail	11.4
2.0 miles	on Overlook Trail	13.4
2.7 miles	on Ray Miller	16.1

and head uphill on the rock-embedded path. Wind along the mountain contours while marveling at the great vistas. After 1.6 miles and a 1000-foot elevation gain, the trail reaches a signed fork on the left. A short detour on the left leads 150 yards to 3,111-foot Sandstone Peak, the highest peak in the Santa Monica Mountains. The side path climbs steps to the multi-colored outcroppings atop the peak.

After savoring the 360-degree views, return to the Sandstone Peak (Backbone) Trail. Zigzag down the slope while overlooking stunning sandstone formations. Pass a non-ending display of weather-carved outcrops. Drop into a small valley surrounded by eroded rock monoliths to a Y-fork at 2.7 miles. The right fork leads 1.3 miles to Split Rock on the Mishe Mokwa Trail. Veer left and walk 30 yards to another Y-fork. To the right, the Tri-Peaks Trail leads a half mile to the massive formation. Follow the valley floor a half mile, parallel to a seasonal drainage, to the second junction with the Tri-Peaks Trail and the Boney Mountain State Wilderness boundary at 3.2 miles.

Continue straight ahead on the Chamberlain (Backbone) Trail. Weave through the rolling terrain on a generally downward slope interspersed with numerous small rises. Stroll through a canopy of scrub oak and manzanita high above the canyon, with vistas across Thousand Oaks to the Los Padres National Forest. Follow a long, downhill, cliff-hugging stretch. Cross a narrow ridge, with the meadows of Serrano Valley on the left and forested Big Sycamore Canyon on the right. Descend to a T-junction at 6 miles with the Old Boney Trail. The left fork leads to Serrano Valley and Big Sycamore Canyon.

Bear right on the Old Boney Trail (staying on the Backbone Trail), with close-up views of the towering mountain peaks from which the trail just descended. Walk down to the canyon floor, parallel to Blue Canyon Creek. Cross stream forks three times to a posted junction with the Blue Canyon Trail at 7.1 miles. The Old Boney Trail bears right, leading to the Danielson Monument and Sycamore Canyon Falls. Continue straight on the Blue Canyon Trail on a gentle downward slope through the riparian corridor. Pass conglomerate boulders and cross the stream five more times. After the fifth crossing, walk through the forested grasslands to the Danielson Ranch on the floor of Big Sycamore Canyon. Pass the picnic area and corrals to Big Sycamore Canyon Trail/Road by the ranch house at 8.1 miles. The right fork leads up canyon to the Hidden Pond Trail and the Satwiwa Native American Indian Cultural Center.

Bear left on the old paved road, heading down canyon amongst sycamores and coast live oaks. Pass the Old Boney Trail on the left and the Wood Canyon Fire Road on the right. Walk 0.2 miles farther to the posted Wood Canyon Vista Trail on the right.

Leave the Big Sycamore Canyon Trail, and take the footpath to the right, staying on the Backbone Trail (Wood Canyon Vista Trail). Weave up the west canyon wall while steadily climbing to magnificent views of the canyon and mountains. After gaining 750 feet in elevation, follow the ridge between two canyons. Cross the level ridge to a T-junction with the Overlook Fire Road on a saddle overlooking La Jolla Valley at 10.2 miles.

Bear left and head up the slope on the Overlook Fire Road. Traverse the upper west rim of Big Sycamore Canyon overlooking La Jolla Valley, Serrano Valley, Big Sycamore Canyon, and one of the best views of the jagged Boney Mountains, all in one sweeping panorama. Follow the north/south-running ridge to the top of the hill and expansive ocean vistas. Descend while enjoying the continuous, far-reaching views. After 2 miles on the Overlook Fire Road is the signed Ray Miller Trail on a left bend. This is the final (westernmost) leg of the Backbone Trail.

Bear right on the footpath, and wind along the contours of the oceanfront mountains. The trail runs along the cliffs and descends at an easy grade. Near the bottom, pass the group camp/upper picnic area, and drop down to the trailhead parking lot. ■

Day Hikes Around Los Angeles

Now in its 5th edition, this book has made the *LA Times Bestseller* list for many years. Residents and travelers alike will find the book essential to discovering an amazing number of hiking opportunities. Despite the imminent presence of the city, there are thousands of acres of natural, undeveloped land with hundreds of miles of trails. Includes 135 hikes and walks within a 50-mile radius of the city.

352 pages • 135 hikes • 5th Edition 2010

Day Hikes Around Ventura County

Ventura County's unique topography includes national forest land, wilderness areas, several mountain ranges, and over 50 miles of coastline. The many communities that lie throughout the county have been thoughtfully integrated within the green space and undeveloped land. This guide includes an excellent cross-section of hikes, from relaxing beach strolls to mountain-to-coast hikes with expansive views.

320 pages • 116 hikes • 3rd Edition 2011

Day Hikes On the Calif. Southern Coast

This guide is a collection of 100 great day hikes along 240 miles of southern California coastline, from Ventura County to the U.S.–Mexico border. The area has some of the most varied geography in the state...a blend of verdant canyons, arid bluffs, and sandy coastline. Discover hundreds of miles of trails in scenic and undeveloped land, despite the expansive urban areas.

224 pages • 100 hikes • 1st Edition 2004

Title	ISBN	Price
Day Hikes On the California Central Coast	978-1-57342-058-7	17.95
Day Hikes On the California Southern Coast	978-1-57342-045-7	14.95
Day Hikes In the Santa Monica Mountains	978-1-57342-065-5	21.95
Day Hikes Around Sonoma County	978-1-57342-053-2	16.95
Day Hikes Around Napa Valley	978-1-57342-057-0	16.95
Day Hikes Around Monterey and Carmel	978-1-57342-036-5	14.95
Day Hikes Around Big Sur	978-1-57342-041-9	14.95
Day Hikes Around San Luis Obispo	978-1-57342-051-8	16.95
Day Hikes Around Santa Barbara	978-1-57342-060-0	17.95
Day Hikes Around Ventura County	978-1-57342-062-4	17.95
Day Hikes Around Los Angeles	978-1-57342-061-7	17.95
Day Hikes Around Orange County	978-1-57342-047-1	15.95
Day Hikes In Yosemite National Park	978-1-57342-059-4	13.95
Day Hikes In Sequoia and Kings Canyon N.P.	978-1-57342-030-3	12.95
Day Hikes Around Sedona, Arizona	978-1-57342-049-5	14.95
Day Hikes On Oahu	978-1-57342-038-9	11.95
Day Hikes On Maui	978-1-57342-039-6	11.95
Day Hikes On Kauai	978-1-57342-040-2	11.95
Day Hikes In Hawaii	978-1-57342-050-1	16.95
Day Hikes In Yellowstone National Park	978-1-57342-048-8	12.95
Day Hikes In Grand Teton National Park	978-1-57342-046-4	11.95
Day Hikes In the Beartooth Mountains Billings to Red Lodge to Yellowstone N.P.	978-1-57342-064-8	15.95
Day Hikes Around Bozeman, Montana	978-1-57342-063-1	15.95
Day Hikes Around Missoula, Montana	978-1-57342-032-7	13.95

These books may be purchased at your local bookstore or outdoor shop. Or, order them direct from the distributor:

The Globe Pequot Press

246 Goose Lane • P.O. Box 480 • Guilford, CT 06437-0480
on the web: www.globe-pequot.com

800-243-0495 DIRECT **800-820-2329** FAX

DAY HIKES ON THE
California Central Coast
Robert Stone
DAY HIKES ON THE
California Southern Coast
100 GREAT HIKES
Robert Stone
DAY HIKES IN THE
Santa Monica Mountains
DAY HIKES AROUND
Sonoma County
95 GREAT HIKES
DAY HIKES AROUND
Napa Valley
88 GREAT HIKES
Robert Stone

DAY HIKES AROUND
Monterey & Carmel
77 GREAT HIKES
Robert Stone
DAY HIKES AROUND
Big Sur
80 GREAT HIKES
Robert Stone
DAY HIKES AROUND
San Luis Obispo
Robert Stone
DAY HIKES AROUND
Santa Barbara
113 GREAT HIKES
Robert Stone
DAY HIKES AROUND
Ventura County
116 GREAT HIKES
Robert Stone

DAY HIKES AROUND
Los Angeles
135 GREAT HIKES
Robert Stone
DAY HIKES AROUND
Orange County
108 GREAT HIKES
Robert Stone
DAY HIKES IN
Yosemite
NATIONAL PARK
80 GREAT HIKES
Robert Stone
DAY HIKES IN
Sequoia & Kings Canyon
NATIONAL PARKS
Robert Stone
DAY HIKES AROUND
Sedona
ARIZONA
100 GREAT HIKES
Robert Stone

DAY HIKES IN
Yellowstone
NATIONAL PARK
82 GREAT HIKES
Robert Stone
DAY HIKES IN
Grand Teton
NATIONAL PARK
72 GREAT HIKES
Robert Stone
DAY HIKES IN THE
Beartooth Mountains
Robert Stone
DAY HIKES AROUND
Bozeman
MONTANA
DAY HIKES AROUND
Missoula
MONTANA

Areas That Allow Dogs on Leash

Santa Monica Mountains National Recreation Area

National Park Service

Arroyo Sequit	Peter Strauss Ranch
Castro Crest	Rancho Sierra Vista/Satwiwa
Circle X Ranch	Rocky Oaks
Deer Creek Canyon	Solstice Canyon
Paramount Ranch	Zuma/Trancas Canyons

Santa Monica Mountains Conservancy

Calabasas Peak	Fryman Canyon
Dixie Canyon	Red Rock Canyon Park
Escondido Canyon	Temescal Gateway Park
Franklin Canyon	Wilacre Park

San Vicente Mountain Park

Marvin Braude Mulholland Gateway Park

City of Malibu

Charmlee Wilderness Park	Malibu Bluffs

L.A. City Recreation and Park District

Coldwater Canyon Park	Runyon Canyon Park
Laurel Canyon Park	Temescal Canyon Park

California State Parks

Leo Carrillo State Park—beach and campground only

Will Rogers State Historic Park— loop road and day-use areas only

Pets are NOT allowed on backcountry trails in the following:

Topanga State Park	Point Mugu State Park
Malibu Creek State Park	Leo Carrillo State Park

County Line Beach

INDEX

LINDA STONE

About the Author

Since 1991, Robert Stone has been writer, photographer, and publisher of Day Hike Books. He is a Los Angeles Times Best Selling Author and an award-winning journalist of Rocky Mountain Outdoor Writers and Photographers, the Outdoor Writers Association of California, the Northwest Outdoor Writers Association, the Outdoor Writers Association of America, and the Bay Area Travel Writers.

Robert has hiked every trail in the Day Hike Book series. With 24 hiking guides in the series, many in their fourth and fifth editions, he has hiked thousands of miles of trails throughout the western United States and Hawaii. When Robert is not hiking, he researches, writes, and maps the hikes before returning to the trails. He spends summers in the Rocky Mountains of Montana and winters on the California Central Coast.